PATERNOSTER THEOLOGICAL MONOGRAPHS

# Kṛṣṇa and Christ

## Body-Divine Relation in the Thought of Śaṅkara, Rāmānuja and Classical Christian Orthodoxy

PATERNOSTER THEOLOGICAL MONOGRAPHS

PATERNOSTER THEOLOGICAL MONOGRAPHS

# Kṛṣṇa and Christ

## Body-Divine Relation in the Thought of Śaṅkara, Rāmānuja and Classical Christian Orthodoxy

Steven Tsoukalas

WIPF & STOCK · Eugene, Oregon

Wipf and Stock Publishers
199 W 8th Ave, Suite 3
Eugene, OR 97401

Krsna and Christ
Body-Divine Relation in the Thought of
Sankara, Ramanuja, and Classical Christian Orthodoxy
By Tsoukalas, Steven

ISBN 13: 978-1-55635-324-6
Publication date 6/1/2011
Previously published by Paternoster, 2006

This Edition reprinted by Wipf and Stock Publishers
by arrangement with Paternoster

## Paternoster Theological Monographs

# Series Preface

In the West the churches may be declining, but theology—serious, academic (mostly doctoral level) and mainstream orthodox in evaluative commitment—shows no sign of withering on the vine. This series of *Paternoster Theological Monographs* extends the expertise of the Press especially to first-time authors whose work stands broadly within the parameters created by fidelity to Scripture and has satisfied the critical scrutiny of respected assessors in the academy. Such theology may come in several distinct intellectual disciplines—historical, dogmatic, pastoral, apologetic, missional, aesthetic and no doubt others also. The series will be particularly hospitable to promising constructive theology within an evangelical frame, for it is of this that the church's need seems to be greatest. Quality writing will be published across the confessions—Anabaptist, Episcopalian, Reformed, Arminian and Orthodox—across the ages—patristic, medieval, reformation, modern and counter-modern—and across the continents. The aim of the series is theology written in the twofold conviction that the church needs theology and theology needs the church—which in reality means theology done for the glory of God.

## Series Editors

David F. Wright, Emeritus Professor of Patristic and Reformed Christianity, University of Edinburgh, Scotland, UK

Trevor A. Hart, Head of School and Principal of St Mary's College School of Divinity, University of St Andrews, Scotland, UK

Anthony N.S. Lane, Professor of Historical Theology and Director of Research, London School of Theology, UK

Anthony C. Thiselton, Emeritus Professor of Christian Theology, University of Nottingham, Research Professor in Christian Theology, University College Chester, and Canon Theologian of Leicester Cathedral and Southwell Minster, UK

Kevin J. Vanhoozer, Research Professor of Systematic Theology, Trinity Evangelical Divinity School, Deerfield, Illinois, USA

# Contents


Acknowledgements xiii
Abbreviations xv

Introduction 1
1. Logistics 1
2. Methodological Reflections 5
3. General Reasons for this Study 21
4. Goal and General Intentions of this Study 23
5. Specific Reasons for this Study 25
5.1. Cases in Point: The Humanity and Deity of Kṛṣṇa 29
5.1.1. Ovey N. Mohammed 29
5.1.2. N. V. George 30
5.1.2.1. Vallabha 33
5.1.2.2. Madhva 35
5.1.2.3. Nimbārka 38
6. Conclusion 39

Chapter 1 Epistemologies of Śaṅkara and Rāmānuja 41
1. A General Survey of Pramāṇa-s in Vedānta Epistemology 41
1.1. Smṛti and Śruti 43
1.1.1. Smṛti 43
1.1.2. Śruti 45
1.2. Śaṅkara's Epistemology 45
1.2.1. Pratyakṣa 46
1.2.2. Anumāna 48
1.2.3. Śabda 48
1.2.3.1. Secular Śabda 48
1.2.3.2. Śruti and Smṛti 49
1.2.4. Other Epistemological Phenomena 53
1.2.4.1. Vidyā 53
1.2.4.2. Śruti and Sāmānādhikaraṇya 53
1.2.4.3. Adhyāsa and Avidyā 54
1.2.5. Summary 55

1.3. Rāmānuja's Epistemology 56
1.3.1. Pratyakṣa and Anumāna 56
1.3.2. Śabda 58
1.3.3. Śruti 59
1.3.4. Śruti and Sāmānādhikaraṇya 61
1.3.5. Summary 62
2. More on Abheda and Bheda 63
2.1. Taittirīya Upaniṣad 2.1 67
3. Summary 70

Chapter 2 Śaṅkara : Nature of Brahman, World, and Soul 71
1. Introduction 71
2. The Nature of Brahman 71
2.1. Para Brahman and Apara Brahman (or Īśvara) 72
2.1.1. Para Brahman 73
2.1.2. Apara Brahman or Īśvara 74
2.1.3. Brahman as Antaryāmin 78
2.1.4. The Cosmic Form 79
2.1.5. Summary 81
3. The Jagat and Jīva-s in Relation to Brahman 81
3.1. The Jagat 81
3.1.1. Brahman and Māyā 82
3.1.2. Līlā 83
3.1.3. Sleep, Dreams and Illusion: An Explanation of the Jagat 84
3.2. The Soul 86
3.2.1. The Jīva not Individual but Brahman 86
3.2.1.1. No Individuality 86
3.2.1.2. Ontological Oneness 87
3.2.2. The Jīva in Mokṣa 91
3.3. The Bhagavad Gītā 93
3.3.1. Abheda and the Brahmavidaḥ 93
3.3.2. "The Field and the Field-Knower" 94
3.3.3. Summary 95
3.4. Summary 95

Chapter 3 Rāmānuja: Nature of Brahman, World, and Soul 97
1. The Nature of Brahman 97
1.1. The Personal Brahman 98
1.1.1. Brahman as Antaryāmin 99
1.1.2. The Cosmic Form 100
1.1.3. Summary / Conclusion 101
2. The Jagat in Relation to Brahman 102
2.1. The Jagat 102
2.1.1. The World and the Antaryāmin 103
2.1.2. Unity in Difference 104
2.1.3. Māyā and Līlā 105
3. The Jīva in Relation to Brahman 107
3.1. The Jīva and the Antaryāmin 107
4. Brahman, the Jagat, and the Jīva: BG 13 and Bheda 109
4.1. 13.1—Identity in Difference with Body and Self 110
4.2. 13.2—Lord, Body and Self 111
4.3. Jagat and Jīva: Body of the Lord 111
5. Mokṣa 112
6. Summary 115

Chapter 4 The Kṛṣṇāvatāra of Śaṅkara and Rāmānuja 117
1. BG 4.5-9 118
1.1. Śaṅkara on BG 4.5-9 118
1.2. BG 4.5 121
1.2.1. Śaṅkara on BG 4.5 121
1.2.2. Rāmānuja on BG 4.5 121
1.3. BG 4.6 123
1.3.1. Śaṅkara on BG 4.6 123
1.3.2. Rāmānuja on BG 4.6 125
1.4. BG 4.7-8 126
1.4.1. Śaṅkara on BG 4.7-8 127
1.4.2. Rāmānuja on BG 4.7-8 129
1.5. BG 4.9 129
1.5.1. Śaṅkara on BG 4.9 129
1.5.2. Rāmānuja on BG 4.9 130
2. BG 7.24-25 131
2.1. Śaṅkara on BG 7.24-25 133
2.2. Rāmānuja on BG 7.24-25 134

3. BG 9.11 135
3.1. The Nature of Prakṛti in the BG 136
3.1.1. Prakṛti in BG 7.4-6 137
3.1.2. Kṛṣṇa and the Jagat 138
3.2. Immediate Context of Mānuṣī Tanu in 9.11 139
3.2.1. BG 9.4a 140
3.2.2. BG 9.4b-6 141
3.2.3. BG 9.7-8,10 143
3.3. The Meaning of Mānuṣī Tanu in BG 9.11 143
3.4. Śaṅkara on BG 9.11 145
3.4.1. Aham / Ahaṁkāra—Ego / Egoism 145
3.4.1.1. Aham / Ahaṁkāra in General 145
3.4.1.2. My Observations: Aham / Ahaṁkāra in BG 7.4-6? 147
3.4.1.3. Śaṅkara on BG 7.4-6 149
3.4.2. Śaṅkara on Mānuṣī Tanu of BG 9.11 150
3.4.2.1. BG 9.4 150
3.4.2.2. BG 9.5 151
3.4.2.3. BG 9.6-10 152
3.5. Rāmānuja on BG 9.11 154
3.5.1. Aham / Ahaṁkāra—Ego / Egoism 154
3.5.1.1. The Positive Side of Aham / Ahaṁkāra 154
3.5.1.2. The Negative Side of Aham / Ahaṁkāra 155
3.5.1.3. Rāmānuja on BG 7.4-6 156
3.5.2. Rāmānuja on Mānuṣī Tanu of BG 9.11 157
3.5.2.1. Rāmānuja's Comments on 9.11 157
3.5.2.2. BG 9.4,7 157
3.5.2.3. Implications for the Mānuṣī Tanu 158
4. Summary of the Meaning of Mānuṣī Tanu 164
4.1. My View 165
4.2. Śaṅkara's View 165
4.3. Rāmānuja's View 168
5. Postscript 169

Chapter 5 The World and God: Traditional Christianity 171
1. The Material Universe 172
1.1. Earlier Confessions and Statements 172

1.1.1. Matter not Eternal 173
1.1.1.1. Irenaeus 174
1.1.1.2. Tatian 175
1.1.1.3. Theophilus 176
1.1.1.4. Tertullian 177
1.1.1.5. Novatian 177
1.1.1.6. Origen 178
1.1.1.7. Cyril 179
1.1.1.8. Eusebius 179
1.1.1.9. Lactantius 180
1.1.1.10. Constitutions of the Holy Apostles 180
1.1.1.11. Theodoret 180
1.1.1.12. Athanasius 180
1.1.1.13. Gregory 181
1.1.1.14. Hilary 181
1.1.1.15. Ambrose 182
1.1.1.16. Augustine 182
2. The Biblical Witness 184
2.1. Genesis 1.1-3 185
2.1.1. Syntax 185
2.1.2. Cultural Background and Overall Biblical, Theological Context 186
2.1.2.1. John 1.1,3 188
2.1.2.2. Colossians 1.15b-16a 189
2.1.2.3. Hebrews 11.3 190
2.1.3. Interpretation of Genesis 1.1-3 192
2.1.3.1. "In the Beginning" 192
2.1.3.2. "God Created the Heavens and the Earth" 193
2.1.3.3. "Now the Earth Was Empty, That Is, Unproductive and Uninhabited" 195
2.1.3.4. Summary 198
3. Summary and Conclusion 198

Chapter 6 Incarnation of Christ: Body-Soul-Divine Relation 201
1. "Lord Jesus Christ" 203
1.1. Romans 10.9,13 203
1.2. First Corinthians 1.8 204

1.3. First Thessalonians 5.2 204
2. "Truly God . . . God the Word" 205
2.1. John 1.1 205
2.2. John 8.58 207
2.3. What Jesus Did, יהוה Did 207
2.3.1. Matthew 8.23-26 207
2.3.2. Matthew 9.2-3, Mark 2.5-7, Luke 5.20-21 208
3. "ὁμοούσιος with the Father" 209
4. "Truly Man . . . ὁμοούσιος with Us according to the Manhood" 209
5. John 1.14: "Truly God and Truly Man" 212
6. Body-Soul-Divine Relationship 215
6.1. Two Natures Possessed in Their Fullness 215
6.2. Two Natures Distinct 216
6.3. "Union" 217
7. Conclusion: Body-Soul-Divine Relationship 220

Chapter 7 Conclusion: Avatāra and Incarnation Compared 223
1. The Words Avatāra and Incarnation 224
2. The Purpose of Avatāra and Incarnation 231
2.1. Brief Preliminary Discussion for Śaṅkara's and Rāmānuja's Views 231
2.2. Śaṅkara and Rāmānuja 232
2.3. Classical Orthodoxy's Atonement: Comparative Conclusions 234
2.4. Once for All / Redemption; Multiple Descents / Liberation; Comparative Conclusions 238
3. Śaṅkara's, Rāmānuja's, and Classical Orthodoxy's Views of God in Relation to the World; the Bodies of Kṛṣṇa and Christ; Identification 241
3.1. Śaṅkara 242
3.2. Rāmānuja 244
3.3. Classical Orthodoxy 245
3.4. Comparative Conclusions 246
4. Conclusion / Reflections for Future Research 259

Bibliography 265
Glossary of Sanskrit Terms 303
General Index 307

# Acknowledgements

I wish to thank my doctoral supervisor, Dr. David Cheetham of the University of Birmingham, for his willingness to accept my thesis as worthy of pursuit, and for his scholarly assistance throughout the dissertation process. To Professor Julius Lipner of Cambridge University, my external examiner, I extend my appreciation for his valuable comments and suggestions. My appreciation also extends to my mentor at Harvard University, Dr. Edwin Bryant, and to my colleague at Asbury Theological Seminary, Dr. Jerry Walls. Both have encouraged me greatly and have taught me much. Dr. John Dennis, my good friend who suggested Birmingham University to me, has also been of great encouragement. But above all I thank my wife, Sandy, who, to mention one among many blessings that have come from her, encouraged me to pursue a doctoral program.

Steven Tsoukalas
October 2006

# Abbreviations

| | |
|---|---|
| AĀ | Aitareya Āraṇyaka |
| ANF | The Ante-Nicene Fathers |
| AU | Aitareya Upaniṣad |
| BG | Bhagavadgītā |
| BGB | Bhagavadgītābhāṣya |
| BGBs | Bhagavadgītābhāṣya-s |
| BP | Bhāgavata Purāṇa |
| BS | Brahmasūtra or Vedāntasūtra |
| BSB | Brahmasūtrabhāṣya |
| BSs | Brahmasūtra-s or Vedāntasūtra-s |
| BU | Bṛhadāraṇyaka Upaniṣad |
| BUB | Bṛhadāraṇyaka Upaniṣad Bhāṣya |
| C | Chalcedonian Creed (451 A.D.) |
| CU | Chāndogya Upaniṣad |
| IU | Īśa Upaniṣad |
| KU | Kaṭha Upaniṣad |
| MBGB | Madhva's Bhagavadgītābhāṣya |
| MBh | Mahābhārata |
| MSB | Madhva's Sūtrabhāṣya |
| MU | Mahānārāyaṇa Upaniṣad |
| MuU | Muṇḍaka Upaniṣad |
| NC | Nicaeno-Constantinopolitan Creed (381 A.D.) |
| NPNF | The Nicene and Post-Nicene Fathers |
| NPNF2 | The Nicene and Post-Nicene Fathers, second series |
| PU | Praśna Upaniṣad |
| RBGB | Rāmānuja's Bhagavadgītābhāṣya |
| RV | Ṛg Veda |
| RVed | Rāmānuja's Vedārthasaṃgraha |
| SBE | Sacred Books of the East, containing the BSB of Śaṅkara (vols. 34 and 38) and the BSB of Rāmānuja (vol. 48) |
| SBGB | Śaṅkara's Bhagavadgītābhāṣya |
| SBGK | Śaṅkara's Bhāṣya on Gauḍapāda's Kārikā |
| SBUB | Śaṅkara's Bṛhadāraṇyaka Upaniṣad Bhāṣya |
| SCUB | Śaṅkara's Chāndogya Upaniṣad Bhāṣya |
| STUB | Śaṅkara's Taittirīya Upaniṣad Bhāṣya |
| SU | Śvetāśvatara Upaniṣad |
| TU | Taittirīya Upaniṣad |
| US | Śaṅkara's Upadeśa Sāhasrī |
| VC | Śaṅkara's Vivekacūḍāmaṇi |
| VP | Viṣṇu Purāṇa |
| YS | Yatīndramatadīpikā by Śrīnivāsadāsa |

# Introduction

## 1. Logistics

Following is a summary of the content of each chapter and the place each chapter holds in the overall aim of this study.

Introduction: I interact with the issue of imposing western philosophical and theological categories on Indian thought, and outline my general and specific reasons, goals, and intentions for this study as concerns the comparison between Śaṅkara's and Rāmānuja's Kṛṣṇāvatāra doctrines and classical Christian orthodoxy's incarnation.

Chapter 1: Epistemologies of Śaṅkara and Rāmānuja. Here I spend a significant amount of time exploring the epistemologies of Śaṅkara and Rāmānuja. The reason for this is that their epistemological methods figure considerably in their worldviews, theologies, and subsequent views of Kṛṣṇāvatāra.

Chapter 2: Śaṅkara: Nature of Brahman, World, and Soul serves to lay a foundation for the later discussion of Śaṅkara's doctrine of Kṛṣṇāvatāra. Examination of who and what Brahman is, what the world of matter is, what the soul is, and how Brahman, the world and the soul relate are indispensable elements for my later analysis of Kṛṣṇāvatāra.

Chapter 3 is entitled Rāmānuja: Nature of Brahman, World, and Soul. Reasons for this chapter are the same as for chapter 2.

Chapter 4, The Kṛṣṇāvatāra of Śaṅkara and Rāmānuja: Body-Soul-Divine Relationship, is a most important part of my thesis. Since the foundational epistemologies and doctrinal teachings of Śaṅkara and Rāmānuja documented in chapters 1, 2 and 3 determine their avatāra doctrines, I therefore call upon my findings from these chapters in order to interact with their doctrines of Kṛṣṇāvatāra, and here the BG and the BGBs of Śaṅkara and Rāmānuja play major roles in exploring what each taught concerning Kṛṣṇāvatāra. Additionally, chapters 1, 2 and 3 prove very important to my further overall analysis of Kṛṣṇāvatāra, for some questions I have are left unanswered by Śaṅkara and Rāmānuja, and some are not raised at all by the two Vedāntins. I therefore draw upon these chapters in order to answer and to raise several important questions relevant to the body-soul-divine relation in Kṛṣṇāvatāra that most naturally arise in the comparison of avatāra and incarnation. In this chapter I also offer my interpretation of BG passages with regard to Kṛṣṇāvatāra.

Chapter 5, The World and God: Traditional Christianity, serves the same purpose for the discussion of Christ's incarnation in chapter 6 that chapters 2 and 3 serve for the avatāra of Kṛṣṇa in chapter 4. That is, just as chapters 2 and 3 are most important to chapter 4, so is the material in chapter 5 most important to chapter 6. I focus upon two statements contained in the NC and explore how the world relates to God. I argue for creatio ex nihilo by way of documenting many statements by early church theologians and by way of exegesis of key biblical texts.

Chapter 6: Incarnation of Christ: Body-Soul-Divine Relation. In this chapter I make a case for the full deity and full humanity of Christ and explore the relationship between matter, Christ's soul / spirit, and his divine nature. I cite certain statements from the NC and the C, and my exegesis of key biblical texts substantiates those statements. I also document in the notes several statements from early church theologians.

Chapter 7: Conclusion: Avatāra and Incarnation Compared. As the title suggests, this chapter contains my conclusion and final comparative analysis. In this chapter I harness the material from the preceding six chapters and draw out major differences between Śaṅkara's and Rāmānuja's doctrines of Kṛṣṇāvatāra and classical orthodoxy's incarnation as regards the body-soul-divine relation and the resulting, and profoundly different, theological / soteriological implications. At the chapter's end I also offer reflections on future research.

By "classical Christian orthodoxy" ("orthodox" coming from the Greek words ὀρθῶς ["upright", "straight", fig. "correct", "true"] and δόξα ["honor", "glory"], meaning, from this tradition's particular viewpoint, giving right honor to God) I mean that tradition which finds itself largely in conformity with the NC (381 A.D.) and the C (451 A.D.), creeds that set the standards for what is to be called orthodox doctrine. I hope to demonstrate that this particular tradition holds to both creatio ex nihilo and Christ as fully God and fully human. Note that though throughout this work I cite certain early church theologians and their teachings concerning one or both these doctrines, they may have (1) existed prior to the times of composition of the NC and the C, and (2) not been in total agreement with the NC and the C with regard to any one of the two doctrines. In light of this I ask the reader to understand that these theologians have nonetheless contributed to classical Christian orthodox doctrine. For example, in the case of Origen, though some (if not many) consider him to be outside the fold of orthodox Christology, with regard to his contribution to creatio ex nihilo in the subsequent formation of the doctrine by the early church, he nonetheless did just that, contribute to it.

A few more matters of concern remain with regard to the nature of this study. First, for the most part I have labored to make it a comparative study that mentions similarities but, in the main, points out intrinsic differences between Śaṅkara's and Rāmānuja's Kṛṣṇāvatāra doctrines and classical Christian orthodoxy's incarnate Christ. For there exist many deep differences between them that significantly outweigh similarities, and many of the similarities cited by scholars are in reality not so when avatāra and incarnation are interpreted within their respective ontologies. Second, I write this dissertation as a Christian scholar committed to the faith tradition of classical orthodoxy, and ask that my readers consider chapters 5 and 6 as secondary to the primary purpose of this study, which is to compare avatāra and incarnation. Note further that in chapters 5 and 6 I give evidence for my view without engaging, in depth, opposing opinions that would come from those who consider themselves to be within the Christian tradition. Third, in my exploration of the two Hindu traditions I do not offer, for the most part, opposing opinions intra each system. The primary purpose is to compare classical Christian orthodoxy's incarnation with my take on the Kṛṣṇāvatāra doctrines of Śaṅkara and Rāmānuja (and subsequently to compare Śaṅkara's and Rāmānuja's Kṛṣṇāvatāra doctrines). Thus, fourth, this study is not so much concerned with intra-tradition debate as it is with inter-tradition debate. Fifth, although this study has as its ultimate goal the comparison of Śaṅkara's and Rāmānuja's Kṛṣṇāvatāra with classical Christian orthodoxy's incarnation of Christ, by way of chapters 1-3 and 5-6, which function as indispensable preliminaries to the ultimate goal, readers may find that these chapters make a contribution to the comparative study of the epistemologies of Śaṅkara and Rāmānuja and the ontologies of all three traditions in a way that stands apart from the ultimate goal. That is to say, these chapters may be considered a work in and of themselves for contribution to epistemology and ontology studies. Sixth, in addition to academicians who may desire to read this work for comparative reasons only, this study can aid those who want to take this comparative study a step farther and enter into interreligious dialogue, however one defines the practice. In connection with this, though I readily admit that my embracing of classical Christian orthodoxy at times evidences a presuppositional slant on my part in the presentation of evidence, some of the comparative categories I choose, and the comparative conclusions I draw (especially in chapter 7), I nonetheless have worked as best I can to leave the discipline of in-depth apologetics to others, both Christian and Hindu, and therefore to function mainly as a phenomenologist who stands outside the two Hindu traditions but labors intensely to understand them through the reading of texts.[1] The only exception to this is found at the end of this work, in chapter 7, where I introduce the issue of historicity and faith in hope that others (including myself

---

[1] See John B. Carman's excellent discussion of the discipline of the phenomenology of religion in his The Theology of Rāmānuja: An Essay in Interreligious Understanding (New Haven and London: Yale University Press, 1974; Bombay: Ananthacharya Indological Research Institute, 1981), 1-23. In another book, Carman, while discussing the phenomenology approaches of W. Brede Kristensen and Gerardus van der Leeuw, explains that the comparative scholar first seeks to understand any given religion's phenomena within its context, and then proceeds to relate those phenomena to other religions. The two scholars differ in certain respects, though. While van der Leeuw's view is to allow his Christianity to form general categories of comparison, a practice I exhibit in this work, Kristensen, writes Carman, "does not make it clear whether one's own religion in any way furnishes the pattern for correlating the phenomena in other religions (Majesty and Meekness: A Comparative Study of Contrast and Harmony in the Concept of God [Grand Rapids, Mich.: William B. Eerdmans, 1994], 31).

in a future work) will explore more deeply the issues I raise.

According to Francis Clooney there is justification for the apologetic task, for there naturally arises after deep penetration of belief systems in the comparative venture an apologetic dimension. He writes,

> The deeper, more difficult, and more acute differences become, the more slender the distinction between a "confessional" theology, where one pronounces and explains the truth of one's positions, and an "apologetic" theology, where one also asserts the error of others' positions. For this reason I speak of an interreligious theology's "confessional and even apologetic" dimension. Strong arguments in favor of one's own tradition often go along with critiques of others' theological positions, and theologies are often confessional and apologetic at the same time, testifying and criticizing, explaining and arguing, persuading and disproving. But even criticism need not be a problem if it is offered respectfully and professionally. That is, the theologian must actually know something about the theological tradition being criticized, become engaged in a receptive dialogue with theologians of that other tradition, admit that areas of disagreement are probably far fewer than areas of consensus, and concede that one's own theology is not beyond criticism. Such is the high price for a useful apologetics today.[2]

I agree with most of what Clooney states above. My one disagreement is with his assertion that the theologian must "admit that areas of disagreement are probably far fewer than areas of consensus". This study hopes to show that there are far more areas of disagreement than consensus when comparing avatāra and incarnation, and even the similarities I list are, when explored deeply, not so similar. Nonetheless, I hope that this study will prove to be most helpful to theologians and apologists of all three traditions because it informs them of important differences between avatāra and incarnation.

Although I have striven to be as exhaustive as is reasonably possible, I am quite sure that I have not exhausted all the implications in this comparative study. Perhaps others will pick up implications and issues I have missed, and this, I hope, in addition to the valuable constructive critiques and interactions that may arise.

I note now some linguistic items. Sanskrit is transliterated only. Greek and Hebrew appear in both original script and transliteration, and in each section or subsection repeated words appear in transliteration only, unless appearing in a new sentence or phrase. Greek and Hebrew are transliterated according to the system used in The New American Standard Exhaustive Concordance of the Bible: Hebrew-Aramaic and Greek Dictionaries (Nashville, Tenn.: Holman,

---

[2] Francis X. Clooney, Hindu God, Christian God: How Reason Helps Break Down the Boundaries between Religions (New York: Oxford University Press, 2001), 11.

1981). More detailed transliteration is not needed since readers will find details sufficient in the arguments presented. Sanskrit is transliterated according to Perry's A Sanskrit Primer, except āi is rendered ai. Also, I use the ending "-s" rather than "s" for many Sanskrit words in the plural occurring in English sentences, due to the fact that many plurals in Sanskrit do not end simply with "s" added to the singular form. For examples, the word for "teacher", ācārya, becomes ācāryās in the nominative plural, and agni (fire) becomes agnayas in the nominative plural. However, in this study I would transliterate them, if used in English sentences, as ācārya-s and agni-s, meaning "teachers" and "fires". There are exceptions with some commonly used terms, such as Upaniṣads and Vedas, with which I do not follow this rule. Lastly, because chapter 4 serves as a prominent part of the dissertation, Sanskrit transliteration is given for a large amount of the texts cited in that chapter, while in other chapters I have placed Sanskrit transliteration only where I feel it is needed.

## 2. Methodological Reflections

In a work such as this the issue of imposing western categories of philosophical thought upon eastern (specifically Indian) thought naturally arises in the minds of some academicians. This imposition may occur by way of presupposing that philosophy and philosophical categories have arisen only in European culture. In a significant book, Richard King states, "The association of systematic thought, theoretical abstraction and philosophy exclusively with European culture is a common feature in the works of many modern western intellectuals."[3] King notes his concern that political, economic and cultural subordination makes "Indian thought and culture particularly vulnerable to manipulation, domination and distortion by western interests", and his general criticism of departments of philosophy in western universities for omitting "non-European modes of thought from 'philosophy'"[4] is well deserved.[5] King's

---

[3] Richard King, Indian Philosophy: An Introduction to Hindu and Buddhist Thought (Washington, D.C.: Georgetown University Press, 1999), 25.

[4] King, Indian Philosophy, 24,243. On the latter criticism, see also pages xiii-xiv.

[5] Though not without valid observations being raised in the effort to counterbalance. For example, Daya Krishna observes that the primary issue that needs to be raised concerns how Indian philosophy "can be regarded a 'philosophy' proper when it is supposed to be primarily concerned with mokṣa, that is, liberation from the very possibility of suffering, which is a quintessentially practical end and has hardly anything theoretical about it". Krishna adds to this the fact that revelation or some superhuman authority overrides both reason and experience, and concludes that

> It is, then, no wonder that Indian philosophy is not taught in the philosophy departments of most western universities, for neither the students nor the teachers in these departments are presumably seeking mokṣa. The relegation of Indian philosophy to departments of Indology and its effective segregation from all active philosophical concerns of the day speaks for itself" ("Comparative Philosophy: What It Is and What It Ought to Be", in Gerald James

motivation for writing his book is "to challenge the parochialism of 'western philosophy' and to contribute to the growth of a relatively new, and much maligned, field known as 'comparative philosophy'".[6] In this way he challenges academics "to think through the implications of a post-colonial approach for the study and practice of philosophy as a cross-cultural phenomenon".[7]

This I applaud, and King has indeed forced me to think through such implications. I also resonate with King's astute observation that "European and Indian cultures have, until the advent of colonialism, developed in relative (though not absolute) isolation from each other". King then follows with this conclusion: "One would expect, therefore, to find particular traditions of intellectual thought within both that are culturally specific" and "broad cultural assumptions within both that differentiate their respective approaches".[8] With

---

Larson and Eliot Deutsch, eds., Interpreting Across Boundaries: New Essays in Comparative Philosophy [Princeton: Princeton University Press, 1988], 74).

J. N. Mohanty, however, disagrees with the common-held thesis that Indian philosophy "is deeply spiritual; that its goal is not simple intellectual juggling but the spiritual transformation of one's nature; that philosophy is a means to attain mokṣa". This view he calls "highly misleading" ("Indian Philosophical Tradition: The Theory of Pramāṇa", in Shlomo Biderman and Ben-Ami Scharfstein, eds., Rationality in Question: On Eastern and Western Views of Rationality [Leiden: E. J. Brill, 1989], 217-18). See also Julius Lipner, "Philosophy and world religions", in Brian Davies, ed., Philosophy of Religion: A Guide to the Subject (London: Cassell, 1998), chapter 11, on the issue of whether there is philosophy proper in Indian tradition.

[6] Indian Philosophy, xiii.

[7] Indian Philosophy. See also the informative essay by Don Howard, "The History That We Are: Philosophy as Discipline and the Multiculturalism Debate", in Anindita Niyogi Balslev, Cross-Cultural Conversation (Initiation) (Atlanta: Scholars Press, 1996), 43-76, wherein Howard traces, briefly though informatively, the beginnings and subsequent adaptation of a Eurocentric view of philosophy (pp. 45-58), due in part to industrial capitalism and European colonial expansion (p. 45). Though Howard states his awareness of Indian philosophy as a recognized discipline (p. 44), thus placing himself outside King's specific criticism, he at one time did not escape King's general criticism. Howard admits his former prejudice when in the past he read a flyer from Lakehead University in Ontario. The flyer advertised a new program in Native American philosophy. His first reaction was that of his colleagues when they, upon hearing of African philosophy, thought it an oxymoron (p. 43). He writes of his thoughts back then: "Religion, yes; mythopoeisis, perhaps—but not philosophy ... But as we were all taught in our own introductory courses, and as we all now teach our beginning students, philosophy is different in kind from poetry and myth" (p. 43). Howard's reasons for this prejudice on his part (in the past) and presently on the parts of other philosophers is (1) their inability to engage in cross-cultural philosophical conversations and (2) that they have defined themselves and their discipline in a certain way, leaving, in the end, an "aversion" and "condescension", as he puts it, toward such phrases (p. 44).

[8] Indian Philosophy, 1.

this I agree as well, though with the stipulation that one must make careful note of what is meant by "particular traditions of intellectual thought" and "broad cultural assumptions". Certainly "rationality" is not included here, for it is, arguably, universal.

On this last point I find myself agreeing in whole with Jonardon Ganeri, who offers this interesting observation: "Forms of rationality are, I maintain, interculturally available even if they are not always interculturally instantiated."[9] He then documents early Indian forms of the practice of reason, specifically those found in the MBh, the Rāmāyaṇa, the Arthaśāstra, and the Nyāyasūtra.[10] Ganeri then explores the role of perception in early Indian thought, and moves to reason, scripture and testimony.[11] "If the objection is simply that 'rationality' is a western concept imperiously misapplied", writes Ganeri, "my response would be that it is no more western than perception, thought, language or morality".[12]

Jack Goody is of the same mindset, in that he has suggested that rationality's roots lie not with Europe as is commonly and popularly thought. In an essay he first states that we need to reconsider the "Great Divide" that "links us with Greece and Rome and them with less 'rational' traditions of human thought".[13] Such a divide, he asserts, is set forth due to a foundational error pertaining to both history and culture. As a corrective he states that the major societies of Eurasia "are all heirs to the great Bronze Age civilizations of B.C.E. 3000, with their various forms of writing and the associated accumulation of knowledge".[14] He subsequently argues that "rationality [which he defines as "the capacity to reason, to apply logic"], and its specialist form, logic [which he defines in part as "a science that deals with the canons of validity of inference and demonstration"], are attributes of all cultures".[15] He then demonstrates that forms of logic were found among the Azande people, and, in particular, the syllogism, so important a part of the philosophy of Aristotle, was found in embryonic form earlier in Mesopotamia, with subsequent emergence in India, China and Japan.[16] Of India Goody states that forms of syllogistic reasoning were acquired even before Western Europe had done so.[17]

---

[9] Jonardon Ganeri, Philosophy in Classical India (London: Routledge, 2001), 3.

[10] Philosophy in Classical India, 7-15.

[11] Philosophy in Classical India, 17-22,35-37.

[12] Philosophy in Classical India, 4. Additionally, R. S. Sugirtharajah notes that "Indians have a well-developed system of śāstra paddhati." This practice utilizes various interpretive tools such as grammar and logical reasoning (Postcolonial Criticism and Biblical Hermeneutics [Oxford: Oxford University Press, 2002], 14). For a view contrary to that of Ganeri, see Mohanty, "Indian Philosophical Tradition".

[13] Jack Goody, "East and West: Rationality in Review", Ethnos (1993): 8.

[14] "East and West", 8.

[15] "East and West", 10.

[16] "East and West", 6,16-25.

[17] "East and West", 24.

In defense of my methodology for this study, I now raise a few observations of my own and substantiate them with the views of others. First, Ganeri's observations coincide exactly with my findings in Śaṅkara's advaita and Rāmānuja's viśiṣṭādvaita. There are indeed philosophical categories in Indian philosophies[18] that are common to western categories of philosophy, especially within the category of epistemology.[19] Reason and perception are two examples, and if one wants to extend this to religious, philosophical epistemology, then add to the epistemological mix verbal authority. Indeed, in a Christian tradition with which I am familiar, the Wesleyan tradition, we find the "quadrilateral": scripture, reason, experience, and tradition. This is similar, category-wise, to some Indian philosophical epistemologies, especially the two I explore in this work.

Second, Śaṅkara and Rāmānuja are not only philosophers, they are also theologians. In fact, I would have no objections if they were considered first and foremost theologians who then secondarily employed philosophy to advance their theologies. But perhaps better they should be categorized as philosophical theologians, and this in the effort to minimize the distinction of the disciplines of theology and philosophy, a distinction most likely brought about in the not too distant past.[20]

Third, the question now arises as to whether or not one might force upon Śaṅkara and Rāmānuja categories of theology not found in their systems. I am not convinced that there must be a prohibition on asking certain questions of Indian philosophies / theologies that arise strictly from categories of thought (such as "identification") from other religious traditions. Nor am I convinced

---

[18] King states that "one might argue that the term 'Indian philosophy' is problematic not only because it presupposes that a particular product of western cultural history (viz. philosophy) can be applied beyond its western context, but also because of the political implications of such a designation" (Indian Philosophy, 24). Though he raises the issue in order to facilitate discussion, King nonetheless uses the phrase "Indian philosophy" throughout his book, and, as is obvious, employs it in his title.

[19] I do not consider in this study the possibility that similarity of categories may have arisen in part from cross-cultural communication in Eurasia due to trade routes for commerce and with military campaigns.

[20] Specifically, eighteenth century Europe. See Howard, "The History That We Are", 45,59. Though noting the noble-mindedness of most academicians who are unaware of the specific European context behind defining the limits and the discipline of philosophy, and who, unaware, have simply bought into that context, in lamenting fashion Howard writes on page 59, "How many of us today, for example, really understand what cultural project is served by the prejudices that lead us, instinctively, to condescend to those more 'backward' universities where religion and philosophy still coexist in one department and to rail against bookstores that insist on shelving books on philosophy and religion in one section."

that the reverse is the case.[21] Gavin Hyman has challenged what he deems modernity's older view of "neutrality" in religious studies, particularly as represented by Ninian Smart, wherein a phenomenological approach that merely reports religious phenomena from the "neutral" perspective was the norm for the discipline.[22] Smart, says Hyman, considered neutrality "the pearl of great price that is to be secured by such methodological procedures as

---

[21] There is a great difference, however, between this and imposing alien philosophical and / or theological hermeneutic grids upon systems that do not belong to the systems themselves, and in so doing emerging with interpretations that are foreign to the related texts. For example, I am quite unenthusiastic about the methodology and conclusions of the Neo-Vedāntin Ramakrishna. His view of all religions as valid paths to God forced him to ascertain Christ as one in a line of avatār a-s (for Ramakrishna's view, see Hal W. French, "Reverence to Christ through Mystical Experience and Incarnational Identity: Sri Ramakrishna", in Arvind Sharma, ed., Neo-Hindu Views of Christianity [Leiden: E. J. Brill, 1988], 68-70). For a first-hand portrayal of the hermeneutic of Ramakrishna, see Swami Akhilananda, Hindu View of Christ (Boston: Branden Press, 1949), chapter 1. Also, S. Radhakrishnan imposes his Neo-Vedāntic hermeneutic upon Christ, viewing Jesus as an avatāra who demonstrated the way for all people to become avatār a-s, that is, to come to recognize their own Christhood. Radhakrishnan, ironically, accuses Christians of taking what was originally an eastern religion and gradually making it conform to the western spirit (see K. P. Aleaz, Jesus in Neo-Vedānta: A Meeting of Hinduism and Christianity [Rani Bagh, Delhi: Kant Publications, 1995], 71). Ishwar Harris observes, "His [Radhakrishnan's] treatment of Jesus, though commendable, robs Jesus of his uniqueness. He is made to look like an eastern seer, a Sanyāsin, and an avatara of Vishnu. Thus, critics are uneasy over his entire enterprise to interpret Jesus and Christianity from a Vedantic perspective" ("Radhakrishnan's View of Christianity", in Sharma, Neo-Hindu Views of Christianity, 174). Prashant Miranda, in answering the question of whether or not Jesus was an avatār a, adopts the perspective of Radhakrishnan (Avatār and Incarnation: A Comparative Analysis [New Delhi: Harman Publishing House, 1990]). As other examples, see K. P. Aleaz, An Indian Jesus from Śaṅkara's Perspective (Calcutta: Punthi Pustak, 1997), and the content throughout, Daniel E. Bassuk's "Six Modern Indian Avatars and the Ways They Understand Their Divinity" (Dialogue & Alliance 1, no. 2 [Summer 1987]: 90-91), wherein Bassuk documents six modern Indian avatāra-s' views of Jesus in relation to their own divinity, and M. Thomas Thangaraj's The Crucified Guru: An Experiment in Cross-Cultural Christology (Nashville: Abingdon Press, 1994). Regarding Thangaraj's work, his epistemological starting point (which he admits on pp. 32-33) is based on his bilingual / bicultural and religious experiences, which find further extension in the multicultural and diverse religious environments of the world in various cities (pp. 19-20,23-24). With this as his starting point, the uniqueness of Jesus, which, along with other New Testament deific titles and recordings of supernatural work on behalf of sinners on the part of Jesus, is relegated to myth and is discarded in favor of a Śaiva Siddhānta conception of guru, rather than avatār a, which, in Thangaraj's view is likewise mythical and not grounded in history. Gurus, though, are grounded in history (p. 122).

[22] Gavin Hyman, "The Study of Religion and the Return of Theology", Journal of the American Academy of Religion 72 (March 2004): 195-219.

'phenomenology', 'structured empathy', 'bracketing', and 'methodological agnosticism' ... 'without introducing the assumptions and slant of the investigator'".[23] This, says Smart, and "'value-free' descriptions are necessary to avoid the imposition of alien interpretive categories into 'other' religions".[24] The challenge to Smart from Hyman, in part, begins to take shape from this question: "Can we really wipe away all our intellectual, cultural, and biographical conditioning in order to think, observe, and write in a white, pristine, and uncontaminated state? Should we not have learned from Kant that the mind always unavoidably interprets and shapes knowledge?"[25] Hyman's answer is that we cannot, and implied is that we should have learned from Kant.[26] Religious data are always interpreted, the data always chosen and

---

[23] "The Study of Religion", 198.

[24] "The Study of Religion", 198.

[25] "The Study of Religion", 199.

[26] Thus in this sense I agree with certain types of liberal theologians' opposition to Smart's value-free descriptions. There is a sense in which liberal theologians would share certain epistemological traits with me. Reason as a universal would be an example, though a limit to this universal would be what Hyman observes from Kant in what follows above, namely that reason is limited in part because reasoning cannot occur outside the boundaries of the particular situations in which we find ourselves. But I may not go as far as Hyman intends here. True, in my particular work, reason and comparison occur within the boundaries of my theological system and the theological systems of Śaṅkara and Rāmānuja. But I would say that truth in reality can be apprehended, that we can know it, and that though truth may be defined by way of one's particular approach and the circumstances that ally themselves with that particular approach, this does not dismiss forthwith the fact that someone may indeed hold certain propositions that are true to reality. There does not have to be a chasm between a belief system (and its tools used to apprehend truth) and truth in reality and as universal. The goal here, then, is to determine which belief system most plausibly enables the acquisition of truth as it really is. On another note, though somewhat related to the preceding, Mark Chapman has outlined a liberal, Kantian approach to doing theology, in which the Kantian Enlightenment, "with its emphasis on criticism [and] on defining the limits of human understanding", leads to an approach that is both critical and open to criticism (Mark D. Chapman, The Future of Liberal Theology [Burlington, Vt.: Ashgate, 2002], 13). I resonate with this. However, where I would differ from Chapman and other liberal theologians specifically concerns the liberal accompanying, and to a certain extent causal, position of rejecting exclusivist claims (see p. 15). One can have the first without the second. This kind of liberalism, then, is defined by Marsh as "the spirit of free and open enquiry" (here "liberal" means that an orthodox traditional evangelical is a "critical traditionalist"; see Clive Marsh, "The Experience of Theological Education: Maintaining a 'Liberal' Agenda in a Post-Liberal Age" in Chapman, The Future of Liberal Theology, 145 n. 6), and he postulates, and rightly so, that "it need not ... be a reductionistic exercise" in the Cupittian sense (p. 144). For a sketch of Don Cupitt's move from liberal to non-realist to postmodern, see Gavin Hyman, "Postmodern Theology: The Apotheosis or Scourge of Liberalism?" in Chapman, The Future of Liberal Theology, 191-207.

reported, from the slant of the investigator whether we choose to acknowledge it or not.[27] Hyman continues then to demonstrate first that "neutrality" is itself not neutral. "It is highly particularist", argues Hyman, "being indissolubly linked with a modern scientific canon of rationality, as numerous scholars have pointed out".[28] Second, the dichotomy Smart gives us, namely neutral fairness as opposed to non-neutral unfairness and ignorance, is questioned by Hyman. One need not be neutral to represent fairly others' views. As an example Hyman states that he need not be neutral in order to critique Smart. He most definitely disagrees with Smart, yet feels he has represented Smart's views accurately and fairly and can proceed to critique them.[29] Additionally, Smart's approach may have distinct roots, or, perhaps, presuppositions. Representing the thought of Graham Ward,[30] Hyman states, "Liberalism, and with it religious studies, eradicates or at least subordinates differences to a higher unity",[31] a phenomenon against which this work of mine argues.

What, then, should constitute comparative philosophical and theological inquiry? I agree with Hyman, who states that "the ideal of the neutral observer is illusory and that the discipline is itself underpinned by certain presuppositions that are themselves more theological than was previously thought."[32] If such theology underpins the old approach, why not replace it with a new theological approach, one "where religions ... can confront and engage with each other on their own terms rather than on the a priori basis of a specious pacifism that turns out to be a covert eradication of differences"[33]? With this as my hermeneutic, I can, for example, both raise and answer the question of whether or not Rāmānuja's Kṛṣṇāvatāra and traditional Christian orthodoxy's Christ possess bodies like the bodies of all humans. This does not constitute a "forcing" of a category upon the Indian theologian, but rather a category from my particular tradition that I wish to pursue in the comparative venture with the Indian theologian. And, in all fairness, he may wish to reverse the case with me. Thus it is not wrong to explore the differences between

---

[27] See Hyman, "The Study of Religion", 199.

[28] "The Study of Religion", listing Gavin D'Costa and Alasdair MacIntyre as examples. Additionally, in my readings of Indian theologians in medieval times (admittedly a Eurocentric category!), I have not found a "neutrality"-based approach. Rather, the intent of documenting or stating other (or, most often, opposing) theological views was in the main to refute them and prove the school or view (darśana) of the investigator superior.

[29] "The Study of Religion", 200.

[30] Graham Ward, "Review Essay: Religionists and Theologians: Toward a Politics of Difference", Modern Theology 16:541-547.

[31] "The Study of Religion", 204. See also page 208, where Hyman suggests that the priorities of similarities and unities that often accompany comparative studies need to be reconsidered.

[32] "The Study of Religion", 215.

[33] "The Study of Religion", 217.

Kṛṣṇa's identification with humanity and Christ's identification with humanity, even though, as a Christian scholar, I am engaging in the comparative venture with "identification" in mind, a theme that one finds specifically in christological studies. To ask these questions and others like them is necessary to the comparative venture and, as Hyman states representing Ward, allows us to "secure the very difference and openness that religious studies prizes".[34] But at the same time this methodology must not be seen as fostering a "ghetto-like" mentality, for my approach of both raising theological categories held essential to my tradition and being open to the reverse guards against this criticism. My approach might be considered kin in some sense to "the liberal 'take'" of the matter, which is "to foster openness in theological exploration", leading to "resisting the temptation to consider theology as largely a matter of learning an insider's language".[35] This temptation will, as Marsh observes, "never be enough theologically to do justice to a God who is said to be incarnate in the world".[36]

Another hotly debated issue closely linked to the imposition of western theological / philosophical categories, and an issue that directly relates to my methodology of biblical interpretation, is that of postcolonial biblical hermeneutics. It is closely linked to our imposition issue because scholars such as Richard King have theorized that western Imperialism as it affects the scholarly discipline known as (western) Orientalism is directly related to the problem of viewing Indian religions from the rationale of western categories,[37]

---

[34] "The Study of Religion", 204. Ward, though, asserts, according to Hyman, that the liberal methodology of religious studies actually undermines "its ethical commitment to difference, otherness, openness, and tolerance" (p. 204).

[35] Marsh, "The Experience of Theological Education", 156.

[36] "The Experience of Theological Education", 156. Marsh insightfully concludes,

> And the resistance to turning theology solely into an insider's discipline entails recognizing the respect which the "other" (the religious other, the disciplinary other, the non-believing other) commands in her or his otherness. Theological education in such a climate will always be even harder than it is already seen to be, for it will require its participants to learn more than a single language (p. 156).

In the all-important context of Christian community, this kind of "theological liberalism", writes Marsh, "seeks to respect the church within the context of a wider web of communal contexts within which, and in relation to which, the Christian undertakes theological reflection" (p. 157).

[37] The criticism does not stop here. Sugirtharajah mentions Edward W. Said's Orientalism (London: Penguin Books, 1985), which charged that "Orientalism" was a vehicle by which certain western power figures dominated, restructured, and held authority over the Orient. Further, knowledge of the "other" culture results in power. Thus the discipline of Orientalism operated on the assumption that studying cultures of the Orient resulted in knowing better how to rule over those other cultures (Sugirtharajah, Postcolonial Criticism and Biblical Hermeneutics, 15). Violence also played a part in the mix (perhaps needless to say). Dipesh Chakrabarty quotes Alexander Dow's multivolume History of Hindostan, published from 1770 to 1772. Dow writes to

as I have briefly documented earlier and as he deeply investigates in another work.[38] Moreover, included in this rationale is what R. S. Sugirtharajah has severely criticized (and in many instances I share his criticisms), namely, European colonialist interpretations of biblical passages in substantiation of the colonialist agenda.[39] Though there are several expressions of postcolonialism,[40] I shall focus upon the postcolonialism documented by Sugirtharajah.

Sugirtharajah's postcolonial hermeneutic alternative is what he labels "a hybridized form of textual interpretation".[41] This includes "critical integration" that "deflates particularisms" and "facilitates redefinitions of identities".[42] Sugirtharajah suggests we read the scores of religious texts in "comparative and inclusive ways" in order to "avoid any kind of sectarian essentializing leading to religious fanaticism".[43] He is careful to state that his way of an inclusive

---

the King: "The success of Your Majesty's arms has laid open the East to the researches of the curious." Chakrabarty states that even at that time "one did not need a Michel Foucault [and Said] to uncover the connection between violence and knowledge" ("Postcoloniality and the Artifice of History: Who Speaks for 'Indian' Pasts?" Representations 37 [Winter 1992]: 5).

38 Richard King, Orientalism and Religion: Postcolonial Theory, India and 'the Mystic East' (London: Routledge, 1999). His discussion of the term "Hinduism" as an invention of western scholars may be of special interest (pp. 96-117). See also Sharada Sugirtharaja, Imagining Hinduism: A Postcolonial Perspective (London: Routledge, 2003). Here Sugirtharaja, working with postcolonial categories, attempts to show how Hinduism has been manufactured through western categories. This critique, argues Sugirtharajah, does not spare Hindu discourse about itself, for it also has been influenced by Orientalism.

39 Postcolonial Criticism and Biblical Hermeneutics. See throughout. See also his Asian Biblical Hermeneutics and Postcolonialism: Contesting the Interpretations (Sheffield: Sheffield Academic Press, 1999). In this latter work Sugirtharajah offers two interpretive tasks that follow closely from the postcolonial agenda. First "is to interrogate the biblical narratives and the interpretations which legitimize and reinscribe colonial interests". Second "is to engage in an emancipatory reading of the texts, informed by a hermeneutic yoked to postcolonial concerns" (pp. 18-19).

40 King mentions at least two on page 191 of his Orientalism and Religion, that of "a romanticized search for the heroic subaltern" and that of "a deconstructionist/Foucauldian stance that remains skeptical of the existence of anything outside of discursive power relation". Subalternity may be characterized as holding to "the demographic difference between the total Indian population and all those whom we have described as the 'elite'" (King, Orientalism and Religion, 190, quoting Ranajit Guha, "On Some Aspects of the Historiography of Colonial India", in Subaltern Studies 1 [Delhi: Oxford University Press, 1982], 8).

41 Postcolonial Criticism and Biblical Hermeneutics, 6.

42 Postcolonial Criticism and Biblical Hermeneutics, 194.

43 Postcolonial Criticism and Biblical Hermeneutics, 204. This is akin to Stanley Samartha's portrayal of the "Christ-against-Religions" attitude that "goes hand-in-hand with tremendous economic power, military strength and political subjugation of

reading of texts is not a superficial acceptance or tolerance of religions, nor a method of defusing religious conflicts.[44] Rather, he describes his methodology as akin to "the Indian attitude, sarvadharmasambhava (acceptance of all religious experience)" which "allows one to accept other sacred texts as complementary disclosures" enabling one "to comprehend the analogous encounters of others, and to recognize and to revere them".[45] In what he calls "a wider textual interweaving",[46] he recommends the hermeneutic of reading the Bible alongside of Hindu holy texts in order to arrive at seeing affinities both in textual and conceptual categories[47] (something against which, to a very large extent, I argue in this work[48]).

But it seems that Sugirtharajah, while engaging in this "wider textual interweaving", nonetheless views the Bible in a certain way peculiar to his postcolonial hermeneutic, which is presuppositional, as we shall see. In his view postcolonial criticism hopes to accomplish several tasks, two of which I now list. First is "scrutiny of the biblical documents for their colonial entanglements". This method gives way to a reconsideration of biblical narratives "not as a series of divinely guided incidents or reports about divine-human encounters, but as emanating from colonial contacts".[49] Second "is to

---

nations". This quotation is cited in Vinoth Ramachandra, The Recovery of Mission: Beyond the Pluralist Paradigm (Grand Rapids, Mich.: William B. Eerdmans, 1996), 4.

[44] Postcolonial Criticism and Biblical Hermeneutics, 204-5.

[45] Postcolonial Criticism and Biblical Hermeneutics, 205. Sugirtharajah's alternate way of reading texts falls into the observation of John McLeod that postcolonial methods of "reading" contest "conventional reading methods and models of interpretation". Conventional reading methods "need to be rethought if our reading practices are to contribute to the contestation of colonial discourses to which postcolonialism aspires. Rethinking conventional modes of reading is fundamental to postcolonialism" (Beginning Postcolonialism [Manchester: Manchester University Press, 2000], 33-34). Stanley Samartha holds a somewhat similar view to Sugirtharajah's sarvadharmasambhava. Ramachandra describes Samartha's view as "an approach that has as its basic premise an understanding of the 'great religious traditions' as embodying different responses to the Mystery of Sat or God (or of Ultimate Reality) so that the distinctiveness of each response, the Christian included, should be stated in such a way as to enhance a 'mutually critical and enriching relationship' among them all" (Ramachandra, The Recovery of Mission, 7). See Ramachandra's critique of Samartha on pages 13-33.

[46] Asian Biblical Hermeneutics and Postcolonialism, 93. See also Sugirtharajah's Voices from the Margin: Interpreting the Bible in the Third World (London: SPCK / Orbis, 1995), 289-403.

[47] Asian Biblical Hermeneutics and Postcolonialism, 93.

[48] I hold that there are textual and conceptual affinities that should be acknowledged, and I note them in this comparative study. However, I argue that many of the affinities are quite superficial when probed deeply. More on this issue later.

[49] The Bible and the Third World: Precolonial, Colonial and Postcolonial Encounters (Cambridge: Cambridge University Press, 2001), 250-51.

engage in reconstructive reading of biblical texts" and "reread biblical texts from the perspective of postcolonial concerns".[50] On these and other tasks Sugirtharajah admits that "The Bible is approached not for its intrinsic authoritativeness or distinctiveness, but because of the thematic presuppositions of postcolonialism, which are influenced by such cultural and psychological effects as hybridity and alienation triggered by colonialism."[51] As a result, "The interest of postcolonial criticism does not lie in the truth of the text but in the central question of its promotion of colonial ideology. The text is studied not for its own sake ... but for those intrinsic textual features which embody colonial codes."[52]

In Postcolonial Criticism and Biblical Hermeneutics the last word Sugirtharajah offers is that "postcolonial biblical criticism should go beyond the Protestant preoccupation with words [due, Sugirtharajah asserts, to the Enlightenment] and texts and scriptures"[53] and, since meaning is crucial but the texts that convey meaning are not,[54] "we should be prepared to give up the very texts themselves".[55] In his context of "Texts, dogmas, and creeds" (in my opinion a specific conservative Christian trilateral) the following statement by Sugirtharajah appears:

> I end with a quotation from a text which advocates both embracement and eventual abandonment, attachment and detachment from text. It comes from an ancient Indian text, The Upanishads. It contains this apparently sacrilegious thought: 'Read, study and ceaselessly ponder the Scriptures; but once the light has shined within you, throw them away as you discard a brand which you have used to light your fire' (Amritanada Upanishad 1).[56]

The implication here is that the Bible, in the end, should be discarded.

I now offer a few points that I hope will answer the overall gist of Sugirtharajah's alternative offering of postcolonial criticism. In doing so I not only address some of Sugirtharajah's statements documented above, but additional statements (here I am not exhaustive) made by Sugirtharajah.

Though many of Sugirtharajah's charges against certain European colonialist interpretations are justified, the alternative he offers leaves little or no hope of setting foot in an epistemological foundation that is stable. Here, though, one might ask why Sugirtharajah would accept this as being a problem!

---

[50] The Bible and the Third World, 252.
[51] The Bible and the Third World, 258.
[52] Asian Biblical Hermeneutics and Postcolonialism, 19.
[53] Postcolonial Criticism and Biblical Hermeneutics, 206.
[54] Postcolonial Criticism and Biblical Hermeneutics, 206-7.
[55] Postcolonial Criticism and Biblical Hermeneutics, 206.
[56] Postcolonial Criticism and Biblical Hermeneutics, 207.

In the process of resonating with a "diasporic hermeneutic" that includes hybridization, Sugirtharajah states, "It is essential to knowledge that there is no stable epistemological point of view, nor a homogenous unique truth."[57] But does not Sugirtharajah hope that his position is recognized by those outside his paradigm or hermeneutic, by those who do hold that there are stable epistemological points of view? If not, why does he engage his readers at all? If so, should not we assume that Sugirtharajah presupposes some sort of stable, or, perhaps, universally plausible epistemological point of view? Further, does not the statement that there are no stable epistemological points of view implicate Sugirtharajah's epistemological point of view?

Additionally, I believe that his overall alternative methodology goes too far by way of solution. In this relation I offer six points.

First, I offer in place of Sugirtharajah's "critical integration" a critical integration of my own.[58] Here one first critically engages the texts involved in comparative study in hope of determining, as best one can in light of the multi-layered and complex exegetical issues involved in "authorial intent", what the authors of the texts had in mind to communicate to readers. Then, the actual integration is the comparative venture itself, not the practice of reading and interpreting texts in an integrative fashion. The integration is the comparative

---

[57] Postcolonial Criticism and Biblical Hermeneutics, 191. On another note, I maintain that if scholars and other spokespeople are going to change the tide of outlandish European colonialist interpretations of the biblical text and European-dominated recordings of histories, offering what I believe is an unstable option on the part of Sugirtharajah does not help the situation any, except perhaps to raise awareness. But awareness due to analysis does not necessarily make this problem disappear. Dipesh Chakrabarty observes that

> insofar as the academic discourse of history—that is, "history" as a discourse produced at the institutional site of the university—is concerned, "Europe" remains the sovereign, theoretical subject of all histories, including the ones we call "Indian," "Chinese," "Kenyan," and so on. There is a peculiar way in which all these other histories tend to become variations on a master narrative that could be called "the history of Europe." In this sense, "Indian" history itself is in a position of subalternity; one can only articulate subaltern subject positions in the name of this history ... [J]ust as the phenomenon of orientalism does not disappear simply because some of us have now attained a critical awareness of it, similarly a certain version of "Europe," reified and celebrated in the phenomenal world of everyday relationships of power as the scene of the birth of the modern, continues to dominate the discourse of history. Analysis does not make it go away ("Postcoloniality and the Artifice of History," 1-2).

[58] Sugirtharajah's postcolonial critique applies to the United States as well as to Europe. On page 34 of Postcolonial Criticism and Biblical Hermeneutics he addresses "The question as to whether the United States is postcolonial or not", citing a few scholars who answer in the affirmative (pp. 34-36). He concludes, "Associating the United States with postcoloniality, captures many of the complicated experiences of contemporary American life" (p. 36). His critique therefore directly concerns me, for I am a citizen of the United States.

study, nothing more, which subsequently involves a "sitting beside" on the parts of the traditions and the meanings of their teachings. Thus, the traditions themselves are not blurred as they sit side by side, their particularisms not deflated, their texts not read in an inclusive way with the other texts but in a way that seeks to understand each tradition within its unique framework. The goal here, then, is integration—the comparison of similarities and differences—leading to religious dialogue and debate in order to see which tradition offers the more plausible and / or correct explanations of the issue(s) at hand.

Second, one of Sugirtharajah's intended goals, a methodology that "deflates particularisms", is itself a particularism.[59] Put another way, how can one escape embracing the particularism of deflating particularisms? One might also apply this line of reasoning in answer to Sugirtharajah's assertion that we read texts in "inclusive ways" in order to "avoid any kind of sectarian essentializing leading to religious fanaticism". Is not reading texts in inclusive ways (as Sugirtharajah understands the practice) itself a particularism? Moreover, is it not an essentialism of a different color?[60] Further, though I disagree with important parts of Sugirtharajah's alternative methodology, there are parts with which I agree, and which I would hope Sugirtharajah believes others who believe in the exclusive truth of Christ's gospel in fact adopt. For example, I for one strive to "comprehend the analogous encounters of others". But though in some cases these encounters are indeed analogous, in many other cases I believe they are merely analogous on the surface, as I seek to demonstrate in later chapters of this work.

Third, Sugirtharajah claims, "postcolonial biblical criticism should go beyond the Protestant preoccupation with words" in texts. Then he states that

---

[59] It is indeed difficult if not impossible to deflate them. Richard King also calls attention to criticisms leveled against Subaltern historians "for reintroducing the problematized notions of autonomous agency and subjectivity that they repudiated in their assault upon elitist historiography". He then quotes Rosalind O'Hanlon, who writes, "At the very moment of this assault upon western historicism the classic figure of western humanism—the self-originating, self-determining individual, who is at once a subject in his possession of a sovereign consciousness whose defining quality is reason, and an agent in his power of freedom—is readmitted through the backdoor in the figure of the subaltern himself, as he is restored to history in the reconstructions of the Subaltern project" (Orientalism and Religion, 191, quoting O'Hanlon, "Recovering the Subject: Subaltern Studies and Histories of Resistance in Colonial South Asia", Modern Asian Studies 22.1, [1988]: 191). The Subaltern project to which O'Hanlon refers is the Subaltern Studies Collective, which King describes as "a group of (mainly diaspora) Indian historians" (Orientalism and Religion, 190).

[60] A charge put forth by O'Hanlon (see King, Orientalism and Religion, 192). Similarly, Linda Alcoff asks postcolonial writers whether or not their narrative gives rise to the empowerment of the oppressed, resulting in yet another domination / dominated situation (King, Orientalism and Religion, 214, representing Alcoff, "The Problem of Speaking for Others", Cultural Critique 20 [1991]: 5-32).

"texts are not crucial but the meanings they convey are".[61] But how is meaning conveyed, if not from words themselves contained in the texts, words that string together to form propositions? (I mention briefly here that even Śaṅkara and Rāmānuja would disagree with Sugirtharajah.[62]) Or perhaps he means that words are important but that one should go beyond an unhealthy or epistemically dangerous preoccupation with them? Whatever the case, according to Sugirtharajah one should, in the end, discard the very texts containing those words. If this is the case, I argue that in the case of classical Christian orthodoxy this would clash with the meaning of, for example, 2 Timothy 3.16, a meaning gathered from this text's words as they are placed to form a proposition. The text translates, "All scripture is God-breathed [or inspired] and profitable for teaching, for reproof, for correction, for instruction in righteousness." One line of argument against Sugirtharajah's thesis is that Sugirtharajah assumes too much of humanity, if not an ultimate perfection in which one is free from wrong-doing again. For the intent of this passage is that the scripture is to be consulted continuously for guidance. The implicit meaning drawn from inference is that the passage, the "text", should not be discarded.[63]

Fourth, Sugirtharajah writes, "The greatest single aim of postcolonial biblical criticism is to situate colonialism at the centre of the Bible and biblical interpretation."[64] In doing this, the focus is placed "on the whole issue of expansion, domination, and imperialism as central forces in defining both the biblical narratives and biblical interpretation".[65] This is a startling aim. Could Sugirtharajah be painting with too broad a brush? I suggest he is. First, I know of several Christian missiologists and missionaries who are advocates of bringing the message of Christ to other cultures without at all changing unique indigenous elements of those cultures, unless there are elements that either directly or indirectly affect converts' relationships with Christ. One may still be Indian, for example, and follow Christ. In other words, as regards biblical interpretation and its application to other cultures, it can be done right.[66] And if

---

[61] Postcolonial Criticism and Biblical Hermeneutics, 206-7.

[62] See as examples chapter 1, section 1.2.3.1, and my discussions of Śaṅkara's and Rāmānuja's ideas on sāmānādhikaraṇya in chapter 1, sections 1.2.4.2 and 1.3.4.

[63] This is also the case with the injunctions found in Deuteronomy 6.1-9. One is to teach the statutes and judgments of the LORD to one's children, and they are to be written "on the doorposts of your house and your gates" (v. 9).

[64] Postcolonial Criticism and Biblical Hermeneutics, 25.

[65] Postcolonial Criticism and Biblical Hermeneutics, 25.

[66] The way to begin to "do it right" is to acknowledge, and address, how some, if not all, postcolonialists view the biblical concept of "God's chosen people". For example, Canaan S. Banana has called upon this concept as the Israelites' "justification for their conquering people in the land they viewed as the 'promised land'" ("The Case for a New Bible", in Sugirtharajah's Voices from the Margin, 73). Further, what needs to be addressed is Sugirtharajah's point that the Bible has been used as "a cultural weapon" by colonizers / missionaries, and that the colonized, as a result, used the Bible to their

it can be done right, perhaps there is in the Bible no colonialist agenda as Sugirtharajah claims? Second, Sugirtharajah is entirely welcome to carry out his stated aim, but I do hope he realizes that there are many biblical exegetes who do not have as an agenda expansion, domination and imperialism. I for one fit into this camp.

Fifth, even with concession of my fourth point, Sugirtharajah may still accuse me of an Enlightenment-influenced method of biblical interpretation, a method he says is shaped by rationalistic thinking.[67] I may have been seduced, asserts Sugirtharajah, "by the modernistic notion of using the rational as a key to open up texts"[68] and have failed "to accept intuition, sentiment, and emotion as a way into the text".[69] With this Sugirtharajah further charges that in large part biblical interpreters display a detachment from the world and its problems and are not concerned with social change.[70] In response, first, I resonate with and employ certain Enlightenment-based epistemological principles, as I have stated in preceding pages. Second, I simply cannot think of any other way of interpreting Sugirtharajah's work than to include the rational. As a matter of fact, I believe I owe it to Sugirtharajah to interpret his book as accurately as is possible, and employing rational methods certainly aids me in this quest. Third, I believe that Sugirtharajah wants me to understand accurately his rationalized thesis. Fourth, intuition and sentiment and emotion have indeed played a part in my interpretation not only of Sugirtharajah's work, but of the Bible as well. In my practice of hermeneutics all three of these are intertwined not only with each other but with rationality as well.

Lastly, contra Sugirtharajah's charge that in large part biblical interpreters display a detachment from the world and its problems and are not concerned with social change, first, it is my intuition that he is incorrect in his general

---

advantage by learning to "master it", as Sugirtharajah states, in order to resist the colonizers (The Bible and the Third World, 108). Sugirtharajah develops this latter theme in detail in his Postcolonial Criticism and Biblical Hermeneutics. For example, Sugirtharajah mentions a novel that is "overlooked in postcolonial discussion" though "relevant to our purpose", Akiki Nyabongo's Africa Answers Back (London: George Routledge & Sons, 1936). According to Sugirtharajah, the novel is about African Abala Stanley Mujungu, who challenges his parents' embracing of western culture introduced by a missionary named Hubert. At school, Mujungu clashes with and bests the missionary on questions of the Bible's recording of certain events and the missionary's interpretations / applications of them (see pp. 19-21).

[67] Postcolonial Criticism and Biblical Hermeneutics, 25.

[68] Curiously, however, Sugirtharajah employs rationality and historical / contextual method when, and for example, he challenges the NRSV's translation of kurios in Matthew 15.22 and 17.15, and when he discusses "Blessed are the poor in spirit" (Matthew 5.3) in the New Revised Standard Version (Postcolonial Criticism and Biblical Hermeneutics, 168-69).

[69] Postcolonial Criticism and Biblical Hermeneutics, 26.

[70] Postcolonial Criticism and Biblical Hermeneutics, 26.

quantification. Second, and here I think I am a microcosmic example of much of Christian biblical scholarship, the so-called "Great Commission" of Matthew 28:19-20 should include, along with evangelism, discipleship that includes teaching others to bring about social change in a positive way.

In closing, Richard King observes that "Much of the contemporary reflection that has gone on within 'postcolonial studies' has been informed by the popularity of post-structuralist and postmodernist theories within western intellectual circles since the 1980s."[71] Interestingly, I find elements in Sugirtharajah's work that are similar to western (if King is correct) elements of postmodernism, and I have addressed some of them in the preceding six points. A few of the elements of postmodernism listed in A. K. M. Adam's introductory work are as follows: the undermining of the "assumption of unshakable truth",[72] turning the tables on a "universalized conception of reason", for it is "nothing other than a power play",[73] "antifoundationalism",[74] no claim of "privileged access to the truth", "a provocative reading of topics" in criticism that is "relative",[75] no one correct or particular interpretation of a text due, in part, to no desire to pursue authorial intent,[76] and, finally, a deconstruction or disassembling of the biblical text by way of (1) calling into question "the presumption that there are things to which our words refer",[77] (2) antifoundationalism, and (3) freedom to interact with texts in ways that are considered abnormal by "institutionally legitimated interpretation".[78] Yet, though related to postmodernism in these respects, postcolonial criticism as represented by Sugirtharajah comes not by way of reaction to western modernity,[79] as does postmodernism, but by way of reaction against colonial

---

[71] Orientalism and Religion, 197. In note 53 on page 252 King states that much material has been published on the issue of the connection between postcolonialism and post-structuralism / postmodernism. King directs the reader to Bart Moore-Gilbert, Postcolonial Theory: Contexts, Practices, Politics (London: Verso, 1997), 223 n. 27, for a bibliography of works.

[72] A. K. M. Adam, What Is Postmodern Biblical Criticism (Minneapolis: Augsburg Fortress Press, 1995), 6.

[73] Page 14.

[74] Page 5, here drawing upon Cornel West's assessment of postmodernism. In addition, Adam lists what is akin to Sugirtharajah's statement documented earlier, "that there is no stable epistemological point of view, nor a homogenous unique truth". Adam writes, "Perhaps this is the most important lesson of postmodern thinking: We cannot guarantee either the correctness or soundness of our thinking by adopting the right method or by starting from the right point. Or, for that matter, by not starting at all" (p. 23).

[75] What Is Postmodern Biblical Criticism, 15.

[76] What Is Postmodern Biblical Criticism, 20.

[77] What Is Postmodern Biblical Criticism, 27.

[78] What Is Postmodern Biblical Criticism, 31-32.

[79] Sugirtharajah admits in another work that postmodernism and postcolonialism "have certain affinities", one of which is "discomfort over modernistic thinking" that spawned

discourses and interpretations of the Bible that have obscured and / or oppressed indigenous readings of texts.[80]

## 3. General Reasons for this Study

"It remains true", Geoffrey Parrinder states, "that very little critical study has been undertaken of the Avatar beliefs of India or comparison between them and Christian doctrines of the Incarnation". Parrinder continues: "[T]here is need for a comparative study to discover how much or little ground exists between beliefs in Avatar and Incarnation. It is remarkable that little has been written in European languages on Avatars and their meaning."[81] He also writes, "The source literature is immense, in Indian and Christian scriptures, and nobody could hope to read it all."[82] Quite true![83]

These observations of Parrinder have led me (an academic interested in Christian-Hindu dialogue) to pursue two paths that in the end become one. First is the obvious—to undertake a critical comparative study of the doctrine of avatāra[84] in Hinduism and the doctrine of incarnation in Christianity in order to

---

"an excessive reverence for reason". Further, "both are offshoots of the crumbling of Western political and cultural hegemony and its imperialistic tendencies". Yet, Sugirtharajah is careful to point out that the alliance between the two ends at a certain point, drawing attention to postmodernism as Eurocentric, its failure "from a third world perspective" to offer a theory of resistance and a transformative agenda, and its distaste for metanarratives (Asian Biblical Hermeneutics and Postcolonialism, 15). On this latter point, Sugirtharajah mentions postcolonialism's use of liberation "as an emancipatory metastory" (Asian Biblical Hermeneutics and Postcolonialism, 15).

[80] For this observation I thank Dr. David Cheetham of the University of Birmingham.

[81] Geoffrey Parrinder, Avatar and Incarnation: The Divine and Human Form in the World's Religions (Oxford: Oneworld Publications, 1997), 7,13-14. See also Ovey N. Mohammed, "Jesus and Krishna", in R. S. Sugirtharajah, ed., Asian Faces of Jesus (New York: Maryknoll, 1993), 9:

> At the turn of the [twentieth] century, the childhoods of Krishna and Jesus were much discussed by Western scholars. Since then, however, the comparison between these two savior figures has received little or no serious attention, even though Krishna has become widely known among Christians since the 1960s and there is great interest in interreligious dialogue.

John Carman states that early in his academic career he desired to research and to write his dissertation on the subject of "a Christian interpretation of the Hindu doctrine of incarnation" (Majesty and Meekness, 8), but, unfortunately for all of us, he never addressed the subject, for he was led to other topics of study.

[82] Avatar and Incarnation, 7.

[83] For a glimpse at this immensity, see Chinmayi Chatterjee, "A Note on the Vaiṣṇavic Concept of Avatāra and Līlā of God", Anvīkṣā 6 (March 1972): 1-11.

[84] This noun comes from the Sanskrit prefix ava (down) and the verb tṛ or tṛī (to cross over). The meaning of avatāra is, therefore, "descent". See Ronald M. Huntington, "Avatāras and Yugas: An Essay in Purāṇic Cosmology", Purāṇa 6 (January 1964): 8,

contribute to the eradication of Parrinder's expressed lacuna. The second is not so obvious. Since the source literature is indeed immense and no one could hope to read it all, I shall narrow my interest to a particular expression of Hinduism, the classical philosophical school known as Vedānta.[85]

Narrowing even further, within this school I concentrate on its two most influential theologians / philosophers, Śaṅkara (c. 788-820 A.D.[86]) and Rāmānuja (c. 1017-1137 A.D.[87]), and their views on the avatāra of Kṛṣṇa.[88] As

---

and Sir Monier Monier-Williams, A Sanskrit-English Dictionary (Delhi: Motilal Banarsidass, 1990), 99. Monier-Williams continues: "(especially of a deity from heaven), appearance of any deity upon earth (but more particularly the incarnations of Vishṇu in ten principal forms, viz. the fish, tortoise, boar, man-lion, dwarf, the two Rāmas, Kṛishṇa, Buddha, and Kalki)". The list varies in other editions or versions of the MBh. For example, Parrinder notes the list of "swan, fish, tortoise, boar, man-lion, dwarf, Rāma with the axe, Rāma, Krishna, and Kalkin", and further notes that in other lists no swan is mentioned and is replaced with yet another Rāma. In later works, such as the BP, the number increases to 22 (Parrinder, Avatar and Incarnation, 22 [the 22 avatāra-s are listed on p. 75]; Julius Lipner, "Avatāra and Incarnation?" in Re-Visioning India's Religious Traditions: Essays in Honour of Eric Lott, ed. David C. Scott and Israel Selvanayagam [Delhi: ISPCK: 1996], 134). Huntington concurs, and states, "Unanimity with regard to the number and identity of the avatāras is not an established fact." Huntington then notes BP 2.7.1-38, "where 24 avatāras are listed" ("Avatāras and Yugas", 9). Huntington also calls attention to a group of 19 in the Garuḍa Purāṇa ("Avatāras and Yugas", 15), and to 39 vibhavas or manifestations of the supreme being in the Ahirbudhnya Saṁhitā (Avatāras and Yugas", 15; see the list, name by name, in Svāmī Ādidevānanda, trans., Yatīndramatadīpikā by Śrīnivāsadāsa [Mylapore: Sri Ramakrishna Math, n.d.], 204 n. 21). See also Chatterjee, "A Note on the Vaiṣṇavic Concept of Avatāra and Līlā of God", 1-5, Alain Daniélou, The Myths and Gods of India: The Classic Work on Hindu Polytheism from the Princeton Bollingen Series (Rochester, Vt.: Inner Traditions International, 1991), 164-87, and Carman, Majesty and Meekness, 210-12. Finally, Lipner states that the Gītagovinda by Jayadeva (twelfth century Sanskrit poem) refers to ten descents of Kṛṣṇa ("Avatāra and Incarnation?", 134).

[85] Vedānta literally means "end (anta) of the Vedas". Thus Vedānta may refer to the Upaniṣads as the concluding (anta) part (or even "goal" or "end") of the ancient Hindu holy literature known as the Vedas, or it may refer to one of the six classical schools of Hindu philosophy that finds its basis in the Upaniṣads. Either way, both definitions revolve around one specific point, namely that the Upaniṣads as a later philosophical corpus are the end, the goal, of the Vedas and the central philosophical treatise that elucidates the teachings of the Vedas. The school of Vedānta, then, concerns itself with the true meaning of the Upaniṣads.

[86] Gavin Flood points out that the exact time of Śaṅkara's life cannot be established with certainty. "Some scholars date him between 788 and 820 CE." See his An Introduction to Hinduism (New York: Cambridge University Press, 1996), 239.

[87] Flood, An Introduction to Hinduism, 136. These are the years given for Rāmānuja's life span as suggested by tradition. Carman questions the "suspicious neatness about the

regards Christianity, though throughout centuries past there have been many essentially different expressions of the doctrine of the incarnation of Christ, I shall concentrate mainly upon the conclusions of what is commonly labeled "classical orthodoxy", specifically the conclusions of the NC and the C. I note here at the outset that the classical orthodoxy of the NC and the C is that to which I adhere.

## 4. Goal and General Intentions of this Study

Jacques Dupuis writes,

> [O]ne thing is certain which needs to be stressed: Inter-religious dialogue in general, and 'Hindu-Christian' dialogue in particular, in order to be sincere and authentic, requires that both partners, while holding to the integrity of their own religious faith, endeavor to enter personally, as far as is possible, into the religious experience and world-view of the other.[89]

My goal is quite specifically that of the suggestion of Dupuis. As a Christian holding to classical orthodoxy, I intend to hold to the integrity of my faith and enter into, as Dupuis suggests, "as far as is possible" through a

---

life span of 120 years", which is "twice the normal span of 60 years". See his The Theology of Ramanuja, 27.

[88] In addition to Indian primary sources concerning various descents, there are also different types of descents. For example, according to Chatterjee, the Viṣvakṣena Saṃhitā mentions five kinds of descents: "Para (absolute state), Vyūha (emanation), Avatāra (incarnation), Antaryāmī (inner controller) and Arcāvatāra (incarnation in the form of image)" ("A Note on the Vaiṣṇavic Concept of Avatāra and Līlā of God", 3). These are further broken down into the categories of primary and secondary, and the latter is again broken down into two categories ("A Note on the Vaiṣṇavic Concept of Avatāra and Līlā of God", 3). For yet other types of descents, see Chatterjee, pages 4-5. Regunta Yesurathnam writes, "Hindus believe that God manifested himself in one thousand and one ways and forms." In the note for this statement he cites the BP: "the incarnations of the Lord are uncountable" ("The Adequacy of the Concept of Avatara for Expounding the Christian Doctrine of Incarnation", Dialogue & Alliance 1, no. 2 [Summer 1987]: 46,51n.20). Yesurathnam gives no book, chapter, and verse for the quote. Needless to say, if one were to undertake a detailed study of all the descents, it would fill several volumes.

[89] Jacques Dupuis, "Interculturation and Inter-religious Dialogue in India Today", in A Universal Faith?: Peoples, Cultures, Religions, and the Christ, comp. Catherine Cornille and Valeer Neckebrouck (Louvain: Peeters Press; Grand Rapids, Mich.: W. B. Eerdmans, 1992), 24. Lott makes a similar statement concerning understanding of the "other" religious tradition: "Our first concern in any valid research must be to understand that religious tradition, as far as possible from the perspective of its adherents" (Eric J. Lott, "The Relevance of Research in Religions: Understanding Avatara as a Test-Case", Bangalore Theological Forum, 10, no. 1 [1978]: 33).

phenomenological and comparative study, the experience and, in particular, the worldviews of both Śaṅkara and Rāmānuja and consequently their modern-day followers. Such a venture, writes Dupuis, is "a pre-required condition for the inter-religious dialogue between persons belonging to the two different faiths".[90] As a result I hope this work will aid both those who embrace conservative Christian perspectives and those that follow Śaṅkarācārya or Rāmānujācārya.

Francis Clooney offers additional advice, which I hope to keep, and articulates his position well:

> If I give an account of my beliefs, I then become accountable to a wider theological community that reaches beyond my own tradition. Even the most devout theologians have to defend their beliefs in a way that is at least minimally well informed about what others believe, and they must articulate their beliefs in a way that is at least potentially intelligible to theological peers in other traditions ... Admitting the intense particularity of their own beliefs and those central to other traditions, theologians must still learn to offer explanations for their faith that still take seriously and respect the theologies and beliefs of other traditions. Theologians of various traditions can consider together a variety of reasonable theological views regarding divine embodiment and thereafter investigate together whether there are reasons that favor one understanding of that embodiment over other such understandings. In this more concrete interreligious conversation ... theologians can find constructive ways to question one another, to argue intelligently among themselves, and to account for their differing conclusions about how and when divine embodiment has occurred and what it means. One can think about the options, sort them out, make comparisons, offer criticisms, and then make judgments about what is convincing and what is not ... But this interreligious theological critique will have to be at least as subtle and complex as the particular theological positions under consideration, as one explores with great respect the web of reasons, practices, beliefs, and pieties that undergird various convictions about God's embodiment.[91]

As mentioned earlier, my aim is to inform thinkers from all three traditions of the intrinsic differences between Śaṅkara's and Rāmānuja's Kṛṣṇāvatāra and classical Christian orthodoxy's incarnate Christ. I leave, however, more in-depth apologetic endeavors to those theologians who wish to pursue them. I hope this work will aid competent apologists of all three traditions to take

---

[90] "Interculturation and Inter-religious Dialogue in India Today", 24. Dupuis instructs the reader to consult Raymond Panikkar, The Intra-Religious Dialogue (New York: Paulist Press, 1978).

[91] Hindu God, Christian God, 126-27.

seriously Clooney's suggestions above, and one in particular, that "Theologians of various traditions can consider together a variety of reasonable theological views regarding divine embodiment and thereafter investigate together whether there are reasons that favor one understanding of that embodiment over other such understandings."

One unfortunate situation we face today is the general lack of in-depth treatises that compare avatāra and incarnation. In this work I explore (1) how the three different ontologies (those of Śaṅkara, Rāmānuja, and classical Christian orthodoxy) come into being through the exegesis of sacred texts and, with Śaṅkara and Rāmānuja, through utilizing certain other epistemological categories such as perception and inference. Then, (2) I document how these ontologies provide the foundation for further exegesis of sacred texts concerning the doctrines of avatāra and incarnation. Differences as well as similarities will be explored throughout in order to facilitate interreligious dialogue / theological critique / comparison that is, to use the words of Clooney, "subtle and complex".

On the parts of Śaṅkara and Rāmānuja, since I intend to focus on how their expressions of avatāra are derived from the exegesis of certain texts deemed authoritative for the Vedānta tradition, I shall investigate which sacred texts are an epistemological given, and why they are. This means that I shall examine their status and, further, how they fare both quantitatively and qualitatively with other epistemological categories such as perception and inference. This I do in chapter 1.

## 5. Specific Reasons for this Study

For someone interested and invested in Christian-Hindu dialogue, epistemologies, theologies and ontologies that are inextricably linked to avatāra and incarnation must be explored in order to understand, as fully as possible, avatāra and incarnation doctrines. This for me is the crux of the matter: The theologies / ontologies represented in the three religious traditions are intrinsically different from each other, and these differences thereby make these traditions' avatāra and incarnation doctrines quite different from one another, contrary to so-called common traits one may discover among them. Eric Lott rightly observes, "An area in religious studies requiring more extensive analysis is that of the relationship between theological formulations and the mythic/symbolic matrix in which they are grounded."[92] Concerning avatāra as a mythic symbol, Lott later states that it is in the bhāṣya-s (commentaries) of the theologians of Vedānta "that we find just how disparate are the conceptual frameworks within which this primal mythic symbol can be placed. The hermeneutical setting becomes determinative of 'avatara's'

---

[92] Eric J. Lott, "The Mythic Symbol Avatara in Indian Conceptual Formulations", Dialogue & Alliance 1, no. 2 (Summer 1987): 3.

meaning."[93] Likewise, Vinoth Ramachandra observes that when comparing avatāra and incarnation in the Hindu-Christian encounter the similarities often cited "are only superficial".[94] He then states that "the concept [of avatāra] must be interpreted within the whole Vedanta framework".[95]

On the other hand, respected indologist John Carman, in the context of Vaiṣṇava Hinduism in comparison to Christian incarnation, has argued that "there are significant similarities, and they are not just on the surface".[96] Carman explains:

> [T]hey [avatāra and incarnation] are expressions of a conception of ultimate reality that is personal and that is in relation to other realities which are distinguished from ultimate reality both by a radical difference in nature (God is infinite; all other beings are finite) and by a great distance between God's holiness and freedom, on the one hand, and the sin and bondage of finite beings, on the other hand. In both cases the act of incarnation or the multiple acts of descent need to be regarded as expressions of a basic quality in the divine nature ...[97]

It seems to me, however, that Carman's observations call for more questions and considerations that, in the end, actually prove my thesis that the many similarities often cited by scholars show themselves as surface similarities after careful probing of what Lott calls "conceptual frameworks". In the above quotation questions arise as to what constitutes, ontologically and functionally, "ultimate reality", "other realities" and "sin and bondage". The answers to these questions not only pose great differences between Vaiṣṇava and Christian ontologies, but also affect significantly what Carman calls attention to, namely the "radical difference in nature" between the "infinite" and the "finite" (and even these two terms need definition). Even in the framework of the Vaiṣṇava conception of avatāra with Rāmānuja, a theologian with whom Carman is well acquainted, ultimate reality differs in major respects from that of classical Christian orthodoxy, and the ramifications that this alone poses for avatāra and incarnation are of tremendous importance, and in turn render so-called

---

[93] "The Mythic Symbol Avatara in Indian Conceptual Formulations", 4. Lott concludes, "[I]t has become clear that this mythic symbol, like any other mythic symbol, has little meaning for believers apart from the conceptual systems within which it is interpreted" (p. 11). On page 50 of his "The Relevance of Research in Religions", Lott states, "Among the various schools of Vedanta there is clearly a significant variety of belief concerning the character of divine Embodiment. This reflects principally a variety of ontological attitudes."

[94] Vinoth Ramachandra, The Recovery of Mission: Beyond the Pluralist Paradigm (Grand Rapids, Mich.: William B. Eerdmans, 1996), 241.

[95] The Recovery of Mission, 241.

[96] Majesty and Meekness, 190.

[97] Majesty and Meekness, 190.

similarities, including those of Carman cited above,[98] only apparent, including the "radical difference in nature" that the Vaiṣṇava's avatāra and the Christian's Jesus are said to share one with the other in relation to finite beings. This radical difference is similar only in category, but different in type. This I hope to demonstrate in chapters that follow.

Lott's and Ramachandra's call to consideration of foundational theological and philosophical elements in examination of various avatāra doctrines therefore must not go unheeded, for, and as I seek to demonstrate in this work, it leads to a more accurate assessment of the issues involved in comparative analyses. In other words, foundations must be explored before proceeding to interpret and compare avatāra and incarnation.[99] Śaṅkara's advaita (non-dualism), also known as kevalādvaita (absolute monism), postulates Brahman as the ultimate and only reality, and therefore the material world as ultimately illusory. Rāmānuja's viśiṣṭādvaita (qualified non-dualism), which R. C. Zaehner labels "non-duality in difference",[100] sets forth Brahman as the ultimate, only reality and the material cause of the world, but the material world as quite real, and the material world as the body of Brahman.[101] The worldview that is the foundation for the NC and the C postulates an ontological and radical dualism between God and the material world.[102] As one might imagine, these result in essential differences not only between the avatāra doctrines of Śaṅkara and Rāmānuja themselves, but between them and classical Christian orthodoxy.[103]

---

98 Carman does, however, acknowledge "significant differences between the Vaishnava Hindu and Protestant Christian concepts of 'descent' or incarnation" (p. 190), and he somewhat probes them in the work cited.

99 Lott, mentioning Rāmānuja's "body of God" doctrine, a doctrine he describes as Rāmānuja's "inner core vision", states, "It is this core vision with its wide-ranging implications that must be seen as determinative of the meaning Ramanuja attaches to so many other doctrines, including that of God's embodiment on earth in his special avatara forms" ("The Mythic Symbol Avatara in Indian Conceptual Formulations", 8). See though, my chapter 4, note 264 for failure on Lott's part to see that the material for Kṛṣṇa's body (in Rāmānuja's theology) stems from the divya rūpa.

100 R. C. Zaehner, Hinduism (Oxford: Oxford University Press, 1966), 100.

101 Rāmānuja asserts that Brahman is the only reality, though in "qualified" ways. First, difference (bheda) exists between Brahman and the world and souls. Second, the latter two are the body of Brahman.

102 In Christian ontology / cosmogony God is wholly other than his creation. It may surprise some to learn that Madhva (1238-1317), a Vedāntin, was a stark dualist (dvaita). He claimed that Brahman, the world of matter, and individual souls are eternally and absolutely real and absolutely distinct from each other, matter and souls being dependent upon the independent Brahman. This ontology is quite similar to that of classical Christian orthodoxy, though Madhva is not so similar with regard to his doctrine of Kṛṣṇāvatāra in comparison to Christ (see section 5.1.2.2).

103 Franklin Edgerton writes concerning the avatāra of Kṛṣṇa in BG 4.7-8, "God condescends to become man Himself ... This is the beginning of the famous system of

In some of the literature written for comparison of the avatāra of Kṛṣṇa and the incarnation of Jesus, though similarities and differences are given, there is much that is superficial, and, may I be so bold to state, naïve concerning similarities. In the words of Julius Lipner, with this practice "the words 'avatāra' and 'incarnation' are comparable as two individuals plucked out of a row of similars, or by way of one-to-one correspondence".[104]

Many times conclusions about similarities leave, in the end, inquisitive readers with many questions unanswered because the conclusions drawn were not based upon adequately fleshed-out issues. Though these conclusions may be true to some extent, without more data they are not satisfying to those who feel the need to probe certain neglected, underlying ingredients they feel are central to the issues at hand. Second, oftentimes the so-called similarities are simply inaccurate due to lack of in-depth considerations.[105] Third, quite often issues that should be raised are not raised. Following are some examples.

---

avatārs or incarnations of God, which became so characteristic of later Viṣṇuism ... No Christian community needs to be told how such a doctrine of a loving God who is born upon earth to save the world can conquer the hearts of men" (The Bhagavad Gītā [Cambridge, Mass.: Harvard University Press, 1972], 155). Though Edgerton, it is true, is here concerned with his interpretation of the BG, the question nonetheless remains as to what the BG postulates as a worldview (or whether or not the BG postulates a combination of several worldviews), and therefore what exactly one means by the claim that Kṛṣṇa had "become man". Edgerton admits that the BG "regards God as immanent in all beings", and that one time it "speaks of the human soul as a part of God", but "Generally God is personally distinct from the human soul" (p. 139). He also states that "The whole material universe is, then, in some sense God's manifest form or material nature" (p. 154). Edgerton, though, does not probe the implications of the actual relation between the humanity of Kṛṣṇa and his deity in the light of these observations. He simply states that Kṛṣṇa appears "in his human aspect", and that "he is in truth a manifestation of the Supreme Deity in human form" (p. 105).

[104] "Avatāra and Incarnation?", 128. This statement by Lipner occurs in the context of his praise for Lott's call to analyze avatāra doctrines within their respective theological and philosophical frameworks. Lipner thus views as "quite proper" the practice of informed methodological comparative analyses of various traditions (p. 129), and states that 'difference" in comparative study has received "bad press", with major foci occurring primarily in the area of similarity (p. 129). Difference, states Lipner, "individuates and completes the context; it endows specificity. It is also potentially highly creative. It can stimulate new thought, initiate integration of ideas, close gaps, and, by exciting wonder or repulsion, create or reinforce a sense of identity" (p. 129).

[105] Moreover, given the vast diversity we see in the legion of religious expressions associated with Hinduism, statements are made in which all of Hinduism seems to be represented in one fell swoop. For example, though a significant popular work, Parrinder's Avatar and Incarnation, at times, paints with too broad a brush by speaking for all of Hinduism, a practice that by nature carries with it generalities that are, in the light of in-depth analysis, inaccurate. I list some examples of this in chapter 7.

### 5.1. Cases in Point: The Humanity and Deity of Kṛṣṇa

#### 5.1.1. OVEY N. MOHAMMED

In an essay entitled "Jesus and Krishna", Ovey N. Mohammed states that in order "to foster and promote what Hindus and Christians have in common, this article attempts to highlight similarities between the notion of salvation offered by Krishna in the Bhagavad Gita and the notion of salvation offered by Jesus in the New Testament".[106] Under the subsection entitled "The Incarnation of God", we read,

> Although Krishna in the Gita is unborn and eternal, he explicitly stated that he incarnates himself in the world "whenever the law of righteousness withers away and lawlessness arises" (4:7). The purpose of his coming into the world from age to age is "for the protection of the good ... and for the setting up of the law of righteousness" (4:8).[107]

Mohammed, immediately after this, states, "Krishna in the Gita is, therefore, true God and true human."[108]

But why, based upon the above statement by Mohammed in which he cites BG passages, should we conclude that Kṛṣṇa is a "true human"? First, I argue in chapter 4, sections 3.3 and 4.1, that although Kṛṣṇa, intra-BG, identifies with humanity is some respects, Kṛṣṇa is nonetheless four-armed. In this respect one is justified in questioning Kṛṣṇa's true identification with all humanity. Second, saṁbhavāmi yuge yuge, "I come into being[109] from age to age" (4.8), does not necessarily suggest this interpretation. In fact, Viṣṇu, as tradition suggests, came into being in the past as fish, tortoise, boar, and man-lion.[110] Buttressing this, in BG 4.5 Kṛṣṇa informs Arjuna that "Many of my births have passed",[111] referring to his past avatāra events. Third, though Mohammed may be speaking for himself as to what he believes the BG teaches, he does not state this in his essay, and seems therefore to neglect the problem of sensitivity to

---

[106] In Sugirtharajah, Asian Faces of Jesus, 9.

[107] In Sugirtharajah, Asian Faces of Jesus, 11.

[108] In Sugirtharajah, Asian Faces of Jesus, 11. See a similar conclusion drawn by Vitaliano R. Gorospe, in his "Krishna Avatara in the Bhagavad Gita and Christ Incarnate in John's Gospel", Dialogue & Alliance 1, no. 2 (Summer 1987): 55. In his discussion of BG 9.11, Gorospe states, "it is believed that Krishna assumes a genuine human nature" (p. 58). Note though that with statements like that of Gorospe it is difficult to know from which perspective "human nature" is defined. Certainly from the point of classical Christian orthodoxy the Kṛṣṇa of the BG cannot be said to possess a true human nature.

[109] Saṁbhavāmi (I come into being) of verse 8 parallels atmānaṁ sṛjāmyaham (I create myself) of verse 7.

[110] See note 84.

[111] bahūni me vyatītāni janmāni.

varying traditions in Hinduism. For example, what would a person familiar with Śaṅkara's advaita say regarding the conclusion that the BG teaches the true humanity of Kṛṣṇa? Speaking for myself, I do not believe that Śaṅkara's advaita teaches true humanity on the part of Kṛṣṇa in light of the fact that the tradition denies the ultimate reality of the material world. Śaṅkara denies, in the ultimate sense, the real, material body of Kṛṣṇa in his avatāra state: "He appears, by virtue of His Maya, to be embodied and born as man."[112] It could be argued, however, that intra-Śaṅkara the "true" humanity of Kṛṣṇa in advaita parallels our "true" humanity in advaita, with true placed in quotes to communicate that the phrase should be interpreted not through a dualist lens (for example, mine) but through a monistic lens. But Mohammed does not state this.[113]

#### 5.1.2. N. V. George

N. V. George lists Geoffrey Parrinder's well known "Twelve Characteristics of Avatar Doctrines"[114] under his own "Common Characteristics of Incarnation[115] in Christianity and Vaishnavism".[116] Of the twelve characteristics, George states, "When we closely examine the above mentioned characteristics, it becomes obvious that they are not simply the characteristics of the avatara doctrine of Vaishnavism only, but they are common characteristics of incarnation in both Vaishnavism and Christianity, though they differ in certain details."[117] But it is, exactly, these certain details that raise serious doubts as to whether some comparisons stated by scholars are in the end as accurate as they appear to be, and whether they are as common as we think.

First, on the positive side, George takes time to outline, albeit briefly, Rāmānuja's system as opposed to Śaṅkara's system, especially the doctrine of God in relation to the world. This, George instructs, accounts for difference between the two Vedāntins. "Unlike Sankara", states George, "Rāmānuja believes that the appearance of God as avatara is real".[118] George follows with

---

[112] A. G. Krishna Warrier, trans., Srīmad Bhagavad Gītā Bhāṣya of Sri Śaṅkarācārya (Mylapore: Sri Ramakrishna Math, 1983), 2,3. Noted from hereon as SBGB.

[113] It is true that BG 9.11 states that Kṛṣṇa has assumed a human form (mānuṣī tanu). Śaṅkara virtually says nothing about this verse in his bhāṣya, except merely to restate what the verse states (SBGB, 304). We should, however, assume that he would interpret this verse in the context of his introductory words, "He appears, by virtue of His Maya, to be embodied and born as man", quoted above.

[114] Parrinder, Avatar and Incarnation, 120-26.

[115] Note George's use of the word incarnation for both traditions. On this, see my chapter 7, section 1, which introduces the issue of interchangeability of the two words.

[116] N. V. George, The Doctrine of Incarnation in Vaishnavism and Christianity (Kashmere Gate, Delhi: Indian Society for Promoting Christian Knowledge [ISPCK], 1997), 125.

[117] The Doctrine of Incarnation in Vaishnavism and Christianity, 125-26.

[118] The Doctrine of Incarnation in Vaishnavism and Christianity, 76.

an extremely important observation: "God's body, according to Rāmānuja, is not really human and it does not belong to the realm of Prakriti [matter].[119] It is a mode of spiritual matter and as such is not limited to time and space. It is free from the laws of human nature."[120]

On the negative side, concerning Rāmānuja's doctrine of God's body not belonging to the realm of prakṛti, he states, "This view agrees with the Bible's narrative about the body of Jesus Christ. The New Testament speaks that Jesus was having a physical body which got glorified after his resurrection ... The glorified body of Jesus was not limited to time and space."[121] The latter two statements are true, but George does not mention that (1) in contrast to Rāmānuja's doctrine of the human form of Kṛṣṇa, Jesus possessed real humanity,[122] the same material that all human beings possess (he does not address and explore the fact that the doctrine of the humanity of the pre-resurrected Jesus is quite different from the Rāmānujan doctrine of the body of Kṛṣṇa), (2) in traditional Christianity the resurrected saints will possess in the afterlife physical bodies that are exactly like the resurrected body of Jesus with which he appeared on earth after his death, making the identity of the earthly Jesus one with the eschatological Jesus (a fact that sets this doctrine apart from those of Śaṅkara and Rāmānuja[123]), and (3) there is in the biblical witness and in the conclusions of classical orthodoxy no evidence that the material from which the resurrected are fashioned will be other than the material that Jesus currently possesses in his humanity. These three points I hope to flesh out in later chapters.

In addition to this prakṛti issue, following is another example of what I consider an extremely important detail not addressed by George. One of George's several "important characteristics of incarnation that are common in Christianity and Vaishnavism"[124] is that "Incarnation is both divine and

---

[119] That is, prakṛti in association with the three guṇa-s: sattva, goodness; rajas, passion; and tamas, darkness. Kṛṣṇa's birth is "unlike ordinary beings whose birth is caused by Karma associated with Prakṛti and its three Guṇas" (Svāmī Ādidevānanda, trans., Śrī Rāmānuja Gītā Bhāṣya [Mylapore: Sri Ramakrishna Math, n.d.], 163). Noted from hereon as RBGB

[120] The Doctrine of Incarnation in Vaishnavism and Christianity, 76.

[121] The Doctrine of Incarnation in Vaishnavism and Christianity, 76.

[122] This statement is made from my viewpoint of classical Christian orthodoxy. Śaṅkara and Rāmānuja would differ from Christian orthodoxy as to the actual makeup of a true human being.

[123] Richard De Smet makes an observation that contrasts the Indian view of avatāra (not limited to Śaṅkara and Rāmānuja) with Christ: "Krishna dies, but does not rise in a glorious humanity. Christ does rise from the dead in a glorious body, a living promise of our own resurrection in him" ("Jesus and Avatāra", in Jerald Gort, et al., eds., Dialogue and Syncretism: An Interdisciplinary Approach [Grand Rapids, Mich.: William B. Eerdmans, 1989], 162).

[124] The Doctrine of Incarnation in Vaishnavism and Christianity, 126.

human".[125] To his credit, George mentions Śaṅkara's position that "incarnation is appearance or illusion".[126] But George's claim that Vaiṣṇavism's "incarnation", as George labels it, "is both divine and human" is not true, at least with regard to Rāmānuja's Kṛṣṇa, as I hope to demonstrate in chapter 4.

Questions of historicity aside,[127] as regards Rāmānuja's Vaiṣṇavism, my

---

[125] The Doctrine of Incarnation in Vaishnavism and Christianity, 127.

[126] The Doctrine of Incarnation in Vaishnavism and Christianity, 126, though under the subsection "Incarnation is real".

[127] "Except Buddha [see n. 84], we do not have any authentic historical record to prove the historicity of the Vaishnava avataras." Yet, George admits, perhaps based on his experience in dialogue with Vaiṣṇava-s, "Even the purely mythological [fish, tortoise, boar, man-lion] avatars also must be treated as real ... [A]vataras of Vaishnavism are real in the sense that they are the manifestations of God" (The Doctrine of Incarnation in Vaishnavism and Christianity, 126). Diana Eck mentions that Kṛṣṇa, though lacking a documented name, date and footnotes, is still a "reality in the lives of people of faith" (Diana L. Eck, Encountering God: A Spiritual Journey from Bozeman to Banaras [New Delhi: Penguin Books, 1995], 90). Geoffrey Parrinder is careful not to affirm dogmatically the historicity of Kṛṣṇa, but affirms that followers of Kṛṣṇa believe him to be historical. See, for example, Avatar and Incarnation, pages 237,273. The fact that Jesus of Nazareth actually existed is not questioned at all by Parrinder, and in fact Eck, shortly after making the aforementioned statement, observes, "I confess that Jesus enables me to see something of God that I do not know in any other way: God truly grounded in the soil of human life and death" (Encountering God, 90). Lipner states that "Hindu apologists have sat more lightly to the historicity of the avatāra" ("Avatāra and Incarnation?", 138). Gorospe notes that people may believe in Kṛṣṇa "without any conviction that such a person ever existed in history" ("Krishna Avatara in the Bhagavad Gita and Christ Incarnate in John's Gospel", 64). John Brockington notes that some draw contrast between Christ and Hindu avatāra-s on the basis of the absence of any historical evidence for the latter. "There may be a limited measure of truth in this", Brockington asserts, "but it completely ignores the fact that for the average Hindu the narratives about Rāma and Kṛṣṇa are far more real—are viewed, that is, as having actually occurred and in that sense being historical—than any of the history of India that has been compiled over the last couple of centuries or so" (Hinduism and Christianity [New York: St. Martin's Press, 1992], 43). Kathleen Healy adds much the same. Though "Hinduism has been called the most searching quest for the divine that the world has known", states Healy, "the Hindu has never been able to find, in the eyes of the West, a true relation between the Absolute and the relative world of time and space ... 'What is history?', asks the Hindu philosopher. 'It is subjective, relative. Even the distant past changes in the perspective of time. Just as human beings have different appearances in different pictures, so God has different appearances in different ages: Krishna and Christ are the same'" (Christ as Common Ground: A Study of Christianity and Hinduism [Pittsburgh: Duquesne University Press, 1990], 104). Brockington and Healy correctly represent the general Hindu view, but it seems to me that the pursuit to answer this question on ontological grounds, that is, on the grounds of what in reality is the case, is not out of line. After all, and as we shall see, perception and reason play important roles in the quest for truth in the philosophies of Śaṅkara and Rāmānuja. If through perception

contention is that though there may be "common characteristics" (such as the simple facts of descent, special revelations of God,[128] deaths of Kṛṣṇa and Christ[129]) between Vaiṣṇavism's avatāra and Christianity's incarnation, when we closely examine them we find that common characteristics, once on the surface clear to some, become seriously blurred, so much as to become not so common. The reason for this is that certain theological categories inextricably linked to the doctrine of incarnation, once considered, are so significant that they throw serious doubt upon hasty conclusions drawn concerning so-called common characteristics. These theological categories are, specifically, (A) the intrinsic nature of (1) deity, (2) matter or the creation, and (3) humanity, and (B) the relationship (both ontological and functional) between them all.

Consider briefly as examples three early major commentators on Vedānta other than Śaṅkara and Rāmānuja—Vallabha, Madhva, and Nimbārka. (With the focus of this work being on Śaṅkara and Rāmānuja, brief consideration of these three philosophers / theologians affords me the opportunity to round out my study a bit more, since many consider Śaṅkara, Rāmānuja, Vallabha, Madhva, and Nimbārka to be the five major commentators on Vedānta.)

5.1.2.1. Vallabha

The theological / philosophical system of Vallabha (1479-1531 A.D.), named śuddhādvaita (pure non-dualism), differs from Śaṅkara's advaita or kevalādvaita, one important reason being that contrary to the thesis of Śaṅkara that māyā causes the jagat-prapañca (world of appearance), Vallabha proposes no connection at all between Brahman and māyā.[130] Brahman therefore is śuddha (pure), untainted by the stain of māyā. Further distancing himself from Śaṅkara, for Vallabha the jagat (world) and jīvātman-s (individual souls) are real in the truest sense (not illusory). They are Brahman in manifestation,[131] aṁśa (part) of Brahman and therefore brahmātmaka (of the nature of Brahman), so much so that "the effect [the world] is non-different [thus

---

one captures events, only to reason from them as if they were past occurrences, why is it then, that history should hold little (if any) sway over matters of such as this? Further, pertinent questions should arise regarding Rāmānuja's stress on the reality of the avatāra of Kṛṣṇa (stressed by him in part if not in whole because of Śaṅkara's doctrine; see chapter 4, sections 1.2.2 and 1.3.2). Given that stress, does it not imply that Kṛṣṇa should be a historical person? Moreover, given the aforementioned, should we not expect hard and reliable external, historical evidence for the existence of Kṛṣṇa as he is portrayed in the BG and thus during the time of the famous Battle of Kurukṣetra?

128 George, The Doctrine of Incarnation in Vaishnavism and Christianity, 127.

129 George, The Doctrine of Incarnation in Vaishnavism and Christianity, 127.

130 See S. Radhakrishnan, Indian Philosophy (Delhi: Oxford University Press, 1989), 2:756, and Mrudula I. Marfatia, The Philosophy of Vallabha (Delhi: Munshiram Manoharlal, 1967), 8.

131 Radhakrishnan, Indian Philosophy, 2:758; Marfatia, The Philosophy of Vallabha, 29.

abheda] from the cause [Brahman]".[132] The relationship, therefore, between Brahman and the world and souls is one of unqualified[133] (aviśiṣta, contra Rāmānuja) advaita,[134] oneness "as the relation of whole (aṁśin) and part (aṁśa) is"[135]; but the relationship, according to Vallabha, is śuddha, without any connection whatsoever with māyā. Moreover, Vallabha is considered a theist. He worships Kṛṣṇa as the Supreme Brahman and as source (the substratum of the universe, in that the universe is a manifestation of Brahman), as the sole object of the scriptures, and promulgates a doctrine of the avatāra of Kṛṣṇa.

Questions now arise when considering the humanity and deity of Kṛṣṇa, questions that are not answered or explored by George[136] or by, for example, Vallabha scholar Mrudula I. Marfatia, at least in one work.[137] Marfatia writes of "the incarnation of the Lord in human form",[138] and also states that "all these different incarnations [as fish, human, etc.] are but His manifestations".[139] In the light of Vallabha's doctrine of the world being the actual manifestation of the nature of Brahman,[140] one is left to wonder about the nature of the human body,[141] or "form",[142] of Kṛṣṇa. If prakṛti is Brahman, what of the body of Kṛṣṇa? Additionally, what is the nature of the human soul and / or spirit of

---

132 Marfatia, The Philosophy of Vallabha, 29. This statement of Marfatia concerns Vallabha's gloss of BS 2.1.14, which reads tadananyatvamārambhaṇaśabdādibhyaḥ, "The non-difference of identity [between Brahman and the world] follows from such terms as 'origin'" (my translation; Sanskrit taken from Pandit Shridhar Tryambak Pāthak, ed., Aṇu-Bhāṣya of Vallabhāchārya [Poona: Aryabhushan Press, 1921], part one, 124). "Thus", states Marfatia, "the world is of the nature of Brahman" (The Philosophy of Vallabha, 29).

133 Marfatia, The Philosophy of Vallabha, 34

134 Marfatia, The Philosophy of Vallabha, 33.

135 Radhakrishnan, Indian Philosophy, 2:760.

136 George includes a brief section on Vallabha (The Doctrine of Incarnation in Vaishnavism and Christianity, 80-81).

137 Nor shall I answer these questions in great depth in this work, as space limits my treatment of Vedānta to two of its theologians. I do hope, however, that some in the future might take up the task.

138 See also page 224.

139 The Philosophy of Vallabha, 133.

140 Marfatia cites Vallabha: "The form or body which He [avatāra] assumes is perceived to be the manifested nature of Br." (The Philosophy of Vallabha, 134). Marfatia states in representation of Vallabha, in the context of avatāra, that "It is the Lord alone who was (existent) in the beginning, who is whatever exists and whatever will be" (The Philosophy of Vallabha, 218).

141 Additionally, Kṛṣṇa is said to possess four arms (Marfatia, The Philosophy of Vallabha, 302). All commentators on the BG admit this, since the BG mentions the four-armed Kṛṣṇa (BG 11.46).

142 "The possession of form or otherwise should not be considered as two aspects of Br. but Br. Itself" (The Philosophy of Vallabha, 276).

Kṛṣṇa (if indeed such categories exist for Vallabha and his followers when considering the makeup of humanity[143])? Even setting issues of the human soul and the human spirit aside for the moment, can Vallabha's Kṛṣṇa be truly human[144] when we consider the nature of his flesh by way of logical inference stemming from Vallabha's doctrine of the relationship between Brahman and matter? Finally, and further positing classical orthodox Christian categories in the exchange, does Vallabha's Kṛṣṇa possess two natures, one truly human and one divine?

#### 5.1.2.2. Madhva

Madhva (1238-1317 A.D.) breaks with any of the kinds of non-dualism of Śaṅkara and Rāmānuja[145] and opts for a system that is "purely dualistic in character",[146] known as dvaita (dualism). Little known in the popular study of Hinduism,[147] the system of dvaita claims that Brahman, the world (jagat or loka) of matter (prakṛti), and individual souls (jīva-s) are eternally and absolutely real and absolutely distinct (bheda) from each other, matter and souls being dependent upon the independent Brahman. Madhva's three-fold ontology of God, individual souls, and the world falls under his theological rubric of independent reality (Viṣṇu) and dependent reality (souls and matter).[148] God, he says, is absolutely independent, separate, from creation.[149] Thus, absolute duality between God and souls and the world is based on the latter two being dependent upon God.[150]

---

[143] "The soul is said to be a part of the Lord" (The Philosophy of Vallabha, 269). In the context of Hindu thought in general, where the emphasis is on the soul being Brahman, this cannot be said to address the human soul per se.

[144] It may be that intra-Vallabha there is ontological identification between Kṛṣṇa and humanity.

[145] Both Rāmānuja and Madhva were very concerned with refutation of Śaṅkara's advaita, but "Madhva himself says little or nothing which may be interpreted as a direct attack upon his predecessor Ramanuja" (Surendranath Dasgupta, A History of Indian Philosophy [Delhi: Motilal Banarsidass, reprint 1992], 4:94-95). Madhva, however, does take issue specifically with Rāmānuja's doctrine of the world and souls as the body of Brahman. Moreover, Rāmānuja would have nothing to say in refutation of Madhva, since the latter was born after Rāmānuja's death.

[146] V. S. Ghate, The Vedānta: A Study of the Brahma-Sūtras with the Bhāṣyas of Śaṅkara, Rāmānuja, Nimbārka, Madhva and Vallabha (Poona: Bhandarkar Oriental Research Institute, 1960), 30.

[147] Though Dasgupta lists a long line of dvaitic ācārya-s (teachers) from the death of Madhva to 1882. See A History of Indian Philosophy, 4:56. Indeed, dvaitic ācārya-s continue to this day.

[148] Svāmī Tapasyānanda, Bhakti Schools of Vedānta (Madras: Sri Ramakrishna Math, n.d.), 144.

[149] S. Subba Rau, trans., The Vedanta-Sutras with the Commentary by Sri Madhwacharya (Madras: Thompson and Co, 1904), 54,187,192.

[150] Tapasyānanda, Bhakti Schools of Vedānta, 148.

Within this three-fold ontology is pañcabheda (five-fold difference), said to form the "skeleton of Madhva's theology".[151] The five differences are between (1) souls and souls, (2) God and souls, (3) God and matter, (4) souls and matter, and (5) matter and matter.[152]

In spite of an ontology that is quite like that of Christianity, Madhva's Kṛṣṇāvatāra "appears as if in a human form".[153] What does this mean? In a section of his BGB, Madhva, seeking to sustain an absolute separation between the Lord and matter, divorces the former from any connection whatsoever with the latter. In his interpretation of BG 9.11 he states, "Those deluded by ignorance of My true nature neglect Me. The words 'they neglect Me who has assumed a human body' should be understood in the sense of 'a form which appears to deluded eyes as human' ... [T]he Lord is not physically embodied."[154] Because of Madhva's vehement denial of illusionism and affirmation of stark realism, this means that Madhva's Lord is not physically embodied essentially as are other human beings. Thus, the form of Kṛṣṇa is solely divine, it being solely "of divine essence", for "It is sheer delusion to regard them [avatāra-s] as of human, animal or other mundane species."[155] This theology of avatāra is confirmed in Madhva's BSB, specifically under BS 2.3.46-50. Unlike souls, which are essentially different from the Lord (in the scheme of pañcabheda), the avatāra-s are of the same essence of Lord,[156] "essential (non-different) parts of the Supreme Being".[157] The soul is again different from the avatāra-s "because of his [the soul's] connection with the gross body", while the avatāra-s are not "limited by bodily existence".[158]

If there is any semblance between the Lord and souls, it is on the basis of the soul being a "reflection" of the Lord. Enter Madhva's doctrine of bimbapratibimba (original / counter-reflection). The essential meaning of bimbapratibimba is that all the objects of the world (including jīva-s and human bodies) resemble Brahman in that they counter-reflect the attributes that

---

151 Tapasyānanda, Bhakti Schools of Vedānta, 144.

152 Tapasyānanda, Bhakti Schools of Vedānta, 144. See also Dasgupta, A History of Indian Philosophy, 4:57.

153 Arvind Sharma, The Hindu Gītā: Ancient and Classical Interpretations of the Bhagavadgītā (London: Duckworth, 1986), 166.

154 B. N. K. Sharma, The Bhagavadgītabhāṣya of Śrī Madhvācārya (Poornaprajna Vidyapeetha, Bangalore: Anandatirtha Pratishthana, 1989), 198.

155 Sharma, The Bhagavadgītabhāṣya of Śrī Madhvācārya, 199. Lott concurs. "Madhva's principal concern", states Lott, "is to show how different the Lord's embodiment is from all other embodied existence" ("The Relevance of Research in Religions", 47). This is due to "the transcendent character of the Lord" (p. 49).

156 The Vedanta-Sutras with the Commentary by Sri Madhwacharya, 148.

157 The Vedanta-Sutras with the Commentary by Sri Madhwacharya, 149 (for BS 2.3.47) and 150-51 (for BS 2.3.48).

158 The Vedanta-Sutras with the Commentary by Sri Madhwacharya, 149-50, for BS 2.3.48.

Brahman possesses. Only in this sense can it be stated that "All this is Brahman." Interestingly enough, this is Madhva's way of explaining a mahāvākya of Śaṅkara, CU 3.14.1: "All this is Brahman." "Brahman", says Madhva, "is spoken of as identical with all, on account of there being all the qualities in Brahman which are predicated of the whole world".[159] Souls and material objects, therefore, are in the bimbapratibimba relationship with the Lord, and therefore are in stark ontological distinction from the Lord.[160] Not so,

---

[159] The Vedanta-Sutras with the Commentary by Sri Madhwacharya, 142, for BS 2.3.29. The comments in his BSB (for BS 2.3.28-29) are foundational to one of Madhva's interpretations of tat tvam asi ("You are That"). The soul is "That" only on the basis of its sharing similar qualities with Brahman. As Sharma states about bimbapratibimba,

> It would be enough to point out here that ... 2.3.29 gives eloquent support to M.'s [Madhva's] particular way of interpreting the language of identity used in describing the relation between Jīva and B[rahman] in Śruti texts like Tat tvam asi from the point of view of the measure of resemblance in respect of his essential attributes of reality, knowledge and bliss, which the Jīvātman bears to the Supreme (B. N. K. Sharma, The Brahmasūtras and Their Principal Commentaries [Delhi: Munshiram Manoharlal Publishers, 1986], 1:49; emphasis for tat tvam asi is original; second emphasis added).

In other literature apart from his BSB, for example his BGB, Madhva lays out a different interpretation of tat tvam asi, this time mainly on grammatical grounds in connection with the phrase before it (sa ātmā, the Self). Madhva says that the student Śvetateku has become arrogant, thinking "I am not a human being. I am either a God or part manifestation of Keshava" (Nagesh D. Sonde, trans., Bhagavad Gita Bhashya and Tatparyanirnaya of Sri Madhva [Bombay: Vasantik Prakashan, 1995], 58-59). It is in this context that his teacher (his father) scolds him. The famous saying "tat tvam asi" therefore becomes "atat tvam asi" ("you are not That") in scolding fashion (Sonde, Bhagavad Gita Bhashya and Tatparyanirnaya of Sri Madhva, 60). Here Madhva takes the Sanskrit of CU 6.8.7, sa ātmātat tvam asi (usually translated "the Self; you are That [tat]"), and reads it as sa ātmā atat tvam asi ("the Self; you are not That")—the compound ātmātat with the application of Sandhi (grammar rules) to contain in actuality the two separate words ātmā atat, here the negative "a" before "tat" (That), thus "not That" (see S. Radhakrishnan, Indian Philosophy, 2:746). In Sanskrit ā can stand alone or it can be an assimilation of ā + a (or a + a). In this case Madhva sees the compound "ātmātat" as a collection of the two words "ātmā atat", which, if placed together, read "ātmātat". Madhva then can confidently claim one of the most popular advaita mahāvākya-s as teaching his doctrine of absolute bheda, where a person is not the Self (Brahman).

[160] In connection with bimbapratibimba is Madhva's doctrine of viśeṣa. Viśeṣa means "particularity". Madhva taught that every substance has an infinite number of particulars. A tree, for instance, though possessing one substance, has a plurality of particulars (it is tall, wide, has a certain scent and shape, possesses branches, etc.). Thus, the attributes must be distinguished from the substance, though one with it. The essential meaning is that all the objects of the world (including jīva-s and human bodies) resemble Brahman only in that they share, or counter-reflect, the attributes that Brahman possesses. Only in this sense can it be stated that "All this is Brahman." As with bimbapratibimba, Madhva does not transfer his doctrine of viśeṣa to his avatāra-Lord

says Madhva, with avatāra-s. Rather, they are parts of the Lord, and thus are of his essential nature.

At least three differences therefore arise between Madhva's Kṛṣṇa and the Christ of traditional Christian orthodoxy. First, there is no human nature to Kṛṣṇa, including no human soul. Second, Kṛṣṇa is solely divine. Third, there is no true identification of Kṛṣṇa with humanity.[161]

5.1.2.3. Nimbārka

Nimbārka (twelfth century) claimed that bhedābheda (difference and non-difference) or dvaitādvaita (dualistic non-dualism) was true to the teaching of śruti (scripture), for śruti teaches difference and non-difference, dualism and non-dualism.

Nimbārka is a pure realist on all levels, unlike Śaṅkara. Kṛṣṇa is Brahman,[162] and as for the relation between Brahman and matter and souls, Brahman is matter and souls, for Brahman "has transformed itself into the world of matter and spirits".[163] Creation, then, is ex deo, and Brahman the material cause of matter and souls. In this sense Nimbārka is understood to be a monist. Just as the spider spins a web and the web remains a part of the spider, so it is that web and spider are one. Further, the essence of the spider pervades the web through and through. Nimbārka is fond of the sun-ray analogy, wherein the sun and its rays are ontologically one in the same way the web is one with the spider. It is in this sense that abheda śruti texts are understood. But there is for Nimbārka a dualism, a difference, between Brahman and the world of matter and souls. Here again the two analogies are used to show that the web and the rays, though one with spider and sun, respectively, are nonetheless different from the spider and the sun. It is in this sense that bheda śruti texts are understood. Nimbārka therefore claims to reconcile the two types of śruti texts, not illogically but with the epistemic ingredients of reason and perception by way

theology, for the avatāra-s are actual parts of the Lord himself. That is, they do not share in the essence of the Lord on the basis of viśeṣa, but truly and ontologically share in his essence.

161 Lott states that for Madhva, God's embodiment is "essentially different from other forms of embodiment ... His embodiments are special creations, described as unique 'manifestations' of the sovereign will" ("The Mythic Symbol Avatara in Indian Conceptual Formulations", 10). See also Lott's "The Relevance of Research in Religions", pages 49 and 50, for similar statements, and his observation that Madhva's doctrine of divine embodiments sets forth the teaching that the embodiments are not subject to the maturation process (p. 50). If true this would further distinguish Madhva's Kṛṣṇa from Christ.

162 Verse 4 of Nimbārka's Daśaślokī reads, "[O]n Kṛṣṇa let us meditate! On Kṛṣṇa, the Brahman" (Geeta Khurana, The Theology of Nimbārka: A Translation of Nimbārka's Daśaślokī with Giridhara Prapanna's Laghumañjūsā [New York: Vantage Press, 1990], 53).

163 Dasgupta, A History of Indian Philosophy, 3:405.

of logical analogies in order to illustrate the truth of śruti. Matter and souls are therefore aṁśa-s of Brahman[164] and are fully pervaded by Brahman,[165] the difference then being in name and form. For example, a snake's coiling posture is different from the snake itself and has no existence apart from the snake. But as Dasgupta states, "The coiled state of the snake ... is nothing but the snake by which it is pervaded through and through."[166] The bodies and souls of human beings in relation to Brahman are to be understood in this way.

I list here briefly some implications for the body-soul-divine relation in Nimbārka's Kṛṣṇāvatāra: (1) The body and soul of Kṛṣṇa are Brahman,[167] for "God is the only reality",[168] yet (2) they are different from Brahman in name and form. (3) Thus there is no ontological distinction between the human body / soul of Kṛṣṇa and Brahman,[169] for creation is ex deo.[170] (4) Related to the teaching that the whole creation consists of God's essence, in a certain sense there is, intra-Nimbārka, identification between Kṛṣṇa and human beings, for "there is no duality involved in the individual soul [and God]".[171] Here one may imply the same for the material body. (5) Yet in another sense there is not identification with all humanity, for Kṛṣṇa is also four-armed.

## 6. Conclusion

Because there is much written that does not probe adequately the issues at hand (and very little that does), for my part as a Christian scholar interested in interreligious dialogue, I intend to understand deeply, and represent accurately, the epistemologies, ontologies, theologies, and subsequent Kṛṣṇāvatāra doctrines of Śaṅkara and Rāmānuja. This is with the hope of facilitating productive dialogue between adherents of the three traditions.

---

164 Dasgupta, A History of Indian Philosophy, 3:412-13.

165 Dasgupta, A History of Indian Philosophy, 3:431.

166 Dasgupta, A History of Indian Philosophy, 3:434.

167 Jadunath Sinha states that "God is nondifferent from His human Incarnations, yet He appears to be different from them" (The Philosophy of Nimbārka [Calcutta: Sinha Publishing House, 1973], 10). Sinha then illustrates this with the coiled snake analogy. The avatāra may appear to be different from God, but is not, just as the coiled snake is in reality not different from the snake (p. 10).

168 Khurana, The Theology of Nimbārka, 122.

169 This is so because "[T]his whole creation ... consists of God's essence" (Khurana, The Theology of Nimbārka, 122). Perhaps for this reason Kṛṣṇa is viewed as a "plenary" (full) avatāra (Khurana, The Theology of Nimbārka, 56). Further, as is characteristic of many avatāra theologies, Kṛṣṇa's avatāra is "sportive" (Khurana, The Theology of Nimbārka, 56), thus a līlāvatāra (Sinha, The Philosophy of Nimbārka, 10). For līlā see my chapter 7, section 2.3.

170 "The whole creation comes into existence from Brahman" (Khurana, The Theology of Nimbārka, 121). This includes the soul (p. 123).

171 Khurana, The Theology of Nimbārka, 123.

When the worldviews and theologies of the three traditions are taken seriously, in turn serious differences result between avatāra and incarnation. Thus chapters 2, 3 and 5 probe the worldviews and theologies of the three traditions, and result in demonstration of deep-rooted differences between avatāra and incarnation in chapters 4 and 6, culminating with commentary on these differences (and others) in my comparative conclusions in chapter 7.

On the surface there is much in common, theologically, between Śaṅkara and Rāmānuja and classical Christian orthodoxy. Belief in God, in some kind of descent of deity, and the existence of the soul and the afterlife are but a few examples. However similar these appear to be, though, there is more difference than meets the eye when they are viewed within the respective worldview or ontology of each.

Finally, though there are differences of categories when comparing Indian philosophy and western philosophy, and though conclusions reached by the two are often drastically different, there are yet some common epistemic ingredients. In many western philosophies and in the philosophies of Śaṅkara and Rāmānuja, perception, reason, and verbal testimony play important roles. With religious philosophies we might also add to the epistemological mix the use of scripture as verbal testimony. In the next chapter I examine the epistemologies of Śaṅkara and Rāmānuja.

# CHAPTER 1

# Epistemologies of Śaṅkara and Rāmānuja

Śaṅkara and Rāmānuja, standing solidly in the orthodox Hindu world because of their acceptance of the Vedic Literature,[1] resolved to explain the problem of the one and the many. They set out to explain the nature of Brahman and how it is that Brahman can be one in relation to the plurality and complexity of, and in, the cosmos. In like fashion Christian theologians endeavored to do the same with regard to God and the world. As mentioned earlier, it is precisely within this category of ontology that one finds the seeds of vital differences when comparing avatāra and incarnation. But it is with epistemology that ontology finds its ground, and for this reason epistemology must be treated first.

## 1. A General Survey of Pramāṇa-s in Vedānta Epistemology

Valid means of ascertaining truth are known as pramāṇa-s, which are most important in the philosophies of India. Śaṅkara and Rāmānuja[2] rely heavily upon pramāṇa-s, for they are central to the pursuit of the knowledge of truth. The three crucial and fundamental pramāṇa-s are pratyakṣa (perception),[3] anumāna (reason) and śruti or āgama (scripture). Śruti also falls under the category of śabda (verbal testimony), which in a broader sense includes language both spoken and written.

Use of pramāṇa-s runs against the stereotype some possess regarding Indian philosophy—that Hindus do not utilize logic and its categories. Śaṅkara and Rāmānuja employed categories that are similar, at least category-wise, to what is properly basic in some western philosophies.[4] Further, in reading their works

---

[1] Though see note 9.

[2] And other early Vedānta philosophers such as Madhva, Vallabha and Nimbārka.

[3] Pratyakṣa may be used in two senses. First is direct sensory perception, that is, perception with the five senses and with the mind in the perception of physical objects. Second, it may refer to "direct vision of the Transcendent" (Eric Lott, Vedantic Approaches to God [New York: Barnes and Noble, 1980], 66). For the purpose of this study I shall use pratyakṣa in the first sense.

[4] See, however, J. N. Mohanty, "Indian Philosophical Tradition: The Theory of Pramāṇa", in Shlomo Biderman and Ben-Ami Scharfstein, eds., Rationality in Question: On Eastern and Western Views of Rationality (Leiden: E. J. Brill, 1989). Here

one cannot progress too far without realizing that they desired to think and to operate within the parameters of the logical application of pratyakṣa, anumāna and śruti.

Leaving for later the details of Śaṅkara's and Rāmānuja's utilization of pramāṇa-s, I wish now to address in general the interrelationship between the pramāṇa-s, specifically as regards the question of one pramāṇa over another. What is the practice of the two Vedāntins when it comes to weighing the importance and therefore the roles of the three pramāṇa-s? For example, does śruti hold sway over pratyakṣa and anumāna? If so, when does it? Is śruti to be believed no matter what one might conclude via pratyakṣa and anumāna?

I hold that with Śaṅkara and Rāmānuja we encounter an "on the one hand ... on the other hand" phenomenon. On the one hand, for these theologians pratyakṣa and anumāna, though important, cannot in and of themselves contribute much by way of the metaphysical or the spiritual, where Brahman can be found. As a result they often state that pratyakṣa and anumāna must defer to the testimony of śruti, especially in the quest to know Brahman intimately. For them, scripture is the "original source for the knowledge and attainment of man's supreme end, the ultimate reality, Brahman".[5] Indeed, one cannot read too far into their bhāṣya-s before noticing an abundance of śruti passages cited as proof for each position. Moreover, the BSs (as smṛti, secondary revelation) themselves command an acceptance of śruti, since 1.1.3-4 states that the knowledge of Brahman and Brahman's work concerning the universe follows from the total agreement of the statements of scripture.[6]

On the other hand, at times they place such a great deal of authority upon pratyakṣa and anumāna that even śruti must not contradict what is perceived and reasoned in everyday experience. In other words, if pratyakṣa and anumāna lead to a certain conclusion, and certain śruti verses seem to contradict that conclusion, then śruti has to be interpreted in harmonious fashion with what is concluded by pratyakṣa and anumāna. Śaṅkara and Rāmānuja, however, place no accusation of error on the part of śruti. Rather, the problem of the meaning of śruti lies with our understanding of it.

Such use of the three pramāṇa-s is not evidence of dishonesty or deceit on the parts of Śaṅkara and Rāmānuja. On the contrary, any religious, philosophically inclined apologist engaged in the interpretation of scripture and in the refutation of other views rightly fluctuates as to where s/he places the greatest weight of evidence for a position. The weight of importance and

---

Mohanty seeks "to caution against the temptation to view pramāṇa theories as near-kins of Western epistemologies" (p. 220).

[5] Julius J. Lipner, The Face of Truth: A Study of Meaning and Metaphysics in the Vedantic Theology of Ramanuja (Albany: State University of New York Press, 1986), 4.

[6] śāstrayonitvāt tat tu samanvayāt. For this observation see Eliot Deutsch and J. A. B. van Buitenen, A Source Book of Advaita Vedanta (Honolulu: The University Press of Hawaii, 1971), 53.

priority for any given pramāṇa varies from issue to issue. That is, there is a harmonization and mutual deference between the three pramāṇa-s with respect to the primary and proper object of knowledge. So, if Brahman is to be known, then śruti many times (not always; see below) is the dominant pramāṇa; if the object of knowledge is empirical or mundane, then śruti often defers to other pramāṇa-s and should be interpreted in the light of what is inferred by these other pramāṇa-s. The issues at hand determine whether the apologist employs scripture alone, scripture working with perception and reason, or reason and / or perception alone.[7]

Finally, even though the two Vedāntins differ with regard to the nature, scope and function of the three pramāṇa-s (and in what contexts, therefore, pratyakṣa and anumāna might defer to śruti), they agree that in the total scheme of things pratyakṣa and anumāna work together with śruti to reach true meaning.

## 1.1. Smṛti and Śruti

Generally, for all Hindus śruti as śabda has as its ground the metaphysical premise that "the universe stems from the eternal word [of God] (Śabdabrahman)".[8] In this sense śruti is not only eternal but is perfectly revealed to humans who first preserved it in oral tradition. Scripture as śabda is most important to Śaṅkara and Rāmānuja. Before I examine śruti, it is important to define smṛti.

### 1.1.1. SMṚTI

The collective term for writings that are considered "tradition" is smṛti. Smṛti is thus secondary revelation as śabda. As such, it is important and holy, but not on the level of śruti, which is scripture.[9] Examples of smṛti include all the

---

[7] The situations, theological questions, and texts with which Śaṅkara and Rāmānuja interact are many, and therefore to conclude that there is priority of one epistemic ingredient over others is too simplistic. One might further question Clooney, then, who states, "It comes as no surprise then that the Vedānta theologians ... defend the priority of scripture over reasoning as the primary source of right knowing" (Francis X. Clooney, Hindu God, Christian God: How Reason Helps Break Down the Boundaries between Religions [New York: Oxford University Press, 2001], 52). This is not the case, it seems to me, with Śaṅkara and Rāmānuja, and again, the supremacy of one pramāṇa over others is dependent upon what the primary object of knowledge is in any given situation.

[8] Frederick L. Kumar, The Philosophies of India: A New Approach (Lewiston, N.Y.: The Edwin Mellen Press, 1991), 475.

[9] Generally speaking, holding to scripture means that a tradition holds to the Vedic Literature, specifically the Ṛg, Yajur, Sāma and Atharva Vedas, Brāhmaṇas, Āraṇyakas, and Upaniṣads. The accepted thesis that the orthodox schools accept only the Vedic Literature as śruti has been challenged relatively recently. See Daya Krishna, Indian

purāṇa-s[10] (ancient tales), itihāsa (legend), and the BSs. Purāṇa-s are religious stories of the heroes and gods of India, a more famous one being the BP, a collection of 18,000 verses extolling the god Viṣṇu, the tenth part of which tells of Kṛṣṇa, an incarnation of Viṣṇu.[11] The MBh, the famous epic work, is an example of itihāsa. Contained within the MBh is a work familiar to all students of Hinduism, the BG.[12] The BSs are a collection of short, esoteric and hard-to-understand theological and philosophical statements written down by the teacher Bādarāyaṇa. The BSs are so difficult to understand that they cannot be grasped by the majority of readers without the aid of bhāṣya-s. Śaṅkara and Rāmānuja wrote bhāṣya-s on the BSs as well as the BG, which, together with bhāṣya-s on the Upaniṣads, constitute what is known as the prasthānatraya, the "three-fold foundation", specifically associated with later Vedānta epistemologies.

---

Philosophy: A Counter Perspective (Oxford: Oxford University Press, 1991), 61-94. Krishna challenges the notion on the grounds that, for example, certain ācarya-s (teachers) have written bhāṣya-s on smṛti literature, such as the BG and the BSs, thereby treating these texts as śruti. He also argues that some ācarya-s have not written bhāṣya-s on traditionally-labeled śruti texts but have written bhāṣya-s on traditionally-labeled smṛti texts, thereby buttressing his challenge concerning the traditional view of what texts comprise śruti.

[10] It is in the purāṇa-s where we find more extensive treatment of Kṛṣṇāvatāra (see Ronald M. Huntington, "Avatāras and Yugas: An Essay in Purāṇic Cosmology", Purāṇa 6 [January 1964]: 8; see also pp. 24-25). My treatment of Kṛṣṇāvatāra, however, focuses largely on the writings of Śaṅkara and Rāmānuja, especially their BGBs. Thus, there is on my part little interaction with purāṇa-s. For an essay on Kṛṣṇāvatāra in the purāṇa-s, see Sukumari Bhattacharji, The Indian Theogony: A Comparative Study of Indian Mythology from the Vedas to the Purāṇas (London: Cambridge University Press, 1970), 301-13.

[11] See Gavin Flood, An Introduction to Hinduism (New York: Cambridge University Press, 1996), 109-13 for a comprehensive description of purāṇa-s.

[12] See Flood, An Introduction to Hinduism, 14. The BG is a part of the MBh, which is classified as itihāsa and ākhyāna (narrative). See also Arthur A. Macdonell, A History of Sanskrit Literature (New York: D. Appleton, 1929), 281. Though Flood's comments that the BG is secondary revelation are technically correct, one should at least acknowledge that with Śaṅkara and Rāmānuja it is treated as if it were śruti, for they wrote bhāṣya-s on the BG (see n. 9). The same should be said of Madhva. See, for example, Sonde's observation that for Madhva, "Mahābhārata has as much importance as the Vedas and the Upanishads" (Nagesh D. Sonde, trans., Bhagavad Gita Bhashya and Tatparyanirnaya of Sri Madhva [Bombay: Vasantik Prakashan, 1995], 32). On another point, for an excellent review of the issue of whether or not the BG is part of the MBh, see Ishanand Vempeny, Kṛṣṇa and Christ: In the Light of Some of the Fundamental Concepts and Themes of the Bhagavad Gītā and the New Testament (Pune: Ishvani Kendra, 1988), 27-40.

### 1.1.2. ŚRUTI

Śruti is primary revelation. It is what was "heard" by the ancient seers and is thus scripture. Śruti may be synonymous with the Vedic Literature—the four Vedas, Brāhmaṇas, Āraṇyakas, and the Upaniṣads.

The four Vedas are Ṛg (hymns to the gods), Yajur (sacrificial texts), Sāma (songs with instructions on recitation), and Atharva (texts of magical spells and incantations). Brāhmaṇas are manuals of rituals, giving information about sacrifices, particularly sacrifices that perpetuate or sustain the universe. Āraṇyakas are forest texts dealing with interpretation of rituals, and serve as an interpretive connection between the Brāhmaṇas and the Upaniṣads. The Upaniṣads are concerned with philosophical questions or truths that underlie the sacrifices contained in the Vedas. The Upaniṣads address the nature of Brahman, the relation between Brahman and the jīvātman, and mokṣa ("liberation" of the soul). The philosophical emphasis of the jīva in relation to Brahman constituted the distinguishing mark between the Upaniṣads and other parts of Vedic Literature, so much so that it led the great Sanskrit scholar Arthur A. Macdonnell to state that "they [the Upaniṣads] really represent a new religion".[13] As we shall see, the great challenge facing Śaṅkara and Rāmānuja was whether or not their systems were true to the Upaniṣads.

## 1.2. Śaṅkara's Epistemology

In Śaṅkara's quest to know ultimate truth, he generally utilizes the three[14] pramāṇa-s—pratyakṣa, anumāna and śruti or āgama. I shall sum up briefly Śaṅkara's overall methodology here, and flesh it out bit by bit as we proceed in sections that follow.

Śaṅkara employs śruti, pratyakṣa and anumāna in the quest to determine the nature of Brahman, the jagat or loka, and the jīva, which in turn influence his doctrine of Kṛṣṇāvatāra. In Śaṅkara's system it is generally thought that pratyakṣa and anumāna cannot in and of themselves bring one to Brahman realization or to the realization that Kṛṣṇa is Brahman. This is due to the limit of the senses and the mind to contemplate a being that is beyond the senses and reason (and therefore is metaphysical). It is here then that śruti holds priority[15]

[13] A History of Sanskrit Literature, 218.

[14] Later proponents of advaita add three more pramāṇa-s to the list: upamāna (comparison), arthāpatti (presumption), and abhāva (negation). See R. Puligandla, Fundamentals of Indian Philosophy (Nashville: Abingdon Press, 1975), 208,307n.45. See also Swami Satprakashananda, Methods of Knowledge According to Advaita Vedanta (London: George Allen & Unwin, 1965), 35, where in place of abhāva he lists anupalabdhi (non-apprehension).

[15] "Among [the certain pramāṇa-s] the priority in terms of importance is clearly with verbal testimony, which, for an Advaitin, mainly means scripture" (Karl H. Potter, Advaita Vedānta up to Śaṃkara and His Pupils [Princeton, N.J.: Princeton University

and is an indispensable ingredient in the epistemological mix. "Brahman", asserts Śaṅkara, is "beyond the range of proofs".[16] This being said, note that at other times this does not prohibit Śaṅkara from making use of pratyakṣa and anumāna working together with śruti,[17] even to the point of placing them on par with śruti, in the quest for Brahman realization.

### 1.2.1. PRATYAKṢA

In simple definition, pratyakṣa occurs when the subject (let us say a person) perceives an object (let us say a jar).[18] Thus, the immediate conclusion,[19] the statement (śabda) "I see the jar", is made when sense-object contact is made between subject and object.

Even though in many places Śaṅkara and Rāmānuja claim that by itself pratyakṣa associated with the jagat cannot in the long run be used to determine the nature of Brahman (and therefore the real nature of Kṛṣṇa) and the jagat and the jīva (śruti accomplishes this), they differ as to how this is so.[20] It is with

---

Press, 1981], 97; see, however, my n. 7). See also Bimal Krishna Matilal, Perception: An Essay on Classical Indian Theories of Knowledge (Oxford: Clarendon, 1986), 32, where he points out that Śaṅkara considers the scriptures "self-validating", that is, they are considered a priori authoritative in all matters of affirmation.

16 Swāmī Mādhavānanda, trans., Vivekacūḍāmaṇi [Crest-jewel of Discrimination] (Calcutta: Advaita Ashrama, 1998), 155, par. 409 (here and throughout I assume this as a work of Śaṅkara, though it has been a subject of debate). Mādhavānanda states in the note, "Proofs—Other than revelation, viz. direct perception and inference."

17 Though this has been a point of division between scholars of Śaṅkara's system, as we shall see later. Note, though, that Padmapāda, a disciple of Śaṅkara and author of a bhāṣya (the Pañcapādikā) on Śaṅkara's BSB, specifically on Śaṅkara's gloss on BS 1.1.1-4 states (I think correctly) in his invocatory verses that Śaṅkara "attaches equal value to reasoning [anumā] ... equally with śruti" (D. Venkataramiah, ed. and trans., The Pañcapādikā of Padmapāda [Baroda: Oriental Institute, 1948], xlvi). Indeed, Padmapāda himself refutes adversarial doctrines on the basis of reasoning (see, for example, Venkataramiah, The Pañcapādikā of Padmapāda, 267).

18 Satprakashananda writes that "perception (pratyakṣa) is two-fold: external and internal" (Methods of Knowledge According to Advaita Vedanta, 35). External perception I describe above. Internal perception is the mental perception of pain, love, hate, joy, etc. See also note 3.

19 As regards pratyakṣa, "All sources of immediate experience ... are included here" (Karl H. Potter, Presuppositions of India's Philosophies [Delhi: Motilal Barnarsidass, 1991], 57).

20 For example, B. N. K. Sharma, a follower of Madhva, writes, "The Advaita school is not in favor of recognizing the absolute validity of Pratyakṣa. According to it, Pratyakṣa (Sense-perception) can only be given a sort of provisional validity (Vyāvahārika-prāmāṇya), which is to be stultified at the dawn of Advaita-Sākṣātkāra [intuition of non-dualism], which puts an end to all world-experiences, together with its dualities" (Śrī Madhva's Teachings in His own Words [Bombay: Bharata Vidya Bhavan, 1979], 43-44).

the role of pratyakṣa that Śaṅkara parts company with Rāmānuja. Śaṅkara's system does not use perception of the world of objects in the same way as his Vedāntic rival. Contrary to the views of Rāmānuja, Śaṅkara holds that what one perceives (by the power of māyā) in the jagat-prapañca is ultimately mithyā (unreal, illusion).[21] Māyā, Śaṅkara teaches, is the śakti (power) of Brahman that

[21] For a contrary view see Bradley Malkovsky, "The Personhood of Śaṁkara's Para Brahman", The Journal of Religion 77 (1997): 555-58. Here he argues for a realist ontology for Śaṅkara's advaita, where the jagat, upon enlightenment, is "relatively real" as compared to the Real (Brahman). This view, according to Malkovsky, does not admit to a total monistic rejection of contingent being. In this way "Advaita means that brahman and the world cannot be added up as parallel entities" (p. 555). "[T]he world is real", states Malkovsky (p. xiii), and upon enlightenment there is a new way of looking at the world, rather than an annihilation of it (p. 556). Thus, an "illusionist ontology" is rejected (p. 558). Malkovsky argues that the way in which Śaṅkara is commonly understood is but a development of post-Śaṅkara Advaitins (see Bradley J. Malkovsky, The Role of Divine Grace in the Soteriology of Śaṃkarācārya [Leiden: Brill, 2001], 49). This common view is well represented in this statement by Nikhilānanda: "The world that is seen extended in time and space [along with its various phenomena] ... are all nothing but the ideas in the mind of the Creator, i.e., Ātman as Īśvara" (Swāmī Nikhilānanda, trans., The Māṇḍūkyopaniṣad with Gauḍapāda's Kārikā and Śaṅkara's Commentary [Calcutta: Advaita Ashrama, 1987], 102 n. 3; noted from hereon as SBGK). Is Malkovsky correct concerning his observation? Consider this statement by Gauḍapāda (as tradition has it, the teacher of Govinda, who was the teacher of Śaṅkara): "Those ["objects" {see previous verse and the commentary of Śaṅkara}] that are cognized within only as long as the thought of them lasts, as well as those that are perceived by the senses and that conform to two points of time, are all mere imaginations" (SBGK, 102 [2.14]). Śaṅkara, in the gloss of this statement by Gauḍapāda, writes, "Ideas perceived within and existing as long as the mind that cognizes them lasts, as well as the external objects related to two points in time, are all mere imaginations" (SBGK, 103). This is characteristic of many other statements in SBGK. For example, "Hence it is established that the objects perceived in the waking state are as much imagination of the mind as those seen in a dream" (p. 105, based upon a similar statement by Gauḍapāda in 2.15 [p. 105]). Further, Gauḍapāda writes, "When the real nature of the rope is ascertained all illusions about it disappear and there arises the conviction that it is the one (unchanged) rope and nothing else; even so is the nature of the conviction regarding the Ātman [i.e., Brahman]" (SBGK, 109 [2.18]; emphases mine). Śaṅkara comments, "When it is determined that it is nothing but the rope alone, then all illusions regarding the rope disappear and the (non-dual) knowledge that there exists nothing else but the rope, becomes firmly established" (SBGK, 109; emphases mine). If tradition is correct in holding that Gauḍapāda was the didactic and spiritual grandfather of Śaṅkara, this is proof that what Malkovsky attributes to later Advaitins actually precedes Śaṅkara (though Malkovsky casts doubt upon the tradition [The Role of Divine Grace in the Soteriology of Śaṃkarācārya, 107]). Malkovsky concedes that Gauḍapāda's Kārikā is "monistic-illusionistic" (The Role of Divine Grace in the Soteriology of Śaṃkarācārya, 107), appearing to be "strongly influenced by Buddhist illusionism" (p. 109), but he casts doubt upon Śaṅkara's authorship of the commentary

causes adhyāsa (superimposition), which in turn causes avidyā or ajñāna (ignorance[22] or wrong knowledge). These are phenomena that will prove to be indispensable in determining the nature of the body of Kṛṣṇa, as I demonstrate in chapter 4.

### 1.2.2. Anumāna

Anumāna is the mode by which we come to a final conclusion from pratyakṣa. For example, as the result of pratyakṣa, the statement "I see the jar" is made when sense-object contact is made between subject and object. Anumāna then enables the subject to pass from the immediate conclusion made with pratyakṣa (I see the jar) to a reasoned or inferred conclusion about the actual relationship between the subject (person) and the jar (object). One then could infer from "I see the jar" to "the jar is real and different from me", as does Rāmānuja. Conversely, one could infer in this same relation that "the jar is ultimately not real", as does Śaṅkara. Later I shall examine the mechanics involved in these conclusions of Śaṅkara and Rāmānuja, but for now I move to our third and last pramāṇa, śabda.

### 1.2.3. Śabda

There are two kinds of śabda, secular and scriptural (śruti or āgama).[23]

#### 1.2.3.1. Secular Śabda

The underlying foundation of secular śabda is that words convey something. This may seem quite obvious and fundamental, but Śaṅkara spends a great deal of time on the nature of words and what they communicate.[24] As part of a

---

on Gauḍapāda's Kārikā (pp. 107-8, see also pp. 17-19, though note that on p. 19 Malkovsky states that Paul Hacker attributes to Śaṅkara authorship of the SBGK). Carman mentions "a modern reinterpretation of the philosophy of Sankara, which collapses the classical distinction between the lower knowledge of a personal Lord who descends to earth and the higher knowledge of the supreme Brahman, whose only human exemplification is in the life of the realized soul already liberated in this life" (John B. Carman, Majesty and Meekness: A Comparative Study of Contrast and Harmony in the Concept of God [Grand Rapids, Mich.: William B. Eerdmans, 1994], 208). Though Carman is specifically addressing the neo-Vedāntism of Radhakrishnan, has Malkovsky been indirectly influenced by Radhakrishnan (through the reinterpretation of Śaṅkara by Richard De Smet and D. M. Datta; see my chapter 4 n. 292)?

[22] And thus the result is stated by Śaṅkara in his bhāṣya on the MuU: "the phenomenal world of duality is a creation of ignorance" (Swāmī Gambhīrānanda, trans., Eight Upaniṣads: With the Commentary of Śaṅkarācārya [Calcutta: Advaita Ashrama, 2000], 2:171).

[23] Satprakashananda, Methods of Knowledge According to Advaita Vedanta, 193.

[24] It is important to note that both Śaṅkara and Rāmānuja considered language itself, especially within śruti, to be of particular importance in determining truth. As Lipner

lengthy section of his BSB, he states, "Just as ants constitute the idea of a row only if they march one after the other, so the letters also constitute the idea of a certain word only if they follow each other in certain order."[25] Words placed together in a sentence therefore convey propositional truth, such as the statements "I am walking" and "I see the jar."

Drawing together my observations concerning pratyakṣa and anumāna in the context of secular śabda, which later will be quite important for my conclusions regarding Śaṅkara's Kṛṣṇāvatāra, Arvind Sharma writes,

> The Advaita definitely denies that there can be any relation at all between two such disparate entities as spirit and matter. But at the same time, it cannot be forgotten that our investigation of experience leads us to the conclusion that they are not only together but are often identified with each other as implied, for example, when a person says "I am walking." Here the act of walking is obviously a feature characterizing the physical body; and yet it is predicated of the person's self which is spiritual. The only explanation conceivable is that their association must be mere appearance or, in other words, that the relation between them is ultimately false.[26]

1.2.3.2. Śruti and Smṛti

As to the importance of śruti as śabda, Śaṅkara states that "the validity of 'Śruti' will hold good in regard to the knowledge of Brahman".[27] Moreover, śruti is authoritative as it pertains to prescriptions for one's caste duty (jātidharma), one's own duty (svadharma). Here we have both the metaphysical (knowledge of Brahman) and the practical (jātidharma) addressed by śruti: "The sacred texts are certainly to be considered absolutely authoritative with regard to Brahman as well as with regard to religious duty

---

observes, "The impression is widespread that questions relating to scriptural hermeneutic and the theory of (sacred) language were of secondary concern for the master Vedāntins; this impression is false" (The Face of Truth, xi).

[25] George Thibaut, trans., Vedānta-Sūtras: With the Commentary by Śaṅkarācārya, in F. Max Müller, ed., Sacred Books of the East (Delhi: Motilal Banarsidass, 1988), 34:210. Noted from hereon as SBE. Note also that at times I will exclude Thibaut's parenthetical remarks in the commentary texts of Śaṅkara and Rāmānuja. If parentheses do appear in the commentary text, they are those of Thibaut. Any insertions on my part are contained in brackets.

[26] Arvind Sharma, "Who Speaks for Hinduism: A Perspective from Advaita Vedanta", Journal of the American Academy of Religion 68 (December 2000): 754.

[27] A. G. Krishna Warrier, trans., Srīmad Bhagavad Gītā Bhāṣya of Sri Śaṅkarācārya (Mylapore: Sri Ramakrishna Math, 1983), 630. Noted from hereon as SBGB. Śaṅkara's statement is in the context of a reply to a pūrvapakṣa (opposing argument) that śruti will prove to be invalid upon the dawn of vidyā, since when vidyā dawns, and all that remains is Brahman as pure consciousness, then śruti indeed will have no real existence.

[dharma[28]]."[29]

Though it is tempting, given Śaṅkara's advaita, to think that he is solely a metaphysician (thus only concerned with viewing the material world as illusory without any proof whatsoever), he proves otherwise.[30] He is quite concerned with the meaning of holy texts: "The comprehension of Brahman is effected by the ascertainment, consequent on discussion, of the sense of the Vedanta-texts,

---

[28] That is, acts prescribed by the sacred texts. A major difference between Śaṅkara and Rāmānuja is the nature of religious duties necessary for "Then therefore the enquiry in to Brahman" (BS 1.1.1) (see Rai Bahadur Śrīsachandra Vidyārṇava, Studies in the Vedānta Sūtras [Allahabad: Sudhindra Natha Vasu, 1919], 30,39), though Rāmānuja believes, with Śaṅkara, that knowledge of Brahman is the ultimate goal and that there are prerequisites to knowledge of Brahman, due to the opening words of the BSs (in 1.1.1), which are atha (then) and atas (therefore) (SBE, 34:12 for Śaṅkara's prerequisites; see also Swami Vimuktananda, trans., Aparokshānubhuti: Or Self-Realization of Sri Sankarāchārya [Calcutta: Advaita Ashrama, 2000], 4-6, pars. 6-8). In his lengthy commentary on BS 1.1.1 Rāmānuja understands Śaṅkara to say that the enquiry into religious duty obtained through reading the Vedas is therefore not a necessary prerequisite to the enquiry into Brahman (George Thibaut, trans., Vedānta-Sūtras: With the Commentary by Rāmānuja, in F. Max Müller, ed., Sacred Books of the East [Delhi: Motilal Banarsidass, 1989], 48:8; noted from hereon as SBE). Rāmānuja believes that religious duty is indeed an absolute prerequisite (taken due to his exegesis of atha and atas in 1.1.1, which call for antecedent conditions) to obtaining knowledge of Brahman. Sacrifices and works connected with one's station in life ("works enjoined on the different castes and asramas" [SBE, 48:18]; see also J. A. B. van Buitenen, trans., Rāmānuja's Vedārthasaṃgraha [Poona: Deccan College Postgraduate and Research Institute, 1956], 281, par. 126 [Sanskrit text p. 156]; noted from hereon as RVed) are performed for obtaining knowledge of Brahman practiced in the form of daily meditation (SBE, 48:16).

[29] SBE, 34:299.

[30] There exists presently the debate over whether Śaṅkara was a metaphysician only, whether he advocated enlightenment through analysis only, or whether he represented a combination of both. See the essays of G. C. Nayak ("Does Śaṅkara Advocate Enlightenment Through Analysis?") and Visvaldis V. Klive ("Analytic Philosophy and Advaita") in S. S. Rao Pappu, ed., Perspectives on Vedānta (Leiden: E. J. Brill, 1988), 18-41. Nayak understands Śaṅkara as advocating linguistic analysis of śruti as a means, but by no means the be-all and end-all, to enlightenment. Nayak leaves room for the ontological and metaphysical in Śaṅkara's view of enlightenment, and seeks a balance between the analytical and the ontological. Klive it seems incorrectly charges Nayak with saying that Śaṅkara utilized linguistic analysis only. Klive, however, was basing his charge on previous essays by Nayak, and not on this essay by Nayak. In this essay Nayak criticizes those who hold that the Advaitin was concerned with mere linguistic analysis (see pp. 19,23, and the notes). I agree with Nayak's view that Śaṅkara was undoubtedly interested in linguistic analysis (evidenced, for example, in Śaṅkara's concern for atha and atas in his exegesis of BS 1.1.1) as a means to enlightenment, though it is neither the only nor final ingredient in the process.

not either by inference or by the other means of right knowledge."[31] Here he places ultimate and sole authority upon śruti for attaining knowledge of Brahman, and consequently Kṛṣṇa's true Self. Yet, Śaṅkara also states, "inference [reasoning] also, being an instrument of right knowledge in so far as it does not contradict the Vedānta-texts,[32] is not to be excluded as confirming the meaning ascertained".[33] "Scripture itself", says Śaṅkara, "allows [this] argumentation". He cites BU 2.4.5: "The Self [using the tool of reason] is to be heard, to be considered."[34] Commenting under BG 18.50 in his BGB, Śaṅkara states that what Kṛṣṇa says about the nature of the self "is affirmed by the Upanishads, and is in accordance with reason [nyāya]".[35] Thus, his epistemology on the one hand exalts the authority of śruti, but in other places we see an importance of analyses of śruti working with anumāna, the former being the means to enlightenment but not without the role of anumāna in determining the meaning of texts.[36]

Finally, we might also add to this epistemological mix the role of sākṣātkāra (intuition), for it is here that Śaṅkara makes some interesting statements leading to the conclusion that in some contexts his sole authority is not śruti. Śaṅkara states in the commentary on BS 1.1.2 that "Scriptural texts, etc., are not, in the enquiry into Brahman, the only means of knowledge ... but Scriptural texts on the one hand, and intuition [sākṣātkāra], etc.,[37] on the other hand"[38] work together for the enquiry into Brahman. Śaṅkara then states that "intuition is the

---

[31] SBE, 34:17. Nayak asks the question, "How are we going to account for such passages in Śaṅkara? ... It is thus that analysis of the meaning of Vedānta passages comes to play a significant role in Śaṅkara for enlightenment" ("Does Śaṅkara Advocate Enlightenment Through Analysis?", 18-19).

[32] Nayak observes that for Śaṅkara the "comprehension or the understanding of the nature of ultimate reality [is] consequent upon the analysis of the meaning of the Vedānta passages" ("Does Śaṅkara Advocate Enlightenment Through Analysis?", 24).

[33] SBE, 34:17. See Lipner, The Face of Truth, 4. Lipner states: "The faith of the Vedāntins was not a blind, irrational faith. Though reason on its own was a treacherous guide in matters theological, directed and illumined by scripture it had a very important part to play" (emphases added).

[34] SBE, 34:17.

[35] SBGB, 599.

[36] Potter states that it is by śruti, then, that the Advaitin must ultimately defend his position, for it is by the śruti that he can oppose what critics would call an irrational system (Advaita Vedānta up to Śaṃkara and His Pupils, 98). Yet, Potter registers a caveat as regards Śaṅkara's view of śruti. Śaṅkara's two-tiered view of reality posits a lower reality and an ultimate reality. In the ultimate sense even śruti must be viewed as mithyā (false or unreal), simply because it (along with pratyakṣa and anumāna) assumes the instrumentality of ignorance (avidyā). In the end, all that exists is Brahman as pure consciousness, so the saying of BU 2.3.6, "neti neti" (not this, not this). See pages 54,96,97.

[37] "Etc." here meaning inference and so on. See SBE, 34:18 n. 1.

[38] SBE, 34:18.

final result of the enquiry into Brahman".[39] (As we shall see, this is one major disagreement between Śaṅkara and Rāmānuja.)

What do we do with such statements of Śaṅkara? A balanced view gathered from the writings of Śaṅkara should not dismiss the high priority given to sākṣātkāra, pratyakṣa and anumāna. It should take them into account, and lead to the conclusion that Śaṅkara was quite comfortable with the "on the one hand ... on the other hand" paradigm. That is, Śaṅkara in places sets ultimate authority upon śruti, yet in other places he puts such emphasis upon other pramāṇa-s (in this case sākṣātkāra, pratyakṣa and anumāna) that they seem to be placed at the very least on par with śruti (if not śruti deferring to the other pramāṇa-s), even when Brahman is the proper object of knowledge. Like Rāmānuja, generally speaking for Śaṅkara the issue of what pramāṇa is primary often depends upon the issue at hand, that is, what the proper object of knowledge is. But there is at times, as I have argued, the sense that pratyakṣa and anumāna hold sway over śruti, even when the proper object of knowledge is Brahman. Note his words in his BGB for BG 18.66 regarding the role of other pramāṇa-s in relation to the śruti: "Even a hundred statements of śruti to the effect that fire is cold and non-luminous won't prove valid. If it does make such a statement, its import will have to be interpreted differently ... Nothing in conflict with the means of valid cognition [pramāṇa-s] or with its own statements may be imputed to śruti."[40] My point here is that even when Brahman is the proper object of knowledge, at times Śaṅkara employs pratyakṣa and anumāna in analogies of everyday affairs in order to make his point concerning the nature of Brahman. One therefore would be amiss to segregate the use of śruti as the lead pramāṇa over pratyakṣa and anumāna, for his argument cannot hold if these are left out of the mix.

For my purpose, what this amounts to is that Śaṅkara, when reaching conclusions concerning the nature of Kṛṣṇa in relation to the human form of Kṛṣṇa, at times uses the other pramāṇa-s in a way that is on par with śruti in order to establish the nature of Kṛṣṇa and the mithyā of the jagat-prapañca (of which the human form is a part). For example, he employs pratyakṣa and anumāna in his rope-snake and conch-silver analogies.[41] I contend that these epistemological foundations influence significantly Śaṅkara's view of the

[39] SBE, 34:18. See also Thomas A. Forsthoefel, Knowing Beyond Knowledge: Epistemologies of Religious Experience in Classical and Modern Advaita (Burlington, Vt.: Ashgate, 2002), 170, wherein he mentions the importance of sākṣātkāra in the epistemologies of various Advaitins.

[40] SBGB, 629-30. On this Satprakashananda comments: "The Śruti is the authoritative source of knowledge in suprasensuous matters, but not in matters within the range of perception. The scriptural text cannot controvert facts of experience ... Vedānta philosophy does not accept the authority of the Śruti against the evidence of perception" (Methods of Knowledge According to Advaita Vedanta, 220).

[41] See chapter 2, sections 3.1.1 and 3.1.3.

body-soul-divine relationship in the person of Kṛṣṇa.

### 1.2.4. Other Epistemological Phenomena

Śaṅkara notes other phenomena that either grow out of the three foundational pramāṇa-s (pratyakṣa, anumāna and śabda) or are associated with them.

#### 1.2.4.1. Vidyā

Even though Śaṅkara oftentimes gives high standing to śruti, he nonetheless gives high standing to vidyā[42] (right knowledge, gained through śruti, pratyakṣa and anumāna[43]). In the process where one states "I see the jar", the conclusion through pratyakṣa and anumāna that "the jar is not real" (mithyā) is symptomatic, in a positive way, of vidyā. In other words, with vidyā one concludes that the jar is not real because reality is advaita—all that exists is Brahman. Once through śruti (and, I might add, other pramāṇa-s) one is made aware of the existence of Brahman as advaita, it remains the task of vidyā to supplement śruti in further enquiry into Brahman and the true nature of Kṛṣṇāvatāra. Thus Śaṅkara, though viewing śruti as authoritative, does not exclude the importance of vidyā. For him śruti and vidyā go hand in hand, and Śaṅkara came to the conclusion that the jar is not real because śruti and other pramāṇa-s teach that it is not real.

#### 1.2.4.2. Śruti and Sāmānādhikaraṇya

Śaṅkara makes use of sāmānādhikaraṇya[44] (correlative predication)—how non-synonymous words of the same case describe the referent that shares the same case—in both secular śabda and śruti. As with the pramāṇa-s examined above, sāmānādhikaraṇya, in an implicit way, plays a role in Śaṅkara's conclusions about Kṛṣṇa.

In Śaṅkara's advaita, śruti and sāmānādhikaraṇya reveal the truth of the fundamental and absolute (i.e., ontological[45]) unity of Being,[46] that Brahman is all there is. "[W]e know", writes Śaṅkara, "that the words 'Brahman' and 'self'

---

[42] Vidyā is knowledge of things as they really are.

[43] SBE, 34:6-7. More technically, "Perception is a two-fold being based either on the sense organs external and internal or on extraordinary concentration of mind ... Inference is of two sorts, Inductive and Deductive" (Vidyārṇava, Studies in the Vedānta Sūtras, 41).

[44] "The abiding of several things in a common substrate" (Thibaut's translation, SBE, 48:79).

[45] As we shall witness, Śaṅkara admits to bheda between Brahman and the world, but only on epistemological and subjective grounds, not ontological grounds.

[46] John Grimes, A Concise Dictionary of Indian Philosophy (Albany: State University of New York Press, 1989), 287.

are synonymous, being used thousands of times in co-ordination".[47] All is Brahman and reality is, ultimately, characterized by abheda. For this Śaṅkara would cite tat tvam asi ("you are That [Brahman]", CU 6.8.7). This mahāvākya ("great saying" from scripture) serves as a foundational hermeneutic for the interpretation of all other scriptural verses, even those verses that imply the reality of the jagat and bheda between the jagat-prapañca (of which the body of Kṛṣṇa is a part) and Brahman. With sāmānādhikaraṇya, since "you" (tvam) and "That" (tat) share grammatically the same case in this Sanskrit phrase, they both point to absolute identity—you are That.[48] Sāmānādhikaraṇya in this foundational verse is then the hermeneutic by which to interpret all apparently contradicting śruti verses implying a subject-object bheda. So in our example of the immediate conclusion (I see the jar) drawn from pratyakṣa, Śaṅkara would ultimately conclude (through the mechanism of anumāna) that the jar only seems to be a jar and only seems to be different from the "I". The reality is that the "I" is Brahman and Brahman is all there is; thus the jar, as far as it has been given a name and a form, is illusory.

1.2.4.3. Adhyāsa and Avidyā

Why does Śaṅkara conclude this? In a famous and pivotal passage that prefaces his BSB, and which is a key, succinct summary of his epistemological conclusions, Śaṅkara states,

---

[47] Swāmī Mādhavānanda, trans., The Brihadāraṇyaka Upaniṣad with the Commentary of Śaṅkarācārya (Calcutta: Advaita Ashrama, 1965), 152-53 (interpreting BU 1.4.10). Noted from hereon as SBUB.

[48] Malkovsky, in his "The Personhood of Śaṁkara's Para Brahman", 555, cites Śaṅkara's comments on BS 1.2.13 and 3.2.6, wherein the referent for "That" is Īśvara. Thus, he argues for no Īśvara-Brahman distinction (Malkovsky, The Role of Divine Grace in the Soteriology of Śaṃkarācārya, 47-49). But whether or not one employs the category of Īśvara-Brahman for Śaṅkara's higher and lower realities, the fact remains that Śaṅkara did indeed posit a Brahman with a double nature (or Brahman apprehended in two forms). In his comments for BS 1.1.11, Śaṅkara cites śruti passages that communicate Brahman's double nature. He writes, "All these passages, with many others, declare Brahman to possess a double nature, according as it is the object either of Knowledge or of Nescience [avidyā]. As long as it is the object of Nescience, there are applied to it the categories of devotee, object of devotion, and the like" (SBE, 34:62). Interesting is this last sentence read in conjunction with another statement made later by Śaṅkara in his BSB: "the highest Lord (parameśvara) also may, when he pleases, assume a bodily shape formed of Māyā, in order to gratify thereby his devout worshippers" (SBE, 34:80). Therefore Śaṅkara's Kṛṣṇāvatāra, even though associated with the supreme Brahman (parameśvara), still operates in the realm of lower Brahman as the object of avidyā, for many passages in the BG relate a subject (devotee) and object (Kṛṣṇa) relationship.

> It is a matter not requiring any proof that the object and the subject whose respective spheres are the notion of the "Thou" and the "Ego" ["I"], and which are opposed to each other as much as darkness and light are, cannot be identified. All the less can their respective attributes be identified. Hence it follows that it is wrong to superimpose upon the subject ["I"]—whose Self [Brahman] is intelligence, and which has for its sphere the notion of the Ego—the object whose sphere is the notion of the Non-Ego, and the attributes of the object, and vice versa to superimpose the subject and the attributes of the subject on the object. In spite of this it is on the part of man a natural procedure—which has its cause in wrong knowledge—not to distinguish the two entities and their respective attributes, although they are absolutely distinct, but to superimpose upon each the characteristic nature and the attributes of the other, and thus, coupling the Real and the Unreal.[49]

In the above Śaṅkara starts with the premise[50] that the "I" (ego, the subject, the "Self") and the "thou" (object acknowledged in pratyakṣa by the ego) are opposed to each other. How so? Latent in this premise is that the "I", which is Brahman, is the only reality. Therefore the "thou", i.e. the jar, has no ultimate reality. Śaṅkara then introduces us to another important phenomenon in his system—adhyāsa. This, he says, is the act of the subject ("I") imposing upon itself the object and the attributes of the object. That is to say, it is an act of avidyā to impose the illusory object (the jar) and its attributes ("jarness") upon the pure and only Self (ego), which is Brahman. In the last sentence above, Śaṅkara states that humans do not make the distinction that the "thou" (jar) has no ultimate reality and that the "I" is the only reality, but couple them in a subject-object relationship that views both the "I" and the "thou" as real.

Is the same the case with Kṛṣṇa? Yes, as I seek to demonstrate in chapter 4, but, in Śaṅkara's estimation, for a very good reason that still harmonizes with his advaita.

### 1.2.5 Summary

Śaṅkara's epistemology includes the use of śruti, pratyakṣa and anumāna (the three pramāṇa-s). Śruti works with pratyakṣa and anumāna (and sākṣātkāra) in the quest for the truth, but in different combinations of emphasis. Though on the one hand pratyakṣa and anumāna defer to śruti, on the other they are

---

[49] SBE, 34:4-5.

[50] Or presupposition? Forsthoefel describes adhyāsa as the "sine qua non of phenomenal interaction" in the epistemology of Śaṅkara (Knowing Beyond Knowledge, 62). Also, see Forsthoefel's work for social dimensions, such as relationship to a guru and caste status, that contribute to the religious experience that helps form Śaṅkara's epistemology (pp. 35-71), and social, cultural ingredients, such as ritual, pilgrimage and myth, that help form Rāmānuja's epistemology (pp. 171-76).

sometimes placed on par (perhaps over?) with śruti, depending on what the proper object of knowledge is (at times even Brahman). I conclude this not only from explicit statements of Śaṅkara, but implicitly as well, through observation of his epistemological method. Thus, in this sense Śaṅkara's epistemology on the one hand should be viewed as determined by certain śruti texts, that is, certain mahāvākya-s that inform his epistemology. But on the other hand, some of his epistemological statements include the charge to see śruti working with the other pramāṇa-s, implying that these other pramāṇa-s inform one's interpretation of śruti texts.

### 1.3. Rāmānuja's Epistemology

"The central idea of Viśiṣṭādvaita as a philosophy of religion is the integration and harmonization of all knowledge obtained through sense-perception, inference and revelation."[51] Evident in this quotation from P. N. Srinivasachari is the uncompromising importance of three pramāṇa-s. Like Śaṅkara, Rāmānuja recognizes pratyakṣa, anumāna and śruti[52] (and secular śabda).[53] Note, however, that though Rāmānuja differs from Śaṅkara in his theological and philosophical conclusions made after employing the three pramāṇa-s, including conclusions made about the nature of the body of Kṛṣṇa, he differs not from Śaṅkara when it comes to the interplay between pratyakṣa and anumāna as they relate to śruti in the quest to know Brahman.

#### 1.3.1. Pratyakṣa and Anumāna

A key factor of importance for later discussion of Kṛṣṇāvatāra is that viśiṣṭādvaita, unlike Śaṅkara's advaita, accepts the reality of the objects of the world as they appear.[54] In other words, and in direct contradiction of advaita, "The objects in nature are [a] given and are not made by thought. It is the

---

[51] P. N. Srinivasachari, The Philosophy of Viśiṣṭādvaita (Madras: The Adyar Library and Research Centre, 1970), 21.

[52] As do, for example, two later significant viśiṣṭādvaita theologians, Vedānta Deśika (1268-1369 A.D.) and Śrīnivāsa (seventeenth century). See Svāmī Ādidevānanda, trans., Yatīndramatadīpikā by Śrīnivāsadāsa (Mylapore: Sri Ramakrishna Math, n.d.), xi-xii. Noted from hereon as YS. In this work Śrīnivāsa explains in depth these three pramāṇa-s (YS, 8-49).

[53] S. Radhakrishnan states that both Śaṅkara and Rāmānuja accept pratyakṣa, anumāna and śruti as pramāṇa-s (Indian Philosophy, 2:488,672). Lipner concurs: "Rāmānuja seems to have accepted only three pramāṇas as valid: perception, inference and the word (i.e. speech/language) as testimony" (The Face of Truth, 26).

[54] As we shall see later, however, Rāmānuja moves beyond this basic realism to postulate that the world is the body of Brahman. This, of course, is the result of Rāmānuja's epistemology, that though pratyakṣa and anumāna have their places, in many circumstances one must appeal to śruti as the final arbiter for how one interprets the jagat in relation to Brahman.

function of thought only to reveal them and not to create them."[55] The objects of the world have a real existence apart from the mind or consciousness of individuals (and these objects co-exist with Brahman on one level of reality, which is ultimate, contrary to Śaṅkara's framework of two levels, which I examine in chapter 2). This is a major difference between Rāmānuja's conclusions rising from pratyakṣa and anumāna and Śaṅkara's conclusions from the use of them. Moreover, Viśiṣṭādvaitins claim that it is quite abnormal to give too great a weight to illusion (and analogies of illusion) in the epistemological venture.[56]

Pratyakṣa's tools are the sense (or sensation) modes of seeing, hearing, tasting, smelling, and touching. For example, someone perceives a jar through seeing it.[57] Pratyakṣa then works with anumāna in drawing certain conclusions. That is, the subject states "I see the jar" when pratyakṣa works with anumāna, then the subject further utilizes anumāna toward the penultimate conclusion that the subject ("I", the self, utilizing the mind) consciously perceives an object (jar). Thereafter, with yet further use of anumāna, the subject concludes that both the subject and the object are real, and that, contra Śaṅkara, there is bheda between the subject and the object. For Rāmānuja phenomenal experience shows this; in actuality, the conscious self (as subject) perceiving something (an object) implies (in the very act of perceiving something) that there is bheda between the subject and the real object[58]:

> If it is the nature of consciousness to be "proof"[59] on the part of a person with regard to something, how can this consciousness which is thus connected with the person and the thing be itself conscious of itself? To explain: the essential character of consciousness or knowledge is that by its very existence it renders things capable of becoming objects ...

---

[55] Srinivasachari, The Philosophy of Viśiṣṭādvaita, 24.

[56] See Srinivasachari, The Philosophy of Viśiṣṭādvaita, 57. Here Srinivasachari accuses advaita of using illusion as an epistemological starting point. This may be true in light of Śaṅkara's preface to his BSB (quoted earlier), where he, before any exposition of text, lays out the workings of adhyāsa. It may be argued, however, that Śaṅkara does so because he feels that the weight of śruti supports the view that only Brahman is real.

[57] Śrīnivāsa states under the heading of pratyakṣa, "The mode of perception is thus: The individual self [ātmā] is joined with the mind (manas), mind with the sense organ, and the sense organ with the object of knowledge ... Therefore when the visual sense is in contact with an object, in the form of a jar etc., ocular knowledge arises in the form 'this is jar'" (YS, 9 [1.14]).

[58] YS, xii. Śrīnivāsa comments, "Hence all apprehensions are likewise true, having for their contents objects affected with difference, because a non-differentiated object is never apprehended (YS, 18 [1.34]).

[59] Rāmānuja is most likely attacking Śaṅkara's introduction to his BSB, where Śaṅkara states that "It is a matter not requiring any proof". For Śaṅkara's statement see section 1.2.4.3.

> [Consciousness] is a particular attribute belonging to a conscious self and related to an object ... as appears from ordinary judgments such as "I know the jar."[60]

As regards anumāna, Rāmānuja says, "reasoning is to be applied only to the support of Scripture".[61] He, then, was not averse to the use of anumāna. In this respect Rāmānuja does not differ significantly with Śaṅkara. Rāmānuja, however, holds that there is no room whatsoever for Śaṅkara's sākṣātkāra, pratyakṣa and anumāna,[62] for all three are put to practice within Śaṅkara's framework of adhyāsa. Nonetheless, though both teachers differ as to conclusions made after appealing to pratyakṣa, anumāna and śruti, both indeed utilize the former two in conjunction with śruti.

How should we understand this when examining the interrelationship between śruti, pratyakṣa and anumāna? We must also ask the question as to whether or not in practice Rāmānuja believed śruti and the language (śabda) of śruti alone were sufficient for liberating knowledge of Brahman. After all, Śaṅkara stated in places that he believed śruti (and its linguistic analysis) alone was the final court of appeal in the inquiry into Brahman. Yet, at other times Śaṅkara placed a great deal of weight upon sākṣātkāra, pratyakṣa and anumāna, stating that they work together for the inquiry into Brahman,[63] and, as I have shown, in places they are viewed at the least as on par with śruti. Rāmānuja also does this. The answer to the above question, then, is that with Rāmānuja we witness the same "on the one hand ... on the other hand" phenomenon as we did with Śaṅkara as pertains to the interplay between śruti, pratyakṣa and anumāna. This is clear in what follows.

### 1.3.2. Śabda

Secular śabda follows closely our discussion above. That is to say, sentences used throughout the day in communication (such as "I know the jar") logically imply bheda between subject and object. In our "I see the jar" statement, Rāmānuja claims that the "I" and the "jar" are obviously different from each other; otherwise one could never perceive the jar in the first place. Thus Rāmānuja concludes through anumāna that there simply is no proof of Śaṅkara's abheda. He argues philosophically that for those who adhere to abheda, various means of parā vidyā (higher knowledge) are utilized for the realization of abheda, yet those very means "have for their object things affected with difference".[64] In other words, Śaṅkara's use of the clay-jar

---

[60] SBE, 48:56.
[61] SBE, 48:426.
[62] Vidyārṇava, Studies in the Vedānta Sūtras, 41, and Lipner, The Face of Truth, 4.
[63] SBE, 34:18.
[64] SBE, 48:39. This applies to the inner workings of Brahman as well:

analogy taken from CU 6.1.4[65] is faulty because, as Rāmānuja argues, "All states of consciousness have for their object something that is marked by difference."[66] What he means here is that even in the clay-jar analogy the very words making up the phrase "clay-jar" imply bheda.[67] On the ground of śabda itself, there is bheda, since sentences themselves set forth propositions by different words, and therefore possess "the power of denoting only such things as are affected with difference".[68] For the language of śruti, and thus CU 6.1.4, it is no different.

As concerns our question as to whether or not Rāmānuja viewed scripture alone as authoritative in the quest to know Brahman, this practice of the perception of language and reasoning from it raises serious doubts that he did. Does not the appeal to everyday language play an important part in determining how the language of scripture functions? If so, then pratyakṣa and anumāna are vital in the quest for knowledge of Brahman, and consequently for true knowledge about the body-soul-divine relation in Kṛṣṇa. That is, since on the grounds of language and its resulting propositions there is bheda between subject and object, and one continues on this basis to conclude that scriptural language implies the same, can we truly say that it was "scripture alone" for Rāmānuja?

### 1.3.3. Śruti

Along with Śaṅkara, Rāmānuja on the one hand maintains the authority of śruti, so one will find an abundance of śruti (and smṛti[69]) in his writings. The

---

> As regards the theory of the Advaitins that the perception of difference is brought about by ignorance only and is not really real, the Supreme Being ... cannot possibly perceive the so-called difference arising from ignorance. It is, therefore, unimaginable that He engages himself in activities such as teaching, which can proceed only from a perception of differences arising from ignorance (Svāmī Ādidevānanda, trans., Śrī Rāmānuja Gītā Bhāṣya [Mylapore: Sri Ramakrishna Math, n.d.], 64; noted from hereon as RBGB).

65 "Just as, my dear, by one clod of clay all that is made of clay is known, the modification [the object made of clay] being only a name, arising from speech, while the truth is that all is clay" (Swami Nikhilananda, trans., The Upanishads [New York: Harper & Row, 1963], 327).

66 SBE, 48:39.

67 Nikhilānanda, who favors the system of Śaṅkara, disagrees. In a note regarding the first clause of CU 6.1.4 ("Just as, my dear, by one clod of clay all that is made of clay is known"), he writes, "Because the effect is non-different from the cause" (The Upanishads, 327 n. 153).

68 SBE, 48:40.

69 Śrīnivāsa states that smṛti such as the MBh, the Rāmāyaṇa, and the Purāṇa-s are authoritative in that they supplement śruti. As such they are considered pramāṇa, but only when those portions of smṛti do not contradict śruti (YS, 44-45 [3.29-31]). In the notes Ādidevānanda asserts that "ordinary men with an imperfect knowledge of the Veda [śruti] can hardly determine the meaning of the Vedānta passages without the help

BSs (smṛti) themselves command an acceptance of scripture.[70] BS 1.1.3-4 states that the knowledge of Brahman and Brahman's work concerning the universe follows from the total agreement of the statements of scripture (śāstrayonitvāt tat tu samanvayāt), and that the authoritative nature of scripture exists because it is the highest aim of man to know Brahman.[71]

Rāmānuja had indeed stated that "Scripture alone is authoritative"[72] and alone "is the source (of the knowledge of Brahman)".[73] But what does this mean concerning other pramāṇa-s such as pratyakṣa and anumāna? As stated before, the answer comes in the form of "on the one hand ... on the other hand".

On the one hand, though pratyakṣa and anumāna have their place in making sense of the world around us and may be used partially and somewhat to explain in analogous fashion such phenomena as bheda and other aspects of Brahman, they cannot lead to knowledge of Brahman. "Brahman, being raised above all contact with the senses, is not an object of perception and the other means of proof [other pramāṇa-s], but [is] known through Scripture only."[74] Before this statement in his BSB, Rāmānuja carefully explains that pratyakṣa and anumāna [75] cannot in and of themselves prove a Brahman that "is in kind different from all other things".[76] Speaking of reasoning, and as mentioned earlier, Rāmānuja concludes that "Reasoning is to be applied only to the support of Scripture."[77] Thus it has been said that when it comes to the knowledge of Brahman, "Rāmānuja rejects any sort of perception or inference as a valid pramāṇa (source of knowledge) of Brahman. On the contrary, he asserts, the sole such pramāṇa is scripture."[78]

---

of a smṛti instituted by a competent and trustworthy person." But, ever cautious, Ādidevānanda immediately follows with, "But, while choosing the help of a smṛti one must be very careful as many a smṛti contains doctrines opposed to the Veda. Hence, one should follow such smṛti which does not contradict the Veda" (YS, 179 n. 26).

[70] S. S. Raghavachar writes, "Ramanuja's conception of the Vedanta sutra [BSs] is that it contains the core of the Upanishads" (Introduction to the Vedarthasangraha of Sree Ramanujacharya [Mangalore: The Mangalore Trading Association, 1957], 21).

[71] SBE, 48:161,174.

[72] SBE, 48:426.

[73] SBE, 48:161 (BS 1.1.3). Deśika argued that though anumāna has its place in the epistemic venture, in that it can be used to buttress one's faith, on its own it cannot lead to knowledge of Brahman. This is left to śruti. (Vedānta Deśika, Nyāyasiddhāñjana with the Saralaviśada of Śrī Raṅgarāmānuja and the Ratnapeṭikā of Sri Kṛṣṇatātayārya [Chennai: Ubhaya Vedānta Granthamala, 1976], 353-56).

[74] SBE, 48:161.

[75] Here Rāmānuja explains that there are two kinds of perception (sense perception and yoga) and two kinds of inference (special and general) (SBE, 48:162).

[76] SBE, 48:160.

[77] SBE, 48:426.

[78] Lipner, The Face of Truth, 4. Note carefully that Lipner is not saying that Rāmānuja rejects perception and reason outright, but only that in and of themselves these fall short

But this should be noted with caution. Though Rāmānuja recognized the absolute authority of śruti, on the other hand he did not discard pratyakṣa and anumāna altogether.[79] As a matter of fact, in what follows Srinivasachari represents Rāmānuja accurately and makes the case that (1) in some sense śruti defers to pratyakṣa, and (2) all three pramāṇa-s work together for the knowledge of Brahman.[80]

> All three pramāṇa-s are coherent and they are not contradictory. Pratyakṣa is the foundation of knowledge, and reasoning is based on it and does not supersede it. Śruti is the consummation of all knowledge, but it cannot be at variance with pratyakṣa. Truth is an eminent criterion ... and the three pramāṇa-s in their integral unity and perfection enable the truth-seeker to know the whole of reality.[81]

This observation of Srinivasachari and my observation made earlier (see concluding par. of section 1.3.2) evidence that it is too simplistic to assert that Rāmānuja always relied solely on śruti when Brahman is the proper object of knowledge. Consider also the following, which buttresses this point.

### 1.3.4. ŚRUTI AND SĀMĀNĀDHIKARAṆYA

Rāmānuja's argument is that (1) everyday language (secular śabda) makes known differentiated beings only; (2) śruti is śabda (revelatory language); (3) Brahman is mentioned in śruti; (4) therefore śruti makes known a differentiated Brahman.[82]

Śabda itself, within śruti, is particularly important in determining truth, and it is exactly here that Rāmānuja makes use of sāmānādhikaraṇya to show bheda both within the unified Brahman (though not Śaṅkara's absolute unity[83]) and between Brahman and the phenomenal world.[84] Rather than the advaita

---

in the quest to know Brahman. Forsthoefel also mentions "Rāmānuja's absolute dependence on scripture for shaping his concept of God" (Knowing Beyond Knowledge, 170).

[79] Eric Lott as well questions whether or not Rāmānuja's professed dependence upon scripture was demonstrated in all matters of interpretation and debate for truth, though Lott's question comes in the context of Rāmānuja's analogical method of the individual self / body, Brahman as Self / world. Here Rāmānuja's "hermeneutical norm" is that of microcosm and macrocosm; that is, just as the self indwells and governs the body and is one with it, so also does Brahman as the Self indwell and govern the world and individual souls as his body. See Lott's Vedantic Approaches to God, 32-34.

[80] Recall that points 1 and 2 are exactly the view of Śaṅkara as I see it.

[81] Srinivasachari, The Philosophy of Viśiṣṭādvaita, 47.

[82] SBE, 48:40-41,78-79. See also Lipner, The Face of Truth, 26.

[83] For Rāmānuja the differentiation occurs on both epistemological and ontological grounds.

[84] See Lipner, The Face of Truth, 29.

view, which states that the predicate in the phrase tat [that] tvam [you] asi [you are] ("That you are", CU 6.8.7) is the subject (tat = tvam), Rāmānuja holds that the subject is differentiated (bheda) from the predicate, as in simple language tvam and tat logically imply bheda. But bheda is carried further to establish Rāmānuja's doctrine of modes or attributes. The predicate tat functions in sāmānādhikaraṇya to convey the idea of one thing (tat or Brahman) being qualified by an attribute (tvam), the meaning therefore being that the individual is a mode or attribute of Brahman (see section 2.1 and the example of Devadatta). Thus, for Rāmānuja the gist of this verse is not to define Brahman (tat) as tvam but to show the relation between the individual (tvam) and Brahman.[85] As is the case with other ingredients in Rāmānuja's epistemology, all this is critical for interacting with Rāmānuja's view of Kṛṣṇāvatāra.

### 1.3.5. Summary

Rāmānuja, like Śaṅkara, makes use of three pramāṇa-s—pratyakṣa, anumāna, and śruti as śabda (and secular śabda)—though without question Rāmānuja differs from Śaṅkara in conclusions made after utilizing the three pramāṇa-s. The result of Rāmānuja's epistemology is that bheda really exists between Brahman and the jagat. This is quite different from the conclusion of Śaṅkara, who holds to abheda in this relation.

For Rāmānuja, on the one hand śruti is the only means of properly defining Brahman and ultimately knowing Brahman (because pratyakṣa and anumāna in and of themselves cannot scripturally define Brahman, nor can they lead one to a deep and profound knowledge of Brahman). But on the other hand pratyakṣa and anumāna are not left in the epistemic dust in the interpretation of śruti as it leads to knowledge of Brahman. Of course Rāmānuja (like Śaṅkara) held to a high view of śruti and made statements to the effect that śruti alone was authoritative for inquiry into Brahman, but pratyakṣa and anumāna also worked together with śruti. Further, and this not necessarily admitted by Rāmānuja, even śruti defers to pratyakṣa and anumāna in the sense of setting a proper foundation for subsequent interpretation of śruti. Therefore, even at certain times (not always) in śruti when Brahman is the proper object of knowledge, śruti alone is not the sole means of determining the nature of Brahman.

In some cases scriptural interpretation hinges on pratyakṣa and anumāna as they relate to secular śabda. One example of this is that since it is perceived and reasoned from common language that the relation of words in sentences implies bheda, so it follows that in śruti we have the same relation of words implying bheda. Rāmānuja then proceeds on this phenomenon to the interpretation of the body-soul-divine relation in the person of Kṛṣṇa, as we shall see in chapter 4.

I conclude, then, that Rāmānuja's epistemology at times gives primary

---

[85] Lipner, The Face of Truth, 36.

importance to śruti, while at other times śruti works with pratyakṣa and anumāna, and this in varying combinations of deference, one to the others.

I now move to the crucial outgrowth of the epistemologies of Śaṅkara and Rāmānuja (an outgrowth that has tremendous implications for the doctrine of avatāra), the question of bheda versus abheda.

## 2. More on Abheda and Bheda

Figuring heavily in the debate concerning the nature of Kṛṣṇa's body as it relates to the divine is the issue of abheda (Śaṅkara's view) versus bheda (Rāmānuja's view).

Śaṅkara and Rāmānuja agree that Brahman is ultimate reality. Where they differ is with regard to ultimate reality as it relates to the jagat and the jīvātman. For Śaṅkara, Brahman as ultimate reality means that ultimately Brahman is the only reality, and that the jagat as we see it is, though in a sense originating in Brahman, ultimately mithyā. For Rāmānuja, Brahman is ultimate reality and a real jagat "has originated from Viṣṇu".[86] Further, though both theologians postulate Brahman as the antaryāmin or indweller of the jagat (as we shall see in chapters 2 and 3[87]) they do so in such ways that keep in step with their abheda and bheda doctrines.

Though (as I demonstrate in the next chapter) Śaṅkara posits a three-fold ontology of Brahman, jagat and jīva-s in the realm of apara brahman (lower Brahman) or Īśvara (the Lord),[88] Śaṅkara's ultimate ontology, and his ultimate hermeneutic lens, is abheda. Ultimately there is only Brahman; there is in reality no difference, no plurality, and the jagat is mithyā and the jīvātman in reality is not "individual", but Brahman. "The fact is", says Śaṅkara, "that the texts aim solely at teaching non-difference".[89]

Why is it that Śaṅkara cannot opt for ultimate bheda in Brahman as

---

[86] RVed, 262, par. 110 (Sanskrit text p. 140), quoting VP 1.1.31. See also RVed, 263. For further support Rāmānuja cites BS 1.1.2: janmādyasya yataḥ ("from whom the birth etc., of this proceed" [van Buitenen's translation, p. 262]).

[87] The doctrine of antaryāmin is sometimes assumed only to be part of Rāmānuja's system, when in reality Śaṅkara also taught it, though not with the amount of theological emphasis that Rāmānuja demonstrated. Interesting is Śaṅkara's opening statement of his BGB, where Warrier notes that he praises Nārāyaṇa, the indweller (antaryāmin) and absolute progenitor of the world (SBGB, 1 n. 1). This should be understood in light of Śaṅkara's doctrine of māyā, "the power by which the Absolute appears as the world" (SBGB, xiii). For example, Śaṅkara states that Kṛṣṇa was born as an aspect of Nārāyaṇa, and that "He appears, by virtue of His Maya, to be embodied and born as man" (SBGB, 2-3).

[88] Thus technically the three-fold ontology is Īśvara, jagat and jīva-s. See Satprakashananda, Methods of Knowledge According to Advaita Vedanta, 75-76. More on this in chapter 2.

[89] SBE, 38:66.

Rāmānuja teaches? One reason is Śaṅkara's epistemological presupposition stated at the opening of his BSB (cited earlier). If adhyāsa is a matter "not requiring any proof" (other than scriptural proof? [see below]), then it follows that because of the error of adhyāsa people believe in a Brahman characterized by bheda. Further, texts teaching bheda must bend to this presupposition and thus be interpreted on the level of the subjective or as some kind of secondary or subservient texts. In a passage where the master Advaitin discusses unfounded arguments that the Vedānta texts teach contradictions about the cause of the world, he writes,

> The creation of the world and similar topics are not at all what Scripture wishes to teach. For we neither observe nor are told by Scripture that the welfare of man depends on those matters in any way ... That all the passages setting forth the creation and so on subserve the purpose of teaching Brahman, Scripture itself declares; compare Ch. Up. 6.8.4, "As food too is an offshoot, seek after its root, viz. water. And as water too is an offshoot, seek after its root, viz. fire. And as fire too is an offshoot, seek after its root, viz. the True."[90]

Śaṅkara also admits later on in the BSB that adhyāsa is a presupposition of his and must be assumed in the reading of śruti:

> The mutual superimposition of the Self and the Non-Self, which is termed Nescience, is the presupposition on which [are based] all the practical distinctions—those made in ordinary life as well as those laid down by the Veda—between means of knowledge, objects of knowledge, and all scriptural texts, whether they are concerned with injunctions and prohibitions or with final release.[91]

Another reason is that Śaṅkara cites texts in śruti such as the analogy of clay (CU 6.1.4) and tat tvam asi (CU 6.8.7) to show that there is ultimately no bheda. From clay all that is made of clay is known, and the effect of the clay (i.e., the thing made of clay) is known only through its name ("jar"), but in reality it is clay alone.[92] So it is with the true Self—"you are That".[93] Then, like

---

[90] SBE, 34:265-66. In his preface to his translation of Śaṅkara's bhāṣya on Gauḍapāda's Kārikā, Nikhilānanda quotes Śaṅkara's introduction to the fourth chapter of the AU: "Here (i.e., the theories and stories of creation), the only fact intended to be conveyed is the realization of Ātman, the rest is but attractive figure of speech; and this is no fault. It seems more reasonable that the Lord, omniscient, omnipotent, did, like a magician, display all this illusion to facilitate explanation or comprehension, inasmuch as stories, although false, are easily understood by all" (SBGK, xxvii-xxviii).

[91] SBE, 34:6.

[92] In Śaṅkara's bhāṣya on the CU we read, "the product [the clay known only through name and form] is not thus different from its material cause [the clay]" (Swāmī

Rāmānuja,[94] Śaṅkara appeals to these texts which to him are clear and thus the standard by which to interpret those texts that seem to teach otherwise.[95]

Does śruti merely assume adhyāsa and not teach it specifically? Because of the weight given to tat tvam asi[96] (and texts such as CU 6.1.4), in Śaṅkara's opinion there seems to be in all bheda śruti texts the presupposition of adhyāsa. (For this reason it is difficult for me to ascertain what Śaṅkara means by "not requiring any proof".) Consider first Śaṅkara's priority and emphasis of tat tvam asi. If from tat tvam asi we gather that there is abheda, then Brahman, argues Śaṅkara, cannot be the object of pratyakṣa. That is to say, there can be no subject-object relationship if only Brahman exists and the self is Brahman. Thus, it must be by adhyāsa that one experiences or perceives bheda between oneself and Brahman. For Śaṅkara, then, philosophical and theological truths "cannot be grasped without the aid of the scriptural passage, 'That art thou'".[97]

Thus, for Śaṅkara, śruti assumes adhyāsa in phenomenological texts (which speak of creation, etc.). Consider next his example regarding supposed bheda between enjoyers and the objects of enjoyment.

> In reality, however, that distinction does not exist ... Viz. Ch. Up. 6.1.4, "As, my dear, by one clod of clay all that is made of clay is known, the modification (i.e. the effect; the thing made of clay) being a name merely which has its origin in speech, while the truth is that it is clay merely ..." The meaning of this passage is that, if there is known a lump of clay which really and truly is nothing but clay, there are known thereby likewise all things made of clay, such as jars, dishes, pails, and so on, all of which agree in having clay as their true nature. For these modifications or effects are names only, while in reality there exists no such thing as

---

Gambhīrānanda, trans., Chāndogya Upaniṣad with the Commentary of Śaṅkarācārya [Calcutta: Advaita Ashrama, 1983], 410; noted from hereon as SCUB).

93 SBE, 34:320-21.

94 Rāmānuja's exegesis of tat tvam asi unfolds under the priority of texts such as "It thought, may I be many" and "Having created, He entered into it" (TU 2.6 and the similar passage in CU 6.2.3; see SBE, 48:130,133,134).

95 This is the claim of Swami Satchidanandendra Sarasvati. See his The Method of the Vedanta (London: Kegan Paul International, 1989), 923-25.

96 See SBE, 34:23. In and of itself, it must be admitted this phrase mentions nothing of superimposition.

97 SBE, 34:23. See also Forsthoefel's brief discussion of Śaṅkara's interpretation of tat tvam asi and his use of the phrase as a hermeneutic device. Śaṅkara, says Forsthoefel, appeals to this mahāvākya in the same way I have described above. Forsthoefel then mentions Rāmānuja's appeal to sāmānādhikaraṇya to answer Śaṅkara, though here he does not mention Śaṅkara's use of sāmānādhikaraṇya for interpretation of tat tvam asi (Knowing Beyond Knowledge, pp. 167-69). For my discussion on Rāmānuja's interpretation of tat tvam asi by way of sāmānādhikaraṇya, see chapter 3, section 3.1.

> modification. In so far as they are names (individual effects distinguished by names) they are untrue; in so far as they are clay they are true.[98]

Rāmānuja counters and takes Śaṅkara to a logical conclusion:

> Now, against all this [i.e. Śaṅkara position], the following objection is raised ... All effects, and all empirical thought and speech about effects, are based on Nescience [avidyā]. Apart from the causal substance, clay, which is seen to be present in effected things such as jars, the so-called effect, i.e. the jar or pot, rests altogether on Nescience ... merely on empirical thought and speech, and are fundamentally false, unreal; while the causal substance, i.e. clay, alone is real ... [But] to whom, [we reply] then, does that imagination belong? Not to Brahman surely whose nature, consisting of pure intelligence, allows no room for imagination of any kind![99] ... This, we reply, is the view of teachers who have no insight into the true nature of aduality ... Knowledge produced by texts such as 'Thou art that' does not put an end to bondage, because it is produced by texts which are the fictitious product of avidyā ... or because it is the product of a process of study which depends on teachers who are the mere creatures of avidyā.[100]

Rāmānuja's apologetic here is two-pronged. First, if Śaṅkara is correct, then Brahman is the abode of avidyā and adhyāsa. It seems, however, that Śaṅkara has no problem with this.[101] Śaṅkara says that the Lord, "by means of Nescience, manifests himself in various ways".[102] And as we saw earlier, Śaṅkara even admits to the role of adhyāsa within śruti. Second, Rāmānuja takes Śaṅkara to the conclusion that the texts themselves are products of avidyā on the reader's part. Moreover, teachers expounding these fictitious texts to students are also the products of avidyā. Thus, to Rāmānuja, Śaṅkara's epistemology is faulty at the outset.

Following is a detailed illustration of how Śaṅkara and Rāmānuja exegete a certain śruti passage, TU 2.1, from their perspectives of abheda and bheda as it

---

[98] SBE, 34:320-21.

[99] Raghavachar argues along these same lines, questioning the ontological status of Śaṅkara's avidyā (Introduction to the Vedarthasangraha of Sree Ramanujacharya, 74-75). His approach follows that of Rāmānuja in other places in his commentary—raising the objection, representing the opponent by offering answers, and then showing those answers to be faulty in light of the opponent's doctrine of Brahman.

[100] SBE, 48:432,436,437,448. Though Rāmānuja utilizes reason to counter Śaṅkara, Gauḍapāda would counter Rāmānuja by stating that non-duality "alone is rational and correct" (SBGK, 157 [3.13]).

[101] Neither does Sarasvati, as is evident from a section in his The Method of the Vedanta entitled "Superimposition and Its Removal do not Affect the Absolute" (pp. 3-4).

[102] SBE, 34:190.

relates to the nature of Brahman.

### 2.1. Taittirīya Upaniṣad 2.1

Describing the nature of Brahman, TU 2.1 reads satyaṁ jñānam anantaṁ brahma ("truth, knowledge, infinite is Brahman"). In Rāmānuja's case the application of sāmānādhikaraṇya, grammatical co-ordination of terms or correlative predication, plays a major role in the understanding of this text, which communicates something about the nature of Brahman.[103] In his appeal to sāmānādhikaraṇya he cites the experts: "According to the experts, sāmānādhikaraṇya is the application to one object of several words in different functions."[104] He therefore concludes that "speech [śabda[105]] can never be a pramāṇa to prove a non-differentiated thing; for speech derives its character of pramāṇa from the peculiar nature of the words and sentences in which it consists".[106] In his commentary on BS 1.1.1 (which is an extensive treatise on his epistemology[107]) Rāmānuja states that sāmānādhikaraṇya denotes "one thing distinguished by several attributes".[108] What this means for the text cited is that Brahman (the subject) is distinguished by the predicates "Truth", "Knowledge", and "Infinite". The predicates, possessing the same case-ending as the subject (neuter nominative or neuter accusative), function in co-ordination "to convey the idea of one thing being qualified by several attributes".[109] Thus Rāmānuja's claim that "the text 'Truth, knowledge, infinite is Brahman', does not prove a substance devoid of all difference"[110] is proven true on the basis of syntactical analysis. His point here is that there is bheda both within Brahman and between Brahman and other objects.[111] Moreover, for Rāmānuja the interpretive conclusions drawn from sāmānādhikaraṇya in śruti texts have for their example conclusions drawn from sāmānādhikaraṇya in secular śabda. For instance, Rāmānuja's example, "Devadatta is young, swarthy, magnanimous and well-bred" means that within Devadatta exist several differentiated attributes. This is the way everyday language operates, and with śruti it is no different. Translating this to the nature of Brahman, Rāmānuja states, "Hence follows that words like truth, knowledge and the like declare that Brahman is differentiated by, for instance, knowledge in the proper

---

[103] Lipner, The Face of Truth, 29-30.
[104] RVed, 200, par. 26 (Sanskrit text p. 86). See also SBE 48:79-80.
[105] RVed (Sanskrit text p. 87).
[106] RVed, 201.
[107] SBE, 48:3-156.
[108] SBE, 48:79.
[109] SBE, 48:79.
[110] SBE, 48:79.
[111] Lipner, The Face of Truth, 29-30,35.

sense of the word."[112]

As far as Śaṅkara is concerned, sāmānādhikaraṇya is a trustworthy venture, and, as we have seen, he employs it. Both theologians, then, make use of sāmānādhikaraṇya, and both even admit to bheda in the texts themselves.[113] Where they differ is with interpretive conclusions after sāmānādhikaraṇya is utilized.

In contrast to Rāmānuja, Śaṅkara's "exegeses show that in the case of correlatively predicated scriptural texts about Brahman our ordinary expectations of the rules of grammar are to be put aside".[114] That is to say, bheda seen in the texts is a necessary phenomenon for the reader because "we cannot help but think and speak differentiatedly of the really non-differentiated Absolute".[115] The texts, then, communicate on our level, but one must look beyond bheda (caused by adhyāsa) in order to see and understand Brahman.[116] Śaṅkara's way of dealing with TU 2.1, then, rests upon what I believe is the lynchpin of his epistemology and exegesis, CU 6.8.7: tat tvam asi. Consequently, the three terms "truth, knowledge, infinite" in TU 2.1 are understood in a way that differs from everyday perceptual usage of sāmānādhikaraṇya. Rather than affirming a Brahman differentiated by the predicates, the passage affirms a description-of-essence relationship between Brahman and three specifying terms[117]:

---

[112] RVed, 199, par. 24 (Sanskrit text p. 85).

[113] Lipner, The Face of Truth, 30.

[114] Lipner, The Face of Truth, 30.

[115] Lipner, The Face of Truth, 30. Here the conclusion is that śabda as language has bheda inherent within it by nature.

[116] As we saw above, this two-tiered structure of texts in part afforded Rāmānuja the opportunity to seize upon the logical conclusion that for Śaṅkara the texts themselves must therefore be a product of māyā and avidyā.

[117] See Julius Lipner, "Śaṅkara on Satyaṃ, Jñānam Anantaṃ Brahma", in P. Bilimoria and J. N. Mohanty, eds., Relativism, Suffering and Beyond: Essays in Memory of Bimal K. Matilal (New Delhi: Oxford University Press, 1997), 301-18. Further, Śaṅkara argues this in his lengthy gloss on TU 2.1: "Brahman is truth, knowledge, infinite—is meant as a definition of Brahman. For the three words beginning with satya are meant to distinguish Brahman which is the substantive" (p. 307 [bibliographic information appears at the end of this note]). Thus, rather than functioning as attributes of Brahman as Rāmānuja would have them, the first three words define Brahman (p. 311). Though Śaṅkara acknowledges that the word brahma is identical to the other three words in case-ending, he argues that because Brahman (brahma) is That which is to be known, that is, "the chief object of knowledge", Brahman is therefore "marked out from [the] other nouns" (p. 307). The first three nouns (satyaṁ jñānam anantaṁ) are therefore descriptive of Brahman—Brahman "is truth, knowledge, and infinite" (p. 318 [on p. 358, interpreting TU 2.6, Śaṅkara states, "That which is satyam, the absolute truth. What is that, again? It is Brahman"]; see Swāmī Gambhīrānanda, trans., Eight Upaniṣads: With the Commentary of Śaṅkarācārya. 2 vols. [Calcutta: Advaita Ashrama, 2000], 1:307-18; vol. 1 noted from hereon as STUB).

> Such as the creator is described in any one Vedānta-passage, viz. as all-knowing, the Lord of all, the Self of all, without a second, so he is represented in all other Vedānta-passages also. Let us consider, for instance, the description of Brahman. There it is said at first, "Truth, knowledge, infinite is Brahman." Here the word "knowledge", and so likewise the statement, made later on, that Brahman desired (2.6), intimate that Brahman is of the nature of intelligence.[118]

In order to substantiate his exegesis, in another place in his BSB Śaṅkara states, "The Self is indeed called by many different names, but is one only."[119] This is reminiscent of the clay / jar teaching of CU 6.1.4 and serves to reinforce the description-of-essence relationship of the non-dual Brahman with predicates of this type in śruti,[120] predicates normally taken by Rāmānuja as attributes of Brahman.

As we see in the above quotation, where Śaṅkara mentions TU 2.6, TU 2.1 must be interpreted in the context of 2.6. He states, "Again—in the passage [Taitt. 2.6], 'May I [Brahman] be many, may I grow forth'—it tells how the Self became many, and thereby declares that the creator is non-different from the created effects."[121] Because of the mention of "created effects", on the surface this text seems to support Rāmānuja, and Rāmānuja is quick to seize upon it as a chief mahāvākya, as we shall see in chapter 3. However, according to Swami Satchidanandendra Sarasvati, Śaṅkara has an interpretation that he feels is faithful to the overall context. After saying that the passage "thereby declares that the creator is non-different from the created effects", Śaṅkara further appeals to the passage that immediately follows. "If he [a man] makes the slightest differentiation in It [Brahman], there is fear for him" (TU 2.7[122]).

---

[118] SBE, 34:264.

[119] SBE, 34:283.

[120] See SCUB, 409-10.

[121] SBE, 34:265. In STUB he argues that Brahman is non-different from created effects, just as the clay is non-different from the pots made from the clay, the difference being only in name and form (pp. 350-52 [interpreting TU 2.6]). In his bhāṣya on the AU Śaṅkara again admits of bheda, though in the context of names and forms. The single Brahman remains, states Śaṅkara, but name and form characterize the one Brahman. He likens this to foam and water. Though there is a perceived difference in the foam and water, the actual difference is due to name and form only (Gambhīrānanda, Eight Upaniṣads, 2:20 [interpreting AU 1.1.1: "In the beginning this was but absolute Self alone. There was nothing else whatsoever that winked. It thought, 'Let Me create the worlds'"]).

[122] Nikhilananda, The Upanishads, 269. "[F]ear crops up for this soul that perceives difference ... [T]hat very Brahman, when perceived through (a sense of) duality and called God, becomes a terror for the (apparently) learned man who knows thus, 'God is different from me, and I am a worldly creature different from God', and who creates the slightest difference" (STUB, 365 [interpreting TU 2.7]).

Thus Śaṅkara sees 2.6 affirming the jagat as we see it—cause and effect on the level of day by day phenomena—but only as a "preliminary device".[123] Sarasvati, in chapter 3 of his The Method of the Vedānta (in which he argues that Śaṅkara belongs to the true tradition of Vedānta), argues for the true interpretation of TU 2.6:

> In the Taittiriya Upanishad, it is first said that the projection of the world consisting of the ether and other elements proceeds from the Absolute. And in the end it is declared that one finds perfect stability, bringing freedom from all fear, in identifying oneself with the Absolute, bereft of all relation with the perceptible and imperceptible aspects of the world (Taitt. 2.7). In all cases of this kind, a doctrine of cause and effect is accepted as a preliminary device to help induce the mind to understand the unity and sole reality of the Self.[124]

In order to see the jagat (including the body of Kṛṣṇa) for what it truly is, one must recognize that the passage culminates with 2.7 and the warning that there is no bheda. If heeded, this in turn leads to mokṣa. Sarasvati goes on to cite CU 6.1.4: "As, my dear, by one clod of clay all that is made of clay is known, the modification being a name merely which has its origin in speech, while the truth is that it is clay merely." He has for his example the great Advaitin himself, who cites this CU passage to sustain his interpretation of TU 2.6.[125]

## 3. Summary

In this chapter I examined the epistemic tools of Śaṅkara and Rāmānuja—pratyakṣa, anumāna, śruti, smṛti, vidyā, sāmānādhikaraṇya, adhyāsa, avidyā, śabda—and conclusions drawn from them by the two Vedāntins, such as bheda, abheda, mithyā, advaita and viśiṣṭādvaita, because each of these play key roles in Śaṅkara's and Rāmānuja's views of Kṛṣṇāvatāra. The material in chapter 4 will evidence this. Yet, there still remain other considerations significant to avatāra, this time more on the theological scope. To these I now proceed, beginning with Śaṅkara's doctrines of Brahman, the jagat, and the jīva.

---

[123] See the next quotation above.

[124] Sarasvati, The Method of the Vedanta, 75.

[125] SBE, 34:266. Śaṅkara learned this from the Kārikā of Gauḍapada. He quotes the Kārikā, section 3.15: "If creation is represented by means of clay, iron, sparks, and other things; that is only a means for making it understood that there is no difference whatever" (SBE, 34:266; see SBGK, 161).

# CHAPTER 2

# Śaṅkara: Nature of Brahman, World, and Soul

## 1. Introduction

Śaṅkara was so great an influence on the Hindu religious mind that to the casual observer he has come to be representative of "what Hinduism teaches". As John Carman observes, "Most of the interpretations and translations of Rāmānuja in western languages at the beginning of the twentieth century tried to correct the prevalent western impression that Śaṅkara's Advaita is identical with the Vedānta, and indeed with all of Hinduism."[1]

Śaṅkara's father died when Śaṅkara was a young boy. His mother raised him as a Brahmin and there are several stories that describe the young Śaṅkara as devoutly religious. It is said that sometime after his mother refused to allow her son to become a sannyāsin (renouncer), he was bathing in a nearby river and seized by a crocodile that would not let him go until he agreed to embark on the path of a sannyāsin. His mother rushed to the scene and agreed that it be so. A tribute to his genius is that he lived only to the age of thirty-two. Even with such a short life he would author many bhāṣya-s and other works and alter the religious thought of millions.[2]

Śaṅkara's view of Brahman, the jagat, and the jīva has direct impact upon his doctrine of Kṛṣṇāvatāra. Put another way, no study of Śaṅkara's Kṛṣṇāvatāra can be thorough without first examining Śaṅkara's teachings of Brahman, the jagat, and the jīva because these directly affect the body-soul-divine relation in Kṛṣṇāvatāra. I begin first with the nature of Brahman.

## 2. The Nature of Brahman

Śaṅkara's advaita has been summarized in the famous Sanskrit phrase brahma

---

[1] John B. Carman, The Theology of Ramanuja: An Essay in Interreligious Understanding (New Haven and London: Yale University Press, 1974; Bombay: Ananthacharya Indological Research Institute, 1981), 199. Although there are many expressions of Hinduism, the popular view of Hinduism is thought to be only that of Śaṅkara. Gavin Flood mentions one scholar who has stated that Śaṅkara's philosophy is the only expression of Vedānta (see Flood's An Introduction to Hinduism [New York: Cambridge University Press, 1996], 239,300n.25).

[2] Some of the material in this paragraph was taken from Flood, An Introduction to Hinduism, 239-40.

satyaṁ jaganmithyā jīvo brahmaiva nāparaḥ (Brahman is real, the world unreal, the soul is none other than Brahman).[3] In his study on the Vedānta, V. S. Ghate states that Śaṅkara's doctrine of Brahman "may be summed up in the four Sanskrit words: 'Brahma satyaṃ jaganmithyā' [Brahman is real; the world is illusion (or not real)]".[4] Further, "It [Brahman] is only intelligence,[5] without form, without qualities, without any limitations of time, space or causality that is real."[6] Thus "Kevalādvaita or absolute monism".[7] Śaṅkara's Brahman, then, is pure intelligence, pure consciousness[8] (cit) and it alone is real. Consequently, this doctrine of Brahman affects Śaṅkara's view of the world and the soul, all of which have further implications for his avatāra doctrine.

Śaṅkara's Brahman is ultimately the one reality. In his kevalādvaita Brahman alone is real, is all there is, and thus there is ultimately no duality. The word "ultimately" is both essential and necessary in understanding Śaṅkara's advaita, for, as we shall see, he does account for Brahman in relation to the perceived world.

### 2.1. Para Brahman and Apara Brahman (or Īśvara)

One important philosophical and doctrinal distinction of Śaṅkara is the dichotomizing of Brahman related to the jagat-prapañca or world of appearance, and Brahman in reality. The first declares that the jagat-prapañca seems real and qualifies Brahman, the second that ultimately what truly and only exists is Brahman. Śaṅkara states, "Brahman is apprehended under two forms; in the first place as qualified by limiting conditions owing to the

---

[3] Malkovsky challenges the notion that this oft-quoted aphorism is from Śaṅkara. He mentions Eliot Deutsch attributing this aphorism to Śaṅkara. The phrase, writes Malkovsky, actually comes from the Bālabodhinī, which is "a spurious work authored by a Pseudo-Śaṃkara" (Bradley J. Malkovsky, The Role of Divine Grace in the Soteriology of Śaṃkarācārya [Leiden: Brill, 2001], 47 n. 7). In this note Malkovsky cites Richard Brooks, "The Meaning of 'Real' in Advaita Vedānta", Philosophy East and West 19 (1969): 385, as a source for this observation.

[4] V. S. Ghate, The Vedānta: A Study of the Brahma-Sūtras with the Bhāṣyas of Śaṅkara, Rāmānuja, Nimbārka, Madhva and Vallabha (Poona: Bhandarkar Oriental Research Institute, 1960), 21. Sanskrit transliterated.

[5] Cit, not buddhi. Cit is "spirit; consciousness; the individual self", while buddhi is intellect (see John Grimes, A Concise Dictionary of Indian Philosophy [Albany: State University of New York Press, 1989], 107,103).

[6] Ghate, The Vedānta, 21.

[7] Ghate, The Vedānta, 21.

[8] Śaṅkara mentions that the word brahman comes from the Sanskrit root bṛh (to be great). He therefore states, "eternal purity, and so on, belong to Brahman" (George Thibaut, trans., Vedānta-Sūtras: With the Commentary by Śaṅkarācārya, in F. Max Müller, ed., Sacred Books of the East [Delhi: Motilal Banarsidass, 1988], 34:14). Noted from hereon as SBE.

multiformity of the evolutions of name and form,[9] i.e. the multiformity of the created world; in the second place as being the opposite of this, i.e. free from all limiting conditions whatever."[10] In his BUB Śaṅkara states something quite similar: "Brahman or the Supreme Self has but two forms, through the superimposition of which by ignorance the formless Supreme Brahman is defined or made conceivable."[11]

### 2.1.1. PARA BRAHMAN

"Vāsudeva [another name for Kṛṣṇa[12]] is all", says Śaṅkara, quoting BG 7.19[13] (see also 11.40, "You are the all"). Para brahman—the highest, supreme Brahman; the Self—is the one Self, and "all this is Self alone" (BU 2.4.6[14]). In his BUB Śaṅkara asserts in strong fashion that "the Self is everything", "everything is the Self", and "there is nothing besides the Self".[15] Further, as we read above, Brahman is "without form, without qualities, without any limitations". Śaṅkara divorces from ultimate Brahman any attributes. To assign attributes to Brahman is to add phenomena to Brahman, something that is

---

[9] In his BUB Śaṅkara writes, "The Lord [Indra] on account of Māyā or diverse knowledge, or (to give an alternative meaning) the false identifications created by name, form and the elements, not in truth, is perceived as manifold, because of these notions superimposed by ignorance" (Swāmī Mādhavānanda, trans., The Brihadāraṇyaka Upaniṣad with the Commentary of Śaṅkarācārya [Calcutta: Advaita Ashrama, 1965], 403-4). Noted from hereon as SBUB. In this text italicized words are from the BU verse that Śaṅkara is interpreting, in this case BU 2.5.19.

[10] SBE, 34:61. Swami Satprakashananda translates the first phrase, "Two kinds of Brahman are stated" (Methods of Knowledge According to Advaita Vedanta [London: George Allen & Unwin, 1965], 255).

[11] SBUB, 330 (interpreting BU 2.3.1).

[12] See Winthrop Sargeant, trans., The Bhagavad Gītā (Albany: State University of New York Press, 1984), 337.

[13] A. G. Krishna Warrier, trans., Srīmad Bhagavad Gītā Bhāṣya of Sri Śaṅkarācārya (Mylapore: Sri Ramakrishna Math, 1983), 265. Noted from hereon as SBGB. Rāmānuja understands this text to teach that "Vasudeva alone is my highest end" (Svāmī Ādidevānanda, trans., Śrī Rāmānuja Gītā Bhāṣya [Mylapore: Sri Ramakrishna Math, n.d.], 259). Noted from hereon as RBGB.

[14] SBGB, 460. Śaṅkara lists this reference as 2.4.8.

[15] SBUB, 358 (interpreting BU 2.4.6). Further, "[T]he Supreme Self is supposed to be the only entity that exists. As the Śruti says, 'One only without a second' (Ch[āndogya Upaniṣad] VI.ii.1) ... for we have spoken at length of the absence of any other entity but the Supreme Self" (SBUB, 722 [interpreting BU 4.4.6]). For Śaṅkara MuU 2.1.4 ("He is the inner Self of all beings" [eṣa sarvabhūtāntarātmā]) "shows the absence of a relative self other than the Supreme Self". Here Śaṅkara quotes other śruti texts for support—MuU 2.2.11[12] ("This universe is but Brahman") and CU 8[7].25.2 ("All this is but the Self")—and concludes, "it is but proper to conclude the identity of the individual self with Brahman" (SBUB, 298-99 [interpreting BU 2.1.20]).

impossible[16] (thus neti neti, "not this, not this") given Śaṅkara's view that Brahman alone is real. Thus, in reality Brahman "is pure consciousness [cit and thus nirguṇa brahman, Brahman without attributes], [and] is in reality unrelated to all empirical experiences",[17] thus "non-dual" (advaitam).[18] As such Brahman is "the Supreme Reality"[19] that is "unmanifest, being adjunctless [i.e., no attributes, nothing connected to Brahman; again, neti neti] and beyond the range of the senses".[20] Following is an example of Śaṅkara's unswerving conviction that śruti teaches advaita.

BG 18.66 has been called India's "verse". It quotes Kṛṣṇa: "Giving up all Dharma [duty], seek refuge in Me, alone; I shall liberate you from all sins; grieve not." The basic setting of the BG is that the great warrior, Arjuna, is faced with the dilemma of whether or not he should fight a fierce battle against his family and countrymen. As a member of the warrior class (a kṣatriya), he is duty-bound to fight; it is his dharma. As he struggles with the dilemma, Kṛṣṇa gives to him spiritual teachings (the soul is eternal, for example) to ease his worry, and finally instructs him to fight. In his bhāṣya on this verse the master Advaitin cites a smṛti text, the Śāntiparva: "There is nothing but I", "Know for certain nothing exists other than Me."[21] Śaṅkara understands this to teach kevalādvaita. In part this is Kṛṣṇa's ground for answering Arjuna's dilemma with "do not grieve",[22] and the basis upon which his command to fight rests. The thrust here is that Kṛṣṇa is asserting ultimate truth to Arjuna—Brahman alone is real. This of course implies that the jagat-prapañca in which Arjuna (and Kṛṣṇa) finds himself is mithyā. But though it is mithyā, it does seem to exist. How does Śaṅkara account for this?

### 2.1.2. Apara Brahman or Īśvara

In Śaṅkara's system certain passages of śruti and smṛti and their linguistic analyses introduce one to apara brahman. This is witnessed by śruti texts speaking of Brahman's attributes (saguṇa brahman). But they are only the means, a stepping stone, to parā vidyā leading to Brahman realization. Other passages of nirguṇa śruti (scriptures affirming Brahman without attributes), according to Lipner viewed by Śaṅkara as "more authoritative",[23] facilitate the existential reality of parā vidyā through sākṣātkāra, which increases as one

---

[16] See Eric Lott, Vedantic Approaches to God (New York: Barnes and Noble, 1980), 71-72.
[17] SBGB, 304.
[18] SBGB, 607.
[19] SBGB, 326.
[20] SBGB, 385.
[21] SBGB, 617. Śaṅkara lists Śāntiparva 329.40; 331.44.
[22] SBGB, 617.
[23] Julius J. Lipner, The Face of Truth: A Study of Meaning and Metaphysics in the Vedantic Theology of Ramanuja (Albany: State University of New York Press, 1986), 30.

progresses toward the realization of para brahman.[24] To a large degree this method is born out of the emphasis Śaṅkara places on his most treasured verse, the mahāvākya "tat tvam asi" (CU 6.8.7), which I examined in chapter 1, section 1.2.4.2, and which I mention briefly in this chapter (section 3.2.1.2).

Despite Śaṅkara's view of para Brahman, where Brahman is viewed as absolutely the only reality, he does account for Brahman in relation to the perceived world. Thus Śaṅkara and his pupils can claim a three-fold ontology of God, the world, and souls. Swami Satprakashananda calls this "a triple existence consisting of individuals (the jīvas), the objective universe (jagat), and their supreme Ruler (Īśvara)".[25] Vital to Śaṅkara's system is his view of Brahman as Īśvara. This doctrine affects significantly Śaṅkara's analysis of Kṛṣṇāvatāra, as I hope to demonstrate in chapter 7. Īśvara is apara Brahman, Brahman in fictitious connection with the world of appearance.[26] Here śruti and smṛti speak of Brahman as saguṇa, but only in relation to the seeming

---

[24] Swami Satchidanandendra Sarasvati, in his The Method of the Vedanta (London: Kegan Paul International, 1989), lays out in detailed fashion Śaṅkara's theological method and argues for the validity of Śaṅkara's system. Sarasvati quotes Śaṅkara in Śaṅkara's bhāṣya on BS 4.3.14 (SBE, 38:401): "Are there two Absolutes, a supreme Absolute and a lower Absolute?" He answers, "Yes, there are two, as is shown by such texts as 'This Absolute, O Satyakama, in its supreme and lower aspects, Is Om' (Praśna, v.2)" (p. 130; see also Swāmī Nikhilānanda, trans., The Māṇḍūkyopaniṣad with Gauḍapāda's Kārikā and Śaṅkara's Commentary [Calcutta: Advaita Ashrama, 1987], 12 [noted from hereon as SBGK], wherein Śaṅkara mentions "the higher and lower Brahman", and p. 114 [2.27], wherein Gauḍapāda writes of para and apara brahman). By this differentiation of para and apara brahman Śaṅkara means nirguṇa brahman and saguṇa brahman. For Advaitins the accusation that the theology of para brahman as well as apara brahman produces an irreconcilable contradiction in śruti is answered with the phenomenon of avidyā (ignorance). Speaking of texts such as CU 3.14.2, where Brahman is said to consist of mind, vital energy, light, etc., Sarasvati anticipates the argument of the pūrvapakṣin (opponent) and asks, "But would not this contradict the texts affirming the non-duality of the Absolute?" He answers, "No. This objection stands refuted because the conditioning adjuncts [mind, vital energy, light] are name and form set up by ignorance [avidyā]" (p. 131). Further, Sarasvati has in his book already established that false attribution (or adhyāsa, superimposition) is a necessary prerequisite to parā vidyā, for parā vidyā cannot exist without its counterpart (just as no concept of light can exist without the concept of dark). Only then can the false attributions, which are attributed to the Absolute, be negated. This, says Sarasvati, is called the "method of false attribution", an epistemological method adopted by Advaitins (p. 43).

[25] Methods of Knowledge According to Advaita Vedanta, 75.

[26] SBE, 34:369. Paul David Devanandan concludes, "It follows, then, that the Īśvara himself is of the 'lower' order of knowledge" (The Concept of Māyā: An Essay in Historical Survey of the Hindu Theory of the World, with Special Reference to the Vedānta [London: Lutterworth Press, 1950], 102).

empirical world through māyā[27] [the power or śakti of Brahman that causes the illusory world].[28]

In his BSB Śaṅkara anticipates the objection that if there is a world of moving objects and Brahman is the only reality that is pure consciousness, how can there even be movement of objects? He answers the objection on the grounds of lower Brahman: "Such objections have repeatedly been refuted by our pointing to the fact of the Lord being fictitiously connected with Māyā, which consists of name and form [i.e. the world of objects] presented by Nescience [or wrong knowledge, avidyā]."[29]

Śaṅkara must have an answer for śruti and smṛti texts that assume the existence of beings and objects other than Brahman. One such text is BG 9.5b: "My Self brings beings into existence and sustains them."[30] I shall go into greater detail later as I explore Śaṅkara's explanation of the jagat (world), but for now I simply mention that Śaṅkara indeed has a framework for his exegesis of such creation texts, and it is that of Īśvara.[31] In BG 9.5 he associates the process of creation with Īśvara. In his BGB Śaṅkara paraphrases the words of Kṛṣṇa: "Behold, the manner of My creative power or of fashioning beings by me as the Lord [Īśvara], i.e. the truth of the Lord's creative process."[32] So much

---

[27] "[I]t is also through this power of māyā that the Absolute, the unrelated nirguṇa Brahman becomes a saguṇa Brahman, the Īśvara" (Devanandan, The Concept of Māyā, 107).

[28] Interesting is Paul Deussen's comment that Śaṅkara's doctrine of lower Brahman "should on the contrary be described as Theism" (The System of the Vedanta [New Delhi: Puja Publications, 1983], 119). Here as well there is room for Śaṅkara to view Brahman through Īśvara as the material cause of the world (see BS 2.2.37-38). There is in this assertion of Śaṅkara in his BSB an implicit rejection of a "maker" of a world from which the material for that world is other than from Brahman. Concerning BS 2.2.37, Śaṅkara states that its purpose "is to make an energetic attack on the doctrine that the Lord is not the material cause, but merely the ruler, i.e. the operative cause of the world; a doctrine entirely opposed to the Vedāntic tenet of the unity of Brahman" (SBE, 34:434). Further, Śaṅkara opposes the view of creation from non-existence. In another work of his he states, "no example can be cited for illustrating the birth of an existing thing from non-existence ... Therefore, existence does not come out of non-existence" (Swāmī Gambhīrānanda, trans., Chāndogya Upaniṣad with the Commentary of Śaṅkarācārya [Calcutta: Advaita Ashrama, 1983], 419; noted from hereon as SCUB).

[29] SBE, 34:369.

[30] SBGB, 299.

[31] "Īśvara, in collaboration with māyā, brings into being this creative manifold" (Devanandan, The Concept of Māyā, 107).

[32] SBGB, 299. In addition, recall my mention of certain śruti and smṛti texts teaching apara brahman or Īśvara for the purpose of facilitating future parā vidyā or higher knowledge of things as they are. Satprakashananda states, "The creative process is intended for the experience and the liberation of the individual souls" (Methods of Knowledge According to Advaita Vedanta, 76). Malkovsky notes this as a hermeneutic of many Advaitins (see Bradley Malkovsky, "The Personhood of Śaṁkara's Para

has this framework of Īśvara affected his understanding of phenomenological texts that he interprets BG 9.7 ("All beings, Arjuna! at the end of a cycle repair to my nature [prakṛtim]"[33]) as "All beings, Arjuna! repair to my lower nature [aparāṁ prakṛtim]."[34]

Another such text is BG 15.16, which reads, "In the world are these two Persons, the perishable and the imperishable. The perishable consists of all beings, the imperishable is the immovable."[35] Interesting is Śaṅkara's preface to this verse and his subsequent interpretation of verses 16-18. In the preface to verse 16 (16.0) in his BGB he states that the Lord is "distinguished by His perishable and imperishable adjuncts[36] [śarāśaropādhi]".[37] He then proceeds in his BGB to set this understanding of the Lord "In the world of transmigratory life [saṁsāra[38]]".[39] Only within this sphere (the sphere of apara brahman where saṁsāra exists), where the māyāśakti of Īśvara operates, must Īśvara be understood to possess śarāśaropādhi.

If it seems to some that Śaṅkara has imposed his presuppositions upon the text, his disciples would argue that he is not without textual warrant for such

---

Brahman", The Journal of Religion 77 [1997]: 550). Malkovsky cites A. G. Krishna Warrier's God in Advaita (Simla: Indian Institute of Advanced Study, 1977) as a source.

[33] SBGB, 301. According to Sargeant, prakṛtim here is "material nature" (The Bhagavad Gītā, 383). This is Śaṅkara's opportunity to call Brahman's material nature "lower", as we shall see above. Rāmānuja interprets prakṛtim as Brahman's body (RBGB, 299).

[34] SBGB, 301; emphasis added. Śaṅkara does not always use the word Īśvara in the negative sense of apara brahman in fictitious connection with the jagat-prapañca. See SBGB, 306 and his commentary on BG 9.13:

> But magnanimous persons having capacious minds adore Me the Lord [Īśvara], Arjuna! 'resorting to a nature that is divine'—marked by restraint of mind and senses, compassion, faith, etc. They are 'single-minded'—having a mind given to nothing other than Me. They know Me to be 'the imperishable source'—the eternal cause, of things like space, etc., and of living beings.

Here, knowing Īśvara in this way is positive and necessary. This affirms Sarasvati's view (the "method of false attribution" mentioned in n. 24) that true knowledge cannot exist without its counterpart. Lower Brahman must be known and recognized if higher Brahman is to have any sort of definition. To counter this, see Malkovsky, "The Personhood of Śaṁkara's Para Brahman", 553-55, wherein Malkovsky argues for "A revised Īśvara-para brahman relation" that, in part, views Īśvara as synonymous with para brahman.

[35] SBGB, 505.

[36] Phenomena or attributes.

[37] SBGB, 505.

[38] This is the continuing cycle of birth, death and rebirth through the "Lord's power of māyā" (bhagavataḥ māyāśaktiḥ). In Śaṅkara's view saṁsāra is mithyā and only exists through aparā vidyā or lower knowledge.

[39] SBGB, 506.

words.[40] BG 15.17 and 15.18 read, respectively, "Distinct from these [perishable and imperishable] is the Supreme Spirit", and, "Since I surpass the perishable and am exalted above the imperishable".[41] The para brahman in Śaṅkara's system is beyond all limiting adjuncts (upādhi), "beyond all name and form",[42] because they are "postulated through nescience [avidyā]".[43]

### 2.1.3. Brahman as Antaryāmin

Rāmānuja is well known for his doctrine of Brahman as antaryāmin, the "inner controller", but Śaṅkara also makes use of the title. This would seem odd given that Śaṅkara denies the ultimate reality of the world of objects, and that by its very nature antaryāmin implies an inner controller of objects. But Śaṅkara stands ready for the challenge of answering this implication.

Interesting is Śaṅkara's opening statement of his BGB, where he praises Nārāyaṇa, whom Warrier notes as God the indweller (antaryāmin), the Lord (bhagavān) who created the jagat.[44] Śaṅkara continues in the opening section to label Nārāyaṇa as the "all-pervading creator" (ādikartā viṣṇuḥ),[45] thus defining what he means by antaryāmin. But Śaṅkara stops here, and therefore one must interpret this in the overall context of his advaita, which postulates immediate realness to the world of objects, yet concludes with an ultimate monism with regard to the world of objects. The meaning of antaryāmin, then, is two-pronged; on the one hand Nārāyaṇa indwells the jagat-prapañca as the Self of all, but on the other hand that Self is ultimately all there is. (Which implies that Kṛṣṇa does not, in the ultimate sense, possess an individual soul.[46])

Immediately following this opening section of his BGB, Śaṅkara, in section two of his introduction, asserts that the antaryāmin is in sovereign control of his "all-pervasive Māyā" (vaiṣnavīṁ māyāṁ).[47] The antaryāmin, then, should also be understood in light of Śaṅkara's doctrine of māyā, the śakti of Brahman that causes the illusion of both names of objects and forms of objects (and I must here include the body of Kṛṣṇa) through avidyā. In this sense Warrier

---

[40] Yet some may argue that he is indeed without warrant. Since BG 15.16 states, "In the world are these two Persons [puruṣau], the perishable and the imperishable", to interpret puruṣa as "adjunct" is textually and etymologically unwarranted. Perhaps this is why (in part) Arvind Sharma states that "Śaṅkara's position is cogent, but only within the framework of his own philosophy after it has been superimposed on the Gītā" (Arvind Sharma, The Hindu Gītā: Ancient and Classical Interpretations of the Bhagavadgītā [London: Duckworth, 1986], 78).

[41] SBGB, 506,507.

[42] Carman, The Theology of Ramanuja, 158.

[43] SBGB, 507.

[44] SBGB, 1 n. 1.

[45] SBGB, 2.

[46] See chapter 7, section 3.4, point six, section C.

[47] SBGB, 3.

defines it as "the power by which the Absolute appears as the world".[48] Illusion, then, would be adhyāsa caused by Brahman's māyā.[49] Śaṅkara's concept of māyā then becomes crucial to his understanding of the avatāra of Kṛṣṇa. He states in the opening section of his BGB that Kṛṣṇa was born as an aspect (aṁśa) of Nārāyaṇa, and in section two that "He appears, by virtue of His Māyā, to be embodied and born as man."[50] Through māyā the avatāra only appears to be real.

With his interpretation of BG 18.46b ("Him from whom all beings have proceeded and by whom all this has been pervaded") Śaṅkara agrees with Rāmānuja that the antaryāmin is the Lord.[51] But Śaṅkara disagrees with Rāmānuja in that Śaṅkara's antaryāmin is Īśvara in the sense described above. Śaṅkara's antaryāmin is inner controller of "all beings" insofar as beings operate in the realm of saṁsāra (and apara brahman), but we are to transcend that ultimately illusory realm and recognize that the para brahman, the Supreme Self, is pure consciousness alone.[52]

### 2.1.4. The Cosmic Form

To many the highlight of the story of the BG comes in chapter 11 when Kṛṣṇa reveals the splendor of his cosmic form only to Arjuna (11.47) in the world of men (11.48). The BG states,

> Behold, Son of Pṛthā,[53] my forms, a hundredfold, rather a thousandfold. Various, divine, and of various colors and shapes ... Behold now the entire universe, with everything moving and not moving, here standing together in my body ... Thus having spoken, O King, the Great Lord of Yoga, Hari (Vishnu), revealed to the son of Pṛthā His majestic supreme form. Of many mouths and eyes, of many wondrous aspects, of many divine ornaments, of many uplifted divine weapons ... If there should be in the sky a thousand suns risen all at once, such splendor would be of the splendor of that Great Being. There the entire universe, standing as one, divided in many ways, the son of Pāṇḍu then beheld in the body of the God of Gods ... With many arms, bellies, faces, eyes, I see Thee everywhere, infinite in form. Not the end, nor the middle, nor yet the

---

48 SBGB, xiii; emphasis mine.

49 Satprakashananda, Methods of Knowledge According to Advaita Vedanta, 124-26.

50 SBGB, 2,3.

51 SBGB, 590.

52 To followers of Rāmānuja it would seem that there would be on the part of Advaitins no need of antaryāmin (or any talk of antaryāmin) when one is merged with the para brahman. Further, the Advaitin would therefore have to place all dialogue of this sort (between Kṛṣṇa and Arjuna) in the realm of saṁsāra, a part of the lower reality that is mithyā and caused by adhyāsa.

53 Arjuna.

beginning of Thee I see, O Lord of all, whose form is the universe [BG 11.5,7,9,10,12,13,16].[54]

How does Śaṅkara deal with the Lord's cosmic form that is described as "thousands, varied, divine [divya], variously coloured and shaped", "the entire world of beings", and "with many a mouth and many an eye", phenomena that strongly imply the real material existence of the cosmic form?

He begins by saying they are divine (11.5), "shaped in heaven [divi bhavāni], i.e., they are not of Prakṛti or Matter [aprākṛta]".[55] Based on this statement one would expect the cosmic form to be para brahman or higher Brahman because of the disassociation of the divine form with prakṛti. This, however, does not appear to be the case. We must explore Śaṅkara's comments at the beginning of the next chapter of the BG to see what he, in the end, says about the cosmic form.

Śaṅkara takes BG 12.1 to be a dichotomy of existence of Brahman (para brahman / apara brahman). The verse reads, "Of those devotees, who, ever integrated, worship You thus [evaṁ] elaborately, and those who worship the Unmanifest, the Imperishable".[56] Evaṁ (thus), says Śaṅkara, "refers to the ideas set forth in the immediately preceding verse", the very end of chapter 11 (11.55), and refers to those "who meditate on You in Your cosmic form", which, interestingly, he describes as "lordly" (aiśvaraṁ, from Īśvara).[57] These are distinguished from "those who ... worship the imperishable Brahman described earlier [in chaps. 2-10[58]]—Brahman who is unmanifest, being adjunctless[59] and beyond the range of the senses".[60] The key here is that Śaṅkara refers his readers to BG chapters 2-10, where he describes a Brahman that is not the cosmic form of chapter 11. This Brahman "is beyond the range of words and is not capable of being described ... [and] not revealed by any means of cognition".[61] Indeed, the best we can do here is recite "neti neti".

How is it, then, that such a glorious appearance in cosmic form—a form, to

---

[54] From Sargeant, The Bhagavad Gītā, 457,459,461,462,464,465,468, on my part with a number of modifications to capitalization and punctuation.

[55] SBGB, 349.

[56] SBGB, 384-85.

[57] SBGB, 384.

[58] SBGB, 384.

[59] Thus this statement about the "imperishable Brahman" should not be confused with Śaṅkara's statement about "the Lord" made in my section 2.1.2 concerning BG 15.16, where in section 16.0 of his BGB he states that the Lord possesses perishable and "imperishable adjuncts". The former is not the same as the latter. There is here, then, a distinction for Śaṅkara. Here he writes of the ultimate Brahman that does not possess adjuncts, whereas in section 16.0 of his BGB, he writes of the Lord that possesses adjuncts.

[60] SBGB, 385; emphases added.

[61] SBGB, 387.

use Śaṅkara's words, "not of Prakṛti"[62] and thus a form that should by definition be associated with the para brahman—should be distinguished from the Unmanifest, the para brahman? Śaṅkara has employed his doctrine of Īśvara (apara brahman) to explain the appearance of the cosmic form in BG chapter 11. The reference in the BG to the cosmic form as divya, which Śaṅkara interprets as "shaped in heaven" (divi bhavāni) must therefore find association with apara brahman.[63]

### 2.1.5. Summary

Śaṅkara concludes that para Brahman alone is real. But Śaṅkara still accounts for the fact that humans perceive a world of objects. These everyday phenomena he explains within the contexts of Īśvara, apara Brahman in fictitious connection with māyā, and with Brahman as antaryāmin who through māyā appears as the world. Śruti texts relating a world of objects, even the cosmic form of Kṛṣṇa in BG chapter 11, are therefore relegated to these contexts. When all is said and done, para brahman is characterized by abheda and para brahman alone is real.

## 3. The Jagat and Jīva-s in Relation to Brahman

Śaṅkara would readily admit that pratyakṣa suggests the reality of the jagat. Therefore Śaṅkara must somehow account for the jagat-prapañca, that is, the appearance of prakṛti and of jīva-s, even though ultimately Brahman alone exists as non-differentiated pure being and consciousness. In other words, he must explain the many in relation to the (ultimately real) one. How does Brahman relate to the jagat and to the jīva? How do the jagat and jīva-s relate to Brahman? These questions are important to ask and to answer if any sense is going to be made of Śaṅkara's theological framework, including his doctrine of Kṛṣṇāvatāra. I begin with the Advaitin's view of the jagat.

### 3.1. The Jagat

Śaṅkara's kevalādvaita is well thought out, and he does in fact account for the jagat-prapañca, not in simple fashion but by a carefully built system that he

---

[62] Unlike Rāmānuja, who believes that his Lord possesses a "non-prakṛtic", anthropomorphic divine form (divya rūpa) from which the material for the body of Kṛṣṇāvatāra is fashioned, Śaṅkara does not set forth a doctrine of avatāra wherein the body is fashioned from a non-prakṛtic substance. Note, however, that Rāmānuja does not associate the divya rūpa with the cosmic form of BG 11, for the latter consists of prakṛti (see RBGB,362).

[63] And from this it follows that to Śaṅkara the concept of heaven finds its identity in the jagat-prapañca and cannot therefore be associated with para brahman, the Brahman that alone exists as pure consciousness.

believes does justice to the overall teaching of śruti.[64] What makes Śaṅkara so interesting is that he had to account for what appears to be the case in everyday experience through pratyakṣa—that there are objects visible to us which appear quite real (including the avatāra). Here the doctrine of māyā plays a most important role.

### 3.1.1. Brahman and Māyā

For the Advaitin the jagat-prapañca is ultimately illusion.[65] There is no ultimate reality to it, for Brahman is truly the only reality. And "Just as a person out of confusion perceives only the snake, leaving aside the rope, so does an ignorant person see only the phenomenal world [jagat] without knowing reality [satyaṁ]."[66] With Śaṅkara māyā is considered primarily to be the śakti of Brahman that causes the jagat-prapañca and it is inextricably linked with avidyā or ajñāna[67] in the phenomenon of bheda in the perception of the phenomenal world. Further, though māyā is the principal cause of the appearance of the illusion, it is not the appearance itself,[68] for it has no being (sat) or non-being (asat), because in the end Brahman is the only reality.[69] Śaṅkara writes, "Māyā is properly called undeveloped or non-manifested since it cannot be defined either as that which is or that which is not."[70]

---

[64] See SBGK, 86-135, chapter 2, entitled "Illusion" by Nikhilānanda. In this lengthy portion of the Kārikā are many noteworthy statements from both Gauḍapāda and Śaṅkara to the effect that the jagat-prapañca is mithyā. Gauḍapāda and Śaṅkara start by declaring that objects in dreams are unreal or false (pp. 86-89 [2.1-4a]), and declare the same concerning objects in the waking state (p. 89, [2.4b and following]). Nikhilānanda, the translator of this work, comes directly to the point in a note: "The world that is seen extended in time and space ... [is] all nothing but the ideas in the mind of the Creator, i.e., Ātman as Īśvara" (p. 102 n. 3).

[65] M. Hiryanna, The Essentials of Indian Philosophy (London: George Allen & Unwin, 1949), 155. There are some Advaitins who object to the term "illusion" to describe the advaita view of the world of appearance, guarding against attempts to define illusion as absolutely void of existence. Such is not the case, they say, for even the illusion has some kind of existence (though see the previous note, and note also that "illusion" is used in translation throughout SBGK). See Satprakashananda, Methods of Knowledge According to Advaita Vedanta, 67. Satprakashananda seems to prefer the term "unreal" in reference to the world.

[66] Swami Vimuktananda, trans., Aparokshānubhuti: Or Self-Realization of Sri Sankarāchārya (Calcutta: Advaita Ashrama, 2000), 50, par. 95.

[67] Because of this link Śaṅkara can also state, "The Vedānta texts declare ignorance [ajñāna] to be verily the material (cause) of the phenomenal world [prapañca]" (Vimuktananda, Aparokshānubhuti, 49-50, par. 94).

[68] K. Satchidananda Murty, Revelation and Reason in Advaita Vedanta (New York: Columbia University Press, 1959), 4.

[69] And thus Brahman is said to be "the root of the universe" (SCUB, 497 [interpreting CU 6.16.3]).

[70] SBE, 34:243.

Māyā cannot be sat, for only Brahman exists. Here Śaṅkara, ever the apologist, anticipates an objection. If Brahman is the only reality, how is there room for motion of something else within this aduality? In other words, how can one believe at the same time the absolute oneness of Brahman, which is pure intelligence, and the motion or action of objects in the jagat-prapañca?[71] Śaṅkara answers with the analogy of a magnet, which lacks motion, yet is capable of moving "other things".[72] Further, as we saw earlier, because of adhyāsa Brahman[73] is "fictitiously connected with māyā".[74] If the connection is fictitious, then māyā cannot be sat.

On the other hand, māyā cannot be asat, for we somehow have to account for its existence. It is here that Śaṅkara maintains that māyā must be associated with Brahman as Īśvara, the personal Lord, and that in this context māyā is still primarily the śakti of Brahman.[75] But Śaṅkara also calls upon SU 4.10: "Know then Prakṛti is Māyā, and the Lord [Īśvara] he who is affected with Māyā." Thus māyā as prakṛti, insofar as it is connected with Brahman, is also the material cause of the world.[76] In the end, however, even though māyā, prakṛti and avidyā are at times linked to the creation as its material cause, it is Brahman that is ultimately responsible for the jagat-prapañca, for Brahman is the ground of the jagat-prapañca.[77]

### 3.1.2. LĪLĀ

The question now arises as to why an undifferentiated Brahman, a being that is pure consciousness, all that really exists, and all-sufficient in and of itself, would need to be associated at all with the jagat, no matter what the explanation of the jagat might be. Śaṅkara writes, "If, then, on the one hand, you assume [creating the world] to serve some purpose of the intelligent highest Self [Brahman], you thereby sublate [remove] its self-sufficiency vouched for by Scripture."[78] In other words, a being that is self-sufficient does not need anything; so to say that creation serves a purpose of Brahman cancels out the claim of śruti that Brahman is self-sufficient. Further, to create implies a motive for creation, and motive is something that ultimate Brahman cannot

---

[71] SBE, 34:369.

[72] Rāmānuja would object to such an analogy, arguing that in advaita there are no "other things". He argues similarly against the Advaitin's analogy of clay as Brahman and thus the cause, and jars as the effect, charging that Śaṅkara is using an unreal effect to play the role of the cause. See chapter 3, section 2.1.3.

[73] Brahman in both higher and lower realms.

[74] SBE, 34:369.

[75] SBE, 34:361-62.

[76] SBE, 34:xxv (Thibaut's introduction). In a note in SBUB Mādhavānanda states that prakṛti is "The primordial stuff out of which the universe has been formed" (p. 338 n. 2).

[77] See note 87.

[78] SBE, 34:356.

possess. BS 2.1.32 reads, "([Ultimate] Brahman is) not (the creator of the world), on account of (beings engaging in any action) having a motive."[79] Further complicating matters, Śaṅkara knows that "if, on the other hand, you affirm absence of motive on its [Brahman's] part, you must affirm absence of activity [of creation] also".[80] But this he cannot do, for experience and scripture imply the existence of the jagat-prapañca.

Śaṅkara answers these dilemmas by employing the analogy of princes and others of high standing who have all they need and have no unfulfilled desires, but still engage in sport or play (līlā) for no purpose whatsoever.[81] He further argues "that the process of inhalation and exhalation is going on without reference to any extraneous purpose, merely following the law of its own nature. Analogously, the activity of the Lord may also be supposed to be mere sport, proceeding from his own nature."[82]

One might here raise pertinent arguments against Śaṅkara, the most obvious being that when princes engage in līlā, even though it be said they have all they need, it logically implies they lack līlā. Śaṅkara answers that on the ground of reason and scripture we simply cannot come to any other conclusion than that of holding to both the all-sufficiency of the Lord and the fact that the Lord engages in līlā. "Nor can his nature be questioned", says Śaṅkara, even if "we might possibly, by close scrutiny, detect some subtle motive, even for sportful action, ... as the Scripture says".[83] Śaṅkara ends his argument with an appeal to śruti. He employs one of his mahāvākya-s, MU 2.1.4: "[Brahman is] the Self of everything",[84] with which he interprets other śruti texts implying creation, and because of which he labels the creation "apparent" as a result of adhyāsa:

> Nor can it be said that he [the Lord] either does not act or acts like a senseless person; for Scripture affirms the fact of the creation on the one hand, and the Lord's omniscience on the other hand. And, finally, we must remember that the scriptural doctrine of creation does not refer to the highest reality; it refers to the apparent world only, which is characterised by name and form, the figments of Nescience [avidyā], and it, moreover, aims at intimating that Brahman is the Self of everything.[85]

### 3.1.3. Sleep, Dreams and Illusion: An Explanation of the Jagat

As seen in the above quotation, for Śaṅkara the jagat exists insofar as it is imagined to exist, and it exists insofar as it is the product of the śakti of

---

79 SBE, 34:356.
80 SBE, 34:356.
81 SBE, 34:356-57.
82 SBE, 34:357.
83 SBE, 34:357.
84 This is also a mahāvākya of Rāmānuja.
85 SBE, 34:357.

Brahman, specifically māyā, the power that causes the jagat-prapañca. But, and again as implied in the above quotation, the jagat is real to a certain, apparent extent.[86] This apparent realness of the jagat is due to Brahman in his mode as Īśvara.[87]

Śaṅkara also employs analogies within the category of sleep, dreams and illusions as explanations of the jagat. For example, in a dream the work of māyā is to make it seem that one is fighting with another person in hand-to-hand combat. The fight is real insofar as one has imagined it (it is an act of adhyāsa), but is not in actuality real. As Gauḍapāda explains, "As are dreams and illusions or a castle in the air seen in the sky, so is the universe viewed by the wise in the Vedānta."[88]

To illustrate this point of the existence of adhyāsa and māyā in the waking state, Śaṅkara appeals to various illustrations. For example, "But what have we to understand by the term 'superimposition?'—The apparent presentation, in the form of remembrance, to consciousness of something previously observed, in some other thing ... 'Mother-of-pearl appears like silver', 'The moon although one only appears as if she were double.'"[89]

Concerning the famous shell-silver analogy,[90] where a person coming upon what is in reality a shell mistakes it for a piece of silver, Śaṅkara writes, "Similarly, in the sentence 'he sees the piece of shell as silver', the word 'shell' simply means the actual shell, whereas the word 'silver' implies the imaginary idea of silver. One merely imagines silver, although there is in fact no silver

---

[86] Satprakashananda notes that there is indeed empirical existence, unlike "a barren woman's son, which is entirely false". Toward this he quotes Śaṅkara's TU bhāṣya. Under TU 2.6 Śaṅkara states, "Relative to the illusory objects [which also, as noted, have some kind of existence], such as mirage, actual water and the like are real" (Methods of Knowledge According to Advaita Vedanta, 67). Here the sense is that in the jagat-prapañca, which is "empirical", "water is said to be true in comparison with water in a mirage which is false" (Swāmī Gambhīrānanda, trans., Eight Upaniṣads: With the Commentary of Śaṅkarācārya [Calcutta: Advaita Ashrama, 2000], 1:358 [Śaṅkara interpreting TU 2.1]; noted from hereon as STUB). The idea here is that the world is real insofar as it is imagined to be real, just as water is imagined to be real in a mirage.

[87] SBE, 34:xxv, and Satprakashananda, Methods of Knowledge According to Advaita Vedanta, 75-76. Further, Brahman is also the sole support, the ground, of both the world of experience and Īśvara (Satprakashananda, Methods of Knowledge, 75).

[88] SBGK, 118 (2.31).

[89] SBE, 34:4,5. Padmapāda defines adhyāsa as "the manifestation of the nature of something in another which is not of that nature". "That (manifestation), it is reasonable to hold, is false (mithyā)" (D. Venkataramiah, ed. and trans., The Pañcapādikā of Padmapāda [Baroda: Oriental Institute, 1948], 8).

[90] What follows may also be said of Śaṅkara's rope-snake analogy. Here a person mistakes a piece of rope for a snake.

there."[91] Swami Satchidanandendra Sarasvati offers these words: "Here what is said is that there is indeed non-existence of silver in the shell, and that the true nature of the silver is shell and nothing else."[92] Thus, regarding Brahman and the jagat, Śaṅkara holds that the jagat (analogous to silver), though appearing real in the confines of adhyāsa and māyā, has as its true nature the pure non-differentiated Brahman[93] (analogous to the shell).

## 3.2. The Soul

From our discussion thus far we have seen that Śaṅkara holds to a hermeneutic of ultimate abheda and mithyā in the category of Brahman in relation to the jagat. The only reality is Brahman, which is pure non-differentiated being. We have also seen that since śruti at the very least implies the existence of the empirical world, Śaṅkara was forced to answer how this is so. This he did in the context of certain epistemic and interpretive categories such as Īśvara, māyā, adhyāsa, and avidyā.

How the jīva relates to Brahman is of particular importance to the study of Kṛṣṇāvatāra, for what is determined here has implications for Kṛṣṇāvatāra and aids in answering specific questions that arise with regard to the body-soul-divine relation.

### 3.2.1. The Jīva not Individual but Brahman

As with śruti implying the existence of the jagat-prapañca, likewise śruti implies the existence of the individual jīvātman or jīva, and a plurality of jīvātman-s or jīva-s. But since the master Advaitin comes to the conclusion that Brahman is all, in the monistic sense, it follows first that what appears to be the individual jīva is in reality not individual, and second that the individual jīva is Brahman: "The existence of Brahman is known on the ground of its being the Self of everyone ... And this Self ... is Brahman."[94] Śaṅkara therefore argues that a plurality of individual jīva-s cannot ultimately exist, because there is no plurality; Brahman is all there is, and therefore the jīva must be Brahman.

#### 3.2.1.1. No Individuality

Individuality resulting in the appearance or thought of a body of flesh is the result of adhyāsa, the act of imposing attributes and flesh upon the Self: "Attributes of the body are superimposed on the Self,[95] if a man thinks of

---

[91] Sarasvati, The Method of the Vedanta, 400. This is Sarasvati's translation of Śaṅkara's commentary of BS 4.1.5. See SBE, 38:344.
[92] The Method of the Vedanta, 401.
[93] See note 87.
[94] SBE, 34:14.
[95] See SBGK, 121. Here Śaṅkara states, "Duality is superimposed upon Ātman through ignorance, like the snake, etc., upon the rope."

himself as stout, lean, fair, as standing, walking, or jumping."[96] Once adhyāsa takes hold, it also gives rise to the views of the jīvātman as individual and different in relation to other jīvātman-s, views that must be "discarded"[97] if mokṣa from saṁsāra is to take place. Śaṅkara's saṁsāra is multi-faceted. Generally speaking it is the cycle of birth, death, and rebirth, but it must be understood as ultimately mithyā. Further, the saṁsāra-state contains in itself the world of multiplicity and has as its seed adhyāsa.[98] Upon attaining mokṣa the jīvātman being subject to saṁsāra (which includes the erroneous idea of a multiplicity of jīva-s) comes to an end, and saṁsāra itself comes to an end.[99]

As a result Śaṅkara sets himself against those who hold to both difference and non-difference (bhedābheda) at the same time.[100] He says, "Should you say that ... the soul is a part of the Lord,[101] we reply that such might be the case if the intention of the texts were to teach difference as well as non-difference. But the fact is that the texts aim solely at teaching non-difference."[102]

3.2.1.2. Ontological Oneness

Śaṅkara employs the example of deep sleep not only as an analogy of oneness with Brahman, but also as the actual state of oneness with Brahman. At the point of deep sleep the jīva enters into a state in which it is not conscious of any limiting adjuncts (physical actions or attributes) and enjoys its non-difference from Brahman.[103] Śaṅkara then anticipates an objection: "This would mean that from the waking and dreaming states to the deep sleep state the soul slips in and out of oneness with Brahman!" Not so, says Śaṅkara:

> It cannot, moreover, be said that the soul is at any time not united with Brahman—for its true nature can never pass away—; but considering that

---

[96] SBE, 34:8-9. In his Pañcapādikā, Padmapāda, in a section on superimposition, states "that the ultimate nature of the individual soul (ātman) alleged to be samsārin (transmigratory being) is one of uniform bliss, the very essence of existence, non-mutable and consciousness entire. And that teaching [i.e., the alleged individual transmigratory soul is really the Absolute Being] conflicts with the notion 'I am the doer', 'I am happy'" (Venkataramiah, The Pañcapādikā of Padmapāda, 3).

[97] See SCUB, 456 (interpreting CU 6.8.1).

[98] SBE, 34:14, 38:69.

[99] SBE, 34:439.

[100] For examples, the bhedābheda of Bhāskara (lived near the time of Śaṅkara) and the Mīmāṁsā school (along with Vedānta, one of the six orthodox philosophical schools; it holds to a plurality of jīva-s and the true existence of the world of objects). Nimbārka, a philosopher within the Vedānta tradition, also taught bhedābheda (see Introduction, section 5.1.2.3).

[101] This is Rāmānuja's view. See Thibaut's remarks in his introduction to Śaṅkara's commentary (SBE, 34:lviii).

[102] SBE, 38:66.

[103] SBE, 38:145.

in the state of waking and that of dreaming it passes, owing to the contact [superimposition] with its limiting adjuncts [attributes], into something else, as it were, it may be said that when those adjuncts cease in deep sleep it passes back into its true nature.[104]

Śaṅkara is saying that during deep sleep the soul is enjoying what it truly is all the time—ontologically one with Brahman. But during the waking and dreaming states this continuing oneness is hidden by limiting adjuncts that māyā places upon the jīva.[105]

Śaṅkara's mahāvākya-s, and those of Advaitins in general, are those texts which affirm the ontological oneness of the jīva with Brahman.[106] Indeed, the puruṣa (synonymous here with jīvātman or jīva) "is the subject of the Upaniṣads".[107] For Śaṅkara the most important verse in the Upaniṣads is CU 6.8.7, where a teacher states to his pupil, "Now that which is that subtle essence, in it all that exists has its self. It is the True. It is the Self, and thou, O Svetaketu, art it." This Upaniṣad's declaration, "tat tvam asi", states that Svetaketu's jīva is Brahman.[108]

---

[104] SBE, 38:145.

[105] Here I register a caveat. Although Śaṅkara mentions the waking and dreaming states in the same breath, he takes time to differentiate between the two. They are not analogous. He has for his authority BS 2.2.29: "And on account of their difference of nature (the ideas of the waking state) are not like those of a dream." Things of which we are conscious in dreams are negated by the waking state. Thus, persons may have dreams of meeting others, but once awakened they know that they wrongly thought these meetings took place. This then differs from the waking state, says Śaṅkara. The context in which Śaṅkara makes this statement concerns various types of Bauddha philosophies. Thibaut, in his discussion of Śaṅkara's view of māyā, states that Śaṅkara has "to reject the idealistic doctrine of certain Bauddha schools according to which nothing whatever exists … for external things, although not real in the strict sense of the word, enjoy at any rate as much reality as the specific cognitional acts whose objects they are" (SBE, 34:xxvi). Sarasvati, an Advaitin, concurs: "In the Vedanta school this is accepted, and interpreted according to the doctrine called Sat-kārya Vāda ["the effect exists prior to its manifestation in a latent state in the cause" (John Grimes, A Concise Dictionary of Indian Philosophy, 325)]. Though the effect is utterly non-existent as effect, it is eternally real as the Absolute, the substratum on which it is projected" (The Method of the Vedanta, 81; see also Satprakashananda, Methods of Knowledge According to Vedanta, 67: "All effects with different names and forms are real only as Pure Existence but unreal in themselves").

[106] Grimes, A Concise Dictionary of Indian Philosophy, 194.

[107] SBE, 34:36.

[108] See Murty, Revelation and Reason in Advaita Vedanta, 90: "It is categorically stated in the Upaniṣad that the real Self [Brahman] ... is the individual soul." See also Julius J. Lipner, "The Self of Being and the Being of Self: Śaṃkara on 'That You Are' (Tat Tvam Asi)", in New Perspectives on Advaita Vedānta: Essays in Commemoration of Professor Richard De Smet, SJ, ed. Bradley J. Malkovsky (Leiden: Brill, 2000). Here

Given Śaṅkara's hermeneutic that the attributes of the body are erroneously superimposed by the subject, and that ultimately all is Brahman, there is no other way to interpret tat tvam asi. In chapter 18 of his US, śloka 197a, Śaṅkara teaches the ontological oneness of the jīva with Brahman: "The word 'That' means the Innermost Self [ātman]; the word 'Thou' thus means [the same thing as] the word 'That.'"[109]

Other mahāvākya-s from śruti include,

> This everything, all is that Self (BU 2.4.6).
>
> But when the Self only is all this, how should he see another, how should he know another, how should he know the knower? (BU 4.5.15)
>
> This Self is Brahman (BU 2.5.19).
>
> I am Brahman (BU 1.4.10).[110]
>
> If a man understands the Self, saying, "I am he",[111] what could he wish or desire that he should pine after the body? (BU 4.4.12)

In other words, the jīva simply is Brahman. Some may argue that it is, from the ultimate point of view, incorrect (in the context of nirvikalpa samādhi, the superconscious state[112]) to use the phrase "the jīva is Brahman", for the

---

Lipner argues on linguistic grounds and on the ground of chapter 18 of Śaṅkara's US that the referent of "That" is Brahman (see Swami Jagadananda, trans., Upadeśa Sāhasrī: A Thousand Teachings, in Two Parts—Prose and Poetry of Śrī Śaṅkarāchārya [Mylapore: Sri Ramakrishna Math, n.d.], 218-87; noted as US).

[109] My translation of the Sanskrit text taken from US, 276. See also Lipner, "The Self of Being and the Being of Self", 63-64, where Lipner's translation of śloka 197 conveys the same meaning. Sanskrit reads tacchabdaḥ pratyagātmārthas tacchabdārthas tvamas tathā.

[110] A verse that is reiterated throughout Śaṅkara's US, and upon which Śaṅkara spends a great deal of time in his BUB (SBUB, 145-74).

[111] Or "I am this" (ayam asmi), that is, the Supreme Self (see SBUB, 738 [interpreting 1.4.12]). In his commentary on the next verse (1.4.13) Śaṅkara declares that the knower of Brahman claims "I am the Supreme Brahman" and concludes that "all is his [the knower's] Self" (SBUB, 740).

[112] See Satprakashananda, Methods of Knowledge According to Advaita Vedanta, 223,250. Additionally, Śaṅkara states, "By the Nirvikalpa Samādhi the truth of Brahman is clearly and definitely realized, but not otherwise" (Swāmī Mādhavānanda, trans., Vivekacūḍāmaṇi [Crest-jewel of Discrimination] [Calcutta: Advaita Ashrama, 1998], 138-39, par. 365; noted from hereon as VC). It seems here that nirvikalpa samādhi is not merely a state at which to arrive, but is a means of attaining the state of absolute oneness with Brahman, as witnessed by the instrumental case (nirvikalpasamādhinā).

sentence assigns a particular, a description, to Brahman, which we simply cannot have in kevalādvaita. Rather, the true Self (Brahman) is neti neti and therefore in the realm of higher Brahman cannot be described.[113] But Śaṅkara could answer that the word jīva means Brahman, and this on the basis of his premier mahāvākya, tat tvam asi, which, when interpreted with his use of sāmānādhikaraṇya, means that the word "you" means "That".[114]

Śaṅkara is quick to add that smṛti also affirms that recognition of the jīva in its ultimate sense is the be-all and end-all of life. He cites the BG: "Having understood this, the understanding man has done with all work, O Bharata."[115] Further, since the BG also affirms that "All is Vasudeva [Brahman]" (vāsudevaḥ sarvam), it follows that the jīva is Brahman. But the jīva in reality is not a part (aṁśa) of Brahman[116]; the jīva is Brahman, there being abheda between Brahman and the jīva. Any bheda between Brahman and the jīva is mithyā. Śaṅkara states, "Those who are knowers of Brahman ... perceive their non-difference from the Lord [īśvarābheda]."[117]

---

[113] Though it may be argued that even neti neti implies description. For this see B. N. K. Sharma, Madhva's Teachings in Hs Own Words (Bombay: Bharatiya Vidya Bhavan, 1979), 112: "Even distinction from all empirical attributes (neti neti) is, after all, a characterization." Moreover, it is no wonder that some have accused Śaṅkara of believing that once the state of Brahman realization has been achieved, there simply is no need for śruti. After all, if śabda cannot legitimately be used to describe Brahman in nirvikalpa samādhi, what then becomes of tat tvam asi? Does it not imply erroneous usage of words as just described?

[114] See chapter 1, section 1.2.4.2. The Advaitin Sureśvara elaborates upon the statement "The space in the pot is the space in the sky." Taken literally this is a false statement, for the actual space in the pot is in the pot, and not in the sky. Therefore one should not take the sentence literally, but in such a way as to interpret it beyond a literal meaning, that is, that the space in the pot and the space in the sky share the same elementary nature. They are identical, and so it is with the intent of tat tvam asi. It is to teach the identity of the jīva as Brahman. I thank Karl H. Potter for bringing this to my attention. See his Advaita Vedānta up to Śaṃkara and His Pupils (Princeton, N.J.: Princeton University Press, 1981), 60.

[115] SBE, 34:36, citing BG 15.20.

[116] As per the philosophy of the bhedābheda Vedāntin Nimbārka (see Madan Mohan Agrawal, The Philosophy of Nimbārka [Gali Manahar, Sadabad {Mathura}: Shrimati Usha Agrawal, 1977], 65).

[117] SBGB, 140. The wording here (īśvarābheda) is interesting given Śaṅkara's doctrine of Īśvara. Though it is possible to interpret Īśvara as synonymous with Brahman, it may be taken another way. Upon realizing one's abheda from Īśvara or apara brahman, one achieves true recognition of the jīva as para brahman. This can be stated because Brahman is, ultimately, the ground of Īśvara. Therefore, realizing abheda between one's self and Īśvara is, ultimately, realization of abheda between one's self and Brahman (the Self).

### 3.2.2. THE JĪVA IN MOKṢA

This subject relates to this study by way of the eschatological relationship between the released jīva and Kṛṣṇa, which I discuss in chapter 7.[118]

For Śaṅkara the recognition of the jīva as Brahman in nirvikalpa samādhi is the object of the Upaniṣads and the terminating point of involvement in the seeming world of multiplicity, the jagat-prapañca. Texts teaching this are many, and they are there for a man[119] even though he "acts intent on external things" and is "anxious to attain the objects of his desire ... and does not thereby reach the highest aim of man".[120] These texts, says Śaṅkara, can "divert him from the objects of natural activity and turn the stream of his thoughts on the inward Self".[121]

In advaita "the individual soul [jīvātman] and the highest Self [paramātman, the Supreme Self, Brahman] differ in name only",[122] just as a jar (here analogous to the jīvātman) is in reality clay (here analogous to Brahman) but finds its seeming bheda in name alone. As śruti states, "Just as, my dear, by one clod of clay all that is made of clay is known, the difference being only a name, arising from speech, while the truth is that all is clay" (CU 6.1.4). "Plurality of Selfs" is therefore "senseless".[123] Indeed, it is Brahman who is hidden in what is erroneously thought of as (in the act of adhyāsa) the individuality of the jīva: "He who knows Brahman which is real, knowledge, infinite, as hidden in the cave" (TU 2.1). The abode of Brahman is the jīva (the cave), and the jīva is Brahman.[124] For this Śaṅkara cites a text that Rāmānuja often cites for his basis of the jagat as Brahman's body: "Having sent forth he entered into it" (TU 2.6).

"Moreover", claims Śaṅkara, "absolute Liberation cannot be achieved apart from the realisation of the nondual Self".[125] Upon understanding the ātman as essentially Brahman (and thus as paramātman), and, vice versa, the paramātman as the ātman, mokṣa is attained. As stated earlier, mokṣa is merging into oneness with Brahman (or going to or becoming Brahman). This

---

118 Section 3.4, point seven.

119 Here I represent the androcentricity of Śaṅkara's time. For examples, in his VC he states, "For all beings a human birth is difficult to obtain, more so is a male body [puṁstvaṁ]; rarer than that is Brāhmaṇahood" (p. 1, par. 2); "The man who, having by some means obtained a human birth, with a male body [pṛṁstvaṁ] and mastery of the Vedas to boot, is foolish enough not to exert himself for self-liberation, verily commits suicide, for he kills himself by clinging to things unreal" (p. 2, par. 4); "What greater fool is there than the man who having obtained a rare human body, and a masculine body [pāuruṣam] too, neglects to achieve the real end of this life?" (p. 3, par. 5).

120 SBE, 34:35.

121 SBE, 34:36.

122 SBE, 34:282.

123 SBE, 34:282.

124 Śaṅkara elaborates upon this in his commentary on TU. See STUB, 305-6.

125 SCUB, 4 (Śaṅkara's introduction).

"merging", however, lest it be understood to imply the passing of one thing to another, thereby logically implying bheda, must be understood as recognizing the already eternal state of the ātman as Brahman. As mentioned earlier, even when one's life is characterized by acknowledgement of the reality of the jagat-prapañca and the jīva as individual (through adhyāsa and avidyā), the reality is that even in these states the jīva is Brahman, though one may not know it. Śaṅkara addresses this in his BUB: "Even before knowing Brahman, everybody, being Brahman, is really always identical with all, but ignorance superimposes on him the idea that he is not Brahman and not all, as a mother-of pearl is mistaken for silver."[126] Thus, it seems first that the stress is not so much on merging but on realization of what one always has been (see just below: "Being Brahman he goes to Brahman" [BU 4.4.6]), and second that merging means realization.

In the state of mokṣa one has entered into (realized) one's own Self, the dissolution of the jagat-prapañca and of the individuality of jīva-s characterizes one's consciousness, and the absolute bliss that is Brahman manifests. "Bliss is Brahman" (TU 3.6.1), and "that man, too, in consequence of his knowledge culminating thus, gets established in the Bliss that is the supreme Brahman; that is to say, he becomes Brahman Itself".[127] In commenting on BS 4.4.15-16 ("The entering is like the flame of a lamp" and "Refers either to deep sleep or union"), Śaṅkara says, "By 'entering into one's own Self' is meant dreamless sleep; according to the text, 'He is gone to his own Self, he sleeps they say' [CU 6.8.1]. 'Union' means blissful isolation,[128] according to the text, 'Being Brahman he goes to Brahman' [BU 4.4.6 (brahmaiva san brahmāpyeti)]."[129] It is fitting, therefore, that the BSs end with an acclamation about those who have reached the world of Brahman, that world of blissful isolation in mokṣa through parā vidyā. Of them it is written, "there is non-return, according to scripture; non-return according to scripture" (BS 4.4.22). For Śaṅkara this BS speaks of "those who through perfect knowledge have dispelled all mental darkness and are devoted to the eternally perfect Nirvāṇa".[130] For them there is "non return", no return into the apparent saṁsāra.

---

[126] SBUB, 147 (interpreting BU 1.4.10, "I am Brahman"). Concerning the role of avidyā or ignorance, Padmapāda asserts, "the non-Brahman nature of the individual self has to be shown as being due to the play of avidyā" (Venkataramiah, The Pañcapādikā of Padmapāda, 4).

[127] STUB, 399.

[128] Or final release.

[129] SBE, 38:414-15.

[130] SBE, 38:419. Śaṅkara states that "the purpose of the science of the Gītā is to set forth the summum bonum, which consists in the total cessation of the transmigratory life [saṁsāra] and its causes. This is brought about by the law of implementation of Self-knowledge [ātmajñāna]" (SBGB, 4).

### 3.3. The Bhagavad Gītā

Essential to the overall discussion of the avatāra of Kṛṣṇa is the BG. The BG is arguably India's most treasured holy book. Though traditionally labeled smṛti, the BG[131] is a work worthy of commentary by Śaṅkara and Rāmānuja. As far as Śaṅkara is concerned, the BG supports his philosophy.

#### 3.3.1. ABHEDA AND THE BRAHMAVIDAḤ

In his comments on passages that applaud the brahmavidaḥ, "knowers of Brahman" (such as 4.10[132]), Śaṅkara mentions several times in his BGB that this knowledge has as a component the realization of abheda: "Those who are knowers of Brahman [brahmavidaḥ], who perceive their non-difference from the Lord [Īśvarābheda]".[133] Becoming a "knower" involves much. One must be brought to the place where one is no longer controlled by adhyāsa and avidyā. One is then able to perceive abheda between one's self and Brahman who was acting as Īśvara. The veil thereby lifted, one comes to the realization that para brahman is all there is and that the jīvātman in the jagat-prapañca was simply mithyā or a dream that disappeared with the dawning of parā vidyā. It is what happens as in the shell-silver analogy. Upon realizing first the shell acting as silver, the consequent realization of the unreality of silver becomes obvious upon seeing the shell for what it really is. And just as in the hand-to-hand combat dream analogy, the realness of the fight is seen as unreal when one awakens from sleep. So it is with the dawn of parā vidyā—the jagat-prapañca associated with Īśvara disappears.

These "knowers" thus affirm BG 7.19, "All is Vasudeva [vāsudevaḥ sarvam]."[134] This verse is taken literally by Śaṅkara. Only Brahman is real; Brahman is all there is. The purport is that the jagat-prapañca has to be transcended, known as having no ultimate reality. Upon this realization the enlightened person takes refuge in the confession, "vāsudevaḥ sarvam."

BG 4.24 states, "The means of the sacrificial offering is Brahman; Brahman is the oblation placed in the fire of Brahman and by Brahman is the sacrifice made." Here Brahman is the sacrifice, the means of the sacrifice, and the fire. In other words, Brahman is all. In Śaṅkara's comments on this verse he states, "all things, in reality, are Brahman".[135] The person of knowledge sees all as nothing but Brahman, "just as in the nacre [mother-of-pearl] one sees the total

---

[131] And the BSs as well. See chapter 1 n. 9 concerning one scholar's challenge to the traditional notion of what constitutes śruti and smṛti.

[132] "Free from passion, fear, and wrath, filled with my power, dependent on Me, and purged by the austerity of knowledge, many have attained my status" (SBGB, 140).

[133] SBGB, 140.

[134] SBGB, 142. See also page 164 (for BG 4.24) and page 470 (for BG 14.2). These are a few examples of several.

[135] SBGB, 163.

absence of silver".[136] Thus, the jagat and jīvātman-s are Brahman.

3.3.2. "THE FIELD AND THE FIELD-KNOWER"

In the BG, for Śaṅkara in what sense are all things Brahman? The answer to this question provides the most basic premise of Śaṅkara's system, and subsequently his ontology on both the penultimate and ultimate levels.

Śaṅkara's ontology is three-fold (Brahman, prakṛti, jīva-s) in the category of apara brahman. That is, all things, including a multiplicity of jīva-s, are recognizable as such because the empirical world appears to be very real,[137] but only in relation to Brahman as Īśvara. The three-fold ontology in relation to Īśvara, and all its accompanying phenomena (māyā, adhyāsa, avidyā), is explained in detail by Śaṅkara in chapter 13 of the BG, which deals with "The Field and the Field-Knower". Śaṅkara mentions that in a previous chapter, chapter 7, "Two prakṛtis, natures, of God have been mentioned. The first, an inferior one, consists of the three constituents[138] ... [and] is the cause of the empirical life."[139] "The second is a superior one ... whose essence is God. By means of these two natures, God is the cause and origination, sustentation, and dissolution of the world."[140] The inferior nature, consisting of the three constituents, is responsible for the ultimately unreal, empirical world,[141] the "field" (kṣetra). Thus, in the context of Īśvara all "things" may be said to be Brahman, but only in such a way as to be within the category of Īśvara. It is in this sense that Śaṅkara understands BG 7.4-5,[142] which reads, "The earth, water, fire, air, space, mind, intellect and the ego-sense constitute My distinctive eight-fold nature. This is my lower nature; but My higher nature, know it to be other than it."[143]

Given this doctrine, Śaṅkara then concludes that on the ultimate ontological level there is no bheda between Brahman and the jagat. But this way of putting it is, in the category of parā vidyā and nirvikalpa samādhi, inadequate and misleading. That is, to speak of Brahman, the jagat and the jīva in this ultimate sense is to create false categories, for in this higher sense Śaṅkara's ontology is one-fold—Brahman is all there is. Therefore it is the "field-knower"

---

[136] SBGB, 162.

[137] SBGB, 303-4.

[138] Or guṇas (qualities). The three constituents are sattva, goodness; rajas, passion; and tamas, darkness.

[139] SBGB, 402.

[140] SBGB, 402.

[141] SBGB, 402-3. Śaṅkara then records possible objections to this and follows with answers that have their ground in the Upaniṣads, smṛti and reasoning (pp. 404-20). Like Rāmānuja, whose comments on BG 13.1-2 are quite lengthy (18 pages), Śaṅkara also devotes much time to verses 1 and 2.

[142] See chapter 4, section 3.4.1.3.

[143] SBGB, 254,255.

(kṣetrajña), i.e. the Self, "who metaphysically [also] is God Himself",[144] that is exhorted to the highest vidyā, the absolute knowledge that realizes abheda. He states, "In the science of the Gītā, difference [bheda] between the field-knower and God is not recognized."[145]

### 3.3.3. SUMMARY

According to Śaṅkara in his BGB, the BG teaches the following: (1) Brahman is ultimately the only reality—Brahman is really all there is.[146] (2) There are two levels of ontology, these being in the categories of apara brahman (Īśvara) and para brahman.[147] (3) The bheda-laden empirical life of jīva-s and the jagat only exists in relation to Īśvara by the power of māyā[148] but vanishes with the dawn of true knowledge.[149] Further, (4) the jīva is not individual; in the higher sense "Indeed the Self is Brahman",[150] that is, the jīva is identical (abheda) with Brahman.[151]

## 3.4. Summary

Śaṅkara believed the jagat was ultimately mithyā. He did account for the existence of the world but only as jagat-prapañca, as a shell is mistaken for silver and a rope for a snake. The experience in the realm of mithyā is real only as experience of an illusion is real, but the illusion has no ultimate existential reality.

Śaṅkara accounted for the temporary existence of the jagat with his doctrine of māyā, defined as the śakti of Brahman that causes the experience of the jagat-prapañca. Knowledge of the jagat-prapañca caused by adhyāsa fictitiously connects Brahman with the jagat-prapañca. This arises from aparā vidyā in connection with Īśvara, or apara brahman. In the end only para brahman exists.

As regards the jīva, Śaṅkara's system as well allows for the existence of the apparent individuality of jīva-s, but only in the context of Īśvara. Ultimately, then, the jīva is Brahman (tat tvam asi, "you are That") and is in reality not individual. The gap between apparent individuality and the ultimate reality that is Brahman again must be bridged, so when avidyā and adhyāsa are overcome

---

144 SBGB, 407,410. See also SCUB, 497: "He who has become entitled to be ... the knower, is none other than the Supreme Deity himself" (interpreting CU 6.16.3).

145 SBGB, 470.

146 SBGB, 162,238,303-4.

147 SBGB, 298-304 (though note that sometimes Īśvara is used in relation to "knowers" who have the ultimate knowledge; see p. 306), 468,505-8.

148 SBGB, 387-88,402-3,506.

149 SBGB, 609. In this sense valid knowledge of Brahman "has no content other than satyam [being], jñānam [knowledge] and ānanda [bliss]" (SBGB, 465).

150 ātmā hi brahma (SBGB, 36,37).

151 "Which all the Upaniṣads have established" (SBGB, 174).

and parā vidyā dawns, one recognizes "tat tvam asi" and one is merged into the bliss that is Brahman. In this state of mokṣa the eternal dreamless state of merging into Brahman[152] becomes an eternal reality, and one is delivered from the much dreaded cycle that is saṁsāra. As Śaṅkara would say in quotation of BS 4.4.22, "No return; No return."

All the aforementioned play an epistemological, theological and soteriological role in the formation of Śaṅkara's Kṛṣṇāvatāra, as we shall see in chapter 4. Now, though, I move to chapter 3 in order to document Rāmānuja's doctrines of Brahman, the jagat, and the jīva, for they also figure significantly in his Kṛṣṇāvatāra, as will be demonstrated in chapter 4.

[152] Gauḍapāda writes, "As on the destruction of the pot, etc., the ether enclosed in the pot etc., merges in the Ākāśa ... similarly the Jīvas merge in the Ātman" (SBGK, 141 [3.4]).

## Chapter 3

# Rāmānuja: Nature of Brahman, World, and Soul

In direct contradistinction to Śaṅkara, Rāmānuja believed that in the sense of viśiṣṭa (qualification) there is bheda between Brahman (the personal Viṣṇu who is the one reality) and real jīvātman-s and real prakṛti. Rāmānuja's doctrine of Brahman as the one reality therefore allows the name of his system to contain the word advaita, though it must be "qualified" in this basic sense: the material universe, both in its cit (sentient) and acit (non-sentient) aspects, is the body of Brahman. Thus Rāmānuja's viśiṣṭādvaita.

Quite important to the issue of the body-soul-divine relation in the person of Kṛṣṇa in Rāmānuja's system is the relationship between Brahman, cit, and acit. Here Brahman is the antaryāmin (inner controller) and śarīrin (indweller) of all; and just as the human body is indwelled by the jīvātman, so also does Brahman indwell the jīvātman and prakṛti.

In this chapter I discuss (1) what Rāmānuja teaches concerning Brahman's essential nature, and (2) Rāmānuja's doctrine of the jagat and jīva-s in relation to Brahman. For the former it is necessary to bring into the discussion the jagat and jīva-s in a general way, then in sections 2, 3 and 4 I offer more detail pertaining to the jagat and jīva-s.

### 1. The Nature of Brahman

Rāmānuja's viśiṣṭādvaita posits a Brahman that is personal. As regards Rāmānuja's answer to the philosophical problem of the one and the many, his Brahman is a qualified "Whole",[1] with the jagat and jīvātman-s forming the body of the one Brahman. Though advaita in this sense, there are internal

---

[1] It is important to note here a very astute observation by Svāmī Ādidevānanda (trans., Śrī Rāmānuja Gītā Bhāṣya [Mylapore: Sri Ramakrishna Math, n.d.], 176). Noted from hereon as RBGB. As concerns the understanding of the term "Brahman" in Rāmānuja's system, he writes (and note especially the last sentence), "It is to be remembered that in Rāmānuja's system 'Brahman' in the primary sense is the 'Whole' with the Supreme Being as the Soul and Ātmans [individual souls] and Matter (Prakṛti) as His body in inseparable union with the Whole. So the word 'Brahman' can, according to the needs of each context, be used to indicate the Supreme Being, the Ātman [individual soul], or Prakṛti [matter or the world]."

divisions within the nature of Brahman[2] since Brahman possesses an infinite amount of auspicious (favorable, propitious) attributes. Thus Brahman is saguṇa. The jagat and jīvātman-s are part of these attributes, insofar as they are prakāra-s (modes) of Brahman. Rāmānuja, however, does acknowledge śruti texts that support the doctrine of the Supreme Brahman as nirguṇa (or guṇa-niṣedha, negation of attributes), though "in the sense that He is not associated with evil attributes", citing the śruti text, "He is free from evil" (CU 8.7.1).[3]

Though Rāmānuja's Brahman is the ultimate reality, Brahman is not the only reality. Viśiṣṭādvaita holds to a Brahman that, although the highest reality, is different from prakṛti and the jīvātman, which are very real. Rāmānuja adds that Brahman comes from the Sanskrit root bṛh, denoting that which possesses the quality of greatness (bṛhattva) and other qualities in inexhaustible fullness.[4] All the above add certain qualifications to Brahman that in the end distinguish Rāmānuja's doctrine of Brahman from that of Śaṅkara. Finally, the personal Brahman is called by such names as "Nārāyaṇa, Īśvara, Bhagavān, Puruṣottama, Viṣṇu, etc.".[5]

## 1.1. The Personal Brahman

Rāmānuja's Brahman is the eternal personal Lord of all, possesses a personal bodily divine form (divya rūpa) that is non-prakṛtic, and yet also has the universe as his body.[6] (I hope to demonstrate in chapter 4 that the human form [mānuṣī tanu] of Kṛṣṇa is fashioned from the divya rūpa, not from the prakṛti that is the material of the universe.) Stressing personality in order to differentiate his Lord from all other entities, Rāmānuja labors to note that

---

[2] Tapasyānanda's Introduction to RBGB, 10. Tapasyānanda mentions that the term viśiṣṭādvaita (also known as "Pan-organistic Non-dualism") "was not coined by Rāmānuja but came to be used by others afterwards". Tapasyānanda does not mention who these others were. Moreover, "As far as [Rāmānuja] is concerned", writes Tapasyānanda, "he is a Vedāntin, and his doctrine is the Vedānta" (RBGB, 10).

[3] RBGB, 426.

[4] George Thibaut, trans., Vedānta-Sūtras: With the Commentary by Rāmānuja, in F. Max Müller, ed., Sacred Books of the East (Delhi: Motilal Banarsidass, 1989), 48:4. Noted from hereon as SBE.

[5] Svāmī Tapasyānanda, Bhakti Schools of Vedānta (Madras: Sri Ramakrishna Math, n.d.), 35.

[6] John B. Carman states, "Rāmānuja vehemently insists that the Supreme Deity Himself has a real and personal bodily form, in addition to His having the entire universe as His body" (The Theology of Rāmānuja: An Essay in Interreligious Understanding [New Haven and London: Yale University Press, 1974; Bombay: Ananthacharya Indological Research Institute, 1981], 173). Yet, as Carman points out, this real bodily form is still "essentially different from everything else" (p. 168). Here Ramanuja sets to guard the Lord from possessing "a defiling material body" (p. 174).

Kṛṣṇa employs "different terms like 'I', 'you', 'these', 'all' and 'we'".[7] For example, BG 2.12 reads, "There never was a time when I did not exist, nor you, nor any of these kings of men. Nor will there be any time in the future when all of us shall cease to be." Rāmānuja asserts that since Kṛṣṇa employs "I" in distinction from "you", "these", and "us", this certainly implies bheda between Kṛṣṇa and others.

### 1.1.1. Brahman as Antaryāmin[8]

The Vaiṣṇava view of Viṣṇu having a personal bodily form,[9] having the universe as his body, and possessing personal attributes in a non-dichotomization of reality (that is, unlike Śaṅkara's two-tiered ontology) sets viśiṣṭādvaita apart from advaita and in the end distinguishes Rāmānuja's Kṛṣṇāvatāra from Śaṅkara's Kṛṣṇāvatāra. And though both Śaṅkara and Rāmānuja share the view that Brahman is antaryāmin, the way Rāmānuja fashions the doctrine is quite different from Śaṅkara.

As mentioned above, in addition to the personal bodily form of Viṣṇu, there is the doctrine that the jagat and jīvātman-s are the body of Brahman. Brahman in this relation functions as the antaryāmin. Brahman as antaryāmin plays a major role in Rāmānuja's system. As antaryāmin, Brahman is "the Self[10] of all beings"[11] and the universe is his body. BG 9.4a ("This entire universe is pervaded[12] by me") forms a basis upon which Rāmānuja launches into Brahman as antaryāmin, buttressing his interpretation with BU 3.7.3 ("He is your Self, the Inner Controller [antaryāmin]"[13]).[14] Here the second phrase of the verse defines the first. And for Rāmānuja the Self (Brahman) therefore dwells within the self and is its antaryāmin. The antaryāmin is also the basis upon which Rāmānuja claims that Brahman is the sovereign controller of the

---

[7] RBGB, 63.

[8] The purpose of this section is mainly to state that Brahman is the inner controller. I shall in the next major sections explore the mechanics of Brahman as inner controller in relation to the world and the soul.

[9] "God is not formless but possessed of a personal form" (Carman, The Theology of Rāmānuja, 167).

[10] There is a distinction in Rāmānuja's theology between the "self" and the "Self". The self is thought of as the jīva or jīvātman, the individual soul; the Self is Brahman, the antaryāmin, Brahman within the self. Note though, that the self may be called Brahman in so far as the self is the body of Brahman. See also n. 1.

[11] RBGB, 354,382; see also 166,249,273,296-97,555,582.

[12] Śrīnivāsa states, "Īśvara is essentially of the nature of vibhu. What is called vibhu is all-pervasiveness [vyāpakatvam]" (Svāmī Ādidevānanda, trans., Yatīndramatadīpikā by Śrīnivāsadāsa [Mylapore: Sri Ramakrishna Math, n.d.], 132 [9.14]; noted from hereon as YS).

[13] Swami Nikhilananda, trans., The Upanishads (New York: Harper & Row, 1963), 211.

[14] RBGB, 297.

universe[15] and the "'Supreme Substratum' of the universe, i.e., supreme support of this universe".[16]

1.1.2. THE COSMIC FORM

Brief discussion of Rāmānuja's interpretation of the cosmic form of BG 11 is necessary for my purpose, not for what it is but for what it is not. Brahman's personal bodily form, the divya rūpa (which is non-prakṛtic in nature and not karmic-caused[17]), is not the cosmic form of BG 11. Rather, the universe as the body of Brahman is the cosmic form and therefore it shares no ontological semblance with the divya rūpa. The divya rūpa is non-prakṛtic, but the cosmic form consists of prakṛti.[18]

The Lord, then, is "the Ancient Person", the Puruṣa who is the universe:[19]

> Behold, Son of Pṛthā, my forms, a hundredfold, rather a thousandfold. Various, divine, and of various colors and shapes ... Behold now the entire universe, with everything moving and not moving, here standing together in my body ... Thus having spoken, O King, the Great Lord of Yoga, Hari (Vishnu), revealed to the son of Pṛthā His majestic supreme form. Of many mouths and eyes, of many wondrous aspects, of many divine ornaments, of many uplifted divine weapons ... If there should be in the sky a thousand suns risen all at once, such splendor would be of the splendor of that Great Being. There the entire universe, standing as one, divided in many ways, the son of Pāṇḍu then beheld in the body of the God of Gods ... With many arms, bellies, faces, eyes, I see Thee everywhere, infinite in form. Not the end, nor the middle, nor yet the

---

15 RBGB, 296.

16 RBGB, 365.

17 SBE, 48:256.

18 RBGB, 361, 362.

19 RBGB, 382. The puruṣa (ancient person or cosmic man) comes from RV 10.90, "the Hymn of Puruṣa". The concept of sacrifice was indispensable to ancient Vedic religion. In the hymn the gods sacrifice a cosmic giant (puruṣa) whose body parts formed the universe. With the theology of macrocosm/microcosm priests through the performance of sacrifice keep the universe functioning; they perpetuate the world. The earthly sacrifices of priests, then, serve to commemorate the earlier cosmic event of the gods and, more importantly, actually regenerate the world anew. For more information, see Gavin Flood, An Introduction to Hinduism (New York: Cambridge University Press, 1996), 48-49, David M. Knipe, Hinduism: Experiments in the Sacred (New York: HarperCollins, 1991), 32-35, and R. C. Zaehner, Hinduism (New York: Oxford University Press, 1966), 43-45. I am indebted to these authors for this information.

beginning of Thee I see, O Lord of all, whose form is the universe [BG 11.5,7,9,10,12,13,16].[20]

Rāmānuja takes great care to stress that the phenomena described as the Lord's cosmic form are many, yet they constitute the one form of the Lord, "this one body of Mine with all mobile and immobile entities".[21] Interpreting (not translating) the two vocatives in the latter part of BG 11.16b (viśveśvara viśvarūpa, "O Lord of all, O form of all"), Rāmānuja states, "O Universal Form, having the universe as your body!"[22] Further, the cosmic form, though personal and visible to Arjuna, is "not limited by time and space because of its being the foundation of the entire universe in the past, present and future".[23] Thus, the cosmic form is infinite, transcends time and space and is real and personal. For this Rāmānuja cites textual support from the BG (10.8,19-21,39,42).[24] It is therefore safe to say that Rāmānuja's doctrine of the personal and real cosmic form is quite different from that of Śaṅkara, who denies any ultimate connection of the cosmic form with para brahman.

1.1.3. SUMMARY / CONCLUSION

For Rāmānuja, Brahman is above all personal and in the highest sense possesses an infinite amount of favorable attributes (saguṇa Brahman). Brahman's essential nature is characterized by bheda, since Brahman possesses attributes. This is evident in the language of śruti and with use of sāmānādhikaraṇya. As demonstrated in chapter 1,[25] Rāmānuja is quick to seize upon TU 2.1, which reads, "Truth, knowledge, infinite is Brahman." Through sāmānādhikaraṇya the words "truth, knowledge and infinite" are predicated of Brahman and thus describe attributes of Brahman. The point Rāmānuja wishes to make is that "truth, knowledge and infinite" are not Brahman, but are possessed by Brahman. Just as the sentence "Arjuna is young, powerful and handsome" communicates that Arjuna possesses these three qualities (and not that "young" or "powerful" or "handsome" are actually Arjuna), so it is with the interpretation of TU 2.1.

Brahman as antaryāmin plays a crucial role in Rāmānuja's theology. As antaryāmin Brahman is the Self of all and within all things. The jagat (including the prakṛti of all human bodies) and jīva-s, then, are the body of

[20] Taken from Winthrop Sargeant, The Bhagavad Gītā (Albany: State University of New York Press, 1984), 457,459,461,462,464,465,468, with modifications to capitalization and punctuation.

[21] RBGB, 358.

[22] RBGB, 364.

[23] RBGB, 360.

[24] RBGB, 362.

[25] Section 2.1.

Brahman.[26] It is in this sense that Rāmānuja interprets such śruti verses as "That you are" (CU 6.8.7), "This everything, all is that Self" (BU 2.4.6), and "I am Brahman" (BU 1.4.10).

Finally, and most important to the issue of the body-divine relation in the person of Kṛṣṇa, Brahman's body, the cosmic form of BG 11, is the material universe with all its components, but is not Brahman's anthropomorphic, non-prakṛtic divya rūpa. Further, and as I shall explain in detail in chapter 4, the body of Kṛṣṇa is not fashioned from ordinary prakṛti—what constitutes the body of the cosmic form of Brahman—but from the non-prakṛtic divya rūpa.

## 2. The Jagat in Relation to Brahman

Exploring the relationship between Brahman and the jagat (or prakṛti) and the jīva is critical to Rāmānuja's anthropology (specifically the relation of each human being's body and soul to the divine). In chapter 4 this leads me to raise crucial questions regarding Kṛṣṇa's identification with humanity.

There are not two categories of ontology in the sense of Śaṅkara's para brahman and apara brahman (or Īśvara), so Rāmānuja's doctrine of a metaphysical separation between Brahman, prakṛti and jīva-s is real and occurs on one, and only one, ontological level. But bheda must be harmonized with both advaita and Brahman as the ultimate reality—"the many" must somehow be reconciled to "the one". Believing that śruti supports his doctrine, Rāmānuja solves this philosophical problem with his qualified non-dualism, or "identity in difference".[27]

### 2.1. The Jagat

Rāmānuja differs significantly from Śaṅkara as regards the interpretation of TU 2.6 (and the similar passage in CU 6.2.3): "He [Brahman] wished, may I be many, may I grow forth ... Having sent forth, he entered into it." As I documented in chapter 1, section 2.1, Śaṅkara appeals to the very next verse for his abheda interpretation of 2.6: "If he [a man] makes the slightest differentiation in It [Brahman], there is fear for him" (TU 2.7). To be sure, Śaṅkara concedes the world of plurality in the word "many", but verse 6 refers only to the jagat-prapañca as a preliminary device to prepare one for the higher knowledge to come. Not so with Rāmānuja.

---

[26] Śrīnivāsa states that Brahman "has everything except Himself and His consciousness as His body" (YS, 122 [9.1]).

[27] See Julius J. Lipner, The Face of Truth: A Study of Meaning and Metaphysics in the Vedantic Theology of Ramanuja (Albany: State University of New York Press, 1986), 37,39,44-45,47,60,84,119-20,135-37,142 (this list taken from his index on p. 180).

### 2.1.1. THE WORLD AND THE ANTARYĀMIN

For Rāmānuja the real world is the body of Brahman and Brahman is the Self, the "ensouler",[28] of all non-spiritual (acetana) entities and spiritual (cetana[29]) entities,[30] which are the prakāra-s of Brahman. As we read in RVed, "His mode of being is that He is modified by all creatures, for His body is constituted by all entities because He is the inner Ruler of all entities ... firstly the non-spiritual [acetana] entities ... and secondly the spiritual [cetana] entities."[31] Further, there is absolutely real bheda between Brahman and objects.[32] TU 2.6 (also CU 6.2.1,3) is a mahāvākya for Rāmānuja, for to him it highlights (1) Brahman as the antaryāmin of the jagat and (2) bheda between Brahman and the jagat, though essential oneness:

> Other texts, again, aim at teaching that the highest Self to whom non-intelligent and intelligent beings stand in the relation of body, and hence of modes, subsists in the form of the world, in its causal as well as its effected aspect,[33] and hence speak of the world in this its double aspect as that which is (the Real); so e.g. "Being only this was in the beginning, one only without a second—it desired, may I be many, may I grow forth—it sent forth fire" ... "Having sent forth that he entered into it."[34]

Whether in a causal or effected condition, Brahman has for his body the jagat.

> The world has its Self in Brahman, in so far as the whole aggregate of intelligent and non-intelligent beings constitutes Brahman's body ... Compare "Abiding within, the ruler of beings, the Self of all"; "He who dwells in the earth, different from the earth, whom the earth does not know, whose body the earth is, who rules the earth within—he is thy Self", etc. [BU 3.7.3,22] ... "Having created that he entered into it; having entered it he became sat and tyat" [TU 2.6] ... (where the 'sat' denotes the

---

[28] Lipner, The Face of Truth, 37.

[29] Both acetana and cetana derive linguistically from acit and cit.

[30] Even other divinities constitute the body of Brahman (see RBGB, 261). See also Eric Lott, Vedantic Approaches to God (New York: Barnes and Noble, 1980), 23, who identifies a "second-order doctrine" of multiple gods in Vedānta. Though Śaṅkara and Rāmānuja may be called theistic, they are so in a specialized sense, Brahman being the supreme deity and ontologically and functionally superior to lower deities.

[31] J. A. B. van Buitenen, trans., Rāmānuja's Vedārthasaṃgraha (Poona: Deccan College Postgraduate and Research Institute, 1956), 213, par. 42 (Sanskrit text p. 95). Noted as RVed.

[32] "The physical world is a real world. It is not an illusory projection" (S. S. Raghavachar, Introduction to the Vedarthasangraha of Sree Ramanujacharya [Mangalore: The Mangalore Trading Association, 1957], 27).

[33] See the next sub-section entitled Unity in Difference.

[34] SBE, 48:140-41.

> individual soul), it follows that the individual soul also has Brahman for its Self, owing to the fact of Brahman having entered into it.—From all this it follows that the entire aggregate of things, intelligent and non-intelligent, has its Self in Brahman in so far as it constitutes Brahman's body.[35]

Rāmānuja further explains that the phrase "Having created that he entered into it" (TU 2.6) should be interpreted as "The highest Self evolved names and forms by entering into matter."[36] With this interpretation Rāmānuja cites BU 1.4.7 for confirmation: "All this was then unevolved; it became evolved by form and name."[37] This is a direct argument against the position of advaita. The "names and forms" are very real, not ultimately mithyā and perceived by avidyā[38] as the Advaitin claims.[39]

At the same time, however, prakṛti is not completely different from Brahman.[40] But neither is the world ultimately mithyā, as in Śaṅkara's advaita. Rather, the relationship between Brahman and prakṛti is one of viśiṣṭādvaita or qualified non-duality. How is it qualified? The answer comes with Rāmānuja's "identity in difference encapsulated by the body-ensouler model".[41]

### 2.1.2. Unity in Difference

Lipner observes that Rāmānuja's viśiṣṭādvaita posits simultaneously a view of Brahman "from above" and "from below".[42] Brahman from above has three aspects that emphasize the identity between Brahman and the jagat, or "the non-difference between Brahman and the world".[43] These are (1) Brahman essentially as the Absolute, (2) Brahman producing the whole aggregate of things (Rāmānuja: "Brahman in his causal condition", that is, as the material cause of the jagat[44]), and (3) Brahman as the whole aggregate of things (Rāmānuja: "Brahman in his effected condition").[45] Brahman from below

---

[35] SBE, 48:133,134.

[36] SBE, 48:141.

[37] SBE, 48:141.

[38] Swami Satchidanandendra Sarasvati, The Method of the Vedanta (London: Kegan Paul International, 1989), 131.

[39] It is easy to see, however, how Advaitins would interpret this portion of CU 1.4.7. They of course make allowance for such śruti statements within the context of Īśvara. This śruti, then, would simply be stating the obvious—as we perceive things from aparā vidyā, the unevolved (undifferentiated) becomes evolved (differentiated).

[40] Though it is completely different from the divya rūpa.

[41] Lipner, The Face of Truth, 37.

[42] Lipner, The Face of Truth, 37.

[43] Lipner, The Face of Truth, 38.

[44] Śrīnivāsa states that Brahman is "the material cause of the universe" (YS, 122 [9.2]; see also p. 129 [9.10]).

[45] Lipner, The Face of Truth, 38. See also my chapter 4, section 3.5.1.3.

emphasizes bheda between Brahman and the jagat.[46] Thus, with Brahman from above and from below we find Brahman as absolute in being while at the same time the cause and effect of a differentiated jagat. This allows for Rāmānuja's Brahman to be both "all" and yet the cause of a real and differentiated jagat, for the jagat is Brahman in the effected condition.[47]

There is yet another way in which the "from above" and "from below" work out in Rāmānuja's viśiṣṭādvaita to answer the question, "How is all this Brahman?" The answer is that the jagat must be Brahman "in so far as the whole aggregate of intelligent and non-intelligent beings constitutes Brahman's body".[48] Rāmānuja's qualifying phrase "in so far as", mentioned throughout his BSB,[49] is a hermeneutical key to recognizing the viśiṣṭa in viśiṣṭādvaita. With this he is able to set forth Brahman as the "all" and the "Self", confirm the ontological oneness between Brahman (the Self) and the jagat, and yet maintain bheda between Brahman and the jagat[50]—thus "identity in difference". In this way Rāmānuja meets head-on the śruti text that states, "This everything, all is that Self" (BU 2.4.6).

### 2.1.3. MĀYĀ AND LĪLĀ

If the world is real and not unreal, what is māyā in Rāmānuja's theological framework? This is an important question to answer, for Rāmānuja's doctrine of māyā, like Śaṅkara's, is a factor in his doctrine of avatāra. Both Rāmānuja and Śaṅkara agree that māyā is the śakti of Brahman. But there are differences between the two theologians. For Śaṅkara it is the power that causes the unreal manifestation of the jagat. For Rāmānuja it is the power that causes the real manifestation of the jagat, including the real manifestation of Kṛṣṇa.[51] Like Śaṅkara, Rāmānuja would say that the jagat and all that is associated with it (including the avatāra) arises from the līlā vibhūti (cosmic sport) of Brahman; but unlike Śaṅkara, Rāmānuja holds that the jagat is very real (note also Brahman's līlā does not remove the responsibility of action on Brahman's part):

---

[46] Lipner, The Face of Truth, 38. This two-aspect Brahman differs from Śaṅkara's two-tiered structure of reality under the rubric of his apara brahman and para brahman in that, fundamentally, Rāmānuja's Brahman operates on one level of real existence, contrary to the unreal realm and the ultimately real realm of Śaṅkara's Brahman.

[47] SBE, 48:399. In his bhāṣya on BS 1.4.23 Rāmānuja makes reference to CU 3.14.1: "All this is Brahman."

[48] SBE, 48:133; emphases added.

[49] See, for example, SBE, 48:84-85,93,101,130,133,134,140.

[50] Though there is an ontological oneness between Brahman and the jagat, there is bheda, and in this way Rāmānuja and his followers are able to maintain that Brahman remains untouched by the imperfections of the jagat in Brahman's universe-body existence (see YS, 131-32 [9.13]).

[51] See my chapter 4, section 1.3.2.

> Consisting of unlimited knowledge and bliss he for ever abides in his uniform nature, engaged in the sport of making this world go round ... undergoing a change into the multiplicity of actual sentient and non-sentient things ... All beings ... are mere playthings of Brahman, and ... the creation and reabsorption of the world are only his sport.[52]

We come now to Rāmānuja's response to the shell-silver and rope-snake analogies, both of which Śaṅkara substantiates in part with CU 6.1.4. In his bhāṣya on BS 2.1.15,[53] Rāmānuja understands the pūrvapakṣin as saying that the shell (the cause) alone is real, though appearing to be silver (the effect, unreal). Likewise, the rope alone is real, and the snake is unreal. This is the meaning, says the pūrvapakṣin, of CU 6.1.4 ("As, my dear, by one clod of clay all that is made of clay is known, the modification being a name merely which has its origin in speech, while the truth is that it is clay merely"): Brahman (the cause) alone is real, and the effects, though appearing real and based on adhyāsa, have no ultimate reality.[54]

Not so, says Rāmānuja. The Advaitin is in reality using his own unreal effect (clay, shell, rope) to play the role of the cause! He forces the Advaitin to this conclusion:

> In order to facilitate the understanding of the truth that everything apart from Brahman is false, we have so far reasoned on the assumption of things such as clay, gold, etc., being real, and have thereby proved the non-reality of all effects. In truth, however, all special causal substances are unreal quite as much as jars [and snakes and silver] are; for they are all of them equally effects of Brahman.[55]

This refutation on the part of Rāmānuja implies another objection: Although the silver is illusory in the place where the shell is, real silver therefore exists elsewhere; otherwise, how could one presume to superimpose it upon the shell?

In this same section concerning BS 2.1.15, Rāmānuja, ever the apologist, takes another line of reasoning. Concerning the Advaitin's "lord of māyā" (who is Īśvara), Rāmānuja states, "Without being conscious of others the lord of Māyā is unable to delude them by his Māyā." In other words, Rāmānuja states that the Advaitin's Brahman must be conscious of others in order to delude them. But if Brahman is conscious of others and others are mithyā because they are "other" than Brahman, then Brahman has to view these others as mithyā.

---

[52] SBE, 48:406; emphasis added.

[53] The BS reads, "The non-difference (of the world) from that (viz. Brahman) follows from what begins with the word arambhana [something taken or touched]" (SBE, 48:430).

[54] SBE, 48:432-35.

[55] SBE, 48:435.

The situation further poses a "catch 22" for the Advaitin's Brahman, for in order to delude them Brahman must be conscious of them, but if conscious of them, Brahman has to enter into a state of lower consciousness. Nonetheless Rāmānuja, in sarcastic tone, concludes, "Surely none but a madman would aim at deluding beings known by him to be unreal!"[56]

Rāmānuja then proceeds to attack the Advaitic view of māyā and līlā. Is māyā real or unreal? No matter what the answer, the Advaitin cannot win. Rāmānuja poses a series of questions and supplies the Advaitin's answers himself:

> Brahman, we [i.e., Rāmānuja] reply, has for its nature unlimited bliss, and hence cannot be conscious of, or affected with, unreal Māyā ... Of what use, we further ask, should an eternal non-real Māyā be to Brahman?—[ans.] Brahman by means of it deludes the individual souls!—But of what use should such delusion be to Brahman?—[ans.] It affords to Brahman a kind of sport or play!—But of what use is play to a being whose nature is unlimited bliss?—[ans.] Do we not then see in ordinary life also that persons in the enjoyment of full happiness and prosperity indulge all the same in play?—The cases are not parallel, we reply. For none but persons not in their right mind would take pleasure in an unreal play.[57]

## 3. The Jīva in Relation to Brahman

In contrast to Śaṅkara, Rāmānuja argues for a real plurality of jīva-s. Jīva-s, though distinct from each other and from Brahman, are pure cit and are of the same substance as Brahman.[58] The individuality of jīva-s in turn must be understood within Rāmānuja's doctrine of antaryāmin. Like the doctrine of the nature of Brahman and like the doctrine of the jagat as it relates to Brahman, Rāmānuja's views on the jīva and its relation to Brahman figure significantly in his doctrine of Kṛṣṇāvatāra.

### 3.1. The Jīva and the Antaryāmin

Once again TU 2.6 plays a large part in Rāmānuja's theology of antaryāmin, this time in relation to the jīva. It reads, "Having sent forth, he entered into it." We have seen that in the relation between Brahman and the jagat, this is a key text teaching that the jagat is Brahman's body and that Brahman is its antaryāmin. Rāmānuja remains consistent with this interpretation when speaking of the jīva: "the individual soul also has Brahman for its Self, owing

---

[56] SBE, 48:441.
[57] SBE, 48:442.
[58] Zaehner, Hinduism, 99.

to the fact of Brahman having entered into it".[59]

Along with Śaṅkara, Rāmānuja admits that the jīva is Brahman, but, and this contrary to Śaṅkara, "in so far as". "Brahman is the Self of all", says Rāmānuja,[60] including jīva-s. And Brahman is also "all", so as not to contradict the clear teaching of śruti: "All this is Brahman" (CU 3.14.1). Rāmānuja's solution to the problem of the one and the many, that is, Brahman and the plurality of jīva-s, is the "in so far as" clause. Regarding the jīva, BS 2.3.46 reads, "And the Smṛti texts declare this."[61] Rāmānuja asserts, "The 'and' in the Sūtra implies that śruti texts also declare that the individual Self is a part of Brahman in so far as it is its body."[62] Moreover, Brahman is the Self of the individual self in so far as the individual self is a prakāra of Brahman: "The individual soul [jīvātmā] is itself ensouled by Brahman, for the soul is a modification [prakāra] of Brahman because it constitutes His body [śarīra [63]]."[64] It is therefore in this sense that Rāmānuja interprets BU 1.4.10: "I am Brahman." This brings us to our next important śruti text, tat tvam asi.

Rāmānuja is consistent with his antaryāmin model in his exegesis of tat tvam asi (CU 6.8.7). In fact, he expounds upon the phrase at length in his bhāṣya on BS 1.1.1.[65] Rāmānuja first states his thesis with refutation of advaita in mind:

> In texts, again, such as "Thou [individual self] art that [Brahman]", the co-ordination [correlative predication] of the constituent parts is not meant to convey the idea of the absolute unity of a non-differentiated substance [that is, thou = that]: on the contrary, the words "that" and "thou" denote a Brahman distinguished by difference.[66]

Context and sāmānādhikaraṇya play a central role in the exegesis.

---

[59] SBE, 48:133,134. As is true in the Brahman-jagat relationship, where Brahman remains untainted by imperfections associated with the jagat (including material human bodies), so it is with Brahman-jīvātman relationships. Śrīnivāsa, after mentioning that the antaryāmin remains with the jīvātman in the latter's states of experiences, asserts that though Brahman as antaryāmin "co-exists with the individual self [jīva], He is untouched by the taints associated with it" (my translation; Sanskrit for "by the taints associated with it" is tad gatadoṣaiḥ; YS, 139 [9.26]). In his BSB Rāmānuja declares that, though a part of Brahman and thus of the same substance as Brahman, Brahman nonetheless remains untouched by imperfections associated with the jīvātman (SBE, 48:562-67).

[60] SBE, 48:376.

[61] SBE, 48:564.

[62] SBE; emphases added.

[63] Thus Brahman is the śarīrin, the possessor of the body.

[64] RVed, 194, par. 17b (Sanskrit text pp. 80-81).

[65] SBE, 48:129-38.

[66] SBE, 48:130.

Rāmānuja states that tat refers to Brahman, but with the texts "It thought, may I be many" and "In that all this world [together with individual jīva-s] has its Self" in mind.[67] Tvam, then, must be interpreted in light of the rule of sāmānādhikaraṇya, which leads him once again to use his popular qualifying clause "in so far as". "Thou", he observes, "stands in co-ordination to 'that'", and "conveys the idea of Brahman in so far as having for its body the individual souls".[68] Statements that utilize sāmānādhikaraṇya, argues Rāmānuja, lay to rest any theory of absolute oneness.[69] With application of sāmānādhikaraṇya the phrase has reference to one object, Brahman, in a "two-fold form", a "doubleness of aspect".[70] The two-fold form is the absolute Brahman and Brahman as the Self of the individual jīva (itself a prakāra of Brahman). Brahman then can be the ultimate and only reality, and all things, jīva-s included, have reality and have being (sat) in Brahman in so far as they are prakāra-s of Brahman.[71] This is the central ingredient in Rāmānuja's viśiṣṭādvaita. By way of "identity in difference" Brahman is all, and the jagat and jīva-s form one organic whole that is Brahman.[72]

### 4. Brahman, the Jagat, and the Jīva: BG 13 and Bheda

In BG chapter 13—entitled in Rāmānuja's BGB "Differentiation of the Known from the Knower"—the first two verses are quite important to Rāmānuja, for his comments on these verses are among the longest (if not the longest) in his whole commentary. It is here that he sets out in detailed fashion to spell out his doctrine of identity in difference as regards Brahman, the jagat, and jīva-s. His argument is fascinating.

Sometimes called the chapter on the Field (kṣetra) and the Field-Knower (kṣetrajña), kṣetra is defined as "an aggregate of earth etc.".[73] This obviously includes the body.[74] Kṣetrajña is the jīva, the individual soul or self.[75] Rāmānuja then employs sāmānādhikaraṇya as his basic ground for identity in difference, first with reference to the jagat (including the body) and the jīva, and then with reference to the Lord and the jagat and the jīva.

---

[67] SBE, 48:130,133,134.

[68] SBE, 48:130.

[69] SBE, 48:134.

[70] SBE, 48:130,134.

[71] See Raghavachar, Introduction to the Vedarthasangraha of Sree Ramanujacharya, 45.

[72] In the introduction to Rāmānuja's BGB, Tapasyānanda states that visiṣṭādvaita "is a philosophy of unity in diversity, one of arriving at the unity that underlies diversity without sublating the latter" (RBGB, 39).

[73] RBGB, 420.

[74] RBGB, 414.

[75] RBGB, 414,420.

### 4.1. 13.1—Identity in Difference with Body and Self

BG 13.1 reads, "This body, O Arjuna, is called the Field, Kṣetra. He who knows it is called the Field-knower, Kṣetrajña, by those who know the self."[76] He asserts that with sāmānādhikaraṇya[77] the perceiving person is one who understands that "in the propositions, 'I am a god', 'I am a man', 'I am fat', 'I am slender' etc.", the body as the kṣetra is distinct (bheda) from the experiencing self (kṣetrajña), the "I". Thus, this person can say, "I know it, the body, as an object." This person is therefore the kṣetrajña, who knows "I" as different from the kṣetra, the object of knowledge.[78]

Still, Rāmānuja must have "identity" in this relationship. To establish this, he continues with "But" (tu[79]): "But this knowledge [of bheda between body and self[80]] which arises by way of co-ordinate predication is justified on the ground that the body is inseparable from oneself; for it constitutes an attribute[81] of the self like cowness of the cow etc."[82] Here he is saying that even with bheda between body and self, there is still a oneness between the two. To illustrate, just before his observation of bheda between body and self, Rāmānuja explains that in the very act of perceiving an object like a pot, the seer thinks, "I am a man who sees it." The seer, then, places the body in identity with the perceiving self, because in this sentence "I" and "man" are in union (proved through sāmānādhikaraṇya) when perceiving the object (the pot).[83] In other words, in the context of secular śabda the sentence "I see the pot" assumes we have oneness between the "I" (soul) and the eyes. Thus we have identity, oneness, between self and body.

---

[76] RBGB, 413.

[77] Translated in RBGB as "co-ordinate predication".

[78] RBGB, 414.

[79] RBGB, 413, Sanskrit text.

[80] Likewise Śrīnivāsa writes of the jīva, "it is different from the body ... it is different from the body as seen in the perception, 'this is my body'" (YS, 103 [8.3]).

[81] Or "particularity" (viśeṣa); Sanskrit text page 413.

[82] RBGB, 414.

[83] RBGB, 414. As discussed earlier, advaita makes use of sāmānādhikaraṇya. For example, M. Hiriyanna states:

> The Advaita definitely denies that there can be any relation at all between two such disparate entities as spirit and matter. But at the same time, it cannot be forgotten that our investigation of experience leads us to the conclusion that they are not only together but are often identified with each other as implied, for example, when a person says "I am walking." Here the act of walking is obviously a feature characterizing the physical body; and yet it is predicated of the person's self which is spiritual (quoted in Arvind Sharma, "Who Speaks for Hinduism? A Perspective from Advaita Vedānta", Journal of the American Academy of Religion 68 [December 2000]: 754, citing Hiriyanna's The Essentials of Indian Philosophy [London: George Allen and Unwin, 1949], 160-61).

Hiriyanna goes on to state that with Advaita the association of the person's self with the body is "mere appearance" and "ultimately false".

### 4.2. 13.2—Lord, Body and Self

BG 13.2 reads, "And know Me [Kṛṣṇa] also as the Field-knower in all Fields, O Arjuna. The knowledge of the Field and its knower is, in My view, the true knowledge."[84] Rāmānuja's argument above for the identity and difference of the body and the self of a person serves as the model for identity in difference between his Lord and the body and the self (note the "yathā ... tatha" ["just as ... in the same manner"] argument below). He also sees in the verse the Lord as antaryāmin (and consequently the body and the self as the Lord's modes[85] [attributes]), for, as the verse states, he is the knower in all fields.[86] Interpreting 13.2, Rāmānuja states,

> Know as Myself the Field-knower also who is the only form of the Knower in all the bodies like divinities, men etc., i.e., know them as ensouled by Me ... Just as [yathā] the body, on account of its being the attribute of the knower [the self], cannot exist separately, and is consequently denoted by way of co-ordinate predication (sāmānādhikaraṇya) with it, in the same manner [tathā] both the Field and the Field-knower, on account of their being my attributes, cannot exist as entities separate from Me, and hence can be denoted as "one with Me" by way of co-ordinate predication.[87]

Sāmānādhikaraṇya is most important in Rāmānuja's BGB. Both secular śabda and śruti as śabda prove viśiṣṭādvaita. In other words sāmānādhikaraṇya demands bheda. Consider the statement, "Rāmānuja is young, handsome, and intelligent." Here Rāmānuja must be differentiated from the words "young, handsome, and intelligent", since these (as different predicated qualities) describe some of the attributes of Rāmānuja. Further, this statement evidences bheda within the nature of Rāmānuja. In like fashion, consider the statement, "Brahman is being (sat), consciousness (cit), and bliss (ananda)." Here Brahman must be differentiated from sat, cit and ananda since these (as different predicated qualities) describe some of the attributes of Brahman.

### 4.3. Jagat and Jīva: Body of the Lord

Just as the body has within it the individual self and thus the two are one, so is the Lord the Self of the world and of the individual self—all being one. For Rāmānuja this is a microcosm of the relationship between Brahman (analogous to the "I" or self) and the jagat and jīva-s (analogous to the body). In other

---

[84] RBGB, 415.

[85] "The relation of the Jīva and Prakṛti to Īśvara is as of body and soul or as a mode (Prakāra)" (RBGB, 429).

[86] The locative sarva kṣetreṣu.

[87] RBGB, 419-20.

words, just as the jīva has for its prakāra the physical body, so does Brahman (the Self of all) have all things as his body.[88] "Both the Kṣetra (Field)", writes Rāmānuja, "and the Kṣetrajña (the Jīva) have the Lord for their Self, because of their being of the nature of the body of the Lord".[89] He then cites śruti passages for proof of his position, one being from BU 3.7.3 ("He is your Self, the Inner Controller").[90] Here Rāmānuja takes "your" to include, through sāmānādhikaraṇya, the body and the jīva in oneness.[91] Additionally, "The world", explains Rāmānuja, "is He Himself".[92] For this view Rāmānuja quotes śruti: "It thought, 'May I become many'" (CU 6.2.3).[93] In this oneness in distinction Brahman enjoys the operation of the real jagat and jīva-s as prakāra-s on the basis of the Self-Body relationship: "It is affirmed that Brahman thus exists of His own Will in a wonderful plurality of modes on account of His having the immovable and movable entities as His Body."[94]

## 5. Mokṣa

Both Śaṅkara and Rāmānuja agree that mokṣa is liberation of the jīva from saṁsāra. But further eschatological considerations create sharp differences between the two theologians and, consequently, sharp differences between their avatāra doctrines (and between them and classical Christian orthodoxy). Following are several important differences between the two teachers.

First, as I have documented, Brahman (in Rāmānuja's view) is not synonymous with bliss (Śaṅkara's view), but is distinct from the state known as

---

[88] See Lott, Vedantic Approaches to God, 32.

[89] RBGB, 420.

[90] RBGB, 420.

[91] RBGB, 420. Verses from the BG are also quoted (10.20, 10.39, 10.42), followed with a refutation of advaita. The view of advaita, states Rāmānuja, employs sāmānādhikaraṇya to set forth the identity of the individual self with Brahman (see my chapter 1, section 1.2.4.2). Further, the individual self is only seen as such (individual) through superimposition (RBGB, 420-21). He then counters advaita in a way similar to his apologetic in his BSB, under 2.1.15 (SBE, 48:436-42). In his BGB he states, "Such interpreters are to be questioned thus" (p. 421). His argument follows and is in effect this: Is the Lord himself, the Supreme Ruler, one who has had his superimposition erased through true knowledge of the Self? If so, then the very act of teaching Arjuna is impossible, for in doing so the Lord is superimposing a false form on Arjuna while in this state of true knowledge! On the other hand, if the Lord's knowledge has not erased superimposition, how can he be expected to teach the true knowledge of the Self? After all, BG 4.34 teaches, "The wise, who have realized the truth, will instruct you in knowledge" (p. 421).

[92] RBGB, 424.

[93] RBGB, 424.

[94] RBGB, 427. See also page 26.

bliss.[95] Śaṅkara's kevalādvaita necessarily postulates a Brahman that is bliss, for Brahman in reality is all there is. Concerning the text "Bliss is Brahman" (TU 3.6.1), Rāmānuja explains to the Advaitin,

> Your assertion that the text "Bliss is Brahman" proves pure bliss to constitute the essential nature of Brahman is already disposed of by the refutation of the view that knowledge constitutes the essential nature of Brahman; Brahman being in reality the substrate only of knowledge. For by bliss we understand a pleasing state of consciousness. Such passages as "consciousness, bliss is Brahman" therefore mean "consciousness—the essential character of which is bliss—is Brahman" ... And in the same way numerous passages teach that Brahman, while having knowledge for its essential nature, is at the same time a knowing subject; so other passages, speaking of Brahman as something separate from mere bliss, show it to be not mere bliss but a subject enjoying bliss; cp. "That is one bliss of Brahman" (Taitt. Up. [TU] II,8,4); "he knowing the bliss of Brahman" (Taitt. Up. [TU] II,9,1).[96]

Second, contrary to Śaṅkara's total and absolute identity of the jīva with Brahman in mokṣa, and the loss of all apparent individuality in abheda, Rāmānuja holds to an I – Thou relationship between each jīvātman (which is the "I" of each person[97]) and the absolute Brahman.[98] In this relationship the jīva does not reach ontological equality with Brahman in "co-existence" (sālokya), but instead enjoys bliss in "communion" (sāyujya) with Brahman and retains its personality.[99] This I – Thou relationship may occur before final liberation, the fruit of which is the enjoyment of Brahman in the here and now in the phenomenal world. But upon final, full release what was enjoyed before in the phenomenal world is heightened with absolute direct experience of Viṣṇu by the jīvātman (released from karmic-induced bodily existence[100]) in the afterlife.

---

[95] See also Lipner, The Face of Truth, 60.

[96] SBE, 48:84; emphases added.

[97] Rāmānuja chides those who think otherwise: "They who are bond to saṁsāra think that the body is the 'I'" (RVed, 297, par. 143 [Sanskrit text pp. 171-73]). That the jīva is the locus of personality is evident in these words: "The common characteristics of the individual self ... are self-consciousness, sentiency, selfhood, illumine oneself for oneself. Sentiency consists in being the locus of consciousness ... And it (the jīva) is different from the body" (YS, 102-3 [8.1,3]). Finally, in his BGB Rāmānuja asserts that "the experiencing self ... is distinct from the body" (RBGB, 414).

[98] Lipner, The Face of Truth, 60.

[99] YS, 120 (8.24), 199n.31.

[100] Concerning the afterlife it appears that Rāmānuja leaves room for the released jīvātman to acquire material bodies according to its own will. This I mention in chapter 4, section 3.5.2.3,2D and chapter 7, sections 3.2 and 3.4, seventh point.

Third, mokṣa is attained by bhakti directed to Viṣṇu. Unlike Śaṅkara, who employs the term bhakti but defines it as "figurative identification",[101] and who is concerned only with bhakti on the lower level with Īśvara,[102] Rāmānuja's framework does not allow for two levels of Brahman. His Lord gives the call in the BG: "To those who are constantly devoted and worship with love I give that knowledge by which they reach me" (10.10).[103] Rāmānuja sees a reciprocal relationship between the Lord who chooses his devotees by his divine grace and those who as a result adore him.[104] The way of bhakti, then, leads to mokṣa "when the ātman [individual soul] in the union of Brahman comes to the fullest realisation of its being", and "perfect bliss comes in the self's perfect realisation of union with its source and goal".[105]

Fourth, Rāmānuja describes the released jīva: "Its being is the being, viz. the character or nature, of Brahman; but this does not mean absolute oneness of nature."[106] Here Rāmānuja is careful not to be misunderstood as postulating advaita. Yet he can at the same time affirm śruti texts such as "I am Brahman" on the basis of Brahman as the Self, the Being of one's own being. The meaning is close meditative, real union with Brahman.[107]

This, then, is what it means to "know" Brahman. It is meditating on the personal Brahman as one's very Self and antaryāmin in loving devotion to

---

[101] George Thibaut, trans., Vedānta-Sūtras: With the Commentary by Śaṅkarācārya , in F. Max Müller, ed., Sacred Books of the East (Delhi: Motilal Banarsidass, 1988), 38:7. Noted from hereon as SBE.

[102] "Śaṅkara does make concessions to the idea of devotion (bhakti) to a personal Lord (Īśvara) as a lower level of knowledge" (Flood, An Introduction to Hinduism, 242).

[103] SBE, 48:16.

[104] "Chosen of Viṣṇu on the basis of his divine grace" is essential to understanding Ramanuja's doctrine of salvation. Carman observes that the goal of bhakti is attained entirely by God's grace in "the acknowledgement that there is no human means to salvation without divine grace" (The Theology of Ramanuja, 222). Interestingly, there arose in the fourteenth century a debate on the role of human cooperation in the mechanics of salvation. The question was this: Does human choice have a role to play in the divine economy? Answers to this question gave rise to two basic schools of thought, named the "cat's way" and the "monkey's way". In the first, a mother cat rescues its young from danger by dashing to the kitten, clasping with her mouth the scruff of the kitten's neck, and carrying the kitten to a safe place. Here there is no cooperation on the kitten's part. In the second, a mother monkey offers her back to her offspring who is in danger. The baby monkey climbs on her back, holds on, and the mother carries it to safety. Here there is cooperation. For this observation I am indebted to David M. Knipe (Hinduism, 63). Rudolf Otto writes of this in his India's Religion of Grace and Christianity Compared and Contrasted, trans. Frank Hugh Foster (London: Student Christian Movement Press, 1930), 56.

[105] Lipner, The Face of Truth, 61.

[106] SBE, 48:100. See YS, 120 (8.24).

[107] The antaryāmin relationship between Brahman and the released jīva continues in mokṣa.

Brahman[108] as both the transcendent and the immanent Being. Rāmānuja's model for this is the relation of the jīva to the body: "Brahman is rather to be meditated upon as being the Self of the meditating Devotee. As the meditating individual soul is the self of its own body, so the highest Brahman is the Self of the individual soul—this is the proper form of meditation."[109] This meditation extinguishes avidyā or ajñāna[110] and is the fruit of parā vidyā that brings mokṣa.[111]

It is no wonder that Rāmānuja's viśiṣṭādvaita, like Śaṅkara's advaita, is ultimately concerned with mokṣa. The bhakta (devotee), says Rāmānuja, is one who has attained "that supreme [state of] bliss which consists in the direct intuition of His [Brahman's] own true nature: and after that [Brahman] does not turn them back into the miseries of Saṁsāra".[112]

## 6. Summary

Rāmānuja holds to a three-fold ontology of Brahman, the jagat, and jīva-s.[113] He sees bheda not only within Brahman himself and within the jagat itself and the jīva itself, but also between Brahman, the jagat, and jīva-s. Within this doctrine of bheda, however, is unity. There is oneness, a whole, which characterizes Rāmānuja's theology of bheda. Thus, Rāmānuja's system may be described as "unity in diversity", "oneness in distinction", "non-duality in difference", or "identity in difference". As Ādidevānanda writes, "Śrī Rāmānuja's system is called Viśiṣṭādvaita, since the attributive elements (matter and selfs) and the substantive element (Īśvara) form a synthetic

---

[108] See Lott, Vedantic Approaches to God, 32.

[109] SBE, 48:717. See also Lott, Vedantic Approaches to God, 48, though Lott mentions that Rāmānuja places restrictions on the analogy, lest it be taken too far. The jīva needs the body to carry out its desires. Not so with Brahman's relation to the jagat and jīva-s (his body), for Brahman does not necessarily need them. Lott (p. 49) quotes part of Rāmānuja's BGB where Rāmānuja comments on BG 9.4-5. The BG reads, "This entire universe is pervaded by Me, in an unmanifest form. All beings abide in Me, but I do not abide in them. And yet beings do not abide in Me. Behold My divine Yoga. I am the upholder of all beings and yet I am not in them. My will alone causes their existence." Rāmānuja comments: "I am the supporter of all beings, and yet I derive no help for Myself whatever from them" (RBGB, 297-98).

[110] For Rāmānuja avidyā or ajñāna on the part of the jīvātman is lack of knowledge about its dependence upon the personal Brahman in a relationship of trust in all matters of life.

[111] The BSs end with 4.4.22: "Non-return, according to Scripture; non-return, according to Scripture" (SBE, 48:770). Both Śaṅkara and Rāmānuja agree that the repetition of the words of this BS signal "the conclusion of this body of doctrine", that is, all the BSs (SBE, 38:419, 48:771).

[112] SBE, 48:770.

[113] See YS, x.

unity."[114] Unity in diversity has śruti for its ground, and Rāmānuja uses the analogy of the relationship between the jīva and the body to conclude that Brahman is the Self of the jagat and jīva-s. The jagat and jīva-s, then, are prakāra-s of Brahman (just as the body is a prakāra for the jīva) in his role as antaryāmin.

With this model Rāmānuja interprets all śruti texts such as "thou art That", "I am Brahman" and "All this is Brahman" in a way quite different from Śaṅkara. Hermeneutically significant here is Rāmānuja's phrase "in so far as". The jīva is called Brahman in so far as Brahman is the Self of the jīva and in so far as the jīva is the body of Brahman. Therefore all is Brahman in so far as all is the body of Brahman. Rāmānuja can then hold to advaita, but it is viśiṣṭa in the sense of "in so far as".

I concluded in chapter 2 that Śaṅkara's doctrines of Brahman, the jagat, and the jīva play major epistemological, theological and soteriological roles in his doctrine of Kṛṣṇāvatāra. I conclude the same here with Rāmānuja's ontology—it determines his Kṛṣṇāvatāra doctrine. With all preliminary considerations complete, I focus attention now on the body-soul-divine relation in the Kṛṣṇāvatāra doctrines of Śaṅkara and Rāmānuja.

[114] YS, xi.

CHAPTER 4

# The Kṛṣṇāvatāra of Śaṅkara and Rāmānuja

In this chapter I (1) offer my exegesis of BG 4.5-9, 7.24-25 and 9.11, wherein follows (2) an examination of Śaṅkara's and Rāmānuja's exegeses and interpretations of the same. Within these sections I (3) intersperse my comments on Śaṅkara's and Rāmānuja's views of the body-soul-divine relation in the person of Kṛṣṇa.[1] Here I shall work largely with their BGBs and cite some of their other bhāṣya-s and / or works where pertinent.

The material herein demonstrates significant differences between the Kṛṣṇāvatāra doctrines of Śaṅkara and Rāmānuja and how these doctrines naturally follow from their epistemologies and theologies examined in previous chapters. Additionally, this chapter serves the wider purpose of providing elements of comparison with the incarnation of Christ for the conclusion of this study (chapter 7).

---

[1] Though there is mention of a person named Kṛṣṇa in RV 8.85.13-14 and in Kauṣītakī Brāhmaṇa 30.9, "there is", according to Huntington, "insufficient detail to link the later Kṛṣṇa with the one referred to in these passages" (Ronald M. Huntington, "Avatāras and Yugas: An Essay in Purāṇic Cosmology", Purāṇa 6 [January 1964]: 25). Mention of Kṛṣṇa as "the son of Devakī" occurs in CU 3.17.6, a citation that is, according to Huntington, an attempt to link this mention of Kṛṣṇa with those of RV 8.85.13-14 and Kauṣītakī Brāhmaṇa 30.9 (Huntington, "Avatāras and Yugas", 25). Huntington further observes that "it is only in the Mahābhārata that a distinct Kṛṣṇa emerges in the role of a human hero, religious teacher, and counsellor of the Pāṇḍavas, and later gradually raised to the level of divinity and even identified with Brahman" ("Avatāras and Yugas", 25-26; Huntington cites as a reference A. D. Pusalker, Studies in the Epics and Purāṇas [Bombay: Bhāratīya Vidyā Bhavan, 1955], 51-52). See also Dasgupta's brief but informative section on the different Kṛṣṇa-s (Surendranath Dasgupta, A History of Indian Philosophy [Delhi: Motilal Banarsidass, reprint 1992], 2:544). Radhakrishnan asserts, "So far as the teaching of the Bhagavadgītā is concerned, it is immaterial whether Kṛṣṇa, the teacher, is a historical individual or not. The material point is the eternal incarnation of the Divine, the everlasting bringing forth of the perfect and divine life in the universe and the soul of man." Radhakrishnan, however, immediately follows this with the observation that there is "ample evidence in favour of the historicity of Kṛṣṇa". He cites as proof of this CU 3.17.6, RV 8 and Kauṣītakī Brāhmaṇa 30.6,9 (S. Radhakrishnan, The Bhagavadgītā: With an Introductory Essay, Sanskrit Text, English Translation and Notes [London: George Allen & Unwin, 1956], 28).

### 1. BG 4.5-9

In the famous avatāra passage in BG 4.5-9, Kṛṣṇa states,

> (5) Many of my births have already occurred, Arjuna, and of you. I know them all. You do not know [them], O oppressor of the foe. (6) Even though I am unborn—being the imperishable Self—even though being the Lord of beings, governing my own material nature, I come into being by my māyā. (7) For whenever a decrease of virtue comes about, O Bharata [Arjuna], a rise of non-virtue, then I give forth myself. (8) For the rescue of the virtuous and for the destruction of evil doers, for the purpose of the establishing of virtue, I come into being from age to age. (9) Thus he who knows truly my divine birth and deeds, having left the material body, he does not go to rebirth; he goes to me, Arjuna.[2]

#### 1.1. Śaṅkara on BG 4.5-9

The BG is the primary text in which Kṛṣṇa is revealed, and the master Advaitin is well aware of the philosophical problem of a Kṛṣṇa revealed in the context of the Battle of Kurukṣetra in what is arguably the most treasured book of the Hindu people. The challenge for him is reconciling this generally accepted-as-historical battle with his kevalādvaita.

Quantitatively speaking, there is not much by way of commentary on the part of Śaṅkara concerning these important verses.[3] There are, however, a few of his preliminary statements worth noting, statements that naturally flow from his epistemology and theology, the latter including his doctrine of Īśvara. Śaṅkara's exegesis of BG 4.5-9 (and consequently other avatāra texts) actually begins with two significant statements in the introduction to his BGB. These statements provide the hermeneutic foundation from which spring both his understanding of this passage and our take, inferentially, on his intent. Without these in place for his readers it would indeed be difficult to ascertain the sense from his commentary alone.

The following statements inform us of the issues of quantity of essence taken in the event of avatāra, the role of māyā in the event, and the "seeming"

---

[2] bahūni me vyatītāni janmāni tava cārjuna tānyahaṁ veda sarvāṇi na tvaṃ vettha paraṁtapa ajo 'pi sann avyayātmā bhūtānām īśvaro 'pi san prakṛtiṁ svām adhiṣṭhāya saṁbhavāmyātmamāyayā yadā yadā hi dharmasya glānir bhavati bhārata abhyutthānam adharmasya tadā 'tmānaṁ sṛjāmyaham paritrāṇāya sādhūnāṁ vināśāya ca duṣkṛtām dharmasaṁsthāpanārthāya saṁbhavāmi yuge yuge janma karma ca me divyam evaṁ yo vetti tattvataḥ tyaktvā dehaṁ punarjanma naiti mām eti so 'rjuna.

[3] Śaṅkara spends just as little time on BG 7.19, "Vāsudeva is all", a rather important verse for his advaita (see A. G. Krishna Warrier, trans., Srīmad Bhagavad Gītā Bhāṣya of Sri Śaṅkarācārya [Mylapore: Sri Ramakrishna Math, 1983], 265). Noted from hereon as SBGB.

reality of the avatāra:

> The primal and all-pervading [viṣṇuḥ] Agent, celebrated as Nārāyaṇa,[4] is held to have been born of Vasudeva from Devaki's womb[5] by an aspect [aṁśa] of Himself as Kṛṣṇa.[6]
>
> The Lord (Bhagavān) is in eternal possession of knowledge, lordliness, executive power,[7] strength, energy and splendour. He has under His control His all-pervasive Māyā [vaiṣnavīṁ māyāṁ] (Illusive Power)[8] or material Nature [mūlaprakṛti], whose essence is the three constituents [triguṇātmikāṁ].[9] Thus, though unborn, immutable, Lord of beings [bhūtānāṁ īśvaraḥ], and, in essence, eternally pure, conscious and free, He appears[10] [lakṣyate], by virtue of His Māyā, to be embodied and born as a man [dehavān iva jātaḥ iva].[11]

---

[4] See W. Douglas P. Hill, The Bhagavadgītā (London: Oxford University Press, 1928), 10-14, for an account of the development of the Kṛṣṇa Vāsudeva-Viṣṇu-Nārāyaṇa doctrines. He concludes that Kṛṣṇa Vāsudeva's identification with Nārāyaṇa is a later development than that of the BG, and that "while the identification of Kṛiṣṇa with Viṣṇu satisfied the desire of the worshiper for a personal Supreme, cosmic Nārāyaṇa met the need of the philosopher [such as Śaṅkara] who preferred to meditate on Vāsudeva as the immanent principle of life" (p. 13).

[5] The MBh and the VP mention the mechanics of the conception of Kṛṣṇa. The conception of Kṛṣṇa occurred when Viṣṇu plucked a black hair from his head (in Sanskrit kṛṣṇa means "black"). The black hair then entered the womb of Devakī. See J. A. B. van Buitenen, trans., The Mahābhārata (Chicago: The University of Chicago Press, 1973), 1:373 (MBh 1.189.31), and Horace H. Wilson, The Vishnu Purana (New York: Garland, 1981), 4:258-59 (VP 5.1).

[6] Or as I translate, "by an aspect of himself, namely [kila] Kṛṣṇa". See also BG 10.41-42.

[7] Knowledge, lordliness, executive power from the Sanskrit jñānaiśvaryaśakti.

[8] Parenthetical remark is that of translator.

[9] See Swāmī Mādhavānanda, trans., Vivekacūḍāmaṇi [Crest-jewel of Discrimination] (Calcutta: Advaita Ashrama, 1998), 39, par. 108, where māyā "is made up of the three guṇas". Noted from hereon as VC.

[10] Or "seems".

[11] SBGB, 2,3. In the Sanskrit phrase svamāyayā dehavān iva jātaḥ iva ... lakṣyate, translated as "by his own māyā he appears as if embodied, as if born", the iva ("as if" or "as it were") is important to the overall meaning. Bradley J. Malkovsky, in his The Role of Divine Grace in the Soteriology of Śaṃkarācārya (Leiden: Brill, 2001), 339, is correct when he calls attention to the ambiguity of iva, stating that it could mean "just so, just, exactly, indeed" (see Sir Monier Monier-Williams, A Sanskrit-English Dictionary [Delhi: Motilal Banarsidass, 1990], 168). However, Malkovsky does not treat what appears to me to be quite important in the passage, specifically the verb lakṣ, which Warrier, Malkovsky, and I translate "appear" (for lakṣ see Monier-Williams' A Sanskrit-English Dictionary, 891). Though "appear" does not necessarily denote an

Implicitly evident in this statement is Śaṅkara's placement of the avatāra of Kṛṣṇa squarely in the context of apara brahman or Īśvara. Several reasons for this follow.

First, Śaṅkara states that Īśvara is in possession of jñāna. But for Śaṅkara para brahman does not possess knowledge. Rather, this higher Brahman is knowledge,[12] an interpretation in harmony with his kevalādvaita. Thus Warrier (an Advaitin) mentions "Kṛṣṇa representing the saguṇa Brahman".[13] I take this to mean Śaṅkara's Īśvara or apara brahman.[14]

Second, Īśvara is in sovereign control of his vaiṣnavī māyā. Śaṅkara comments on BG 14.6 as he represents Kṛṣṇa: "I am the master [īśvaraḥ īśanaśīlaḥ] of all beings from Brahmā down to a tuft of grass."[15] This statement lends to the necessity of Kṛṣṇa as Īśvara in Śaṅkara's jagat-prapañca. For Śaṅkara the gods and the material world are relegated to the lower order of being, which ultimately is mithyā.

Third, Kṛṣṇa's vaiṣnavī māyā is his mūlaprakṛti, the essence of which are the triguṇa-s. Again, for Brahman to possess any attributes necessitates an apara brahman or Īśvara.

Fourth, and connected to the first reason above, Śaṅkara assigns further attributes to the bhūtānāṁ īśvara (such as lordliness, executive power, strength,

---

unreal appearance, as perhaps Malkovsky might argue, I take it to mean "to seem (or "was perceived") as if embodied". J. A. B. van Buitenen translates as follows: "This Blessed Lord was perceived as born, as it were, as an embodied person, as it were, by virtue of his own power of illusion" (The Bhagavadgītā in the Mahābhārata [Chicago: University of Chicago Press, 1981], 10). Malkovsky cites this translation of van Buitenen in a note after stating that most translators favor the "as if" or "as it were" sense (The Role of Divine Grace in the Soteriology of Śaṃkarācārya, 339). Malkovsky cites Murty's interesting observation on Śaṅkara's Kṛṣṇāvatāra. Malkovsky writes, "Ultimately Śaṁkara's 'as if' (iva) [now quoting Murty] 'implies that the appearance of an avatāra is an illusion in a double sense', the illusion of an incarnation in a world that is itself an illusion" (The Role of Divine Grace in the Soteriology of Śaṃkarācārya, 341 n. 220, quoting S. Murty, Revelation and Reason in Advaita Vedānta [Delhi: Motilal Banarsidass, 1974], 278-79).

[12] See my overview of Śaṅkara's exegesis of TU 2.6 in chapter 1, section 2.1.

[13] SBGB, xiii. Warrier points the reader to BG 14.27. In BG 14.27 Kṛṣṇa claims that he functions as the ground of Brahman ("I am the ground [pratiṣṭhā] of Brahman"). Interestingly, Śaṅkara in the bhāṣya equates Kṛṣṇa with "the inner Self" (pratyagātman). Warrier, in his introduction, does not mention this. The pratyagātman, writes Śaṅkara, "is the ground of the Supreme Self" (SBGB, 488). The import here is that the saguṇa brahman, the apara brahman as represented by Kṛṣṇa, is nevertheless one with the para brahman in an advaitic whole (SBGB, 488). Following this, Śaṅkara offers an alternative interpretation. The word "Brahman" in BG 14.27 refers to saguṇa brahman, while the "I" in the text is the Supreme Self, the para brahman.

[14] Kṛṣṇa, whether in the context of his being the "inner Self" or not, still operates in the realm of apara brahman.

[15] SBGB, 138.

energy, splendour, unborn, immutable, eternally pure, conscious and free), attributes which are not assigned to the para brahman, excepting the statement neti neti.

Fifth, by māyā Kṛṣṇa "seems" to be embodied or born as a man. Thus, Śaṅkara implicitly relegates the avatāra of Kṛṣṇa to the jagat-prapañca.

## 1.2. BG 4.5

In BG 4.5 Kṛṣṇa states that many avatāra events of his (as Viṣṇu) have already taken place. Kṛṣṇa also claims to know all of Arjuna's births.[16]

### 1.2.1. ŚAṄKARA ON BG 4.5

Śaṅkara knows here that Kṛṣṇa speaks, though we should understand this as Nārāyaṇa speaking as Kṛṣṇa, who is one of several avatāra-s of this "all-pervading Agent". Kṛṣṇāvatāra, then, is not unique, whether within the one cycle of the four yuga-s or within the whole eternal and megacosmic cyclical phenomenon, wherein the four yuga-s are endlessly repeated. Moreover, Kṛṣṇa assigns to himself certain abstract attributes such as "eternally pure" (nityaśuddha), "awake" (buddha), "free" (mukta), and "unimpaired cognitive powers" (anāvaraṇajñānaśaktiḥ), attributes not acknowledged in the context of para brahman, for there we find only neti neti. The context of para brahman necessitates, in Śaṅkara's advaita, nirguṇa brahman, not saguṇa brahman as is evidenced here. The setting, then, of the avatāra passage of BG 4.5-9 is that of Īśvara, thereby rendering the human form mithyā.

### 1.2.2. RĀMĀNUJA ON BG 4.5

Prior to 4.5, in the commentary on 4.4 Rāmānuja asks significant questions as regards the body-divine relationship in the person of Kṛṣṇa:

> Can the birth of the Lord ... be of the same nature as that of the gods, men etc., who are subject to Karma? Or can it be false [mithyā] like the

---

[16] By itself this statement does not necessarily imply omniscience. However, Vempeny argues that this text in conjunction with others in the BG (for example 7.26, 11.3, 13.12) demonstrates that Kṛṣṇa is omniscient (Ishanand Vempeny, Kṛṣṇa and Christ: In the Light of Some of the Fundamental Concepts and Themes of the Bhagavad Gītā and the New Testament [Pune: Ishvani Kendra, 1988], 78). In addition to BG 4.5, Vitaliano R. Gorospe adds BG 7.26 to Kṛṣṇa's claim of omniscience, and adds that Kṛṣṇa claims to possess "all wisdom", citing 10.38, 11.18, 15.15, and 16.39 ("Krishna Avatara in the Bhagavad Gita and Christ Incarnate in John's Gospel", Dialogue & Alliance 1, no. 2 [Summer 1987]: 56). Finally, Madhusūdana Sarasvatī, a sixteenth century Advaitin in the tradition of Śaṅkara, believes that Kṛṣṇa is omniscient due to the latter's knowledge of all of Arjuna's births (Sisir Kumar Gupta, Madhusūdana Sarasvatī on the Bhagavad Gītā: Being an English Translation of his Commentary, Gūḍhārtha Dīpikā [Delhi: Motilal Banarsidass, 1977], 78).

> illusions of a magical show? Or could it be real [satya]? ... If His birth is real, what is the mode [prakāra] of His birth?[17] What is the nature of His body?[18] What is the manner of His birth ... What is the cause of His birth? To what end is He born?[19]

Rāmānuja also makes a few key statements in his introduction to his BGB. I shall mention them briefly before moving to BG 4.5.

Based upon his epistemology and exegesis of certain mahāvākya-s in other places, Rāmānuja strongly asserts the reality of the material world and says of his Lord,

> His nature and qualities transcend all thought and words. He dwells in the divine and imperishable supreme heaven which abounds in manifold, wondrous and countless objects, means and places of enjoyment ... His sportive delight brings about the origination, sustentation and dissolution of the entire cosmos [jagat] filled with multifarious, variegated and innumerable objects.[20]

Rāmānuja then claims the absolute reality of past avatāra events and states that his Lord "shaped His own figure [svarūpa[21]] into the likeness of the various kinds of creatures without giving up His own supreme nature, and got incarnated [avatīrya[22]] in the worlds of creatures".[23] He follows with an apologetic regarding the avatāra of Kṛṣṇa, stressing the actual visible nature of the descent: "He incarnated [avatīrya] on earth as Śrī Kṛṣṇa. He thus became

---

[17] Rāmānuja, like Śaṅkara, holds that Kṛṣṇa was born in the womb of Devakī.

[18] M. Dhavamony, in his essay "Hindu 'incarnations'", Studia Missionalia 21 (1972): 148, states, "Who is Krishna? ... Does the prehistory of Krishna of the Bhagavadgītā indicate that he is a humanized god or that he is a deified man? Indologists, both native and foreign, have discussed this problem in great detail." Curiously, Dhavamony offers no sources to substantiate this last statement.

[19] Svāmī Ādidevānanda, trans., Śrī Rāmānuja Gītā Bhāṣya (Mylapore: Sri Ramakrishna Math, n.d.), 159. Noted from hereon as RBGB.

[20] RBGB, 43.

[21] Carman translates svarūpa as "essential nature" (John B. Carman, The Theology of Rāmānuja: An Essay in Interreligious Understanding [New Haven and London: Yale University Press, 1974; Bombay: Ananthacharya Indological Research Institute, 1981], 169). Van Buitenen translates "proper form" (J. A. B. van Buitenen, trans., Rāmānuja's Vedārthasaṃgraha [Poona: Deccan College Postgraduate and Research Institute, 1956], 265, par. 113 [Sanskrit text p. 144]; noted from hereon as RVed). In section 3.5.2.3 I discuss the meaning of svarūpa as including the divya rūpa.

[22] The gerund of ava and tṛī.

[23] RBGB, 43; Sanskrit text page 41. The theme of not abandoning the essential nature is repeated in RBGB, 240, this time specifically with regard to the avatāra of Kṛṣṇa.

the visible object for the sight of all men."[24] Finally, Rāmānuja states that Kṛṣṇa "had taken upon Himself a mortal human form [martya]".[25] Whether or not this human form was truly human I answer later.

As for the commentary on 4.5, Rāmānuja's gloss is quite short, but he is sure to stress, perhaps specifically against Śaṅkara, "the reality of the Lord's birth [janmanaḥ satyatvam]".[26] He then states that in verse 6 "The mode of incarnation [avatāraprakāraṁ], the reality of His body [dehayāthātmyaṁ] ... are explained".[27]

## 1.3. BG 4.6

Kṛṣṇa here claims that he is God. Further, he is avatārin as well as avatāra.[28] Being unborn, the imperishable Self, he is the Lord of beings, he is Viṣṇu. Unlike ordinary beings who are born again and again "from the power of prakṛti" (prakṛter[29] vaśāt) under the control of Kṛṣṇa (BG 9.8),[30] his birth is not necessitated by karma through avidyā māyā[31] (the power of ignorance) in saṁsāra. As deity he is in sovereign control of the universe by virtue of his own māyā, which here I take to be power, by which he takes birth according to his own will.

### 1.3.1. ŚAṄKARA ON BG 4.6

In his BGB under 4.6, Śaṅkara, again representing what Kṛṣṇa would claim, states, "resorting to, i.e. mastering, My 'power of becoming' [prakṛtiṁ māyāṁ], I take birth or appear to become embodied".[32] BG 3.27 explains that all actions (whether by gods or human beings) are performed "by the guṇa-s of

---

[24] RBGB, 43. Sanskrit for the second sentence: sakalamanujanayanaviṣayatāṁ gataḥ.
[25] RBGB, 44.
[26] RBGB, 159; emphasis mine.
[27] RBGB, 159; emphasis mine.
[28] See Hill, who states concerning verse 5, "Kriṣṇa declares that he, though in reality God who knows no birth nor change, has many times been born; Lord of all creatures, he creates himself" (The Bhagavadgītā, 10). I thank Julius Lipner for the comment that Kṛṣṇa is avatārin as well as avatāra. In other words, explains Lipner, the individual known as Kṛṣṇa is the Supreme Being ("Avatāra and Incarnation?", in Re-Visioning India's Religious Traditions: Essays in Honour of Eric Lott, ed. David C. Scott and Israel Selvanayagam [Delhi: ISPCK, 1996], 130).
[29] May be viewed as a genitive of apposition: "from the power which is prakṛti."
[30] See S. Radhakrishnan, The Bhagavadgītā: With an Introductory Essay, Sanskrit Text, English Translation and Notes (London: George Allen & Unwin, 1956), 153-54.
[31] Radhakrishnan, The Bhagavadgītā, 241.
[32] SBGB, 138. Radhakrishnan labels this interpretation by Śaṅkara "not satisfactory" (The Bhagavadgītā, 154). This is evident in the parenthetic insertion in his translation of verse 6: "I come into (empiric) being" (p. 153).

prakṛti". Here in 4.6 we find that it is Kṛṣṇa who is sovereign over prakṛti,[33] so much so that it is he who governs his own material nature (prakṛtiṁ svām adhiṣṭhāya).[34] Thus, Kṛṣṇa's apparent embodiment, though similar to embodiments of others in that they too are apparent, differs in one very important sense: Kṛṣṇa is embodied of his own choice, "by my own power of becoming" (ātmamāyayā,[35] instrumental case) as Warrier translates, whereas others are born due to, and corresponding to, the law of karma. Swami Swarupananda, a modern Advaitin, states, "He does not come into being as others do, bound by Karma, under the thraldom of Prakṛti (Nature). He is not tied by the fetters of the Guṇas—because He is the Lord of Māyā."[36] Kṛṣṇa therefore is "eternally pure" (nityaśuddha) and born, writes Śaṅkara, "even in the absence of merit [dharma] and demerit [adharma]",[37] which implies Kṛṣṇa's sinlessness.

In 4.6 māyā and prakṛti are synonymous. On this point we read in SU 4.10: "Know, then, that prakriti is māyā, and the great Lord [Īśvara] the possessor of māyā."[38] This lends weight to Śaṅkara's statement in the introduction to his BGB, quoted earlier: "He has under His control His all-pervasive Māyā [vaiṣnavīṁ māyāṁ] (Illusive Power) or material Nature [mūlaprakṛti]." Radhakrishnan, commenting on Śaṅkara's view of Īśvara as the cause of the world, states that "the causation of the world is traced to māyā or prakṛti which is the power of Brahman conceived as Īśvara".[39] Thus it is that Kṛṣṇa, representative of Īśvara, utilizes his māyā that is prakṛti (and his "power of becoming") to appear as embodied.[40] Śaṅkara continues: "Thus am I born, as it

---

[33] See R. C. Zaehner, The Bhagavad-Gītā: With a Commentary Based on the Original Sources (London: Oxford University Press, 1973), 183.

[34] Vempeny's interpretation concurs with mine. The avatārin is in control of his own birth, unlike other beings whose births are necessitated by karma (Kṛṣṇa and Christ, 256).

[35] Hill translates "by my delusive power" (The Bhagavadgītā, 138; see also p. 32), though he does not mean delusion in the sense of Śaṅkara. The extent of the delusion is that some do not recognize that Kṛṣṇa is God in human form (pp. 32-33). Hill points his readers to BG 7.25.

[36] Swami Swarupananda, Śrīmad-Bhagavad-Gītā (Calcutta: Advaita Ashrama, 1847, thirteenth revised edition, 1982), 99.

[37] SBGB, 137.

[38] māyāṁ tu prakṛtiṁ viddhi māyinaṁ tu maheśvaram. Sanskrit transliteration taken from S. Radhakrishnan, ed., The Principal Upaniṣads (New York: Harper & Brothers, 1953), 734. Unless otherwise noted, from hereon all transliteration from the Upaniṣads is taken from this source.

[39] Radhakrishnan, The Principal Upaniṣads, 711.

[40] "By My own Māyā: My embodiment is only apparent and does not touch My true nature" (Swarupananda, Śrīmad-Bhagavad-Gītā, 99). Madhusūdana Sarasvatī states in his interpretation of BG 4.6 that the Lord "just simulates embodiment", and that Kṛṣṇāvatāra "is only an appearance and not reality" (Gupta, Madhusūdana Sarasvatī on

were, by virtue of My power of becoming and not in fact, as is the [same] case for the world [loka]."[41] Here the phenomenal world, the jagat-prapañca, including the avatāra of Kṛṣṇa, is "not in fact" (na paramārthatas, not in reality[42]), due to the power or māyā of Īśvara.[43]

### 1.3.2. RĀMĀNUJA ON BG 4.6

Rāmānuja begins his gloss once again reiterating that in the avatāra event Kṛṣṇa loses nothing of his essential nature, and, like Śaṅkara, admits what is undeniable in the text: "I am born of My free will [ātmamāyayā]."[44] Later on in this lengthy commentary he mentions that Kṛṣṇa's essential nature has as an attribute the reality of "being free from sins [apāpmatva]".[45]

As the sovereign Lord he creates, "by governing My own nature [svabhāvam adhiṣṭhāya]",[46] his avatāra form "similar to the configuration of gods, men [devamanuṣyādisajātīya]".[47] Svabhāvam is most likely the divya rūpa, for immediately Rāmānuja follows with a description of the form (rūpa) of his Lord[48] that is reminiscent of the description given to the anthropomorphic divya rūpa in paragraph 134 of RVed. Sajātīya is translated as "similar to the configuration" by Ādidevānanda. The question now is whether or not this means "absolutely identical" or "similar but not identical". Though the word jātīya means "belonging to any species or genus or tribe or order or race of",[49] the prefix sa is responsible for the ambiguity. It can mean "similarity" as well as "equality" or "possessing".[50] Since there is nothing in the commentary for

---

the Bhagavad Gītā, 80). He reiterates the apparentness of Kṛṣṇāvatāra in his glosses on BG 4.7 and 4.9 (p. 81).

[41] SBGB, 138.

[42] Monier-Williams, A Sanskrit-English Dictionary, 588. C. Sadanandam states regarding Śaṅkara's comments on BG 4.6, "This stand of Śankara appears to deny the reality of Avatāra" (The Doctrine of Avatāra [Delhi: New Bharatiya Book Corporation, 2002], 44).

[43] As I state in chapter 1, for Śaṅkara māyā is the śakti of Brahman that causes the mithyā of both names of objects and forms of objects through avidyā (see section 1.2.1). I disagree with Hill, who states, "Śaṅkara uses the word māyā in his monistic system as equivalent to that ignorance whereby the individual falsely attributes existence to the objects of experience" (The Bhagavadgītā, 32; emphasis mine).

[44] RBGB, 159-60. Śrīnivāsa concurs, stating, avatārāṇāmicchaiva hetuḥ, na tu karma "The cause of the descent is the will alone, but not karma" (Svāmī Ādidevānanda, trans., Yatīndramatadīpikā by Śrīnivāsadāsa [Mylapore: Sri Ramakrishna Math, n.d.], 138 [9.25]; noted from hereon as YS).

[45] RBGB, 161; Sanskrit text page 160.

[46] RBGB, 159 (my translation from Sanskrit text).

[47] RBGB, 161; Sanskrit text page 160.

[48] RBGB, 160.

[49] Monier-Williams, A Sanskrit-English Dictionary, 418.

[50] Monier-Williams, A Sanskrit-English Dictionary, 1111.

this verse that elucidates the exact meaning of sajātīya, one must look elsewhere for statements by Rāmānuja in order to flesh it out. For example, in a passage in RVed he states that the body of Kṛṣṇa "is not of the stuff common bodies are made of".[51] The meaning, then, is "similar but not identical".

Rāmānuja's Kṛṣṇa in his essential nature is as BG 4.6 confesses—ajas or unborn. For proof he cites śruti: "'Being unborn, he is born in various forms' (Tai[tirīya] Ā[raṇyaka] 3.12.7)."[52] This leads Rāmānuja to conclude that Kṛṣṇa's birth is different from those of others, theirs being the outcome of karma, but his of his own free will and not necessitated by karma, due to his perfect essential nature. As the later viśiṣṭādvaita theologian Śrīnivāsa taught, "The cause of the descents is the will [of the Lord] only, and not karma."[53]

Interesting is the number of times Rāmānuja, in this section of his BGB, employs certain terms to indicate or reiterate the ultimate reality of Kṛṣṇa's avatāra. He uses saṁbhavāmi (I am born) three times, janman (birth) or jan (its verbal form) five times, rūpa (form) three times,[54] sṛjāmyaham (I give forth myself) once, and bahudhā (various forms) once. Perhaps for this reason Ādidevānanda adds a comment of his own to the end of Rāmānuja's comments on 4.6: "All this elaboration is meant to refute the doctrine of mere apparency of incarnations as taught by the Advaitins. Rāmānuja, as stated in his Introduction to the Bhāṣya, upholds the absolute reality of incarnations."[55]

### 1.4. BG 4.7-8

The enclitic particle hi (for) serves to introduce the reasons for Kṛṣṇa's avatāra. When there is a decrease in dharma, Kṛṣṇa comes to rescue (paritrāṇāya[56]) the virtuous and to destroy evil doers. The goal (evidenced by artha, "aim", "purpose", in the compound dharmasaṁsthāpanārthāya) of these reasons is to establish virtue.

The concluding verbal phrase in 4.7, "I give forth (sṛjāmi)[57] myself", is virtually synonymous with the concluding phrases of 4.6 and 4.8, where the verbal phrase used is saṁbhavāmi ("I come into being"). "From age to age [yuge yuge]" (4.8) does not limit the avatāra of Kṛṣṇa to a once-per-four-yuga-cycle appearance, but leaves open the possibility of several descents within fourfold cycles. Adding weight to this, both sṛjāmi and saṁbhavāmi are in the

---

[51] Page 265, par. 113 (Sanskrit text p. 144). I shall have more on this in section 3.5.2.3.

[52] RBGB, 161. Sanskrit on page 160: ajāyamāno bahudhā vijāyate.

[53] YS, 138 (9.25). My translation of avatārāṇāmicchaiva hetuḥ, na tu karma.

[54] Two other times to denote essential nature.

[55] RBGB, 161.

[56] Dative from pari and the verb trā.

[57] See Swami Ramakrishnananda's "I body Myself" in his God and Divine Incarnations (Mylapore: Sri Ramakrishna Math, n.d.), 127.

present tense and can be interpreted as habitual,[58] especially in light of the repetitive use of the locative yuge.

### 1.4.1. ŚAṄKARA ON BG 4.7-8

Concerning this vital passage in Śaṅkara's bhāṣya, Arvind Sharma states that Śaṅkara spends very little time treating the avatāra of Kṛṣṇa:

> In viewing the Gītā as a harmonious whole in the light of one's philosophy, one may tend to overlook thematic transitions which occur within the text. Śaṅkara seems to do that when the theme of incarnation is introduced in the Fourth Chapter. It is true that in his Preface to his commentary on the Gītā he comments on Kṛṣṇa's status as an avatāra,[59] like Rāmānuja. But when the key text [4.7-8] appears and is followed by IV:9 ... Śaṅkara treats the subject rather skimpily.[60]

Sharma is correct in his observation. Śaṅkara's comments for the most part are merely a reiteration of the content of verses 7-8, except to add in verse 7 that Kṛṣṇa's avatāra occurs māyayā ("through Māyā"[61]),[62] this itself being a reiteration of what is stated in BG 4.6.

Interesting is Warrier's translation of sṛjāmi in 4.7 and of Śaṅkara's reiteration of this verb in his bhāṣya. Though Warrier is in step with several modern translators and commentators on the translation of saṁbhavāmi as "I take birth" (v. 6) and "I am born" (v. 8),[63] Warrier, in the fashion of advaita,

---

[58] An option of the present tense. See William Dwight Whitney, Sanskrit Grammar: Including both the Classical Language, and the Older Dialects, of Veda and Brahmana (Cambridge, Mass.: Harvard University Press, sixteenth issue [1987] of the second edition [1889]), 278.

[59] Quoted in my section 1.1.

[60] Arvind Sharma, The Hindu Gītā: Ancient and Classical Interpretations of the Bhagavadgītā (London: Duckworth, 1986), 45-46.

[61] Warrier's translation of the dative.

[62] And except to add that the virtuous ones of verse 8 are "those who tread the path of morality".

[63] Ādidevānanda, "I am born" and "am I born" (RBGB, 159,162), Radhakrishnan, "I come into (empiric) being" and "I come into being" (The Bhagavadgītā, 153,155), Hill, "I come into being" (The Bhagavadgītā, 138), Zaehner, "I come to be" and "I come into being" (The Bhagavad-Gītā, 58), Edgerton, "I come into being" (Franklin Edgerton, The Bhagavad Gītā [Cambridge, Mass.: Harvard University Press, 1972], 23), Miller, "I come into being" and "I appear" (Barbara Stoler Miller, trans., The Bhagavad Gita: Krishna's Counsel in Time of War [New York: Bantam Books, 1986], 50), Deutsch, "I come into being" (Eliot Deutsch, The Bhagavad Gītā [New York: Holt, Rinehart and Winston, 1968], 55), and Sargeant, "I come into being" (Winthrop Sargeant, The Bhagavad Gītā [Albany: State University of New York Press, 1984], 206,208).

translates the verb sṛjāmi in verse 7 as "I project",[64] a translation that is certainly acceptable,[65] but, arguably, different from some other translations. Radhakrsihnan translates "I send forth (create, incarnate)",[66] Hill "I create",[67] Zaehner "I generate",[68] Miller "I create",[69] and Edgerton and Deutsch "I send forth".[70] Taken in light of the overall advaitic worldview, this carries the meaning of a projecting forth on the part of Īśvara in the context of the jagat-prapañca an appearance of flesh that is from the perspective of para brahman or ultimate Brahman mithyā, an appearance "not in fact".

The one possibility of similarity here is Zaehner's "I generate", but the resemblance is purely superficial. Zaehner states that his translation is "more accurate" than those of Edgerton, Radhakrishnan and Hill.[71] In this section Zaehner does not commit to stepping on the sides of Śaṅkara or Rāmānuja[72] (he only reports their commentary[73]; he is careful to note under verse 6 that Śaṅkara's understanding of māyā, unfortunately misunderstood by some to mean world illusion, "means illusion from the point of view of Absolute Reality ... Empirically it is real"[74]). Surely the verb sṛj can mean "let loose", "let go", "produce", and in this sense "generate", but we are not sure why Zaehner translates it so; nor are we sure why he states that Edgerton, Radhakrishnan and Hill are less accurate in their renderings of the verb, because he offers here no lexical or contextual proof. But if we take other statements made by Zaehner in other parts of his work, such as Rāmānuja being "nearest to the mind of the author of the Gītā",[75] and interpret in this light Zaehner's comments in various places that Kṛṣṇa is God incarnate,[76] it is unlikely that by "generate" he means "project" in the sense of Warrier or

---

[64] SBGB, 138-39.

[65] Sṛj also carries the meaning of "let go", "let loose", "emit" and "create" (Monier-Williams, A Sanskrit-English Dictionary, 1245). The first three meanings are arguably akin to Warrier's rendering, that is, strictly lexically speaking.

[66] The Bhagavadgītā, 154.

[67] The Bhagavadgītā, 138.

[68] The Bhagavad-Gītā, 58.

[69] The Bhagavad Gita, 50.

[70] Edgerton, The Bhagavad Gītā, 23; Deutsch, The Bhagavad Gītā, 55.

[71] The Bhagavad-Gītā, 184.

[72] Zaehner states in the introduction that both philosophers "almost invariably read their own philosophical and theological views into the text, however forced and incongruous this may turn out to be" (The Bhagavad-Gītā, 4). Zaehner does admit, however, that Rāmānuja's bhāṣya is "so much nearer in spirit to the Gītā" (p. 3; see also p. 8).

[73] The Bhagavad-Gītā, 183-84.

[74] The Bhagavad-Gītā, 183. See also page 8, where Zaehner states that Śaṅkara taught that the world of diversity and multiplicity is "ultimately an illusory appearance".

[75] The Bhagavad-Gītā, 8; see also page 3.

[76] The Bhagavad-Gītā, 21,120,219,243,273,278.

Śaṅkara.[77] Evidencing this are Śaṅkara's comments concerning BG 4.9 (see section 1.5.1).

### 1.4.2. Rāmānuja on BG 4.7-8

Ādidevānanda translates sṛjāmi in verse 7 as "I incarnate",[78] wanting to keep in step with viśiṣṭādvaita and Rāmānuja's constant reiteration (in his introduction and in his commentary on 4.5-6) of the reality of the avatāra of Kṛṣṇa. Rāmānuja closes his gloss of verse 7 with ātmānaṁ sṛjāmi—"I incarnate Myself."[79]

In the comments on verse 8 Rāmānuja employs rūpa four times, once in the sense of affording the virtuous ones "the opportunity to behold My form and acts and to converse (pradarśana) with Me",[80] a clear indication of the reiteration yet again of the reality of the avatāra event.

## 1.5. BG 4.9

The one who understands that Kṛṣṇa (1) has come in numerous past avatāra-s (v. 5), (2) is unborn, (3) is the imperishable Self and the Lord of beings who governs his own material nature, (4) comes into being by his own māyā (v. 6), and (5) gives forth himself for the rescuing of the virtuous and for the destruction of the wicked, is no more subject to the dreaded saṁsāra but "is liberated" (mucyate[81]).

### 1.5.1. Śaṅkara on BG 4.9

Commenting on BG 4.9 and thus connecting the appearance of Kṛṣṇa's birth to the realm of Īśvara, Śaṅkara states, "My birth [janma], having the nature of an appearance [māyārūpaṁ],[82] ... [is] divine and lordly, and not material [divyaṁ aprākṛtaṁ eśvaraṁ]."[83] Here, grammatically speaking, the guṇa-strengthened eśvaram[84] stems from Īśvara. Warrier's translation of māyārūpam as "the

---

[77] Since he seems to favor Rāmānuja's take on the BG rather than Śaṅkara's (see n. 72).

[78] RBGB, 162.

[79] RBGB, 162.

[80] RBGB, 163.

[81] From the verb muc, from which derives mokṣa.

[82] In his BSB Śaṅkara states that "the highest Lord (parameśvara) also may, when he pleases, assume a bodily shape formed of Māyā, in order to gratify thereby his devout worshippers" (George Thibaut, trans., Vedānta-Sūtras: With the Commentary by Śaṅkarācārya, in F. Max Müller, ed., Sacred Books of the East [Delhi: Motilal Banarsidass, 1988], 34:80). Noted from hereon as SBE.

[83] SBGB, 139. See also "Hindu 'incarnations'", 153, where Dhavamony quotes Śaṅkara on BG 4.9: "My birth is an illusion (māyā)." Sadanandam states, "His [Śaṅkara's] attitude is summed up in his comments on [the] ninth verse, 'my birth is an illusion'" (The Doctrine of Avatāra, 44).

[84] Emphasizing quality.

nature of an appearance" is correct, considering Śaṅkara's system, for here Śaṅkara employs the word māyā not in the primary sense in which he uses it (the power responsible for mithyā), nor in a secondary sense of māyā being prakṛti, but in another secondary sense, meaning mithyā itself.[85] The reason for this is that māyā, in the compound māyārūpam, is not prakṛti ( aprākṛtam), as seen in the above quotation. Finally, the possessive compound māyārūpaṁ, in the neuter accusative singular, qualifies janma, which is neuter. Also qualifying janma are divyaṁ, aprākṛtaṁ and eśvaraṁ. The meaning, then, is that Kṛṣṇa's birth must be viewed as divine, lordly and not material. That is to say, the birth is divine by virtue of occurring in the realm of Īśvara, but from the ultimate point of view not material. Kṛṣṇa's avatāra is, in the ultimate sense, mithyā. Dhavamony quotes A. Mahadeva Sastry's translation of Śaṅkara's BGB, which is quite interesting, more to the point concerning the first phrase (the second phrase perhaps a bit more interpretive than Warrier's translation), and concurs with my thesis that Kṛṣṇāvatāra occurs in the context of Īśvara: "My birth is an illusion (māyā). It is divine, peculiar to Īśvara, not of ordinary nature (aprākṛiti)."[86] As Swarupananda states, "He who knows the great truth—that the Lord though apparently born is ever beyond birth."[87]

### 1.5.2. RĀMĀNUJA ON BG 4.9

Rāmānuja once again stresses the fact that Kṛṣṇa's divine birth (janma divyam), mentioned in 4.9, is not like other beings. Unlike them, Kṛṣṇa's birth is not caused by karma and has no association with prakṛti in connection with the three guṇa-s.[88] In stark contradistinction to Śaṅkara, who states that knowledge of Kṛṣṇa's birth having the nature of an appearance leads to mokṣa,[89] Rāmānuja states that true knowledge of Kṛṣṇa's divine birth leads to mokṣa.[90]

---

[85] This sense of the word is often represented as Śaṅkara's only definition of māyā. Madhusūdana Sarasvatī uses the word in this sense in his interpretation of BG 4.6, stating that the simulated embodiment of the Lord "is nothing but the same cosmic principle, Māyā" (Gupta, Madhusūdana Sarasvatī on the Bhagavad Gītā, 80).

[86] Dhavamony states that Śaṅkara's view of incarnation (Dhavamony's term) is "illusory from the ultimate point of view" ("Hindu 'incarnations'", 154).

[87] Śrīmad-Bhagavad-Gītā, 101

[88] RBGB, 163. Tirukkurukai Piran Pillan, "Rāmānuja's disciple and younger cousin" (John B. Carman, Majesty and Meekness: A Comparative Study of Contrast and Harmony in the Concept of God [Grand Rapids, Mich.: William B. Eerdmans, 1994], 102), once stated of his Lord, "his incarnate bodies have not even a whiff of the faults of material nature" (Carman, Majesty and Meekness, 194; quoted from John Carman and Vasudha Narayanan, The Tamil Veda: Pillan's Interpretation of the Tiruvaymoli [Chicago: University of Chicago Press, 1989], 88 [Tiruvaymoli 3.5.6]).

[89] SBGB, 139.

[90] RBGB, 163.

2. BG 7.24-25

Here Kṛṣṇa states,

> [Though I am] unmanifested, the unintelligent imagine me as entered into manifestation [only], not knowing my higher being—imperishable, highest of all. Covered by yoga-maya, I am not manifest to all. This world, deluded, does not recognize me, birthless, imperishable.[91]

In words reminiscent of BG 4.6a Kṛṣṇa describes himself as the unmanifested,[92] imperishable and Supreme Being. The unintelligent or undiscerning do not recognize this, seeing only his manifestation in the jagat, and believing of Kṛṣṇa that he exists in saṁsāra as do other beings.[93] The reason for this is that many are deluded. Owing to the fact that it is Kṛṣṇa who is in sovereign control of prakṛti and the triguṇātmikā (see BG 7.12-14[94]), it is he who deludes according to his will (see BG 9.8). Just as he is in control of the jagat and all its phenomena, and just as he is in control of his own māyā (BG 4.6), he controls as well the yoga-māyā, which conceals his true being from the deluded.

What is yoga-māyā? Translations / interpretations vary. Zaehner has it as "creative power and the way I use it", arguing that it "corresponds to the way the two words have been used in the Gītā hitherto".[95] Radhakrishnan translates

---

[91] avyaktaṁ vyaktim āpannaṁ manyante mām abuddhayaḥ paraṁ bhāvam ajānanto mamāvyayam anuttamam nāhaṁ prakāśaḥ sarvasya yogamāyāsamāvṛtaḥ mūḍho 'yaṁ nābhijānāti loko mām ajam avyayam.

[92] Kṛṣṇa should not be confused with those avyakta bhūtāni (unmanifest beings) of BG 2.28. It is true that the BG teaches the jīva is eternal, and in this sense avyakta bhūtāni share something in common with him. But, as 2.27 states, these are born again even after death, and taken in conjunction with the theological premise of 4.6, in which Kṛṣṇa's birth or avatāra does not take place according to karma associated with the triguṇātmikā, the avyakta bhūtāni are not avyakta in the same sense that Kṛṣṇa is avyakta. Thus the meaning following above.

[93] "[F]ools think He is a human being like everyone else, here today and gone tomorrow" (Zaehner, The Bhagavad-Gītā, 253).

[94] "And the states of being which are sattvic, and which are rajasic and tamasic, know them from me ... By these three guṇa-produced states of being all this world is deluded ... Truly, divine is my guṇa-produced māyā" (ye caiva sāttvikā bhāvā rājasās tāmasāśca ye matta eveti tān viddhi ... tribhir guṇamayair bhāvair ebhiḥ sarvam idaṁ jagat mohitaṁ ... daivī hy eṣā guṇamayī mama māyā).

[95] The Bhagavad-Gītā, 253. However, Deutsch states, "The term yoga is used extensively in the Gītā and in a number of different senses" (The Bhagavad Gītā, 6), but then adds that "yoga is sometimes employed in the Gītā as a synonym for 'divine power.' When Krishna, as the Lord, speaks of his yoga (as in Chapters X and XI) he does not mean his 'way' or 'path' but his 'creative power'" (Deutsch, The Bhagavad Gītā, 7). Zaehner admits on page 254 that māyā also means "deceit" in PU 1.16.

"creative power"[96] and offers no commentary of his own. Edgerton renders the phrase "magic trick of illusion",[97] and offers no commentary, except to allude to BG 7.13-14.[98] Hill translates "power of delusion",[99] offers interpretations of others in the notes, but offers no personal explanation of the phrase in the commentary.[100] Miller has "magic of my discipline", and in the glossary offers no explanation as to why she adds "discipline",[101] and Deutsch offers "power of illusion",[102] explaining the translation and interpretation in the introduction.[103] Monier-Williams offers a number of possible meanings for the word māyā in the RV: "illusion, unreality, deception, fraud, trick, sorcery, witchcraft, magic ... an unreal or illusory image, phantom, apparition".[104] For the compound yoga-māyā we read, "magic ... the Māyā or abstract power of meditation ... the power of God in the creation of the world personified as a deity".[105] In sum, the phrase, since it appears only here in the BG, is difficult to grasp in both translation and meaning.[106] Zaehner, however, seems to be correct when he interprets the compound in light of the use of both words in the BG. Arguably the word yoga carries the meaning of (or is somehow associated with[107]) "discipline".[108] Further, in 9.5 yogam aiśvaram means "lordly power", and in

---

Speaking of those to whom the world of Brahmā belongs, PU 1.16 reads, "in whom there is no crookedness, no falsehood or deceit" (na yeṣu jihmam anṛtaṁ na māyā ceti).

[96] Bhagavadgītā, 223.

[97] The Bhagavad Gītā, 40. Zaehner states that Edgerton "avoids the issue" (The Bhagavad-Gītā, 254), most likely meaning by this that Edgerton offers no commentary.

[98] The Bhagavad Gītā, 152.

[99] The Bhagavadgītā, 171.

[100] The Bhagavadgītā, 77.

[101] The Bhagavad-Gita, 74,166. Perhaps because yoga carries with it the idea of disciplined meditation (see Deutsch, The Bhagavad Gītā, 6).

[102] The Bhagavad Gītā, 75.

[103] The Bhagavad Gītā, 7.

[104] A Sanskrit-English Dictionary, 811.

[105] A Sanskrit-English Dictionary, 857.

[106] Other translations include "the wizardry I apply" (Kees W. Bolle, The Bhagavadgītā: A New Translation [Berkeley: University of California Press, 1979], 91), "veil of mystery" (Bede Griffiths, River of Compassion: A Christian Commentary on the Bhagavad Gita [New York: Continuum, 1987], 145, and Juan Mascaró, trans., The Bhagavad Gita [New York: Penguin Books, 1962], 76), "veiled in my Maya" (Swami Prabhavananda and Christopher Isherwood, The Song of God: The Bhagavad-Gita [New York: Mentor Books, 1951], 73), and "covered by maya" (P. Lal, The Bhagavadgita [Delhi: Orient Paperbacks, 1965], 51).

[107] See BG 5.5a, wherein the meaning is "by the followers of yoga" (yogais).

[108] In 2.39,48,50; 4.1-3,38,41,42; 5.1,5b,6,7; 6.2,12,16-17,19,20,29,33,36,37,41,44; 7.1; 8.10,12,27; 10.7b; 12.1,6; 13.24; 18.33,75. The word does not always carry this meaning. For examples, in 2.53, 6.3ab,4,23 the meaning "union" is possible, and in 9.22 the meaning is "secure possession". For the list of verses here and throughout this chapter I am indebted to Bolle, The Bhagavadgītā.

10.7a,18 and 11.8 the meaning is "power". The meaning of yoga-māyā in 7.25, then, is "[my] power and the discipline used to exercise it". This coincides with SU 4.10, where the great Īśvara (maheśvaram) is called the māyin, the possessor,[109] the controller, of māyā.[110]

### 2.1. Śaṅkara on BG 7.24-25

Śaṅkara's bhāṣya once again contains only a short paragraph for each verse, but he makes certain he interprets verse 24 in the context of (1) Īśvara in relation to the para brahman, and (2) the "appearance" of Kṛṣṇa's avatāra. Concerning point one, Śaṅkara interprets Kṛṣṇa saying, "The unmanifest or unrevealed, now become manifest or revealed—so, they deem Me, the ever-present Lord [Īśvara]—they, those who do not discriminate." Śaṅkara then immediately asserts that those who do not discriminate are "ignorant of My supreme aspect as the higher Self [paramātman]".[111] Here the paramātman should be viewed as synonymous with Śaṅkara's para brahman. On this point Warrier concurs: "Śaṅkara says Brahman is the paramātmā."[112] Concerning point two, Śaṅkara states of those who are ignorant of the paramātman, "they deem [manyante[113]] me now manifest".[114] Though Śaṅkara here states not explicitly that "they deem" is a supposition on the part of the ignorant that Kṛṣṇa in his avatāra is in the ultimate sense real, this is the implication.

How is this so? Yogamāyāsamāvṛtas (covered by yoga-māyā) in verse 25 is translated by Warrier as "Veiled by the delusive power of My Yoga-Maya".[115] Śaṅkara understands yoga-māyā as follows: "Yoga is the union with, the connection with, the guṇa-s [sattva, rajas, tamas[116]]; thus [this] is the māyā, or

---

[109] Evidenced by the possessive suffix in.

[110] Radhakrishnan directs attention to RV 6.47.18, where "Indra is declared to have assumed many shapes by his māyā", and to BU 2.5.19, which in part reads, "Indra (the Lord) goes about in many forms by his māyās (magical powers)" (Radhakrishnan, The Principal Upaniṣads, 83,208).

[111] SBGB, 268.

[112] SBGB, xiii.

[113] Or "they think", "they suppose".

[114] SBGB, 269.

[115] SBGB, 269.

[116] Śaṅkara, speaking of māyā, states, "She has her guṇas as rajas, tamas, and sattva" (VC, 40, par. 110). Concerning sattva in connection with māyā, it is instrumental in self-realization and in revealing the jagat-prapañca for what it truly is: "The reality of the Ātman becomes reflected in sattva and like the sun reveals the entire world of matter." Concerning rajas, from it "mental modifications such as attachment and grief are continually produced", thus veiling the para brahman. About tamas Śaṅkara states, "Ignorance, lassitude, dullness, sleep, inadvertence, stupidity, etc. are attributes of tamas" (VC, 43, par. 117; 40, par. 111; and 42, par. 116). "Pure sattva", writes Śaṅkara, "is (clear) like water, yet in conjunction with rajas and tamas it makes for

yoga-māyā."[117] Warrier translates as follows: "Yoga being the combination, i.e., fabrication of Prakṛti's constituents, and this combination being Māyā."[118] I suggest Śaṅkara views yoga-māyā as māyā, the delusive power in connection with the guṇa-s, which are the essence of prakṛti (see BG 3.27). It is this "fabrication", due to avidyā on the part of the deluded that leads to the illusory manifestation of the jagat. Swarupananda states it another way, with māyā being illusion, not delusive power: "Yoga-Māyā, i.e., illusion born of Yoga or the union of the three Guṇas."[119] Again, the implication, regardless of which interpretation one adopts, is that Kṛṣṇāvatāra is ultimately mithyā.

### 2.2. Rāmānuja on BG 7.24-25

Whereas Śaṅkara saw in these verses the illusory realm as the veil over the true nature of Brahman, Rāmānuja, in realist fashion, interprets them in the sense that the human form is the veil that hides the higher nature of Kṛṣṇa.

He begins the commentary on verse 24 with a reiteration of the text itself—the ignorant (ajānantas) are unaware of the higher nature (paraṁ bhāvam)[120]—and yet once again asserts that Kṛṣṇa has descended (avatīrṇa) without abandoning his own (higher, divine[121]) nature (ajahatsvabhāva).[122] In further contradistinction to Śaṅkara's view of the ultimate mithyā of the avatāra of Kṛṣṇa, Rāmānuja states that the purpose[123] of the avatāra is for "the refuge of all" (sarvasamāśrayaṇīyatvāya).[124]

For verse 25, though Kṛṣṇa is covered (samāvṛtas) by yoga-māyā, Rāmānuja states that he is "associated with a human form" (sadhāraṇamanuṣyatva) and

---

transmigration [saraṇa]" (VC, 43, par. 117). See also P. T. Raju, The Philosophical Traditions of India (London: George Allen & Unwin, 1971), 180, for the functions of the three guṇa-s in Śaṅkara's advaita.

117 My translation of yogaḥ guṇānāṁ yuktiḥ ghaṭanaṁ. Zaehner translates, "the māyā (sc. delusion) which consists in association with the constituents" (The Bhagavad-Gītā, 253).

118 SBGB, 269; emphasis mine.

119 Śrīmad-Bhagavad-Gītā, 175.

120 RBGB, 263.

121 So the translation of ajahatsvabhāva by Ādidevānanda (RBGB, 263).

122 RBGB, 263. Moreover, the ignorant, writes Rāmānuja, believe Kṛṣṇa was born as are ordinary men, by karma (RBGB, 263).

123 Ādidevānanda translates "has incarnated as the son of Vasudeva, without abandoning My divine nature ... in order that I may be the refuge of all". Purpose is seen in the phrase sarvasamāśrayāṇīyatvāya ajahatsvabhāva eva vāsudevasūnuḥ avatīrṇa: "For the purpose of being the refuge of all, without abandoning his own nature, the very offspring of Vāsudeva was incarnated." Here āśrayāṇīyatvāya is the dative form of āśrayāṇīyatva(m) and can be translated as a dative of purpose (see Whitney, Sanskrit Grammar, 96).

124 RBGB, 263.

has "assumed a human form" (manuṣyatvasaṁsthānam[125]).[126] These two compounds suggest that the human form of Kṛṣṇa is to Rāmānuja quite real.

## 3. BG 9.11

Following the style of the previous sections, I offer first my interpretation of BG 9.11 and follow with assessment of the interpretations of Śaṅkara and Ramanuja.

The verse reads, "The deluded despise me, having assumed a human form [mānuṣīṁ tanum], not knowing my higher being, the great Lord of beings."[127]

As regards this verse, none of the commentators mentioned thus far resolve to answer the question of the status of the body or form of Kṛṣṇa as it relates to his divine nature. But if, as Deutsch states, the BG "is to have a consistent teaching",[128] how does one view the human form of Kṛṣṇa in relation to his "higher nature"? In his introductory essay entitled "Krishna as an Avatāra",[129] Deutsch assumes a consistent teaching on the part of the BG and states something rather significant:

> But if one takes this doctrine of Krishna as an avatāra literally, one must acknowledge that it is simply inconsistent with the rest of the teaching about the nature of the Divine and the world which is put forward by the Gītā. Nature, or prakṛti, the Gītā suggests, is indifferent to the moral concerns of man ... Further, according to the general Hindu cosmological scheme which the poem accepts (VIII, 16-19; IX 7-10), the world always runs a course from dharma to adharma and finally to a state of dissolution (pralaya), after which the cycle recommences ... To complicate the picture even further, this "lower nature" of the Divine, which is subject to growth and decay, is referred to as māyā—that which results from the creative power of the Divine, and that which is "illusory" when seen as independent of the Divine.[130] Now it would certainly be odd if the Lord were to enter into his own lower nature whenever it goes

---

[125] At the end of a compound, sthāna denotes "being in the state of" (see Monier-Williams, A Sanskrit-English Dictionary, 1263). "Assumed a human form" (manuṣyatvasaṁsthānam), as translated by Ādidevānanda here, differs from BG 9.11, wherein we read mānuṣīṁ tanum āśritam (having assumed a human form). It is a bit curious to me why Rāmānuja did not simply adopt here the language of BG 9.11.

[126] RBGB, 264.

[127] avajānanti māṁ mūḍhā mānuṣīṁ tanum āśritam paraṁ bhāvam ajānanto mama bhūtamaheśvaram.

[128] The Bhagavad Gītā, 18.

[129] The Bhagavad Gītā, 18-20.

[130] In the second chapter, Arjuna is told not to grieve, and this on the basis of the self being immortal and the body only a passing phenomenon—here today and gone tomorrow.

astray—this lower nature, which is controlled by Him, is an illusion when seen as separate from Him, and is destined to dissolve—in order to adjust it for the benefit of those living beings whose primary duty is precisely to overcome all attachment to it![131]

My points here are (1) that Deutsch displays an awareness of the principle of interpreting avatāra passages in light of the overall context of the document in which they appear, and (2) that he seriously considers implications for the body-divine relation in the person of Kṛṣṇa. Now, since I, Like Deutsch, assume a consistent teaching on the part of the BG, I wholeheartedly concur with his principle of interpretation.[132] Moreover, with it I now offer my interpretation of BG 9:11 and draw certain conclusions for the body-divine relation in Kṛṣṇa, but with preliminary consideration of one important aspect of teaching on the BG's part, since it directly addresses my purpose for the interpretation of 9.11. The question of the body-divine relation in the person of Kṛṣṇa rests upon what the BG teaches about prakṛti—meaning matter, material nature, or the material world—and its relationship to the higher nature of Kṛṣṇa. I turn first to this teaching before examining BG 9.11.

### 3.1. The Nature of Prakṛti in the BG

The word prakṛti appears in BG 3.27,29,33, 4.6, 7.4,5,20, 9.7,8,10,12,13, 11.51, 13.19,20,23,29, and 18.59. Derivatives appear in 3.5, 13.21, 18.40 (prakṛtija), 13.19, 14.5 (prakṛtisaṁbhava), and 13.21, 15.7 (prakṛtistha).[133]

Meanings throughout, including those of the derivatives, are as follows: The natural material world as a power itself producing the three guṇa-s, or as the primal causal substance (3.27,29, 13.19,20,21,23, 14.5, 15.7), the natural material world that is a part of Kṛṣṇa on a cosmological level (4.6, 7.4, 9.7,8,10), Kṛṣṇa's higher, spiritual nature (7.5,[134] 9.13), the fleshly nature of

---

[131] The Bhagavad Gītā, 18-19. As a result Deutsch concludes, "If the Gītā is to have a consistent teaching, then, we must look for a deeper psychological or allegorical meaning in this doctrine of divine descent, and it is not too difficult to find one" (p. 19). The meaning Deutsch offers is that a man can overcome his bondage to the world by recognizing that there is more to him than is immediately assumed, and that is one's higher self. The goal, then, is "an awakening to one's own higher potential" (p. 20).

[132] Deutsch also states, "The main philosophical-religious position of the Bhagavad Gītā is that of a 'personalized monism' or a 'non-dualistic theism'" (The Bhagavad Gītā, 4). Thus Deutsch seems to favor Rāmānuja's viśiṣṭādvaita over the advaita of Śaṅkara (pp. 175-76). Zaehner follows suit: "God is the One: but He is not a One who obliterates and nullifies the manifold: rather He binds the many together in a coherent whole since the whole is his body" (The Bhagavad-Gītā, 39-40).

[133] Bolle, The Bhagavadgītā, 289-90.

[134] prakṛtiṁ parām (higher nature) here synonymous with paraṁ bhāvam (higher being) of 9.11 and daivīṁ prakṛtim (divine nature) of 9.13.

humanity (3.5,33, 7.20, 9.12,[135] 13.29, 18.40,[136]59[137]),[138] and one's normal state of mind or natural state after being terrified (11.51).

Prakṛti, in two instances listed above, is used to refer to Kṛṣṇa's higher, spiritual nature. And as we shall now see with BG 7.5, this higher nature sharply contrasts with the lower nature of Kṛṣṇa. Further, in what follows it is of interest to comment upon prakṛti as the guṇa-producing natural material world, as the primal causal substance, and as the natural material world that is a part of Kṛṣṇa on a cosmological level.

### 3.1.1. PRAKṚTI IN BG 7.4-6

How is prakṛti a part of Kṛṣṇa? After stating in BG 7.3 that hardly anyone knows him in truth (in his higher nature, 7.5), Kṛṣṇa follows in 7.4 by saying something quite significant: "Earth, water, fire, wind, sky, mind, intelligence and self consciousness [ahaṁkāra], so this, my material nature, eightfold divided."[139] This nature (prakṛti), says Kṛṣṇa, is his lower (aparā) nature (7.5).

BG 7.5b and 7.6 place 7.4 in the context of cosmogony. Beginning with 7.5 in its entirety and proceeding to 7.6 we read,

> [5] This [the material nature] is lower, but know my other nature as highest, consisting of spiritual beings, O Arjuna, by which this universe is sustained. [6] In[140] these [the higher and lower natures] all beings have their origins. Thus, understand! I am the origin and also the dissolution of the whole universe.[141]

Some of the modern commentators mentioned thus far interpret 7.4-5 within the framework of cosmogony and / or individuals as microcosm and the Lord as macrocosm, and all of them mention nothing of body-divine relationship in the sense that I am pursuing it.[142]

Indeed, BG 7.6 addresses cosmological issues, that is, the origin of all things. But pressing here for my purpose is the question of how to interpret the singular nearer demonstrative pronoun etad, which heads off the verse, and

---

[135] Here the āsurīṁ prakṛtiṁ (demonic nature).

[136] Used in synonymous parallelism with svabhāva (one's innate nature) of 18.41.

[137] Synonymous with svabhāva (one's innate nature) of 18.41.

[138] All these except 7.20 and 9.12 Zaehner interprets as "Nature", the upper case "N" signifying the material world.

[139] bhūmir āpo 'nalo vāyuḥ khaṁ mano buddhir eva ca ahaṁkāra itīyaṁ me bhinnā prakṛtir aṣṭadhā.

[140] I use italics here to indicate that I have taken liberty to add this word.

[141] apareyam itas tv anyāṁ prakṛtiṁ viddhi me parām jīvabhūtāṁ mahābāho yayedaṁ dhāryate jagat etadyonīni bhūtāni sarvāṇīty upadhāraya ahaṁ kṛtsnasya jagataḥ prabhavaḥ pralayas tathā.

[142] Radhakrishnan, The Bhagavadgītā, 214; Zaehner, The Bhagavad-Gītā, 245; Hill, The Bhagavadgītā, 75,76,166 in the notes; Edgerton, The Bhagavad Gītā, 152.

which I have translated "In these", that is, both the higher and the lower natures. Being singular, the pronoun may refer to the higher nature only, which is the closest antecedent in the preceding verse (5),[143] and not to both natures.[144] However, the singular etad may be translated in the plural, as I have done, if it appears in compounds (etadyonīni), as Zaehner and Edgerton note.[145] If one were to take this passage in isolation from the rest of the BG then perhaps the most natural way to read etad would be in the singular and referring to the closest antecedent, that being the "higher nature" (parām prakṛtiṁ) of verse 5. But the verse appears not in a vacuum, and should be interpreted in light of, for example, 9.7-8, where we read, "All beings ... enter into my material nature at the end of a cosmic cycle, and I send them forth again at the beginning of a cosmic cycle. Relying on my own material nature, I send forth again and again this entire multitude of beings, which is powerless, from the will of my material nature."[146] If in verse 7 all beings enter into Kṛṣṇa's material nature at the end of a cosmic cycle, we may presume that at the beginning of the next all beings proceed out of the material nature and from (or by), as verse 8 states, the will of Kṛṣṇa's material nature (prakṛtim). The meaning, then, of 7.4-6 is that the entire creation has its origin in the material (lower) nature of Kṛṣṇa as well as the higher nature; not the higher nature alone, as this is prohibited by 9.7-8 in conjunction with etad in 7.6 referring to the two antecedents in 7.5.

### 3.1.2. Kṛṣṇa and the Jagat

Note again that in the text at hand this eternal relationship between Kṛṣṇa and the jagat occurs at the cosmological level, not in the context of avatāra as such. This is the also case with the foundational cosmogony of the BG found in 8.16-22. Here the cyclical nature and extent of time and history(ies) are mentioned (vv. 16-17,19). Verse 18 asserts that "from the Unmanifest all manifestations originate".[147] This Unmanifest is the primal causal substance, and is prakṛti.[148]

---

[143] As translated / interpreted by Edgerton (The Bhagavad Gītā, 96), Sargeant (The Bhagavad Gītā, 324) and Prabhavananda and Isherwood (The Song of God, 70).

[144] The pronoun referring to both natures as translated / interpreted by Zaehner (The Bhagavad-Gītā, 246), Hill (The Bhagavadgītā, 74,166), Lal (The Bhagavadgita, 48) and Deutsch (The Bhagavad Gītā, 73,149n.4 for chapter 7). Radhakrishnan steps on neither side, translating "Know that all beings have their birth in this", and closes his gloss with "God includes the universe within Himself, projects it from and resumes it within Himself, that is, His own nature" (The Bhagavadgītā, 215). With "nature" being singular and with neither "lower" nor "higher" before it, it is difficult to determine where Radhakrishnan falls on the issue. Perhaps he senses ambiguity. In the translation Bolle follows suit (The Bhagavadgītā, 85), as does Miller (The Bhagavad-Gita, 72).

[145] Zaehner, The Bhagavad-Gītā, 246; Edgerton, The Bhagavad Gītā, 95-96.

[146] sarvabhūtāni ... prakṛtiṁ yānti māmikām kalpakṣaye punas tāni kalpādāu visṛjāmy aham prakṛtiṁ svām avaṣṭabhya visṛjāmi punaḥ punaḥ bhūtagrāmam imaṁ kṛtsnam avaśaṁ prakṛter vaśāt.

[147] avyaktād vyaktayaḥ sarvāḥ prabhavanti.

Above this Unmanifest primal prakṛti, however, is another Unmanifest (v. 20) which does not pass away like the manifestations of prakṛti at the end of the cosmic cycle. This Unmanifest is the "Imperishable" (v. 21), the "Supreme Spirit" (puruṣaḥ paraḥ, v. 22).

This title of puruṣa para is later in the BG absorbed by Kṛṣṇa. I have already discussed BG 7.4-6, where the sense is that the jagat originates in Kṛṣṇa's lower and higher natures. The material world, then, is a part of Kṛṣṇa. In this sense Kṛṣṇa is all things, but not in the sense of advaita. Rather, Kṛṣṇa is the material cause of an ultimately real material jagat, and Kṛṣṇa as Brahman is sovereign over the primal prakṛti that is in reality part of him. In the BG a cause of the jagat is prakṛti, the primal causal substance and Kṛṣṇa's lower nature (so in this sense Kṛṣṇa is the material cause of the jagat). But his higher nature, consisting of spiritual beings, is also part of the cosmogony. The mechanism of this material cause on the part of Kṛṣṇa is given in a few passages in the BG, and 2.17 is the first of these. Here Kṛṣṇa states that it is "That by which all this was spun out (tatam)".[149] The "That" is the neuter, the "Indestructible" (avināśi), which I take, following Zaehner, to be Brahman.[150] Later in BG 8.22 it is the masculine puruṣaḥ paraḥ "by which all this was spun out (tatam)", while in 9.4 Kṛṣṇa states explicitly that it is he who spun out (tatam) the entire universe. In the last two instances in the BG it is again Kṛṣṇa who spun (tatam) out the universe (11.38, 18.46).

### 3.2. Immediate Context of Mānuṣī Tanu in 9.11

I interpret the mānuṣī tanu of Kṛṣṇa in light of both the larger and immediate contexts of the BG, and in light of certain śruti passages. The larger context I have discussed above. Immediate contextual considerations now follow.

---

[148] Radhakrishnan, The Bhagavadgītā, 233. Zaehner labels it "pradhāna, 'primal matter' or 'undifferentiated primal Nature' of the Sāṁkhya system" (The Bhagavad-Gītā, 266), with which terminology the BG "is permeated through and though" (p. 139). Sāṁkhya postulates a dualism in which eternal primal matter or prakṛti and the eternal spirit(s) or puruṣa are clearly distinct, the latter being the pure, immutable and highest reality and the former the ever-changing primal cause of consciousness, ego, mind, the senses, motor organs, subtle elements, and gross elements (Zaehner, The Bhagavad-Gītā, 140). Sāṁkhya and the BG may be close relatives in the contexts of cosmogony and person. Antonio T. de Nicolás, however, states that although there may be mention of the term sāṁkhya in the BG, it does not mean that the BG is specifically referring to the Sāṁkhya system. De Nicolás, though, admits to "ontological parity" between prakṛti and puruṣa (Avatāra: The Humanization of Philosophy through the Bhagavad Gītā [New York: Nicolas Hays, 1976], 244-45).

[149] tad ... yena sarvam idaṁ tatam.

[150] The Bhagavad-Gītā, 130. I am also indebted to Zaehner for the following information (The Bhagavad-Gītā, 130).

3.2.1. BG 9.4a

As mentioned above, in the BG it is Kṛṣṇa who has "spun out" (tatam) the universe. Translating tatam as "spun out"[151] in BG 2.17, 8.22, 11.38 and 18.46 keeps in thematic step with BG 7.6, also discussed above, wherein the jagat and all individuals have their origins in the two natures of Kṛṣṇa. I translate mayā tatam idaṁ sarvaṁ jagat in BG 9.4 as "this entire universe was spun out by me". This theme of "spinning out" the universe is reminiscent of two passages in the Upaniṣads:

> As a spider moves along the thread, as small sparks come forth [vyuccaranti] from the fire, even so from this Self come forth [vyuccaranti] all breaths, all worlds, all divinities, all beings. [BU 2.1.20][152]

> As a spider sends forth [srjatẹ] and draws in (its thread), as herbs grow on the earth, as the hair (grows) on the head and the body of a living person, so from the Imperishable arises here the universe. [MuU 1.1.7][153]

In other words, the effect shares the same substance as the cause. This leads to the next point.

---

[151] Interesting are several translations reading "pervaded" instead of "spun out" (or its equivalent) for the past passive participle tatam (from the root tan). Among the translations thus far listed, Zaehner renders the verb as "was spun", and Bolle as "stretched forth". Deutsch, Sargeant, Radhakrishnan, Edgerton, Hill, Miller, Prabhavananda and Isherwood, and Lal translate "pervade". Obviously Rāmānuja will follow the meaning of pervade, and define it in the context of the antaryāmin. In a note Hill mentions John Davies and J. C. Thomson translating "expanded" and "spread out", respectively. Monier-Williams does not list "pervade" as an option (A Sanskrit-English Dictionary, 435).

[152] sa yathorṇanābhiś tantunoccaret, yathāgneḥ kṣudrā visphuliṅgā vyuccaranti, evam evāsmād ātmanaḥ sarve prāṇāḥ, sarve lokāḥ sarve devāḥ, sarvāni bhūtāni vyuccaranti. Translation taken from Radhakrishnan, The Principal Upaniṣads, 190. See also TU 3.1, wherein we read taṁ hovāca, yato vā imāni bhūtāni jāyante, yena jātāni jīvanti, yat prayanty abhisaṁviśanti, tad vijijñāsasva, tad brahmeti. "That, verily, from which these beings are born, that, by which, when born they live, that into which, when departing, they enter. That, seek to know. That is Brahman" (Radhakrishnan, The Principal Upaniṣads, 553; translation is from Radhakrishnan, who interprets this as Brahman as the material cause of the world in the function of Īśvara).

[153] yathorṇa-nābhiḥ sṛjate gṛhṇate ca, yathā pṛthivyām oṣadhayas sambhavanti, yathā sataḥ puruṣāt keśalomāni tathākṣarāt sambhavatīha viśvam. Translation taken from Radhakrishnan, The Principal Upaniṣads, 673. My thanks to R. C. Zaehner (The Bhagavad-Gītā, 130) for these cross-references.

3.2.2. BG 9.4b-6

This passage is pivotal to the interpretation of the nature of the mānuṣī tanu of verse 11. It reads,

> [4b] matsthāni sarvabhūtāni na cāhaṁ teṣv avasthitaḥ [5] na ca matsthāni bhūtāni paśya me yogam aiśvaram bhūtabhṛn na ca bhūtastho mamātmā bhūtabhāvanaḥ [6] yathākāśasthito nityaṁ vāyuḥ sarvatrago mahān tathā sarvāṇi bhūtāni matsthānīty.
>
> [4b] All beings reside in me, and I do not reside in them. [5] On the other hand[154] beings do not reside in me. Behold my lordly activity, sustaining beings and not dwelling in [them], my Self causing beings to come into existence. [6] As the mighty wind, blowing everywhere, resides eternally in space, so all beings reside in me.

The purport of this passage is difficult to ascertain, for there appears to be a contradiction. In 4b Kṛṣṇa states that all beings reside in him. But on the other hand they do not (v. 5). It is unlikely that we are left with contradiction, due to the close proximity of verse 4b to verses 5 and 6, the latter wherein Kṛṣṇa offers a clear analogy to drive home the intended points.

But what are the intended points? There is a "tongue-in-cheek" genre to the passage, as seen in the transition from verse 4b to verse 5. The phrase "reside in me" (matsthāni) in verse 4b portrays an ontological reality. All beings are indeed a part (aṁśa) of Kṛṣṇa, as we have seen—in the cosmogony of the BG all beings eternally reside in him, arise out of him, and once again enter into him. Then a shift occurs. Verse 5 emphasizes the "otherness" of Kṛṣṇa. Though all material phenomena actually arise out of Kṛṣṇa's very being, "on the other hand they do not reside in me [matsthāni]". This is strange given the BG's teaching of the immanence of Kṛṣṇa in all things (10.20, 15.13-15, 17.6, 18.61).[155] But here matsthāni, used in verse 4 to assert cosmogony, is now used figuratively in negated form to emphasize that Kṛṣṇa is not tainted or touched by any guṇic or karmic connection with the material world (neither does he need the material world in order for him to exist), for in 9.8 all beings arise from the power of Kṛṣṇa's material nature (prakṛti), and, as I have explained, Kṛṣṇa is sovereign over it and, as eternally God, does not eternally come into being out of the necessitating circumstances of karma associated with prakṛti (BG 4.6; see section 1.3). To drive home this point of otherness, Kṛṣṇa, in the

---

[154] Taking ca as disjunctive. See Monier-Williams, A Sanskrit-English Dictionary, 380.

[155] See BU 3.7.3: "He who resides in the earth, the interior of the earth, whom the earth does not know, of whom the earth is the body, who controls the earth within, this one is the Self, the inner controller, imperishable" (yaḥ pṛthivyāṁ tiṣṭhan pṛthivyā antaraḥ yam pṛthivī na veda yasya pṛthivī śarīram yaḥ pṛthivīm antaro yamayati eṣa ta ātmāntaryāmy amṛtaḥ).

remainder of verse 5, reiterates verse 4b and points to the fact that his ātman does not dwell in beings, in the sense that Kṛṣṇa's paramātman is other than prakṛti, and that other beings are born of his māyā or power that is prakṛti and dependent upon him for their existence.[156]

BG 13.12-16 provides a key correlative passage that illustrates and lends support to this interpretation. Brahman is a paradox, for Brahman is neither sat nor asat (v. 12), appearing to possess the guṇa-s of the senses yet free from them, unattached yet supporting all, enjoying the guṇa-s yet not (v. 14), both inside and outside everything (v. 15),[157] undistributed yet distributed in beings (v. 16). This reiterates the theme of paradoxical Brahman found in IU 5: "It moves and It does not move; It is far and It is near; It is within everything and It is outside everything."[158]

As regards immediate context for this interpretation of BG 9.4b-5, the verse that follows provides an analogy to reinforce the themes of paradox and otherness. Though the eternal mighty wind blows everywhere and seems to be the entirety of space, space itself is greater than it is, for it resides in space (yet space does not need the wind to exist). In this way, Kṛṣṇa states, all beings

---

[156] Hill holds the same interpretation (The Bhagavadgītā, 79,182nn.1-3). He states on page 182 n. 2 that "in view of the fact that Kṛiṣṇa as adhyātma is said to dwell in the heart of every being, it is strange to find the statement that his Self (ātman) dwells not in beings ... Kṛiṣṇa is probably emphasizing the fact of ātman's real isolation, in spite of an apparent indwelling, as explained by the simile in the following śloka". Radhakrishnan agrees: "The Supreme is the source of all phenomena but is not touched by them ... Though He creates existences, God transcends them to such a degree that we cannot even say that He dwells in them" (The Bhagavadgītā, 239). Radhakrishnan states of verse 5a (which he translates "And (yet) the beings do not dwell in Me"), "Even the idea of immanence of God is, strictly speaking, untenable. All existences are due to His double nature but as His higher proper nature is ātman which is unconnected with the work of prakṛti, it is also true that beings do not dwell in Him nor He in them" (Radhakrishnan, The Bhagavadgītā, 239; emphases mine). Edgerton's interpretation is similar, though he adds a teaching from the RV: "The dictum that the First Principle is more than all existing things, that the universe is only a part thereof, is at least as old as the 'Puruṣa' hymn of the Rig Veda [10.90.3,4], in which the entire universe is derived from only one-quarter of the cosmic Purusa [sic] or 'Person'" (The Bhagavad Gītā, 149). Zaehner offers little by way of his own commentary, stating instead the views of Śaṅkara and Rāmānuja, though pointing to an important cross-reference in BG 13.14-16 (The Bhagavad-Gītā, 275), to which I allude above.

[157] Within the BG the fact of the immanence of Brahman must not negate the transcendence of Brahman. For example, in BG 7.7 Kṛṣṇa states, "There is not any other thing whatsoever that is higher than me" (mattaḥ parataraṁ nānyat kiṁcid asti). See Vempeny, Kṛṣṇa and Christ, 72-74 for a treatment of the BG's theme of the immanence and transcendence of Kṛṣṇa. In addition to BG 7.7, Kṛṣṇa is called "(of) the God of Gods" (devadevasya, BG 11.13).

[158] tad ejati tan naijati tad dūre tad vad antike tad antarasya sarvasya tad u sarvasyāsya bāhyataḥ.

reside in him. Strongly suggesting the themes of paradox and otherness is the textual addition of the following to verse 6 in the Kāśmīr recension: evaṁ hi sarvabhūteṣu carāmyanabhilakṣitaḥ bhūtaprakṛtimāsthāya saha caiva vinaiva ca[159]—"Indeed thus I move about unnoticed in all beings, maintaining [their] material nature, thus both with [them] and without [them]." Whether this is original or added commentary, it nonetheless reinforces the above interpretation.

The general meaning, then, for BG 9.4b-6 is as follows. In verse 4b we are told that all things material reside in Kṛṣṇa; thus, in light of my previous discussion in sections 3.1.1 and 3.1.2, all things are, ontologically, an aṁśa of Kṛṣṇa. Yet the otherness of Kṛṣṇa is preserved by what we read in verse 5. Here the BG's portrayal of the paradoxical Brahman (see 13.12-16) is affirmed lest the transcendence of Brahman be lost, for "on the other hand" Kṛṣṇa's paramātman is beyond prakṛti. Finally, both elements—all things in Kṛṣṇa and the otherness of Kṛṣṇa—are illustrated in verse 6. Here all beings are in Kṛṣṇa just as the wind is in space, but the wind owes its existence to the space in which it dwells, making space greater and other than the wind.

### 3.2.3. BG 9.7-8,10

In section 3.1.1 I discussed BG 9.7-8: "All beings ... enter into my material nature at the end of a cosmic cycle, and I send them forth again at the beginning of a cosmic cycle. Relying on my own material nature, I send forth again and again this entire multitude of beings, which is powerless, from the will of my material nature." In verse 10 Kṛṣṇa announces that he is the "supervisor" (adhyakṣa), one who is sovereign over the entire process of "all things moving and unmoving" (sacarācara) that come from prakṛti (here meaning his own material nature), said to be the cause (hetu). Therefore all things come from the material nature of Kṛṣṇa. The effect—the universe and all its components—is Kṛṣṇa. The jagat in the BG remains real, finding its eternity in, dependence on, and subjection to, Kṛṣṇa, and yet it is Kṛṣṇa, coming from his own material nature.

## 3.3. The Meaning of Mānuṣī Tanu in BG 9.11

In the light of the preceding, I interpret the mānuṣī tanu of Kṛṣṇa as follows. I also list some implications that logically follow.

First, the mānuṣī tanu is not touched in any way by the triguṇātmikā. In this sense the mānuṣī tanu is pure and untainted, sinless and not bound by karma in saṁsāra.

Second, the mānuṣī tanu comes into being in form as the result of the will of

---

159 Transliterated from the Sanskrit from Rao Bahadur P. C. Divanji, Critical Word-Index to the Bhagavadgītā (Bombay: New Book Co., 1946), 207. I am indebted to Zaehner for introducing the variant (The Bhagavad-Gītā, 276).

Kṛṣṇa.

Third, though the mānuṣī tanu comes into being in its intended form by the will of Kṛṣṇa, the prakṛti from which it is fashioned is eternal. (Prakṛti arises from Kṛṣṇa at the beginning of cosmic cycles and draws back into him at the dissolution of the universe at the end of cosmic cycles.) Note, however, that though Kṛṣṇāvatāra and other beings are fashioned from the same prakṛti, Kṛṣṇa's prakṛtic body has no guṇic or karmic connection, that is, it comes into being by the will of Kṛṣṇa alone.

Fourth, since the material world and all its phenomena are indwelled by Kṛṣṇa, the actual flesh of Kṛṣṇa, then, is itself indwelled by Kṛṣṇa. Though it might not necessarily follow, I raise this next point as a question: In this context, could the implication be that a blurring of a clear distinction of the human and divine natures occurs in the person of Kṛṣṇa? In other words, if the body in all its individual components is itself indwelled by the divine, is there a real separation between the two? BG 7.8 (I am the taste in the waters ... I am the light in the sun and the moon") interpreted in light of BU 3.7.3-23 (especially vv. 16-23, where the supreme Self dwells in the breath, speech, eye, ear, mind, skin, understanding, and semen[160]) further elaborates upon the extent of this indwelling, which seems to be a pervading rather than a union of divine and human.

Fifth, since the material world is Kṛṣṇa, a further (perhaps clearer) blurring of the distinction of the two natures—human and divine—arises. If prakṛti is Kṛṣṇa's material nature and it is Kṛṣṇa on a cosmic level, then the body of Kṛṣṇa is divine. The mānuṣī tanu would in this sense be wholly divine.[161]

Sixth, the mānuṣī tanu of BG 9.11 is four-armed. In the eleventh chapter of the BG Kṛṣṇa reveals his cosmic form to Arjuna. Arjuna, delighted yet terrified, is no longer able to behold Kṛṣṇa in this state, and asks Kṛṣṇa to take the form (rūpa) in which he previously[162] appeared (11.45) throughout the BG, that is,

---

[160] Radhakrishnan, The Principal Upaniṣads, 228-30.

[161] Though see M. Dhavamony, "Hindu 'incarnations'", 146, wherein Dhavamony states that Kṛṣṇa "assumes really a human nature", but then states on page 148 that Kṛṣṇa "is a divinized man".

[162] BG 11.45 translates "cause me to see that form, O God" (tad eva me darśaya deva rūpaṁ) and states nothing about the form appearing "throughout" the BG. However, many of the translators translate / interpret the phrase as meaning the form that Kṛṣṇa has throughout the BG. Sargeant translates as "Cause me to see that form, O God, in which Thou originally appeared" (The Bhagavad-Gītā, 497), Deutsch as "Show me, O Lord, that other form of Thine" (The Bhagavad Gītā, 100), Hill as "show me that other form, O Lord" (The Bhagavadgītā, 213), Radhakrishnan as "Show me that other (previous) form of Thine, O God" (The Bhagavadgītā, 286), Edgerton as "Show me, O God, that same form of Thine (as before)!" (The Bhagavad Gītā, 60), Zaehner as "Show me, then, God, that [same human] form [I knew]" (The Bhagavad-Gītā, 318; brackets original), Miller as "Show me, God, the form I know" (The Bhagavad-Gita, 107), Bolle as "Show me that one usual form of yours" (The Bhagavadgītā, 141), and

his "four-armed form" (rūpacaturbhuja, 11.46). Kṛṣṇa obliges, and states that this rūpacaturbhuja is "my form" (rūpam idaṁ, 11.49). The text then states that the four-armed form is "his own form" (svakaṁ rūpaṁ, 11.50) and, once again, his "human form" (though this time mānuṣaṁ rūpaṁ, 11.51).

To conclude, in some respects (third [first half], fourth and fifth above) Kṛṣṇa, intra-BG, identifies with humanity, for human beings themselves (both soul and body) are both indwelled by Kṛṣṇa and fashioned from the same eternal prakṛti that is Kṛṣṇa (though the very act of Kṛṣṇa coming into being is not guṇic- or karmic-caused). Yet, Kṛṣṇa is four-armed, and in this sense one is justified in questioning the extent of identification between Kṛṣṇa and all of humanity.

## 3.4. Śaṅkara on BG 9.11

Before exploring what Śaṅkara states about the mānuṣī tanu in 9.11, I shall offer my comments and document his comments on aham and ahaṁkāra in BG 7.4-6,25 and thereafter document his comments on BG 9.4-10, for both passages serve as preliminary to the interpretation of mānuṣī tanu.

### 3.4.1. Aham / Ahaṁkāra—Ego / Egoism

Because Kṛṣṇa in BG 9.11 states "The deluded despise me (māṁ, accusative of aham), having assumed a human form", I consider now the metaphysical reality of the "I" (aham) of Kṛṣṇa, both in the BG (in many places due to its narrative genre) and in the BGB of Śaṅkara.

#### 3.4.1.1. Aham / Ahaṁkāra in General

For example, BG 7.25 reads "I [ahaṁ] do not stand revealed to all."[163] In his BGB Śaṅkara writes, "I [ahaṁ] am not revealed to the whole world."[164] Is it not logical, given Śaṅkara's philosophy, that even in the midst of the jagat-prapañca, and thus in the context of Īśvara in which Kṛṣṇa speaks and acts, the ultimate aham is the ātman and is in actuality the para brahman? That is, does not the aham that is Brahman persist[165] through the mithyā of the jagat-prapañca and Kṛṣṇa's avatāra?

Surprisingly, in the writings of Śaṅkara ahaṁkāra or egoism is for the most part a negative phenomenon or is associated with the jagat-prapañca. Leaving for a later section the implications this carries regarding the doctrine of the avatāra of Kṛṣṇa, I shall here only discuss what we can find in Śaṅkara

Prabhavananda and Isherwood as "Show me now your other Form, O Lord" (The Song of God, 96).

163 SBGB, 269.

164 SBGB, 269.

165 Not only on the part of Kṛṣṇa, but for all. Thus the declaration found in BU 1.4.10, "I am Brahman" (aham brahmāsmi).

explicitly as regards ahaṁkāra.

Ahaṁkāra is characterized by one's sense of "I" and "mine", and obviously takes place within the sphere of the jagat-prapañca. Ahaṁkāra is therefore an instrument that keeps one bound to the empirical world. In this sense we have in Śaṅkara a distinction between the jīva and the ātman, the former being individual (and plagued by "I-mine") and entangled in the realm of prakṛti (which is not-self) and the latter being the pure conscious self that is Brahman. P. T. Raju observes, "According to Śaṅkara, the ātman is not the same as the I-consciousness (ahamdhī). The I-consciousness is only the ego (ahaṁkāra), which knows, acts, and also calls itself the son of so and so, and so on."[166] In other words, ahaṁkāra takes place in the context of perception of the jagat-prapañca.[167] Moreover, "It is through 'I-ness' or the ego-consciousness", writes Satprakashananda, "that the immutable self becomes more or less identified with the mental processes, the bodily organs ... and the physical conditions".[168] Evidence for this lies in statements such as "I remember" and "I was eloquent."[169] Thus it is that ahaṁkāra

> is the knot that ties together the conscious spirit and the unconscious matter, in other words, the self and the not-self. So there is an intermingling of the two. The knower becomes identified with the known and the known with the knower. It is not easy to discriminate one from the other. The light of consciousness transmitted through "I-ness" makes the mental states, the organs, and the body appear to be conscious in themselves. So it is said: "My mind knows this to be true", "As far as the eyes can see", "My hands work day and night", "My body feels tired".[170]

In his VC Śaṅkara states,

> [I]t is egoism [ahaṁkāra] which, identifying itself with the body, becomes the doer or experiencer, and in conjunction with the guṇas such as the sattva, assumes the three different states [waking, sleeping, dreaming]. When sense-objects are favorable it becomes happy, and it becomes miserable when the case is contrary. So happiness and misery are characteristics of egoism, and not of the ever-blissful Ātman.[171]

Śaṅkara's advice concerning ahaṁkāra rings polemically stronger in a

---

[166] The Philosophical Traditions of India, 182.

[167] See Satprakashananda, Methods of Knowledge According to Advaita Vedanta, 53, where ahaṁkāra is involved in "every external perception".

[168] Methods of Knowledge According to Advaita Vedanta, 234.

[169] Methods of Knowledge According to Advaita Vedanta, 234.

[170] Methods of Knowledge According to Advaita Vedanta, 234.

[171] Page 37, paras. 104,105.

particular section of his VC. For example, he labels ahaṁkāra wicked (durātman) and an enemy (śatru) "which appears as a thorn sticking in the throat of a man taking his meal"[172] and counsels to give up all attachment and sense of duality, the activities of ahaṁkāra.[173]

In the BG the word appears in 2.71, 3.27, 7.4, 12.13, 13.5,8, 16.18, 17.5 and 18.17,53,58,59.[174] Behind these translations is the basic foundation of "I". In 3.27 the cause is directly stated—the guṇa-s of prakṛti (prakṛti here meaning material nature): "Actions are in every instance performed by the guṇa-s of material nature; the ego-deluded self thus thinks, 'I am the doer.'"[175] It generally carries the meaning of self-consciousness, self-awareness, ego, and self-centeredness[176] in negative contexts such as the sense of "I and mine" in the performance of actions and attachment to material things (2.71, 3.27, 12.13, 13.5,8, 16.18, 17.5, 18.17,53,58,59). This, then, is the meaning behind all actions of everyone.

3.4.1.2. My Observations: Aham / Ahaṁkāra in BG 7.4-6?

Kṛṣṇa's actions, however, seem to be exempt from my above observation, for Kṛṣṇa, as we have seen, is not born out of the necessitating circumstances of triguṇātmikā. Nor does he exhibit a sense of attachment in the performance of actions. As a matter of fact, he counsels Arjuna not to perform actions in this way.

Kṛṣṇa states in BG 7.3,5 that hardly anyone knows his higher nature. Then he states in 7.4 concerning his lower nature, "Earth, water, fire, wind, sky, mind, intelligence and self consciousness [ahaṁkāra], so this, my material nature, eightfold divided."[177] None of the major commentators herein consulted ask what is for my purpose this significant question touching on the subject of

---

[172] Pages 114,117, paras. 299,307.

[173] Pages 117-18, par. 308, though here Śaṅkara employs the simpler aham instead of ahaṁkāra. The sense of "I-ness", however, is not always used by Śaṅkara in this negative sense. For example, the "I" may refer to the eternally existing Self (see Swami Jagadananda, trans., Upadeśa Sāhasrī: A Thousand Teachings, in Two Parts—Prose and Poetry of Śrī Śaṅkarāchārya [Mylapore: Sri Ramakrishna Math, n.d.], 219, [18.4-5]; noted from heron as US). Note also this statement from Śaṅkara: "It is reasonable that of the two ideas, 'I am Existence-Brahman' and 'I am an agent' ... , the one owing its origin to Ignorance [ajñāna] should be given up" (US, 220 [18.6,7]). In this statement "I am Existence-Brahman" (sadbrahmāhaṁ) is positive, but the other statement, "I am an agent" (karomi), is viewed in the negative sense.

[174] Bolle, The Bhagavadgītā, 264,287.

[175] prakṛteḥ kriyamāṇāni guṇaiḥ karmāni sarvaśaḥ ahaṁkāravimūḍhātmā karthāham iti manyate.

[176] Bolle, The Bhagavadgītā, 264.

[177] bhūmir āpo 'nalo vāyuḥ khaṁ mano buddhir eva ca ahaṁkāra itīyaṁ me bhinnā prakṛtir aṣṭadhā.

ahaṁkāra belonging to Kṛṣṇa's lower, material nature[178]: If ahaṁkāra here is possessed by Kṛṣṇa's lower nature and in 7.5 the lower nature is clearly distinguished[179] from Kṛṣṇa's "other" (anyā) or higher (parā) nature (prakṛti), what do we make of this in the context of the body-soul-divine relation in the person of Kṛṣṇa, especially in BG 9.11? Further, should we understand ahaṁkāra on the part of Kṛṣṇa in the same negative sense described above?

First, I have (or rather the context has) ruled out any possibility of BG 7.4 stating anything about Kṛṣṇa's avatāra per se,[180] even though Kṛṣṇa in his avatāra makes this statement.[181] Second, even though all beings arise from both natures, the primary emphasis of the passage, signaled by the tu (but) of verse 5, is on the higher nature, from which (along with the lower nature) all beings have their origins (v. 6). Buttressing this is Zaehner's reference to BG 3.42 in conjunction with KU 6.7-8.[182] BG 3.42 reads in part, "the mind is higher than the senses, but higher than the mind is intelligence; but what is higher than intelligence is he [the ātman; see next verse, dehinam, the embodied one, v. 40[183]]".[184] This is taken directly from KU 2.3.7,[185] which reads, "Higher than the senses is the mind; above the mind is intelligence[186]; above intelligence is the great self; above the great [self] is the unmanifest."[187] Moreover, BU 2.5.15 stresses the highest Self (ātmā) as "the Lord of all beings (bhūtānām adhipatiḥ)", and that in this Self the whole universe is held together, a cosmological and theological theme in direct comparison to BG 7.7b ("On me all this [universe] is strung like many jewels on a thread"[188]). Third, Kṛṣṇa as

---

[178] Nor does Arvind Sharma. See The Hindu Gītā, 57-61.

[179] Evidenced by the tu (but) in verse 5: apareyam itas tv [from tu] anyāṁ prakṛtiṁ ... parām. "This [iyaṁ, the material nature of v. 4] is inferior, but my other nature is highest."

[180] So Hill, who states that "the seventh Reading [chapter] is concerned with the two 'natures' and the manifestation of prakṛti" (The Bhagavadgītā, 183 n. 2).

[181] See sections 3.1.1 and 3.1.2.

[182] The Bhagavad-Gītā, 177. In my sources the reference is KU 2.3.7-8.

[183] Zaehner states that by "he" is meant the ātman, and that "practically all other commentators both ancient and modern take this to mean the ātman which occurs in the following stanza (cf. dehinam, 'embodied [self]', in verse 40)" (The Bhagavad-Gītā, 177; brackets are Zaehner's).

[184] indriyebhyaḥ paraṁ manaḥ manasas tu parā buddhir yo buddheḥ paratas tu saḥ.

[185] Though the BG substitutes buddhi for sattva and stays with para (higher) throughout, while the KU employs para, uttama, and adhi.

[186] sattva. Radhakrishnan translates "above the mind is its essence (intelligence)". He then states in the note, "sattva: essence. Intelligence constitutes the essence of the mind" (Radhakrishnan, The Principal Upaniṣads, 643). See Monier-Williams, A Sanskrit-English Dictionary, 1135, which substantiates Radhakrishnan's translation and note.

[187] indriyebhyaḥ param mano manasas sattvam uttamam sattvād adhi mahān ātmā mahato 'vyaktam uttamam.

[188] mayi sarvam idaṁ protaṁ sūtre maṇigaṇā iva. See BG 9.5,13.

avatāra is not associated ontologically with the triguṇātmikā, nor bound by karma. Regardless of one's philosophical persuasion, most all agree that the BG de-emphasizes (the extent of de-emphasis depending on one's philosophical system) prakṛti (matter) and elevates the ātman. Therefore, in light of the emphasis on the higher nature of Kṛṣṇa and his ontological separation with prakṛti in conjunction with the three guṇa-s and triguṇātmikā, I argue that BG 7.4 speaks not directly to the body-soul-divine relationship. Further substantiating this is the passage's aim of cosmogony rather than probing the human-divine aspect of Kṛṣṇa. Consequently, though BG 7.4 does not communicate Kṛṣṇa's personal utilization of ahaṁkāra (often employed negatively throughout the BG), it appears that ahaṁkāra, in both the negative and positive senses, ultimately comes from Kṛṣṇa, as it is part of Kṛṣṇa's lower nature.

But though the passage does not speak directly to the body-soul-divine relationship of Kṛṣṇa, one may still infer indirectly from the passage certain implications. For example, there is still in the text the unquestionable reality of one aham ("I") that persists in the claim on the part of Kṛṣṇa that all beings have their origin in the two natures. And since there is nothing in the text that states that the material nature of Kṛṣṇāvatāra was created from anything other than the basic prakṛti from which all beings originate (though, as noted, the mechanics—karmic versus non-karmic—of origin differ when comparing the birth of Kṛṣṇa to the births of other beings), the "I" of Kṛṣṇa is therefore connected with the cosmological lower nature (though also with the higher nature). I conclude therefore that in the context of cosmogony the "I" on the part Kṛṣṇa is ontologically the same "I" in his non-avatāric state, and that this "I" or aham, though not understood in the sense of attachment in the performance of actions, nonetheless should be accounted for.

### 3.4.1.3. Śaṅkara on BG 7.4-6

Śaṅkara also does not see the passage directly addressing the issue of the human-divine relation in the person of Kṛṣṇa, but interprets in the context of cosmogony in a negative setting.

He sets the passage in the jagat-prapañca in which Īśvara exercises his power (aiśvarī māyāśaktiḥ).[189] Speaking of the ignorant, he states, "Thus ahaṁkāra is the unmanifest yoked with ignorance (or nescience)."[190] Ahaṁkāra, then, is that which is exercised by ignorant human beings, not Kṛṣṇa—this is in step with the BG's use of ahaṁkāra.[191] To be sure, Brahman as Īśvara must be seen as the ground upon which ahaṁkāra is manifested in ignorant humanity, but again, the text is placed in the context of cosmogony,

---

[189] SBGB, 255.

[190] My translation of ahaṁkāra iti avidyāsaṁyuktaṁ avyaktam (SBGB, 254).

[191] See, for examples, Śaṅkara's comments on ahaṁkāra in SBGB, 523-24 (for BG 16.18) and 605-6 (for BG 18.53).

not avatāra where questions of human-divine are directly answered.

The lower nature (v. 5) Śaṅkara labels "impure" (aśuddhā) and "the essence of bondage" (saṁsārabandhanātmikā).[192] But the higher nature he labels "the field-knower" (kṣetrajña).[193]

As for verse 6, Śaṅkara interprets the singular etad as plural, thus referring to both the lower and higher natures of Īśvara, who is the cause of the world (jagatkāraṇa).[194]

Nonetheless, just as I concluded with my interpretation of BG 7.4-6 in the previous section, it seems that Śaṅkara also has to admit to an "I" persisting in Kṛṣṇa in both the lower and higher nature. The "I" that persists in the lower nature persists in the jagat-prapañca. For Śaṅkara this "I" is in reality the supreme Self of the higher nature, the paramātman, in the apparent humanity of Kṛṣṇa.

### 3.4.2. Śaṅkara on Mānuṣī Tanu of BG 9.11

Warrier translates 9.11 as follows: "Fools deride Me, who have assumed a human body; for, they are unaware of My transcendent status as the great Lord of beings."[195]

Śaṅkara, representing Kṛṣṇa, states, "As I have assumed a human body (mānuṣīṁ tanuṁ), I function as a human being [manuṣya]."[196] He adds that fools "fail to discriminate" and "know nothing about My 'transcendent'—exalted—status, the truth of the Supreme Self [paramātman]".[197]

This is the gist of his short paragraph on this verse, and reading in isolation this relatively short commentary for so important a verse leaves the reader unsatisfied as regards the meaning of the mānuṣī tanu. But since Śaṅkara comments on BG 9.4-10, these immediate preceding verses serve to flesh out, implicitly, his commentary on 9.11 and the meaning of mānuṣī tanu. To this I now turn. In what follows I document Śaṅkara's glosses on each of the verses, draw conclusions based upon them, and offer what I think are logical implications for his view of the mānuṣī tanu.

#### 3.4.2.1. BG 9.4

Warrier translates mayā tatam idaṁ sarvaṁ jagad avyaktamūrtinā matsthāni sarvahūthāni na cāhaṁ tesyavsthitah in 9.4 as "The entire world has been pervaded by Me in My Unmanifest form. All beings dwell in Me, but I dwell

---

[192] SBGB, 255.

[193] SBGB, 255. See Vempeny, Kṛṣṇa and Christ, 73, wherein he observes that for Śaṅkara "the transcendent nature is the same as the Kṣetrajña of [BG] chapter 13".

[194] SBGB, 256.

[195] avajānanti māṁ mūḍhā mānuṣīṁ tanum āśritam paraṁ bhāvam ajānanto mama bhūtamaheśvaram.

[196] SBGB, 304.

[197] SBGB, 304.

not in them."[198] Here the ahaṁkāra or "I-consciousness" is evident in Kṛṣṇa, but in what sense? In a positive sense, so it seems (see also next section). Śaṅkara writes, "'By Me'—by that supreme form of My being all this world has been pervaded. That form of My being is Unmanifest [avyakta]—beyond the range of the senses of perception [karaṇāgocarasvarūpeṇa]."[199] Here the "I" of Kṛṣṇa must be the para brahman, for (1) it is this avyakta of which Śaṅkara speaks in BG 8.20, and of which he specifically terms "Unmanifest, being beyond the range of the senses",[200] and (2) because further along in the bhāṣya for 9.4 he represents Kṛṣṇa as saying "I am the Self of beings" (bhūtānāṁ ahaṁ ātmā[201]).

In his comments for 9.4 Śaṅkara writes the phrase karaṇāgocarasvarūpeṇa. As mentioned above, Warrier translates this phrase as "beyond the range of the senses of perception". It is possible that by rūpa Śaṅkara means "appearance",[202] so the purport is "beyond the range of the senses of appearance". The jagat in BG 9.4, then, is the jagat-prapañca in Śaṅkara's system. Perhaps lending weight to this is Śaṅkara's comment that all beings "are said [ucyante] to exist in Me".[203] The meaning here is that in reality there are no actual beings, but nonetheless it is said that they exist.

### 3.4.2.2. BG 9.5

Warrier translates na ca matsthāni bhūtāni paśya me yogam aiśvaram bhutabhṛn na ca bhūtastho mamātmā bhūtabhāvanaḥ as "Neither do beings exist in Me—behold My sovereign Yoga! My Self brings beings into existence and sustains them, yet does not dwell in them."[204]

Once again Īśvara plays a vital part in the exegesis. Śaṅkara writes, again representing Kṛṣṇa, "Behold the manner of my creative power (yoga) or of fashioning of beings by Me as the Lord (Īśvara)."[205] Thus all beings, all things, must be seen within the context of the jagat-prapañca. Śaṅkara opts for the total separation of the paramātman as "unassociated with all things [asaṁsargitvāt asaṅgatāṁ]", citing BU 3.9.26 for support—"Detached, the Self cleaves not" (asaṅgo na hi sajjate).[206] I am forced to conclude once again that, implicitly (due to the context of Īśvara), the mānuṣī tanu of Kṛṣṇa in 9.11 is ultimately mithyā.

Because of this non-attachment of the paramātman from all things empirical

---

198 SBGB, 298.
199 SBGB, 298.
200 avyaktaḥ anindriyagocaraḥ (SBGB, 288); similar to karaṇāgocarasvarūpeṇa.
201 SBGB, 298.
202 Monier-Williams, A Sanskrit-English Dictionary, 886.
203 SBGB, 298-99.
204 SBGB, 299.
205 SBGB, 299.
206 SBGB, 299.

(and ultimately mithyā), Śaṅkara is careful to note the basis upon which Kṛṣṇa employs the phrase "My Self" (mama ātmā), for it has potential negative implications regarding his usual way of understanding ahaṁkāra (that is, the "I-mine" sense). He guards against this by stating, "Why then is it stated 'My Self'? Analysing the conglomerate of body, senses and so forth, and superimposing the I-sense (ahaṅkāraṁ) on it, the Lord uses the expression 'My Self' as in common parlance, and not, like the deluded world."[207]

3.4.2.3. BG 9.6-10

Warrier translates:

> [6] Just as the vast (expanse of) air, eternally subsists in space while moving everywhere, even so know that all beings exist in Me. [7] All beings, Arjuna! at the end of a cycle repair to My nature, at the beginning of the (next) cycle, I loose them forth. [8] Resorting, again and again, I loose forth this entire multitude of bound beings, swayed by and dependent on that nature. [9] Those actions, Arjuna! bind Me not; I am as it were, indifferent (to them all), being unattached to them. [10] Due to Me, the Supervisor, Nature gives birth to the world of mobile and immobile (beings). For this reason, Arjuna! it revolves in manifold ways.[208]

Commenting on verse 6, Śaṅkara is careful to maintain the absolute otherness of the para brahman from the jagat-prapañca. He admits, along with the text, that Kṛṣṇa states "all beings exist in Me", but Śaṅkara adds "without cleaving [asaṁśleṣeṇa] to Me".[209]

In verse 7 Śaṅkara states, "All beings, Arjuna! repair to my lower nature [aparā prakṛti]."[210] Adding "lower" to the verse in the gloss evidences Śaṅkara's desire to place this within the context of Īśvara, for he continues on to say that the aparā prakṛti consists of the triguṇātmikā.[211]

In admitting that beings come from the aparā prakṛti of Kṛṣṇa, Śaṅkara remains consistent in the interpretation of verse 8. Here he writes that all beings are "dependent" (avaśa) upon the aparā prakṛti due to avidyā.[212] Here I interpret Śaṅkara saying that all beings, because of avidyā, are bound in the

---

207 SBGB, 300.

208 SBGB, 302: yathākāśasthito nityaṁ vāyuḥ sarvatrago mahān tathā sarvāṇi bhūtāni matsthānītyupadhāraya sarvabhūtāni kāunteya prakṛtiṁ yānti māmikām kalpakṣaye punastāni kalpādāu visṛjāmyaham prakṛtiṁ svāmavaṣṭabhya visṛjāmi punaḥ punaḥ bhūtagrāmamimaṁ kṛtsnamavaśaṁ prakṛtervaśāt na ca māṁ tāni karmāṇi nibadhnanti dhanaṁjaya udāsīnavadāsīnamasaktaṁ teṣu karmasu mayā 'dhyakṣeṇa prakṛtiḥ sūyate sacarācaram hetunā 'nena kāunteya jagadviparivartate.

209 SBGB, 300.

210 SBGB, 301.

211 SBGB, 301.

212 SBGB, 301.

ultimately unreal realm of Īśvara.

In the preface to his interpretation of verse 9, Śaṅkara anticipates a pūrvapakṣa: "If so [that is, if what Śaṅkara just said is true], You, the supreme Lord [parameśvara], fashioning beings unequally, are subject to righteousness and its opposite, the causes of these inequalities."[213] Śaṅkara answers with verse 9. He states that the action of creation of all beings on the part of Kṛṣṇa does not bind Kṛṣṇa, because Kṛṣṇa is, as the text communicates, "indifferent" (udāsīnavat), "unattached" (asaktam) to that action.[214] The conclusion is "ātmanaḥ avistriyatvāt"—"the Self is immutable".[215] Further, to guard the parameśvara from ahaṁkāra in the negative sense, Śaṅkara has his Lord assert, "The thought, 'I do them' [ahaṁ karomi] [that is, 'I perform creative works'] does not occur to Me."[216]

For verse 10 Śaṅkara states that Kṛṣṇa's "māyā, consisting of the three constituents [triguṇātmikām] or nescience [avidyā], gives birth to the world of beings".[217] But then Śaṅkara begins once again to assert the otherness of the para brahman. Immediately he cites BU 6.11, where "The one God [eko devas] is hidden in all beings ... and is beyond constituents."[218] He concludes that "the one Lord [eko devas] ... is in reality unrelated to all empirical experiences [paramārthaḥ sarvabhogānabhisambandhinaḥ]."[219]

What do Śaṅkara's comments on BG 9.6-10 imply for the mānuṣī tanu? First, even though Kṛṣṇa's birth is not associated with karma or triguṇātmikā, the mānuṣī tanu must be part of the jagat-prapañca. Second, since the jagat-prapañca is ultimately mithyā, it is logical to conclude that the mānuṣī tanu is ultimately mithyā. Third, since the para brahman is for Śaṅkara purely other than prakṛti in the context of his kevalādvaita, and the para brahman "is in reality unrelated to all empirical experiences", the mānuṣī tanu must be viewed as having no ultimately real relationship to the para brahman, who is the only and truly existing being. Fourth, if all beings because of avidyā are bound in the illusory realm of Īśvara, what does this communicate regarding the actual relationship between Arjuna and Kṛṣṇa? To be sure, Śaṅkara, keeping with the teaching of BG 4.8 (Kṛṣṇa comes in every age for the protection of the virtuous), would readily admit that it is for the sake of those who are thus bound that Kṛṣṇa descends. But I am forced to conclude that with Śaṅkara's advaita there is no ultimately real relationship between Arjuna and Kṛṣṇa, because, fifth, ultimately there is no Kṛṣṇa, and sixth, Arjuna "metaphysically

---

213 SBGB, 301-2.
214 SBGB, 302.
215 SBGB, 302.
216 SBGB, 302.
217 SBGB, 303.
218 SBGB, 303: eko devaḥ sarvabhūteṣu gūḍhaṣ ... kevalo nirguṇaśca.
219 SBGB, 303-4.

[also] is God Himself",[220] (he will realize this if he becomes a kṣetrajña). Śaṅkara states, "In the science of the Gītā, difference [bheda] between the field-knower and God is not recognized."[221]

## 3.5. Rāmānuja on BG 9.11

In this section I shall examine the question of the "I" (aham) in Rāmānuja's viśiṣṭādvaita and explore Rāmānuja's interpretation of the mānuṣī tanu in BG 9.11.

### 3.5.1. AHAM / AHAṀKĀRA—EGO / EGOISM

Ahaṁkāra for Rāmānuja does not carry the same negative connotations attributed to it by Śaṅkara. But there are indeed implications of a different sort for Rāmānuja (which I address later) that derive from his sense of both the positive and negative connotations of aham / ahaṁkāra.

#### 3.5.1.1. The Positive Side of Aham / Ahaṁkāra

In the context of discussing the "I" for ordinary humans, Rāmānuja so disagreed with Śaṅkara that he devoted sections to it in his massive commentary on BS 1.1.1. In it he states a pūrvapakṣa, which holds Śaṅkara to the ultimate unreality of ahaṁkāra,[222] and then proceeds to refute the pūrvapakṣa.[223] For Rāmānuja ahaṁkāra proves bheda, for the "I", says Rāmānuja, "proves itself as the knowing subject",[224] and this, of course, in a real subject-object relationship. Further, representing a man who desires mokṣa and thus asks, "May I ... enter on free possession of endless delight?" Rāmānuja concludes, "were it a settled matter that release consists in the annihilation of the I, the same man would move away as soon as release were only hinted at".[225] Contra Śaṅkara he concludes, "Hence, what constitutes the inward Self is not pure consciousness but the 'I' which proves itself as the

---

220 SBGB, 407,410. Śaṅkara stated, "All these [śruti] passages, with many others, declare Brahman to possess a double nature, according as it is the object either of Knowledge or of Nescience [avidyā]. As long as it is the object of Nescience, there are applied to it the categories of devotee, object of devotion, and the like" (SBE, 34:62; see my chapter 1, n. 48).

221 SBGB, 470.

222 George Thibaut, trans., Vedānta-Sūtras: With the Commentary by Rāmānuja, in F. Max Müller, ed., Sacred Books of the East (Delhi: Motilal Banarsidass, 1989), 48:36-38. Noted from hereon as SBE.

223 SBE, 48:61-67. See also pages 47-61.

224 SBE, 48:67.

225 SBE, 48:58.

knowing subject."[226] Thus, true knowledge is that which acknowledges the inward Self as the "I", and by which reasons a subject-object relationship between the "I" and other objects, including other jīvātman-s.

The para brahman or paramātman enjoys I-consciousness in a subject-object relationship with the material world. In his BSB Rāmānuja, as argued above, establishes the fact that "the 'I' constitutes the essential nature of the Self", and that, as an example, another being, the ṛṣi Vāmadeva, "enjoyed the consciousness of the personal 'I'".[227] Rāmānuja then states that "the highest Brahman ... is spoken of in an analogous way ... 'May I be many, may I grow forth' (Kh. Up. [CU] VI,2,3)".[228] This I-consciousness also occurs on the part of Kṛṣṇa in, for example, BG 7.24, where Rāmānuja represents Kṛṣṇa as saying "They do not know that it is I [aham], who is worshipped through all the rites, who is the Lord of all, that has incarnated as the son of Vasudeva."[229]

3.5.1.2. The Negative Side of Aham / Ahaṁkāra

Yet on the other hand we encounter in Rāmānuja the phenomenon that the material world is viewed as lower in importance compared to that of the Self. After stating the above—that even the para brahman enjoys I-consciousness—Rāmānuja anticipates a philosophical problem regarding ordinary beings, and asks, "But if the 'I' (aham) constitutes the essential nature of the Self, how is it that the Holy One teaches the principle of egoity (ahaṁkāra) to belong to the sphere of objects ... (Bha. Gī. [BG] XIII,5)?"[230] By asking the question Rāmānuja displays his awareness of the BG's assertion of the negative side of the ahaṁkāra, which I discussed earlier in section 3.4.1.1. He answers the question by first reasserting "that the 'I' constitutes the essential nature of the Self", and then moves on to explain that "within the sphere of the Objective, he [the Holy One] means that principle which is called ahaṁkāra, because it causes the assumption of Egoity on the part of the body which belongs to the Not-self".[231] For Rāmānuja, when the 'I' has for its sole object the body, this constitutes avidyā and ahaṁkāra in this negative sense.[232]

---

[226] SBE, 48:67. The jīvātman remains in a subject-object relationship even in the final eschatological state of mokṣa, which is dwelling forever as a conscious subject in perfect communion with Viṣṇu, the object of all affections. See also pages 70-71.

[227] SBE, 48:71.

[228] SBE, 48:71.

[229] RBGB, 263.

[230] SBE, 48:71-72.

[231] SBE, 48:72. Rāmānuja's comments on BG 13.5-6 state the same. The ahaṁkāra "originates in the Kṣetra [kṣetrārambha]". Further, desire, hatred, etc. (v. 6) "originate from the association of the self with the Kṣetra [ātmanaḥ kṣetrasaṁbandhaprayuktāni]" (RBGB, 433).

[232] This differs from Śaṅkara's general view of avidyā. Though there is similarity between Śaṅkara and Rāmānuja in the sense that one of avidyā-'s symptoms is association of the material with the Self, the difference lies in the fact that another

3.5.1.3. Rāmānuja on BG 7.4-6

In section 3.4.1.2 I came to the conclusion that there is a non-avatāric "I" in the person of Kṛṣṇa that persists in his claim that the lower and higher natures are his, and that the jagat has its origin in both his lower and higher natures. For Rāmānuja the language of Kṛṣṇa implies this as well. Implications for Rāmānuja as regards the body-soul-divine relation in the person of Kṛṣṇa follow in a later section (3.5.2.3,1). Suffice it now only to document what Rāmānuja states regarding this passage, and I document only what becomes important for the later discussion of implications.

In the commentary on verse 4 the Viśiṣṭādvaitin admits that prakṛti belongs to Kṛṣṇa.[233] By this is meant that prakṛti is actually an aṁśa of Kṛṣṇa, for Rāmānuja echoes the words of Kṛṣṇa in verse 5: "This is My lower Prakṛti."[234] Rāmānuja, in harmony with 4.5, then distinguishes between the lower prakṛti and the higher prakṛti, the latter "more preeminent" (pradhāna bhūtāṁ).[235] Yet, and nonetheless, under verse 6 (where Kṛṣṇa, speaking cosmologically, thus also as Viṣṇu, uses aham: "I am the origin and also the dissolution of the whole universe") Rāmānuja declares that the entire universe (kṛtsnajagat) has its origination in the two prakṛti-s (prakṛtidvayayonitva), which in turn (once again representing Kṛṣṇa) have their "origin in Me" (madyonitva).[236] For further proof of the validity of his gloss, Rāmānuja cites VP 6.4.38-39: "What was described by Me as Prakṛti in its dual form of the manifest and the unmanifest, and the Puruṣa do merge in the Supreme Self, and the Supreme Self is the support of all."[237] I must mention as well a comment by Rāmānuja under BG 4.7, for it pertains to my purpose: "[E]verything constitutes the body of the Supreme Person ... Therefore all terms used in common parlance for different things denote Him only."[238] The same is found in RVed.[239]

The main point for all this is that since the "I" on the part of Kṛṣṇa is the "I" of his non-avatāric state as Viṣṇu, and since with this "I" Kṛṣṇa mentions that the lower material nature is his, the material world must come from the being of Kṛṣṇa / Viṣṇu himself. That is, the material world shares the same substance as Kṛṣṇa in his non-avatāric state as Viṣṇu (though not Viṣṇu-divya rūpa).

---

symptom of avidyā for Śaṅkara is the erroneous assumption that the material world is ultimately real. Rāmānuja will not traverse that far.

233 RBGB, 246.

234 RBGB, 247. Sanskrit on page 246: iyaṁ mama aparā prakṛtiḥ.

235 RBGB, 247.

236 RBGB, 247.

237 RBGB, 248.

238 RBGB, 249, this latter statement due to the following verse (4.8) in the BG: "I am the taste in the waters; I am the light in the sun and the moon."

239 Names of other objects such as gods denote the Supreme because he is the antaryāmin (RVed, 278; see also p. 254).

### 3.5.2. Rāmānuja on Mānuṣī Tanu of BG 9.11

As is the case with Śaṅkara, Rāmānuja's commentary on 9.11 is relatively short and does not delve into the ontological issue of the body-soul-divine relationship in the person of Kṛṣṇa. Therefore I shall first document Rāmānuja's comments on 9.11, and then move to interpreting those comments in the light of what Rāmānuja teaches concerning 9.4,7 and in the light of previous material discussed, for it is there that Rāmānuja addresses cosmological and ontological issues.

#### 3.5.2.1. Rāmānuja's Comments on 9.11

Again Rāmānuja claims that Kṛṣṇa has taken on the mānuṣī tanu so that he might become the refuge of all (sarvasamāśrayaṇīyatvāya).[240] Rāmānuja then interprets the part of the verse reading "The deluded despise me ... not knowing my higher being [paraṁ bhāvam]" as follows, and again representing Kṛṣṇa: "They consider Me to be a man [manuṣya] like themselves."[241] The deluded do not consider the para bhāva of Kṛṣṇa, from which flow compassion and other wonderful qualities, and think of him only as a man.[242] And yet this very nature—the para bhāva—is the cause of Kṛṣṇa's taking on the mānuṣī tanu.[243]

#### 3.5.2.2. BG 9.4,7

Ādidevānanda translates mayā tatam idaṁ sarvaṁ jagad avyaktamūrtinā matsthāni sarvabhūthāni na cāhaṁ tesyavsthitaḥ in 9.4 as "This entire universe is pervaded by Me, in an unmanifest form. All beings abide in Me, but I do not abide in them."[244] The Sanskrit of verse 7, sarvabhūtāni kāunteya prakṛtiṁ yānti māmikām kalpakṣaye punastāni kalpādāu visṛjāmyaham, is translated "All beings, O Arjuna, enter into My Prakṛti at the end of a cycle of time. Again I send these forth at the beginning of a cycle of time."[245]

Rāmānuja interprets the first clause of verse 4 in terms of the antaryāmin. The entire universe that is composed of "sentient and non-sentient beings" (cetanācetanātmakaṁ) is "pervaded by Me, the inner controller" (mayā antaryāmiṇā tatam).[246] He cites BU 3.7.3 for support ("He [that is, the antaryāmin of vv. 1,2] who dwells in the earth ... the inner controller [antaryāmin]").[247] Further, Rāmānuja states that the antaryāmin also dwells in the jīvātman, the individual self, and that all cetanācetanātmaka serve as the

---

[240] RBGB, 302.
[241] RBGB, 302.
[242] RBGB, 302.
[243] RBGB, 302.
[244] RBGB, 296.
[245] RBGB, 299.
[246] RBGB, 296.
[247] Radhakrishnan, The Principal Upaniṣads, 225. Sanskrit for the BU: yaḥ pṛthivyāṁ tiṣthan. Citation in RBGB, 297.

body of the antaryāmin.

The phrase "All beings abide in Me" Rāmānuja takes as "all beings rest [sthitāni] in Me", that is, they are dependent upon the Lord[248] because they form the body of the Lord.[249] This should be taken in the context of the greater cosmology and not for the avatāra. This correlates with his comment under verse 7, wherein he mentions that prakṛti constitutes the body of the Lord.[250] For support he cites Manu 1.5.8. Speaking of the universe, "He produced it out of His body."[251]

The statement "I do not abide in them" means "I do not depend on them [ahaṁ na tadāyattasthitiḥ]."[252] The meaning here is that the Lord (again, on a cosmological level) does not depend upon prakṛti for his existence.[253] But the Lord in a very important sense depends upon some sort of prakṛti for the avatāra. This I now discuss.

3.5.2.3. Implications for the Mānuṣī Tanu

Implications for the mānuṣī tanu of Kṛṣṇa follow from answers to the following. First, what is the nature of the "I" of Kṛṣṇa and where do we locate the "I" in the body-soul-divine relationship? Second, does Kṛṣṇa identify ontologically with humanity?

1. The Nature of the "I" and Its Location. Exploring this issue means exploring first the two states of existence of Viṣṇu—pre-avatāra and avatāra.

Concerning the first, there is in Viṣṇu a union of both a paramātman and a divya rūpa. I postulate that the locus of personality is found in the paramātman and not the divya rūpa, for there is nothing to suggest in the writings of Rāmānuja that the divya rūpa has in and of itself any personality. All that is said of it is that it is non-prakṛtic in nature. Moreover, I make this conclusion based upon Rāmānuja's body-self relationship in each ordinary being. Here the locus of the personality of each being is the jīvātman, as we have seen ("Hence, what constitutes the inward Self is not pure consciousness but the 'I' which proves itself as the knowing subject"), in a subject-object relationship, and that it is the essence of avidyā for an individual to state "I am this body alone."

---

[248] This is stated as well in the bhāṣya under 9.6.

[249] RBGB, 296.

[250] RBGB, 299.

[251] RBGB, 299. See G. Bühler, trans., The Laws of Manu, in F. Max Müller, ed., Sacred Books of the East (Delhi: Motilal Banarsidass, 1989), 25:5, for the creation account (and the cosmic egg) to which Rāmānuja refers. See also an account of the cosmic egg that is the abode of Viṣṇu, "the Lord of the universe", and where he "assumed a perceptible form", in Fitzedward Hall, ed., The Viṣṇu Purāṇa (New York: Garland, 1981), 1:38-39.

[252] RBGB, 296.

[253] matsthitāu taiḥ na kaścit upakāra ityarthaḥ: "There is no help derived from them for My existence" (RBGB, 296 [Sanskrit], 297 [translation]). In the bhāṣya under 9.6 Rāmānuja writes of "the Lord [bhagavataḥ], who is independent of all others [sarveṣāṁ sthitiḥ]" (p. 299).

Certainly it would be an exercise in avidyā on the part of the anthropomorphic Viṣṇu if he were to do the same! Even further, on the basis of Rāmānuja's sāmānādhikaraṇya the "I" is the subject in, for example, the statements "I am a man" and "I am fat." For Rāmānuja sāmānādhikaraṇya reveals the body as a prakāra of the jīvātman, and the jīvātman as the experiencing self or the "I".[254] Similar "I" statements made by Viṣṇu, then, must be interpreted in the same way if Rāmānuja is to remain consistent.

Concerning the second, in Kṛṣṇāvatāra we have, basically, the paramātman and the mānuṣī tanu. Again I suggest that the locus of the personality of Kṛṣṇa is found in the paramātman, for two reasons. First, if my above thesis that the divya rūpa is void of personality is correct, and we know that the mānuṣī tanu is fashioned from the divya rūpa, it follows then that the locus of personality stems not from the mānuṣī tanu. Second, if Rāmānuja is to remain consistent, the same paradigm of self-as-the-"I" (analyzed with sāmānādhikaraṇya) must apply to Kṛṣṇa. That is to say, Kṛṣṇa's statements involving "I" on his part must be paradigmatic of those on the parts of ordinary beings (there is nothing in the BG or Rāmānuja's writings that suggest otherwise).

But though the locus of the "I" in Kṛṣṇa is situated in the paramātman, is it a locus in relation to a true human nature?

2. Does Kṛṣṇa Identify Ontologically with Humanity? I answer no (see A and C below), at least not before final release (see section D). Obviously this in turn influences how I view the nature of the body of Kṛṣṇa as well as the body's relation to the divine in Kṛṣṇa.

In postulating that there is no ontological identification between Kṛṣṇa's humanity and that of human beings, it is necessary to discuss briefly (A) from where the material for Kṛṣṇa's body comes, and (B) Rāmānuja's anthropology, for it is key in determining the difference between Kṛṣṇa's body and those of ordinary human beings.

A. The Material of Kṛṣṇa's Body. Kṛṣṇa's body comes from the divya rūpa, the "divine form". As I mentioned briefly in chapter 3,[255] the divine form is not the ordinary jagat, which forms the body of the antaryāmin. Nor is it in toto the body of Kṛṣṇāvatāra, for Rāmānuja admits, quoting VP 5.17.33, that Kṛṣṇa is aṁśāvatāraṁ Viṣṇoḥ, "the incarnation of a portion of Viṣṇu".[256] Rather, the divya rūpa is God's "particular bodily form", as Carman puts it.[257] In his BSB Rāmānuja states that "He [the Supreme] possesses a divine form [divya rūpa], peculiar to itself, not derived from the original element [aprākṛta], not karmic."[258] Important here is that the divine form is not made of prakṛti, the

---

[254] See my chapter 3, section 4.1.

[255] Section 1.1.

[256] RBGB, 501. See Wilson, The Vishnu Purana, 5:7.

[257] The Theology of Rāmānuja, 167.

[258] My translation of sa cāprākṛtākarmanimittasvāsādhāraṇadivyarūpa. Sanskrit transliteration taken from Julius J. Lipner, The Face of Truth: A Study of Meaning and

material from which all other beings are formed, that is, the material that comes out of Viṣṇu, as evidenced by the "I" in language communicating that the lower material nature is Viṣṇu.[259] Nor is it karmic, that is, it does not come into being as all other beings do as a result of their karma. Rāmānuja thus establishes the doctrine that the Lord in his divine form is not tainted by any impurities or evils that befall ordinary beings, including gods.[260] Rather, Rāmānuja ascribes to the supreme person a host of glorious attributes. These are found in section 134 of RVed.[261] Unfortunately, though Lipner notes that it is wise on Rāmānuja's part, Rāmānuja says nothing about the actual nature of this material "non-prakṛtic substance".[262]

As noted earlier, Rāmānuja lays stress upon the fact that the Lord manifests "without abandoning his essential nature". There is something more tangible to the essential nature of Viṣṇu than mere abstract categories of attributes. Carman observes that Rāmānuja is "willing to expand the concept of God's essential nature (svarūpa) to include God's [personal] form [the divya rūpa]".[263] If Carman is correct, the thesis is plausible that the divya rūpa is somehow carried into the avatāra of Kṛṣṇa, though the divya rūpa is itself not exhausted by Kṛṣṇāvatāra because, as Rāmānuja states, the Lord assumes a human form without abandoning his essential nature and is a manifestation of a portion of Viṣṇu. This accords with Lipner's observation that without exhausting the divya rūpa, the "divine avatāric form is a particular manifestation or expression of the supernal form [divya rūpa] itself, both being non-prakṛtic in nature".[264]

The following quotes from Rāmānuja, when taken together, are evidence that the body of Kṛṣṇa comes from the divya rūpa. "This essential form [svābhāvikam rūpam] of his, the most compassionate Lord, by his mere will individualises as a shape human [manuṣya] or divine or otherwise, so as to

---

Metaphysics in the Vedantic Theology of Ramanuja (Albany: State University of New York Press, 1986), 167 n. 38. See SBE, 48:256 for Thibaut's translation.

259 See section 3.5.1.3.

260 Even the gods, such as Brahmā, are subject to rebirth due to their karma (RVed, 265, par. 113 [Sanskrit text p. 144]).

261 Sanskrit text pages 164-65; English translation pages 289-91.

262 The Face of Truth, 95.

263 The Theology of Rāmānuja, 169; emphasis mine. Lipner agrees with Carman that the divya rūpa is "an aspect of Brahman's proper form" (The Face of Truth, 96).

264 The Face of Truth, 96. Curiously, Lott makes no mention of the divya rūpa in one of his key essays on avatāra in the Vedānta of Śaṅkara, Rāmānuja and Madhva. Rather, he seems first to suggest, implicitly, the view that the material for Kṛṣṇa's body comes from the same material that forms the universe in Rāmānuja's universe-as-God's-body model (Eric J. Lott, "The Relevance of Research in Religions: Understanding Avatara as a Test-Case", Bangalore Theological Forum, 10, no. 1 [1978]: 43-46). Then at the end of the article Lott more strongly implies this view and concludes that "the stage is set for a real incarnation of God in material human nature" (p. 53). This, of course, misses entirely what I and Lipner conclude.

render it suitable to the apprehension of the devotee and thus satisfy him."[265] Here the svābhāvika rūpa need not necessarily be the divya rūpa,[266] nor need it be, necessarily, in this next statement by Rāmānuja. In a passage in RVed he states that Viṣṇu, whom he titles the Supreme Brahman, "descends ... in his own proper form [svarūpa] to help[267] the entire universe".[268] However, most telling is this comment now following, and when the previous two statements are read in its light, the thesis is proved that Kṛṣṇa's body stems from the divya rūpa: "[H]is body in his incarnation [avatāra] as a god etc., is not of the stuff [na prākṛta, that is, "not derived from the original element"[269]] common bodies are made of."[270] From where else could the material for the body come, if not from the divya rūpa? I conclude, then, along with Carman[271] and Lipner, that the material from which the body of Kṛṣṇāvatāra comes is the "non-prakṛtic" (though in a mysterious[272] way still a material substance) divya rūpa.

B. Rāmānuja's Anthropology. Each human being's material nature comes from prakṛti that is actually an aṁśa of Kṛṣṇa and forms the body (not the divya rūpa) of the Lord because the Lord indwells the material nature of human beings. Further, the jīvātman of each human is the body of the Lord since it

---

265 SBE, 48:241.

266 Though Lipner believes it is (The Face of Truth, 96).

267 My translation of upakāra.

268 RVed, 265, par. 113 (Sanskrit text p. 144). Rāmānuja reiterates this later in the paragraph.

269 See Monier-Williams, A Sanskrit-English Dictionary, 703.

270 RVed, 265, par. 113 (Sanskrit text p. 144).

271 See his Majesty and Meekness, 198, where he writes representing the "Vaishnava Hindu": "The embodiment is real, but it consists of a special pure matter unlike ordinary material bodies." Though Carman immediately connects this statement with the statement that this special pure material body is different from that of ordinary bodies that are karmic in outcome, thus establishing the non-prakṛtic = non-karmic connection, it seems that it does not end here. The body is still of a "special pure matter". From where does this body come, if not the divya rūpa?

272 Lipner, as I stated above, observes that Rāmānuja "wisely says nothing" about the exact nature or makeup of the non-prakṛtic divya rūpa (The Face of Truth, 95). I have confirmed this in my reading of the materials of Rāmānuja. Lipner further states in the notes that Rāmānuja's followers "less wisely ... speculated and even argued about its nature" (p. 167 n. 41). That the divya rūpa is of an actual material substance may be assumed from the debates between Rāmānuja's followers. Moreover, one can gather from, for example, RVed that the divya rūpa is anthropomorphic (Lipner, "anthropomorphic and male in appearance" [The Face of Truth, 94]). Just before paragraph 134 Rāmānuja states, "The Author of the [Brahma] Sūtras declares that the Supreme Brahman [para brahman] has form [rūpavattvaṁ] in the sūtra 'within, on account of the instruction of His properties' [BS 1.1.21: antastaddharmopadeśāt]." He then proceeds in paragraph 134 to describe the para brahman as "gloriously visible", with "long eyes", "forehead" and "nose", "fingers" and "[finger]nails", "feet", etc. (RVed, 289-90).

also is indwelled by the paramātman. So in each human being we have, then, the material nature indwelled by the paramātman and the jīvātman indwelled by the paramātman.

C. Conclusions. Rāmānuja declares that Kṛṣṇa is free from sins, not born from prakṛti in connection with the three guṇa-s nor from prakṛti itself. Further, with Rāmānuja the avatāra of Kṛṣṇa is real (as is the jagat), appears in (or has assumed) a mortal human form that is similar to men, and this without abandoning his essential nature. But to reiterate Rāmānuja's question quoted earlier, "What is the nature of His body?" Is it, as Lipner asks, "the real thing?"[273]

Because the material for Kṛṣṇāvatāra comes from the divya rūpa and is non-prakṛtic, ontological identification with humanity is therefore missing. Perhaps if Rāmānuja postulated that the material for the body of Kṛṣṇāvatāra came from ordinary prakṛti, he would be well on his way to a doctrine of identification. But it is not the case that he was ontologically all that humanity is. Nor can it be stated that Kṛṣṇa is human at all, but "solely Divine"[274] (but perhaps not fully so?[275]), for the divya rūpa is, ontologically, strictly divine. These conclusions are intra-Rāmānuja. That is, even within Rāmānuja's own theology and without imposing categories of my own concerning the nature of a human being, there is no ontological identification. Each ordinary human is, materially speaking, prakṛtic, while Kṛṣṇa is, materially speaking, non-prakṛtic (in the sense described above).

One might state that there is for Rāmānuja no theological or soteriological reason for Kṛṣṇa being fully human as are all humans, though every reason for the distance between Kṛṣṇa and humanity. The emphasis lay not on a substitutionary atonement for sins as much as for a didactic discourse on Kṛṣṇa's true, supreme nature, and for Kṛṣṇa as the true object of devotion. Rāmānuja made "the out-of-the-way avatāra nature", as Lipner puts it, "a transparent disguise for the transcendent Reality within, and as such, to his mind, the fitting focus of devotion".[276]

Lastly I raise some questions that unfortunately cannot be answered directly from a reading of Rāmānuja's works. They nonetheless are of importance for my purpose.

---

[273] The Face of Truth, 103. Lipner continues, "Compared to the Incarnation in traditional Christian teaching, according to which the Son took real flesh in the humanity of Jesus, the answer is 'No'" (p. 103). Clooney also admits that, although real, Rāmānuja's avatāra does not embody in the same sense as humans, and documents concurring conclusions from viśiṣṭādvaita theologians (see Francis X. Clooney, Hindu God, Christian God: How Reason Helps Break Down the Boundaries between Religions [New York: Oxford University Press, 2001], 113,115,116,118).

[274] Carman raises this as a possible implication (The Theology of Rāmānuja, 185).

[275] "The incarnation of a portion of Viṣṇu" (RBGB, 501).

[276] The Face of Truth, 104.

If both sentient and non-sentient reality are indwelled by Viṣṇu,[277] is the mānuṣī tanu (material nature) of Kṛṣṇa itself pervaded or indwelled by the paramātman or para brahman, the antaryāmin? If so, does the mānuṣī tanu constitute Brahman's (Viṣṇu's) body (in the universe-as-God's-body sense) and is it a prakāra of Brahman as is the case with all human bodies?

Since bheda is significant to Rāmānuja's system, are both the body and the soul of Kṛṣṇa indwelled separately by Viṣṇu as is true with all humans ("the whole aggregate of intelligent and non-intelligent beings constitutes Brahman's body"[278])?

Does Kṛṣṇa's mānuṣī tanu even possess a jīvātman?[279] If so, we would have, in this context, identification with humanity at least by way of analogy (analogy only, because the mānuṣī tanu is non-prakṛtic). If not, then we would have in Kṛṣṇa one who does not identify with humanity even in this respect, for he would not, in his humanity, possess a jīvātman.

Would Kṛṣṇa's jīvātman be Brahman "in so far as" it is indwelled by the antaryāmin? And if so, would Kṛṣṇa confess BU 1.4.10, "I am Brahman" or CU 6.8.7, tat tvam asi, on that basis? Further, if Kṛṣṇa possesses a jīvātman, is it of the same substance as Brahman, as are the souls of all humans?[280] If Kṛṣṇa does not possess a jīvātman, does the paramātman replace the jīvātman in the mānuṣī tanu?

Finally, since we have in the person of Kṛṣṇa both a mānuṣī tanu (consisting perhaps of a jīvātman but definitely a body) and a divine nature consisting of the paramātman, are these two natures mixed, separated or united? Is the first option most likely true since in Rāmānuja's theology the paramātman pervades all things?

D. Identification in Final Release? In the category of identification with eschatological ends in view, do Viṣṇu's devotees who have attained final mokṣa dwell eternally in his presence as jīvātman-s that are void of any material, bodily form? Or is it the case that at final release from the prakṛtic body there is identification between devotees and Viṣṇu's anthropomorphic divya rūpa?

With regard to the latter question Lipner states, "Rāmānuja allows for the liberated ātman to assume at will, in furtherance of its power and enjoyment, non-prakṛtic, apparently anthropomorphic, bodies."[281] But with regard to the former it seems that the decision is left to the released jīvātman-s as to whether or not they would assume the bodies. Following is an account of what happens to the jīvātman of the devotee at death, followed by a brief examination of the

---

[277] As discussed throughout chapter 3.

[278] SBE, 48:133.

[279] For reasons why I raise these questions see chapter 3, sections 2 through 4 and their subsections.

[280] See my chapter 3, section 3.

[281] The Face of Truth, 119.

jīvātman assuming or not assuming bodies in the afterlife.

In Rāmānuja's theology full mokṣa comes only with the fall of the body.[282] Before final mokṣa the body that is shed is a prakṛtic body, for in the highest state the jīvātman is "abiding in Its essential nature free from the contact with the Prakṛti".[283] Further, the soul at final mokṣa seems to be made anew. In his BSB under BS 4.4.1 Rāmānuja quotes CU 8.12.3: "Thus does that serene being, having risen from the body and having approached the highest light, manifest itself in its own form."[284] From this Rāmānuja concludes "that on approaching the highest light [Brahman] the soul connects itself with a new form only then brought about".[285] Then, according to Vaiṣṇava theologian Śrīnivāsa, when one reaches Brahman one may obtain non-prakṛtic anthropomorphic forms. "The liberated one", states Śrīnivāsa, "is one who ... assumes a non-material, divine figure with four arms, ... who then salutes the lotus-feet of Bhagavān [Viṣṇu], ... [and] who when questioned, 'Who art thou?' replies, 'I am a mode of Brahman' ... The released individual self ... can assume manifold forms and wander all over the worlds."[286] (Note that this dialogue between the released jīvātman and Viṣṇu assumes an I – Thou relationship between Viṣṇu and his devotees.) Rāmānuja's BSB under BS 4.4.10-14 goes into some detail concerning the eschatological bodies of the released soul.[287] Under 4.4.10,11 he records two opinions held by others as to the question of whether or not the released soul may have a body, each scholar in turn citing texts to prove his thesis. One scholar says yes, the other no. But then, under 4.4.12 Rāmānuja concurs with the opinion of Bādarāyaṇa, specifically that the released soul may be with or without a body. This view, says Rāmānuja, "satisfies both kinds of texts".[288] Finally, in this state the released jīvātman lives eternally, being capable, if it wishes, of "making many bodies its own",[289] even at the time of the recreations and dissolutions of the universe.[290] In chapter 7 I have more on this subject.

### 4. Summary of the Meaning of Mānuṣī Tanu

In this section I summarize my view, Śaṅkara's view, and Rāmānuja's view of

---

[282] RBGB, 213.

[283] RBGB, 286. In his BSB, for example under BS 4.4.2 (SBE, 48:756-57), Rāmānuja is careful to state that the released soul is free from connection with the prakṛtic body in association with karma, making room, it seems, for his doctrine of the freed soul assuming non-prakṛtic bodies in the afterlife.

[284] SBE, 48:755.

[285] SBE, 48:756.

[286] YS, 117-20 (8.23,24).

[287] SBE, 48:763-65.

[288] SBE, 48:763.

[289] SBE, 48:765.

[290] RBGB, 461,499. See BG 14.2.

the mānuṣī tanu of Kṛṣṇa.

## 4.1. My View

The mānuṣī tanu of Kṛṣṇa comes into being as the result of the will of Kṛṣṇa. Kṛṣṇa is sinless because his form has no connection with prakṛti as it relates to the triguṇātmikā. This is not to say that the mānuṣī tanu of Kṛṣṇa has no connection at all with prakṛti, but only to say that there is no connection with prakṛti as it relates to the triguṇātmikā. I have argued that Kṛṣṇa's body is fashioned from eternal prakṛti, but that, unlike ordinary beings and gods, the mānuṣī tanu arising from prakṛti is, as the text affirms, protected from any association with evil or impurity, even though it is said that Kṛṣṇa's birth took place from the womb of Devakī.

I also concluded that the mānuṣī tanu is fashioned from eternal prakṛti and is itself indwelled by Kṛṣṇa, the antaryāmin, the implication being that there is a confusion of the human and the divine, no clear separation of the two natures, in the person of Kṛṣṇa. On yet another front, that being that the material world is Kṛṣṇa, there arises further blurring, if not eradication, of two natures in Kṛṣṇa. Prakṛti is Kṛṣṇa's material nature—it is Kṛṣṇa / Viṣṇu. The implication is that the body of Kṛṣṇa is wholly divine. Here there is identification of Kṛṣṇa with humanity, for human beings' material nature comes from eternal prakṛti that is indwelled by Viṣṇu and is Viṣṇu.

The issue of the "I" of Kṛṣṇa, however, carries with it certain implications concerning whether or not Kṛṣṇa possesses a jīvātman as do all human beings. The "I" is definitely that of Viṣṇu, that is, the "I" of Kṛṣṇa carries over from the pre-avatāric state. But it is uncertain whether or not Kṛṣṇa possesses a jīvātman in addition to the locus of personality that is Viṣṇu. If not, there is lack of identification between Kṛṣṇa and humanity. If so, further questions arise: What would constitute the locus of personality? Is it the jīvātman as is the case with all human beings? Is it Viṣṇu?

Finally, the mānuṣī tanu of BG 9.11 is four-armed, the implication being that Kṛṣṇa is not similar to humans who have two arms.[291] (Yet if one accepts my observation, mentioned above, that the mānuṣī tanu of Kṛṣṇa is itself indwelled by Viṣṇu and is fashioned from eternal prakṛti that is Viṣṇu, at least on this front there is on the part of Kṛṣṇa identification with humanity, intra-BG, because Viṣṇu indwells all things and is all things, including the material nature of humans.)

## 4.2. Śaṅkara's View

Śaṅkara also finds it necessary to affirm that Kṛṣṇa's birth in the womb of

---

[291] None of the commentators cited in this chapter mention this implication, nor do they offer any comment otherwise.

Devakī comes about by his own will and is not associated with karma or triguṇātmikā. But for Śaṅkara Kṛṣṇa's birth occurs in the realm of Īśvara and therefore the jagat-prapañca. For this reason Śaṅkara believes Kṛṣṇa "appears to be embodied and born as a man". The avatāra of Kṛṣṇa is therefore ultimately mithyā.[292] There is ultimately no real flesh to Kṛṣṇāvatāra and

---

[292] Richard De Smet writes that "the transcendent Brahman-Ātman ... alone is Real in the supreme sense of the term (paramārthataḥ). The rest, including the human body of Krishṇa, is un-Real" ("Jesus and the Avatāra", in Jerald Gort, et al., eds., Dialogue and Syncretism: An Interdisciplinary Approach [Grand Rapids, Mich.: Eerdmans, 1989], 160). De Smet also states that the transcendent Brahman "is not really embodied in Krishṇa, but only 'as if' (iva)" (p. 160). De Smet's use of upper case "R" for "Real" is interesting. "Real" equals the transcendent Brahman, whereas "un-Real"—used for the jagat, including avatāra—means "not Brahman", in the sense that Brahman is so utterly transcendent that it cannot be ontologically linked to the jagat. The jagat is "real" (note lower case "r"), but only relatively real within a realist ontology that De Smet believes is characteristic of Śaṅkara's advaita (see directly below). Thus, the jagat is not "Real", that is, not Brahman.

De Smet, D. M. Datta and Bradley Malkovsky advance the thesis that Śaṅkara's advaita proposes a realist ontology. Malkovsky, in his article "The Personhood of Śaṁkara's Para Brahman" (The Journal of Religion 77 [1997]: 541-62), specifically argues this on pages 555-58 (see also his The Role of Divine Grace in the Soteriology of Śaṃkarācārya, 47-50). Key to his hermeneutic of Śaṅkara on this point is the "transcendence of brahman, besides which no other being can exist in a like manner" ("The Personhood of Śaṁkara's Para Brahman", 555). Though admitting that advaita always postulates a denial of dualism, it "need not entail a total monistic rejection of contingent being" (p. 555). Given this, Malkovsky moves on to cite Datta's observation that, contrary to many that see in Śaṅkara's system the total banishing of the material realm after enlightenment, the jagat remains, and at enlightenment one's perception of it changes. Here a negation of the world takes place but not in pure monist fashion, and there is a "transformation, re-organisation and revaluation" of the jagat (p. 556, citing D. M. Datta, "Some Realistic Aspects of the Philosophy of Śaṁkara", in Recent Indian Philosophy, ed. Kalidas Bhattacharya [Calcutta: Progressive Publishers, 1963], 1:344-45). "Thus", Malkovsky concludes, "according to Datta, in the state of non-dual awareness the world is not negated but rather perceived to be in brahman" (p. 556; Datta, in the quotation cited, states that the jagat is perceived "as the manifestation of Brahman"). Malkovsky then moves to the observations of De Smet, who argues for realism on the basis of Śaṅkara's use of language. Since Śaṅkara's reference point of the jagat is the infinite Brahman, Śaṅkara's "value-oriented" (rather than ontological-oriented) language allows him to be "a radical valuationist who measures everything to the absolute Value, the Brahman, and declares its unequality to it rather than the degree of its participation in it" (p. 556). The jagat, then, has reality, but not to the same degree as that of Brahman (p. 557). In this sense the jagat and the phenomena of the jagat are "relatively real" (p. 558).

With such a realist view, implications still arise for Śaṅkara's Kṛṣṇāvatāra, implications that are still in conflict with Rāmānuja and / or classical orthodoxy. The supreme transcendence of Brahman, which translates to "besides which no other being

ultimately no real body-divine relation in the person of Kṛṣṇa. Additionally, in the context of Īśvara Śaṅkara's Kṛṣṇa is an aṁśāvatāra, that is, an avatāra that embodies a part of the deity, as found in Śaṅkara's introduction to his BGB (see my section 1.1). This could lead to the conclusion that Śaṅkara's Kṛṣṇāvatāra is not fully divine.[293]

One may in a very loose sense see ontological identification between Kṛṣṇa's "humanity" and the "humanness" of other human beings[294] in the

---

can exist in a like manner", relegates to a lesser quality and value the existence of avatāra in the sense that the avatāra is "relatively real" when set over against Brahman. If Kṛṣṇāvatāra is relatively real, then the body-divine relation in Kṛṣṇāvatāra must be viewed as relatively real (thus De Smet's observation that the transcendent is not really embodied in Kṛṣṇa?). And since ultimate Brahman, as Śaṅkara admits, is unrelated to all empirical experiences and beyond the range of the senses (see SBGB, 304,385), does this not place Kṛṣṇāvatāra in a lower reality that divorces from ultimate Brahman all actions on Kṛṣṇa's part, including suffering, pain, and the like? Moreover, ultimately, and at enlightenment, the Kṛṣṇāvatāra, though relatively real, must be seen to have been a product of lower knowledge (see "The Personhood of Śaṁkara's Para Brahman", 556). For classical orthodoxy it is in fact higher knowledge (if I may use the phrase) that leads to confession of Christ as true God and true man, and true knowledge of him comes, in part, by acknowledging the reality of his suffering. Finally, if, as Datta observes, in the state of non-dual awareness the jagat is seen as a manifestation of Brahman, Śaṅkara's Kṛṣṇāvatāra cannot be said to be truly human from the point of view of classical orthodoxy. Thus, on this point, whether one takes a realist or monist view, true humanity on the part of Kṛṣṇa is lacking.

[293] Parrinder comments that "followers of Śankara have had difficulty with this notion, since it is generally held that Krishna was the full and perfect Avatar of Vishnu. So the annotator Ānandagiri said that 'part' meant in an illusory form created by the Lord's own will" (Geoffrey Parrinder, Avatar and Incarnation: The Divine and Human Form in the World's Religions [Oxford: Oneworld Publications, 1997], 51; see also Sadanandam, The Doctrine of Avatāra, 44, and Lott, "The Relevance of Research in Religions", 42). Here Parrinder cites "A. M. Śāstri, The Bhagavad-Gītā with the Commentary of Śrī Śankarachāryā, 5th edn., 1961", 3. S. Murty, in his Revelation and Reason in Advaita Vedānta, 8, does not consider Śaṅkara's Kṛṣṇa to be an aṁśāvatāra. He states, "the word 'partially' can only mean that though God incarnated in Kṛṣṇa, he has not ceased to be the creator and sustainor of the universe ... Though he became Kṛṣṇa, he was not exhausted in the form of Kṛṣṇa". The view that Kṛṣṇa is but an aṁśāvatāra may come from RV 10.90.2-3: "Three quarters of the supreme Being is unmanifest, and only one quarter is manifest" (taken from Timothy C. Tennent, Building Christianity on Indian Foundations [Delhi: ISPCK, 2000], 338).

[294] However, Ramakrishnananda, a disciple of the neo-Vedāntin Ramakrishna, states, perhaps alluding to BG 7.24-25, "Further, He [Kṛṣṇa] declares, 'Ordinary fellows like Duryodhana and others insult Me by regarding Me merely as a man. But I am not really a man', and that was shown in the eleventh chapter of the Gita, when He made known His universal form to Arjuna. So, although He was appearing as a man, He was not a man" (God and Divine Incarnations, 135). Mithyā does not seem to be the context in which Ramakrishnananda makes this statement; rather, the universal form of BG 11 is

context of lower Brahman. First, like other human beings who are not material in the ultimately real sense, Kṛṣṇa is not, ultimately, really material. Second, like other human beings who are in reality only the ātmanbrahman, Kṛṣṇa is in reality only the ātmanbrahman. But as just mentioned, this must be understood in a loose sense, indeed perhaps in an erroneous sense, for ultimately there should not even be talk of identification between Kṛṣṇa and humanity, as this itself implies existence of two entities, a phenomenon quite averse to Śaṅkara's ultimate monistic whole. In the ultimate sense, then, identification does not even exist.

As for the "I" of Kṛṣṇa, we see that it operates in the realm of lower Brahman and the jagat-prapañca. But, as I concluded, the "I" on Kṛṣṇa's part also operates in this lower realm with reference by Kṛṣṇa to his higher nature. In other words, Kṛṣṇa speaks in I-ness about his higher nature. The problem, it seems to me, is that with Śaṅkara the notion of "I" is eradicated in the state of parā vidyā. But does not Kṛṣṇa possess parā vidyā? If so, why is he (1) speaking with I-ness, and (2) why does he acknowledge objects that exist in the jagat-prapañca? As we saw in section 3.5.1.1, Rāmānuja picks up on this dilemma on Śaṅkara's part.

## 4.3. Rāmānuja's View

Like Śaṅkara, Rāmānuja affirms that Kṛṣṇa's birth in the womb of his mother comes about by his own will and is not associated with karma and triguṇātmikā. But unlike Śaṅkara, according to Rāmānuja Kṛṣṇa's mānuṣī tanu is real. Further, like Śaṅkara in the absolute sense, there is for Rāmānuja no ontological identification between Kṛṣṇa and ordinary human beings, at least in the here-and-now. (There is no need for it in Rāmānuja's theology [just as there is no need in Śaṅkara's system; and Śaṅkara's "loose sense" identification is most likely a consequence he never explicitly intended].) The non-prakṛtic divya rūpa is the material from which the mānuṣī tanu of Kṛṣṇa is fashioned, which is quite different from the ordinary prakṛti from which all human bodies are fashioned. The solely divine nature of the divya rūpa also leads to the conclusion that the mānuṣī tanu of Kṛṣṇa is solely divine and therefore not human (though human beings may be said to be solely divine, but only in that [1] they are the body of God and that [2] they are fashioned, in all aspects, out of God).

Kṛṣṇa speaks in "I" language in both the cosmological and avatāric settings. I am quite certain that Kṛṣṇa's "I" is the pre-avatāric Viṣṇu. It is not clear, however, whether or not Kṛṣṇa possesses a jīvātman as do all human beings. If

---

the context. I take this to mean, therefore, that according to Ramakrishnananda Kṛṣṇa does not identify with humanity in the lower reality of Īśvara (in which, as discussed, the cosmic form appeared). He is beyond identification with humanity, as the universal form implies.

not, there is yet another category in which there is no identification with humanity. If so, this raises further questions. Is Kṛṣṇa's jīvātman indwelled by Viṣṇu? Is the jīvātman of Kṛṣṇa the locus of personality?

## 5. Postscript

This ends my treatment of Śaṅkara's and Rāmānuja's epistemologies, theologies and doctrines of Kṛṣṇāvatāra. In the next chapter I outline the relation of matter to God in the thought of classical Christian orthodoxy, and in chapter 6 I probe the two natures of Christ in light of the material discussed in chapter 5. This I do in order to proceed to the main purpose of this work, found in chapter 7, which is a comparison of the theological and soteriological implications, similarities, and differences between Śaṅkara's Kṛṣṇa, Rāmānuja's Kṛṣṇa, and the Christ of classical Christian orthodoxy.

CHAPTER 5

# The World and God: Traditional Christianity

In this chapter I focus upon two statements contained in the NC and exegete certain biblical texts that I, along with theologians of my tradition, consider to be evidence for these statements.[1] The two statements are as follows. Πιστεύομεν εἰς ἕνα ΘΕΟΝ ΠΑΤΕΡΑ παντοκράτορα, ποιητὴν οὐρανοῦ καὶ γῆς, ὁρατῶν τε πάντων καὶ ἀοράτων (pisteuomen eis hena theon patera pantokratora, poiētēn ouranou kai gēs, horatōn te pantōn kai aoratōn): "We believe in one God the Father almighty, maker of heaven and earth, and of all things visible and invisible." Καὶ εἰς ἕνα κύριον 'ΙΗΣΟΥΝ ΧΡΙΣΤΟΝ ... δι' οὗ τὰ πάντα ἐγένετο (kai eis hena kurion Iēsoun Christon ... di' hou ta panta egeneto): "And in one Lord Jesus Christ, ... by [or through[2]] whom all things were made."[3]

I explore two themes[4] by way of cosmogony and theology creatio ex nihilo and God as ontologically other than the material world. Creatio ex nihilo

[1] I assume that the creeds reflect and represent orthodoxy already present in the biblical witness. As Philip Schaff writes, "The Bible is the Word of God to man; the Creed is man's answer to God. The Bible reveals the truth in popular form of life and fact; the Creed states the truth in logical form of doctrine" (The Creeds of Christendom: With a History and Critical Notes [New York: Harper and Row, 1931; Grand Rapids, Mich.: Baker Book House, 1985], 2:3). Here Schaff distinguishes between the Bible as the Norma Normans ("norming norm") and the creeds as Norma Normata ("normed norm"). See Harold O. J. Brown, Heresies: The Image of Christ in the Mirror of Heresy from the Apostles to the Present (Grand Rapids, Mich.: Baker Book House, 1984), 133-34.

[2] The Greek preposition δία (dia). I treat this briefly in section 2.1.2.1.

[3] Greek text is taken from Schaff, The Creeds of Christendom, 2:57. From hereon the Greek text for both creeds is taken from this source. Therefore I shall not cite source, volume and page numbers pertaining to both NC and C. On another note, it is not within the scope of this dissertation to deal specifically with text critical issues regarding NC and C. For these issues I refer the reader to Schaff, The Creeds of Christendom, and J. N. D. Kelly, Early Christian Creeds, 3rd ed. (New York: Longman, 1972).

[4] The doctrine of the human soul I relegate to notes. The general consensus of the early church is that all human souls had a beginning. This coincides with the statement of the NC that God is the maker "of all things ... invisible". It is not the object of this work to detail the various nuances, for example various ideas of distinction (or not) between the human soul and spirit, of early church theologians in this doctrinal area. Rather, the focus shall be on the creation and thus beginning of the human soul / spirit.

receives the bulk of attention, since the latter category, though not the only option,[5] most naturally and logically flows from it. I hope to show in the following chapter that these two themes play an important role in the christological category of the body-soul-divine relation regarding the person of Jesus, and therefore also figure significantly in the final chapter's comparison of avatāra and incarnation.

## 1. The Material Universe

The first issue is whether or not matter is eternal, and, if not eternal, how it came to be. The first clause of the NC reads, "I believe in one God the Father almighty, maker [ποιητὴν, poiētēn] of heaven and earth, and of all things visible and invisible." The choice of ποιητὴς (poiētēs) over κτίστης (ktistēs, creator) is interesting, for it might, for some, imply in the bringing into existence of all things merely a framer of eternally preexistent matter rather than a creator of all things ex nihilo.[6] I now raise several observations as regards poiētēs in the phrase "maker of Heaven and earth".

### 1.1. Earlier Confessions and Statements

The creed keeps with traditional language of some of the early church theologians. For examples, Irenaeus in his Against Heresies (180 A.D.) mentions "the Father Almighty, who has made [πεποιηκότα, pepoiēkota[7]] heaven and earth".[8] Theophilus (c. 150 A.D.) confesses that God is "craftsman and Maker [ποιητὴς, poiētēs], because He is creator [κτίστης, ktistēs] and

[5] For example, God could have created ex nihilo and then fused himself to creation, thereby becoming ontologically one with it. Though I am not aware of such a worldview existing in the world of ideas, it still is a possible choice.

[6] I assume that the early church theologians were well aware that the New Testament employs poiētēs (maker) and ktistēs (creator) or their verbal forms when speaking of creation of the heavens and the earth. For example, Acts 14.15 and Revelation 14.7 employ ποιέω (poieō) and Revelation 4.11 and 10.6 use κτίζω (ktizō) to communicate that God created the heavens and the earth. Nonetheless, whether "made" or "create", early church theologians, for approximately 230 years before the NC, and after the NC, embraced creatio ex nihilo, as I hope to show above.

[7] The perfect participle from ποιέω (poieō).

[8] Schaff, The Creeds of Christendom, 2:13. See Against Heresies, I.10.1, in Alexander Roberts and James Donaldson, eds., The Ante-Nicene Fathers (reprint, Grand Rapids, Mich.: Wm. B. Eerdmans Publishing Company, 1977), 1:330. Noted from hereon as ANF. In note 126 I mention some early church apologists' efforts to include in their doctrine of creation a Logos (or Word) theology (diverse as they are), specifically the mediative role of the Son in the creative act of God (see Hubert Cunliffe-Jones, ed., A History of Christian Doctrine [Philadelphia: Fortress Press, 1980], 44).

maker [poiētēs] of the universe".[9] Lucian (300 A.D.) employs poiētēs,[10] as do Eusebius of Caesarea (325 A.D.),[11] Cyril of Jerusalem (c. 350 A.D.),[12] and Epiphanius (374 A.D.).[13] Regarding Latin documents translating "maker" or "creator", in Irenaeus' Against Heresies we read "fabricatorem",[14] while Tertullian's (c. 160 - c. 230 A.D.) De Virginibus Velandis, chapter 1, reads "conditorem".[15] Novatian's (of Rome, 210-280 A.D.) De Trinitate, in which is contained De Regula Fidei, has "conditorem".[16] Origen (c. 185 - c. 254 A.D.) has "creavit".[17] Interesting is the received form of the Apostles' Creed in both the Greek and Latin texts: ποιητὴν οὐρανοῦ καὶ γῆς (poiētēn ouranou kai gēs) and creatorem cœli et terrœ,[18] where "maker" and "creator" are therefore synonymous.

### 1.1.1. MATTER NOT ETERNAL

With the following evidence from early church theologians up to Augustine I hope to demonstrate that the NC's confession "maker of heaven and earth", interpreted in the context from which it was framed, means that the universe was created out of nothing. Gerhard May states that the development of what would become the church doctrine of creatio ex nihilo began in the latter half of the second century. The conclusion that matter is created by God, writes May, "is reached at almost the same time by Tatian and Theophilus of Antioch, and soon with Irenaeus the doctrine of creatio ex nihilo achieves its essentially permanent form".[19] May argues that the doctrine of a creatio ex nihilo began to be established when early church theologians thought it essential to answer the challenge of Gnosticism's various cosmologies.[20]

---

[9] Greek text: δημιουργὸς δὲ καὶ ποιητὴς διὰ τὸ αὐτὸν εἶναι κτίστην καὶ ποιητὴν τῶν ὅλων (dēmiourgos de kai poiētēs dia to auton einai ktistēn kai poiētēn tōn holōn). Taken from Robert M. Grant, trans., Theophilus of Antioch Ad Autolycum (London: Oxford University Press, 1970), 6 (I.4). See ANF, 2:90 (Theophilus to Autolycus, I.4).

[10] In Lucian's creed in Schaff's The Creeds of Christendom, 2:26.

[11] Schaff, The Creeds of Christendom, 2:29.

[12] Schaff, The Creeds of Christendom, 2:31.

[13] Schaff, The Creeds of Christendom, 2:33.

[14] Schaff, The Creeds of Christendom, 2:15; ANF, 1:417 (III.4.2).

[15] Schaff, The Creeds of Christendom, 2:17.

[16] Schaff, The Creeds of Christendom, 2:21.

[17] Schaff, The Creeds of Christendom, 2:22 (De Principiis; see ANF, 4:240 [Preface, 4]).

[18] Schaff, The Creeds of Christendom, 2:45.

[19] Gerhard May, Creatio Ex Nihilo: The Doctrine of 'Creation out of Nothing' in Early Christian Thought, trans. A. S. Worrall (Edinburgh: T&T Clark, 1994), 148.

[20] This leads to two further observations on May's part. First, this does not mean that there was, though arguably, at the beginning of this period a universal consensus. See May's treatment of Justin Martyr and Athenagoras (Creatio Ex Nihilo, 120-39). Further, May observes that at the time of Tatian, and after him, other Christian teachers were "under the influence of Middle Platonism" and still propagating its principles in their

1.1.1.1. Irenaeus

In Against Heresies Irenaeus specifically argues for creatio ex nihilo. The heretics, he says,

> believe not that God ... formed all things[21] ... out of what did not previously exist ... They do not believe that God (being powerful, and rich in all resources) created matter itself ... While men, indeed, cannot make anything out of nothing, but only out of matter already existing, yet God is in this point preeminently superior to men, that He Himself called into being the substance of His creation, when previously it had no existence.[22]

If we take as authentic one of the Fragments from the Lost Writings of Irenaeus, we have an apologetic by Irenaeus that matter is not eternal. He holds

---

doctrines of creation (p. 150). Second, May observes that the use of the phrases "to create out of non-being" or "to create out of nothing" does not necessarily mean creatio ex nihilo. For an example of the former, May cites Xenophon's statement in Memorabilia where parents "bring forth their children out of non-being". May asserts, "Naturally that does not mean that the children come to be out of nothing, and it will occur to no one to understand the statement in terms of a creatio ex nihilo" (p. 8). Rather, "Only when the formula is seen from the train of thought to be an intentional antithesis of the idea of world-formation [see nn. 21,30], is it to be taken as a testimony to the doctrine of unconditional creation" (p. 8). As an example of the latter, May states that "Philo could speak of the creation of the world 'out of nothing' and at the same time suppose the preexistence of matter" (p. 152). May states, however, that Philo is "remarkably vague" in his statements about the creation of the cosmos, and that Philo does not specifically answer the question concerning the eternal or non-eternal nature of matter, though, in May's opinion, Philo's negative statements about matter lead one to think that God did not create formless matter beforehand (see pp. 9-21).

[21] The doctrine of "world-formation", as May puts it (Creatio Ex Nihilo, 74,147), where formless matter is created ex nihilo and then formed into objects, is a part of several early church theologians' cosmogonies. I shall not treat the subject of world-formation in depth, for the issue at hand is creatio ex nihilo, which is part of world-formation. See note 30 for a brief description of May's two types of world-formation doctrines.

[22] ANF, 1:370 (II.10.2,3). The Latin text starting from "While men": quoniam homines quidem de nihilo non possunt aliquid facere, sed de materia subjacenti: Deus autemquam homines hoc primo melior, eo quod materium fabricationis suæ cum ante non esset ipse adinvenit. Taken from W. Wigan Harvey, ed., Sancti Irenæi: Episcopi Lugdunensis, Libros Quinque, Adversus Haereses (Cantabrigiæ: Typis Academicis, 1857), 1:274. See Against Heresies, ANF, 1:347 (I.22.1): "[T]here is one God Almighty, who made all things by His Word, and fashioned and formed, out of that which had no existence, all things which exist."

in contempt "certain men" who maintain "that matter itself is uncreated".[23]

Illustrating the logical outcome of creatio ex nihilo, namely God as wholly other,[24] note Irenaeus' reasoning. "All things", states Irenaeus, "were both established and created by Him who is God over all". Speaking of Christ and quoting John 1.3, Irenaeus asserts that "All things were made by Him, and without Him was not anything made."[25] He continues, affirming that the created order is distinct from God:

> But the things established are distinct from Him who has established them, and what have been made from Him who has made them. For He is Himself uncreated, both without beginning and end, and lacking nothing. He is Himself sufficient for Himself; and still further, He grants to all others this very thing, existence; but the things which have been made by Him have received a beginning.[26]

1.1.1.2. Tatian

Tatian[27] (110-172 A.D.) speaks of the Lord of the universe as the "necessary ground [ὑπόστασις, hupostasis] of all being" and the Logos as "having first created for Himself the necessary matter ... For[28] matter is not, like God, without beginning, nor, as having no beginning, is of equal power with God; it is begotten, and not produced by any other being, but brought into existence by

---

[23] ANF, 1:573. In the notes we read, "Harvey considers this fragment to be a part of the work of Irenæus referred to by Photius under the title De Universo, or de Substantia Mundi. It is to be found in Codex 3011 of the Bodleian Library, Oxford."

[24] Creatio ex nihilo in a theistic context naturally leads to the doctrine of God as wholly other. The ontological "otherness" of God was at times taken for granted by the theologians of the early church due to creatio ex nihilo, though at other times they labored to state the obvious, as I shall document on two occasions, above with Irenaeus and later above with Augustine.

[25] Against Heresies, III.8.3 (ANF, 1:421).

[26] Against Heresies, III.8.3 (ANF, 1:422). This includes the human soul. In Against Heresies, II.24.1 (ANF, 1:411), Irenaeus argues first against the doctrine that souls pass from body to body in a transmigratory way (see also II.23.1-5). Though after death they continue to exist, he asserts that "they do not pass from body to body". In the very next section (II.24.2) Irenaeus argues that human souls have a beginning (as do all created things, see II.24.3); they are created, "and on this account are inferior to Him who formed them, inasmuch as they are not unbegotten".

[27] May states that "Tatian is the first Christian theologian known to us who expressly advanced the proposition that matter was produced by God (Creatio Ex Nihilo, 150).

[28] Greek text for this and what follows: οὔτε γὰρ ἄναρχος ἡ ὕλη καθάπερ καὶ ὁ θεός, οὔτε διὰ τὸ ἄναρχον ἰσοδύναμος τῷ θεῷ, γενητὴ δὲ καὶ οὐχ ὑπὸ ἄλλου γεγονυῖα, μόνου δὲ ὑπὸ τοῦ πάντων δημιουργοῦ προβεβλημένη (oute gar anarchos hē hulē kathaper kai ho theos, oute dia to anarchon hisodunamos tō theō, genētē de kai ouch hupo allou gegonuia, monou de hupo tou pantōn dēmiourgou probeblēmenē). Taken from May, Creatio Ex Nihilo, 149 n. 7.

the Framer of all things alone".[29]

1.1.1.3. Theophilus

"Theophilus", states May, "speaks in settled terminology of creation 'out of nothing': 'God has created everything out of nothing into being'".[30] In a direct apologetic against those who hold that nature is eternal, and against the Platonist view that "matter as well as God is uncreated", Theophilus asserts that God is greater than human artists who create from already existing materials: "God is more powerful than man, in this way—out of things that are not he creates and has created all things."[31] In three other instances in his Ad Autolycum that are worthy of mention, Theophilus claims that "He made all things out of nothing",[32] "He creates out of nothing",[33] and "He created you out of nothing."[34]

---

[29] ANF, 2:67 (Address of Tatian to the Greeks, chapter 5).

[30] May, Creatio Ex Nihilo, 156, quoting Theophilus in Ad Autolycum I.4 (see ANF, 2:90). Greek text reads τὰ πάντα ὁ θεὸς ἐποίησεν ἐξ οὐκ ὄντων εἰς τὸ εἶναι (ta panta ho theos epoiēsen ex ouk ontōn eis to einai) (Grant, Theophilus of Antioch Ad Autolycum, 6 [I.4]). May cautions his readers that the phrase ἐκ μὴ ὄντος (ek mē ontos, "out of nothing" or "out of non-being") need not necessarily mean creatio ex nihilo. It is therefore the context, he argues, in which the phrase occurs that determines meaning. Since, as May states, Theophilus criticizes the Platonist view of "world-formation" (Creatio Ex Nihilo, 158), his use of the phrase carries the meaning of creatio ex nihilo. Note that May writes of two types of world-formation doctrines: world-formation out of eternally preexisting matter ("the world-formation idea of the Greek philosophers"), and world-formation out of matter created ex nihilo. May understands Theophilus as teaching the latter (Creatio Ex Nihilo, 162-63).

[31] δυνατώτερός ἐστιν ὁ θεὸς τοῦ ἀντηρώτου, οὕτως καὶ τὸ ἐξ οὐκ ὄντων ποιεῖν καὶ πεποιηκέναι τὰ ὄντα (dunatōteros estin ho theos tou antērōtou, houtōs kai to ex ouk ontōn poiein kai pepoiēkenai ta onta). Greek text taken from Grant, Theophilus of Antioch Ad Autolycum, 26 (II.4). See ANF, 2:95.

[32] ἐξ οὐκ ὄντων τὰ πὰντα ἐποίησεν (ex ouk ontōn ta panta epoiēsen) (Grant, Theophilus of Antioch Ad Autolycum, 38 [II.8]). See ANF, 2:98.

[33] ἐξ οὐκ ὄντων ποιῇ (ex ouk ontōn poiē) (Grant, Theophilus of Antioch Ad Autolycum, 46 [II.13]). See ANF, 2:99.

[34] ἐποίησέν σε ἐξ οὐκ ὄντος (epoiēsen ex ouk ontos) (Grant, Theophilus of Antioch Ad Autolycum, 12 [I.8]). Here Theophilus writes of the resurrection and appeals to his reader to put his faith in God in the here and now, otherwise it will be reckoned to him as unbelief. He then proceeds to illustrate how humanity puts its trust in things it sees in everyday life, and, if so, how much more appropriate it is to place faith in God, who "created you out of nothing". Theophilus then states that God "molded you out of a small moist substance, even out of the smallest drop [here referring most likely to sperm], which itself, formerly, was not [ἥτις οὐδὲ αὐτὴ ἦν ποτε (hētis oude autē ēn pote)]" (Grant, Theophilus of Antioch Ad Autolycum, 12 [I.8]). See ANF, 2:91.

### 1.1.1.4. Tertullian

Tertullian states concerning the "conditorem mundi" in On Prescription Against Heretics, "qui universa de nihilo produxerit".[35] Tertullian also discusses Hermogenes' doctrine of creation from eternally preexisting matter, with which he disagrees,[36] arguing that God made all things ex nihilo[37]: "So also He will be first, because all things are after Him; and all things are after Him, because all things are by Him; and all things are by Him, because they are of nothing."[38] Interesting as well is Tertullian's theological assessment that to be God necessarily postulates creatio ex nihilo. He states that Hermogenes

> does not appear to acknowledge any other Christ as Lord, though he holds Him in a different way; but by this difference in his faith he really makes him another being,—nay, he takes from Him everything which is God, since he will not have it that He made all things of nothing. For ... he learned there from the Stoics how to place Matter (on the same level) with the Lord, just as if it too had existed ever both unborn and unmade.[39]

### 1.1.1.5. Novatian

Though in Novatian we find neither explicit statements regarding creatio ex nihilo nor a polemic against those who hold matter as eternal, we do find strong implicit teaching in Novatian that leads to the conclusion that he affirmed creatio ex nihilo and matter as non-eternal. In his De Trinitate Novatian states concerning God, "there could have been nothing beyond Himself",[40] "nothing is more ancient than He",[41] and "thus He is declared to be one, having no equal ... because there cannot be two infinites".[42] Moreover, Novatian, quoting Psalm

---

[35] Schaff, The Creeds of Christendom, 2:19; ANF, 3:249 (chapter 13); T. Herbert Bindley, ed., Tertulliani: De Praescriptione Haereticorum (New York: Oxford, 1893), 48.

[36] Against Hermogenes, chapters 2-14 (ANF, 3:477- 85), 19-23 (ANF, 3:488-91), and 33 (ANF, 3:496).

[37] Against Hermogenes, chapters 15-17 (ANF, 3:485-87) and chapter 34 (ANF, 3:496). This includes the soul / spirit ("For when we acknowledge that the soul originates in the breath of God, it follows that we attribute a beginning to it ... it had both birth and creation" [A Treatise on the Soul, chapter 4 {ANF, 3:184}]).

[38] Against Hermogenes, chapter 17 (ANF, 3:486). Latin text: sic et primus erit, quia omnia post illum; sic omnia post illum, quia omnia ab illo; sic ab illo, quia ex nihilo. Taken from Frédéric Chapot, trans., Tertullien: Contre Hermogène (Latour-Maubourg, Paris: Les Éditions du Cerf, 1999), 124.

[39] Against Hermogenes, chapter 1 (ANF, 3:477). Tertullian reasons that God cannot be Lord over matter if matter is co-equal with God (Against Hermogenes, 3:482 [chapter 9]).

[40] ANF, 5:612 (chapter 2).

[41] ANF, 5:612 (chapter 2).

[42] ANF, 5:612 (chapter 2); 5:614-15 (chapter 4).

148.5, asserts that the Lord "spake, and all things were made", and follows this assertion with "what is not born [that is, God] cannot be changed; for only those things undergo change which are made".[43]

1.1.1.6. Origen

In De Principiis Origen specifically rejects the idea that matter is co-eternal with God.[44] He states in Book II of this work, "I cannot understand how so many distinguished men have been of the opinion that this matter ... was uncreated, i.e., not formed by God himself, who is the Creator of all things[45] ... saying [instead] that matter is uncreated, and co-eternal with the uncreated God."[46] In the very next section Origen cites Psalm 148.5 and The Shepherd of Hermas in order to substantiate creatio ex nihilo.[47] In this latter work we read, "there is one God, who created [κτίσας, ktisas[48]] and put in order all things, and who brought [ποιήσας, poiēsas[49]] into being all things from non-existence".[50] Here ποιέω (poieō), from which derives ποιητὴς (poiētēs), is

---

[43] ANF, 5:613,614 (chapters 3,4).

[44] ANF, 4:252.

[45] Including souls: "All souls, and all rational natures, whether holy or wicked, were formed or created, and all these, according to their proper nature, are incorporeal; but although incorporeal, they were nevertheless created, because all things were made by God through Christ" (De Principiis, I.7.1 [ANF, 4:262]).

[46] ANF, 4:269 (II.1.4). However, as Cunliffe-Jones writes, "Origen's cosmology ... requires him to believe that God must always have a universe related to himself. It follows that there has been a created world (not necessarily this particular world) from all eternity and that there will be a created world of some kind forever. This does not mean that the universe is a second uncreated principle alongside God ... It is contingent and wholly dependent, but linked with the Creator through his direct image, the Logos" (A History of Christian Doctrine, 73-74). This is understood against the backdrop of the influence of Platonist ideas upon Origen, where pre-creation (before creation in actuality) is seen as an archetypal idea (p. 73).

[47] ANF, 4:270 (II.1.5).

[48] Aorist active participle from κτίζω (ktizō).

[49] Aorist active participle from ποιέω (poieō).

[50] εἷς ἐστὶν ὁ Θεός, ὁ τὰ πάντα κτίσας καὶ καταρτίσας, καὶ ποιήσας ἐκ τοῦ μὴ ὄντος εἰς τὸ εἶναι τὰ πάντα (heis estin ho theos, ho ta panta ktisas kai katartisas, kai poiēsas ek tou mē ontos eis to einai ta panta). Taken from J. B. Lightfoot and J. R. Harmer, eds., The Apostolic Fathers: Revised Greek Texts with Introductions and English Translations (London: Macmillan and Co., 1891; Grand Rapids, Mich.: Baker Book House, 1984), 318 (first mandate [ἐντολὴ α΄ {entolē a}]). The Latin text reads unus est deus, qui omnia creavit atque conposuit et fecit ex eo quod nihil erat, ut essent uniuersa. Taken from Henri Crouzel et Manlio Simonetti, trans., Origène: Traité Des Principes (Latour-Maubourg, Paris: Les Éditions du Cerf, 1978), 1:244. On the caution of reading out of ek mē ontos creatio ex nihilo (and whether to translate the phrase as "out of non-being" or "out of nothing"), see May, Creatio Ex Nihilo, pages 6-18, especially pages 17-18. Thus, May states concerning those who quote from The

used in a context of creation out of nothing.

1.1.1.7. Cyril

For Cyril there is nothing explicit in his writings to suggest that matter is eternal. In his Catechetical Lectures he mentions the Son of God, "By whom all things were made, nothing having been excepted from His creation."[51] Cyril does make many statements to the effect that God is the creator of the universe[52] and is "alone unbegotten",[53] the implication being that matter is not eternal.

1.1.1.8. Eusebius

In his Oration of Constantine Eusebius writes that God is "above all existence" and "has no origin, and therefore no beginning, being the originator [or beginning] of all things which receive existence".[54] Consequently nature is not the first cause of all things,[55] and it is "folly", asserts Eusebius, "to compare created with eternal things, which latter have neither beginning nor end, while the former, having been originated and called into being ... of necessity have an end".[56] Finally, with this statement Eusebius explicitly denies that matter is eternal: "Since, then, nothing exists without a cause, of necessity the cause of existing substances preceded their existence. But since the world and all things that it contains exists, and are preserved, their preserver must have had a prior existence."[57]

---

Shepherd of Hermas, "Only when advanced reflection had recognized the divine creation as creatio ex nihilo, were the sayings of Hermas also understood in that sense and taken as welcome witness to the doctrine of creation out of nothing" (May, Creatio Ex Nihilo, 27). May cites Irenaeus, Against Heresies, IV.20.2, as "[t]he first reference of this kind" (May, Creatio Ex Nihilo, 27 n. 108). However, in light of the previous statement made by Origen, specifically that he is puzzled by the opinion of distinguished men that matter is uncreated, I take his citation of The Shepherd of Hermas as evidence of his assertion of creatio ex nihilo.

[51] Philip Schaff and Henry Wace, eds., The Nicene and Post-Nicene Fathers, second series (reprint, Grand Rapids, Mich.: Wm. B. Eerdmans Publishing Company, 1976), 7:70, Catechetical Lectures, XI.22. Noted from hereon as NPNF2.

[52] Catechetical Lectures in NPNF2, 7:20 (IV.4), 35 (VI.9), 36 (VI.11), 70-71 (XI.21-24). Cyril also applies to Christ the title "maker of the world" and states that "Christ made all things" (XI.21-24).

[53] Catechetical Lectures, IV.4 (NPNF2, 7:20). Souls, then, are created by God (Catechetical Lectures, IV.18 [NPNF2, 7:23], IV.4 [NPNF2, 7:20]).

[54] Chapter 3 (NPNF2, 1:562).

[55] NPNF2, 1:564 (chapter 6).

[56] NPNF2, 1:571 (chapter 14).

[57] NPNF2, 1:569 (chapter 11).

1.1.1.9. Lactantius

Lactantius' (260-330 A.D.) lengthy diatribe against the poets and philosophers in his The Divine Institutes contains the statement that God "made all things out of nothing".[58] He addresses Cicero's belief that matter has a nature all its own and that "it is not probable that the matter from which all things arose was made by divine providence". Lactantius continues to quote Cicero's analogy of a builder who does not create the materials from which he builds, but uses already existing materials. In answer to this, Lactantius appeals to human weakness. The builder is simply not able to create the materials from which he erects, for he is not God. God, however, is able to do this, and in fact has done it.[59]

1.1.1.10. Constitutions of the Holy Apostles

In the Constitutions of the Holy Apostles, a compiled treatise dating "no later than the fourth century",[60] we read, "As, therefore, we believe Moses when he says, 'In the beginning God made the heaven and the earth'; and we know that He did not want matter, but by His will alone brought those things into being which Christ was commanded to make."[61] The work continues to affirm that God made souls and bodies out of nothing.[62]

1.1.1.11. Theodoret

In Ecclesiastical History Theodoret (b. c. 390 A.D.) speaks of the eternally preexistent Christ against those (particularly the Arians) who would state that Christ had a beginning. His argument takes this form: "If, then, all things were made by Him, how is it that He who thus bestowed existence on all, could at any period have no existence Himself? ... [A]ll things were made by Him, and were called by Him out of the non-existent into being."[63]

1.1.1.12. Athanasius

In On the Incarnation of the Word Athanasius (c. 293-373 A.D.) rejects certain views of creation,[64] specifically Epicurean (chance or fortuitous generation), Platonic (preexistent matter) and Gnostic (by a demiurge). These, according to

[58] II.9 (ANF, 7:53).
[59] II.9 (ANF, 7:53).
[60] Introduction of Professor Riddle, quoted in ANF, 7:388.
[61] V.1.7 (ANF, 7:441). See a similar statement in VII.2.12: "who didst bring all things out of nothing into being by Thy only begotten Son" (ANF, 7:487).
[62] V.1.7 (ANF, 7:441).
[63] I.3 (NPNF2, 3:36).
[64] In part Athanasius relies upon perception as a valid means of ascertaining truth. In section 2 he appeals to the distinction of the parts of the human body and a distinction between the sun and the moon and the earth in order to postulate a preexistent cause, that is, God (NPNF2, 4:37).

Athanasius, are vain speculations,[65] for "out of nothing, and without its having any previous existence, God made the universe to exist through His word".[66] He (as Origen did) quotes from The Shepherd of Hermas: "First of all believe that God is one, which created and framed all things, and made them to exist out of nothing."[67] Later in On the Incarnation of the Word Athanasius states that Christ "at the beginning also made all things out of nought".[68] In his Against the Arians Athanasius states that "the things originated had not the power of being eternal. For they are out of nothing [ἐξ οὐκ ὄντων, ex ouk ontōn], and therefore were not before their origination".[69]

### 1.1.1.13. Gregory

Gregory of Nyssa (d. c. 395 A.D.) affirms that "the creation was not in the beginning, and was not with God, and was not God".[70] Matter and its qualities were created by God the Word,[71] and the "Divine will [is] a sufficient cause to the things that are, for their coming into existence out of nothing".[72] Finally, "the universe", asserts Gregory, "took being from nothing".[73]

### 1.1.1.14. Hilary

In his On the Trinity Hilary of Poitiers (d. c. 367 A.D.) quotes 2 Maccabees 7.28, stating, "For all things, as the prophet says, were made out of nothing[74]; it was no transformation of existing things, but the creation into a perfect form of the non-existent."[75] Later in this same work he writes, "all things were made out of nothing".[76] Hilary goes to great philosophical and biblical lengths to establish the eternity of God alone and the origin of all things in time. He does

---

[65] On the Incarnation of the Word, section 3 (NPNF2, 4:37).

[66] On the Incarnation of the Word, section 3 (NPNF2, 4:37).

[67] On the Incarnation of the Word, section 3 (NPNF2, 4:37).

[68] On the Incarnation of the Word, section 20 (NPNF2, 4:47).

[69] I.8.29 (NPNF2, 4:323). As for the soul, Athanasius viewed it as created by God. Referring to Genesis 1.26 he writes, "For the soul is made after the image of God, as divine Scripture also shows, when it says in the person of God: 'Let us make man after our Image and likeness'" (Against the Heathen, II.34 [NPNF2, 4:22]).

[70] Against Eunomius, VIII.5 (NPNF2, 5:208).

[71] Against Eunomius, II.7 (NPNF2, 5:111).

[72] On the Making of Man, XXIII.5 (NPNF2, 5:414). Gregory specifically rejects transmigration of souls (On the Soul and the Resurrection [NPNF2, 5:453-55], On the Making of Man, XXVIII.1-8 [NPNF2, 5:419-20]), and answers with his doctrine of both body and soul coming into existence at the same time (On the Making of Man, XIX.1-3 [NPNF2, 5:420-21]).

[73] On the Making of Man, XXIII.5 (NPNF2, 5:414).

[74] The Greek of 2 Maccabees 7.28 reads οὐκ ἐξ ὄντων ἐποίησεν (ouk ex ontōn epoiēsen).

[75] On the Trinity, IV.16 (NPNF2, 9:76).

[76] On the Trinity, V.4 (NPNF2, 9:86).

this in the context of refuting heretics' views of the Son coming into being in time, which they based upon Proverbs 8.22. Speaking of the creation, "things existing in time", Hilary asserts, "cannot possibly be fitted to indicate eternity".[77] Citing Psalm 33.6 ("By the word of the Lord were the heavens established, and all their power by the breath of His mouth"), he further argues that creation came not "from the blending and commingling of some kind of matter, but from the breath of the mouth of God".[78]

1.1.1.15. Ambrose

Ambrose (c. 339-397 A.D.), posing a question, the answer to which is God, states, "Who commanded the world to come into being out of no matter and no substance? Look at the heaven, behold the earth ... But if God made all these things out of nothing (for 'He spake and they were made, He commanded and they were created' [Ps. 148.5]), why should we wonder".[79]

1.1.1.16. Augustine

In his Confessions Augustine (354-430 A.D.) argues for formless matter being created ex nihilo; from this formless matter God made all things. This doctrine of world-formation Augustine addresses somewhat in Books XI[80] and XIII,[81] but it is in Book XII that we find a lengthy treatment of the issue. I include now some statements from this Book. "[B]efore Thou didst form and separate this formless matter, there was nothing".[82] "Why, therefore, may I not consider the formlessness of matter—which Thou hadst created without shape, whereof to make this shapely world ... ?"[83] "[O]ut of nothing didst Thou create heaven and earth."[84] "Thou, O Lord, hast made the world of a formless matter, which matter, out of nothing."[85] Finally, matter "is preceded by the eternity of the Creator, so that there might be out of nothing that from which something might be made".[86]

---

[77] XII.37 (NPNF2, 9:227).
[78] On the Trinity, XII.39 (NPNF2, 9:228).
[79] On Belief in the Resurrection, II.64 (NPNF2, 10:184). Ambrose also rejects the doctrine of transmigration of souls (On Belief in the Resurrection, II.65,127-31 [NPNF2, 10:184,195-96]). In this same work it is implied that human bodies and souls have a beginning (II.64-65 [NPNF2, 10:184]).
[80] Philip Schaff, ed., The Nicene and Post-Nicene Fathers, first series (reprint, Grand Rapids, Mich.: Wm. B. Eerdmans Publishing Company, 1974), 1:165-66 (Confessions, XI.5.7, 6.8). Noted from hereon as NPNF.
[81] XIII.2.3, 3.4 (NPNF, 1:190-91). See also XIII.23.48 (NPNF, 1:206).
[82] XII.3.3 (NPNF, 1:176).
[83] XII.4.4 (NPNF, 1:177).
[84] XII.7.7 (NPNF, 1:177).
[85] XII.8.8 (NPNF, 1:178).
[86] XII.29.40 (NPNF, 1:188). See also The City of God, XII.25 (NPNF, 2:243). Whether considering his earlier creatiani view (wherein the soul of each human was created

Augustine also confesses that created things are ontologically distinct from God.[87] In his Concerning the Nature of Good, Against the Manichaeans we read, "God made all things which He did not beget of himself,[88] not of those things that already [that is, eternally] existed, but of those things that did not exist at all, that is, out of nothing."[89] Further, unlike created things, God stands outside of relation to time in the human sense. For Augustine, with God "the whole [of time—past, present and future] is present", unlike the created order, which stands in relation to time.[90] The transcendence of God therefore implicitly follows from this concept. Immediately following the confession that God stands outside any relation to time, Augustine addresses the hypothetical question, "What was God doing before He made heaven and earth?"[91] Augustine answers that since God is the creator of all times, and before the universe was created "there was no time", the question "What did God do then" is moot, "for there was no 'then' when time was not".[92] Further, "Neither do you [God] by time precede time."[93] The implication of the above points is as follows: If all created things stand in relation to time and God is the creator of all times, there is therefore no "time" (which can only exist if created) in relation to God prior to the creation of time. The above question, therefore, does not apply. Further, God therefore had to exist prior to the creation of time, and consequently all created things. Therefore God is other than his creation.

---

afresh by God out of nothing), or his later traduciani view (wherein from the soul of the first man Adam [created out of nothing] the soul is passed on by parental descent), Augustine taught that the human soul was created by God (Confessions, XII.20 [NPNF, 1:183]). In his On the Soul and its Origin, written against the Pelagians, Augustine asserts that the human soul is created by God "out of nothing" and "not out of Him". That is, the soul is not of the substance of God (I.4 [NPNF, 5:316-17]). For the two views, see the note by J. G. Pilkington (NPNF, 1:183) and an "Extract from Augustine's Retractions" (NPNF, 5:310).

[87] Confessions, VII.11.17 (NPNF, 1:110).

[88] Augustine strictly forbids creatio ex deo (see also Confessions, XII.7.7 [NPNF, 1:177] and Concerning the Nature of Good, Against the Manichaeans, chapter 27 [NPNF, 4:357]).

[89] Chapter 26 (NPNF, 4:356). Augustine cites Romans 4.17, 11.36 and Psalm 148.5 for proof of his position. The human soul / spirit also is not of the substance of God (On the Soul and Its Origin, 1.4 [NPNF, 5:316], II.4 [NPNF, 5:332], III.3 [NPNF, 5:344]), was created out of nothing (On the Soul and Its Origin, I.4 [NPNF, 5:316-17]), and therefore had no existence prior to birth (On the Soul and Its Origin, II.10{VI} [NPNF, 5:335], II.11{VII} [NPNF, 5:336], II.12{VIII} [NPNF, 5:336], III.9{VII} [NPNF, 5:347], III.10 [NPNF, 5:347]).

[90] Confessions, XI.11.13 (NPNF, 1:167).

[91] Confessions, XI.12.14 (NPNF, 1:167).

[92] Confessions, XI.13.15 (NPNF, 1:168).

[93] Confessions, XI.13.16 (NPNF, 1:168).

## 2. The Biblical Witness

As evidenced in all the above, early church theologians utilized perception, reason and scripture to conclude / defend the doctrine of creatio ex nihilo. In their writings we certainly find appeals to perception and reason standing alone.[94] Yet, as is the case with Śaṅkara and Rāmānuja, scripture was of great importance to the early church. Moreover, it was scripture in the "tradition of the apostles manifested throughout the whole world"[95] that quite often was a central epistemic tool.[96]

In what follows I offer my exegesis of important biblical texts that I and other exegetes / theologians of my tradition take to teach the doctrine of creatio ex nihilo. I also document certain statements and themes of orthodox early

---

[94] I cite two more examples each from Irenaeus and Tertullian. Irenaeus spends the whole of chapter 10 of Book II of Against Heresies refuting the heretics on the grounds of perception and reason. In the quotation cited earlier ("While men, indeed, cannot make anything out of nothing, but only out of matter already existing, yet God is in this point preeminently superior to men, that He Himself called into being the substance of His creation, when previously it had no existence") there is appeal to perception that is inextricably linked to reason toward a conclusion. Immediately after this, Irenaeus comes to the conclusion that the doctrine under discussion "is incredible, infatuated, impossible, and untenable" (ANF, 1:369-70). In chapter 12 of the same, the whole of it (and it is rather lengthy) is spent taking the heretics to logical conclusions that prove their doctrines illogical on their own grounds (ANF, 1:371-73). Tertullian, in Against Hermogenes, will not allow Hermogenes to remain logically consistent in the latter's attempt to teach that matter is co-equal with God while at the same time stating that matter is somehow inferior to God (ANF, 3:479-82 [chapters 5-8]). In refutation of Hermogenes' teaching, Tertullian, relying on perception and reason, states, "Now we lay down this principle, that what is eternal cannot possibly admit of diminution and subjection, so as to be considered inferior to another co-eternal being" (ANF, 3:483 [chapter 11]). In refutation of Hermogenes' doctrine "that Matter was reformed for the better—from a worse condition", thus making "the better a copy of the worse", Tertullian states, "Nobody ever found himself in a barber's looking glass look[ing] like an ass instead of a man" (ANF, 3:500 [chapter 40]).

[95] ANF, 1:415 (Irenaeus, Against Heresies, III.3.1).

[96] Irenaeus states in the preface of Book III in Against Heresies, "I shall adduce proofs from the Scriptures [so that] ... thou mayest receive from me the means of combating and vanquishing those who, in whatever manner, are propagating falsehood" (ANF, 1:414). In the end, states Irenaeus, "these men do now consent neither to Scripture nor to tradition" (ANF, 1:415 [III.2.2]). Tertullian also appeals to scripture and tradition. He states that where there is diversity of doctrine, there must logically be a perversion of the scriptures as well as their expositions. He continues, "[S]o to ourselves also integrity of doctrine could not have been accrued, without integrity in those means by which doctrine is managed. Now, what is there in our Scriptures which is contrary to us? ... What we are ourselves, that also the Scriptures are (and have been) from the beginning. Of them we have our being" (ANF, 3:261-62 [On Prescription against Heretics, chapter 38]).

church theologians up to the time of Augustine.

## 2.1. Genesis 1.1-3

The first three verses of Genesis read על־פני המים [3] ויאמר אלהים יהי אור ויהי־אור את השמים ואת הארץ [2] והארץ היתה תהו ובהו וחשך על־פני תהום ורוח אלהים מרחפת בראשית ברא אלהים (bereshith bara elohim eth hashamayim ve eth ha arets [2] ve ha arets hayethah tohu vabohu vechoshek al-pene tehom veruach elohim merachepheth al-pene hammayim [3] vayomer elohim yehi or vayehi-or). Verse 1 and its precise connection, syntactically (and cosmologically), with verses 2 and 3 has been debated, as have the meanings of certain words in verses 1-3. Where one lands on these issues obviously determines whether one takes verse 1 as communicating creatio ex nihilo or not.

### 2.1.1. SYNTAX

The syntactical issue involves the precise relationship of 1.1 to the next verse(s).[97] Gordon J. Wenham lists four possibilities.[98] First is to understand verse 1 as temporal and in subordination to verse 2, the main clause: "In the beginning when God created ... the earth was without form".[99] Second is to see the relationship of verse 1 as temporal and subordinate to verse 3, the main clause (with verse 2 as parenthetic): "In the beginning when God created ... (now the earth was formless) God said".[100] With the third option (my view) verse 1 serves as a title to the entire chapter and serves also as the main clause that summarizes verses 2-31. Here a translation would read, "In the beginning God created the heavens and the earth." All following verses then supply details for the summary statement. A loose paraphrase of verse 1 and the introduction to verse 2 would read, "In the beginning God created all things. Here is how he did it."[101] The final option, Wenham's view, is to understand verse 1 as "a main clause describing the first act of creation". Verses 2 and 3

---

[97] Writing of the introductory verses of Genesis, Speiser states, "syntax determines the meaning, and the precise meaning of this passage happens to be of far-reaching significance" (E. A. Speiser, Genesis [Garden City, N.Y.: Doubleday, 1964], 11-12).

[98] The following options and quotations are taken from Gordon J. Wenham, Genesis 1-15, Word Biblical Commentary (Waco, Tex.: Word, 1987), 11.

[99] Wenham (Genesis 1-15, 11) mentions the medieval Jewish scholar Ibn Ezra as the first to promote this view. This view, states Wenham, "has attracted little support since, apart from Gross (VTSup 32 [1981] 131-45)".

[100] As viewed by the medieval Jewish interpreter Rashi and modern scholars such as Bauer, Bayer, Herrmann, Humbert, Lane, Loretz, Skinner, and Speiser (list taken from Wenham, Genesis 1-15, 12).

[101] The view taken by Driver, Gunkel, Procksch, Zimmerli, von Rad, Eichrodt, Cassuto, Schmidt, Westermann, Beauchamp, and Steck (taken from Wenham, Genesis 1-15, 12).

then "describe subsequent phases in God's creative activity".[102]

In all four options the central concern is the syntactical function of the introductory waw (ו, v) of verse 2 or verse 3. With option one the waw of verse 2 introduces something simultaneous with the idea of verse 1.[103] In option two the same idea of simultaneity occurs, though this time the waw of verse 3 functions to introduce something simultaneous with idea of verse 1, with the waw in verse 2 being explanatory.[104] With option three the waw of verse 2 is initial, introducing the beginning of a long section that places certain details upon the title (v. 1) of the chapter (in this sense it may be understood as an explanatory waw). Option four sees the waws of verses 2 and 3 as initial, but introducing, each in turn, an event subsequent to the first creative act of verse 1.[105]

### 2.1.2. Cultural Background and Overall Biblical, Theological Context

In order to offer a plausible option that Genesis 1.1-3 teaches creatio ex nihilo, I consider the theological underpinnings of the Old Testament and the New Testament as a whole. This of course includes consideration of extra-biblical cosmologies and cosmogonies as background to the text as well as other statements made in the Old Testament and in the New Testament.[106] In turn this implies that I presuppose the Bible as a coherent whole and that interpretation of Genesis 1.1-3 should proceed along this line.

Against the cosmological and cosmogonical grain of the surrounding nations, Israel's God did not come into being through a process involving "the chaotic primordial ground of the universe".[107] Theogony was not part of the theology of the Old Testament. Indeed, Israel was commanded to view its God as alone existing in the beginning, as is evidenced by Isaiah 41.4b: "I, the Lord,[108] am the first, and with the last; I am he."[109] The idea here is the sole

---

[102] Modern interpreters holding this view are Wellhausen, König, Heidel, Kidner, Ridderbos, Young, Childs, Hasel, Gispen, and Notter (Wenham, Genesis 1-15, 13).

[103] See E. Kautzsch, ed., Gesenius' Hebrew Grammar (Oxford: Oxford University Press, 1985), 501.

[104] Or parenthetical or interruptive. See Bruce K. Waltke and M. O'Connor, An Introduction to Biblical Hebrew Syntax (Winona Lake, Ind.: Eisenbrauns, 1990), 649.

[105] Wenham mentions that this view, wherein "a god first created matter, the primeval ocean, and then organized it, has many Egyptian parallels".

[106] Irenaeus, in the context of God not being "in need of other instruments for the creation of those things which are summoned into existence", thus implying creatio ex nihilo, cites John 1.3, Psalms 33.9 and 148.5, and Genesis 1.1 (Against Heresies, II.2.5 [ANF, 1:361-62]).

[107] Walther Eichrodt, Theology of the Old Testament, trans. J. A. Baker (Philadelphia: Westminster, 1967), 2:99.

[108] I translate Lord (with "small caps") from the Hebrew יהוה, YHVH.

[109] אני יהוה ראשון ואת־אחרנים אני־הוא (ani YHVH rishon ve eth-acheronim ani-hu).

existence of יהוה (YHVH, the LORD) over against any other powers (see Isa. 44.6,8). Irenaeus develops this theme in his Against Heresies. Writing of "God, the Creator, who made the heaven and the earth, and all things that are therein", he claims that there is no power higher than he is, nor is there a power after him, clearly implying God's sole existence from all eternity before "commanding all things into existence".[110] Further, Walther Eichrodt points out that in the context of covenant, where YHVH "is the central and uniquely powerful figure",[111] Israel's strict monotheism is set apart from the polytheisms of the surrounding nations. Noteworthy is that in various other cosmogonies and cosmologies gods come into being through some sort of cosmic process in league with eternally preexisting matter, and that the objects of the world are formed from these as well.[112]

Thus it is that some have viewed the opening verses of Genesis as a polemic against the creation myths of surrounding nations,[113] particularly as recorded in the Babylonian creation account, Enūma eliš. Here the primordial Apsu and Mummu-Tiamat, from their waters, beget all the gods.[114] The words enūma eliš are actually the first words of this creation epic, meaning "When on high",[115] corresponding to the traditional way to title Genesis, בראשית (bereshith, "In the beginning"). Mark F. Rooker points out that numerous scholars have observed that no other cosmology of the ancient Near East opens with such words as the Hebrew "in the beginning God created". He then asks why this is so. "Part of the answer", he states, "surely lies in the fact that these mythologies all assume preexisting matter when the god(s) begin to create".[116] On this latter point we observe that in Enūma eliš Apsu and Tiamat[117] serve as the preexistent material from which all things were created. It is interesting that Proverbs 8.22-24 talks of wisdom existing from all eternity, and that wisdom, possessed by YHVH, existed "when there were no deeps" (באין־תהמות, be en-tehomoth), the point

[110] ANF, 1:359 (Against Heresies, II.1.1).

[111] Theology of the Old Testament, 2:98.

[112] Theology of the Old Testament, 2:98.

[113] See, for example, Gerhard F. Hasel, "The Polemic Nature of the Genesis Cosmology", Evangelical Quarterly 46 (1974): 81-102.

[114] James B. Pritchard, ed., Ancient Near Eastern Texts Relating to the Old Testament (Princeton: Princeton University Press, 1969), 61-62.

[115] Pritchard, Ancient Near Eastern Texts, 60.

[116] Mark F. Rooker, "Genesis 1:1-3: Creation or Recreation?" Bibliotheca Sacra 149 (October-December): 423,424.

[117] There is and has been debate over whether or not the Hebrew תהום (tehom, "the waters" of Gen. 1.2) is cognate to Tiamat. See Wenham, Genesis 1-15, 16. David Toshio Tsumura argues "that it is phonologically impossible to conclude that tĕhôm 'ocean' was borrowed from Tiamat" ("Genesis and Ancient Near Eastern Stories of Creation and Flood", in Richard S. Hess and David Toshio Tsumura, eds., I Studied Inscriptions from before the Flood: Ancient Near Eastern, Literary, and Linguistic Approaches to Genesis 1-11 [Winona Lake, Ind.: Eisenbrauns, 1994], 31).

being that YHVH alone existed "in the beginning".

In the hope to show that it is a plausible option to see creatio ex nihilo in the Bible, other biblical and biblically related texts that I and other Christians of my tradition utilize in conjunction with Genesis 1.1-3 now come to the fore, such as John 1.1,3, to which I now turn.[118]

2.1.2.1. John 1.1,3

The NC reads in part, "And in one Lord Jesus Christ ... by [or through] whom all things became" (δι᾽ οὗ τὰ πάντα ἐγένετο, di' hou ta panta egeneto). When this latter phrase, and note especially the verb egeneto, is read in the light of John 1.1,3, there are plausible grounds for creatio ex nihilo. In John 1.1,3 we read ἐν ἀρχῇ ἦν ὁ λόγος, καὶ ὁ λόγος ἦν πρὸς τὸν θεόν, καὶ θεὸς ἦν ὁ λόγος ... πάντα δι᾽ αὐτοῦ ἐγένετο, καὶ χωρὶς αὐτοῦ ἐγένετο οὐδὲ ἕν ὃ γέγονεν (en archē ēn ho logos, kai ho logos ēn pros ton theon, kai theos ēn ho logos ... panta di' autou egeneto, kai chōris autou egeneto oude hen ho yegonen): "In the beginning was the Word, and the Word was with God, and the Word was God ... All things were made through / by him, and without him not one thing was made that came into being."

The first phrase, "in the beginning", is identical to the opening of Genesis in the LXX, placing John 1.1 in the context of "the beginning". The use of the imperfect active indicative ἦν (ēn), occurring in the first clause of John 1.1 as well as in each of the following clauses, signifies past tense with continuous action. I argue this on both grammatical and contextual grounds. First, grammatically, viewing the imperfect active as past tense with continuous action is certainly an option. Second, and perhaps most important, contextual method on the part of the Gospel of John lends weight to this interpretation of the imperfect ēn. That is, viewing the prologue of the Gospel (1.1-18) as a snapshot of the whole, subsequent portions of the Gospel then function as a commentary to, or illustration of, the themes in the prologue. John 8.58 is a illustrative commentary on 1.1,3, and the theological theme I wish to pursue is "God always existed – everything else came into being."

In John 1.1,3 the stark differentiation between the verbs εἰμί (eimi, "I am", from which ēn comes) in 1.1 and γίνομαι (ginomai, "I become", from which egeneto and gegonen come) in 1.3 is most telling. The logos is associated with eimi (I am), while "all things" (panta) are associated with ginomai, which verb, in Genesis 1 (LXX), is the verb applied to the things that were created.[119]

---

[118] In addition to the following passages, note also Psalm 148.4, where "the waters that are above the heavens" (והמים אשר מעל השמים, ve hammayim asher me al hashamayim) were created (בָּרָא, br') at the command of יהוה (YHVH) (v. 5).

[119] See Genesis 1.3,5,6,8,9, etc. My thanks to Raymond E. Brown for this observation regarding Genesis 1 (The Gospel According to John I-XII [New York: Doubleday, 1966], 6). See also Genesis 2.4: αὕτη ἡ βίβλος γενέσεως οὐρανοῦ καὶ γῆς, ὅτε

Perpetual, eternal existence characterizes the logos, but coming into being characterizes the universe by use of ginomai. This theme is illustrated or commented upon in John 8.58. Here Jesus states πρὶν ᾿Αβραὰμ γενέσθαι [infinitive of ginomai] ἐγὼ εἰμί (prin abraam genesthai egō eimi), "before Abraham came into existence, I am". Abraham "became", but Jesus always existed. The theme of God associated with eimi and everything else associated with ginomai has its background in the Old Testament. Of particular importance is the LXX rendering of Psalm 90.2 (LXX 89.2): πρὸ τοῦ ὄρη γενηθῆναι καὶ πλασθῆναι τὴν γῆν καὶ τὴν οἰκουμένην καὶ ἀπὸ τοῦ αἰῶνος ἕως τοῦ αἰῶνος σὺ εἶ (pro tou horē genēthēnai kai plasthēnai tēn gēn kai tēn oikoumenēn kai apo tou aiōnos heōs tou aiōnos su ei). "Before the mountains came into being, and the earth and the world were formed, from ages to ages you are." With su ei, the second person form of ego eimi, in contrast to genēthēnai, an infinitive of ginomai, the meaning conveyed is that before anything came into being, before anything else, God "is".

In John 1.3 all things came to be through / by the eternally preexistent logos. The preposition dia is understood as a genitive of agency (thus "through" or "by"), wherein the logos is the means (with, of course, the Father and the Spirit in the triune economy, though not expressed here) of the creation of all things, for "apart from him", states the text, "not one thing came to be which came to be".[120]

All the above offer reasons why my tradition confesses that John 1.1-3 implies, strongly, creatio ex nihilo, for all things "became", while the Word who was God always "was".

### 2.1.2.2. Colossians 1.15b-16a

In the context of the doctrine of creation, John 1.3 is reminiscent of Colossians 1.15b-16a[121] ("He is the firstborn [πρωτότοκος, prōtotokos] over all creation [πάσης κτίσεως, pasēs ktiseōs], for by him all things were created [ἐν αὐτῷ ἐκτίσθη τά πάντα, en autō ektisthē ta panta]"), where Jesus is the enthroned one and preeminent one and is confessed as creator. I hope to show that this passage also strongly implies creatio ex nihilo.

Enthronement and preeminence are two shades of meaning to prōtotokos, usually translated "firstborn". Old Testament background affirms enthronement and preeminence. For enthronement, see the LXX of Psalm 88.26 (Heb. 89.28; Eng. 89.27), where the LORD states of David, "I will make him my firstborn

---

ἐγένετο (hautē hē biblos geneseōs ouranou kai gēs, hote egeneto), "this is the book of the generation of heaven and earth, when it [they] became".

120 See Clement of Alexandria, Paedagosus, 1.7. Speaking of Jesus, Clement states, "without whom nothing was" (ANF, 2:224). See also III.5 (ANF, 2:279), and his Stromata, VI.7 (ANF, 2:493) and VI.16 (ANF, 2:513).

121 As are Acts 14.15 (cf. Exod. 20.11), Revelation 4.11, 10.6 (cf. Exod. 20.11) and 14.7. See note 6.

[prōtotokos, Heb. בכור, bekor], the highest of the kings of the earth." In this enthronement motif clause B parallels and enhances clause A. Thus, God, in making David his firstborn, enthrones David over all kings. For preeminence, see Exodus 4.22 wherein the LORD claims, "Israel is my firstborn [prōtotokos, Heb. bekor]." The choice of Israel over Egypt (and, implied, all nations) makes Israel preeminent. The interpretation that Jesus is the firstborn "over all creation" is therefore plausible for Colossians 1.15. In light of the enthronement and preeminence of Christ, I translate pasēs ktiseōs as a genitive of rank. Absolute lordship over all creation, which would be less probable if matter were co-eternal with him, is the idea. In verse 16 (as in John 1.3) Jesus is the focal point in the creation of all things[122] by the triune God. The Greek en autō ektisthē ta panta I translate "by him all things were created". Here en autō is a dative of means, due in part to the passive ektisthē that follows. This is virtually the same as that which is confessed in the NC: "By whom all things became."

2.1.2.3. Hebrews 11.3

The text reads as follows: πίστει νοοῦμεν κατηρτίσθαι τοὺς αἰῶνας ῥήματι θεοῦ, εἰς τὸ μὴ ἐκ φαινομένον τὸ βλεπόμενον γεγονέναι (pistei nooumen katērtisthai tous aiōnas rhēmati theou, eis to mē ek phainomenon to blepomenon gegonenai). "By faith we understand that the universe was fitted by the word of God, so that what is seen has not come from any visible phenomena." Though not a specific assertion of creatio ex nihilo, "that is practically what is implied", observes F. F. Bruce.[123] Bruce further states concerning this verse,

> Thus "the visible came forth from the invisible" (NEB) ... Greek speculation about the formation of the ordered world out of formless matter had influenced Jewish thinkers like Philo and the author of the Book of Wisdom; the writer to the Hebrews is more biblical in his reasoning and affirms the doctrine of creatio ex nihilo, a doctrine uncongenial to Greek thought. The faith by which he accepts it is faith in

---

[122] Note the remark of Hilary of Poitiers: "All things were created in Him and through Him [most likely referring to Col. 1.16] ... Again, nothing that was made in Him was made without Him" (On the Trinity, II.20 [NPNF2, 9:57]).

[123] F. F. Bruce, The Epistle to the Hebrews (Grand Rapids, Mich.: Wm. B. Eerdmans, 1964), 281. Athanasius cites Hebrews 11.3 in order to place scriptural authority on his doctrine of creatio ex nihilo (On the Incarnation of the Word, section 3 [NPNF2, 4:37]). See also Gregory of Nyssa, On the Making of Man, XXIII.1,3 (NPNF2, 5:413), where he cites Hebrews 11.3 in the context of creation having a beginning, and later claims,

> For in that case too, argumentative men might by plausible reasoning upset our faith, so that we should not think that statement true which Holy Scripture delivers concerning the material creation, when it asserts that all existing things have their beginning of being from God. For those who abide by the contrary view maintain that matter is co-eternal with God.

> the divine revelation; the first chapter of Genesis is probably uppermost in his mind ...[124]

Note also that it is by the "word of God" that the universe comes into being (not through any preexisting matter[125]), recalling Psalm 33.6 ("By the word of יהוה [YHVH] the heavens were made [עשה, 'sh]")[126] and Psalm 148.4-5,7.[127] On this latter passage, of interest is that "the waters" (המים, hamayim) are commanded to praise YHVH (v. 4) "because He commanded and they were created [ברא, br']" (v. 5). In verse 7 people are commanded to praise YHVH "from the earth ... and all deeps [תהמות, tehomoth]". Here תהם (tehom), the word for "deep" in Genesis 1.2, is listed among a somewhat long list of created things (vv. 7-12) that are to praise YHVH "because his name alone is exalted"

---

[124] The Epistle to the Hebrews, 281.

[125] Gregory of Nyssa writes, "God, when creating all things that have their origin by creation, neither stood in need of any matter on which to operate, nor of instruments to aid Him in His construction" (Against Eunomius, II.7 [NPNF2, 5:111]). By stating that God was not in need of any instruments in His act of creation, Gregory does not mean that Christ was excluded, for he proceeds in this very section to assert that the Word of John 1 took part in creation.

[126] "Word theology" was a part of several early church theologians' cosmogonies. Though not in the context of discussing Hebrews 11.3, it is with Psalm 33.6 that Irenaeus develops his Word theology, wherein the Word of God, the logos, takes part in the creation process. In his Against Heresies, I.22.1 (ANF, 1:347), he states "the rule of truth which we hold ... that there is one God Almighty, who made all things by His Word, and fashioned and formed, out of that which had no existence, all things which exist". He follows immediately with quotations from Psalm 33.6 and John 1.3. See also Against Heresies, II.2.5 (ANF, 1:361-62), III.8.3 (ANF, 1:421), and IV.32.1 (ANF, 1:506). Theophilus expounds a Word theology in his Theophilus to Autolycus, II.10 (ANF, 2:97-98), as do Origen in De Principiis, IV.1.30 (ANF, 4:377), Hippolytus in Against the Heresy of One Noetus, section 13 (ANF, 5:228), Cyprian in The Treatises of Cyprian, Treatise XII, Second Book, Testimonies, 3 (ANF, 5:516), Novatian in A Treatise of Novatian concerning the Trinity, chapter 17 (ANF, 5:626-27), Lactantius in his The Divine Institutes, IV.8-9 (ANF, 7:107), Victorinus in On the Creation of the World (ANF, 7:342), Eusebius of Caesarea in his Church History, I.2 (NPNF2, 1:82-83), Athanasius in Against the Heathen, III.46 (NPNF2, 4:28-29), To the Bishops of Egypt, II.13 (NPNF2, 4:230), Against the Arians, II.18.31 (NPNF2, 4:364-65) and III.30.61 (NPNF2, 4:429), Gregory of Nyssa in his Against Eunomius, II.7 (NPNF2, 5:111), II.9 (NPNF2, 5:116) and The Great Catechism, chapter 1 (NPNF2, 5:476), Jerome in his Letter to Pammachius against John of Jerusalem, section 15 (NPNF2, 6:432), Ambrose in his Of the Holy Spirit, II.9 (NPNF2, 10:127), III.11 (NPNF2, 10:147), Of the Christian Faith, IV.4.46-47 (NPNF2, 10:268), and Augustine in Confessions, XI.7-9 (NPNF, 1:165-66) and Acts or Disputation against Fortunatus the Manichaean, "First Day", section 13 (NPNF, 4:116).

[127] Ambrose cites this text in the context of creatio ex nihilo (On the Resurrection, II.64 [NPNF2, 10:184]).

(v. 13b). The implication here is not only that the tehom is itself created and thus not eternally preexistent, but that there is no other power or being that can claim coexistence and cooperation with YHVH in the creative act. Implicitly, if not explicitly, this counters the notion of any preexistent primordial "deep" taking part in creation. Though it is not possible to determine with certainty that the writer of Hebrews had these texts in mind when writing this phrase, one is able, if one presupposes the Bible as a unified whole, to call upon these Old Testament texts in order to interpret Hebrews 11.3 as setting forth creatio ex nihilo.

### 2.1.3. Interpretation of Genesis 1.1-3

My interpretation (and the interpretations of some others within my tradition) of Genesis 1.1-3 as teaching creatio ex nihilo does not rest entirely upon the passage itself, but upon the passage in conjunction with what the rest of the canon has to say regarding creation. Therefore in the three previous sections I have examined three other passages. Now I move to my interpretation of Genesis 1.1-3.

My view of Genesis 1.1 (stated earlier in passing in section 2.1.1) is that it serves partly as a title and partly as a summary statement. Verses 2 and 3 (and the following verses) then function to supply certain details to the title / summary statement. It is important that the verse serves not only as a title, but also as an integral part of the text. With this I wish to guard against the text starting, in actuality, with verse 2, which might therefore diminish the import of בראשית (bereshith), ברא (bara), and השמימ ואת הארצ (hashamayim ve eth ha arets).

#### 2.1.3.1. "In the Beginning"

The phrase בראשית (bereshith) is absolute, that is, "In the beginning (when all that is was created[128])." Some have noted the lack of the definite article following the preposition ב (be) and have concluded that verse 1 should be understood as a construct[129] and therefore not in the absolute sense, and some have noted that the current vocalization of בראשית, namely בְּרֵאשִׁית (bereshith), makes the phrase a construct and a dependent clause. Thus the assertion is that verse 1 should start with "When" and not "In the beginning", for the latter would translate from the Hebrew בָּרֵאשִׁית (bareshith), a vocalization not found

---

[128] Origen interprets this first phrase as "before all things" (De Principiis, II.9.1 [ANF, 4:290]). See also III.6.8 (ANF, 4:347-48). Gregory of Nyssa states that the creation starts "from a manifest beginning", whereas God does not (Against Eunomius, I.26 [NPNF2, 5:69]). The same is implied in Irenaeus (Against Heresies, II.28.3 [ANF, 1:400]) and Ambrose (Of the Holy Spirit, II.1 [NPNF2, 10:115], On the Mysteries, chapter 3 [NPNF2, 10:318]).

[129] See Wenham, Genesis 1-15, 12.

in the text.[130] Against these two arguments, and thus in defense of an absolute reading of bereshith, it is possible that an anarthrous construction be understood as absolute and thus not in the construct state, such as found, for example, in Isaiah 46.10, where we read מגיד מראשית אחרית (maggid mereshith acharith, "Declaring the end before the beginning"). Here the vocalized mereshith lacks the article, as do other temporal phrases (see Isa. 40.21; 41.4,26; Gen. 3.22; 6.3,4; Mic. 5.1; Hab. 1.12)[131] not necessarily understood as constructs and possessing the sense of an absolute beginning.[132] Finally, Sailhamer comments that ראשית (reshith) carries in biblical Hebrew the sense of "a starting point of specific duration as in 'the beginning of the year' (rē'šîṯ haššānāh; Deut 11:12) ... In opening the account of Creation with the phrase 'in the beginning' ... the author has marked Creation as the starting point of a period of time".[133]

2.1.3.2. "God Created[134] the Heavens and the Earth"

The text says nothing about God creating out of eternally preexistent (or coexistent) matter;[135] indeed, it is silent on this issue.[136] Though silence does

---

[130] Speiser, Genesis, 12, though Speiser acknowledges the fact that "vocalization alone should not be the decisive factor in this instance. For it could be (and has been) argued that the vocalized text is relatively late and should not therefore be unduly binding" (p. 12).

[131] Wenham, Genesis 1-15, 12. John H. Sailhamer writes, "An example such as Isa 46:10, then, is crucial in that it shows the article is not necessary for the absolute state" (Genesis, in Frank E. Gaebelein, ed., The Expositor's Bible Commentary [Grand Rapids, Mich.: Zondervan, 1990], 2:21).

[132] Speaking of Isaiah 46.10, Wenham states that "it may well have an absolute sense". Wenham continues, "and the analogous expression מראשׁ in Proverbs 8:23 certainly refers to the beginning of all creation. The context of בראשׁית standing at the start of the account of world history makes an absolute sense highly appropriate here" (Genesis 1-15, 12).

[133] Genesis, 20.

[134] The LXX reads ποιέω (poieō) here and for all occurrences (11) of ברא (br') in Genesis (John William Wevers, Notes on the Greek Text of Genesis [Atlanta: Scholars Press, 1993], 1). However, note that in Genesis 14.19,22 the LXX renders קנה (qnh, in the phrase "possessor of heaven and earth") as κτίζω (ktizō). Brown-Driver-Briggs lists "create" as the meaning of qnh in Genesis 14.19,22 (Francis Brown, S. R. Driver, and Charles A. Briggs, The New Brown-Driver-Briggs-Gesenius Hebrew and English Lexicon: With an Appendix Containing the Biblical Aramaic [Peabody, Mass.: Hendrikson, 1979], p. 888).

[135] Speiser, Genesis, 13. Gregory of Nyssa explains, "For 'God said', [Moses] tells us, 'Let there be light, and there was light' ... without any mention either of matter or of any instrumental agency" (Against Eunomius, II.7 [NPNF2, 5:111]).

[136] Wenham, Genesis 1-15, 14. Augustine, however, interprets the phrase "heaven and earth" as formless matter due to verse 2, where it states that "the earth was invisible and without form" (Augustine translation in Confessions, XII.12.15 [NPNF, 1:179]). See

not mean that the text lacks the implication of creation out of eternally preexistent matter, this silence may be more important than might be assumed, for its very silence in the crowd of ancient Near Eastern cosmological voices that shout creation from preexistent matter should be noted. Nahum M. Sarna writes, "Precisely because of the indispensable importance of preexisting matter in the pagan cosmologies, the very absence of such mention here is highly significant. This conclusion is reinforced by the idea of creation by divine fiat without reference to any inert matter being present."[137]

Appealing to ברא (br') alone will not suffice for proving creatio ex nihilo, for br' is not a word that is exclusively reserved for creation of the heavens and the earth; it is used, for example, for the creation of Israel (Isa. 43.15).[138] Coming to the conclusion of creatio ex nihilo involves appeal to other ancient Near Eastern texts (Sarna and von Rad[139]) and biblical texts / theological themes in conjunction with Genesis 1.1-3. In addition to Sarna's observation above (and von Rad's in n. 139), I add the following. First, God alone is eternal but all things came into existence. This I discussed in the exegesis of John 1.1,3. Further, Psalm 90.2 (LXX 89.2), which I addressed in combination with John 1.1,3 and 8.58, implies that creation came into existence but God existed eternally. Second, the phrase "heavens and earth" is idiomatic of "everything".[140] Thus, though in Genesis 1.2,3 and following we find

---

also XII.8.8 (NPNF, 1:178), XII.13.16 (NPNF, 1:180), and XII.29.40 (NPNF, 1:188). In this latter citation we read that "the matter of things was first made, and called heaven and earth". Augustine's interpretation therefore does not set Genesis 1.1 as a title and summary statement, after which the following verses supply details of the title / summary statement. Rather, he views the relationship between the first three verses as an order of events beginning with verse 1.

137 Nahum M. Sarna, Genesis, JPS Torah Commentary (Philadelphia: Jewish Publication Society, 1989), 5. I am indebted to Rooker for this quote ("Genesis 1:1-3: Creation or Recreation?", 418).

138 Wenham, Genesis 1-15, 14.

139 "It is correct to say that the verb 'bārā', 'create', contains the idea both of complete effortlessness and creatio ex nihilo, since it is never connected with any statement of the material ... It is amazing to see how sharply little Israel demarcated herself from an apparently overpowering environment of cosmological and theogonic myths" (Gerhard von Rad, Genesis, trans. John H. Marks [London: SCM Press, 1963], 47). In this sentence "little" is not an adverb but an adjective, thus "little Israel". Tsumura calls "the creation by divine fiat in Genesis unique in the ancient Near East", and further states that "the creation in the Genesis story is quite different from the idea of 'order out of chaos', though the latter is often called 'creation'" ("Genesis and Ancient Near Eastern Stories of Creation and Flood", 31-32).

140 Wenham, Genesis 1-15, 15. Wenham points his readers to J. Krašovec, Der Merismus im Biblisch-Hebräischen und Nordwestsemitischen, Biblica et orientalia 33 (Rome: Biblical Institute Press, 1977), 16-25.

"organization",[141] it is possible to conclude that Genesis 1.1 is interested in claiming that everything came into being by God.[142]

### 2.1.3.3. "Now[143] the Earth Was Empty, That Is, Unproductive and Uninhabited[144]"

I have here followed Tsumura, who states,

> The expression tōhû wābōhû, which is traditionally translated in English as "without form and void" (RSV) or the like, is often taken as signifying the primeval "chaos", in direct opposition to "creation".[145] I have

---

[141] Not organization of eternally preexistent materials. In my view "organization", especially in Genesis 1.3-31, involves (in addition to creatio ex nihilo) the setting up of the theological paradigm "Rulers over Kingdoms". Here the phenomena listed in day 4 rule over the phenomena of day 1, day 5 over day 2, day 6a (vv. 24-25) over day 3, day 6b (אדם, adam, vv. 26-31) over all the preceding, and in day 7 YHVH rules over all the preceding (2.2). God, then, created out of nothing all the phenomena that make up the rulers and kingdoms and organized the whole into this theological paradigm. It is within this paradigm that I understand the phrase "image of God" (Gen. 1.26-27) to mean rulership. That is, the primary meaning of "image" from this passage is humankind's rulership over the created realm, with YHVH ruling over the entire system. For this interpretation of image, see D. J. Clines, "The Image of God in Man", Tyndale Bulletin 19 (1968): 53-103, especially 80-85. I am indebted to Tsumura, "Genesis and Ancient Near Eastern Stories of Creation and Flood", 34 nn. 39,40, for directing me to this article.

[142] In commenting on Genesis 1.1, Theophilus, in his Theophilus to Autolycus, states, "God created the heavens and the earth, and all that is therein" (II.10 [ANF, 2:98]). His comment on Genesis 1.1-2 involves proclaiming "that matter, from which God made and fashioned the world, was in some manner created, being produced by God" (II.10 [ANF, 2:98]). Athanasius cites Genesis 1.1 to evidence his claim that creation was not out of already existing matter, but out of nothing (On the Incarnation of the Word, section 3 [NPNF2, 4:37]).

[143] The LXX reads δέ (de) which may be taken as contrastive, terminative, or signaling a series of thoughts or events. I opt for the latter understanding of de.

[144] LXX reads ἀόρατος καὶ ἀκατασκεύαστος (aoratos kai akataskeuastos), "unseen and unorganized". In the following clause darkness reigned (Wevers, Notes on the Greek Text of Genesis, 1-2), implying that land was not seen, and that it was yet to be organized, a phenomenon that does not occur until verse 3. It might make for an interesting study to view "unorganized" in the light of the thesis in note 141 above.

[145] In De Principiis (IV.1.33 [ANF, 4:379]) Origen writes of those who believe that God shaped the world out of formless matter: "Very many, indeed, are of the opinion that the matter of which things are made is itself signified in the language used by Moses in the beginning of Genesis." He cites Wisdom of Solomon ("a work", states Origen, "which is certainly not esteemed authoritative by all") 11.17 as a text from which those of this opinion come to this conclusion: "For your almighty hand created the world out of formless matter" (ἡ παντοδύναμος σου χεὶρ καὶ κτίσασα τὸν κόσμον ἐξ ἀμόρφου ὕλης, hē pantodunamos sou cheir kai ktisasa ton kosmon ex amorphou hulēs). It

> demonstrated, however, that the phrase tōhû wābōhû has nothing to do with primeval chaos; it simply means 'emptiness' and refers to the earth in a "bare" state, without vegetation and animals as well as without humans. This "unproductive and empty, uninhabited" earth becomes productive with vegetation and inhabited by animals and humankind by God's fiats.[146]

In another article, but still as proof of the above, Tsumura suggests that the Ugaritic thw may be a better choice for a cognate of תהו (tohu), and gives an example of a Ugaritic text using thw, which is translated "desert(s)". The text translates, "And my appetite is an appetite of the lion(s) in/of the desert [thw]."[147] He then proceeds to offer the Arabic bahiya, "used to describe the 'empty' or 'vacant' state of a tent or house which contains nothing or little furniture or goods",[148] as a possible cognate to בהו (bohu), in the light of the lack of definite etymologies from ancient Akkadian and / or Phoenician and / or Egyptian languages.[149]

If Tsumura is correct, the view that Genesis 1.2 speaks of a primordial or primeval chaos is incorrect.[150] Tsumura lists Westermann's three groups of meanings for tohu. The word appears twenty times in the Old Testament and can mean (1) "desert" or "wasteland" (Deut. 32.10; Job 6.18, 12.24; Ps. 107.40), (2a) the threat of devastation from which a "desert-like state" results (Isa. 24.10, 34.11, 40.23, 45.19; Jer. 4.23), (2b) a state opposing and preceding creation (Gen. 1.2; Isa. 45.18; Job 26.7), and (3) "nothingness" in the sense of lack of something (1 Sam. 12.21 [2x]; Isa. 29.21, 40.17, 41.29, 44.9, 49.4,

---

appears, however, that Jerome holds to a primeval chaos (though not necessarily eternal) from which the Spirit produced "the infant world". This statement is couched in an explanation of the gloomy depths of Genesis 1.2 in order to set forth an explanation of Christian baptism. The production of the form of the earth from the gloomy depths, writes Jerome, is "a type of the Christian child that is drawn from the laver of baptism" (Letter LXIX,To Oceanus, section 6 [NPNF2, 6:145]). See also Jerome's The Dialogue against the Luciferians, section 6 (NPNF2, 6:322), where Genesis 1.2 (where the Spirit moves over the surface of the waters) is cited to show that the Spirit is involved in Christian baptism.

146 "Genesis and Ancient Near Eastern Stories of Creation and Flood", 33.

147 David Toshio Tsumura, "The Earth in Genesis 1", in Hess and Tsumura, I Studied Inscriptions from before the Flood, 310-11, citing M. Dietrich, O Loretz, and J. Sanmartín, Die keilalphabetische Texte aus Ugarit, 1.5 (corresponding to C. H. Gordon's Ugaritic Textbook 67): 1:14-16.

148 Tsumura cites E. W. Lane's Arabic-English Dictionary, 260,269 and following, for the above meanings.

149 "The Earth in Genesis 1", 313-14,315-16.

150 Sailhamer also challenges the primeval chaos view and opts for the view Tsumura suggests. See Sailhamer, Genesis, 27-28.

59.4).[151] Tsumura disagrees with Westermann's meaning in 2b and suggests alternative understandings of the three texts listed, specifically "a desert-like place" or "an empty place" (that is, "uninhabited").[152]

In addition to Genesis 1.2, tohu and bohu appear in Jeremiah 4.23 and Isaiah 34.11.[153] In Jeremiah, when the phrase is interpreted in the context of 4.23-28, there occurs an inclusio with the words "earth" and "heavens" in verses 23 and 28. In verse 23 "the earth" is תהו ובהו (tohu ve bohu), corresponding to the earth "drying up" (אבל, 'bl, cf. Isa. 24.4) in verse 28. In turn, "the heavens" in verse 23 are "without light", corresponding to the heavens being dark in verse 28. Unproductiveness rather than chaos[154] is the gist. In Isaiah 34.11 tohu and bohu appear in parallelism in the context of God's wrath against nations. On God's day of vengeance (v. 8), "He [the LORD] will extend over it [the land] a line of desolation [tohu] and stones of emptiness [bohu]" (v. 11). The point, once again, is that the land will not be fit to accommodate inhabitants, as is evident in the context of the verses both preceding and following Isaiah 34.11.

In light of the preceding, tohu ve bohu in Genesis 1.2 is understood as the initial act of creation[155] and the earth being bare with no vegetation and creatures, including human beings (see Gen. 2.5), that is,[156] as the second clause of the verse reads, "darkness was over the surface of the deep".[157] Since Genesis 1.6 and subsequent verses imply that water covered the entire earth, I therefore conclude that "unproductiveness" and "non-habitation" in verse 2 are a direct result of this water-covered landmass.[158] Verse 3 then follows with God's divine fiats, which bring forth the several phenomena listed in verses 3-27.[159]

---

[151] Tsumura, "The Earth in Genesis 1", 316.

[152] Tsumura, "The Earth in Genesis 1", 317-18 (for Job 26.7), 318-19 (for Isa. 45.18).

[153] The following information on these two passages comes from Tsumura, "The Earth in Genesis 1", 321-26.

[154] Lactantius writes, "Nor are the poets to be listened to, who say that in the beginning was a chaos, that is, a confusion of matter and the elements ... For they believe that He [God] can produce nothing, except out of materials already existing" (The Divine Institutes, II.9 [ANF, 7:53]).

[155] "[T]he context suggests that this was the initial state of the created earth rather than a state brought about as a result of God's judgment on the earth or land (cf. Jer 4.23; Isa 34.11)" (Tsumura, "The Earth in Genesis 1", 327).

[156] See the next note.

[157] "That is" because Genesis 1.2a ("the earth was unproductive, uninhabited") is synonymously paralleled by (and enhanced by) 1.2b ("darkness was over the surface of the deep").

[158] See Tsumura, "Genesis and Ancient Near Eastern Stories of Creation and Flood", 28-29,33.

[159] It is in this way that I understand Isaiah 45.18, which reads "He [God] did not create it [the earth] to be empty [tohu], but formed it to be inhabited [לשבת, lashebeth]."

### 2.1.3.4. Summary

Interpreted in cultural and overall biblical contexts, it is plausible that the opening verse of Genesis implies creatio ex nihilo. Genesis 1.1 serves both as a title to the chapter and summary statement. In the absolute beginning[160] God created everything (ex nihilo).[161] Verse 2 then follows with an explanatory waw, that is, verse 2 begins a long list of details explaining the summary statement. With verse 2 we find that the earth is in a bare, empty state with no vegetation or creatures. Verse 3 then begins to list all the phenomena that God, by his divine decree, establishes upon the earth[162] and in the heavens.[163]

## 3. Summary and Conclusion

Several theologians before, during and after the formulation of the NC stood upon the doctrinal platform of creatio ex nihilo. The phrases of the NC, specifically "I believe in one God the Father almighty, maker of heaven and earth" and "And in one Lord Jesus Christ ... by whom all things were made", should therefore be interpreted within the framework of creatio ex nihilo. Further, the general consensus of the early church was that human souls were created out of nothing, for "all things" includes all human souls.

In this chapter I offered my exegesis of Genesis 1.1-3 and several other pertinent, related texts. Presupposing the Bible as a coherent whole, the related texts served to aid my interpretation of Genesis 1.1-3 teaching creatio ex nihilo. Several early church theologians also interpreted Genesis 1.1-3 as setting forth

---

160 Hilary of Poitiers writes, "Survey the universe, note well what is written of it, In the beginning God made the heaven and the earth. The word beginning fixes the moment of creation; you can assign its date to an event which is definitely stated to have happened in the beginning" (On the Trinity, II.13 [NPNF2, 9:56]).

161 Augustine views Genesis 1.1-2 as teaching creatio ex nihilo. See, for example, his Confessions, XII.7.7 (NPNF, 1:177).

162 Eusebius of Caesarea embraces this interpretation in his Church History, I.2 (NPNF2, 1:82).

163 Athanasius states, "And what Moses relates, 'Let there be light' ... is, I think, according to what has gone before [II.18.31], significant of the will of the Agent. For things which once were not but happened afterwards from external causes, these the Framer counsels to make" (Against the Arians, III.30.61 [NPNF2, 4:427]). Earlier in Against the Arians (III.30.60 [NPNF2, 4:426]) Athanasius writes that "things originate only, since also by nature these things once were not, but afterwards came to be [ἐπιγέγονε, epigegone]". This occurs in the context of Athanasius claiming that with Christ the scripture states "He was" (John 1.1), perhaps alluding to the contrast between εἰμί (eimi) and γίνομαι (ginomai) that I pointed out in my comments on John 1.1,3. Gregory of Nyssa states, "For thus the mighty Moses in the record of creation instructs us about the Divine power, ascribing the production of each of the objects that were manifested in the creation to the words that bade them be. For 'God said', he tells us, 'Let there be light, and there was light'" (Against Eunomius, II.7 [NPNF2, 5:111]).

creatio ex nihilo.

I consider next the doctrine of the body-soul-divine relation in the person of Christ, a doctrine that finds its foundation in the material outlined in this chapter.

CHAPTER 6

# Incarnation of Christ: Body-Soul-Divine Relation

The last chapter and this chapter contribute to the all-important comparative discussion that follows in chapter 7, for they establish the classical Christian orthodox ground upon which the comparative conclusions of chapter 7 rest.

In this chapter I examine certain significant biblical passages in conjunction with relevant statements from the C and NC in order to explore the issues of the deity and humanity of Christ and the resultant body-soul-divine, human-divine relation in the person of Christ as believed by orthodox early church theologians. I also document in the notes relevant statements from early church theologians, who are representative of orthodoxy, up to the time of Augustine.[1] I do not debate whether the humanity of Christ is a dichotomy or a trichotomy (or neither). Such debate is beyond the scope of this work. What is important for my purpose is (1) whether or not biblical passages in conjunction with the creeds and orthodox early church theologians state that the body and human soul / spirit of Christ are ὁμοούσιος (homoousios, of the same nature or substance) with all human beings, (2) whether or not the body and soul / spirit of Christ originate from material that is ontologically other than God and created ex nihilo, (3) how the human-divine relationship originated, and (4) how the human nature relates to the divine nature.

The council of Nicaea was convened in part to settle whether or not the scriptures confess Jesus as God the Son, and then to explain how Christ as God relates to God the Father.[2] The C attempted to settle the issue of how Christ's two natures related to each other. The C and NC pronounced that Christ is of the same nature (homoousios) as the Father, yet they are two separate persons.

---

[1] Though I do not document exhaustively the influence of the Athanasian Creed upon the C, see the Athanasian Creed, articles 29-37 in Philip Schaff, The Creeds of Christendom: With a History and Critical Notes (New York: Harper and Row, 1931; Grand Rapids, Mich.: Baker Book House, 1985), 2:68-69.

[2] This paragraph, the following paragraph, much of the exegesis of biblical passages, and exploration of theological themes throughout this chapter are taken or adapted from my Knowing Christ in the Challenge of Heresy: A Christology of the Cults, a Christology of the Bible (Lanham, Md.: University Press of America, 1999), with permission from University Press of America. I also assume Pauline authorship for the following three biblical citations, and a traditional view of authorship for other New Testament writings.

By doing so they rejected the Arian position that Christ is of a different nature (ἑτεροούσιος, heteroousios) than the Father, a being who was created by the Father in time.

The general consensus is that the C does not speculate on how the two natures of Christ relate, but only states what should not be confessed, i.e., the two natures are not confused, not changed, not divided, and not separated (the "four negatives"). However, I think it can be shown that to a certain extent the C explains how the two natures relate. For example, the creed states that Christ is "to be acknowledged in two natures ... the distinction of natures being by no means taken away by the union". Here the term "union" (ἕνωσις, henōsis) is chosen in addition to the four negatives. Further, the creed states that "the property of each nature [is] preserved" in this union.

What led to the formation of the C were a number of suggestions from theologians as to the relationship of the two natures of Christ. For example, Apollinaris (d. c. 390 A.D.) held that Jesus did not have a human soul, and that the logos (the divine nature) replaced the human soul in the person of Christ. The Nestorian position[3] held that there were two distinct persons in Jesus, thus ending in a split of the God-man.[4] In the C both these positions were rejected. Additionally, both before and after the C the Monophysite[5] position claimed

---

[3] I phrase it this way because it is not absolutely certain that Nestorius (patriarch of Constantinople in 428 A.D.) himself actually held the position. Many scholars feel Nestorius was not treated fairly, and that his position was orthodox. Nonetheless, I label the position "Nestorianism" with the understanding that whether or not Nestorius taught it, it was still pronounced heretical.

[4] Thus the C's statement (two times, in addition to "one and the same Christ"), "one and the same Son". Hilary of Poitiers confessed Christ as "one and the same person" (On the Trinity, X.22, in Philip Schaff and Henry Wace, eds., The Nicene and Post-Nicene Fathers, second series [reprint, Grand Rapids, Mich.: Wm. B. Eerdmans Publishing Company, 1976], 9:187; noted from hereon as NPNF2), as did Irenaeus (Against Heresies, III.17.4, in Alexander Roberts and James Donaldson, eds., The Ante-Nicene Fathers [reprint, Grand Rapids, Mich.: Wm. B. Eerdmans Publishing Company, 1977], 1:445; noted from hereon as ANF). Augustine writes that "the human nature assumed into real union with the person of the Word of God, that is, of the only Son of God ... [I]n His union to the human nature which He has assumed, He is still properly called the Son of God; for which reason the same person is the Son of God" (Letter CLXIX2.7, in Philip Schaff, ed., The Nicene and Post-Nicene Fathers, first series [reprint, Grand Rapids, Mich.: Wm. B. Eerdmans Publishing Company, 1974], 1:541; noted from hereon as NPNF; see also Enchiridion, chapter 36 [NPNF, 3:249]).

[5] From μόνος (monos) and φύσις (phusis). I speak here of the Monophysitism of Eutyches (c. 380-456 A.D.), who refused to admit two natures after the union, and refused to admit that Jesus was homoousios with humanity according to the manhood. Rather, Eutyches taught that the humanity of Christ was absorbed into His divinity. Though the Monophysites were not called by this specific designation until after the C was formulated, I nonetheless use the term throughout to refer to the Eutychian doctrine

Christ had a single nature, that both deity and humanity were somehow fused into one nature. Here the implication is that Christ is a divinized man and thus not truly human.

The C (the NC confesses portions of the following) confesses Jesus Christ as the Son of God, God the Son. He as God the Son eternally preexisted and then united to his eternal deity a full human nature through the virgin conception and birth, brought about by the agency of God the Holy Spirit. In the one person of Jesus Christ are two natures—God and humanity—each possessed by Christ in their fullness. The two natures of Christ are not confused, changed, divided or separated, but rather are united in one person.

## 1. "Lord Jesus Christ"

Both the C and the NC utilize the phrase κύριος Ἰησοῦς Χριστός (kurios Iēsous Christos), in part to convey the sense of deity.[6] In what follows I offer a few passages from the New Testament that I hope will demonstrate why the C and the NC came to this conclusion.

### 1.1. Romans 10.9,13

These two verses read, "That if you confess with your mouth Jesus as Lord [κύριος, kurios], and believe in your heart that God raised him from the dead, you will be saved ... For 'whoever will call upon the name of the Lord [kurios] will be saved.'" It is possible to conclude here that Paul labels Christ as God the Son. He equates Jesus, whom he calls "kurios" with יהוה (YHVH) in Joel 2.32.[7] Paul states in verse 9 that in order to have eternal life, one must confess Jesus as kurios. He then quotes Joel 2.32: "Everyone who calls upon the name of YHVH will be saved." Here Paul places kurios in place of YHVH in his Old Testament quotation of Joel. What is significant is not necessarily Paul's usage per se of kurios for the Hebrew YHVH,[8] but that Paul, in such close proximity to his labeling of Jesus as kurios in verse 9, would then proceed to quote an Old

of one nature. Also, note that some other Monophysites rejected Eutyches' absorption theory, but still held to only one nature in Christ.

[6] "Lord" denotes Christ's humanity as well, since the "one and the same Son, our Lord Jesus Christ" (NC) is stated to be "truly God and truly man" (NC).

[7] Hebrew text and LXX, 3.5.

[8] This is not surprising given the LXX's rendering of YHVH as kurios. According to Murray J. Harris, YHVH is found "some 6,823 times in the Hebrew Bible" (he cites Francis Brown, S. R. Driver, and Charles A. Briggs, The New Brown-Driver-Briggs-Gesenius Hebrew and English Lexicon: With an Appendix Containing the Biblical Aramaic [Peabody, Mass.: Hendrikson, 1979], 217b). The LXX renders YHVH as kurios 6,156 times, and as θεός (theos) only 353 times (Murray J. Harris, Jesus as God: The New Testament Use of Theos in Reference to Jesus [Grand Rapids, Mich.: Baker Book House, 1992], 24-25).

Testament text where YHVH is used. The parallel of "confessing" Christ as kurios in verse 9, and "calling upon" the name of YHVH in verse 13 renders plausible the thesis that Paul possessed a high Christology—that for Paul, Christ is YHVH the Son.

### 1.2. First Corinthians 1.8

"Who shall also confirm you to the end, blameless in the day of our Lord Jesus Christ." "In the day of the Lord"[9] is the consummation of the ages. Paul, it is assumed, is familiar with the Old Testament's teaching of "the day of Yahweh",[10] which is prophetic of this consummation. Isaiah 13.6 tells of this great day of Yahweh: "Wail, for the day of יהוה [YHVH][11] is near! It will come as destruction from the Almighty." In telling of the judgment of Christ to come, and by his use of the stock phrase "the day of YHVH" in application to Christ,[12] it is, again, possible to conclude that Paul views the incarnate Lord of glory as YHVH the Son.[13]

### 1.3. First Thessalonians 5.2

Paul again mentions "the day of the Lord". With both encouragement and admonition, Paul begins to close his first letter to the Thessalonians, stating, "For you yourselves know full well that the day of the Lord will come like a thief in the night."

But it is verse 3 that firmly and directly sets this reference to Christ[14] into the contexts of Isaiah and Jeremiah. Paul states in 1 Thessalonians 5.3: "While they are saying, 'Peace and safety!' then destruction will come upon them suddenly like birth pangs upon a woman with child; and they shall not escape." Isaiah 13.6-9 speaks of "the day of יהוה [YHVH]" (vv. 6,9) with the nuance of the judged "writhing like a woman in labor" (v. 8). Isaiah 26.17-18 also speaks of the eschatological judgment of YHVH (see vv. 19,21), and the reaction of the judged as one writhing in labor pains. This will all take place, as Isaiah states,

---

9 τῇ ἡμμέρᾳ τοῦ κυρίου (tē hēmera tou kuriou).

10 יום יהוה (yom YHVH).

11 LXX ἡ ἡμέρα κυρίου (hē hēmera kuriou).

12 See also Philippians 1.6; 2.16. The phrase used by Paul in 1 Corinthians 1.8 (see Phil. 1.6,10) is that of the LXX's translation of the Hebrew יום יהוה (yom YHVH) in Isaiah 13.6.

13 See also 2 Peter 3.10.

14 Κύριος (kurios) in 5.2 refers to Christ. Only a few verses earlier Paul speaks of the "Lord himself" descending from heaven (4.16, a clear reference to the Son). Moreover, 2 Thessalonians 1.7 mentions "the Lord Jesus" being "revealed from heaven with His mighty angels". Paul then states that these events will occur "on that day". These observations, coupled with the fact that in the Pauline corpus "the Lord Jesus" is certainly distinguished from "God our Father" or "God the Father", lend weight to the conclusion that "Lord" in 1 Thessalonians 5.2 is a reference to Christ.

"In that day" (27.1,2,12,13[15]). In Jeremiah 6.14 the theme of people speaking falsely with the words "Peace, peace", when in reality there is no peace,[16] is reminiscent of Paul's statement in 1 Thessalonians 5.3. Moreover, in Jeremiah 6.24 the nuance of birth pains once again arises in the context of the judgment of YHVH.[17]

Once again Paul attributes to Christ that which is thematic and expressive of YHVH in the Old Testament, indicating Paul's high Christology. In short, the themes listed above from the Old Testament that directly relate to YHVH are in turn applied to Christ by Paul.

## 2. "Truly God ... God the Word"

These two phrases of the C (θεὸν ἀληθῶς, θεὸν λόγον; theon alēthōs, theon logon) appear, respectively, near the beginning and near the end of the creed.

### 2.1. John 1.1

The Greek reads Ἐν ἀρχῇ ἦν ὁ λόγος, καὶ ὁ λόγος ἦν πρὸς τὸν θεόν, καὶ θεὸς ἦν ὁ λόγος (en archē ēn ho logos, kai ho logos ēn pros ton theon, kai theos ēn ho logos). Clause A communicates the eternal preexistence of the λόγος, clause B the eternal preexistence of the λόγος with the Father,[18] and clause C that the logos is ontologically (and eternally) theos. (My interpretation of all three clauses communicating "eternal" preexistence is seen in the use of ēn, which I explained in chapter 5, section 2.1.2.1.[19]) Clause C warrants

---

[15] The context here is one of deliverance. In the same way, Paul speaks of deliverance of the Lord's people on "the day of the Lord" (see 1 Thess. 4.17; 5.9,10).

[16] See also Jeremiah 8.11.

[17] See also Jeremiah 4.31, 22.23, 30.6 and their surrounding contexts. In the two Isaiah passages and the Jeremiah passage discussed above, there is, of course, the reality of the judgment (and deliverance, see Isaiah 27) of the nation of Israel, thus an immediate and not eschatological judgment. Yet, there is in these texts (Paul uses the Jeremiah passage to refer to eschatological judgment) the ultimate fulfillment of that immediate judgment, which is the eschatological judgment. Thus, the prefillment in the immediate judgmental sense points to the ultimate fulfillment at the consummation of the ages.

[18] See 1 John 1.2, where it is stated that the "Word of Life", which I take to refer to Jesus, was "with the Father" (πρὸς τὸν πατέρα, pros ton patera).

[19] Ambrose, speaking of Arius, writes of "was": "'In the beginning was the Word, and the Word was with God, and the Word was God. The same was in the beginning with God.' 'Was,' mark you, 'with God.' 'Was,' see, we have 'was' four times over. Where did the blasphemer find it written that He 'was not.' ... The extension of the 'was' is infinite. Conceive any length of time you will, yet still the Son 'was'" (Of the Christian Faith, I.8.56 [NPNF2, 10:209]). Hilary of Poitiers, in like fashion, explains, "In the beginning was the Word. What means this In the beginning was? He ranges backward over the spaces of time, centuries are left behind, ages are cancelled. Fix in your mind

detailed consideration in order to affirm the "Truly God ... God the Word" confession in the C.

With the third clause, theos ēn ho logos, the issue at hand is the use of theos and its consequent meaning. That theos in clause C functions differently from θεόν in clause B is obvious due to its being in the nominative case rather than the accusative (as in clause B).[20] Further, in clause C theos precedes the verb ēn and therefore functions as an anarthrous, qualitative predicate nominative, describing the essence, or nature, of the logos. Philip B. Harner, in his "Qualitative Anarthrous Predicate Nouns: Mark 15:39 and John 1:1", makes a convincing case that the logos is theos, that is, that the preincarnate Christ is ontologically God because "anarthrous predicate nouns preceding the verb may function primarily to express the nature or character of the subject".[21] Raymond E. Brown concurs, stating that "the translation 'The Word was God' is correct. This reading is reinforced when one remembers that in the Gospel as it now stands, the affirmation of i 1 is almost certainly meant to form an inclusion with xx 28, where at the end of the Gospel Thomas confesses Jesus as 'My God' (ho theos mou)".[22] Further, it is possible that Thomas here echoes an Old Testament passage wherein a confession that יהוה (YHVH) is "my God and my Lord" is made (Ps. 35.23). Though the Hebrew text for this verse reads אלהי ואדני (elohay va adonay it is YHVH who is addressed (see 35.1,10, especially vv. 22 and 24). The LXX of this Psalm (34.23) reads the same as the Greek in John's Gospel, though the order of phrases is reversed.[23] John's point, then, may very well be that by mentioning Thomas' confession, that is, Thomas' use of an Old Testament confession praising YHVH, it demonstrates John's belief that Jesus is God the Son.

---

what date you will for this beginning; you will miss the mark, for even then He, of Whom we are speaking, was ... For his was has no limit of time and no commencement; the uncreated Word was in the beginning" (On the Trinity, II.13 [NPNF2, 9:56]).

[20] Further, the omission of the article before theos when it could have been included is evidence that John wanted his readers to distinguish between the persons of the Father and the Son. See E. C. Colwell's "A Definite Rule for the Use of the Article in the Greek New Testament", Journal of Biblical Literature 52 (1933): 12-21. On page 17 Colwell lists the number of occurrences of predicate nouns that appear before the verb. Of the 112 examples in the New Testament, 15 have the article (97 do not have the article, one of which is John 1.1). This, of course, is a small percentage. Yet, it still shows that John was well within the rules of grammar to use the article with *theos* in 1.1c. Raymond E. Brown writes that "by omitting the article it [John 1.1c] avoids any suggestion of personal identification of the Word with the Father" (The Gospel According to John I-XII, The Anchor Bible [New York: Doubleday, 1966], 1:24).

[21] Journal of Biblical Literature 92 (1973): 75.

[22] The Gospel According to John I-XII, 1:5.

[23] John 20.28: ὁ κύριός μου καὶ ὁ θεός μου (ho kurios mou kai ho theos mou); Psalm 34.23: ὁ θεός μου καὶ ὁ κύριός μου (ho theos mou kai ho kurios mou).

## 2.2. John 8.58

If in the Gospel of John the prologue (1.1-18) functions to introduce the reader to themes that are fleshed out as the Gospel unfolds, John 8.58 puts more flesh on the claim that "the Word was God". John 8.58 reads, "Jesus said to them, 'Truly, truly, I say to you, before Abraham came into being, I am.'"

The first thing to note is Jesus' use of the phrase ἐγὼ εἰμί (egō eimi, "I am"). It stands alone, without a predicate. That is, in John 8.58 "I am" is absolute, for there is no predicate phrase[24] that could possibly be implied from the context.

Second is the way Jesus as God is distinguished from the created order, which I have already discussed in chapter 5, section 2.1.2.1.

Third, and the crux of my concern here, is what the phrase "I am" means. Simply put, it is "in the style of deity".[25] It is representative of the "I am" statements in the LXX[26] that are attributed to יהוה (YHVH). In Deuteronomy 32.39 YHVH states, "Behold, Behold, that I am [egō eimi]." Isaiah 41.4c, 43.10a, and 46.4a read, in order, "I, God, the first, and to all the things coming, I am [egō eimi]", "You are my witnesses ... that you may know ... that I am [egō eimi]", and "I am [egō eimi], and until you grow old, I am [egō eimi]" (see also Isa. 45.18). John opens his Gospel with a declaration of the pre-existent deity of the Son (1.1), and continues that witness in John 8.58.

## 2.3. What Jesus Did, יהוה Did

In addition to the statements above, which are more direct in communicating the deity of Christ, there are in the New Testament many texts that witness Jesus doing what יהוה (YHVH) did, and in that way evidencing the deity of Christ. In section 1 and its subsections I examined a few biblical passages where Paul applies to Jesus that which belongs to YHVH. And, as seen in the previous section, in John 8.58 Jesus says what YHVH in the Old Testament says. Now I shall explore a few biblical passages in the synoptic gospels in the hope to substantiate the present theme.

### 2.3.1. Matthew 8.23-26

In this pericope Jesus "stills the storm", a theme reminiscent of the Old Testament wherein יהוה (YHVH) is the "storm stiller". In Psalm 89.9 YHVH rules the swelling of the sea. Christians of my tradition see in this parallelism that Jesus is the YHVH who rules the sea. Further, when the contexts of Psalm 107 and Matthew 8 are considered, we notice similar themes: those in ships

---

[24] See Brown, The Gospel According to John I-XII, 1:533.

[25] Leon Morris, The Gospel According to John (Grand Rapids, Mich.: Eerdmans, 1971), 473. See also Brown's excellent discussion on egō eimi in his The Gospel According to John I-XII, 1:533-38.

[26] Morris, The Gospel According to John, 473 n. 116.

(Ps. 107.23; Matt. 8.23), distress and crying out to the Lord (Ps. 107.27-28, crying out to YHVH; Matt. 8.25, crying out to Jesus), and YHVH stilling the storm (Ps. 107.29; Matt. 8.26). It therefore may be argued that Matthew sees Jesus as the YHVH of Psalm 107.[27]

2.3.2. MATTHEW 9.2-3, MARK 2.5-7, LUKE 5.20-21

In Mark 2.5 Jesus says to the paralytic, "My son, your sins are forgiven" (see Matt. 9.2; Luke 5.20). Here the functional implies the ontological. By Christ forgiving sins he is taking upon himself only what יהוה (YHVH) can do, thereby implicitly claiming to be YHVH in the ontological sense.[28] The Jews follow Jesus' pronouncement with a pronouncement of their own, "He is blaspheming; who can forgive sins but God alone?" God alone can forgive sins: "I, even I, am the one who wipes out your transgressions for my own sake; and I will not remember your sins" (Isa. 43.25). In Isaiah, to forgive sin is the prerogative of YHVH the Redeemer, the Holy One of Israel (Isa. 43.14). In Matthew, Mark and Luke, to forgive sin is the prerogative of the Son of Man, who is YHVH the Son, Redeemer, the Holy One of Israel.[29]

---

[27] In Matthew 14.33 (note the similar theological theme of Jesus ruling the sea in 14.22-27) Jesus, by his actions in fulfillment of that which only Yahweh can do, is rightly worshipped and does not rebuke the disciples for their act of devotion. Thus, ἐγὼ εἰμί (egō eimi) here should be regarded as Jesus' self-identification as "I am", the egō eimi of Deuteronomy 32.39, Isaiah 41.4, 43.10, etc. (LXX), and not understood as communicating, as many translations have it, "It is I." D. A. Carson notes concerning the translation "It is I": "Although the Gr. egō eimi can have no more force than that ["It is I"], any Christian after the Resurrection and Ascension would also detect echoes of 'I am,' the decisive self-disclosure of God" (Matthew, in Frank E. Gaebelein, ed., The Expositor's Bible Commentary [Grand Rapids, Mich.: Zondervan, 1984], 8:344). Brown is sure of it being another instance of an "I am" claim: "That Matthew intends more than a simple 'It is I' is suggested by the profession of faith from the disciples (Matt xiv 33), 'Truly, you are God's Son!'" (The Gospel According to John I-XII, 1:538).

[28] For other occurrences of this theme, D. A. Carson, in his Matthew, 325, directs the reader to Philip B. Payne, "Jesus' Implicit Claim to Deity in His Parables", Trinity Journal [1981]: 3-23. See also Tsoukalas, Knowing Christ in the Challenge of Heresy, chapters 2,4,5,6 and 7.

[29] The first chapter of Matthew confesses Jesus as "God with us" who has come to "save his people from their sins". (See Matt. 1.21,23; cf. Ps. 130.8, where it is YHVH who does this. Further, note "his people", a covenantal possession theme where the people belong to Jesus; not merely ancestral lineage but possession in the covenant sense set squarely in the context of the divine presence [thus "God with us"] with echoes of Isaiah 43:1-7.) One of the ways Jesus is "God with us" is to forgive sins. Further, the final verses of Matthew (28.16-20) serve as an inclusion with the claim of "God with us" in 1.23. In 28.16-20 Jesus appears on a mountain (v. 16), is worshiped (v. 17), gives commands from the mountain and promises his presence (vv. 19-20). All these are prerogatives of deity.

### 3. "**ὁμοούσιος** with the Father"

Both the C and NC contain the phrase ὁμοούσιον[30] τῷ πατρὶ (homoousion tō patri, one substance, or one essence, with the Father).[31]

In John 1.1c the grammatical function of θεός (theos) speaks to the essential nature of the λόγος (logos), as I have previously shown. John 1.1b speaks of the Father (τὸν θεόν, ton theon), with whom the logos was for all eternity. Against the backdrop of monotheistic belief, the logos shares in the nature of the Father; as the Father is deity, so is the Son. And since, as I have documented in the previous chapter, there is in traditional Christian belief nothing co-eternal with God, the logos, who is co-eternal with the Father, must therefore, and once again in a monotheistic context, be essentially deity. Indeed, with traditional Christian monotheism all the biblical passages speaking of Christ's deity must carry this implication.

### 4. "Truly Man ... **ὁμοούσιος** with Us according to the Manhood"

The C confesses that Jesus is ὁμοούσιος (homoousios) with humanity. It further states that Jesus is "in all things like unto us [κατὰ πάντα ὅμοιον ἡμῖν, kata panta homoion hēmin]".[32] The claim here is that what each human being is, ontologically, Jesus is.[33] In other words, there is between Christ and

---

[30] In the NC specifically to refute Arianism, which opted for ἑτεροούσιος (heteroousios, of a different substance), or semi-Arianism's ὁμοιούσιος (homoiousios, of like substance).

[31] R. V. Sellers, in his The Council of Chalcedon: A Historical and Doctrinal Survey (London: SPCK, 1961), 213, notes that Cyril of Alexandria (412-444 A.D.), who exercised great influence on the C (along with Pope Leo and his Tome), confesses that Jesus Christ is ὁμοούσιος ... τῷ θεῷ (homoousios ... tō theō), the same substance ... with God. Hilary of Poitiers confesses the same of Christ, "Who is of the substance of the Father" (On the Trinity, V.35, [NPNF2, 9:96]; see also On the Councils, XXVII.69-71 [NPNF2, 9:22-23]).

[32] After kata panta homoion hēmin the C is careful to insert the qualifying phrase χωρὶς ἁμαρτίας (chōris hamartias, without sin).

[33] Irenaeus forcefully argues for the true manhood of Christ in his Against Heresies, in III.19.1, where Jesus "had become that which we also are", and in V.1.1 (ANF, 1:448-49,526-27). Pope Leo writes of Jesus being "very God" (see also Ambrose's "very God of very God" [Of the Christian Faith, I.17.108 {NPNF2, 10:219}; see also I.17.115-17, I.18.118 {NPNF2, 10:220}, V.2.27 {NPNF2, 10:287}]) and "very man" in the context of Christ's work of atonement (Sermon XXI, section 2 [NPNF2, 12:129]), as did Irenaeus (Against Heresies, III.19.1 [ANF, 1:448-49]). Athanasius argues that Christ was "sent to us and assuming our body which is mortal" (Against the Arians, I.12.47 [NPNF2, 4:334]), that "He takes unto Himself a body, and that of no different sort from ours ... But He takes a body of our kind" (On the Incarnation of the Word, section 8 [NPNF2, 4:40]), that "the Saviour having in very truth become Man, the salvation of the whole man was brought about ... body and soul alike" (Letter LIX to Epictetus, section 7

humanity full identification.[34]

The biblical text is the foundation upon which the early church confessed Jesus' true humanity.[35] Jesus was born of a woman (Gal. 4.4) who was a virgin (Matt. 1.18-23). Though he had no human father in the biological sense, the church nonetheless infers his full humanity by virtue of the fact that Jesus developed from conception in the womb of a human mother just as all human beings do. The genealogies in Matthew and Luke, where Jesus' human ancestry is mentioned, also evidence his humanity. Further, his full, complete humanity[36] is emphasized by the writer of Hebrews, where it is stated that Christ "likewise"[37] shared in our flesh and blood (2.14) and was made like his brethren "in all things [κατὰ πάντα, kata panta]"[38] (2.17), a phrase duplicated in the C.

In the prologue to the Gospel of John "the Word became [ἐγένετο, egeneto] flesh" (1.14). His flesh, his humanity, "became" at a certain point in time[39] at the conception, just as all other human beings experience. Further, in his first epistle John may have encountered a type of docetic separationism that

---

[NPNF2, 4:572]; see also On the Incarnation of the Word, sections 4,5 [NPNF2, 4:38]), and that the body of Christ was "human by nature, and the body of the Lord was a true one" (Letter LIX to Epictetus, section 7 [NPNF2, 4:573]). Novatian declares that Christ "was manifested in the substance of the true body" (De Trinitate, chapter 11 [ANF, 5:620]).

[34] The doctrine of identification must, however, be limited in certain respects. For example, in Hebrews 4.15 we read that Christ is "without sin" (χωρὶς ἁμαρτίας, chōris hamartias).

[35] See for example Hilary of Poitiers, On the Trinity, X.24 (NPNF2, 9:188).

[36] Thus the phrase ἐκ ψυχῆς λογικῆς καὶ σώματος (ek psuchēs logikēs kai sōmatos, of a rational soul and body) in the C, against the Apollinarians. See also the Athanasian Creed, article 32: "of a rational soul and human flesh subsisting" (ex anima rationali et humana carne subsistens). Pope Leo, in his Tome, 2, writes of the "flesh which he assumed from a human being, and animated with the spirit of rational life" (quoted in Sellers, The Council of Chalcedon, 238). Ambrose writes, "He took upon Himself a soul [and] He also took the affections of a soul" (Of the Christian Faith, II.7.56 [NPNF2, 10:230]). Theodoret declares that Christ has "a reasonable soul" (Dialogues, dialogue 1 [NPNF2, 3:172]). Hilary of Poitiers includes in the humanity of Christ a human soul (On the Trinity, X.20,22,57 [NPNF2, 9:186,187,198,]; Psalm LIII, sections 8,14 [NPNF2, 9:245,247]), as, for examples, do Tertullian (On the Flesh of Christ, chapter 10 [ANF, 3:530-31]), Origen (De Principiis, IV.1.31 [ANF, 4:378]), and Augustine (Letter CLXIX2.8 [NPNF, 1:541]), who also writes of the rational part (along with the irrational part) of the soul (On the Gospel of John, XXIII.6 [NPNF, 7:153]).

[37] Implying real human conception and birth (see F. F. Bruce, The Epistle to the Hebrews [Grand Rapids, Mich.: Wm. B. Eerdmans Publishing Co., 1964], 48).

[38] kata panta may also be translated "in every respect".

[39] The implication of the aorist tense for the verb γίνομαι (ginomai). See Morris, The Gospel According to John (Grand Rapids, Mich.: Wm. B. Eerdmans Publishing Co., 1971), 102.

threatened belief in the real and true humanity of Christ.[40] He thus wrote, "Every spirit that confesses that Jesus Christ has come in the flesh is from God" (1 John 4.2). In his second epistle we read, "For many deceivers have gone out into the world, those who do not acknowledge Jesus Christ as coming in the flesh. This is the deceiver and the antichrist" (2 John 7). From these texts (read in conjunction with other canonical passages) we may infer that Jesus was truly a human being. Jesus also referred to himself as a man (John 8.40), and others refer to him as a man (John 1.30; Acts 2.22; Rom. 5.15; 1 Tim. 2.5).

Additionally, the church infers that Jesus is truly human from what Jesus did. Jesus, as humans do, "became twelve" (Luke 2.42). As a boy of twelve he also was in subjection to his parents (Luke 2.51). After this we are told that Jesus increased in wisdom and age (Luke 2.52). He experienced the physical wants of the body: thirst (John 19.28), hunger (Matt. 4.2), and need for rest because he grew tired (John 4.6). He experienced the emotions that characterize humanity. Reacting to the death of Lazarus, Jesus was "deeply moved in spirit" and "Jesus wept" (John 11.33,35). And, of course, he died. He died just as all human beings do (John 19.33).

Traditional orthodoxy also affirms, due to scriptural testimony, that the resurrected, ascended, and soon-coming Jesus is truly human. After the resurrection[41] he appeared to his disciples, and on one occasion comforted them

---

[40] "Separationism" meaning a separation of Jesus from the "Christ". Whether it be that of Cerinthus or that of teachers within the community is uncertain. For the former option one has to rely in part upon Irenaeus' description of Cerinthus' teaching (included with the description is his relating the story of the apostle John fleeing a bath house because Cerinthus, "an enemy of the truth", had entered; see Against Heresies, 3.4). In Against Heresies Irenaeus sums up Cerinthus' teaching: Jesus the man is separate from the Christ, and the Christ descended upon Jesus at his baptism, but later departed from Jesus before the crucifixion. According to Glenn W. Barker (1 John in Frank E. Gaebelein, gen. ed., The Expositor's Bible Commentary, 12:295) several early exegetes advance this as a most probable occasion for the epistle, among them B. F. Westcott (The Epistles of St. John: The Greek Text with Notes and Essays [London: Macmillan, 1883], xxxiv). Later exegetes, however, find some problems with this thesis, and advance the latter view mentioned above. For example, Barker notes that "internal evidence strongly suggests" that error arose within the church community (1 John 2.19), not from someone outside, and that though some common Cerinthian heretical elements may be noted in the epistle, there are differences as well. For example, there is no mention of any "Supreme God", a theological theme found in Cerinthus, and no mention of divine emanations or aeons, of which Christ was among the lowest (see Barker, 1 John, 295). Whether Cerinthian or not, it nonetheless seems to be a type of docetic separationism that plagued the community.

[41] Christ's is the proto-resurrection, after which is patterned the resurrection of all believers in Christ. Classical orthodoxy's linear-history based eschatology culminates in the bodily resurrection of all believers in Christ, who will live in the "New Jerusalem", which, when reading the descriptions of it in Revelation 21-22 in light of Genesis 2-3, is the New Eden. In addition to the linear view of history, bodily existence on a new earth

by his humanity, for they thought they saw a spirit: "See my hands and my feet that it is I myself; touch me and see, for a spirit does not have flesh and bones as you see that I have" (Luke 24.39). On another occasion he invited Thomas to touch his hands and side (John 20.27) which had been wounded at his crucifixion. This strongly suggests the continuance of his humanity and the union of his humanity with his deity even through the resurrection. Before his ascension to the right hand of the Father, Jesus appeared to his disciples, instructed them, and "was lifted up while they were looking on" (Acts 1.9). Immediately after his ascension, "two men in white clothing stood beside [the apostles]; and they also said, 'Men of Galilee ... this Jesus ... will come in just the same way as you have watched him go into heaven'" (Acts 1.10-11).[42] Presently, in his resurrected and ascended state Jesus is a man (1 Tim. 2.5).

### 5. John 1.14: "Truly God and Truly Man"

John 1.14 evidences this phrase in the C and is a biblical passage frequently called upon by early church theologians to demonstrate that Jesus is both God and man[43] or truly God and truly man.[44]

For orthodox theologians, John 1.14 succinctly substantiates the classical

distinguishes this eschatology from the eschatologies of Śaṅkara and Rāmānuja. Classical orthodoxy affirms a renewing of all creation (see Rom. 8.21), which places much emphasis on the importance of the material world (see Athanasius, On the Incarnation of the Word, section 37: "by His death has ... all creation been ransomed" [NPNF2, 4:56]).

[42] For traditional orthodoxy the theological and soteriological implications of Christ being human are immeasurable. Christ is the second Adam. As such he has done what Adam could not do and therefore is advocate before the Father as perfect humanity (both in the moral and quantitative senses), reconciling his people to God by his life, death and resurrection. By, in and through Christ all believers will be restored to the humanity they were intended to be. Further, Christ is true Israel, doing what Israel as a nation failed to do. Believers in Christ, therefore, are incorporated "in him" through faith and participate in him as true Israel.

[43] Ignatius, To the Ephesians, chapter 7 (ANF, 1:52); Origen, Against Celcus, VI.68 (ANF, 4:604); Tertullian, Against Praxeas, chapter 15 (ANF, 3:610-11); Dionysius of Alexandria, Extant Fragments, I.1.6 (ANF, 6:84); Athanasius, On the Opinion of Dionysius, sections 8,9 (NPNF2, 4:179), To the Bishops of Egypt, 2.17 (NPNF2, 4:232), Against the Arians, I.11.41,44-45 (NPNF2, 4:330,332-33), II.14.1 (NPNF2, 4:348), II.20.53 (NPNF2, 4:377), III.26.29 (NPNF2, 4:409); Augustine, Letter CCXIX, section 1 (NPNF, 1:572).

[44] Ignatius, To the Trallians, chapter 9 (ANF, 1:70); Irenaeus, Against Heresies, V.18.2 (ANF, 1:546); Tertullian, On the Flesh of Christ, chapter 18 (ANF, 3:537); Novatian, De Trinitate, chapters 13,24 (ANF, 5:622,634-35); Theodoret, Dialogues, dialogue 1 (NPNF2, 3:162-164,172-73, esp. dialogue 2, NPNF2, 3:214); Athanasius, Against the Arians, III.26.31-32 (NPNF2, 4:410-11); Augustine, On the Gospel of John, XXIII.6 (NPNF, 7:152).

orthodox christological confession that Jesus is θεὸν ἀληθῶς καὶ ἄνθρωπον ἀληθῶς (theon alēthōs kai anthrōpon alēthōs), truly God and truly man: "And the Word became flesh, and dwelled among us, and we beheld his glory, glory as of the only begotten from the Father, full of grace and truth." The Word who always was, the Word who always was with the Father, the Word who always was God (John 1:1), has now taken to himself, in union with his deity, humanity in the one person of Jesus Christ.

As the eternal[45] Word, He can never stop being God. Most importantly for my purpose, the phrase "the Word became flesh" does not mean that the Word changed to humanity, for, and as just mentioned, the preincarnate Christ eternally existed as God the Son. However, his flesh, states the text, "became" (ἐγένετο, egeneto), which indicates coming into existence.[46] Further, "flesh" (σάρξ, sarx) in John 1.14 emphasizes the human nature (sarx is an anarthrous predicate nominative, qualitative in force, in the phrase ὁ λόγος σὰρξ ἐγένετο, ho logos sarx egeneto) that the eternal Word as God united to himself. From this text classical orthodoxy has argued that God the eternal Word united with himself full humanity when his flesh "became"[47] in the womb of the virgin by the agency of God the Holy Spirit[48] (Matt. 1.18,20).

The next two phrases, "and dwelled among us, and we beheld his glory", are covenantal, implying the deity of the Son. First, God in the person of Christ is

---

45 See my comments on ἦν (ēn) in chapter 5, section 2.1.2.1.

46 See my comments on γίνομαι (ginomai) in chapter 5, section 2.1.2.1. Athanasius asserts that "He according to His manhood is said to have been made" (Against the Arians, II.15.12 [NPNF2, 4:354]), and that "He became man" (Against the Arians, II.21.60 [NPNF2, 4:381]).

47 See Athanasius' attack on certain ones who teach that the Word "changed" into humanity (which they held to be coessential with the logos [Letter LIX to Epictetus, section 4] {NPNF2, 4:571-72}). Later in this same letter Athanasius states, "He has become flesh not by being changed into flesh, but because He assumed on our behalf living flesh, and has become Man. For to say 'the Word became flesh' is equivalent to saying 'the Word has become Man'" (section 8 [NPNF2, 4:573]). Yet, the two phrases were not considered by some to be synonymous. There was debate over "Word-man" Christology versus "Word-flesh" Christology, the former relating the logos with full humanity, but the latter relating the logos with flesh. Regarding the latter's emergence in various expressions, it was not considered orthodox teaching, in that it proposed a Christ not fully human (see J. N. D. Kelly, Early Christian Creeds, 3rd ed. [New York: Longman, 1972], 281,282,283,285,287,289,290,291, 301,302,304,310,319,322).

48 "His body not being of a man, but of a virgin alone" (Athanasius, On the Incarnation of the Word, section 37 [NPNF2, 4:56]). "Him the Apostle [Paul] has affirmed to have been afterwards 'made' of a woman, in order that the making might be understood not of the Godhead, but of the putting on of a body—'made of a woman', then, by taking on of flesh" (Ambrose, Of the Christian Faith, I.14.94 [NPNF2, 10:216-17]; see also Ambrose, Of the Christian Faith, III.4.26,34 [NPNF2, 10:246,247]). "[B]y His Incarnation He might take to Himself from the Virgin the fleshly nature" (Hilary of Poitiers, On the Trinity, II.24 [NPNF2, 9:59]).

"dwelling" (indicating the divine presence[49]) with his people. The Gospel means to convey that with the person of Christ we have the Old Testament tabernacle of God among men. The Greek verb ἐσκήνωσεν (eskēnōsen), translated "dwelled" in John 1.14, comes from the noun σκηνή (skēnē), "tabernacle". Second, in the Old Testament, God's presence was "His glory" revealed in the cloud in the tabernacle: "Then the cloud covered the tent of meeting, and the glory of יהוה (YHVH) filled the tabernacle [LXX skēnē]" (Exod. 40.34). Ezekiel 37.26-27 speaks of the time when YHVH will make an everlasting covenant with his people (v. 26) and will dwell with his people[50] and be their God (v. 27). This, asserts John's Gospel, is fulfilled in Christ. In Christ ("as of the only begotten") is the glory of YHVH himself: he has "tabernacled" among us.

The phrase "full of grace and truth" is also covenantal and may imply in the strongest sense the deity of Christ. These words of John to describe Jesus are directly attributed to YHVH in Exodus 34.6 just after YHVH descends in the cloud (see 34.5). When YHVH dwelled with Moses on mount Sinai, he described himself as "full of grace and truth" (רב־חסד ואמת, rab-chesed ve emeth; see also 2 Sam. 2.6, Neh. 9.17, Ps. 25.10, Joel 2.13, Jon. 4.2).[51]

---

[49] In the Old Testament the characteristic that set the nation of Israel apart from all other nations was the "divine presence". YHVH was with his people. He was with his people in various ways. As Eichrodt points out, the presence of YHVH among his people may be manifested by the malak Yahweh (מלאך יהוה, "the angel of YHVH") who is YHVH himself (see Gen. 16.11,13), the kebod Yahweh (כבוד־יהוה, "the glory of YHVH") in the form of a cloud (Exod. 24.16,17; see Luke 1.35), and the pene Yahweh (פני יהוה, "the face of YHVH"), indicative of the presence of YHVH (Exod. 33.14). See Walther Eichrodt, Theology of the Old Testament, trans. J. A. Baker (Philadelphia, Pa.: The Westminster Press, 1967), 2:24,30,37-38.

[50] There is in the Old Testament an indissoluble link between the "presence" and the covenant (Ezek. 37.26-27).

[51] "Only Begotten" (which I have not treated in the NC and C) in John 1.14 means "unique". Jesus is God the Father's unique Son. First, the Greek word μονογενής (monogenēs) derives from μόνος (monos, alone, only) and γένος (genos, kind). Christ is "one of a kind", or unique. Second, the context supports this, for in verse 12 John intentionally calls believers "the children [τέκνα, tekna, children, not υἱοί, huioi, sons] of God". John sets apart the one who is the only begotten and thus the unique Son of God from those who become children of God. The language of the NC and the C suggests "begotten" in the sense of eternal generation of the logos (from the Father, thus "begotten, not made" (NC) and "begotten of the Father before all ages" (C). If I am correct in this assessment of the NC and the C, and if such language stems from either John 1.14 or Hebrews 1.5, it is not warranted. As just discussed, monogenēs in John 1.14 sets forth Christ as God's unique Son. Hebrews 1.5 with its use of the phrase "today I have begotten you" suggests enthronement, as does Psalm 2.6-8, to which Hebrews 1.5 alludes.

## 6. Body-Soul-Divine Relationship

With the preceding sections I sought to demonstrate, albeit briefly, the traditional orthodox understanding that Jesus is both deity and humanity, I focus now on the actual relationship of deity and humanity in the person of Christ. For this the C provides much insight that will prove useful to the comparative discussion in chapter 7.

### 6.1. Two Natures[52] Possessed in Their Fullness

The C confesses that Christ is "consubstantial [ὁμοούσιον, homoousion] with the Father according to the Godhead, and consubstantial [homoousion] with us according to the manhood". Though the C does not specifically state that "The two natures[53] are possessed in their fullness", I note here two observations that virtually establish this confession. First is the implication is that since the Father is assumed to be fully God and human beings are fully human, Christ, being ὁμοούσιος (homoousios) with both, possesses both natures in their fullness.[54] Moreover, and perhaps more explicitly as regards his "full" humanity, Christ, it is stated, is "in all things like unto us".[55] Second, the C does

---

[52] The phrase in the C, ἐν δύο φύσεων ... γνωριζόμενον (en duo phuseōn ... gnōrizomenon, made known [or being acknowledged] in two natures), may stem from Basil of Seleucia in November 448 A.D. (Sellers, The Council of Chalcedon, 122,216). As for the issue of whether this phrase should be read with ἐν (en) or ἐκ (ek), see Schaff, The Creeds of Christendom, 2:64 n. 4, and Sellers, The Council of Chalcedon, 120,122,144-51,177,198,215-17,258,260,286,289,298,311,332-36. Ambrose also writes of "the existence in Christ of both natures, Godhead and Manhood" (Of the Christian Faith, I.14.91 [NPNF2, 10:216]).

[53] The C states "two natures" in opposition to Monophysitism.

[54] As select examples, Ambrose speaks of Christ as "perfect and true God" and "possessing the fullness of Divinity" (Of the Christian Faith, I.8.61,65 [NPNF2, 10:231]), and Hilary of Poitiers states that in Christ is "full and perfect divinity" and "true God" (On the Trinity, XI.48 [NPNF2, 9:217], V.35 [NPNF2, 9:96]).

[55] The Greek of this phrase, κατὰ πάντα ὅμοιον ἡμῖν (kata panta homoion hēmin), is very much like that of Hebrews 2.17: κατὰ πάντα τοῖς ἀδελφοῖς ὁμοιωθῆναι (kata panta tois adelphois homoiōthēnai). Here redemption is the focus. In traditional orthodox theology the full humanity of Christ is indispensable if atonement is to have its full salvific effect (thus the urgency of the early church to answer, at Chalcedon, the theologies of Apollinaris, Nestorianism, and Monophysitism). In Hebrews 2.17 Christ "had to be made like his brothers in every respect in order that (ἵνα, hina) he might become a merciful and faithful high priest in things pertaining to God, to make atonement for the sins of the people". Pope Leo argued much the same (To Pulcheria Augusta, XXXI.2 [NPNF2, 12:44-45]; see also Leo's Tome, 2, mentioned in Sellers, The Council of Chalcedon, 228-29), as did Irenaeus (Against Heresies, III.19.1-3 [ANF, 1:448-49], III.22.1 [ANF, 1:454]), Athanasius (Against the Arians, I.11.43 [NPNF2, 4:331], I.12.50 [NPNF2, 4:336], II.14.7-9 [NPNF2, 4:351-53]; On the Incarnation of the Word, sections 8-10 [NPNF2, 4:40-41]; Letter LIX to Epictetus, sections 6-7 [NPNF2,

state[56] that Christ is "complete ... in Godhead and complete ... in manhood [τέλειον ... ἐν θεότητι καὶ τέλειον ... ἐν ἀνθρωπότητι, teleion ... en theotēti kai teleion ... en anthrōpotēti]",[57] which I take to mean fully God and fully man.[58]

## 6.2. Two Natures Distinct

I note a particular conclusion of the previous chapter: The material world (created ex nihilo) is not of the substance of God. God is therefore ontologically other than his creation, including souls. The C states that there is in the person of Christ a "distinction of natures". The distinction of the two natures therefore

4:572]), Ambrose (Of the Christian Faith, III.1.6, 2.7-8 [NPNF2, 10:243]; Of the Holy Spirit, I.9.107 [NPNF2, 10:107]), Tertullian (On the Flesh of Christ, chapter 10 [ANF, 3:530-31]), and Theodoret (Dialogues, dialogue 1 [NPNF2, 3:173]).

56 In line with the Athanasian Creed, article 32: "Perfect God and perfect man" (perfectus Deus: perfectus homo).

57 In his letter to John of Antioch, Cyril of Alexandria uses the same phrase when he writes that Jesus Christ is τέλειος ὢν ἐν θεότητι καὶ τέλειος ἐν ἀνθρωπότητι (teleios ōn en theotēti kai teleios en anthrōpotēti) (Sellers, The Council of Chalcedon, 212).

58 There are several reasons why I conclude this. First, the following clause seems to reiterate, though in synonymous fashion, the same: "Truly God and truly man". Second is the theological, apologetic and polemic context. Against the backdrop of Apollinarianism, Monophysitism, and Nestorianism, which in their different ways threatened, in the minds of the formulators of the C, the true humanity of Christ, it is more likely that teleion carries a quantitative sense (fully human, human in totality) rather than a moral (i.e., morally perfect) sense. Thirdly, and finally, lexically teleion may carry the quantitative sense (see Walter Bauer's A Greek-English Lexicon of the New Testament and Other Early Christian Literature, trans. William F. Arndt and F. Wilbur Gingrich, second edition [Chicago: The University of Chicago Press, 1979], 809, and Gerhard Kittel and Gerhard Friedrich, eds., Theological Dictionary of the New Testament, trans. Geoffrey W. Bromily [Grand Rapids, Mich.: Eerdmans, 1972], 8:78). See also Pope Leo's statement in his Sermon XXIII,section 2: "complete in what was his [God's] own, complete in what was ours" (NPNF2, 12:133). See Ambrose's "'He took upon Him the form of a servant' ... means that He took upon Him all the perfections of humanity in their completeness" (Of the Christian Faith, V.8.108 [NPNF2, 10:298]) and Hilary's "perfect according to fashion of human form, born a man after the likeness of ourselves ... neither the less man because born of God, nor the less God because Man born of God ... The use of the word 'form' to describe both natures compels us to recognize that He truly possessed both" (On the Trinity, X.21,22 [NPNF2, 9:187]). Hilary further states, "He is perfectly God the Word, and perfectly Christ the Man" (On the Trinity, X.52 [NPNF2, 9:196]). Lactantius writes that Christ is both God and man, and that as to his humanity Christ was "made in the likeness of man himself" (The Divine Institutes, IV.11 [ANF, 7:109-10]; see also IV.12,13,16 [ANF, 7:110-13,116-18]).

is a distinction that is in a strict sense ontological. The human nature possesses nothing in common with the nature of deity, and vice versa.[59]

## 6.3. "Union"

The C provides answers to the question of how the two natures of Christ do not relate to each other, and how they do relate to each other. For the former, it does so with the "four negatives". That is, it sets the boundaries one is not to cross. The two natures are "without confusion [ἀσυγχύτως, asungutōs], without change [ἀτρέπτως, atreptōs],[60] without division [ἀδιαιρέτως, adiairetōs], and without separation [ἀχωρίστως, achōristōs]".[61] With regard to the latter, the two natures are related by way of "union" (ἕνωσις, henōsis).[62]

---

[59] Athanasius battles those who held that the body of Jesus was coessential with the deity of the logos. This opinion Athanasius deems "unsound", and "from the divine Scriptures we discover nothing of the kind. For they say that God came in a human body" (Letter LIX to Epictetus, section 4 [NPNF2, 4:571]). Further, at the resurrection "the Body was not the Word, but Body of the Word" (Letter LIX to Epictetus, section 6 [NPNF2, 4:572]). Athanasius states also that Christ, according to his deity, "is other than all" and "other than all things" (Against the Arians, II.21.60 [NPNF2, 4:381]). Ambrose writes, "He took on Him that which He was not" (Of the Holy Spirit, I.9.107 [NPNF2, 10:107]). Pope Leo expresses the union of the two natures, "remaining what He was and assuming what He was not" (Sermon XXI, section 2 [NPNF2, 12:129]). Hilary of Poitiers tells of "the Form of God ... becoming that which It was not" (Psalm LIII, section 8 [NPNF2, 9:245]), and Augustine declares that "He became man who was God, by receiving what He was not" (On the Gospel of John, XXIII.6 [NPNF, 7:152-53]).

[60] Against Monophysitism. Sellers states that the first two negatives (and perhaps the third and fourth) were used by Cyril of Alexandria to teach the orthodox view of the human and divine in the person of Christ (The Council of Chalcedon, 215 and the notes).

[61] Against Nestorianism.

[62] Augustine frequently refers to the union, and does so with the example of humanity as a microcosm. For examples, "For just as the soul is united to the body in one person so as to constitute man, in the same way is God united to man in one person so as to constitute Christ ... In the person of man, therefore, there is a combination of soul and body; in the person of Christ there is a combination of the Godhead with man; for when the Word of God was united to a soul having a body, He took into union with Himself both the soul and the body" (Letter CXXXVII.3.11 [NPNF, 1:477]). "For just as in every man ... the soul and body constitute one person, so in Christ the Word and His human soul and body constitute one person" (Letter CLXIX2.8 [NPNF, 1:541]). "Union" of the two natures was used extensively by Pope Leo (for example, Sermon XXII, sections 1-2 [NPNF2, 12:132-33]). In this sermon Leo emphasizes the union and distinction of natures as necessary for the accomplishing of salvation on the part of Christ. See also Leo's Letter XXXV to Julian, section 3: "True man was united to God" (NPNF2, 12:49). This is stated in the context of the union being most necessary if Christ is to be mediator

Taken together, there is then a union, a joining, of the two natures, and that union or joining is not to be characterized by certain expressions of mixture or separation that would either cause the one person of Christ to be viewed as non-human (if the natures are mixed) or two persons (if the natures are separated to that extent).

The C states, "the distinction of natures being by no means taken away by the union, but rather the property of each nature being preserved, and concurring in one person".[63] The distinction of natures should not lead to any

---

between God and humanity. Leo then follows with the teaching that with Christ "God and man had co-existed in both natures forming one true Person" (Letter XXXVto Julian, section 3; NPNF2, 12:50). Leo, of course, had his predecessors as regards the doctrine of "union" as well as the soteriological connection of the true humanity of Christ with the act of atonement. For example, see Irenaeus, Against Heresies, V.1.1, wherein he writes of Christ, who is "very man ... redeeming us by His own blood" (ANF, 1:527), and Athanasius' On the Incarnation of the Word, section 18: "God, the Word Himself, Who was united with the body" (NPNF2, 4:45-46). Later in this same treatise Athanasius writes of "the union of the Word with it [Christ's body]" (section 20 [NPNF2, 4:47]). Note that though Irenaeus, and Hippolytus, wrote of a "comingling" and "comixture" of the two natures in Christ (see Irenaeus' Against Heresies, IV.20.4 [ANF, 1:488] and Hippolytus' Treatise on Christ and Antichrist, section 4 [ANF, 5:205]), Sellers observes that "these teachers are utterly opposed to the conception of the 'confusion' of the natures: like the Alexandrians, they use the term 'mixture'—which, clearly, has reached them from the East—only in order to enforce the doctrine of the indivisibility of the union of the divine and human elements in Jesus Christ" (The Council of Chalcedon, 188 n. 3). This seems correct, for, at least with Hippolytus, in the very section cited above he writes of "the Word of God ... uniting His own power with our mortal body". With Augustine we find the same language of comingling, though he similarly uses it in the sense of a real union with no mixture or confusion (On the Trinity, IV.20.30 cf. Letter CXXXVII.3.11 [NPNF, 3:85 cf. 1:477]). Ambrose writes of "the union of two natures, Godhead and Manhood, in Christ" (Of the Christian Faith, III.9.59 [NPNF2, 10:251]), Novatian of "both sides [God and man] woven in and grown together, and associated in the same agreement of both substances, by the binding to one another of a mutual alliance—man and God" (De Trinitate, chapter 24 [ANF, 5:635]; though here Novatian speaks of a "mingling", see above on Irenaeus and Hippolytus), and Hilary of Poitiers writes that Christ has "con-joined the nature of His own flesh to the nature of the eternal Godhead" (On the Trinity, VIII.13 [NPNF2, 9:141]), asserting that the flesh of Christ (whom he labels "the whole Son") was "united to the glory of the Word" (On the Trinity, IX.38 [NPNF2, 9:167]; see also IX.39 [NPNF2, 9:108]).

[63] Athanasius at the least hints at this. In his Letter LIXto Epictetus, section 6, he states that "the incorporeal Word made his own the properties of the Body, being His own Body" (NPNF2, 4:572). (Implied here is that the logos is the locus of the personality, which could be likened to the view that the "I" on the part of Kṛṣṇa is ontologically the same "I" that persists in his non-avatāric state. See my conclusion in chapter 4, section 3.4.1.2, what I deem to be Śaṅkara's implicit view in chapter 4, section 3.4.2.1, and what I deem to be Rāmānuja's implicit view in chapter 4, section 3.5.2.3.) The Second Letter of Cyril to Nestorius contains the phrase, "the difference of the natures having

type of formulations that grant solely to one of Christ's two natures any action or saying on the part of Christ. Rather, any saying or act of Christ, though performed by Christ by virtue of one of the natures, is performed by the one person of Christ.[64]

---

been in no wise taken away by reason of the union" (οὐχ ὡς τῆς τῶν φύσεων διαφορᾶς ἀνῃρημένης διὰ τὴν ἕνωσιν, ouch hōs tēs tōn phuseōn diaphoras anēremenēs dia tēn henōsin). Tertullian, in his Against Praxeas, chapter 27, states, "the property of each nature is so wholly preserved" (ANF, 3:624). On this theme see Sellers, The Council of Chalcedon, 148,194n.3,217. It is likely that the framers of the C drew these phrases from these two theologians, as well as Pope Leo, who stated, "each of the natures retains its proper character without defect" (Tome, 3; quoted in Sellers, The Council of Chalcedon, 230,238). Ambrose writes of the deity and humanity of Christ, where "both are One Person, perfect in respect of each, without any changeableness in the Godhead, as without any taking away from the fullness of the Manhood" (Of the Christian Faith, III.8.54 [NPNF2, 10:250]). Theodoret argues the same (Dialogues, dialogue 1 [NPNF2, 3:162-63]). Hilary of Poitiers, though not in exactly the same wording, states, "But the Father's nature, with which He was in natural unity, was not affected by this assumption of flesh" (On the Trinity, IX.38 [NPNF2, 9:167]). Hilary later confesses Christ as "one and the same person, not by loss of the Godhead, but by assumption of the manhood" (On the Trinity, X.22 [NPNF2, 9:187]; see also X.62 [NPNF2, 9:199]). Augustine writes, "In the first place, I wish you to understand that the Christian doctrine does not hold that the Godhead was so blended with the human nature in which he was born of the virgin." Additionally, "Let my reader, however, guard against borrowing his idea of the combination of properties of material bodies, by which two fluids when combined are so mixed that neither preserves its original character" (Letter CXXXVII.2.4, 3.11 [NPNF, 1:474,477]). Theodoret quotes Cyril of Alexandria: "Then before the incarnation there is one Very God, and in manhood He remains what He was and is and will be; the one Lord Jesus Christ must not be separated into man apart and into God apart, but recognising the difference of the natures and preserving them unconfounded with one another, we assert that there is one and the same Christ Jesus" (Dialogues, dialogue 2 [NPNF2, 3:214]).

64 Though Tertullian (Against Praxeas, 27 [ANF, 3:624]) states that "the two substances acted distinctly", and thus he may be construed to be promulgating proto-Nestorianism, he almost immediately after this statement affirms, "In one Person they no doubt are well able to be co-existent." Sellers defends this view, that is, that Tertullian cannot be teaching a Nestorianist doctrine (The Council of Chalcedon, 202-3). Ambrose writes in such a way that he attributes to each nature that which is spoken and performed by each nature, but is careful to imply, at the least, that the one person is speaking or performing. For example, "He cried: 'My God, My God, why hast Thou forsaken Me?' As being man, therefore, He speaks ... As man, therefore He is distressed, as man He weeps, as man He is crucified" (Of the Christian Faith, II.7.56 [NPNF2, 10:230], emphases mine; see also On the Decease of Satyrus, section 11 [NPNF2, 10:162-63] and the following section, wherein Ambrose takes great care to clarify that the Son is one person). Hilary claims individual functions proper to each nature, but that the Christ "was one" (On the Trinity, IX.11 [NPNF2, 9:159]).

## 7. Conclusion: Body-Soul-Divine Relationship

In light of creatio ex nihilo, which I discussed in the previous chapter, and in light of my observations in this chapter, I conclude here with certain implications concerning the body-soul-divine relation in the person of Christ. But for now I simply mention them, for I comment upon them in the next chapter, wherein I compare avatāra and incarnation.

First, a body made up of matter that is ontologically other than the divine characterizes the body-divine relation. Moreover, since the world is not permeated (to the point of divinization) by God (an implication, though not a necessary implication, of being ontologically other), the humanity of Christ is therefore not permeated by the divine to the point that the divine actively divinizes and thus changes the essentially human nature of Christ. Second, the material of Christ's body is finite, not eternal, and created ex nihilo indirectly by way of descent from Mary back to Adam and Eve.[65] Third, the human soul / spirit of Christ is created ex nihilo and is ontologically other than the divine. Fourth, the humanity of Christ, including the human soul / spirit of Christ, through conception in and birth from a woman, is of the same substance as all human beings. Fifth, the humanity and the divine in the person of Christ are joined in "union", without any mixture or separation (as described earlier in section 6.3).[66] Sixth, the humanity of Christ is both real and true. Seventh,

---

[65] As are all human beings after Adam and Eve. Pope Leo writes, "True man was united to God and was not brought down from heaven as a pre-existing soul, nor created out of nothing as regards the flesh" (Letter XXXVto Julian, section 3 [NPNF2, 12:49]). In other documents he writes of "that flesh which he assumed from a human being" (Tome, 2; quoted in Sellers, The Council of Chalcedon, 238), and of "the Word of God taking to Himself flesh from the Virgin's womb" (Sermon XLVI, section 2 [NPNF2, 12:159]). Irenaeus also argues for the true humanity of Christ coming from his birth in the womb of Mary (Against Heresies, III.22.1 [ANF, 1:454]) and writes of Jesus' "generation as to His human nature from Mary" (Against Heresies, III.19.3 [ANF, 1:449]). Athanasius writes against those who hold other than that Jesus' humanity stemmed from birth from Mary (Letter LIX to Epictetus, sections 2,4 [NPNF2, 4:571]) and later states, "That then which was born of Mary was according to the divine Scriptures human by nature, and the body of the Lord was a true one; but it was this, because it was the same as our body, for Mary was our sister inasmuch as we all are from Adam" (Letter LIX to Epictetus, section 7 [NPNF2, 4:573]). From Ambrose's Of the Christian Faith: "To us, then, was born that which was not before—that is, a child of the Virgin, a body from Mary" (III.8.55 [NPNF2, 10:250]). Hilary writes that Christ's life "springs from a human origin ... as He by His own act assumed a body from the Virgin" (On the Trinity, X.21,22 [NPNF2, 9:187]). Hippolytus: "For whereas the Word of God was without flesh, He took upon Himself the holy flesh by the holy Virgin" (Treatise on Christ and the Antichrist, section 4 [ANF, 5:205]). Tertullian declares that the flesh of Christ was of Mary (On the Flesh of Christ, chapter 20 [ANF, 3:538]).

[66] Obviously there is the sense that the two natures, by virtue of the two natures being ontologically different, are "separate" natures, but by this the C means "distinct" and not

Christ is sinless.

---

separate in what it deemed to be heretical ways. In other words, the natures are indeed separate, distinct, but they are joined, "unioned" if you will, in a very specific way in the one, unified person of Christ.

## CHAPTER 7

# Conclusion: Avatāra and Incarnation Compared

With the exploration of the doctrines of Brahman, the world and the soul in the philosophies and theologies of Śaṅkara and Rāmānuja now complete, and with the same accomplished concerning classical Christian orthodoxy, it remains to explore and to summarize, comparatively, the theological and soteriological implications, similarities and differences between the Kṛṣṇāvatāra doctrines of Śaṅkara and Rāmānuja and classical Christian orthodoxy's incarnation of Christ.

As I stated in the introduction, though there are similarities, when examined in light of the contexts of the philosophical / theological paradigms of the three traditions, several of these similarities are in the end superficial. In other words, the philosophical / theological ingredients of the three traditions in the end shape and therefore nuance "similarities" to such an extent as to render them quite different. The aim of this chapter is to demonstrate, explicitly, this thesis.

Parrinder's remarks quoted earlier in the introduction need to be repeated here. He states "that very little critical study has been undertaken of the Avatar beliefs of India or comparison between them and Christian doctrines of the Incarnation". He adds that "there is need for a comparative study to discover how much or little ground exists between beliefs in Avatar and Incarnation" and concludes, "It is remarkable that little has been written in European languages on Avatars and their meaning."[1] Though I agree with Parrinder that very little critical study has been done, I disagree with his statement that "a" comparative study is needed to fill the lacuna. I do not believe that any single study can do justice to the vast amount of differences that exist between the scores of Hindu avatāra-s and the scores of ācārya-s and their doctrinal formulations regarding these avatāra-s, and between these and Christianity's incarnation. Having combed literature available on avatāra and incarnation, I maintain that there is indeed much that remains to be explored. True, there are several works of a general nature, both by way of books (including Parrinder's book) and shorter essays, but the need remains for in-depth, critical, and more narrowly-focused studies in this much neglected field.

In this work I have labored to fill, in part, Parrinder's lacuna (the one with

---

[1] Geoffrey Parrinder, Avatar and Incarnation: The Divine and Human Form in the World's Religions (Oxford: Oneworld Publications, 1997), 7,13-14.

which I agree) by narrowing the legion of choices of avatāra subjects to just two (three if one counts my interpretation of the BG's doctrine of Kṛṣṇāvatāra), namely the Kṛṣṇāvatāra doctrines of Śaṅkara and Rāmānuja, in comparison with classical orthodoxy's incarnation (which in turn is, admittedly, a choice of tradition among many others in christological studies[2]). The narrow focus of this study has enabled me to probe the epistemologies and ontologies of the three traditions and in turn interpret avatāra and incarnation within these matrixes. The latter cannot be done properly without the former. I have demonstrated that Śaṅkara's non-dualism carries with it both explicit and implicit ramifications upon his doctrine of Kṛṣṇāvatāra (chapters 2 and 4). I have done the same with Rāmānuja's qualified non-dualism (chapters 3 and 4) and with classical Christian orthodoxy's incarnation (chapters 5 and 6). I proceed now to the comparative implications of this aforementioned preliminary and necessary work, beginning with the issue of "similarity or not?" between the words avatāra and incarnation.

## 1. The Words Avatāra and Incarnation

It is not uncommon to find the words used interchangeably by scholars. Following are a few among many other examples. Ādidevānanda translates

---

[2] See, for example, John Macquarrie, Jesus Christ in Modern Thought (London: SCM Press, 1990). Here Macquarrie documents several modern christologies, including Kantian Rationalist Christology (pp. 175-91), Humanistic Christology (pp. 192-211), Idealist Christology (pp. 212-34), Hegelian Christology (pp. 235-50), Positivist Christology (pp. 251-68), and numerous other christological alternatives from the nineteenth and twentieth centuries (pp. 235-50,269-335). It is quite possible that many of the theologians representing these modern expressions would come to different conclusions regarding the theological and soteriological implications I draw between Kṛṣṇa and Christ. For example, Kant's archetype Christ is "an unchanging timeless pattern who has pre-existed in the minds of rational beings" and who is distinct from the human Jesus of Nazareth (p. 185). Jesus, then, as "a concrete example of the life well pleasing to God" (p. 185) is unlikely to atone for sin in the way classical orthodox theologians take atonement. To quote Kant, Jesus was "a godly-minded teacher" and "completely human", "not", writes Macquarrie representing Kant, "a supernatural person". Macquarrie suggests that "it may well require the concrete example to bring about that 'change of heart' [for all of us] of which Kant speaks" (p. 186). This is not far from the thought of John Hick and the six scholars who contributed to The Myth of God Incarnate, a work that Hick edited and to which he contributed (Philadelphia: The Westminster Press, 1977). They as well would view as incorrect my choosing of categories of comparison. According to them the categories are actually mythical and erroneously attributed to Jesus and his work by church establishment in the formative centuries of its doctrinal development. Jesus, believes Hick, was "a man of God" who was "overwhelmingly conscious of the reality of God", but not literally God the Son (p. 172).

avatāraprakāraṁ as "mode of incarnation".[3] Flood refers to avatāra-s as incarnations.[4] Zaehner refers to Kṛṣṇa as God incarnate.[5] Dhavamony uses avatāra and incarnation synonymously throughout an essay.[6] Parrinder makes mention of avatāra-s as incarnations throughout his popular book.[7] Rudolf Otto states that "India possessed doctrines of incarnation long before Christianity."[8] Note the title of Daniel E. Bassuk's book, Incarnation in Hinduism and Christianity.[9] Malkovsky refers to Śaṅkara's Kṛṣṇāvatāra as "the incarnation of Kṛṣṇa".[10] Finally, but not exhaustively, a few articles in a relatively recent published work use the words avatāra and incarnation interchangeably.[11] I suggest that if the words are used interchangeably, it should be done with great care. Take the following as an example.

Christians, whether in an evangelistic setting, in the setting of interreligious dialogue where the aim is accurate communication of the views of two or more religious traditions, or in a setting where there is a combination of both the above, may find it necessary to use the term avatāra in reference to Christ, the reason being that seeking such common ground enhances evangelistic / interreligious relations. Telugu Christians, for example, use the term in song lyrics.[12] But Christians should do so with care, taking time to make distinctions between the incarnation of Christ and Hindu avatāra-s.

---

[3] Svāmī Ādidevānanda, trans., Śrī Rāmānuja Gītā Bhāṣya (Mylapore: Sri Ramakrishna Math, n.d.), 159. Noted from hereon as RBGB.

[4] Gavin Flood, An Introduction to Hinduism (New York: Cambridge University Press, 1996), 118.

[5] R. C. Zaehner, The Bhagavad-Gītā: With a Commentary Based on the Original Sources (London: Oxford University Press, 1973), 21,120,219,243,273,278.

[6] M. Dhavamony, "Hindu 'incarnations'", Studia Missionalia 21 (1972): 127-69.

[7] Avatar and Incarnation. See especially the statements, "It [Kṛṣṇāvatāra] was a real incarnation" (p. 42) and "The Avatars are divinity incarnate" (p. 121).

[8] Rudolf Otto, India's Religion of Grace and Christianity Compared and Contrasted, trans. Frank Hugh Foster (London: Student Christian Movement Press, 1930), 105.

[9] Atlantic Highlands, N.J.: Humanities Press International, 1987.

[10] Bradley J. Malkovsky, The Role of Divine Grace in the Soteriology of Śaṃkarācārya (Leiden: Brill, 2001), 336-44.

[11] Arvind Sharma, ed., Neo-Hindu Views of Christianity (Leiden: E. J. Brill, 1988). See the following essays: H. W. French, "Reverence to Christ through Mystical Experience and Incarnational Identity: Sri Ramakrishna", 68,69; Arabinda Basu, "Sri Aurobindo on Christ and Christianity", 187.

[12] See Julius Lipner, "Avatāra and Incarnation?", in Re-Visioning India's Religious Traditions: Essays in Honour of Eric Lott, ed. David C. Scott and Israel Selvanayagam [Delhi: ISPCK, 1996], 139, who in turn points to Eric Lott, "The Relevance of Research in Religions: Understanding Avatara as a Test-Case", Bangalore Theological Forum 10, no. 1 (1978): 36. Lott documents some of the lyrics: Manala rakṣimpa Krīstu manuja-avatāru-ḍayye, vinare yo narulārā, "Listen mankind! It was to save us that Christ became a human Avatāra" ("The Relevance of Research in Religions", translation in n. 3).

Julius Lipner, however, is not so permissive, asserting that though Christians use the term avatāra, "this does not mean that the usage is legitimate, for the usage could be misguided in a number of ways".[13] Lipner continues: "One must be able to raise questions about the validity of inter-religious transfers—granted that such transfers regularly occur—otherwise there would be no such thing as confused or distorted usage."[14] He then suggests that "substituting avatāra for Incarnation is conceptually and linguistically inadmissible and religiously highly dubious" and adds (and this is the main thrust of my thesis), "Each term carries substantial emotional and theological freight that is unique."[15] This, says Lipner, allows for the two terms to coexist in informative and creative interreligious interaction, with each term retaining its "initial specificities [that] may be respected within a unitive framework of discourse".[16] Lipner still leaves room, though, for Christian use of "avatāra" if it were to refer to "divine theophanies in other subjects".[17]

Indian theologian Y. D. Tiwari is adamantly against the use of avatāra in reference to Christ. "The question is often asked", he writes, "'Should we use Hindu philosophical terms to express Christian thought?' I am afraid I am conservative here ... Words like Avatar ... are better avoided."[18] Though he admits that some terms may be adopted, such as mukti (salvation, liberation), it is good practice, in general, not to utilize religious language from other religions. "A wide use of Hindu terms will weaken the Christian message", Tiwari asserts, adding that "We cannot be theologically accurate if we use these

---

[13] "Avatāra and Incarnation?", 139.

[14] "Avatāra and Incarnation?", 139.

[15] "Avatāra and Incarnation?", 139. See also Vinoth Ramachandra, The Recovery of Mission: Beyond the Pluralist Paradigm (Grand Rapids, Mich.: William B. Eerdmans, 1996), 243, wherein, after listing a few important differences between avatāra and incarnation, he asserts, "to translate avatara as incarnation is to invite confusion". Ninian Smart might disagree with Lipner and Ramachandra. Smart states,

> It is true that some scholars are highly contextualist in their approach to comparisons. Given a highly organic view of cultural [and theological?] systems, it is possible to hold that even apparent likenesses turn out to be unlikenesses ... However, I am sure that these limitations upon comparison are, to say the least, exaggerated. To take such contextualism too seriously would destroy all use of general words such as "sacrifice" and "devotion" across cultures ("The Inner Controller: Learning from Ramanuja", in Scott and Selvanayagam, Re-Visioning India's Religious Traditions, 148).

Though I consider myself "highly contextualist" in my approach to comparative theology, such an approach on my part need not "destroy all use of general words", for I hold that avatāra and incarnation may be used interchangeably, for example, in the context of evangelism / apologetics (see section 4).

[16] "Avatāra and Incarnation?", 139.

[17] "Avatāra and Incarnation?", 139.

[18] "From Vedic Dharma to the Christian Faith", in R. S. Sugirtharajah and C. Hargreaves, eds., Readings in Indian and Christian Theology, vol. 1 (Delhi: ISPCK, 1993), 137.

terms."[19]

As an example of using avatāra in reference to Christ, John Brockington calls attention to Jesuit missionary Roberto de Nobili (1577-1656), who labeled Christ a mānuṣāvatāra (human descent) in order to distinguish him from the avatāra-s of Viṣṇu, which he labeled devāvatāra-s (divine descents), specifying that Christ was truly human, whereas devāvatāra-s were not. That is, they assumed only a human body and not "body and soul together as one reality" as was the case with Christ.[20]

I maintain that the content that fills the words "avatāra" and "incarnation" in advaita, viśiṣṭādvaita, and traditional Christian orthodoxy should be carefully outlined before using the words in an interchangeable manner. In other words, if some desire to use the two terms interchangeably they should carefully outline differences between Christ and the Hindu avatāra under consideration.[21] I hold this position because in a certain sense Christ is a "descent" of God, and because in certain senses the Kṛṣṇāvatāra-s of Śaṅkara and Rāmānuja are "incarnations" or "enfleshments" of some sort within their respective frameworks. To reiterate, then, where interchangeability becomes problematic is when the words and their content are not carefully nuanced.

Robin Boyd concurs, but not first without a brief discussion of the issues. He asks whether or not the term avatara should be employed with regard to the incarnation of Jesus.[22] The question has raised debate for those divided on the issue. Boyd mentions those who favor the term in application to Jesus, such as Sundar Singh, Bishop Appasamy and V. Chakkarai, theologians, states Boyd, "whose natural affiliations are with the bhakti strand of Indian thought".[23] Yet,

---

[19] "From Vedic Dharma to the Christian Faith", 137.

[20] John Brockington, Hinduism and Christianity (New York: St. Martin's Press, 1992), 41.

[21] See Regunta Yesurathnam, "The Adequacy of the Concept of Avatara for Expounding the Christian Doctrine of Incarnation", Dialogue & Alliance 1, no. 2 (Summer 1987): 51. Yesurathnam concurs with Robin Boyd, citing Boyd words, "The concept of avatara may be used to describe the person of Christ—provided it is not the only concept that is used, and provided it is used with full Christian content." I interact with Boyd above. Also, Diana Eck, recalling a conversation with a Hindu, used the term avatāra in reference to Jesus, but mentions that the term as it relates to incarnation in this context "is only approximately accurate" (Diana L. Eck, Encountering God: A Spiritual Journey from Bozeman to Banaras [New Delhi: Penguin Books, 1995], 81).

[22] Robin Boyd, Khristadvaita: A Theology for India (Madras: The Christian Literature Society, 1977), 145.

[23] Boyd, Khristadvaita, 145. Yesurathnam mentions that these theologians, however, are quite careful to use the term avatāra with "deep Christian interpretation" in application to Jesus ("The Adequacy of the Concept of Avatara for Expounding the Christian Doctrine of Incarnation", 50). This is true of Appasamy (A. J. Appasamy, The Gospel and India's Heritage [London: Society for Promoting Christian Knowledge, 1942], 256-61), but in other places Appasamy applies the term "incarnation" to avatāra without

"Those whose philosophical and spiritual affinities lie with advaita Vedanta" reject the application, states Boyd. Here he lists as examples Brahmabandhava Upadhyaya and Swami Abhishiktananda.[24] Boyd then notes possible reasons against using the term to describe Jesus: multiple avatāra-s, little or no stress laid upon the historicity of avatāra-s, difference in purpose, difference in character (especially as Christ compares to Kṛṣṇa in relation to the latter's actions in the Purāṇa-s), and the human-divine relation.[25] Despite these, these bhakti theologians, observes Boyd, nonetheless employed the term avatāra in reference to Jesus,[26] but not without careful consideration of the differences.[27] Boyd nears the end of his discussion with mention of Klaus Klostermaier's view that Hinduism naturally advocates multiple avatāra-s, and that therefore the term should not be allowed in Christian theology,[28] but against this thesis he cites I. T. Ramsey, who made the point that classical Christian orthodoxy adopted many words and phrases from the non-Christian world.[29] Boyd concludes with a statement of his own: "The concept of avatara may be used to describe the person of Christ—provided it is not the only concept that is used, and provided it is used with full Christian content."[30]

When in dialogue with Hindus, then, perhaps some proper phrases referring to Christ might be īśvarāvatāraviśeṣaivapūrṇamanuṣya, "a full human being (arising) from a unique specific / particular descent of the Almighty", or īśvarāvatāraviśeṣaivamanuṣyasatya, "a real human being (arising) out of a unique specific / particular descent of the Almighty".[31] These phrases add

---

much thought, it seems, to the various systems in which the latter is found. For example, he defines avatāra as God coming "down into a human being" and God taking "birth as a man" (p. 252).

[24] Boyd, Khristadvaita, 145. Note, though, that Upādhyāy at one time stated, "The truths of the Hindu philosopher must be baptized and used as stepping stones to the Catholic faith ... It must assume the Hindu garment which will make it acceptable to the people of India. This change can only be effected by Indian Missionary Orders who preach the sacred Faith in the language of the Vedanta" (cited in J. Russell Chandran, "The Development of Christian Theology in India", in Sugirtharajah and Hargreaves, Readings in Indian and Christian Theology, 8).

[25] Khristadvaita, 145-46.

[26] Khristadvaita, 146.

[27] Khristadvaita, 147. Boyd states that Chakkarai, in his Jesus the Avatār, mentions the acute difference that Jesus' humanity continues for eternity, through his resurrection and ascension, a teaching not found in the theologies of avatāra-s (p. 147). I make this observation in section 3.4, section E of the sixth point, and in the seventh point.

[28] Khristadvaita, 148. See also Lott, "The Relevance of Research in Religions", 36 n. 4.

[29] Khristadvaita, 148.

[30] Khristadvaita, 148.

[31] For Christians this could be an important missiological point. That is, in addition to the evangelistic endeavor, where these phrases could be used, even after conversion to Christianity Indian people, by use of these phrases, retain, in form, an aspect of their

satya, pūrṇa or viśeṣa, and eva, emphasizing the realness, fullness or specificity, and uniqueness of the humanity, something that de Nobili did not do explicitly. The phrases also replace deva, which can mean one of many gods, with Īśvara.[32]

Consider the following as evidence for careful expression of content. From the point of view of classical orthodoxy, advaita's avatāra and viśiṣṭādvaita's avatāra doctrines do not commit to an actualization of true humanity,[33] while traditional classical orthodoxy's incarnation does.[34] Further, in the contexts of the theologies of Śaṅkara and Rāmānuja, and again from the point of view of classical orthodoxy, there is no need for full ontological identification with humanity, no need for true humanity, on the part of Kṛṣṇa, for the soteriological emphasis lies more importantly in the recognition of the transcendent One (who descends to show the way) behind the apparent humanity.[35] In the context of traditional orthodox Christianity, there is need for full ontological identification, real "enfleshment", for vital to the atoning redemptive process is that the incarnate God the Son, the Christ, is fully and truly human.[36] To conclude here, (1) given these theological / soteriological underpinnings connected with Christ and Kṛṣṇa, (2) in light of how the two Vedāntins' worldviews and epistemologies examined in chapters 1, 2 and 3 either determine or affect their theologies and soteriologies of Kṛṣṇa documented in chapter 4, and (3) in light of the worldview of classical Christian orthodoxy and

---

"hindutva" (by this I mean "Indian-ness"), though obviously the theological content is different.

[32] My thanks to Julius Lipner for suggesting these Sanskrit compounds.

[33] See chapter 4, sections 3.4.2 and 3.5.2 and their subsections.

[34] See chapter 6, sections 4 and 5.

[35] For Śaṅkara see chapter 2, section 3.2.2; for Rāmānuja see chapter 3, section 5. Additionally, Julius Lipner notes that the BP refers to Kṛṣṇa as "apparently human". BP 1.1.20 reads "bhagavān gūḍhaḥ kapaṭamānuṣaḥ: the Lord remained hidden as an illusory man" ("Avatāra and Incarnation?", 138,143n.32). In his Hindus: Their Religious Beliefs and Practices (London: Routledge, 1994), 313, Lipner translates kapaṭamānuṣaḥ as "a 'counterfeit man'". Lipner notes this in the context of the avatāra not being "constituted from real 'matter', that is, from prakṛti, in the way, say, ordinary empirical beings are. This is because, unlike ordinary empirical beings, the avatāra is not in any way the consequence or expression of past karma" (p. 313). Though the same is true with the Kṛṣṇāvatāra-s of Śaṅkara and Rāmānuja, when, however, Rāmānuja's Kṛṣṇa is further considered (that is, in addition to the karmic-caused issue), there is, ontologically, no material identity between the body of Kṛṣṇa and the bodies of other empirical beings.

[36] See chapter 6 n. 55. Moreover, just as important to the atonement is that Christ dies a real death. The fourth of Parrinder's "Twelve Characteristics of Avatar Doctrines" is "The Avatars finally die" (Avatar and Incarnation, 121). This cannot truly be said of Śaṅkara's avatāra. In the context of ultimate reality the death of Kṛṣṇa is only "so-called", for it is mithyā, though for some, in the context of saṁsāra Kṛṣṇa does indeed die.

its doctrine of the incarnation discussed in chapters 5 and 6, discretion should be exercised when using the terms avatāra and / or incarnation.

Timothy Tennent describes the "working definitions" of avatāra and incarnation as used by Brahmabāndhav Upādhyāy (1861-1907), an Indian Christian theologian and apologist, definitions that, according to Tennent, are "applicable throughout the writings of Upadhyay".[37] Tennent quotes Upādhyāy: "Incarnation means that God, a Being of Infinite, uncompounded, independent nature, enters into a personal union with a human nature, so that the actions of the assumed nature become His personal actions and derive their dignity from Him."[38] Tennent then offers his own words concerning avatāra: "The word 'avatār' may be more broadly defined as a 'descent' or a Divine 'coming down into the world' without necessarily distinguishing what the nature, extent or limitations of this descent may be."[39] Adding to these observations, the point I wish to make is that according to classical Christian orthodoxy the incarnation must include a full and true human nature in a "once for all times" context.[40] With Śaṅkara's and Rāmānuja's avatāra-s we do not find a "once for all times" schema; nor do we find limitations that the avatāra should possess a real and true human nature;[41] nor do we find limitations that avatāra-s should come only

---

[37] Timothy C. Tennent, Building Christianity on Indian Foundations (Delhi: ISPCK, 2000), 323. Note that Tennent may not necessarily agree with the view that the two terms should not be used interchangeably.

[38] Building Christianity on Indian Foundations, 323; emphases mine.

[39] Building Christianity on Indian Foundations, 323.

[40] As Upādhyāy would have it (see Sophia: A Monthly Catholic Journal 2, no. 2 [Feb. 1895]: 11). This in contrast to BG 4.7-8, where the divine comes into being "from age to age". See Tennent, Building Christianity on Indian Foundations, 324.

[41] Upādhyāy did state that "Rāmā, Krishna and other avatārs were God made flesh" (Sophia: A Monthly Catholic Journal 4, no. 10 [Oct. 1897]: 10, quoted in Tennent, Building Christianity on Indian Foundations, 326). Though this may be technically true, one must still ask whether or not the flesh was ultimately real and / or whether or not the flesh was truly human, that is, was it of the same substance as other humans. In this context, though speaking of avatāra-s in general, Diana Eck observes, "The avatara is a divine descent, God coming 'down' into this world, but yet as God. It is not really incarnation with the full meaning of taking on the body of flesh and blood" (Encountering God, 90). In Tennent's book, in the context of exploring Upādhyāy's observation that both Christ and Kṛṣṇa come into being of their own will, Tennent, representing the conclusions of Upādhyāy, makes a very astute observation with which I agree, and then follows with an observation that needs more comment on my part. He writes, "This is not to equate the varying cosmic and soteriological motives which may have given rise to such a free act of condescension [agree], but [Upādhyāy] is merely making the point that both Christ and Krishna are viewed as taking on human flesh as an act of divine freedom" (p. 326). On this latter statement, I have demonstrated that, for example, with Rāmānuja's Kṛṣṇāvatāra it is not human flesh that Kṛṣṇa possesses. Upādhyāy would have been correct in stating that Kṛṣṇa is viewed by some as taking on human flesh, excluding Rāmānuja and his followers.

in "human forms".

These are simply some general observations concerning avatāra and incarnation. What follow are several points more deeply explored that lend weight to these general observations.

## 2. The Purpose of Avatāra and Incarnation

Loosely speaking, in the context of purpose there are similarities between avatāra and incarnation: God, for a purpose,[42] descends[43] to humanity in self-revelation through a miraculous birth,[44] God takes the "form" of a human being, teaches humanity moral and spiritual truths, expects a response to these truths, and, if the response is positive, rescues humanity from sins or from some kind of negative human predicament.

### 2.1. Brief Preliminary Discussion for Śaṅkara's and Rāmānuja's Views

Traditionally the general and overarching purpose of the avatāra event of Kṛṣṇa is that of rescue. In the eternally cyclical cosmological setting of the four yuga-s (ages), satya or kṛta (golden), treta (silver), dvāpara (bronze), and kali

---

[42] Compare BG 4.8 ("For the rescue of the virtuous and for the destruction of evil doers, for the purpose of the establishing of virtue, I come into being from age to age") with Mark 10.45 ("The Son of Man has not come to be served, but to serve, and to give his life as a ransom for many").

[43] Lipner states, "Let us not be put off by the language of 'descent', common to both [i.e., Christian and Hindu] traditions." He then cites in a note the statement in the Nicene Creed: "Who ... came down from heaven" ("Avatāra and Incarnation?", 131,141n.13).

[44] The MBh (which contains the BG) does not address whether or not Kṛṣṇa's birth is from a virgin. It does, though, tell of a miraculous conception. The conception of Kṛṣṇa occurred when Viṣṇu (in the text he is called Hari) plucked a black hair from his head. The black hair then entered the womb of Devakī, and Kṛṣṇa (in the text he is called Keśava) was born (see J. A. B. van Buitenen, trans., The Mahābhārata [Chicago: The University of Chicago Press, 1973], 1:373, MBh 1.189.31). In other literature it is implied that his birth is not from a virgin. In the VP Kṛṣṇa is the eighth conception of Vāsudeva and Devakī in the same way mentioned above (Horace H. Wilson, The Vishnu Purana [New York: Garland, 1981], 4:258-59, VP 5.1). The BP also states that Kṛṣṇa is the eighth conception of Vāsudeva and Devakī, but not by way of a black hair of Viṣṇu. Rather, Kṛṣṇa's conception occurred this way: "the Lord entered into the heart of Vasudeva, as a result of which this great devotee shone with extraordinary brilliance. Then Devakī conceived the Lord in her own heart, transferred there by the noble Vasudeva" (Swami Venkatesananda, The Concise Śrīmad Bhāgavataṁ [Albany: State University of New York Press, 1989], 236-37, Book 10, chapter 2). Swami Prabhupāda, founder-ācārya of the International Society for Krishna Consciousness, embraces the BP version of the conception of Kṛṣṇa (A. C. Bhaktivedanta Swami Prabhupāda, Kṛṣṇa: The Supreme Personality of Godhead. A Summary of Śrīla Vyāsadeva's Śrīmad Bhāgavatam, Tenth Canto [New York: The Bhaktivedanta Book Trust, 1970], 9-12).

(iron), the world progresses from purity to licentiousness, from knowledge to ignorance, thus decreasing in virtue. Kṛṣṇa states, "Truly whenever a decrease of virtue [or duty, law] comes to be ... an emerging of unlawfulness, then I give forth myself. For the rescue of the righteous and for the destruction of evil doers, for the purpose of establishing righteousness, in age after age I come into being"[45] (BG 4.7,8).[46]

However, it must be noted that though there is a purpose in the coming of an avatāra, the creation and dissolution of the universe—and all the history in between, at the beginning and end of the four-yuga-cycle—is in reality the līlā of God.[47] As Bede Griffiths explains, "In the Hindu tradition the avatara is conceived as a play, a lila of God. All creation is a play and human life is a play of God."[48]

## 2.2. Śaṅkara and Rāmānuja

Both Śaṅkara and Rāmānuja do not depart from the above view. In the introduction to his BGB Śaṅkara opens with an explanation of the decrease in virtue and knowledge "Due to lapse of long periods of time" (see BG 4.2[49]). He continues: "Therefore, with a view to ensuring the well-being of the world, the primal all-pervading Agent, celebrated as Nārāyaṇa, is held to have been born of Vasudeva from Devaki's womb."[50] Rāmānuja follows suit. Paraphrasing Kṛṣṇa in his BGB on BG 4.7-8, he states that "whenever the Dharma taught by the Vedas ... declines, and Adharma, its opposite, increases, then I ... incarnate Myself ... So I am born from age to age in the forms of gods, men, etc., for protecting them".[51]

The rescue has for its end mokṣa of the ātman from the fetters of saṁsāra. BG 18.66 reads, "Abandoning all duties, in me alone take refuge; I shall release you from all wrong."[52] For Śaṅkara the emphasis is on knowledge as the

---

[45] yadā yadā hi dharmasya glānir bhavati ... abhyutthānam adharmasya tadā 'tmānaṁ sṛjāmyaham paritṛāṇāya sādhūnāṁ vināśāya ca duṣkṛtām dharmasaṁsthāpanārthāya saṁbhavāmi yuge yuge.

[46] See my chapter 4, section 1.4.

[47] For Śaṅkara see chapter 2, section 3.1.2; for Rāmānuja see chapter 3, section 2.1.3 and chapter 4, section 1.2.2.

[48] Bede Griffiths, River of Compassion: A Christian Commentary on the Bhagavad Gita (New York: Continuum, 1995), 68-69. Though see my section 2.3. For a somewhat detailed but not exhaustive treatment of līlāvatāra-s, see Chinmayi Chatterjee, "A Note on the Vaiṣṇavic Concept of Avatāra and Līlā of God", Anvīkṣā 6 (March 1972): 1-11.

[49] sa kāleneha mahatā yogo naṣṭaḥ. "With time here long, this yoga was lost."

[50] A. G. Krishna Warrier, trans., Srīmad Bhagavad Gītā Bhāṣya of Sri Śaṅkarācārya (Mylapore: Sri Ramakrishna Math, 1983), 2. Noted from hereon as SBGB.

[51] RBGB, 162-63.

[52] sarvadharmān parityajya mān ekaṁ śaraṇaṁ vraja ahaṁ tvā sarvapāpebhyo mokṣayiṣyāmi.

ultimate means,[53] and for Rāmānuja worship in the form of devotion (bhakti) to Kṛṣṇa[54] in the all-important context of abandoning all sense of attachment in the performance of one's dharma.[55] For Śaṅkara the ātman is ultimately essentially pure, for it is Brahman. For Rāmānuja the ātman, though of the substance of Brahman and pure, nonetheless is associated with imperfections, though Brahman remains untouched by them.[56]

Parrinder's eighth of "Twelve Characteristics of Avatar Doctrines" is "The Avatar comes with work to do."[57] Of this there is no doubt. However, when this statement is expressed in the context of Śaṅkara's Kṛṣṇāvatāra it takes on a meaning all its own and thus quite different from Rāmānuja and Christian orthodoxy. In the context of Śaṅkara's jagat-prapañca it is surely the case that the avatāra comes with work to do, for the avatāra seems to appear in this realm for the purpose of bringing parā vidyā to those who presently live in a state of aparā vidyā.[58] But one must ask this question: Is this "work" ultimately real? Taking into consideration Śaṅkara's two realms[59]—that of Īśvara or apara brahman and that of the para brahman[60]—and the criticisms leveled against

---

[53] SBGB, 616-20. "Only the unaided knowledge of the Self (ātmajñāna) is the cause of liberation" (p. 618); "Therefore only pure knowledge is a means to mokṣa" (p. 620). Śaṅkara has as a ground for this BG 4.36,37: "By this raft of knowledge you will go beyond sin." "So does the fire of knowledge reduce all works to ashes." See also US chapter 2, wherein via hypothetical discussion between guru and student Śaṅkara teaches knowledge as the ultimate means. Warrier, however, does state that bhakti is a means to jñāna.

[54] RBGB, 242. Knowledge is a means to bhakti (p. 116).

[55] RBGB, 598-600. Thomas A. Forsthoefel states that bhakti (in the context of dharma) is "the direct means of salvation" in Rāmānuja's system (Knowing Beyond Knowledge: Epistemologies of Religious Experience in Classical and Modern Advaita [Burlington, Vt.: Ashgate, 2002], 173). Rāmānuja also offers abandonment as a way to release from sins (RBGB, 599).

[56] See chapter 3 n. 59.

[57] Avatar and Incarnation, 124.

[58] Eric Lott states, "For Sankara the avatara is thought to function primarily at a didactic or revelatory level: it is a means of enlightenment. It reveals the truth lying behind the veil of illusion which obscures ultimate reality" ("The Mythic Symbol Avatar in Indian Conceptual Formulations", Dialogue & Alliance 1, no. 2 [Summer 1987]: 4). In another place Lott states, "Śankara finds it necessary to take the concept of Avatāra as having pragmatic value, but seriously ambiguous ontological status" ("The Relevance of Research in Religions", 38). Lott mentions that other Vedāntins like Rāmānuja and Madhva "have little doubt about its ontological reality" (p. 38).

[59] See chapter 2, section 2.1 and its subsections.

[60] Parrinder's eleventh characteristic is "Avatars reveal a personal God" (Avatar and Incarnation, 125). Parrinder is careful to note "how uneasy the monists are with the Avatar doctrine" (p. 125), and then proceeds to prove his thesis of Avatars revealing a personal God with his interpretation of the BG. The heading therefore is misleading. It should have read something to the effect of "The Avatar of the BG, in my interpretation,

Śaṅkara's two realms by Rāmānuja,[61] it appears that the similarity of "work" between his Kṛṣṇāvatāra and the Kṛṣṇāvatāra of Rāmānuja is not so similar, both as to actual ultimate means of the purpose (just discussed) and to actual reality of the purpose itself. Moreover, as I mentioned in chapter 2,[62] in His BUB Śaṅkara stated that the supreme Brahman has two forms, and that through superimposition and by ignorance the supreme formless Brahman is made conceivable. If by Kṛṣṇa one comes to know Brahman, it seems one does this through superimposition by ignorance as a preliminary stage.

Śaṅkara and Rāmānuja differ here as to purpose and reality. Classical orthodoxy differs from Śaṅkara and Rāmānuja in certain ways. To this I now turn.

### 2.3. Classical Orthodoxy's Atonement: Comparative Conclusions

Christian orthodoxy would agree with Rāmānuja that both Christ and Kṛṣṇa came with work to do, but there are at least two critical differences to explore—redemption versus liberation, and an ultimately redemptive purpose versus ultimately līlā.

In Kersey Graves' book, The World's Sixteen Crucified Saviors, he lists an amazing 346 similarities between Christ and Kṛṣṇa, several quite superficial, and several quite careless.[63] As an example of the latter, one of the similarities reads, "The necessity of atoning for sin is taught in the religion of each." Further, Christ and Kṛṣṇa are each "selected as the victim for the atoning sacrifice".[64] This is unfortunate. From the perspective of traditional orthodoxy in comparison to the Kṛṣṇāvatāra doctrines of Śaṅkara and Rāmānuja, can there be similarity between Christ and Kṛṣṇa in this regard?[65] Within the linear

---

reveals a personal God." Additionally, Śaṅkara's Īśvara is, according to Śaṅkara, personal, but is he ultimately real? If not, can the Kṛṣṇāvatāra of Śaṅkara be said to reveal, in the ultimate and true sense, a personal God?

[61] See my chapter 1, section 1.3.1, and chapter 3, section 2.1.3 where Rāmānuja's criticism is implicit.

[62] Section 2.1.

[63] Kersey Graves, The World's Sixteen Crucified Saviors (New Hyde Park, N.Y.: University Books, 1971), 256-73.

[64] Graves, The World's Sixteen Crucified Saviors, 256. Graves fleshes out these statements on pages 294-96. On page 294 Graves quotes the BG but gives no chapter and verse listing: "He [Kṛṣṇa] spent his time working miracles, resuscitating the dead, healing lepers, restoring the deaf and the blind ... and in proclaiming his divine mission to redeem man from original sin." I am not aware of such a statement in the BG or in other traditional Hindu literature.

[65] Another example of a careless statement on Graves' part is, "A Spirit or Ghost was the author of the conception of each" (p. 257). An example of a superficial similarity is, "God is sent down from heaven in each case in the form of a man" (p. 256). As I have demonstrated, one must carefully explore what "form" and "man" mean. Further, what

worldview of classical orthodox Christianity the ultimate purpose of the incarnation is redemption through the atonement and rescue from sin and its ultimate consequences—God in the person of Christ came in "the fullness of time ... in order that he might redeem those under the law" (Gal. 4.4).[66] Sin is rooted in the inherent sinful nature (Rom. 5.12-19) of human beings (both soul and body), and in the act of substitutionary atonement Christ suffered in crucifixion and died for the sins of his people (John 1.29; Matt. 1.21). Faith in Christ's person and work then leads to devotion and service to Christ on the part of Christians.

A theology of redemption in this sense cannot be attributed to Kṛṣṇa. On this point concerning the difference between the work of avatāra and the work of Christ, John Brockington correctly observes,

> Yet, however divine and merciful Kṛṣṇa is shown as being in the texts and in the theologies derived from them, he is not a redeemer or saviour in the sense of personally taking on himself the responsibility of the human race and saving it from the consequences of sin. His involvement in the human condition never goes as far as Christ's.[67]

Otto states, "It is not the essential difference between Christ and Krishna and Rāma that he is a 'mediator' only, for they were mediators too ... But that Christ was a 'propitiator' is the profoundest meaning of his coming."[68] And Vitaliano Gorospe admits that "Krishna assumes that human suffering must be transcended, but he does not take upon himself the sufferings of humanity for

---

does Graves mean when he states that both Kṛṣṇa and Christ were "sent"? In the case of Kṛṣṇa, who sent him? Lipner is quite correct when he writes that "there is a rational if not logical connection between Incarnation and Trinity", whereas in the Vaiṣṇava tradition (and, I might add, in the advaita tradition), "there seems to be no correspondence, theologically, to the Trinitarian dimension" ("Avatāra and Incarnation?", 133). In the comparison of the three traditions in this study, only with traditional orthodox Christianity do we find a "sending", by another, of the one who descends.

[66] My emphasis of contrast is on redemption, not on Christ's coming in the fullness of time; Hindus certainly can claim the latter for Kṛṣṇa in the context of the yuga-s.

[67] Hinduism and Christianity, 27. Clooney mentions certain later Vaiṣṇava theologians who found the need theologically to separate avatāra-s from any sort of suffering. Rather than actually suffering, the avatāra-s are exhibiting "dramatic gestures", as actors do on stage, for the benefit of their devotees (Francis X. Clooney, Hindu God, Christian God: How Reason Helps Break Down the Boundaries between Religions [New York: Oxford University Press, 2001], 118).

[68] India's Religion of Grace and Christianity Compared and Contrasted, 105. Brockington also notes this about Otto in his Hinduism and Christianity, 41-42.

salvation."[69] John Carman, representing the thought of the Vaiṣṇava, states that "the avatar does not accomplish his work by sacrificing himself".[70]

Regarding atonement and līlā, Griffiths, after making the observation that in the Hindu view avatāra and creation and human life are a play of God (quoted earlier in section 2.1), immediately states, "Though there is something to be said for this view, it is obviously inadequate. When you think of all the terrible suffering in the world and the agonies which people endure, it is not enough to say that God is playing with them. The crucifixion is not a play at all; it is totally different."[71] Griffiths adds that within the New Testament one finds meaning and purpose with human history, that each person has a "place in the plan of God", and that purpose and meaning are revealed in Christ and "in the historic events of his life and death and resurrection". This, he states, "is the doctrine of incarnation".[72]

Hindus, however, could answer this observation of Griffiths in a number of ways. I shall mention two. First, Vivekananda, an Advaitin, appeals to līlā for the denial of any need for repentance, thus implicitly denying any need for the crucifixion of Christ for sins: "It is all play. Play! That is all. You are the almighty God playing ... The whole universe is a vast play. All is good because all is fun ... Do not repent! ... We make mistakes; what of that? That is all in fun. They go crazy over their past sins, moaning and weeping and all that. Do not repent!"[73] Second, and perhaps more telling of Griffiths' possible misunderstanding of the term līlā, which in English is translated (unfortunately?) "sport", with Rāmānuja the term and its meaning reveals a Brahman who, according to Lipner, is not irresponsible or uncaring. Lipner notes Rāmānuja's illustration of an "unrivalled world-emperor, who, wanting for nothing, plays a ballgame purely for sport". The illustration does not communicate aloofness on the emperor's part. Rather, the emperor engages in the ballgame for non-competitive, as opposed to competitive, sport. Sport of this type is, in Lipner's words, "not consciously gainful or self-interested", signifying activity that is "unselfish". Further, this does not imply

---

[69] Vitaliano R. Gorospe, "Krishna Avatara in the Bhagavad Gita and Christ Incarnate in John's Gospel", Dialogue & Alliance 1, no. 2 (Summer 1987): 64. See also Eck: "Jesus took on suffering himself, experiencing suffering and death as all of us do" (Encountering God, 90).

[70] John B. Carman, Majesty and Meekness: A Comparative Study of Contrast and Harmony in the Concept of God (Grand Rapids, Mich.: William B. Eerdmans, 1994), 199.

[71] River of Compassion, 69. Griffiths does spend some time comparing differences between avatāra and incarnation (pp. 67-69).

[72] River of Compassion, 69.

[73] Swami Chetanananda, ed. and comp., Meditation and Its Methods: According to Swami Vivekananda (Hollywood: Vedanta Press, n.d.), 94,95.

"imperfection in its agent".[74] Rāmānuja's Brahman, therefore, would be quite different from the Brahman described above by Griffiths.

However, though līlā might be understood in Lipner's quite insightful sense, there are still some observations to be made within that sense. For example, though classical orthodoxy would agree with Rāmānuja on the "general theme of work" and the reality of it, it would differ sharply from Rāmānuja as to the definition of the work and thus the real purpose of the work. At this point the two traditions diverge so drastically that it makes any similarity of "rescue" (1) superficial and (2) void of any real theological complexity, and therefore void of deep meaning and ultimately misleading. As Clooney aptly observes with the later Vaiṣṇava theologian Vedānta Deśika, the activity of avatāra is real but is void of any suffering on the part of the avatāra. Any suffering is relegated to "dramatic gestures" on the part of the avatāra.[75] Deśika's Adhikaraṇasarāvali with the Adhikaraṇacintāmaṇi of Vaiśvamitraśrīvaradaguru and the Sārārtharatnaprabhā of Uttamur T. Vīrarāghavācārya[76] contains Deśika's Adhikaraṇasarāvali and two commentaries on it by Vaiśvamitraśrīvaradaguru and Vīrarāghavācārya. Deśika writes of the avatāra and his "dramatic gestures throughout his divine descents".[77] Vīrarāghavācārya comments that there is no suffering on the part of the avatāra-s, and that "suffering is simply dramatic gesture".[78] Vaiśvamitraśrīvaradaguru admits the same, stating that the Lord's feelings of grief are like those of an actor on stage.[79] Thus, though Clooney states that the purpose of the activities of avatāra-s is "bringing humans into proximity with a God involved in human activities", he admits that there is no theology of suffering in atonement for the sins of followers. Demonstrating respect for Vaiṣṇava tradition, Clooney further observes,

> But in any case one can rightly observe that this Vaiṣṇava position does not attribute redemptive power to the suffering itself. The deeds of Kṛṣṇa and Rāma are deeply effective because of the powerful way in which God communicates through these actions and transforms the "audience" of devotees but not because God is suffering as humans suffer.[80]

Upādhyāy adds, though not specifically in connection with the Vaiṣṇava tradition,

---

[74] Julius J. Lipner, The Face of Truth: A Study of Meaning and Metaphysics in the Vedantic Theology of Ramanuja (Albany: State University of New York Press, 1986), 92-93.

[75] Hindu God, Christian God, 115-18. See my note 67.

[76] Chennai: Ubhaya Vedānta Granthamala, 1974.

[77] Page 125 (verse 65).

[78] Page 126.

[79] Page 125.

[80] Hindu God, Christian God, 119.

What the Gītā teaches and what Christians teach about divine descent are completely different. The Gītā teaches that the Lord descends from period to period to punish wrongdoers, protect the virtuous and establish dharma. But the Christians say that the Lord, having assumed human nature, has given up his life but once for the atonement of sin. Jesus cannot be said to be an avatār in the way this word is used in accordance with the Gītā teaching. The nature of his appearance is completely different.[81]

Orthodoxy also differs sharply from Śaṅkara as to both purpose and reality of the work. As the NC states, Jesus "came down from heaven for our salvation ... was crucified ... suffered and was buried". As is the case with Rāmānuja's system, there is no theology of atonement in Śaṅkara. There cannot be, for, first, and as I outlined in chapter 1,[82] Śaṅkara's epistemology grounds him in establishing the ultimate unreality of the world of appearance. Since this is the case, a lack of a theology of atonement is not surprising. Further, there is in his system a līlāvatāra that takes place within the confines of lower reality, and this līlāvatāra I therefore take to be ultimately mithyā,[83] just as a shell might appear to be silver.[84] Upādhyāy concurs with my observation that with Śaṅkara's advaita Kṛṣṇāvatāra must be viewed in the context of Brahman in fictitious connection with the world of appearance through māyā.[85] Tennent, representing the thought of Upādhyāy as regards advaita, states, "Thus, any avatār, full [pūrṇāvatāra] or partial [aṁśāvatāra], is ultimately an expression of māyā and, unlike Christ, has only a contingent or dependent existence."[86]

### 2.4. Once for All / Redemption; Multiple Descents / Liberation; Comparative Conclusions

Brockington states, "In its orthodox form, as laid down at the Councils of Nicaea and Chalcedon, the Christian doctrine of the Incarnation states that Jesus was God incarnate, the Second Person of the Triune God living a human life. It is axiomatic that there cannot be another divine incarnation, for in all respects Christ is unique."[87] In this statement the uniqueness of Christ is asserted within the explicit context of Jesus being God incarnate. But Brockington also states that orthodoxy claims that Christ is unique "in all

[81] Quoted in Tennent, Building Christianity on Indian Foundations, 333.
[82] Section 1.2 and its subsections.
[83] Section 1.2 and its subsections.
[84] See chapter 2, sections 3.1.3 and 3.3.1.
[85] My observation is based on my discussion in chapter 2, section 3.1 and its subsections, especially 3.1.1.
[86] Building Christianity on Indian Foundations, 335.
[87] Hinduism and Christianity, 24.

respects". Whether or not Brockington had in mind the doctrine of redemption I cannot tell. But if not in the above statement, then certainly in this following statement by Brockington do we find the doctrine of the uniqueness of Christ in the context of redemption: "From the Christian side, the uniqueness of Christ has always been part of traditional belief and this can be attested within the New Testament in the assertion that Christ 'has appeared once for all at the climax of history to abolish sin by the sacrifice of himself' (Hebrews 9:26)."[88]

This latter quote leads me to conclude that when examining the philosophical and theological settings of the three traditions, elements that distinguish avatāra from incarnation come to the fore. First, the linear worldview of history in Christian theism more comfortably facilitates (though some say not necessarily[89]) a "once for all" incarnation event for Christ. Yet,

---

[88] Hinduism and Christianity, 40.

[89] See Bassuk, Incarnation in Hinduism and Christianity, 179. Bassuk states that Thomas Aquinas, in his Summa Theologiae, set forth the possibility of multiple incarnations of the Son had God so chosen. Aquinas did indeed teach this (Summa Theologiae, "The Incarnate Word", question 3, article 7). Further, Bassuk correctly observes that Aquinas postulated that the Father or the Holy Spirit could have incarnated, since they possessed the power to do so (Bassuk, p. 179; Aquinas, "The Incarnate Word", question 3, article 5), but misses that Aquinas taught that it was more fitting that the Son should incarnate (question 3, article 8). Bassuk draws upon Quentin Quesnell, "Aquinas on Avatars" (Dialogue and Alliance 1, no. 2 [Summer 1987], 33-42), wherein Quesnell cites several of Aquinas' observations and takes him to certain conclusions of his own, including the thesis that it is indeed possible that there could be multiple incarnations. For a rebuttal to the thesis that the Son can undergo multiple incarnations, see Brian Hebblethwaite, "The Impossibility of Multiple Incarnations", Theology CIV, no. 821 (September / October 2001): 323-34. Here Hebblethwaite argues philosophically and logically that since there is one metaphysical subject, the Son, that incarnated, and that since the incarnate Son is one person, to postulate multiple incarnations for the one metaphysical subject results in a split personality in that subject. Considering Christian eschatology, if multiple incarnations were true, Hebblethwaite asserts, it would result in "the simultaneous existence of a number of risen humans each alleged to be the incarnate Son of God" (p. 326). The point here is that the one metaphysical subject is split, and the multiple incarnations "would have to be the same person". Hebblethwaite also expresses his astonishment at Aquinas' theory of the possibility of multiple incarnations of the Son, and argues against it on these grounds. I add, in addition to Hebblethwaite's arguments, one more objection to the impossibility of multiple incarnations, specifically the Old Testament background of the firstborn son in the family compound of the patriarch, from which the New Testament imagery of the incarnate firstborn Son of God is patterned. Jesus, as the firstborn of the Father, corresponds to the Old Testament teaching of one firstborn son for each father in that father's family compound. The point here is that Jesus, who cannot be replaced as firstborn because he was perfect, is the one firstborn in the one Father's family compound, which will one day be the new heaven and new earth spoken of in the Book of Revelation (see Jesus' statement, "In my Father's house [i.e., family compound] are

the cyclical worldview of history on the parts of Śaṅkara and Rāmānuja more comfortably facilitates a theology of multiple descents.[90] In this sense the avatāra-'s purpose is temporary.[91] Second, given that incarnation is placed in the context of the redemption of humanity through blood atonement, and that enfleshment is a theological and soteriological necessity on the part of Christ,

---

many dwelling places" [John 14.2]). Thus, on exegetical grounds there cannot be more than one firstborn Son of the Father. See also Diogenes Allen, "Incarnation in the Gospels and the Bhagavad Gita", Faith and Philosophy 6, no. 3 (July 1989): 242,256-57, wherein he documents the thesis of Simone Weil that the Word has manifested in human forms in other religions, though Jesus' incarnation differs in certain aspects, namely in his suffering and with his continual possession of his humanity. The implication here is that the other manifestations die and do not continue to possess humanity. This appears to be a middle ground, solution to, or refutation of Hebblethwaite's argument. Such, though, is not the case, for there still remains Hebblethwaite's charge of multiple personalities in association with the Word. The problem with Allen's and Weil's multiple manifestations (and therefore multiple personalities) in association with the Word is furthered when one considers the eschaton, for who will Jesus be known as? Jesus who was at one time also Kṛṣṇa and whatever other manifestations of the Word came into being at times in the past? As an aside, how would Allen and Weil account for Rāmānuja's doctrine of the divya rūpa, where the anthropomorphic form of Viṣṇu is continual? Could it be that they are faced with yet another manifestation of the Word existing simultaneously with Jesus? If so, there would indeed be two different though simultaneous bodily existences of the Word, unless of course Allen or Weil took the view that Rāmānuja and his followers are in error concerning the divya rūpa, or that the divya rūpa cannot be considered a manifestation of the Word since the category applies only to historic persons.

[90] See Parrinder's sixth characteristic: "Avatars are repeated" (Avatar and Incarnation, 122). I suppose that in a sense a Hindu could challenge the thesis that Hinduism presents a strictly cyclical view. Could it not be said that even though eternally-occurring four-yuga cycles exist, these eternally-occurring four-yuga cycles continue on and on, in linear fashion? But even if this were the case, there still remains a sharp difference between this and Christian orthodoxy (see section 3.4, seventh point, C).

[91] Others have stated that its need is dispensable. See Yesurathnam, "The Adequacy of the Concept of Avatara for Expounding the Christian Doctrine of Incarnation", Dialogue & Alliance 1, no. 2 (Summer 1987): 48. Here Yesurathnam cites the observations of Bishop Sabhapathy Kulandran in his Grace: A Comparative Study of the Doctrine in Christianity and Hinduism (London: Lutterworth Press, 1964), 149 and following. I do not necessarily agree with this thesis. It seems to me that the doctrine of multiple avatāra-s cannot, on its own ground, dismiss any avatāra event as dispensable, for each event is important in the age in which it occurs. Lott also disagrees. Reacting to the Christian claim that only when there is a unique incarnation can there be the doctrine of all-sufficiency, he states that "there is logically no reason to deny that each Avatāra is just as much a full divine revelation, or a perfect vehicle of divine redemption in the Age in which it occurs. And except for the lingering influence of karma and the continuation of matter and souls in inconceivably subtle form, each Age can be thought of as complete" ("The Relevance of Research in Religions", 51).

full identification is inextricably woven into the redemptive process (see Heb. 2.14-17[92]). Yet, the traditional avatāra events of Viṣṇu are not exclusively those of persons, and even when they are, at least for Śaṅkara's Kṛṣṇa and Rāmānuja's Kṛṣṇa, there is no real humanity from the perspective of classical orthodoxy—Śaṅkara's epistemology within his advaita[93] and Rāmānuja's doctrine of the divya rūpa in connection with Kṛṣṇāvatāra[94] lead to this conclusion. This also may be due to the fact that with avatāra there is not so much a need for identification with humanity in the redemptive process as there is for a message of liberation, the way of mokṣa[95] for the jīva or ātman, and this by way of recognition of or devotion to the transcendent nature hidden by apparent humanity. In comparing Christianity to advaita in this category, the former underscores the need for individuals to realize that they have fallen short of the glory of God and are in need of redemption, while the latter underscores the necessity of the avatāra to make the soul realize its eternal oneness with Brahman.[96] Third, a deep difference between orthodoxy's Christ and the BG's and our two Vedāntins' Kṛṣṇa is that the former comes to save evil doers, while the latter comes to destroy them, as is stated in BG 4.8.[97]

### 3. Śaṅkara's, Rāmānuja's, and Classical Orthodoxy's Views of God in Relation to the World; the Bodies of Kṛṣṇa and Christ; Identification

Parrinder's first of "Twelve Characteristics" reads, "In Hindu belief the Avatar is real". He further explains, "That is, it is a visible and fleshly descent of the divine to the animal or human plane."[98] What would Śaṅkara have said in response to these statements? I believe he would affirm the statements, but, in light of his epistemology, only with the greatest of care lest he be judged for crediting ultimate reality to the material world. That is, he would have affirmed these statements, but only if he were allowed to put the words real, visible, fleshly, animal, human, and plane in quotes or somehow carefully qualify his statements in the light of his advaita.[99]

---

92 See chapter 6 n. 55.

93 See chapter 1, section 1.2 and its subsections.

94 See chapter 4, section 3.5.2.3,2A-C.

95 Śrīnivāsa taught that "Śrīkṛṣṇāvatāra descended for the purpose of teaching the way of mokṣa." My translation of mokṣopāyadarśānārtham avatīrṇaḥ śrīkṛṣṇāvatāraḥ (Sanskrit from Svāmī Ādidevānanda, trans., Yatīndramatadīpikā by Śrīnivāsadāsa [Mylapore: Sri Ramakrishna Math, n.d.], 138 [9.23]; noted from hereon as YS).

96 See Yesurathnam, "The Adequacy of the Concept of Avatara for Expounding the Christian Doctrine of Incarnation", 50.

97 See Appasamy, The Gospel and India's Heritage, 258.

98 Avatar and Incarnation, 120.

99 This even if one agrees with Richard De Smet, D. M. Datta, and Bradley Malkovsky that Śaṅkara's system proposed a realist ontology. For a description of this view, see notes 21 and 48 of chapter 1, and note 292 of chapter 4.

Further, though the avatāra may be "real", one must ask the question, "Real what?" That is, is the avatāra really human? Parrinder's third characteristic is "The lives of Avatars mingle divine and human." He then comments, "The Avatars are divinity incarnate."[100] But one must ask in what sense this occurs. If I am correct about Rāmānuja's Kṛṣṇāvatāra, the person of Kṛṣṇa is solely divine. And, again, what would Śaṅkara say about such a statement? Would he have to place mingle divine and human in quotation marks?

### 3.1. Śaṅkara

As I have demonstrated in chapter 2,[101] Śaṅkara's kevalādvaita necessitates the ultimate unreality of the jagat and all phenomena associated with it. In the context of kevalādvaita, where the material world is ultimately illusory, there is primarily no need for theological focus on coming in the flesh.[102] And as I have documented in chapter 4, the mānuṣī tanu of Kṛṣṇa, though "real" from the empirical point of view as a dream is real, is ultimately mithyā[103] and has no real relationship with higher Brahman.[104] In the administration of māyā Kṛṣṇa "seems" to be embodied or born as a man.[105] Thus, the avatāra of Kṛṣṇa is for Śaṅkara relegated to the jagat-prapañca in the realm of Īśvara or apara brahman.

As for the doctrine of identification of Kṛṣṇa with humanity, though it is true that with Śaṅkara the jagat, in the realm of Īśvara, is of Brahman (creation is ex

---

[100] Avatar and Incarnation, 121.

[101] Section 3.1 and its subsections.

[102] And I might conclude this for those scholars (like De Smet, Datta, and Malkovsky) who see in Śaṅkara a realist ontology. That is, if the jagat is seen as "relatively real" in comparison to the "Real" (Brahman), the focus for coming in the flesh is thus relegated to relative importance, paling in comparison to the Real.

[103] See chapter 4, section 3.4.2 and its subsections, especially the implications for the mānuṣī tanu at the end of section 3.4.2.3, first, second and fifth points. Malkovsky explores Śaṅkara's possible views on the body of Kṛṣṇa in his The Role of Divine Grace in the Soteriology of Śaṃkarācārya (Leiden: Brill, 2001), 336-44. He offers three options. First is that Kṛṣṇa possesses a normal human body (but not fashioned in accordance with past karma), second that Kṛṣṇa has a body that is unique, different from those of others, and third is that Kṛṣṇa is "a mere appearance of a human body" (pp. 343,344). Malkovsky, though, concludes, "But perhaps for Śaṃkara the question as to whether the Lord was really incarnated or only appeared to be incarnated was after all of only secondary importance" (p. 344).

[104] See chapter 4, the end of section 3.4.2.3 (implications for the mānuṣī tanu), third point.

[105] "Krishna was not a real embodiment of God's ultimate being, but was merely an 'as if' embodiment ... Krishna was only 'as if' embodied, that in truth his body was but a veil of illusion" (Lott, "The Mythic Symbol Avatar in Indian Conceptual Formulations", 5).

deo in the sense that Brahman is ultimately the material cause of the jagat[106]), against the true reality that is para brahman Kṛṣṇāvatāra is not real. His humanity and his deity in connection with his humanity are not real in the ultimate sense. But, as discussed earlier, in a very loose sense it might be said that Kṛṣṇāvatāra identifies fully with human beings intra-Śaṅkara[107] in the realm of lower Brahman. That is to say, the mānuṣī tanu is as "real" as are other bodies of human beings[108]: "Thus am I born, as it were, by virtue of My power of becoming and not in fact, as is the [same] case for the world [loka]."[109] In the ultimate and more important sense, however, there is no identification between Kṛṣṇa and humanity, for in the ultimately real there is only the monistic One that is Brahman as pure consciousness. In other words, in the ultimate sense there simply can be no identification, since (1) this implies two entities, (2) no talk of identification should ever arise, and (3) seeming identification in lower Brahman is ultimately unreal. We must therefore understand that this seeming identification occurs within the context of Īśvara or apara brahman. And given that the realm of Īśvara is of no ultimate importance save for the fact that it serves to accommodate those who have not

---

[106] See Śaṅkara's comments on BS 2.2.37. Śaṅkara states that the purpose of this sūtra "is to make an energetic attack on the doctrine that the Lord is not the material cause, but merely the ruler, i.e. the operative cause of the world; a doctrine entirely opposed to the Vedāntic tenet of the unity of Brahman" (George Thibaut, trans., Vedānta-Sūtras: With the Commentary by Śaṅkarācārya, in F. Max Müller, ed., Sacred Books of the East [Delhi: Motilal Banarsidass, 1988], 34:434). This differs sharply from classical orthodoxy. Clooney states,

> Śaṃkara's point is to criticize the idea of a maker God as an instance of poor reasoning, on grounds that may be summarized as follows. There is no coherent way to understand the variety of creation if a perfect Lord is the single, perfect efficient cause of it all. This perfect maker would make a world that is perfect like himself; there cannot be a coherent account of the relationship between a perfect maker God and the changing, effected world. Prime matter cannot be controlled by a God external to it ... Such a God would be limited in power or knowledge, in proportion to the finite world he seems to be making (Hindu God, Christian God, 55).

[107] See my chapter 4, section 4.2. Lott concurs, though without specifically mentioning identification in his essay: "His [Kṛṣṇa's] embodiment, according to Sankara's interpretation, exemplifies the truth beyond all embodiments. What was true with dramatic clarity of the divine embodiment is essentially true of every embodied self" ("The Mythic Symbol Avatar in Indian Conceptual Formulations", 5). Note, though, that in chapter 4 I mention the possibility of identification on the part of Śaṅkara's Kṛṣṇa in the very loose sense, taken in the context of lower Brahman. In the ultimate sense there is no identification.

[108] In another essay Lott makes essentially the same statement as that in the previous note. Speaking of Śaṅkara's Kṛṣṇāvatāra, Lott writes, "what is true of the divine embodiment is essentially true of every embodied self" ("The Relevance of Research in Religions", 40).

[109] SBGB, 138.

yet experienced parā vidyā, Kṛṣṇāvatāra is therefore of no ultimate importance when the true reality that is para brahman is considered. This lack of ultimate importance for Kṛṣṇāvatāra manifests in Śaṅkara's eschatology, for neither in the here-and-now nor at the dawning of mokṣa, where the jīva realizes its true state, that of complete identity with Brahman,[110] must there be for Śaṅkara a pressing concern for the reality of Kṛṣṇāvatāra.

### 3.2. Rāmānuja

With Rāmānuja, though his viśiṣṭādvaita assures the reality of the material world[111] and therefore likewise assures the reality of the avatāra of Kṛṣṇa,[112] it does not postulate a true humanity for Kṛṣṇa, nor a complete identification of Kṛṣṇa with human beings, at least in the here-and-now.[113] Though Rāmānuja's viśiṣṭādvaita views the jagat as the body of Brahman,[114] who is the antaryāmin and the śarīrin,[115] the mānuṣī tanu of Kṛṣṇa is not fashioned from the fundamental prakṛti that makes up the jagat, including the material makeup of human beings.[116] Rather, the material for the tangible body of Kṛṣṇa stems from the divya rūpa, the divine anthropomorphic form of Viṣṇu that is made up of a mysterious "non-prakṛtic substance" peculiar to Viṣṇu alone.[117] It is quite possible, therefore, that Rāmānuja's Kṛṣṇa is solely divine. It is in this context of the divya rūpa that I also note the doctrine that in Kṛṣṇāvatāra Viṣṇu comes in the person of Kṛṣṇa without any loss of essential nature, including his eternal deity.[118] Yet, just as is the case with Śaṅkara, the question arises as to whether or not Rāmānuja's Kṛṣṇāvatāra is fully divine, that is, whether or not Kṛṣṇa is the fullness of God, for, as documented in chapter 4,[119] Kṛṣṇa is the incarnation of a portion of Viṣṇu.

The lack of need for complete identification of Kṛṣṇa with humanity is in

---

[110] See chapter 2, section 3.2 and its subsections.

[111] See chapter 3, section 2.1 and its subsections.

[112] See, for example, chapter 4, sections 1.2.2 and 1.3.2.

[113] See chapter 4, section 3.5.2.3,2D.

[114] It is partly in this sense of indweller that the world has its origin in lower and higher natures (prakṛti). In BG 7.4-6 the "I" of Kṛṣṇa persists in his claim that all prakṛti belongs to him, that is, in the sense that prakṛti, both lower and higher, is the body of Viṣṇu. But in another sense the jagat is actually a part of Viṣṇu. The material world, then, is Viṣṇu. See chapter 4, section 3.5.1.3 for a treatment of this.

[115] See chapter 3, sections 1.1.1, 2.1.1, 4.2 and 4.3.

[116] Brockington is careful and nuances this statement concerning Rāmānuja's doctrine of avatāra: "He [Viṣṇu] has therefore made himself accessible to his devotees by descending into the world in a form like theirs" (Hinduism and Christianity, 10; emphasis mine).

[117] See chapter 4, section 3.5.2.3,2A.

[118] See chapter 4, section 1.3.2.

[119] Section 3.5.2.3,2A.

one sense consistent with Rāmānuja's eschatology. On the one hand the eschatological emphasis is on mokṣa for the jīva, and there is a dissolution of the flesh of individuals after death. But in another sense, and on the other hand, the afterlife consequent upon mokṣa concerns individual spiritual existence of the jīva in the presence of Viṣṇu but with the addition of the possibility of each individual soul assuming various bodies at will.[120] It is not clear in Rāmānuja's writings where the material for these bodies comes from; that is to say, whether it is the divya rūpa or the material of Brahman in the usual mode of material cause of the world or perhaps some other substance, we cannot be sure. However, there is legitimate cause to reason that there is not really identity between the bodies of released souls and Viṣṇu, for the divya rūpa is peculiar to Viṣṇu alone,[121] even though released souls' embodiments are made of non-prakṛtic substances.[122]

Finally, though Rāmānuja has stated that in the creation and dissolution of the universe released and embodied souls do not suffer,[123] this cannot be said of the creation itself, for at the end of every four-yuga age the creation suffers dissolution.

### 3.3. Classical Orthodoxy

First, there is no ontological likeness between God and matter, or the world, for God is wholly other than his creation. Second, matter is not eternal. These two points I have documented in depth in chapter 5.[124] Third, matter is real, a point that is strongly implied in the Bible and subsequently in the writings of early church theologians. Fourth, as the NC confesses, Christ "was made man" and "was incarnate by the Holy Ghost of the virgin Mary". The body of Christ is fashioned from the womb of a true human being.[125] I concur with certain early church theologians who stated that by way of descent from Mary to Adam the material for Christ's body is fashioned from real matter created ex nihilo,[126] and

---

[120] See chapter 4, section 3.5.2.3,2D.

[121] See chapter 4, section 3.5.2.3,2A. I do not agree, therefore, with the statement by Carman (if representing Rāmānuja's Vaiṣṇava thought) that "The descent of the avatar is part of and continuous with the process of emanation in which all 'creation', all finite reality, is spread out, constituting the cosmic body of God" (Majesty and Meekness, 200). Since the divya rūpa is peculiar to God alone, and therefore a physical phenomenon in addition to the cosmic body of God, the descent of the avatāra, who gains his materiality from the divya rūpa, cannot be part of the process of emanation in connection with the universe as God's body (see my chapter 3, section 1.1 and n. 6, and chapter 4, section 3.5.2.3,2A).

[122] See chapter 4, section 3.5.2.3,2D.

[123] See chapter 4, section 3.5.2.3,2D.

[124] See section 1.1 and its subsections and section 2 and its subsections.

[125] See chapter 6, sections 4 and 5.

[126] See chapter 6 n. 65.

that therefore his humanity is wholly other than his divine nature.[127] Fifth, as the C teaches, Christ's body is just as human as is every human being's body, for Christ is "ὁμοούσιος [homoousios] with us according to the Manhood".[128] Sixth, in the person of Christ is a true and full human nature; he is, as the C asserts, "truly man".[129] Seventh, the true and full humanity of Christ was created and exists in union (C) with his nature as God the Son.[130] There is, then, a real relationship between deity and humanity in the person of Christ. Eighth, the nature of deity within the person of Christ is not diminished whatsoever by way of the union (C), and thus it is that classical orthodoxy confesses that Christ is fully divine (C).[131] Finally, there is a permanent relationship between the human nature and the divine nature in the person of Christ.

Christ therefore fully identifies with humanity.[132] There is also a soteriological and eschatological necessity behind this identification. Christ needed to be human as are all human beings, the purpose being that of atonement for the sins of humanity.[133] Following from this is the concept of resurrection of the faithful, where there is a resurrection of the body—the whole person. The NC speaks of "the resurrection of the dead and the life of the world to come". Within a linear view of history, God's people will live forever in God's place and in God's presence, the place (the world) being recreated and enduring forever.[134]

### 3.4. Comparative Conclusions

There are surface similarities common either to all three traditions or to two of

---

[127] See chapter 6 n. 59.
[128] See chapter 6, section 4.
[129] See chapter 6, section 5.
[130] See chapter 6, section 6 and its subsections.
[131] See chapter 6, section 6.1. Philippians 2:7 and the kenosis of Christ are a text and christological theme cited either to deny Christ as fully God or to convey that in the incarnation God "emptied" himself of glory, majesty, certain divine prerogatives, etc. (Carman calls upon this latter option in his hypothetical Christian-Hindu dialogue, representing the Christian [Majesty and Meekness, 201]). I argue elsewhere, however, that the "emptying" does not occur in the context of the pre-existent Son becoming human, as is commonly interpreted by several conservative Christian theologians and other theologians, with varying degrees of implications. Rather, the context is the earthly existence of the incarnate Son. The emptying, or kenosis, then, is the cross event, and is taken directly from Isaiah 53, specifically verse 12, where "he poured out himself to death". See Steven Tsoukalas, Knowing Christ in the Challenge of Heresy: A Christology of the Cults, a Christology of the Bible (Lanham, Md.: University Press of America, 1999), 98-104.
[132] See chapter 6, section 4.
[133] See chapter 6 n. 55.
[134] See chapter 6 nn. 41,42.

the three traditions. Yet, the dissimilarities theologically and epistemologically intrinsic to the surface similarities must be considered before final conclusions are drawn.

By way of surface similarities, we find first that avatāra and incarnation occur in the wombs of Devakī and Mary because of the divine will.[135] Second, all the texts examined assert that both Kṛṣṇa and Christ are sinless.[136] Third,

---

[135] For Jesus, see, for example, the various passages that speak of God the Father "sending" his Son. The phraseology of the Son being sent appears in Matthew 10.40, Mark 9.37, and Luke 9.48. There are multiple references in the Gospel of John (see, for example, 3.17; 5.30,36,37; 6.29,38,39,40,44,57; 7.16,28,29; 8.16,18,26,42; 9.4; 12.44, etc.). It appears outside the Gospels (Rom. 8.3; Gal. 4.4; 2 Cor. 8.9; 1 John 4.9,10,14). We may add to this Jesus' own witness that He has "come into the world" (see John 9.39; 12.46), and Martha's confession: "I believe that you are the Christ, the Son of God who comes into the world" (John 11.27). This material is taken from Tsoukalas, Knowing Christ in the Challenge of Heresy, 28-29.

[136] For Rāmānuja see chapter 4, section 1.3.2; for Śaṅkara see chapter 4, section 1.3.1; for Christ see chapter 6 nn. 32,34. Lipner also observes, "It is only the unenlightened self that produces karma and is reborn" ("Avatāra and Incarnation?", 138), a statement with which Śaṅkara and Rāmānuja would agree, therefore implying Kṛṣṇa's sinlessness as a doctrine for both Vedāntins.

Some have argued (depending, of course, on one's definition of sin) that the Kṛṣṇa presented in the BP is not sinless. Interesting is Bhagavan Das' quotation of a passage from the BP: "The precepts of the great are generally sound, but not their example. They too transgress the Law and commit willful sins ... Follow the good in their example and not the bad" (Krishna: A Study in the Theory of Avataras [Chaupatty, Bombay: Bharatiya Vidya Bhavan, 1962], 59; Das gives no book and verse reference for this quotation from the BP). In the BP the sexual acts of Kṛṣṇa are recorded, and some Christian missionaries / theologians have commented upon these in effort to show the superiority of Christ over Kṛṣṇa, among them Brahmabāndhav Upādhyāy. Upādhyāy several times made reference to the sexual immorality of Kṛṣṇa in the BP. I refer the reader to a series of articles in Sophia: A Monthly Catholic Journal, specifically, volumes 3 no. 1 (Jan. 1896), 3 no. 2 (Feb. 1896), 3 no. 5 (May 1896), 4 no. 2 (Feb. 1897), and 4 no. 6 (June 1897). My thanks to Timothy C. Tennent, in his Building Christianity on Indian Foundations, 319-22, for these references. Tennent observes that later on Upādhyāy distanced himself from the issue of the sexual immorality of Kṛṣṇa by giving a lecture on Kṛṣṇāvatāra (entitled Śrīkṛṣṇatattva, "The Truth about the Honorable Kṛṣṇa") specifically and exclusively within the context of Śaṅkara's advaita. The lecture is void of any polemic against Kṛṣṇa's sexual encounters (Building Christianity on Indian Foundations, 330). For a historical account of Upādhyāy's earlier and later views of Kṛṣṇa, see Julius J. Lipner, Brahmabandhab Upadhyay: The Life and Thought of a Revolutionary (Delhi: Oxford University Press, 1999). For the early Upādhyāy, see pages 145-47, and note that in this section Lipner observes that the early Upādhyāy made a moral distinction between the Kṛṣṇa of the BG and the Kṛṣṇa of the BP (p. 146). For the later Upādhyāy, including his Śrīkṛṣṇatattva lecture, see pages 325-42.

there is common to Rāmānuja and classical orthodoxy the teaching of an afterlife. Finally, and it is here that I shall spend the majority of my time, in all three traditions we find a body-soul-divine relation in Kṛṣṇa and Christ along with consequent "deity veiled in flesh" motifs.

However, there are dissimilarities—stark dissimilarities—that prove the above similarities either misleading or empty of any deep theological penetration and meaning.

First, though I do not wish to enter into debate on the issue of whether or not Christ could sin, and the reasons for one view or the other in comparison to Kṛṣṇa,[137] I do need to note one doctrinal reason why Kṛṣṇa was confessed as sinless. It is because his form had no connection whatsoever with prakṛti as it relates to the triguṇātmikā. This is not to say that the mānuṣī tanu of Kṛṣṇa has no connection at all with prakṛti, but only to say that there is no connection with prakṛti as it relates to the triguṇātmikā.[138] With orthodoxy the reason why Christ is, essentially, sinless is many times not explicitly delineated in the New Testament text. Of course he is God the Son, surely he was conceived by the agency of the Holy Spirit, and theologians certainly call upon these and other reasons to infer the "why" of it all. My point here is that in many cases the why of it all is implicit in the New Testament. But there is a "why" that is explicit in the New Testament: The sinlessness of Christ is inextricably linked to the doctrine of atonement. As I mentioned earlier, this "why" sets Christ apart from Kṛṣṇa. On another point (but related to the triguṇātmikā doctrine), whereas all other beings are born resultant of their karma,[139] Kṛṣṇa is not; rather, Kṛṣṇa chooses by his own will to be an avatāra. For traditional orthodoxy, there is no cause-effect, or karmic, law by which humans come into existence (though

---

According to Flood the composition of the BP, including its accounts of Kṛṣṇa's love-making with the gopī-s (cowgirls), took place by the fourth century A.D., so one could argue that the BP was in existence by the times of Śaṅkara and Rāmānuja (Flood, An Introduction to Hinduism, 120; by the sixth century according to Tennent [Building Christianity on Indian Foundations, 319], who cites A. L. Herman, Hinduism [Oxford: Westview Press, 1991], 20, though note that it may be as late as the tenth century before we have any recording of eroticism on the part of Kṛṣṇa; Lipner mentions ninth century extant versions ["Avatāra and Incarnation?", 133-34]). However, in my reading of the sources for both Śaṅkara and Rāmānuja, I have not found any citations of the BP in reference to the sexual life of Kṛṣṇa. It is, therefore, difficult, indeed impossible, to include any of these BP passages in their views of Kṛṣṇāvatāra.

137 At least for now it shall remain to be further explored!

138 Lipner, rightly, notes that confession of Kṛṣṇa as aprākṛta (not under nature's thrall, as Lipner translates) does not necessarily mean that Kṛṣṇa is not constituted from natural elements. It means, rather, that one is not bound by the karmic-caused / related cycle of rebirth (Brahmabandhab Upadhyay, 336). Thus, concerning avatāra-s, reasons for any lack of a real material body or a material body not made of the elements from which other bodies are made must rest on other grounds.

139 See chapter 4, section 1.3 and its subsections, and section 1.5.2.

there is the sense of cause-effect when one considers inherited sin from Adam). Rather, human beings come into being solely by the will of God. Further, contrary to the unitarian nature of Viṣṇu in the decision-making process for the descent of Kṛṣṇa, with classical Christian Trinitarian orthodoxy the will of the Father is involved. Here the preincarnate logos is sent by the Father to incarnate by the agency of the Holy Spirit.

Second, for Śaṅkara Kṛṣṇāvatāra is ultimately not real, and the relationship between Arjuna and Kṛṣṇa is ultimately unreal. Higher or ultimate Brahman alone is real, and, further, is "unrelated to all empirical experiences"[140] and "beyond the range of the senses".[141] He differs, therefore, from Rāmānuja and classical orthodoxy, for Rāmānuja holds to a real Kṛṣṇāvatāra[142] (and a real world) and orthodoxy to a real incarnation (and a real world) where Jesus comes into the range of the senses to reveal the Father.[143] (It is true, though, that only with Christian orthodoxy do we find both a real relationship between deity and humanity and a relationship between deity and real humanity.) For Śaṅkara the birth in the womb of Devakī is not ultimately real,[144] and, moreover, what does Kṛṣṇa's sinless life really mean in the context of advaita, where there is no ultimate reality to the actions of Kṛṣṇa? Further, Śaṅkara must speak of Kṛṣṇa's sinlessness, other deeds, and other attributes only in the context of saguṇa Brahman or lower Brahman, for according to him higher Brahman is "without form, without qualities, without any limitations". Kṛṣṇa, then, must not only reveal himself in the context of lower Brahman, but any talk of him whatsoever must be undertaken in the realm of lower Brahman.

Third, this second consideration seriously challenges the notion of total similarity of both Kṛṣṇa and Christ as "veiled in flesh". Here I concentrate only

---

[140] In spite of this, several authors miss the point when they assert in a general way that avatār a-s live the same life as all humans. See, for example, Appasamy, The Gospel and India's Heritage, page 253. Writing of the doctrine of avatāra he states, "He understands our difficulties, for He has lived the same life as we have."

[141] See chapter 2, section 2.1.1. Additionally, note that Śaṅkara stated, "All these [śruti] passages, with many others, declare Brahman to possess a double nature, according as it is the object either of Knowledge or of Nescience [avidyā]. As long as it is the object of Nescience, there are applied to it the categories of devotee, object of devotion, and the like" (SBE, 34:62; see my chapter 1 n. 48 and chapter 2 n. 52).

[142] As regards the Kṛṣṇāvatāra doctrines of Śaṅkara and Rāmānuja, Lott observes, "It is precisely in responding to this problem of the reality of God's embodiment that one finds the most striking divergence between the Vedantins" ("The Mythic Symbol Avatar in Indian Conceptual Formulations", 4).

[143] See John 14.9.

[144] Parrinder's second of his "Twelve Characteristics" is "The human Avatars take worldly birth" (Avatar and Incarnation, 121). This statement should have been nuanced carefully by Parrinder in light of his concise treatment of Śaṅkara earlier in Avatar and Incarnation (pp. 50-51), wherein he documents Śaṅkara's comments about avatāra, and states that Śaṅkara "seems to deny the reality of incarnation" (p. 50).

upon a comparison within the category of the body-divine relation, not in the categories of purpose or reason for veiling. BG 7.25 ("Covered by yoga-māyā, I am not manifest to all. This world, deluded, does not recognize me, birthless, imperishable") communicates the "veiling" of Kṛṣṇa's deity.[145] Similarly, among Christian theologians it is not uncommon to find the christological motif of Christ's humanity veiling his deity. But the similarity begins to shrink when one considers that Śaṅkara's Kṛṣṇāvatāra, although real in the context of Īśvara and the jagat-prapañca, is ultimately not real. That is, there is ultimately no real flesh involved in a "veiling", for since the para brahman is for Śaṅkara purely other than prakṛti in the context of his kevalādvaita, and the para brahman "is in reality unrelated to all empirical experiences", the mānuṣī tanu must be viewed as having no ultimate real relationship to the para brahman. Further, with Śaṅkara an "aspect" of the deity is veiled (again in the context of Īśvara), not full deity (see fifth, below). With Rāmānuja there is veiling of eternal deity by flesh and a real relationship between the flesh and the divine, but the flesh that veils is not the flesh that all humanity shares, since the flesh of Rāmānuja's Kṛṣṇāvatāra comes from the divya rūpa. Rāmānuja would be similar to orthodoxy in that eternal deity is veiled, that there is absolute reality to the veiling in flesh, and that there is a real relationship between the flesh and the deity, but he differs substantially from orthodoxy when the veiling is compared with identification in mind and with careful definition of "flesh". Further, in light of his assertion in his BGB that Kṛṣṇa is the incarnation of a portion of Viṣṇu, it may very well be that Rāmānuja would have difficulty with orthodoxy's Christ being fully God. So Śaṅkara and Rāmānuja differ from one another on the grounds of the reality of the flesh, real flesh concealing deity, flesh in a real relationship with the divine, and identification of Kṛṣṇa with humanity (if one adopts the "loose sense" of identification in Śaṅkara). They differ from classical orthodoxy as well, where Christ's flesh is real and human on all accounts, has a real relationship with deity, conceals full deity (these three points differing from Śaṅkara, the first and possibly third differing from Rāmānuja), and that Christ identifies with the flesh of all humanity (differing therefore from Rāmānuja and Śaṅkara). (For my reading of the BG and the dissimilarities between avatāra and incarnation that implicitly raise differences concerning the "veiling in the flesh" of the three traditions, see sixth, A-E below.)

Fourth, as for identification Śaṅkara's advaita (only in the loose sense) and orthodoxy, each considered within its respective system, share the view of identification with humanity, whereas Rāmānuja offers no identification of Kṛṣṇa with humanity. However, ultimately (and thus in the real sense) in Śaṅkara's system there is no identification. In Rāmānuja's theology Kṛṣṇa is

---

[145] See chapter 4, section 2 and its subsections.

arguably solely divine,[146] and this in the effort on Rāmānuja's part to divorce Viṣṇu from any connection whatsoever with a defiled material body.[147] This, of course, differs significantly from orthodoxy's view of the two natures of Christ. There is with Christ full identification with humanity, and any attempt on orthodoxy's part and the Bible's part to divorce Christ from a defiled material body is not done by making Christ's body other than the bodies of human beings or other than the material from which the world was fashioned, but by confessing Christ as sinless. And when the identification doctrines of Śaṅkara and orthodoxy are compared from the views of orthodoxy and Śaṅkara's ultimate sense, there is no identification with humanity even on the part of Śaṅkara's Kṛṣṇa.

Fifth, though Rāmānuja and classical orthodoxy share the view that the deity is not diminished in Kṛṣṇāvatāra or Christ, with Śaṅkara this seems not to be the case. In his introduction to his BGB, he states that "the primal and all-pervading Agent, celebrated as Nārāyaṇa, is held to have been born of Vasudeva from Devaki's womb by an aspect [aṁśa] of Himself as Kṛṣṇa".[148] Though I theorize that Śaṅkara could say that the divine is not diminished in the context of the para brahman, where the ātmanbrahman of Kṛṣṇa is the only reality (though all he could say of the para brahman is the statement neti neti), it appears he could not have admitted as much in the context of Īśvara.[149] Note also that for Rāmānuja, although Kṛṣṇa is the incarnation of a portion of Viṣṇu, he nonetheless confesses that the deity is not diminished in Kṛṣṇāvatāra, though deity exists at the expense of true humanity. With Christ, the nature of deity in all fullness exists in union with true and full humanity. Within the theological category of the divine-human relation, the three views are not similar at all to each other, and if there were any similarity, it would exist purely on a semantic surface level.

Sixth, with my interpretation of the BG, several dissimilarities occur between avatāra and incarnation. (In what follows I shall, in places, interact with the views of Śaṅkara and Rāmānuja.)

(A) I have argued that the mānuṣī tanu of Kṛṣṇa is fashioned from eternal

---

[146] Though Śaṅkara's Kṛṣṇa may be solely divine, this is so within the category of the Self as ātmanbrahman alone being real and the body being illusory. I make the statement above about Rāmānuja's Kṛṣṇa in the category of a real body-divine relation. With this category in mind Śaṅkara differs markedly from Rāmānuja.

[147] See chapter 3 n. 6.

[148] SBGB, 2. I translate the phrase aṁśena kṛṣṇaḥ kila as "by an aspect of himself, namely Kṛṣṇa".

[149] Lott interprets Śaṅkara's statement, "born of Vasudeva from Devaki's womb by an aspect [aṁśa] of Himself", in a similar fashion: "What Śankara intended by this 'part of himself' description is to deny that the supreme Self's whole being was involved in the revelatory event" ("The Relevance of Research in Religions", 42). Lott, though, does not specifically use the term Īśvara in relation to Śaṅkara's lower reality.

prakṛti.[150] This differs sharply from all three traditions. With Śaṅkara there is, ultimately, no prakṛti. Further, the confession of prakṛti as eternal, in the context of ultimate reality, that is, Brahman, would have been quite distasteful to the Advaitin. With Rāmānuja the material for the mānuṣī tanu comes from the divya rūpa, the divine anthropomorphic form of Viṣṇu that is non-prakṛtic in nature. Moreover, if the divya rūpa is eternal, then the material that forms the mānuṣī tanu of Kṛṣṇa is eternal. With classical orthodoxy matter is not eternal but is created by God ex nihilo. Thus, the flesh of Christ "became" in the womb of the virgin.

(B) the mānuṣī tanu is itself indwelled by Kṛṣṇa, who is the antaryāmin.[151] There is, then, a confusion of the human and the divine, no clear separation of two natures in the person of Kṛṣṇa, unlike the person of Christ in classical orthodoxy. Since the mānuṣī tanu of Kṛṣṇa is itself indwelled by Kṛṣṇa, there is at least one category, intra-BG, where ontological identification of Kṛṣṇa with humanity occurs. If Kṛṣṇa indwells all things,[152] including the material nature of humans, then there is identification—both the human form of Kṛṣṇa and those of all humans are indwelled by Kṛṣṇa. For Rāmānuja the question of whether or not Brahman really indwells the mānuṣī tanu, which, as we have seen, is fashioned from the divya rūpa, is not answered directly by him.[153] As for Śaṅkara's view, the question is from the ultimate point of view, that of parā vidyā, not of ultimate concern.[154] Further, it might be said, in light of Śaṅkara's doctrine of the jīvātman, that the para brahman, which is ultimately the only reality, indwells the mānuṣī tanu as the ātmanbrahman of Kṛṣṇa, but only in the jagat-prapañca of Īśvara and thus in a "negative" sense, for individuality resulting in the appearance or thought of a body of flesh is the result of adhyāsa, the act of imposing attributes and flesh upon the Self.[155] One might then further postulate that there is a "separation" of the two natures, but in the advaitic sense, that is, a separation on the ontological level due to the ultimate unreality of the mānuṣī tanu. Ultimately, though, there can be no discussion of two natures, separation or not, confusion or not.

(C) Does Kṛṣṇa possess a jīvātman or not? If so, is this jīvātman the same as all jīvātman-s in humans? The BG never answers these questions.[156] When

---

[150] See chapter 4, section 3 up to and through subsection 3.3.

[151] See chapter 4, section 3.3, fourth point.

[152] See BG 10.20, 15.13-15, 16.18, 17.6, 18.61.

[153] For more discussion see chapter 4, section 3.5.2.3,2C.

[154] See chapter 2, sections 3.3.1 and 3.3.2.

[155] See chapter 2, section 3.2.1 and its subsections.

[156] Though note Richard De Smet's conclusion concerning Rāmānuja's Kṛṣṇa: "Krishna does not appear to have a distinct human ātman or puruṣa, but his sole Ātman is the Lord's" ("Jesus and Avatāra", in Jerald Gort, et al., eds., Dialogue and Syncretism: An Interdisciplinary Approach [Grand Rapids, Mich.: William B. Eerdmans, 1989], 160). In probing certain questions concerning a possible jīvātman in Kṛṣṇa, De Smet asks, "Are there two puruṣas in Krishna, as in every other man [according to Sāṁkhya

some options are considered, however, there arise stark dissimilarities between avatāra and incarnation. (1) If Kṛṣṇa possesses a jīvātman as do all humans, then there occurs identification with humanity in the intra-BG anthropological sense. But in this category the identifications of Kṛṣṇa and Christ, when compared each from their respective systems, are not the same. The jīvātman of Kṛṣṇa would be pervaded by the para brahman,[157] whereas in Christ, due to identification with humanity, there is a distinct human soul[158] that is not divinized by the deity.[159] Further, the jīvātman of Kṛṣṇa would also have to come ex deo,[160] whereas Christ's human soul would be created ex nihilo.[161] (2) If Kṛṣṇa possesses a jīvātman, but that jīvātman is the para brahman, that is, Kṛṣṇa's deity nature is in place of the human jīvātman, then obviously no identification occurs with humanity, unless of course all the jīvātman-s of humans are the para brahman. Classical orthodoxy, however, rejected outright the doctrine that the logos replaced the human soul of Jesus, and would have rejected the doctrine that the logos as deity dwells in all humans in the place of their souls. With Śaṅkara the jīvātman (the individual soul) exists only, and seemingly, in the realm of Īśvara or lower Brahman.[162] Therefore, though Śaṅkara never directly answered the question of whether or not Kṛṣṇa possessed a "human" soul in the context of Īśvara, one may assume, indirectly from the evidence, that in the ultimate sense neither Kṛṣṇa nor humans, as they appeared so, possessed jīvātman-s. Instead the para brahman, the true Self and the absolutely one pure consciousness that persists in Kṛṣṇa[163] and others, is the only reality and any individuality as regards souls is rejected. In this sense there is no identification, for identification implies two entities. This is far removed

---

anthropology], both lodged in his dual 'gross and subtle' body? But in that case, his lower and properly human puruṣa would be ignorant like theirs, attributing to himself the births and the pleasures and pains of his adjoined body. He would then also be in need of salvation" (p. 158). De Smet also asks, "Is he not theandric?" He follows, "The answer depends on understanding the Sāṅkhya conception of man well. In sāṅkhya, there is no union, substantial or instrumental, between puruṣa and body; but only close nearness" (pp. 158-59). De Smet also concludes that there is no hypostatic union of puruṣa and body in the person of Kṛṣṇa (p. 159). For avatāra in general, and that compared to Christ, De Smet observes, "Vishnu as Krishna many times assumes a creaturely body which does not seem to require a creaturely ātman. The Logos as Jesus takes a body animated by a human soul once for all" (p. 161).

[157] See chapter 4, section 3.3, fourth point.

[158] See chapter 5 nn. 4,26,37,45,53,69,72,79,86,89.

[159] See chapter 6, sections 6.2 and 6.3, and n. 62.

[160] See chapter 4, sections 3.1.1, 3.2.2 (implied), and 3.2.3.

[161] See chapter 6, section 7, in light of chapter 5, section 1.1 and its subsections and section 2 and its subsections.

[162] See chapter 2, section 3.2.1 and its subsections.

[163] See chapter 4, section 3.4.1.3. Note that Rāmānuja accuses Śaṅkara of "annihilation of the I" in release. See chapter 4, section 3.5.1.1.

from the doctrine of identification found in classical orthodoxy, for many reasons, but for now one particular reason I wish to emphasize. Śaṅkara stated that "the Ātman also is never affected by the turbidity of misery, etc., falsely attributed to it by the ignorant".[164] In this category there is a profound difference between Śaṅkara's Kṛṣṇāvatāra and Christ. Whereas the true Self of Kṛṣṇa is divorced from any misery or pain, in the New Testament we read that Jesus, upon notification of the death of Lazarus, "was deeply moved in spirit" and that he "wept"[165] (John 11.33,35). Further, Jesus experienced pain when he was crucified.[166] In the system of Rāmānuja, if Kṛṣṇa possessed a jīvātman it might itself be pervaded by the antaryāmin.[167] If this were the case, there would be identification in this sense (though not in the sense of the material that formed the body of Kṛṣṇa, as has been discussed). This would not only differ radically from Śaṅkara (ultimately there is no jīvātman), but also from orthodoxy's view that the human soul of Christ, within the strict category of the union of two natures, is itself not pervaded by the nature of deity.[168] On the other hand, if with Rāmānuja there were no jīvātman in Kṛṣṇa (but only the para brahman, from which we can be sure Kṛṣṇa derives his "I"[169]) then there would be in this sense no identification of Kṛṣṇa with humanity. This would differ from orthodoxy as well, for Christ possessed a human soul.

(D) Prakṛti, both higher and lower, is Kṛṣṇa.[170] Richard De Smet asserts the same. Writing about the mahad brahman, the "great Brahman", in the BG, De Smet states that it "stands for the totality of prakriti which comprises both material nature ... and all the ātmans or dehins [embodied spirits] or jīvas, i.e. all the conscious entities. These [i.e., the ātman-s or jīva-s], indeed, constitute

---

[164] Swāmī Nikhilānanda, trans., The Māṇḍūkyopaniṣad with Gauḍapāda's Kārikā and Śaṅkara's Commentary (Calcutta: Advaita Ashrama, 1987), 151.

[165] Lipner observes the difference between Christ and Kṛṣṇa in the latter's lack of concern for Arjuna's emotional response at the thought of fighting against his relatives and countrymen. Lipner calls attention to BG 2.10, where Kṛṣṇa, "as if laughing", reacts to Arjuna's angst. "Krishna", Lipner writes, "could not be a Man of Sorrows in the way Jesus was perceived to be, and has never been thus described" ("Avatāra and Incarnation?", 143n.33,138).

[166] See chapter 6, section 4.

[167] See chapter 3, sections 3 and 4 and their subsections for reasons why I raise this.

[168] One might indeed raise an objection to my observation, citing the category of the indwelling of the Holy Spirit, who is God, in the person of Christ. First, my observation as it stands does not occur in this category, but rather in the strict category of the union of the two natures. Second, as regards the indwelling of the Spirit in Christ, pervading in the Hindu sense is not the purport, but rather a dwelling with Christ in the person of Christ.

[169] See chapter 4, sections 3.5.1.1 and 3.5.1.3.

[170] See chapter 4, sections 3.1.1 and 3.2.3. Further, in section 3.4.1.2 of chapter 4 I argue that Kṛṣṇa's "I" persists when in BG 7.4-6 he speaks of lower and higher prakṛti belonging to him.

the higher (parā) as opposed to the lower (aparā) prakriti. This complete prakriti 'is mine', says Krishna".[171] From the view of orthodoxy this leads to an eradication of any ontological distinction of two natures in Kṛṣṇa,[172] that is, an eradication of any distinction between the matter of the body and the divine, since the body arises ex deo. Prakṛti, both higher and lower, is Kṛṣṇa.[173] The implication is that the body / soul of Kṛṣṇa is wholly divine and is fashioned ex deo.[174] This, of course, differs immensely from classical Christian orthodoxy's two natures of Christ, the humanity coming from matter created ex nihilo[175] rather than creatio ex deo.

(E) In my reading of the BG and with my understanding of Śaṅkara and Rāmānuja, there are no soteriological / eschatological reasons for Kṛṣṇa's resurrection in a human bodily form in conjunction with his divine nature. Nor is there need for eternal existence in a true human bodily form in conjunction with his divine nature. Speaking generally of Kṛṣṇa and comparing him to Christ, Richard De Smet writes of this important difference: "Krishna dies, but does not rise in a glorious humanity. Christ does rise from the dead in a glorious body, a living promise of our own resurrection in him."[176] Likewise Ramachandra states, "In the Incarnation he who is the source and sustainer of our humanity has entered once and for all into our historical experience to take that humanity for ever into his own eternal life."[177] With the BG (and with Śaṅkara and Rāmānuja) the emphasis is upon the final and ultimate liberation of the ātman, not the present deha (body), and that within the context of a cyclical view of history(ies) in eternally occurring yuga-s, a phenomenon which of course accommodates the doctrine of multiple avatāra-s[178] and emphasizes the need for one's ultimate liberation in order to avoid yet another bodily existence. With the person of Christ, classical orthodoxy affirms an everlasting union of both humanity (body and soul) and deity in his resurrected state,[179] not, as Ramachandra states, "a casting off of the human and the

---

[171] Richard De Smet, "Towards an Indian View of the Person", in Contemporary Indian Philosophy, ed. Margaret Chatterjee (London: George Allen & Unwin, 1974), 66.

[172] See chapter 4, section 3.3, fifth point. Additionally, with De Smet's dichotomy of the material as the lower nature and the jīva-s as the higher nature, the distinction appears to be of type rather than of kind (ontological).

[173] See chapter 4, section 3.1 and its subsections, and section 3.2.3.

[174] See chapter 4, section 3.2.1.

[175] Based on chapters 5 and 6.

[176] "Jesus and Avatāra", 162.

[177] The Recovery of Mission, 242.

[178] See chapter 4, section 1.4. Lott agrees. See his "The Relevance of Research in Religions", 51: "[I]t is the traditional Vedantic (and generally Indian) doctrine of a repeated cycle of creation, preservation and dissolution, each cycle completing an Age, that made necessary the idea of a number of Avatāras."

[179] See chapter 6, section 4.

resumption of the divine".[180] This in turn necessitates emphasis on the regeneration of both soul and body for believers in Christ, the ultimate fulfillment of which is enjoyed in the resurrection in the last days, and that within a singular and linear view of history that accommodates a single, unique incarnation.

(F) The mānuṣī tanu of BG 9.11 is four-armed.[181] This brings into question the true identification of Kṛṣṇa with all of humanity, not only from the standpoint of orthodoxy, but intra-BG as well.

Seventh is the issue of identification in the afterlife or eschaton. With Śaṅkara we might very well question whether there is in the ultimate sense an afterlife per se, for we have, ultimately, no "before afterlife", since ultimately life in the world of appearance is illusory and the so-called individual soul is in reality Brahman. In other words, in order to have an afterlife, there must be ultimately real existence in a life before the afterlife. Further substantiating this, though there is language in Śaṅkara's writings of one merging with Brahman, what is really the case is that upon true knowledge persons (assuming it is appropriate to use the term) realize that they are indeed what they always were—Brahman. Thus, identification of Brahman with individual souls (if I may employ individuality) always has been (thus, how can there be an afterlife?) and always will be. Śaṅkara's view thus differs from both Rāmānuja and classical Christian orthodoxy. He differs from Rāmānuja in that with Rāmānuja there is identity of the soul with Brahman in the afterlife, but only in so far as the released soul is a mode of Viṣṇu and is ensouled by Viṣṇu.[182] Thus, for Rāmānuja there is in a qualified sense difference (bheda) between Viṣṇu and released souls. There also exists an I – Thou relationship between Viṣṇu and released souls,[183] and worship of the former by the latter. Further, these souls may obtain at will bodies in the afterlife (I explore this in depth below). Śaṅkara differs dramatically from Christian orthodoxy in a few ways. First, with orthodoxy there is (as with Rāmānuja) a difference between God and his subjects. Second, there exists the I – Thou relationship as characteristic of this difference (again as with Rāmānuja; Śaṅkara cannot in the ultimate sense claim this[184]). Third (and yet again as with Rāmānuja), God's subjects worship

[180] The Recovery of Mission, 242.

[181] See chapter 4, section 3.3, sixth point, and section 4.1, final point.

[182] See chapter 4, section 3.5.2.3,2D.

[183] See chapter 3, section 5, and chapter 4, section 3.5.2.3,2D.

[184] See chapter 4, section 3.4.2.3, fourth point. Further, it may be argued that "I" for Śaṅkara is not ultimately a personal "I", for the Self in nirvikalpa samādhi is not conscious of self-ness, as we saw in Śaṅkara's analogy of deep sleep (see chapter 2, section 3.2.1.2). With this point there is further distinction between Śaṅkara's system and the systems of Rāmānuja and classical Christian orthodoxy. Lott asserts that in Śaṅkara's system, at the point of mokṣa "neither emulation of the way of Krishna in his avatara-life, nor faithfulness and receptiveness to his disclosure, nor any kind of relational attitude can remain ... There is no longer relationship but identity of being"

him eternally. Fourth (and unlike the other two traditions), with classical orthodoxy any identification between God and humanity occurs with the Son as the second person of the triune God.

Following on this last point is a further severe difference[185] between the two Vedāntins' Kṛṣṇāvatāra-s and classical orthodoxy's Christ, which I elaborated upon in the sixth point, section E above, and wish to elaborate further upon here: there is for Kṛṣṇāvatāra no body-divine identity carried into the eschaton. This is to say, Kṛṣṇa as Kṛṣṇa was, both in body and deity, does not exist in the eschaton.[186] Rather, for Rāmānuja he seems to be absorbed back into the identity of Viṣṇu-divya rūpa, where in this form Viṣṇu eternally relates to his devotees. With Śaṅkara the "body"-divine relation in Kṛṣṇāvatāra is dissolved by way of true knowledge of ultimate reality, Brahman, where all that exists is Brahman, who is pure consciousness. In contrast, classical Christian orthodoxy holds to a continuing of the identity of Jesus from his pre-resurrection state into and through the resurrected and ascended state. The body before the resurrection remains at the eschaton the same body,[187] though at the resurrection the state of that body changed—what was once mortal became immortal and glorified.[188]

---

("The Mythic Symbol Avatar in Indian Conceptual Formulations", 5,6). In another place Lott observes that for Śaṅkara any form of being, including avatāra, "will be superseded by that intuited Experience of the identity of Selfhood that lies veiled behind the divine embodiment" ("The Relevance of Research in Religions", 42).

185 For which I am indebted to V. Chakkarai, Jesus the Avatār (Madras: Christian Literature Society for India, 1930), 137-39.

186 In Vaiṣṇava thought this seems to be reserved for another avatāra, namely Kalkī (see Carman, Majesty and Meekness, 200).

187 See John 2.19-22. Here Jesus states, "Destroy this temple and in three days I shall raise it up" (v. 19). John, in verse 21, interprets "this temple" as "his body".

188 See 1 Corinthians 15.51-54. Immediately before these verses Paul establishes contrastive states of existence, pre- and post-resurrection (vv. 42-50). He then proceeds in verses 51-54 to state that the dead in Christ will "be changed", that they will be raised, and that mortality will put on immortality. If this is the case with the dead in Christ, and Christ is the prototype of the resurrection, then we can assume that what Paul in this passage says of believers is true of Christ as well. Additionally, that there is a continuing of the "I" of the resurrected is not particularly clear in this passage, though it may be inferred from the motif of the dead being raised. Further, when this passage is interpreted in light of other passages, the case for identity continuing at and through the resurrection is strengthened. For example, Jesus states that all the dead who are in graves will hear his voice and will rise. Jesus then follows with the assertion that those who had committed good works will be resurrected to life, but that those who committed evil deeds will be resurrected to judgment (John 5.28-29). Here there is strong implication that there is no re-creation of a new "I", for it is absurd to think that a new "I" will answer for an "I" it never was in the first place. Moreover, it is reasonable that the "I" of resurrected persons will be the same "I" that existed before the resurrection because this is the case with Christ (inferred, for example, in John 5.28-29).

As far as Rāmānuja is concerned, he asserts that the released soul may or may not possess bodies. Each released soul may obtain at will multiple bodies of a non-prakṛtic nature if it so chooses. The released soul enjoys this type of existence eternally and does not suffer or cease to exist at the dissolution of the universe.[189] In this way, observes Lipner, "There is scope here for points of contact between Rāmānuja's picture of the liberated state and the Christian understanding of the resurrection of a (spiritual) body in the eschaton."[190] However, at another point in his work Lipner states that unlike the Christian view of the eschaton, "Vedānta lacks the concept of an eschaton in which the whole created order finds its historical consummation", and that Rāmānuja "cannot say in the spirit of a Paul that ... 'the creation itself will be set free from its bondage to decay and obtain the glorious liberty of the children of God' (Romans 8:18f.)".[191]

In light of the above concerning Rāmānuja I now offer a few observations.

(A) As I mentioned in section 3.2 of this chapter, it is not clear that there is full identification between Viṣṇu's divya rūpa and the released soul's non-prakṛtic anthropomorphic bodies. That is, it is not clear that the material for the various bodies that a released soul may obtain is of the same material as the divya rūpa.

(B) By way of similarities, there seems to be, to use Lipner's phrase, a point of contact between Rāmānuja and Christian orthodoxy on a few points. (However, while citing these similarities one must suspend for the moment differences concerning [1] the nature of matter, the soul and the "I", [2] the number of bodies assumed by each soul [multiple in Rāmānuja; singular in Christian orthodoxy], and, if Śrīnivāsa correctly represents Rāmānuja, the fact that the bodies possess four arms,[192] [3] the option of possessing or not possessing bodies [Rāmānuja's view], and [4] the fact that with Christianity [not with Rāmānuja] there is a resurrection of the savior which corresponds to the resurrected of the faithful.) First, if Śrīnivāsa is correct in teaching that the jīva "recollects the objects experienced in the past"[193] (and that therefore we might assume the same with past events), with Rāmānuja and orthodoxy the "I" of the person endures in continuity with the past.[194] Second, both traditions make way for a bodily existence in the afterlife. Third, this existence is eternal.

(C) If Lipner is correct in his observation cited above (citing Rom. 8.18), there is in Rāmānuja a lack of concern for the eternal existence of the creation

---

[189] See chapter 4, section 3.5.2.3,2D.

[190] The Face of Truth, 172 n. 47.

[191] The Face of Truth, 131.

[192] See chapter 4, section 3.5.2.3,2D.

[193] YS, 104 (8.5).

[194] With orthodoxy this is implied in several New Testament texts, such as Romans 14.10-12, where believers, at the eschaton, will stand before the judgment seat of God and give accounts for themselves. See also note 188.

in linear fashion, including its redemption and existence as such eternally. Here Rāmānuja differs sharply from Christian orthodoxy, but is in league somewhat with Śaṅkara, though only in the sense that both Vedāntins ultimately see the creation as unworthy of an eternal and once for all same-identity-and-memory-of-past-history redemption (in their unique ways).[195]

## 4. Conclusion / Reflections for Future Research

Though I hold that the terms avatāra and incarnation may be used interchangeably, I suggest that it be done with great care. As I have established, while there are surface similarities between avatāra and incarnation, when probed sufficiently these similarities are not so similar.[196] Conversely, it is for this very reason that some contend that when the two words and their contents are compared in the contexts of their respective epistemologies / theologies / cosmologies / cosmogonies, the differences in the end render each term appropriate only for its respective tradition.

I suspect that where one lands on this issue has to do, in part, with what one desires to accomplish both during and after comparative study. I now mention two possible scenarios that differ from each other in some senses, though this by no means exhausts the possibilities.[197]

First, for reasons that may be purely academic, and solely with the practice of the discipline of "comparative study for comparative study's sake" in mind (and therefore void of any vested interests, except the aforementioned), it might be most appealing for scholars to highlight differences between avatāra and incarnation and conclude that the two terms therefore should not be used

---

[195] It may be stated that our two Vedāntins believe in an eternal redemption of creation, but on two fronts that differ from Christian orthodoxy. First, redemption, if the term is used at all, is seen within the creation-dissolution-creation context eternally occurring in yuga-s. Second, in this context there seems to be no "same identity" and "memory of past history" understanding, except to say that there is in Śaṅkara and Rāmānuja creational same identity in that the multiple creations find their essential identity in God. In representing the theology of Rāmānuja, Lipner, in his The Face of Truth (pp. 60, 75-79), disagrees with my conclusion that the liberated soul does not possess memories of past histories in saṁsāric conditions. Lipner comes to a different conclusion (though admitting that Rāmānuja does not specifically address this issue; see p. 79 and p. 164 n. 32), inferred from other theological concepts that are clear in the writings of Rāmānuja, particularly the liberated soul sharing in the all-knowingness of the Lord (p. 79). If this "sharing" is the case, argues Lipner, then we may assume a memory-of-past-histories-in-saṁsāric-conditions on the part of the liberated soul (p. 79).

[196] I must say here that in light of some religious traditions' (for examples, Islam and Judaism) critiques, if not outright disdain, of even the concept of divine descent, one might still appreciate, in whatever ways one wishes, various Hindu avatāra traditions and their emphases on divine descent.

[197] For representatives of the options that follow, see section 1.

interchangeably. End of study; no more to add. This, in and of itself, is a worthwhile venture, for it makes known to those scholars who in the past have drawn hasty "similarity" conclusions as regards Christ and Kṛṣṇa that such conclusions are, after careful analysis, not warranted.[198] Further, it serves as a scholarly word of caution to those who are beginning a comparative study of their own on this topic. And still further, it opens the way for scholars to demonstrate otherwise—that after careful analysis there are indeed similarities even when exploring deeply the categories I have brought to the fore in this study (though, frankly, I do not see how this can be demonstrated when comparing avatāra to classical orthodox Christology).

Second, some scholars, Christian and Hindu, might undertake an academic comparative study of avatāra and incarnation with the further goals of apologetics and evangelism in mind. This is something in which I am interested, and though I stated earlier that I hope to see others take on this task, I hope to engage this goal in the future, both in writing and in face to face conversations. Such an undertaking, though, not only involves the issue of whether or not to use the two terms interchangeably, but several other issues as well. To these I now turn.

Concerning the debate over the interchangeability of the two terms in the evangelistic / apologetic context, it seems to me that there are basic reasons for holding to each option. Those (here I include the Christian, the Advaitin, and the Viśiṣṭādvaitin) who want to use the terms interchangeably (again, only after careful delineation of differences) would want to do so for "common ground" reasons. This is my view. Missiologically (which includes both apologetics and evangelism) speaking from my tradition, I hope to "connect" in some way with the Hindu by utilizing language with which we are both familiar. This includes not only the use of the word avatāra, but other Sanskrit words as well. Here issues of inculturation arise, with which, in turn, much deeper considerations arise. What we have here is not an exercise of accommodation whereby communication of views alone takes place with use of similar terminology, but a deeper issue, launched from the observation of missiologist David Bosch: "The Christian Faith never exists except as 'translated' into a culture."[199] Using the word avatāra, then, how do I communicate the distinct and radically-different-than-avatāra Christian theological and soteriological content of the incarnation of Christ to a Hindu in a way that the Hindu is able to understand it

[198] This statement assumes a classical orthodox Christology in theological / soteriological comparison with the Kṛṣṇāvatāra doctrines of Śaṅkara and Rāmānuja. See note 2 for mention of several alternative christologies from which different conclusions might be drawn.

[199] See David J. Bosch, Transforming Mission: Paradigm Shifts in Theology of Mission (Maryknoll, N.Y.: Orbis Books, 1991), 447.

and make an informed decision?[200] Further, once the Christian gospel is accepted, the incarnation accepted, how does one go about further inculturation in social and theological contexts?[201] On the other hand, and within this same evangelistic / apologetic context, there may be those who hold (erroneously, I suggest) that since the content that accompanies the two terms is vastly different, the two terms must not exist in an interchangeable way, ever. With this view, for missiological reasons the two terms, because of the content that accompanies each, must stand apart. This view values maintaining a level of otherness since this otherness must be confessed upon true conversion. In my estimation the positive side of this view is, indeed, the maintenance of otherness, which I feel is important. However, this otherness need not flavor the initial approach to the evangelized by the evangelist to such an extent that common ground is erased or not acknowledged. Interchange of terms is possible as a common ground, though again, with careful explanation of content.

Regardless of what view one accepts, a much larger and more important issue concerns truth. For those who wish to carry comparative study to apologetic / evangelistic venues, the question of which tradition is the more plausible, or which tradition teaches ultimate (and pragmatic) truth on the matter, comes to the fore. This issue in turn involves many more questions. What is one's view of "truth"? And this, in turn, involves the all-important sub-question of whether or not there is a particular system of belief in which the truth of the matter at hand can be found, that is, whether or not what is ontologically the case is found in any particular belief system. This, specifically, is the concern for the question, "Kṛṣṇāvatāra or the incarnation of Christ?" In which belief system is the real truth of the matter found? In other words, who, Kṛṣṇa or Christ, is the answer? Who, in the end, is the answer for the human predicament? And this, of course, is predicated upon establishing just what the human predicament is. For example, is the human problem in reality one of escaping the cycle of birth-death-rebirth? Or is the real human problem deep-rooted sin, for which the savior must atone?[202]

---

200 This presupposes a certain attitude on my part, namely "to accept the co-existence of different faiths and to do so not grudgingly but willingly" (Bosch, Transforming Mission, 483). Bosch continues: "We cannot possibly dialogue with or witness to people if we resent their presence or the views they hold" (p. 483).

201 Bosch observes a relatively recent shift in this process—going from the idea of the missionary as the sole agent of change, to the idea and practice where the missionary works in conjunction with those of the culture (see Transforming Mission, 453).

202 Carman alludes to this and other issues when he states that, in the context of understanding the similarities and differences between avatāra and incarnation, "what cannot be decided in this effort at understanding is whether and in what respects the similarities or the differences are more important" (Majesty and Meekness, 190). Perhaps in the "effort at understanding" this is possible, but Carman continues, stating, "Such a decision [about which similarities and differences are more important] calls for

Further, is the belief system coherent? And does the belief system conform to what is in reality (universally and objectively) the case? Indeed, are these questions possible to answer? Yet even here there are further issues and questions that confront us: Are the religious documents that inform us reliable? How so? Does this even matter?—If so, why? If not, why? Can the documents' recorded events and mention of persons be historically confirmed? Did the Kṛṣṇa revealed in the BG really exist? Did the Jesus of classical Christian orthodoxy really exist? Do these questions matter? If so, why do they matter? If not, why not?

It seems to me that historical matters are of grave importance, specifically the question of the historicity of the incarnation and resurrection of Christ. If his incarnation and resurrection really did occur, then these established facts would be my epistemological ground for knowing the answer to the above question; they would constitute the foundation for an order of knowing that is universally and objectively grounded in God's self-revelation of himself in

---

a theological assessment grounded in faith" (p. 190). (For a rebuttal of this paradigm, see Thomas F. Torrance, Space, Time and Resurrection [Grand Rapids, Mich.: William B. Eerdmans, 1976], 19, wherein Torrance argues that the objective reality of God revealed in Christ in space and time "does not allow us to make 'faith' itself the ground of our 'belief'". Torrance concludes, "The only proper ground of faith is the reality to which it is correlated as to its objective pole.") Later, Carman is explicit concerning the doctrine of the atonement of Christ, a doctrine, he says, and rightly so, "Many Christian interpreters of Hinduism regard ... as the major difference between the Christian doctrine of incarnation and the Hindu concept of avatara" (Majesty and Meekness, 201). Carman concludes that "it is a difference that can be evaluated in opposite ways" (p. 201; among the questions I hope to answer in a future work [see next paragraph and the note] is, "Though it can be evaluated in opposite ways, can it truly be evaluated in opposite ways?"). Among Carman's concluding remarks later in the chapter is his assessment that "Christians and Hindus can easily come to different conclusions about the importance of the similarities and the significance of the differences" (p. 209). Carman does mention the "theme of Rama and Sita's suffering" recorded in the Rāmāyaṇa, though that suffering "is only a minor part in the Hindu understanding of God's descent as avatar". But then Carman suggests (and I suggest that for Christians these are key missiological points), "That does not mean, however, that it is impossible for Christians of Hindu background or for Hindus who ponder the gospel story to appreciate the sacrificial significance of the crucifixion, for both their ancient traditions and their current ritual practice make a great deal of actual and symbolic sacrifice" (p. 202). For Hindus Carman has in mind the cutting off of Viṣṇu's head by a snapping bowstring that was gnawed through by ants, the gods sacrificing Viṣṇu in order to rescue the earth from demons, Viṣṇu's identification as the Cosmic Person, and, finally, Viṣṇu's expansion from dwarf to giant in order to win back the world for the gods by taking three great strides (pp. 202-3; in n. 15 Carman cites the following references for these acts involving Viṣṇu: Śathapathā Brāhmaṇa XIV.1.1.1 and following, I.2.5.5 and following, and I.9.3.9, respectively).

Christ and in history.[203]

Another topic for future study that might build upon my work concerns the debate between De Smet, D. M. Datta, and Bradley Malkovsky—three scholars among others who advance the thesis that Śaṅkara's advaita proposes a realist ontology[204]—and those like myself and the majority of Śaṅkara scholars who posit the more traditional view, that is, that the material world and its phenomena are ultimately not real. Though further studies are needed with reference to this ontology question alone in order to settle that matter (if indeed it can ever be settled!), further studies also must be undertaken in order to probe the implications that arise for Śaṅkara's Kṛṣṇāvatāra when a realist ontology is attributed to the great Advaitin.

Finally, more careful, in-depth work remains to be done on the subject of avatāra-s on individual bases. Because of the work of Parrinder and some others, there are adequate studies on the topic as a whole, but they serve only a limited purpose; they are informative in a general way. Yet, one might argue that general studies of this sort do more harm than good. Perhaps in the future more scholars will find the study of avatāra as intriguing and captivating as I find it, and will labor to produce rich works on individual avatāra-s; and perhaps someone might make it a project to collect these individual works into a series of volumes. Then, perhaps, some might also set out to compare these avatāra-s with the Christ of classical Christian orthodoxy. Only time will tell.

---

[203] After completing this dissertation, and before the publication of it in the form of this book, a contributed chapter of mine entitled "Krishna and Christ: The Body-Divine Relation in the Human Form" was published in Catherine Cornille, ed., Song Divine: Christian Commentaries on the Bhagavad Gita (Leuven, Belgium: Peeters Publishers, and Grand Rapids: Wm. B. Eerdmans, 2006). Near the end of the essay appears the subsection entitled "Historicity and Faith", in which I take as a starting point Thomas F. Torrance's epistemology found in his Space, Time and Resurrection and Reality and Evangelical Theology (Downers Grove, Ill.: InterVarsity Press, 1999). Therein I argue, albeit briefly, for the historicity of Christ against the lack of documentation for the historicity of Kṛṣṇa as supreme Deity. I further argue that without this historical element there can be no real relationship between God and people.

[204] See notes 21 and 48 of chapter 1, and note 292 of chapter 4.

# Bibliography

## Bhāṣya-s and Other Primary Sources in Sanskrit


Abhyankar, Vasudev Shastri. Śrībhāṣya of Rāmānujāchārya. Bombay: Government Central Press, 1914.

Aitareya Upaniṣad with Śaṅkarabhāṣya. Pune: Ananda Ashram, 1980.

Anantarangācārya, N. S., ed. Śaraṇāgatigadyam [of Rāmānuja with Sudarśana Sūri's] Vyākhyā. Bangalore: N. S. Anantarangācārya, 1879.

Annangarācārya, P. B., ed. Śrī-Bhagavad-Rāmānuja-Granthamālā [complete works in Sanskrit]. Kāñcīpuram: Granthamālā Office, 1956.

Āpte, V. G. Rāmānuja's Gītābhāṣya, Edited with the Tātparyacandrikā of Veṅkatanāṭha. Vol. 92, Ānandāśrama Sanskrit Series. Bombay: Ānandāśrama Press, 1923.

______. Śaṅkara's Gītābhāṣya, with Ānandagiri's Gloss. Vol. 34, Ānandāśrama Sanskrit Series. Bombay: Ānandāśrama Press, 1936.

Āśramin, Nṛsiṃha. Advaita Dīpikā with the Advaita Dīpikā Vivaraṇa of Śrī Nārāyanāśrama. 3 vols. Varanasi: Sampurnanand Sanskrit Vishvidyalaya, 1984.

Bhagavad-Gītā with Śaṅkarabhāṣya. Pune: Ananda Ashram, 1902.

Brahmasūtra with Śaṅkarabhāṣya. Vol. 3, Works of Śankarāchārya in Original Sanskrit. Delhi:Motilal Banarsidass, n.d.

Brihadāranyaka Upaniṣad with Śaṅkarabhāṣya. Pune: Ananda Ashram, 1982.

Chāndogya Upaniṣad with Śaṅkara bhāṣya. Pune: Ananda Ashram, 1983.

Deśika, Vedānta. Adhikaraṇasarāvali with the Adhikaraṇacintāmaṇi of Vaiśvamitraśrīvaradaguru and the Sārārtharatnaprabhā of Uttamur T. Vīrarāghavācārya. Chennai: Ubhaya Vedānta Granthamala, 1974.

______. Nyāyapariśuddhi with the Nyāyatattvaprakāśikā of Śrī Vātsyavīrarāghavācārya. Chennai: Ubhaya Vedānta Granthamala, 1978.

______. Nyāyasiddhāñjana with the Saralaviśada of Śrī Raṅgarāmānuja and the Ratnapeṭikā of Sri Kṛṣṇatātayārya. Chennai: Ubhaya Vedānta Granthamala, 1976.

Dhupakar, Ramchandra, and Bakre, Mahadeva Shastri, eds. Brahmasūtraśaṃkarabhāṣyam. Bombay: Tukaram Javaji, 1902.

Dvivedin, V. P., ed. Brahmasūtra with a Commentary by Bhāskarācārya. Chowkhamba Sanskrit Series 209. Benares: Vidya Vilas Press, 1915.

Goyandaka, K., ed. Bhagavad-Gītā with Śaṅkarabhāṣya. Gorakhpur: Gita Press, 1988.

Īśa Upaniṣad with Śaṅkarabhāṣya. Pune: Ananda Ashram, 1980.

Kaṭha Upaniṣad with Śaṅkarabhāṣya. Pune: Ananda Ashram, 1981.

Kena Upaniṣad with Śaṅkarabhāṣya. Pune: Ananda Ashram, 1985.

Māṇdūkya Upaniṣad and Gauḍapādīyakārikā with Śaṅkarabhāṣya. Pune: Ananda Ashram, 1984.

Mayeda, Sengaku, ed. Śaṅkara's Upadeśasāhasrī. Tokyo: Hokuseido Press, 1973.

Muṇḍaka Upaniṣad with Śaṅkarabhāṣya. Pune: Ananda Ashram, 1904.

Parāśara Bhaṭṭar. Bhagavadguṇadarpaṇākhyam Śrīviṣṇusahasranāmabhāṣyam.

Kāñcīpuram: P. B. Annangarācārya, 1964.

Pāthak, Pandit Shridhar Tryambak, ed. Aṇu-Bhāṣya of Vallabhāchārya, Poona: Aryabhushan Press, 1921.

Praśna Upaniṣad with Śaṅkarabhāṣya. Pune: Ananda Ashram, 1980.

Rāmānuja. Brahmasūtra-Śrībhāṣya of Śrī Bhagavad Rāmānuja with the Śrutaprkāśikā of Śrī Sudarśanasūri. 2 vols. Chennai: Visishtadvaita Pracharini Sabha, 1989.

Sadhale, Shastri G. S. The Bhagavad-Gītā with Eleven Commentaries. 3 vols. Bombay: Gujarati Printing Press, 1935-1938.

Śaṁkara. The Brahma-Sūtra Śaṁkara Bhāṣya with the Commentaries of Bhamatī, Kalpataru, and Parimala. 2 vols. Delhi: Parimal, 1981.

Sanshodhitam, H., ed. Brahma-sūtra with Śrī Nimbārkabhāṣya. Kashi Sanskrit Series 66. Benares: Vidya Vilas Press, 1989.

Śrīpatipaṇḍitācārya. The Śrīkara Bhāṣya, Being the Viraśaiva Commentary on the Vedānta Sūtras. Edited by C. Hayavadana Rao. Bangalore: Bangalore Press, 1936.

Sudarśana Sūri. [Commentary on Rāmānuja's] Śrībhāṣya. 2 vols. New Delhi: Government of India, 1967.

_______. [Commentary on Rāmānuja's] Vedārthasaṃgraha. Vṛndāvana, 1978 Śaka.

Śvetāśvatara Upaniṣad with Śaṅkarabhāṣya. Pune: Ananda Ashram, 1982.

Taittirīya Upaniṣad with Śaṅkarabhāṣya. Pune: Ananda Ashram, 1977.

Ten Principal Upaniṣads with Śaṅkarabhāṣya. Vol. 1, Works of Śankarāchārya in Original Sanskrit. Delhi:Motilal Banarsidass, 1987.

Viraraghavacharya, Uttamur. Bhāṣyārtha Darpaṇa [Sanskrit commentary on Rāmānuja's Śrībhāṣya]. 2 vols. Madras: Uttamur Viraraghavacharya, 1963-1964.

## Bhāṣya-s and Other Primary Sources in Translation

Ādidevānanda, Svāmī, trans. Śrī Rāmānuja Gītā Bhāṣya. Mylapore: Sri Ramakrishna Math, n.d.

_______, trans. Yatīndramatadīpikā by Śrīnivāsadāsa. Mylapore: Sri Ramakrishna Math, n.d.

Alston, A. J. The Thousand Teachings of Śaṁkara. London: Shanti Sadan, 1990.

Bhashyam, K. Śaraṇāgati Gadya [of Rāmānuja]. Madras: Ubhaya Vedanta Granthamala, 1959. Text and translation with translation of Sudarśana Sūri's commentary.

_______. Vedanta Deepa [of Rāmānuja]. 2 vols. Madras: Ubhaya Vedanta Granthamala, 1957-1959. Tamil translation by Uttamur Viraraghavacharya.

Bose, Roma. Vedānta-Pārijāta-Saurabha of Nimbārka and Vedānta-Kaustubha of Śrīnivāsa (Commentaries on the Brahma-Sūtras). 3 vols. Calcutta: Royal Asiatic Society of Bengal, 1940.

Buitenen, J. A. B. van, trans. Rāmānuja's Vedārthasaṃgraha. Pune: Deccan College Postgraduate and Research Institute, 1956.

_______, trans. Rāmānuja on the Bhagavadgītā. Delhi: Motilal Banarsidass, 1968. Condensed rendering of Rāmānuja's Gītābhāṣya, with notes.

Carman, John, and Narayanan, Vasudha. The Tamil Veda: Pillan's Interpretation of the Tiruvaymoli. Chicago: University of Chicago Press, 1989.

Deśika, Vedānta. Śrīmadrahasyatrayasāra. Translated by M. R. Rajagopala Ayyangar. Salem, India: Literary Press, n.d.

Gambhīrānanda, Swāmī, trans. Bhagavadgītā with the Commentary of Śaṅkarācārya. Calcutta: Advaita Ashrama, 1984.
_______, trans. [Śaṅkara's] Brahma-Sūtra Bhāṣya. Calcutta: Advaita Ashrama, 1983.
_______, trans. Chāndogya Upaniṣad with the Commentary of Śaṅkarācārya. Calcutta: Advaita Ashrama, 1983.
_______, trans. Eight Upaniṣads: With the Commentary of Śaṅkarācārya. 2 vols. 5th and 12th Impressions. Calcutta: Advaita Ashrama, 2000.
_______, trans. Śvetāśvatara Upaniṣad with the Commentary of Śaṅkarācārya. Calcutta: Advaita Ashrama, 1986.
Gokhale, Dinkar Vishnu, ed. The Bhagavad-Gītā with the Commentary of Śrī Śaṅkarācārya. 2nd ed. Poona: Oriental Book Agency, 1950.
Govindacharya, Alkodavilli. Śrī Bhagavad-Gītā: With Rāmānuja's Commentary in English. Madras, 1898.
Grimes, John. The Vivekacudamani of Sankaracarya Bhagavatpada: An Introduction and Translation. Burlington, Vt.: Ashgate, 2004.
Gupta, Sisir Kumar. Madhusūdana Sarasvatī on the Bhagavad Gītā: Being an English Translation of His Commentary, Gūḍhārtha Dīpikā. Delhi: Motilal Banarsidass, 1977.
Hohenberger, A. Rāmānuja's Vedāntadīpa: Seine Kurzauslegung der Brahmasūtren des Bādarāyaṇa. Bonn: Selbstverlag des Orientalischen Seminars der Universität Bonn, 1964.
Jagadananda, Swami, trans. Upadeśa Sāhasrī: A Thousand Teachings, in Two Parts—Prose and Poetry of Śrī Śaṅkarāchārya. Mylapore: Sri Ramakrishna Math, n.d.
_______. Vakyavritti of Sri Sankaracharya. Mylapore: Sri Ramakrishna Math, n.d.
Karmarkar, Raghunath Damodar, ed. and trans. Gauḍapāda-Kārikā. Poona: Bhandarkar Oriental Research Institute, 1973.
_______, ed. and trans. Śrībhāṣya of Rāmānuja. Poona: University of Poona, 1962.
Khurana, Geeta. The Theology of Nimbārka: A Translation of Nimbārka's Daśaślokī with Giridhara Prapanna's Laghumañjūsā. New York: Vantage Press, 1990.
Krishnamacharya, Pandit V., and Narasimha, Ayyangar, M. B. Vedāntasāra of Bhagavad Rāmānuja. Vol. 83, 2nd ed., Adyar Library Series. Madras: Adyar Library and Research Centre, 1979.
Leggett, Trevor. Śaṅkara on the Yoga-sūtra-s. 2 vols. London: Routledge & Kegan Paul, 1981.
Mādhavānanda, Swāmī, trans. The Brihadāraṇyaka Upaniṣad with the Commentary of Śaṅkarācārya. Calcutta: Advaita Ashrama, 1965.
_______, trans. [Śaṅkara's] Vivekacūḍāmaṇi (Crest-jewel of Discrimination). Calcutta: Advaita Ashrama, 1998.
Mahadevan, T. M. P., trans. The Hymns of Śaṅkara. Delhi: Motilal Banarsidass, 1986.
Mayeda, Sengaku, trans. A Thousand Teachings: The Upadeśasāhasrī of Śaṅkara. Tokyo: University of Tokyo Press, 1979.
Narasimha, Ayyangar, M. B. Vedāntasāra of Rāmānuja. Madras: Adyar Library, 1953.
Nikhilananda, Swami, trans. The Māṇḍūkyopaniṣad with Gauḍapāda's Kārikā and Śaṅkara's Commentary. Calcutta: Advaita Ashrama, 1987. Śaṅkara's commentary on Gauḍapāda's Kārikā.
_______. Self-Knowledge ([Śaṅkara's]Ātmabodha). New York: Ramakrishna-Vivekananda Center, 1980.
Otto, Rudolf. Siddhānta des Rāmānuja. Jena: Eugen Diederichs, 1917. German

translation of BSB 1.1.1.

Parāśara Bhaṭṭar. Commentary on the Śrī Viṣṇu Sahasranāmam. Translated by K. E. Parthasarathy. Madras: Ganesh & Co., n.d. With the commentary of Śaṅkara.

_______. Sri Vishnu Sahasranama Bashya. Translated by L. Venkatarathnam Naidu. Tirupati: Tirumala Tirupati Devasthanams, 1965.

Parthasarathy, K. E. , trans. [Śaṅkara's] Commentary on the Śrī Viṣṇu Sahasranāmam. Madras: Ganesh & Co., n.d. Also contains the commentary of Parāśara Bhaṭṭar.

Raghavachar, S. S. Vedārthasaṃgraha [of Rāmānuja]. Mysore: Sri Ramakrishna Ashrama, 1956.

Rajagopala, Ayyangar, M. R. The Gadya-Traya of Rāmānuja. Madras: M. R. Ayyangar Rajagopala, n.d.

_______. Vedartha Sangraha [of Rāmānuja]. Madras: : M. R. Ayyangar Rajagopala, 1956.

Rangacharya, M., and Varadaraja, Aiyangar, M. B. The Vedānta Sūtras with the Śrī Bhāshya of Rāmānuja. 3 vols. Madras: Education Publishing, 1961-1965.

Rau, S. Subba, trans. The Vedanta-Sutras with the Commentary by Sri Madhwacharya. Madras: Thompson and Co, 1904.

Sampatkumaran, M. R., trans. The Gitabhashya of Ramanuja. Mumbai: Ananthacharya Indological Research Institute, 1985.

_______, trans. The Gitabhashya of Ramanuja. Madras: Professor M. Rangacharya Memorial Trust, 1969.

Śastri, A. Mahādeva, trans. The Bhagavad-Gītā with the Commentary of Śrī Śaṅkarācārya. Madras: V. Ramaswamy Sastrulu and Sons, 1972.

Sharma, B. N. K. The Bhagavadgītabhāṣya of Śrī Madhvācārya. Poornaprajna Vidyapeetha, Bangalore: Anandatirtha Pratishthana, 1989.

Sonde, Nagesh D. trans. Bhagavad Gita Bhashya and Tatparyanirnaya of Sri Madhva. Bombay: Vasantik Prakashan, 1995.

Śrīnivāsadāsa. Yatīndramatadīpikā. Madras: Sri Ramakrishna Math, 1949.

Tapasyananda, Swami, trans. Saundarya-Lahari of Śrī Śankarāchārya. Mylapore: Sri Ramakrishna Math, n.d.

_______. Śivānandalaharī or Inundation of Divine Bliss of Śrī Śankarāchārya. Mylapore: Sri Ramakrishna Math, n.d.

Thibaut, George, trans. The Vedānta-Sūtras: With the Commentary by Rāmānuja. 1904. Reprint. Vol. 48, Sacred Books of the East. Delhi: Motilal Banarsidass, 1989.

_______. Vedānta-Sūtras: With the Commentary by Śaṅkarācārya. 1904. Reprint. Vols. 34,38, Sacred Books of the East. Delhi: Motilal Banarsidass, 1988.

Venkataramiah, D., ed. and trans. The Pañcapādikā of Padmapāda. Baroda: Oriental Institute, 1948.

Vimuktananda, Swami, trans. Aparokshānubhuti: Or Self-Realization of Sri Sankarāchārya. Calcutta: Advaita Ashrama, 2000.

Warrier, A. G. Krishna, trans. Srīmad Bhagavad Gītā Bhāṣya of Sri Śaṅkarācārya. Madras: Sri Ramakrishna Math, n.d.

## Translations of Śruti and Smṛti

Arnold, Sir Edwin. Bhagavadgita. New York: Dover Publications, 1993.

Besant, Annie, trans. The Bhagavad-Gītā. Wheaton, Ill.: Theosophical Publishing

House, 1998.
Bhattacharya, Abhibhusan, trans. The Varāha-Purāṇa. Ramnagar, Varanasi: All-India Kashiraj Trust, 1981.
Bolle, Kees W. The Bhagavadgītā: A New Translation. Berkeley: University of California Press, 1979.
Bühler, G., trans. The Laws of Manu. 1886. Reprint. Vol. 25, Sacred Books of the East. Delhi: Motilal Banarsidass, 1989.
Buitenen, J. A. B. van, trans. The Bhagavadgītā in the Mahābhārata. Chicago: The University of Chicago Press, 1981.
______, trans. The Mahābhārata. 2 vols. Chicago: The University of Chicago Press, 1973-1975.
Dimmitt, Cornelia, and Buitenen, J. A. B. van, eds. and trans. Classical Hindu Mythology: A Reader in the Sanskrit Purāṇas. Philadelphia: Temple University Press, 1978.
Doniger, Wendy, trans. The Laws of Manu. New Delhi: Penguin India, 1991.
Griffith, Ralph, trans. The Hymns of the Ṛg-Veda. 2 vols. Delhi: Low Price Publications, 1995.
Hall, Fitzedward, ed. The Viṣṇu Purāṇa. New York: Garland, 1981.
Hume, Robert Ernst, trans. The Thirteen Principle Upanishads. 2nd ed. Delhi: Oxford University Press, 1984.
Iyer, Venkitasubramonia, S., trans. The Varāha-Purāṇa. 2 vols. Edited by J. L. Shastri. Delhi: Motilal Banarsidass, 1985.
Johnson, W. J. The Bhagavad Gita. Oxford: Oxford University Press, 1994.
Lal, P. The Bhagavadgita. Delhi: Orient Paperbacks, 1965.
Limaye, V. P., and Vadekar, R. D. Eighteen Principal Upaniṣads. Poona: Vaidika Samsodhana Mandala, 1958.
Mascaró, Juan, trans. The Bhagavad Gita. New York: Penguin Books, 1962.
Miller, Barbara Stoler, trans. The Bhagavad Gita: Krishna's Counsel in Time of War. New York: Bantam Books, 1986.
Müller, F. Max, trans. The Upanishads. 1900. Reprint. Vol. 1, Sacred Books of the East. Delhi: Motilal Banarsidass, 1988. Part I: Chāndogya-Upanishad, Talavakāra-Upanishad, Aitareya Āraṇyaka, Kaushītaki-Brāhmaṇa-Upanishad, Vājasaneyi-Saṁhitā-Upanishad.
______. The Upanishads. 1884. Reprint. Vol. 15, Sacred Books of the East. Delhi: Motilal Banarsidass, 1989. Part II: Kaṭha-Upanishad, Muṇḍaka-Upanishad, Taittirīyaka Upanishad, Brihadāraṇyaka-Upanishad, Śvetāśvatara-Upanishad, Praśna-Upanishad, Maitrāyaṇa Brāhmaṇa-Upanishad.
______. Vedic Hymns. 1891. Reprint. Vol. 32, Sacred Books of the East. Delhi: Motilal Banarsidass, 1988. Part I: Hymns to the Maruts, Rudra, Vāyu and Vāta.
Narasimhan, Chakravarthi V., trans. The Mahābhārata. New York: Columbia University Press, 1998.
Narayan, R. K. The Ramayana. New York: Penguin Books, 1977.
Nikhilananda, Swami, trans. The Upanishads. New York: Harper & Row, 1964.
Oldenberg, Hermann, trans. Vedic Hymns. 1897. Reprint. Vol. 46, Sacred Books of the East. Delhi: Motilal Banarsidass, 1988. Part II: Hymns to Agni (Mandalas I-V).
Prabhavananda, Swami, and Isherwood, Christopher, trans. The Song of God: The Bhagavad-Gita. New York: Mentor Books, 1951.
Radhakrishnan, S., ed. The Principal Upaniṣads. New York: Harper & Brothers, 1953.

Sargeant, Winthrop, trans. The Bhagavad Gītā. Albany: State University of New York Press, 1984.

Stanford, Ann. The Bhagavad Gita: A New Verse Translation. New York: Herder and Herder, 1970.

Sukthankar, Vishnu S., et al., eds. The Mahābhārata. Poona: Bhandarkar Oriental Research Institute, 1947.

Telang, Kāshināth Trimbak, trans. The Bhagavadgītā, with the Sanatsujātīya [of the Mahābhārata] and the Anugītā [of the Mahābhārata]. 1882. Reprint. Vol. 8, Sacred Books of the East. Delhi: Motilal Banarsidass, 1983.

Thomson, J. Cockburn. The Bhagavad-Gita: Or, a Discourse between Krishna and Arjuna on Divine Matters. Hertford: Stephen Austin, 1855.

Venkatesananda, Swami. The Concise Śrīmad Bhāgavatam. Albany: State University of New York Press, 1989.

Yogi, Maharishi Mahesh. The Bhagavad Gita. New York: Penguin Books, 1969.

Wilson, Horace H. The Vishnu Purana. 5 vols. New York: Garland, 1981.

## Modern Hindu-Related Translations-Commentaries

Bhave, Acharya Vinoba. Talks on the Gita. Kashi: Akhil Bharat Sarva Seva Sangh Prakashan, 1959.

Deutsch, Eliot. The Bhagavad Gītā. New York: Holt, Rinehart and Winston, 1968.

Edgerton, Franklin. The Beginnings of Indian Philosophy: Selections from the Rig Veda, Atharva Veda, Upaniṣads, and Mahābhārata. Cambridge, Mass.: Harvard University Press, 1965.

_______. The Bhagavad Gītā. Cambridge, Mass.: Harvard University Press, 1972.

Griffiths, Bede. River of Compassion: A Christian Commentary on the Bhagavad Gita. New York: Continuum, 1987.

Hill, W. Douglas P. The Bhagavadgītā. London: Oxford University Press, 1928.

Johnston, Charles. Bhagavad Gita: "The Songs of the Master". Flushing, N.Y.: Charles Johnston, 1908.

Lamotte, Etienne. Notes sur la Gītā. Paris: Geuthner, 1929.

Minor, Robert N. Bhagavad-Gītā: An Exegetical Commentary. New Delhi: Heritage, 1982.

Radhakrishnan, S. The Bhagavadgītā: With an Introductory Essay, Sanskrit Text, English Translation and Notes. London: George Allen & Unwin, 1956.

_______. The Brahma Sūtra: The Philosophy of Spiritual Life. New York: Harper & Brothers, 1960.

Roy, Anilbaran. The Gita: With Text, Translation and Notes, Compiled from Aurobindo's Essays on the Gita. Pondicherry: Sri Aurobindo Ashram, 1954.

Swarupananda, Swami. Śrīmad-Bhagavad-Gītā. 13th ed. Calcutta: Advaita Ashrama, 1982.

Zaehner, R. C. The Bhagavad-Gītā: With a Commentary Based on the Original Sources. London: Oxford University Press, 1973.

## Avatāra and Incarnation (avatāra alone or avatāra and incarnation compared)

Akhilananda, Swami. Hindu View of Christ. Boston: Branden Press, 1949.

Aleaz, K. P. Jesus in Neo-Vedānta: A Meeting of Hinduism and Christianity. Rani Bagh, Delhi: Kant Publications, 1995.

_______. An Indian Jesus from Śaṅkara's Perspective. Calcutta: Punthi Pustak, 1997.

Allen, Diogenes. "Incarnation in the Gospels and the Bhagavad Gita". Faith and Philosophy 6, no. 3 (July 1989): 241-59.

Appasamy, A. J. The Gospel and India's Heritage. London: Society for Promoting Christian Knowledge, 1942. Pages 247-64 contain an essay on avatāra and incarnation.

Bassuk, Daniel E. Incarnation in Hinduism and Christianity. Atlantic Highlands, N.J.: Humanities Press International, 1987.

_______. "Six Modern Indian Avatars and the Ways They Understand Their Divinity". Dialogue & Alliance 1, no. 2 (Summer 1987): 73-92.

Basu, Arabinda. "Sri Aurobindo on Christ and Christianity". In Neo-Hindu Views of Christianity, edited by Arvind Sharma. Leiden: E. J. Brill, 1988.

Bessant, Annie. Avataras. Chicago: The Theosophical Press, 1923.

Bhaktipāda, Kīrtanānanda Swami. Christ and Krishna. Moundsville, W.Va.: Bhaktipada Books, 1985.

Brent, Peter. Godmen of India. Chicago: Quadrangle Books, 1972.

Carman, John B. "Avatar and Incarnation: Two Conceptions of Divine Condescension". In his Majesty and Meekness: A Comparative Study of Contrast and Harmony in the Concept of God. Grand Rapids, Mich.: William B. Eerdmans, 1994. See chapter 10 (pp. 188-212).

Chakkarai, V. Jesus the Avatār. Madras: Christian Literature Society for India, 1930.

Chatterjee, Chinmayi. "A Note on the Vaiṣṇavic Concept of Avatāra and Līlā of God". Anvīkṣā 6 (March 1972): 1-11.

Chidananda, Swami. "The Esoteric Meaning of Ten Avataras". The Yoga Vedanta Forest University Weekly 4 (July 2, 1953): 729-30.

Clooney, Francis X. Hindu God, Christian God: How Reason Helps Break Down the Boundaries between Religions. New York: Oxford University Press, 2001. I list this source here because it is an important work for the study of how the divine relates to embodiment.

Das, Bhagavan. Krishna: A Study in the Theory of Avataras. Chaupatty, Bombay: Bharatiya Vidya Bhavan, 1962.

deNicolás, Antonio T. Avatara: The Humanization of Philosophy through the Bhagavad Gītā. New York: Nicolas Hays, 1976.

De Smet, Richard. "Jesus and the Avatāra". In Dialogue and Syncretism: An Interdisciplinary Approach, edited by Jerald Gort, Hendrik Vroom, Rein Fernhout, and Anton Wessels. Grand Rapids, Mich.: William B. Eerdmans, 1989.

_______. Krishna the Cowherd: Or, A Study of the Childhood of Shrī Krishna. Theosophical Publishing House, 1917.

Dhavamony, M. "Hindu 'incarnations'". Studia Missionalia 21 (1972): 127-69.

_______. "Krishna Avatara as Revelation of God in the Bhagavadgita". In Research Seminar on Non-Biblical Scriptures, edited by D. S. Amalorphavadass. Bangalore: National Biblical, Cathetical and Liturgical Center, 1974.

French, H. W. "Reverence to Christ through Mystical Experience and Incarnational Identity: Sri Ramakrishna". In Neo-Hindu Views of Christianity, edited by Arvind Sharma. Leiden: E. J. Brill, 1988.

George, N. V. The Doctrine of Incarnation in Vaishnavism and Christianity. Kashmere Gate, Delhi: Indian Society for Promoting Christian Knowledge (ISPCK), 1997.

Gorospe, Vitaliano R. "Krishna Avatara in the Bhagavad Gita and Christ Incarnate in John's Gospel". Dialogue & Alliance 1, no. 2 (Summer 1987): 53-72.

Graves, Kersey. The World's Sixteen Crucified Saviors. New Hyde Park, N.Y.: University Books, 1971.

Huntington, Ronald M. "Avatāras and Yugas: An Essay in Purāṇic Cosmology". Purāṇa 6 (January 1964): 7-39.

Jaccoliot, Louis. Christna et le Christ. Paris, 1877.

Jones, John P. India's Problem, Krishna or Christ. New York: Fleming H. Revell, 1903.

Lipner, Julius. "Avatāra and Incarnation?" In Re-Visioning India's Religious Traditions, edited by David Scott and Israel Selvanayagam. Delhi: SPCK, 1996.

Lott, Eric. "The Mythic Symbol Avatara in Conceptual Formulations". Dialogue & Alliance 1, no. 2 (Summer 1987): 3-12.

_______. "The Relevance of Research in Religions: Understanding Avatara as a Test Case". Bangalore Theological Forum 10, no. 1 (1978): 33-53.

Miranda, Prashant. Avatār and Incarnation: A Comparative Analysis. New Delhi: Harman Publishing House, 1990.

Moffitt, John. "Incarnation and Avatara: An Imaginary Conversation". Journal of Ecumenical Studies 14 (1977): 261-87.

Mohammed, Ovey N. "Jesus and Krishna". In Asian Faces of Jesus, edited by R. S. Sugirtharajah. Maryknoll, N.Y.: Orbis Books, 1993.

Parrinder, Geoffrey. Avatar and Incarnation: The Divine and Human Form in the World's Religions. Oxford: Oneworld Publications, 1997.

Quesnell, Quentin. "Aquinas on Avatars". Dialogue & Alliance 1, no. 2 (Summer 1987): 33-42.

Ramakrishnananda, Swami. God and Divine Incarnations. Mylapore: Sri Ramakrishna Math, n.d.

Reddy, V. Madhusudan. Avatarhood and Human Evolution. Hyderabad: Institute of Human Study, 1972.

Sadanandam, C. The Doctrine of Avatāra. Delhi: New Bharatiya Book Corporation, 2002.

Shinn, Larry D. "Behind the Avatara Krishna: Bhagavan in the Bhagavata Purana". Dialogue & Alliance 1, no. 2 (Summer 1987): 13-32.

Vempeny, Ishanand. Kṛṣṇa and Christ: In the Light of Some of the Fundamental Concepts and Themes of the Bhagavad Gītā and the New Testament. Anand, India: Gujarat Sahitya Prakash; and Pune: Ishvani Kendra, 1988.

Yesurathnam, Regunta. "The Adequacy of the Concept of Avatara for Expounding the Christian Doctrine of Incarnation". Dialogue & Alliance 1, no. 2 (Summer 1987): 43-52.

## Indian Philosophy and Theology

Agrawal, Madan Mohan. The Philosophy of Nimbārka. Gali Manahar, Sadabad

(Mathura): Shrimati Usha Agrawal, 1977.
_______. The Philosophy of Non-Attachment. New Delhi: Motilal Banarsidass, 1982.
Aleaz, K. P. Christian Thought through Advaita Vedānta. Delhi: ISPCK, 1996.
_______. The Relevance of Relation in Śaṅkara's Advaita Vedānta. Delhi: Kant Publications, 1996.
_______. The Role of Pramāṇas in Hindu-Christian Epistemology. Calcutta: Punthi-Pustak, 1991.
_______. "Vedic-Vedantic Vision in Indian Christian Theology of Nature". Bangalore Theological Forum 25 (1993): 25-40.
Alston, A. J., ed. Śaṅkara on Creation. London: Shanti Sadan, 1985.
_______. Śaṅkara on the Absolute. London: Shanti Sadan, 1980.
_______. Śaṅkara on Enlightenment. London: Shanti Sadan, 1989.
_______. Śaṅkara on the Soul. London: Shanti Sadan, 1985.
Antony, Fr. "Is Rāmānuja a Pantheist?" Indian Ecclesiastical Studies 5.4 (October 1966): 283-313.
Balasubramanian, R. Some Problems in the Epistemology and Metaphysics of Rāmānuja. Madras: University of Madras, 1978.
Bharadwaj, Krishna Datta. The Philosophy of Rāmānuja. New Delhi: Sir Shankar Lall Charitable Trust Society, 1958.
Bhatt, S. R. Studies in Rāmānuja Vedānta. New Delhi: Heritage, 1975.
Bhattacharji, Sukumari. The Indian Theogony: A Comparative Study of Indian Mythology from the Vedas to the Purāṇas. London: Cambridge University Press, 1970.
Bhattacharya, Kalidas. Philosophy, Logic and Language. Bombay: Allied, 1965.
Borelli, John. "Vijñānabhikṣu and the Re-Assertion of Difference-in-Identity Vedānta". Philosophy East and West 28 (1978): 425-37.
Bowen, Paul, ed. Themes and Issues in Hinduism. London: Cassell, 1998.
Brooks, Richard. "The Meaning of 'Real' in Advaita Vedānta". Philosophy East and West 19 (1969): 385-98.
Buch, Manganlal A. The Philosophy of Shankara. Baroda: Good Companions, 1988.
Buitenen, J. A. B. van. Rāmānuja on the Bhagavadgītā. The Hague: H. L. Smits, 1953.
Carman, John Braisted. The Theology of Rāmānuja: An Essay in Interreligious Understanding. 1974. Reprint. Bombay: Ananthacharya Indological Research Institute, 1981.
Carpenter, J. Estlin. Theism in Medieval India. Hibbert Lectures, 2nd series, 1919. London: Williams & Norgate, 1921.
Cave, Sydney. Redemption: Hindu and Christian. London: Oxford University Press, 1919.
Chatterjee, S. C., and Datta, D. M. An Introduction to Indian Philosophy. Calcutta: University of Calcutta, 1960.
Chatterji, Kamala. "Brahman's Creation of the World". Journal of the Indian Academy of Philosophy 24 (1985): 62-68, and 25 (1986): 1-12.
Chattopadhyaya, S. K. "The Concept of Adhyāsa and the Vedānta of Śaṅkara". Indian Philosophical Quarterly 6 (1978): 81-99, 683-96.
Chennakesavan, Sarasvati. Concept of Mind in Indian Philosophy. Reprint. Delhi: Motilal Banarsidass, 1991.
Chethimattam, John B. Consciousness and Reality: An Indian Approach to Metaphysics. Bangalore: Dharmaram College, 1967.

Clooney, Francis X. "Devatādhikaraṇa: A Theological Debate in the Mīmāṃsā and Vedānta Traditions". Journal of Indian Philosophy 16 (1988): 277-98.

_______. "Evil, Divine, Omnipotence, and Human Freedom: Vedānta's Theology of Karma". Journal of Religion 69 (1989): 530-48.

_______. "From Truth to Religious Truth in Hindu Philosophical Theology". In Religious Truth, edited by Robert Neville. Albany: State University of New York Press, 2000.

_______. "Śaṅkara's Theological Realism: the Meaning and Usefulness of Gods (Devatā) in the Uttara Mīmāṃsā Sūtra Bhaṣya". In New Perspectives on Advaita Vedānta: Essays in Commemoration of Professor Richard De Smet, SJ, edited by Bradley J. Malkovsky. Leiden: Brill, 2000.

_______. Theology after Vedānta: An Experiment in Comparative Theology. Albany: State University of New York Press, 1993.

_______. "Vedānta Deśika's 'Definition of the Lord' (Īśvarapariccheda) and the Hindu Argument about Ultimate Reality". In Ultimate Realities, edited by Robert Neville. Albany: State University of New York Press, 2000.

_______. "What's a God? The Quest for the Right Understanding of devatā in Brahmaṇical Ritual Theory". International Journal of Hindu Studies 1 (1997): 337-85.

Coomaraswamy, Ananda K. "Angel and Titan: An Essay in Vedic Ontology". Journal of the American Oriental Society 55 (1935): 373-419.

Damodaran, K. Indian Thought: A Critical Survey. London: Asia Publishing House, 1967.

Daniélou, Alain. The Myths and Gods of India: The Classic Work on Hindu Polytheism from the Princeton Bollingen Series. Rochester, Vt.: Inner Traditions International, 1991.

Das Gupta, Shashi Bhusan. Aspects of Indian Religious Thought. Calcutta: A. Mukherjee, 1957.

Dasgupta, Surendranath. A History of Indian Philosophy. 5 vols. Reprint. Delhi: Motilal Banarsidass, 1992.

Date, V. H. Vedānta Explained. Delhi: Munshiram Manoharlal, 1973.

Datta, D. M. The Six Ways of Knowing. Calcutta: University of Calcutta, 1972.

_______. "Some Realistic Aspects of the Philosophy of Śaṁkara". In Recent Indian Philosophy, edited by Kalidas Bhattacharya. Calcutta: Progressive Publishers, 1963.

De Smet, Richard V. "Advaitavāda and Christianity". The Divine Life 35 (June 1973): 237-39.

_______. "Early Trends in the Indian Understanding of Man". Philosophy East and West 22 (1972): 259-68.

_______. "Forward Steps in Śaṅkara Research". Darshana International 26 (1987): 33-46.

_______. "The Fundamental Antinomy of Śrī Śaṅkarācārya's Methodology". Oriental Thought 2 (1956): 1-9.

_______. "Gītā/Gospel Convergencies". Sevartham 14 (1989): 13-19.

_______. "Is the Concept of 'Person' Congenial to Śaṅkara Vedānta?" Indian Philosophical Annual 8 (1972): 199-205.

_______. "Māyā or Ajñāna?" Indian Philosophical Annual 2 (1966): 220-25.

_______. "Moksha—Deliverance". The Divine Life 34 (1972): 372-73.

_______. "Origin: Creation and Emanation". Indian Theological Studies 15 (1978): 266-

79.
_______. "Questioning Vedānta". Indian Philosophical Annual 7 (1971): 97-105.
_______. "Rāmānuja, Pantheist or Panentheist?" Annals of the Bhandarkar Oriental Research Institute (1977-1978): 561-71.
_______, and Neuner, J., eds. Religious Hinduism. 3rd ed. Allahabad: St. Paul Publications, 1968.
_______. "Śaṅkara Vedānta and Chriastian Theology". Review of Darshana 1 (1980): 33-48.
_______. "Some Governing Principles in Indian Philosophy". Philosophical Quarterly 34 (1962): 249-58.
_______. "The Theological Method of Śaṃkara". Ph.D. diss., Pontifical Gregorian University, 1953.
_______. "Theological Method and Vedānta". Oriental Thought 4 (1960): 20-35.
_______. "Towards an Indian View of the Person". In Contemporary Indian Philosophy, edited by Margaret Chatterjee. London: George Allen & Unwin, 1974.
Deussen, Paul. The Philosophy of the Upanishads. Delhi: Oriental Reprint, 1979.
_______. The System of the Vedānta. New Delhi: Puja Publications, 1983.
Deutsch, Eliot. Advaita Vedānta: A Philosophical Reconstruction. Honolulu: University Press of Hawaii, 1980.
_______, and Buitenen, J. A. B. van. A Source Book of Advaita Vedānta. Honolulu: The University Press of Hawaii, 1971.
Devanandan, Paul David. The Concept of Māyā: An Essay in Historical Survey of the Hindu Theory of the World, with Special Reference to the Vedānta. London: Lutterworth Press, 1950.
Devaraja, N. K. An Introduction to Śaṅkara's Theory of Knowledge. Delhi: Motilal Banarsidass, 1962.
Dhar, Mohini Mohan. Krishna the Charioteer: Or, the Teachings of Bhagavad Gītā. London: Theosophical Publishing House, 1917.
Dhavamony, Mariasusai. Classical Hinduism. Roma: Pontifica Universitas Gregoriana, 1982.
Dube, Manju. Conceptions of God in Vaiṣṇava Philosophical Systems. Varanasi: Sanjay, 1984.
Feuerstein, G. "The One and the Many: A Fundamental Philosophical Problem in the Principal Upanishads". Hinduism 88 (1980): 1-10.
Forsthoefel, Thomas A. Knowing Beyond Knowledge: Epistemologies of Religious Experience in Classical and Modern Advaita. Burlington, Vt.: Ashgate, 2002.
Fort, A. O. "The Concept of Sākṣin in Advaita Vedānta. Journal of Indian Philosophy 12 (1984): 277-90.
Frazer, Robert W. Indian Thought. London: T. F. Unwin, 1915.
Frenz, A., ed. Grace in Śaiva Siddhānta, Vedānta, Islam and Christianity. Arasaradi, Madurai: Tamil Nadu Theological Seminary, 1975.
Ganeri, Jonardon. Philosophy in Classical India. London: Routledge, 2001.
Ghate, V. S. The Vedānta: A Study of the Brahma-Sūtras with the Bhāṣyas of Śaṅkara, Rāmānuja, Nimbārka, Madhva and Vallabha. Poona: Bhandarkar Oriental Research Institute, 1960.
Gispert-Sauch, G. "Shankaracharya and our Theological Task". Vidyajyoti: Journal of Theological Reflection (September 1978): 348-55.
Glasenapp, Helmuth von. "Parallels and Contrasts in Indian and Western Metaphysics".

Philosophy East and West 3 (1953-1954): 223-31.
Gonda, Jan. Change and Continuity in Indian Religion. Delhi: Munshiram Manoharlal, 1985.
_______. Notes on Brahman. Utrecht: J. L. Beyers, 1950.
_______. Viṣṇuism and Śivaism: A Comparison. London: Athlone, 1970.
Grant, Sara. "Christian Theologizing and the Challenge of Advaita". In Theologizing in India, edited by M. Amaladoss. Bangalore: Theological Publications in India, 1981.
_______. "Śaṅkara's Conception of Śruti as a Pramāṇa". In Research Seminar on Non-Biblical Scriptures, edited by D. S. Amalorpavadass. Bangalore: National Biblical, Catechetical and Liturgical Centre, 1974.
Griffiths, Bede. Vedanta and Christian Faith. Los Angeles: The Dawn Horse Press, 1973.
Grimes, John. A Concise Dictionary of Indian Philosophy. Albany: State University of New York Press, 1989.
_______. "Radhakrishnan and Śaṅkara's Māyā". The Scottish Journal of Religious Studies 10 (1989): 50-56.
_______. "Śaṅkara's Siren of Śruti". Journal of Dharma 17 (1992): 196-202.
Gupta, Bina. Perceiving in Advaita Vedānta: Epistemological Analysis and Interpretation. Columbia, Mo.: Associated University Presses, 1991.
Hacker, Paul. "Eigentümlichkeiten der Lehre und Terminologie Śaṅkaras: Avidyā, Nāmarūpa, Māyā, Īśvara". Zeitschrift der Deutschen Morgenländischen Gesellschaft 100 (1950): 246-86.
_______. "Die Idee der Person im Denken Vedānta-Philosophen". Studia Missionalia 18 (1963): 30-52.
_______. "Relations of Early Advaitins to Vaiṣṇavism". Weiner Zeitshcrift für Kunde Süd-und Ostasiens 9 (1965): 147-54.
_______. "Śaṅkara's Conception of Man". Studia Missionalia 19 (1970): 123-31.
Halbfass, Wilhelm. India and Europe: An Essay in Philosophical Understanding. Delhi: Motilal Banarsidass, 1990.
_______, ed. Philology and Confrontation: Paul Hacker on Traditional and Modern Vedānta. Albany: State University of New York Press, 1995.
_______. Tradition and Reflection: Explorations in Indian Thought. Albany: State University of New York Press, 1991.
Harrison, Max Hunter. Hindu Monism and Pluralism. London: Humphrey Milford, Oxford University Press, 1932.
Hartshorne, Charles. "Theism in Asian and Western Thought". Philosophy East and West 28 (1978): 401-11.
Heimann, Betty. Facets of Indian Thought. New York: George Allen & Unwin, 1964.
Herman, A. L. "Indian Theodicy in Śaṅkara and Rāmānuja on Brahma Sūtra II.1.32-36". Philosophy East and West 21 (1971): 265-81.
Hiriyanna, M. "Definition of Brahman". Journal of the Ganganatha Jha Research Institute 2 (1945): 287-92.
_______. The Essentials of Indian Philosophy. London: George Allen & Unwin, 1960.
_______. Outlines of Indian Philosophy. London: George Allen & Unwin, 1932.
Hirst, Jaqueline. "The Place of Bhakti in Śaṅkara's Vedānta". In Love Divine, edited by Karel Werner. Richmond, Surrey: Curzon Press, 1993.
Hogg, A. G. Karma and Redemption. Madras: Christian Literature Society, 1970.
Indich, William M. Consciousness in Advaita Vedānta. Delhi: Motilal Banarsidass,

1980.

Ingalls, Daniel H. H. "Sankara's Arguments against the Buddhists". Philosophy east and West 3 (January 1954): 291-306.

_______. "The Study of Śaṁkarācārya". Annals of the Bhandarkar Oriental Research Institute 33 (1952): 1-14.

Isayeva, Natalia. Shankara and Indian Philosophy. Albany: State University of New York Press, 1993.

Islam, Kazi Nurul. A Critique of Śaṅkara's Philosophy of Appearance. Allahabad: Vohra, 1988.

_______. "Māyā and Avidyā: An Analysis of a Controversy". Journal of the Indian Academy of Philosophy 22 (1983): 57-61.

Iyer, K. Sundarama. Vedānta: Its Doctrine of Divine Personality. Srirangam: Vani Vilas Press, 1926.

Javadekar, A. G. "Ascending Scale of the Advaita Vedānta". Annals of the Bhandarkar Oriental Research Institute 58-59 (1977-1978): 659-66.

Johanns, P. Vers le Christ par le Vedānta. 2 parts. Louvain: Museum Lessianum, 1932.

Keith, Arthur Berriedale. 2 vols. The Religion and Philosophy of the Veda and Upanishads. 1925. Reprint. Westport, Conn.: Greenwood Press, 1971.

King, Richard. "Brahman and the World: Immanence and Transcendence in Advaita Vedānta: A Comparative Perspective". The Scottish Journal of Religious Studies 12 (1991): 107-26.

_______. Early Advaita Vedānta and Buddhism. Albany: State University of New York Press, 1995.

_______. Indian Philosophy: An Introduction to Hindu and Buddhist Thought. Washington, D.C.: Georgetown University Press, 1999.

Kinsley, D. The Divine Player: A Study of Kṛṣṇa Līlā. Delhi: Motilal Banarsidass, 1979.

Klive, Visvaldis V. "Analytic Philosophy and Advaita". In Perspectives on Vedānta, edited by S. S. Rao Pappu. Leiden: E. J. Brill, 1988.

Krishna, Daya. Indian Philosophy: A Counter Perspective. Oxford: Oxford University Press, 1991.

Kulandran, Sabapathy. Grace: A Comparative Study of the Doctrine in Christianity and Hinduism. London: Lutterworth Press, 1964.

Kumar, Frederick L. The Philosophies of India: A New Approach. Lewiston, N.Y.: The Edwin Mellen Press, 1991.

Kumarappa, Bharatan. The Hindu Conception of Deity. Delhi: Inter-India, 1979.

Kumoi, Shozen. "On the Īśvara-vāda: Its Assertion and Criticism". Journal of Indian and Buddhist Studies 14 (28) (March 1966): 936-42.

Lacombe, Olivier. L'Absolu selon le Védânta: Les Notions de Brahman et d'Atman dans les systèmes de Cankara et Râmânoudja. Paris: Librairie Orientaliste Paul Geuthner, 1937.

_______. La Doctrine morale et métaphysique de Rāmānuja. Paris: Adrien-Maisonneuve, 1938. Text and French translation of BSB 1.1.1.

Larson, G. J. Classical Sāṃkhya: An Interpretation of Its History and Meaning. 2nd ed. Delhi: Motilal Banarsidass, 1979.

Lazarus, F. K. Rāmānuja and Browne: A Study in Comparative Philosophy. Bombay: Chetana, 1962.

Lester, Robert. "Rāmānuja and Śrī Vaiṣṇavism: The Concept of Prapatti or Śaraṇāgati". History of Religions (University of Chicago) 5 (Winter 1966): 266-82.

Lipner, Julius J. "The Christian and Vedāntic Theories of Originative Causality: A Study in Transcendence and Immanence". Philosophy East and West 28 (1978): 53-68.
_______. The Face of Truth: A Study of Meaning and Metaphysics in the Vedāntic Theology of Rāmānuja. Albany: State University of New York Press, 1986.
_______. Hindus: Their Religious Beliefs and Practices. London: Routledge, 1994.
_______. "Philosophy and world religions". In Philosophy of Religion: A Guide to the Subject, edited by Brian Davies. London: Cassell, 1998.
_______. "Śaṃkara on Metaphor with Reference to Gītā 13.12-18". In Indian Philosophy of Religion, edited by R. W. Perrett. Dordrecht: Kluwer Academic, 1989.
_______. "Śaṅkara on Satyaṃ Jñānam Anantaṃ Brahma". In Relativism, Suffering and Beyond: Essays in Memory of Bimal K. Matilal, edited by P. Bilimoria and J. N. Mohanty. New Delhi: Oxford University Press, 1997.
_______. "The Self of Being and the Being of Self: Śaṁkara on 'That You Are' (tat tvam asi)". In New Perspectives on Advaita Vedānta: Essays in Commemoration of Professor Richard De Smet, SJ, edited by Bradley J. Malkovsky. Leiden: Brill, 2000.
Lott, Eric. "The Conceptual Dimensions of Bhakti in the Rāmānuja Tradition". Scottish Journal of Religious Studies 2, no. 1 (1981): 97-114.
_______. God and the Universe in the Vedāntic Theology of Rāmānuja. Madras: Rāmānuja Research Society, 1976.
_______. Vedantic Approaches to God. New York: Barnes and Noble, 1980.
Loy, David. Nonduality. New Haven, Conn.: Yale University Press, 1988.
Macnicol, Nicol. Indian Theism: From the Vedic to the Muhammadan Period. 2nd ed. Delhi: Munshiram Manoharlal, 1968.
_______. "Some Hindrances to Theism in India". The Indian Interpreter 7, no. 2 (July 1912): 81-88.
Mahadevan, T. M. P. "The Idea of God in Advaita". Vedānta Kesari 8 (1966): 35-38.
_______. Superimposition in Advaita Vedānta. Delhi: Sterling, 1985.
Mainkar, T. G. A Comparative Study of the Commentaries on the Bhagavadgītā. Delhi: Motilal Banarsidass, 1969.
Maitra, S. K. "Schools of Vedānta Philosophy". In Studies in the History of Indian Philosophy. Vol. 1 edited by D. Chattopadhyaya. Calcutta: K. P. Bagchi, 1978.
Majumdar, Abhay Kumar. Sāṅkhya Conception of Personality or a New Interpretation of the Sāṅkhya Philosophy. Calcutta: University of Calcutta, 1930.
Malkovsky, Bradley J., ed. New Perspectives on Advaita Vedānta: Essays in Commemoration of Professor Richard De Smet, SJ. Leiden: Brill, 2000.
_______. "The Personhood of Śaṁkara's Para Brahman". The Journal of Religion 77 (1997): 541-62.
_______. The Role of Divine Grace in the Soteriology of Śaṃkarācārya. Leiden: Brill 2001.
Manalapuzhavila, Antony. Nature and Origin of the World according to Rāmānuja. Alwaye, India: St. Joseph's Pontifical Seminary, 1966.
Marcaurelle, Roger. Freedom through Inner Renunciation: Śaṅkara's Philosophy in a New Light. Albany: State University of New York Press, 2000.
Marfatia, Mrudula I. The Philosophy of Vallabha. Delhi: Munshiram Manoharlal, 1967.
Masih, Y. Shankara's Universal Philosophy of Religion. Delhi: Munshiram Manoharlal, 1987.
Matesz, Donald A. "Karma and Mokṣa in Vedānta: Reality and Appearance". In The

Dimensions of Karma, edited by S. S. Rama Rao Pappu. Delhi: Chanakya, 1987.
Matilal, Bimal Krishna. Perception: An Essay on Classical Indian Theories of Knowledge. New York: Oxford University Press, 1986.
Mayeda, Sengaku. "The Advaita Theory of Perception". Wiener Zeitschrift für die Kunde Süd- und Ostasiens 12-13 (1968-1969): 221-39.
_______. "On the cosmological View of Śaṁkara". Adyar Library Bulletin 39 (1975): 186-204.
_______. "Śaṁkara and Sureśvara: Their Exegetical Method to Interpret the Great Sentence 'Tat Tvam Asi'". Adyar Library Bulletin 44-45 (1980-1981): 147-60.
Modi, P. M. "Philosophical Ideas of the Gītā, with Special Reference to Śaṁkara's Interpretation". Gujarat Research Society Journal 12 (1950): 123-40.
Mohanty, J. N. "Indian Philosophical Tradition: The Theory of Pramāṇa". In Rationality in Question: On Eastern and Western Views of Rationality, edited by Shlomo Biderman and Ben-Ami Scharfstein. Leiden: E. J. Brill, 1989.
Monier-Williams, Sir Monier. Brahmanism and Hinduism: Or, Religious Thought and Life in India. 4th ed. London: John Murray, 1891.
Mukerji, A. C. Nature of Self. Allahabad: Indian Press, 1938.
Mumme, Patricia Y. The Śrīvaiṣṇava Theological Dispute: Maṇālamāmuni and Vedānta Deśika. Chennai: New Era, 1988.
Murti, T. R. V. "The Two Definitions of Brahman in the Advaita". In Studies in Indian Thought, edited by Harold Coward. Delhi: Motilal Banarsidass, 1983.
Murty, K. Satchidananda. Revelation and Reason in Advaita Vedānta. New York: Columbia University Press, 1959.
Nakamura, H. Early Vedānta Philosophy. Tokyo: Iwanami Shoten, 1950.
Nayak, G. C. "Does Śaṅkara Advocate Enlightenment Through Analysis?" In Perspectives on Vedānta, edited by S. S. Rao Pappu. Leiden: E. J. Brill, 1988.
O'Flaherty, Wendy Doniger. Karma and Rebirth in Classical Indian Traditions. Berkeley: University of California Press, 1980.
Organ, Troy Wilson. The Self in Indian Philosophy. London. Mouton, 1964.
Pandey, R. R. "The Advaitic Theory of Causation". East and West 28 (1978): 291-98.
Pandey, Sangam Lal. Pre-Śaṁkara Advaita Philosophy. Allahabad: Darshan Peeth, 1983.
Panikkar, Raimundo. The Unknown Christ of Hinduism: Towards and Ecumenical Christophany. Revised and enlarged. Maryknoll, N.Y.: Orbis Books, 1981.
Pappu, S. S. Rao, ed. Perspectives on Vedānta. Leiden: E. J. Brill, 1988.
Pappu, S. S. Rama Rao, ed. The Dimensions of Karma. Delhi: Chanakya, 1987.
Paradkar, M. D. "Field of Observation of Śaṅkarāchārya". Journal of the University of Bombay 25 (1956): 42-131.
_______. Perspectives on Vedānta: Essays in Honor of Professor P. T. Raju. Leiden: E. J. Brill, 1988.
Pereira, José. Hindu Theology: Themes, Texts and Structures. Delhi: Motilal Banarsidass, 1976.
Potter, Karl H., ed. Advaita Vedānta up to Śaṃkara and His Pupils. Princeton: Princeton University Press, 1981.
_______. Presuppositions of India's Philosophies. Delhi: Motilal Banarsidass, 1991.
_______. "Śaṃkarācārya: The Myth and the Man". JAAR Thematic Studies 48 (1982): 111-25.
Prabhupāda, A. C. Bhaktivedanta Swami. Kṛṣṇa: The Supreme Personality of Godhead.

A Summary of Śrīla Vyāsadeva's Śrīmad Bhāgavatam, Tenth Canto. 2 vols. New York: The Bhaktivedanta Book Trust, 1970.
Puligandla, R. Fundamentals of Indian Philosophy. Nashville: Abingdon Press, 1975.
Radhakrishnan, S., and Raju, P. T. Concept of Man. London: George Allen & Unwin, 1960.
_______. Indian Philosophy. 2 vols. Delhi: Oxford University Press, 1989.
Raghavachar, S. S. Introduction to the Vedarthasangraha of Sree Ramanujacharya. Mangalore: The Mangalore Trading Association, 1957.
_______. Śrī Rāmānuja on the Upanishads. Madras: Professor M. Rangacharya Memorial Trust, 1972.
Raghavan, V. "The Viṣṇupurāṇa and Advaita". Adyar Library Bulletin 39 (1975): 294-99.
Raju, P. T. The Philosophical Traditions of India. London: George Allen & Unwin, 1971.
_______. Structural Depths of Indian Thought. New Delhi: South Asian, 1985.
Rambachan, Anantanand. Accomplishing the Accomplished: The Vedas as a Source of Knowledge in Sankara. Honolulu: University of Hawaii Press, 1991.
_______. "The Value of the World as the Mystery of God in Advaita Vedanta". Journal of Dharma 14 (1989): 287-97.
Ranade, R. D. The Bhagavadgītā as a Philosophy of God-Realisation. Bombay: Bhāratīya Vidyā Bhavan, 1982.
_______. A Constructive Survey of Upanishadic Thought: Being an Introduction to the Thought of the Upanishads. Bombay: Bhāratīya Vidyā Bhavan, 1986.
_______. Vedānta: The Culmination of Indian Thought. Bombay: Bhāratīya Vidyā Bhavan, 1970.
Reichenbach, Bruce R. "Karma, Causation, and Divine Intervention". Philosophy East and West 39 (1989): 135-49.
_______. The Law of Karma: A Philosophical Study. Honolulu: University of Hawaii Press, 1990.
Roy, Kamala. Concept of Self. Calcutta: Firma K. L. Mukhopadhyay, 1966.
Rukmani, T. S. "Śaṅkara's Views on Yoga in the Brahmasūtrabhāṣya in the Light of the Authorship of the Yogasūtrābhāṣya-vivaraṇa". Journal of Indian Philosophy 21 (1993): 395-404.
Sarasvati, Swami Satchidanandendra. The Method of the Vedānta. London: Kegan Paul International, 1989.
Sarma, Deepak. An Introduction to Madhva Vedanta. Burlington, Vt.: Ashgate, 2003.
Sarma, V. A. "The Language of Śaṅkara's Advaita". Vedānta Kesari 61 (1970): 386-90.
Sastri, Kokileswar. "Brahman in Śaṃkara Vedānta". Calcutta Oriental Journal 1 (December 1933): 117-22.
_______. An Introduction to Adwaita Philosophy. 2nd ed. Calcutta: University of Calcutta, 1926.
_______. "Vidyā and Avidyā". Calcutta Oriental Journal 1 (April, June, July, September, 1934): 253-57, 283-85, 303-308, 351-58.
_______. "The World in Śaṃkara Vedānta". Calcutta Oriental Journal 1 (October, November 1933): 25-30, 41-46.
Sastri, S. Laxminarasimha. "The Place of Viṣṇu according to Śrī Śaṁkarācārya". Kalyāṇa Kalpataru 33 (1972): 308-13.
Satprakashananda, Swami. Methods of Knowledge According to Advaita Vedanta.

London: George Allen & Unwin, 1965.
Satyanand, Joseph. Nimbārka: A Pre-Śaṁkara Vedāntin and His Philosophy. Christnagar Varanasi: Vishwa Jyoti Gurukul, 1994.
Schoonenberg, Piet. "Gott als Person und Gott als das unpersönlich Göttlich: Bhakti und Jñāna". In Transzendenzerfahrung, Vollzugshorizont des Heils: Das Problem on indischer und christlicher Tradition, edited by G. Oberhammer. Vienna: Institut für Indologie der Universität Wien, 1978.
Schuhmacher, Stephan, and Woerner, Gert, eds., The Encyclopedia of Eastern Philosophy and Religion. Boston: Shambhala, 1989.
Schultz, Walter. "The Contribution of Advaita Vedanta to the Quest for an Effective Reassertion of the Eternal". Journal of Dharma 16 (1991): 387-97.
Sen Gupta, Anima. A Critical Study of the Philosophy of Rāmānuja. Vol. 55, Chowkhamba Sanskrit Studies. Varanasi: Chowkhamba Sanskrit Studies Office, 1967.
_______. The Evolution of the Sāṁkhya School of Thought. 2nd ed. Delhi: Munshiram Manoharlal, 1986.
_______. "The Meanings of 'That thou art'". Philosophy East and West 12 (1962): 125-34.
Sharma, Arvind. The Experiential Dimension of Advaita Vedānta. Delhi: Motilal Banarsidass, 1993.
_______. The Hindu Gītā: Ancient and Classical Interpretations of the Bhagavadgītā. London: Duckworth, 1986.
_______. Philosophy of Religion and Advaita Vedānta: A Comparative Study in Religion and Reason. University Park: Pennsylvania State University Press, 1995.
_______. The Study of Hinduism. Columbia: University of South Carolina Press, 2003.
Sharma, B. N. K. The Brahmasūtras and Their Principal Commentaries. 3 vols. New Delhi: Munshiram Manoharlal Publishers, 1986.
_______. Madhva's Teachings in Hs Own Words. Bombay: Bhāratīya Vidyā Bhavan, 1979.
Sharma, Chandradhar. Indian Philosophy: A Critical Survey. London: Rider & Company, 1960. American Edition Published by Barnes & Noble, 1962.
Sharma, Paduranga. "Shankara's View of Space, Time and Ether". Journal of the Indian Academy of Philosophy 24 (1985): 1-12.
Sharma, R. N. Indian Philosophy. Delhi: Orient Longman, 1972.
Sharpe, Eric J. The Universal Gītā: Western Images of the Bhagavadgītā. London: Gerald Duckworth, 1985.
Shastri, M. D. "A History of the Word 'Īśvara' and Its Idea". Proceedings of the All-India Oriental Conference 7 (1935): 487-503.
Sheridan, Daniel P. The Advaitic Theism of the Bhāgavata Purāṇa. Delhi: Motilal Banarsidass, 1986.
Sheth, Noel. "Śaṅkara on How Effects Pre-exist in Their Cause". International Philosophical Quarterly 7 (1967): 298-304.
Shrivastava, S. N. L. Śaṁkara on God, Religion, and Morality". Philosophy East and West 7 (1957-1958): 91-106.
Siegel, Lee. "Theism in Indian Thought". Philosophy East and West 28 (1978): 419-23.
Sinari, Ramakant A. The Structure of Indian Thought. Delhi: Oxford University Press, 1984.
Singer, Milton, ed. Krishna: Myths, Rites, and Attitudes. Chicago: The University of

Chicago Press, 1966.
Singh, Ram Pratap. "The Individual Self in the Vedānta of Śaṁkara". Philosophical Quarterly 23 (1950-1951): 227-34.
_______. "Radhakrishnan's Substantial Reconstruction of the Vedānta of Śaṁkara". Philosophy East and West 16 (1966): 5-32.
_______. "Śaṁkara and Bhāskara". Philosophical Quarterly 19 (1956): 75-81.
_______. The Vedānta of Śaṅkara: A Metaphysics of Value. Jaipur: Bharat Publishing House, 1949.
_______. "Vedāntic Worldview of Śaṁkara". Prabuddha Bhārata 54 (1949): 364-71.
Sinha, Jadunath. Outlines of Indian Philosophy. Calcutta: Sinha Publishing House, 1963.
_______. The Philosophy of Nimbārka. Calcutta: Sinha Publishing House, 1973.
Sircar, M. L. "The Philosophy of Bhāskara". Philosophical Quarterly 3 (1927): 107-39.
Skoog, Kim. "Śaṁkara on the Role of Śruti and Anubhava in Attaining Brahmajñāna". Philosophy East and West (1989): 67-74.
Smart, Ninian. Doctrine and Argument in Indian Philosophy. London: George Allen & Unwin, 1964.
Srinivasachari, P. N. Idea of Personality. Madras: Adyar Library and Research Centre, 1951.
_______. The Philosophy of Bhedābheda. Madras: The Adyar Library and Research Centre, 1972.
_______. The Philosophy of Viśiṣṭādvaita. Madras: The Adyar Library and Research Centre, 1970.
Strydonck, J. M. van. "Śaṅkara's Theism in His Yoga-Sūtra-Bhāṣya-Vivaraṇa". Orientalia Lovaniensia Periodica 18 (1987): 121-35.
Sukhtankar, Vasudev Anant. The Teachings of the Vedānta according to Rāmānuja. Vienna: Adolf Holzhausen, 1908.
Swain, A. C. "Śaṃkara's Attitude towards the Accounts of Creation". Vedānta Kesari 56 (1969): 230-33.
Syed, M. H. "Grace and the Law of Karma". Vedānta Kesari 34 (1947-1948): 89-90.
Taber, John. "Revelation, Reason and Idealism in Śaṅkara's Vedānta". Journal of Indian Philosophy 9 (1981): 283-307.
Tagore, Rabindranath. Personality. London: Macmillan, 1961.
Tapasyānanda, Svāmī. Bhakti Schools of Vedānta. Madras: Sri Ramakrishna Math, n.d.
Tola, Fernando, and Dragonetti, Carmen. "Anāditva or Beginninglessness in Indian Philosophy". Annals of the Bhandarkar Oriental Research Institute 61 (1980): 1-20.
Upadhyaya, K. N. "Śaṅkara on Reason, Scriptural Authority and Self-Knowledge". Journal of Indian Philosophy 19 (1991): 121-32.
Urquhart, W. S. Vedānta and Modern Thought. London: Oxford University Press, 1928.
Varadachari, K. C. Idea of God. Tirupati: Sri Venkatesvara Oriental Institute, 1950
_______. Sri Ramanuja's Theory of Knowledge. Tirupati: Tirumalai-Tirupati Devasthanams Press, 1956.
Vidyārṇava, Rai Bahadur Śrīśachandra. Studies in the Vedānta Sūtras. Allahabad: Sudhindra Nātha Vasu, 1919.
Venkatasubbarao, P. S. "Grace in Dvaita Vedānta". Kalyāṇa Kalpataru 17 (1951-1952): 504-7.
Vetter, Tilmann. "Zur Bedeutung des Illusionismus bei Śaṅkara". Wiener Zeitschrift für die Kunde Süd- und Ostasiens 12-13 (1968-1969): 407-23.

Vidyarthi, P. B. Knowledge, Self and God in Ramanuja: A Study in the Theoretical Foundations of the Theism of Ramanuja. New Delhi: Oriental Publishers and Distributors, 1967.

Vivekananda, Swami. Essentials of Hinduism. Mayavati: Advaita Ashrama, 1947.

Warrier, A. G. Krishna. The Concept of Mukti in Advaita Vedānta. Madras: Madras University, 1981.

_______. God in Advaita. Simla: Indian Institute of Advanced Study, 1977.

_______. "The Śvetāśvatara Upaniṣad and the Vedāntic Schools". Proceedings of the Indian Philosophical Congress 28 (1953): 261-70.

Wilkins, W. J. Hindu Mythology: Vedic and Purāṇic. Calcutta: Thacker, Spink & Co., 1900.

Wyschogrod, Edith. "The Concept of the World in Śaṅkara: A Reply to Milton K. Munits". Philosophy East and West 25 (1975): 301-8.

Yamunacharya, M. Rāmānuja's Teachings in His Own Words. Vol. 111, Bhavan's Book University. Bombay: Bhāratīya Vidyā Bhavan, 1963.

Yandell, Keith. "On Interpreting the Bhagavadgītā". Philosophy East and West 32 (1982): 37-46.

Young, Katherine K., ed. Hermeneutical Paths to the Sacred Worlds of India. Atlanta: Scholars Press, 1994.

Young, R. F. Resistant Hinduism: Sanskrit Sources on Anti-Christian Apologetics in Early Nineteenth-Century India. Vienna: Publications of the de Nobili Research Library, 1981.

Zachner, R. C. Philosophies of India. New York: Pantheon Books, 1951.

## Christology

Alexander, Archibald A. B. "The Johannine Doctrine of the Logos". Expository Times 36 (1924-25): 394-99, 467-72.

Alldrit, N. S. F. "The Logos Outside St. John". In Studia Evangelica, edited by Elizabeth A. Livingstone. Texte und Untersuchungen 126. Berlin: Akademie Verlag, 1982.

Argyle, Aubrey W. The Christ of the New Testament. London: Carey Kingsgate Press, 1952.

_______. "The Logos of Philo: Personal or Impersonal?" Expository Times 66 (1954-55): 13-14.

Austin, Michael R. "Salvation and the Divinity of Jesus". Expository Times 96 (1985): 271-75.

Avis, Paul, ed. The Resurrection of Jesus Christ. London: Darton, Longman & Todd, 1993.

Bacon, Benjamin W. "Jesus as Lord". Harvard Theological Review 4 (1911): 204-28.

Balthasar, Hans Urs von. The Glory of the Lord. Vol. 1, Seeing the Form. Translated by Erasmo Leiva-Merikakis. San Francisco: St. Ignatius Press, 1982.

Barr, James. "The Word Became Flesh: The Incarnation in the New Testament". Interpretation 10 (1956): 16-23.

Barton, Stephen A., and Stanton, Graham, eds. Resurrection: Essays in Honour of Leslie Houlden. London: SPCK, 1994.

Bauckham, Richard. "The Sonship of the Historical Jesus in Christology". Scottish

Journal of Theology 31 (1978): 245-60.
Beasley-Murray, Paul. "Colossians 1:15-20: An Early Christian Hymn Celebrating the Lordship of Christ". In Pauline Studies: Essays Presented to Professor F. F. Bruce on His 70th Birthday, edited by Donald A. Hagner and Murray J. Harris. Grand Rapids, Mich.: William B. Eerdmans, 1980.
Benoit, Pierre. "The Divinity of Jesus in the Synoptic Gospels". In his Jesus and the Gospel. 2 vols. Translated by Benet Weatherhead. London: Darton, Longman & Todd, 1973-74.
Berkey, Robert F., and Edwards, Sarah A., eds. Christological Perspectives: Essays in Honor of Harvey K. McArthur. New York: Pilgrim Press, 1982.
Bertram, Georg. "Praeparatio evangelica in der Septuaginta". Vetus Testamentum 7 (1957): 225-49.
Betz, Hans Dieter. "Jesus as Divine Man". In Jesus and the Historian: Written in Honor of Ernst Cadmann Colwell, edited by F. Thomas Trotter. Philadelphia: The Westminster Press, 1968.
_______. "Gottmensch II". In Reallexikon für Antike und Christentum, edited by Theodor Klauser. 12 vols. Stuttgart: Anton Hiersemann, 1950.
Bieler, Judwig. Theios Anēr: Das Bild des 'gottlichen Menschen' in Spätantike und Früchristentum. 2 vols. Reprint. Darmstadt: Wissenschaftliche Buchgesellschaft, 1967.
Black, Matthew. "The Christological Use of the Old Testament in the New Testament". New Testament Studies 18 (1971-72): 1-14.
_______. Jesus and the Son of Man". Journal for the Study of the New Testament 1 (1978): 4-18.
Bligh, John. "The Origin and Meaning of Logos in the Prologue of St. John". Clergy Review 40 (1955): 393-405.
Bockmuehl, Markus. This Jesus: Martyr, Lord, Messiah. Edinburgh: T&T Clark, 1994.
Boismard, Marie-Émil. "The Divinity of Christ in Saint Paul". In Son and Saviour: The Divinity of Jesus Christ in the Scriptures, edited by A. Gelin. Dublin: Helicon Press, 1962.
Boobyer, G. H. "Jesus as 'Theos' in the New Testament". Bulletin of the John Rylands Library 50 (1968): 247-61.
Boring, M. Eugene. Truly Human / Truly Divine: Christological Language and the Gospel Form. St. Louis: CBP Press, 1984.
Breuning, Wilhelm. Jesus Christus der Erlöser. Unser Glaube: Christliches Selbstverständnis Heute 4. Mainz: Matthias-Grünewald Verlag, 1968.
Brown, Harold O. J. Heresies: The Image of Christ in the Mirror of Heresy from the Apostles to the Present. Grand Rapids, Mich.: Baker Book House, 1984.
Brown, Raymond E. The Birth of the Messiah: A Commentary on the Infancy Narratives in Matthew and Luke. Garden City, N.Y.: Doubleday & Company, 1977.
_______. The Death of the Messiah: From Gethsemane to the Grave. A Commentary on the Passion Narratives in the Four Gospels. Anchor Bible reference Library. New York and London: Doubleday and Geoffrey Chapman, 1994.
_______. Jesus, God and Man: Modern Biblical Reflections. New York: Macmillan, 1967.
_______. The Virginal Conception and Bodily Resurrection of Jesus. New York: Paulist Press, 1973.
Bruce, F. F. "The Humanity of Jesus Christ". Journal of the Christian Brethren

Research Fellowship 24 (1973): 5-15.
_______. "Jesus is Lord". In Soli Deo Gloria: New Testament Essays in Honor of William Childs Robinson, edited by J. McDowell Richards. Richmond: John Knox Press, 1968.
Bultmann, Rudolf. "The Christology of the New Testament". In his Faith and Understanding, edited by Robert W. Funk. Translated by Louise Pettibone Smith. New York: Harper & Row, 1969.
_______. Jesus and the Word. Translated by L. P. Smith and E. H. Lantero. New York: Scribner's, 1958.
Bury, R. G. The Fourth Gospel and the Logos-Doctrine. Cambridge: W. Heffer & Sons, 1940.
Cahill, P. Joseph. "The Johannine Logos as Center". Catholic Biblical Quarterly 38 (1976): 54-72.
Caird, George B. "Jesus and Israel: The Starting Point for New Testament Christology". In Christological Perspectives: Essays in Honor of Harvey K. McArthur, edited by Robert F. Berkey and Sarah A. Edwards. New York: Pilgrim Press, 1982.
Ceroke, Christian P. "The Divinity of Christ in the Gospels". Catholic Biblical Quarterly 24 (1962): 125-39.
Chilton, Bruce D., and Evans, Craig A. Studying the Historical Jesus: Evaluations of the State of Current Research. New Testament Tools and Studies 19. Leiden: Brill, 1994.
Coffrey, D. "The Pre-Existent and Incarnate Word". Faith and Culture 8 (1983): 62-76.
Craddock, Fred B. The Pre-existence of Christ in the New Testament. Nashville: Abingdon Press, 1968.
Craig, Clarence T. "The Identification of Jesus with the Suffering Servant". Journal of Religion 24 (1944): 240-45.
Craig, William L. "The Bodily Resurrection of Jesus". In Gospel Perspectives: Studies of History and Tradition in the Four Gospels, edited by R. T. France and D. Wenham. 2 vols. Sheffield: JSOT Press, 1980-81.
Crawford, R. G. "Is Christ Inferior to God?" Evangelical Quarterly 43 (1971): 203-9.
Cullmann, Oscar. The Christology of the New Testament. Translated by Shirley C. Guthrie and Charles A. M. Hall. Philadelphia: The Westminster Press, 1959.
Davis, Stephen T. Risen Indeed: Making Sense of the Resurrection. London: SPCK, 1993.
_______; Kendall, Daniel; and O'Collins, Gerald. The Incarnation. Oxford: Oxford University Press, 2001.
Dodd, C. H. "Atonement". In his The Bible and the Greeks. London: Hodder & Stoughton, 1935.
Dulière, W. L. "Theos—Dieu et Adonai—Kurios: Conséquences de l'addtion d'un Jésus-Kurios dans la terminologie chrétienne". Zeitschrift für Religions—und Geistesgeschichte 21 (1969): 193-203.
Dunn, James D. G. Christianity in the Making. Vol. 1. Jesus Remembered. Grand Rapids, Mich.: William B. Eerdmans, 2003.
_______. Christology in the Making: A New Testament Inquiry into the Origins of the Doctrine of the Incarnation. Philadelphia: The Westminster Press, 1980.
_______. "Paul's Understanding of the Death of Jesus". In Reconciliation and Hope: New Testament Essays on Atonement and Eschatology Presented to L. L. Morris on His $60^{th}$ Birthday, edited by Robert Banks. Exeter: Paternoster Press, 1974.
Elwell, Walter. "The Deity of Christ in the Writings of Paul". In Current Issues in

Biblical and Patristic Interpretation: Studies in Honor of Merrill C. Tenney Presented by His Former Students, edited by Gerald F. Hawthorne. Grand Rapids, Mich.: William B. Eerdmams, 1975.

Fairbairn, Donald. Grace and Christology in the Early Church. Oxford: Oxford University Press, 2003.

Farmer, William R. "An Historical Essay on the Humanity of Jesus Christ". In Christian History and Interpretation: Studies Presented to John Knox, edited by W. R. Farmer, C. F. D. Moule, and R. R. Niebuhr. Cambridge: Cambridge University Press, 1976.

Fitzmyer, Joseph A. "Another View of the 'Son of Man' Debate". Journal for the Study of the New Testament 4 (1979): 58-68.

_______. "The Ascension of Christ and Pentecost". Theological Studies 45 (1984): 409-40.

France, R. T. Jesus and the Old Testament: His Application of Old Testament Passages to Himself and His Mission. London: Tyndale Press, 1971.

_______. "Worship of Jesus: A Neglected Factor in Christological Debate". In Christ the Lord: Studies in Christology Presented to Donald Guthrie, edited by Howard H. Rowdon. Leicester, England: Inter-Varsity Press, 1982.

Fuller, Reginald H. The Formation of the Resurrection Narratives. New York: MacMillan, 1971.

_______. The Foundations of New Testament Christology. London: Lutterworth Press, 1965.

_______. "Pre-Existence Christology: Can We Dispense with It?" Word and World 2 (1982): 29-33.

_______. "The Theology of Jesus or Christology? An Evaluation of the Recent Discussion". In Christology and Exegesis: New Approaches, edited by Robert Jewett. Semeia 30. Decatur, Ga.: Scholars Press, 1985.

Funk, Robert W., and Hoover, Roy W. The Five Gospels: The Search for the Authentic Words of Jesus. New York: Macmillan, 1993.

Goulder, Michael, ed. Incarnation and Myth: The Debate Continued. London: SCM Press, 1979.

Grant, Frederick C. "The Divinity of Christ". Religion in Life 18 (1949): 483-92.

Haag, Herbert. "'Son of God' in the Language and Thinking of the Old Testament". In Jesus, Son of God?, edited by Edward Schillebeeckx and Johannes-Baptist Metz. New York: Seabury Press, 1982.

Hahn, Ferdinand. The Titles of Jesus in Christology: Their History in Early Christianity. Translated by Harold Knight and George Ogg. London: Lutterworth Press, 1969.

Hall, Douglass John. The Cross in Our Context: Jesus and the Suffering World. Minneapolis: Fortress Press, 2003.

Hamerton-Kelly, Robert G. Pre-Existence, Wisdom, and the Son of Man: A Study of the Idea of Pre-Existence in the New Testament. Society for New Testament Studies Monograph Series 21. Cambridge: Cambridge University Press, 1973.

Hanson, Anthony T. Grace and Truth: A Study in the Doctrine of the Incarnation. London: SPCK, 1975.

_______. Jesus Christ in the Old Testament. London: SPCK, 1965.

_______. The New Testament Interpretation of Scripture. London: SPCK, 1980.

Harrington, Wilfrid J. "The Man Christ Jesus". Milltown Studies 14 (1984): 1-17.

Harris, J. Rendel. "Athena, Sophia and the Logos". Bulletin of the John Rylands Library 7 (1922-23): 56-72.

Harris, Murray J. Jesus as God: The New Testament Use of Theos in Reference to Jesus. Grand Rapids, Mich.: Baker Book House, 1992.
Hebblethwaite, Brian. "The Impossibility of Multiple Incarnations". Theology CIV, no. 821 (September / October, 2001): 323-34.
_______. The Incarnation. Cambridge: Cambridge University Press, 1987.
Hengel, Martin. The Son of God: The Origin of Christology and the History of Jewish-Hellenistic Religion. Translated by John Bowden. Philadelphia: Fortress Press, 1976.
_______. Studies in Early Christology. Edinburgh: T&T Clark, 1995.
Herbert, Gabriel. "Hope Looking Forward: The Old Testament Passages Used by the New Testament Writers as Prophetic of the Resurrection of Jesus Christ". Interpretation 10 (1956): 259-69.
Hick, John, ed. The Myth of God Incarnate. Philadelphia: The Westminster Press, 1977.
Higgins, A. J. B. "The Old Testament and Some Aspects of New Testament Christology". In Promise and Fulfillment: Essays Presented to Professor S. H. Hooke, edited by F. F. Bruce. Edinburgh: T&T Clark, 1963.
Hogg, A. G. "The God That Must Needs Be Christ Jesus". International Review of Missions 6 (January 1917): 62-73.
Holladay, Carl R. Theios Anēr in Hellenistic Judaism: A Critique of the Use of This Category in New Testament Christology. Society of Biblical Literature Dissertation Series 40. Missoula, Mont.: Scholars Press, 1977.
Hooker, Morna D. Jesus and the Servant: The Influence of the Servant Concept of Deutero-Isaiah in the New Testament. London: SPCK, 1959.
Hultgren, Arland J. Christ and His Benefits: Christology and Redemption in the New Testament. Philadelphia: Fortress Press, 1987.
_______, comp. New Testament Christology: A Critical Assessment and Annotated Bibliography. Westport, Conn.: Greenwood Press, 1988.
Hurst, L. D., and Wright, N. T., eds. The Glory of Christ in the New Testament: Studies in Memory of George Bradford Caird. New York: Oxford University Press, 1987.
Hurtado, Larry W. Lord Jesus Christ: Devotion to Jesus in Earliest Christianity. Grand Rapids: William B. Eerdmans, 2003.
Jeremias, Joachim. The Central Message of the New Testament. London: SCM Press, 1965. See pages 71-96 for a discussion of the Johannine Logos.
_______. "Zu Phil ii7: EAUTON EKENŌSEN". Novum Testamentum 6 (1963): 182-88.
_______. "Zum Logos-Problem". Zeitschrift für die Neutestamentliche Wissenschaft 59 (1968): 82-85.
Johnson, Luke T. The Real Jesus. San Francisco: Harper, 1995.
Johnston, George. "New Testament Christology in a Pluralistic Age". In Biblical Studies: Essays in Honour of William Barclay, edited by Johnston R. McKay and James F. Miller. London: William Collins and Sons, 1976.
Käsemann, Ernst. "The Saving Significance of the Death of Jesus in Paul". In his Perspectives on Paul, translated by Margaret Kohl. London: SCM Press, 1971.
Kim, Seyoon. The "Son of Man" as the Son of God. Wissenschaftliche Untersuchungen zum Neuen Testament 30. Tübingen: J. C. B. Mohr (Paul Siebeck), 1983.
Knox, John. The Humanity and Divinity of Christ: A Study of Pattern in Christology. Cambridge: Cambridge University Press, 1967.
Ladd, George E. I Believe in the Resurrection of Jesus. Grand Rapids, Mich.: William B. Eerdmans, 1975.
Lamarche, Paul. Christ Vivant: Essai sur la Christologie du Nouveau Testament. Lectio

Divina 43. Paris: Éditions du Cerf, 1966.

Langkammer, Hugolinus. "Zur Herkunft des Logostitels im Johannesprolog". Biblische Zeitschrift 9 (1965): 91-94.

Lapide, Pinchas. The Resurrection of Jesus: A Jewish Perspective. Translated by Wilhelm C. Linss. London: SPCK, 1983.

Lindars, Barnabas. New Testament Apologetic: The Doctrinal Significance of the Old Testament Quotations. Philadelphia: The Westminster Press, 1961.

Lindeskog, Gösta. "Theoskristologien i Nya Testament". Svensk Exegetisk Årsbok 37-38 (1972-73): 222-37.

Lohmeyer, Ernst. Kyrios Jesus: Eine Untersuchung zu Phil. 2,5-11. 2nd ed. Sitzungsberichte

der Heidelberger Akademie der Wissenschaften, Philosophisch-historische Klasse 4. Heidelberg: Carl Winter, Universitätsverlag, 1961.

Machen, J. Gresham. The Virgin Birth of Christ. New York: Harper & Brothers, 1932.

MacLeod, David J. "The Creation of the Universe by the Word: John 1:3-5". Bibliotheca Sacra (April-June 2003): 187-201.

_______. "The Eternality and Deity of the Word: John 1:1-2". Bibliotheca Sacra 160 (January-March 2003): 48-64.

Macquarrie, John. Jesus Christ in Modern Thought. London: SCM Press, 1990.

_______. "The Pre-existence of Jesus Christ". Expository Times 77 (1966): 199-202.

Maly, Eugene H. "Jesus is Lord!" The Bible Today 61 (1972): 842-50.

Marshall, I. Howard. "The Divine Sonship of Jesus". Interpretation 21 (1967): 87-103.

_______. The Work of Christ. Grand Rapids, Mich.: Zondervan, 1969.

Martin, Ralph P. "Jesus Christ". In The International Standard Bible Encyclopedia, edited by Geoffrey W. Bromily. 4 vols. Grand Rapids, Mich.: William B. Eerdmans, 1979.

Mastin, B. A. "The Imperial Cult and the Ascription of the Title Theos to Jesus (John xx.28)". In Studia Evangelica 6, edited by Elizabeth A. Livingstone. Texte und Untersuchungen 112. Berlin: Akademie-Verlag, 1973.

May, Eric. "The Logos in the Old Testament". Catholic Biblical Quarterly 8 (1946): 438-47.

McArthur, Harvey K. "Christological Perspectives in the Predicates of the Johannine Ego Eimi Sayings". In Christological Perspectives: Essays in Honor of Harvey K. McArthur, edited by Robert F. Berkey and Sarah A. Edwards. New York: Pilgrim Press, 1982.

McCullough, J. C. "Jesus Christ in the Old Testament". Biblical Theology 22 (1972): 36-47.

McDonald, Hugh D. "The Humanity of Jesus". Journal of the Christian Brethren Research Fellowship 24 (1973): 16-23.

_______. Jesus—Human and Divine: An Introduction to New Testament Christology. Grand Rapids, Mich.: Baker Book House, 1968.

Meier, John P. A Marginal Jew: Rethinking the Historical Jesus. 2 vols. New York: Doubleday, 1991/1994.

Metzger, Bruce M. "The Meaning of Christ's Ascension". In Search the Scriptures: New Testament Studies in Honor of Raymond T. Stamm, edited by Jacob M. Meyers, et al. Gettysburg Theological Studies 3. Leiden: E. J. Brill, 1969.

_______. "The Punctuation of Rom. 9:5". In Christ and Spirit in the New Testament: In Honour of Charles Francis Digby Moule, edited by Barnabas Lindars and Stephen S.

Smalley. Cambridge: Cambridge University Press, 1973.
Meyer, Ben F. The Aims of Jesus. London: SCM Press, 1979.
Mollat, Donatien. "The Divinity of Christ in Saint John". In Son and Saviour: The Divinity of Jesus Christ in the Scriptures, edited by A. Gelin. Dublin: Helicon Press, 1962.
Moltmann, Jürgen. The Way of Jesus Christ. London: SCM Press, 1990.
Morris, Leon. The Atonement: Its Meaning and Significance. Downers Grove, Ill.: Inter-Varsity Press, 1983.
Morris, T. V. The Logic of God Incarnate. Ithaca, N.Y.: Cornell University Press, 1986.
Moule, C. F. D. "The Ascension—Acts 1:9". In his Essays in New Testament Interpretation. Cambridge: Cambridge University Press, 1982.
_______. "The Manhood of Jesus in the New Testament". In Christ, Faith and History: Cambridge Studies in Christology, edited by S. W. Sykes and J. P. Clayton. Cambridge: Cambridge University Press, 1972.
_______. "The Pre-existence of Christ in the Light of the Experience of New Testament Christians". Theologia Evangelica 8 (1975): 173-90.
_______. The Sacrifice of Christ. Philadelphia: Fortress Press, 1964.
Nash, Ronald. Is Jesus the Only Savior? Grand Rapids, Mich.: Zondervan, 1994.
Neyrand, Georges. "Le Sens de 'Logos" dans le prologue de Jean. Un essai". Nouvelle Revue théologique 106 (1984): 59-71.
O'Collins, Gerald. Christology: A Biblical, Historical, and Systematic Study of Jesus. Oxford: Oxford University Press, 1995.
_______. Interpreting Jesus. Introducing Catholic Theology 2. Ramsey, N.J.: Paulist Press, 1983.
Osborne, Grant R. "Christology and New Testament Hermeneutics: A Survey of the Discussion". In Christology and Exegesis: New Approaches, edited by Robert Jewett. Semeia 30. Decatur, Ga.: Scholars Press, 1985. N.J.: Paulist Press, 1983.
Payne, Philip B. "Jesus' Implicit Claim to Deity in His Parables". Trinity Journal [1981]: 3-23.
Perry, Victor. "Does the New Testament Call Jesus God?" Expository Times 87 (1975-76): 214-25.
Pertiñez, J. "La Preexistencia de Cristo". Mayeutica 3 (1977): 329-47.
Placher, William C. Jesus the Savior: The Meaning of Jesus Christ for Christian Faith. Louisville, Ky.: Westminster John Knox Press, 2001.
Pollard, T. E. Fullness of Humanity: Christ's Humanness and Ours. Sheffield: Almond Press, 1982.
Radcliffe, Timothy. "My Lord and My God: The Locus of Confession". New Blackfriars 65 (1984): 52-62.
Rahner, Karl. "On the Theology of the Incarnation". Vol. 4, Theological Investigations. Translated by Kevin Smyth. New York: Crossroad, 1982.
_______, and Thüsing, Wilhelm. A New Christology. Translated by David Smith and Verdant Green. New York: Seabbury Press, 1980.
Riesner, Rainer. "Präexistenz und Jungfrauengeburt". Theologische Beiträge 12 (1981): 177-87.
Ringgren, Helmer. Word and Wisdom: Studies in Hypostatization of Divine Qualities and Functions in the Ancient Near East. Lund: Håkan Ohlssons Boktryckeri, 1947.
Robinson, John A. T. "Ascendancy". Andover Newton Quarterly 5, no. 2 (1964): 5-9.
_______. "Resurrection in the New Testament". In The Interpreter's Dictionary of the

Bible, edited by George A. Buttrick. 4 vols. Nashville: Abingdon Press, 1962.
Sabourin, Leopold. Christology: Basic Texts in Focus. New York: Alba House, 1984.
Sachsse, Eugen. "Die Logoslehre bei Philo und bei Johannes". Neue Kirchliche Zeitschrift 15 (1904): 747-67.
Sanders, E. P. The Historical Figure of Jesus. London: Penguin Books, 1993.
Sanders, J. N. "Word, the". In The Interpreter's Dictionary of the Bible, edited by George A. Buttrick. 4 vols. Nashville: Abingdon Press, 1962.
Schillebeeckx, Edward. Christ: An Experiment in Christology. Translated by Hubert Hoskins. New York: Crossroad, 1981.
Schmitt, J. "Christ Jesus in the Apostolic Church". In Son and Saviour: The Divinity of Jesus Christ in the Scriptures, edited by A. Gelin. Dublin: Helicon Press, 1962.
Schnackenburger, Rudolf. "Logos-Hymnus und johanneischer Prolog". Biblische Zeitschrift 1 (1957): 69-109.
Segal, Alan. "Pre-existence and Incarnation: A Response to Dunn and Holladay". In Christology and Exegesis: New Approaches, edited by Robert Jewett. Semeia 30. Decatur, Ga.: Scholars Press, 1985.
Segalla, Giuseppe. La Cristologia del Nuovo Testamento: Un saggio. Studi biblici 71. BresciaL Paideia, 1985.
Sellers, R. V. The Council of Chalcedon: A Historical and Doctrinal Survey. London: SPCK, 1961.
Shires, Henry M. Finding the Old Testament in the New. Philadelphia: The Westminster Press, 1974.
Stanton, Graham N. Gospel Truth? New Light on Jesus and the Gospels. London: HarperCollins, 1995.
Stott, John R. W. The Cross of Christ. Downers Grove, Ill.: InterVarsity Press, 1986.
Stuhlmacher, Peter. "Eighteen Theses on Paul's Theology of the Cross". In his Reconciliation, Law, and Righteousness, translated by Everett R. Kalin. Philadelphia: Fortress Press, 1986.
Taylor, Vincent. "Does the New Testament Call Jesus God?" In his New Testament Essays. London: Epworth Press, 1970.
_______. Jesus and His Sacrifice: A Study of the Passion-Sayings in the Gospels. London: MacMillan, 1937.
_______. The Person of Christ in New Testament Teaching. New York: St. Martin's Press, 1958.
Thangaraj, M. T. The Crucified Guru: An Experiment in Cross-Cultural Christology. Nashville: Abingdon Press, 1994.
Tobac, É. "La Notion du Christ-Logos dans la littératur johannique". Revue d'histoire ecclésiastique 25 (1929): 213-39.
Torrance, Thomas, F. The Incarnation: Ecumenical Studies in the Nicene-Constantinopolitan Creed, A.D. 381. Edinburgh, The Handsel Press, 1981.
Tsoukalas, Steven. Knowing Christ in the Challenge of Heresy: A Christology of the Cults, a Christology of the Bible. Lanham, Md.: University Press of America, 1999.
Vellanickal, Matthew. "Jesus as the Word in the New Testament". Jeevadhara 1 (1971): 152-68.
Wainwright, A. W. "The Confession of 'Jesus is God' in the New Testament". Scottish Journal of Theology 10 (1957): 274-99.
Williams, J. Herbert. The Divinity of Christ in the New Testament. New York: Charles Scribner's Sons, 1923.

Wilkins, M. J., and Moreland, J. P., eds. Jesus Under Fire: Modern Scholarship Reinvents the Historical Jesus. Grand Rapids, Mich.: Zondervan, 1995.

Westermann, Claus. The Old Testament and Jesus Christ. Translated by Omar Kaste. Minneapolis: Augsburg Publishing House, 1970.

Witherington, Ben. The Christology of Jesus. Minneapolis: Fortress Press, 1990.

Worgul, George S. "Prolegomenon to Jesus as the Word of God: A Note". Biblical Theology Bulletin 9 (1979): 115-20.

Wright, N. T. Books about Jesus. 2nd ed. Oxford: Oxford Summer School in Religious Studies, 1996.

_______. Christian Origins and the Question of God. Vol. 1. The New Testament and the People of God. Minneapolis: Fortress Press, 1992.

_______. Christian Origins and the Question of God. Vol. 2. Jesus and the Victory of God. Minneapolis: Fortress Press, 1996.

_______. The Resurrection of the Son of God. Minneapolis: Fortress Press, 2003.

_______. Who Was Jesus? London: SPCK, 1992.

Wuest, Kenneth S. "The Deity of Jesus in the Greek Texts of John and Paul". Bibliotheca Sacra 119 (1962): 216-26.

Zedda, Silverio. "Gesù storico alle origini della cristologia del Nuovo Testamento". Sacra Doctrina 16 (1971): 433-48.

## General Works

Abhishiktananda, Swami. Hindu-Christian Meeting Point. Delhi: ISPCK, 1984.

Adam, A. K. M. What Is Postmodernism? Minneapolis: Fortress Press, 1995).

Alcoff, Linda. "The Problem of Speaking for Others". Cultural Critique 20 (1991): 5-32.

Alston, William P. Epistemic Justification: Essays in the Theory of Knowledge. Ithaca, N.Y.: Cornell University Press, 1989.

_______. Perceiving God: The Epistemology of Religious Experience. Ithaca, N.Y.: Cornell University Press, 1991.

Amaladoss, Michael. "Dialogue and Mission: Conflict or Convergence?" International Review of Mission 75, no. 299 (July 1986): 222-41.

Ariarajah, Wesley: Hindus and Christians: A Century of Protestant Ecumenical Thought. Grand Rapids, Mich.: William B. Eerdmans, 1991.

Ashcroft, Bill. Post-Colonial Transformation. London: Routledge, 2001.

_______; Griffiths, Gareth; and Tiffin, Helen. The Empire Writes Back: Theory and Practice in Post-Colonial Literatures. London: Routledge, 1989.

_______; _______; _______. Key Concepts in Post-Colonial Studies. London: Routledge, 1998.

_______; _______; _______. The Post-Colonial Studies Reader. London: Routledge, 1995.

Attridge, Derek; Bennington, Geoff; and Young, Robert, eds. Post-Structuralism and the Question of History. Cambridge: Cambridge University Press, 1987.

Badham, Paul. Christian Beliefs about Life After Death. London: Macmillan, 1976.

Barker, Glenn W. 1 John. In The Expositor's Bible Commentary. Vol. 12 edited by Frank E. Gaebelein. Grand Rapids, Mich.: Zondervan, 1981.

Barnard, L. W. Justin Martyr. Cambridge: Cambridge University Press, 1967.

Basham, A. L. The Origins and Development of Classical Hinduism. Edited and completed by Kenneth G. Zysk. New York: Oxford University Press, 1989.
Bauer, Walter. A Greek-English Lexicon of the New Testament and Other Early Christian Literature. Translated by William F. Arndt and F. Wilbur Gingrich. 2nd ed. Chicago: The University of Chicago Press, 1979.
Best, Steven, and Kellner, Douglas. Postmodern Theory. New York: The Guilford Press, 1991.
Bindley, T. Herbert, ed. Tertulliani: De Praescriptione Haereticorum. New York: Oxford, 1893.
Bissoondoyal, B. Hindu Scriptures. Port Louis, Mauritius: G. Gangaram, 1979.
Bosch, David J. Transforming Mission: Paradigm Shifts in Theology of Mission. Maryknoll, N.Y.: Orbis Books, 1991.
Boyd, Robin. An Introduction to Indian Christian Theology. Delhi: ISPCK, 1994.
_______. Khristadvaita: A Theology for India. Madras: The Christian Literature Society, 1977.
Bracken, J. The Divine Matrix: Creativity as Link between East and West. Maryknoll, N.Y.: Orbis Books, 1995.
Brockington, John. Hinduism and Christianity. New York: St. Martin's Press, 1992.
Brown, Raymond E. The Gospel According to John I-XII. New York: Doubleday, 1966.
Brown, Francis; Driver, S. R.; and Briggs, Charles A. The New Brown-Driver-Briggs Gesenius Hebrew and English Lexicon: With an Appendix Containing the Biblical Aramaic. Peabody, Mass.: Hendrikson, 1979.
Bruce, F. F. The Epistle to the Hebrews. The New International Commentary on the New Testament. Grand Rapids, Mich.: Wm. B. Eerdmans, 1964.
Bruck, M. von. The Unity of Reality: God, God-Experience and Meditation in the Hindu-Christian Dialogue. Translated by James V. Zeitz. New York: Paulist Press, 1991.
Brueggeman, Walter. Texts under Negotiation. Minneapolis: Fortress Press, 1993.
Buitenen, J. A. B. van. "A Contribution to the Critical Edition of the Bhagavadgītā". Journal of the American Oriental Society 85 (1965): 99-109.
Burnett, David. Clash of Worlds: A Christian's Handbook on Cultures, World Religions, and Evangelism. Nashville: Thomas Nelson, 1992.
Carman, John B. Majesty and Meekness: A Comparative Study of Contrast and Harmony in the Concept of God. Grand Rapids, Mich.: William B. Eerdmans, 1994.
Carson, D. A. Matthew. In The Expositor's Bible Commentary. Vol. 8 edited by Frank E. Gaebelein. Grand Rapids, Mich.: Zondervan, 1984.
Case, Margaret H. Seeing Krishna: The Religious World of a Brahman Family in Vrindaban. New York: Oxford University Press, 2000.
Chakrabarty, Dipesh. "Postcoloniality and the Artifice of History: Who Speaks for 'Indian' Pasts?" Representations 37 (Winter 1992): 1-26.
Chapman, Mark D., ed. The Future of Liberal Theology. Burlington, Vt.: Ashgate, 2002.
Chapot, Frédéric, trans. Tertullien: Contre Hermogène. Latour-Maubourg, Paris: Les Éditions du Cerf, 1999.
Cheetham, David. John Hick: A Critical Introduction and Reflection. Burlington, Vt.: Ashgate, 2003.
Chetanananda, Swami, ed. and comp. Meditation and Its Methods: According to Swami Vivekananda. Hollywood: Vedanta Press, n.d.
Childs, Peter, and Williams, Patrick. An Introduction to Post-Colonial Theory. London:

Prentice-Hall, 1997.
Chrisman, L. and Parry, B., eds. Postcolonial Theory and Criticism. Suffolk: D. S. Brewer, 2000.
Clines, D. J. "The Image of God in Man". Tyndale Bulletin 19 (1968): 53-103.
Clooney, Francis X. "Comparative Theology: A Review of Recent Books (1989-95)". Theological Studies 56, no. 3 (1995): 521-550.
_______. "The Interreligious Dimension of Reasoning about God's Existence". International Journal of the Philosophy of Religion 46, no. 1 (1999): 1-16.
_______. "The Task of Philosophy at the Meeting Points of Cultures". In The Role of the Philosopher Today, edited by Anand Amaladass. Chennai: T. R. Publications for Satya Nilayam Publications, 1993.
Colwell, E. C. "A Definite Rule for the Use of the Article in the Greek New Testament". Journal of Biblical Literature 52 (1933): 12-21.
Complete Works of Swami Vivekananda. 8 vols. Calcutta: Advaita Ashrama, 1985.
Coomaraswamy, Ananda K. "Mahābhārata and Ītihāsa". Annals of the Bhandarkar Oriental Research Institute 18 (1937): 211-12.
Copeland, E. Luther. A New Meeting of the Religions: Interreligious Relationships and Theological Questioning. Waco, Tex.: Baylor University Press, 1999.
Cornille, Catherine and Neckebrouck, Valeer, comps. A Universal Faith?: Peoples, Cultures, Religions, and the Christ. Louvain: Peeters Press; Grand Rapids, Mich.: W. B. Eerdmans, 1992.
Coward, Howard, ed. Hindu-Christian Dialogue: Perspectives and Encounters. Maryknoll, N.Y.: Orbis Books, 1989.
_______, ed. Life after Death in World Religions. Maryknoll, N.Y.: Orbis Books, 1997.
_______, ed. Modern Indian Responses to Religious Pluralism. Albany: State University of New York Press, 1987.
Cox, James. "Faith and Faiths: The Significance of A. G. Hogg's Missionary Thought for a Theology of Dialogue". Scottish Journal of Theology 32 (1979): 241-55.
_______. "The Influence of A. G. Hogg over D. G. Moses: A Missionary Message for India". Religion and Society 27, no. 4 (December 1980): 66-79.
Crouzel, Henri, et Manlio Simonetti, trans. Origène: Traité Des Principes. Latour Maubourg, Paris: Les Éditions du Cerf, 1978.
Cullmann, Oscar. Immortality of the Soul or Resurrection of the Dead? London: Epworth Press, 1958.
Cunliffe-Jones, Hubert, ed. A History of Christian Doctrine. Philadelphia: Fortress Press, 1980.
Cuttat, Jacques-Albert. The Encounter of Religions: A Dialogue between the West and the Orient, with an Essay on the Prayer of Jesus. Translated by Pierre de Fontnouvelle with Evis McGrew. New York: Desclee, 1960.
Daniel, David. The Bible in English: Its History and Influence. New Haven, Conn.: Yale University Press, 2003.
D'Costa, Gavin, ed. Christian Uniqueness Reconsidered. Maryknoll, N.Y.: Orbis Books, 1990.
_______. The Meeting of Religions and the Trinity. Edinburgh: T&T Clark, 1981.
Deshpande, V. W. The Impact of Ancient Indian Thought on Christianity. New Delhi: APH Publishing Corporation, 1996.
Deutsch, Eliot, ed. Culture and Modernity: East-West Philosophic Perspectives. Honolulu: University of Hawaii Press, 1991.

Devaraja, N. K. Hinduism and Christianity: Brahmananda Keshab Chandra Sen Memorial Lectures on Comparative Religion Delivered at Calcutta University. New York: Asia Publishing House, 1969.

Dhavamony, Mariasusai. Hindu-Christian Dialogue: Theological Soundings and Perspectives. Amsterdam: Rodopi, 2002.

_______. Hindu Spirituality. Documenta Missionalia 25. Roma: Editrice Pontificia Univerita' Gregoriana, 1999.

_______. La Spiritualité Hindoue. Bibliothèque de Spiritualité 14. Paris: Beauchesne, 1997.

DiNoia, J. The Diversity of Religions: A Christian Perspective. Washington: Catholic University of America, 1992.

Divanji, Rao Bahadur P. C. Critical Word-Index to the Bhagavadgītā. Bombay: New Book Co., 1946.

Dodd, C. H. The Interpretation of the Fourth Gospel. Cambridge: Cambridge University Press, 1953.

Donaldson, Laura E. "Postcolonialism and Biblical Reading: Introduction". Semeia: An Experimental Journal for Biblical Criticism 75 (1996): 1-14.

D'Sa, Francis, ed. Word-Index to the Bhagavadgītā. Pune: Institute for the Study of Religion, 1985.

_______, ed. Word-Index to Śaṅkara's Gītābhāṣya. Pune: Institute for the Study of Religion, 1985.

Dube, Musa. Postcolonial Feminist Interpretation of the Bible. St. Louis: Chalice Press, 2000.

Dupuis, Jacques. "Interculturation and Inter-religious Dialogue in India Today". In A Universal Faith?: Peoples, Cultures, Religions, and the Christ, compiled by Catherine Cornille and Valeer Neckebrouck. Louvain: Peeters Press; Grand Rapids, Mich.: W. B. Eerdmans, 1992.

_______. Jesus Christ at the Encounter of World Religions. Translated by Robert R. Barr. Maryknoll, N.Y.: Orbis Books, 1991.

_______. Toward a Christian Theology of Religious Pluralism. Maryknoll, N.Y.: Orbis Books, 1998.

Duraisingh, Christopher, and Hargreaves, Cecil. India's Search for Reality and the Relevance of the Gospel of John. Delhi: ISPCK, 1975.

Eck, Diana L. Encountering God: A Spiritual Journey from Bozeman to Banaras. New Delhi: Penguin Books, 1995.

Eichrodt, Walther. Theology of the Old Testament. 2 vols. Translated by J. A. Baker. Philadelphia: The Westminster Press, 1967.

Eliade, Mircea. Patterns in Comparative Religion. Translated by Rosemary Sheed. New York: New American Library, 1958.

Fakirbhai, Dhanjibhai. Kristopanishad (Christ-Upanishad). Bangalore: The Christian Institute for the Study of Religion and Society, 1965.

Farquhar, J. N. The Crown of Hinduism. London: Oxford University Press, 1930.

Farrer, A. Faith and Speculation. London: A. & C. Black, 1967.

Feenstra, Ronald J., and Plantinga Jr., Cornelius, eds. Trinity, Incarnation and Atonement. Notre Dame: University of Notre Dame Press, 1989.

Fish, Stanley. Doing What Comes Naturally. Durham, N.C.: Duke University Press, 1989.

_______. Is There a Text in This Class? Cambridge, Mass.: Harvard University Press,

1980.
Flood, Gavin. An Introduction to Hinduism. New York: Cambridge University Press, 1996.
Ford, David F. The Modern Theologians: An Introduction to Christian Theology in the 20th Century. 2 vols. New York: B. Blackwell, 1989.
Forman, Robert K. C., ed. Religions of the World. 3rd ed. New York: St. Martin's Press, 1993.
Foucault, Michel. "What Is an Author?" In Language, Counter-Memory and Practice, edited by Donald F. Bouchard and translated by Donald F. Bouchard and Sherry Simon. Ithaca, N.Y.: Cornell University Press, 1977.
Fowler, Robert. Let the Reader Understand. Minneapolis: Fortress Press, 1992.
_______. "Postmodern Biblical Criticism". Forum 5, no. 3 (1989): 3-30.
Gairdner, W. H. T. God as Triune, Creator, Incarnate, Atoner. Madras: Christian Literature Society, 1916.
Gallagher, Susan VanZanten. Postcolonial Literature and the Biblical Call for Justice. Jackson: University Press of Mississippi, 1994.
Gandhi, Leela. Postcolonial Theory: A Critical Introduction. Edinburgh: Edinburgh University Press, 1998.
Garbe, Richard. India and Christendom. Translated by Lydia G. Robinson. LaSalle, Ill.: Open Court, 1959.
Gawronski, Raymond. Word and Silence: Hans Urs von Balthasar and the Spiritual Encounter between East and West. Grand Rapids, Mich.: William B. Eerdmans, 1995.
Geach, Peter. God and the Soul. London: Routledge & Kegan Paul, 1969.
Geertz, C. The Interpretation of Cultures. New York: Basic Books, 1973.
Goodchild, Philip, ed. Difference in Philosophy of Religion. Burlington, Vt.: Ashgate, 2003.
Goulder, Michael, ed. Incarnation and Myth: The Debate Continued. London: SCM Press, 1979.
Govindacharya, A. The Life of Rāmānujāchārya. Madras: S. Murthy, 1906.
Grant, Robert M., trans. Theophilus of Antioch Ad Autolycum. London: Oxford University Press, 1970.
Grenz, Stanley J., and Franke, John R. Beyond Foundationalism: Shaping Theology in a Postmodern Context. Louisville, Ky.: Westminster John Knox Press, 2001.
Griffiths, Bede. Christ in India: Essays towards a Hindu-Christian Dialogue. New York: Charles Scribner's Sons, 1966.
Griffiths, Paul J.. An Apology for Apologetics. Maryknoll, N.Y.: Orbis Books, 1991.
_______. Problems of Religious Diversity. Oxford: Blackwell, 2001.
Grillmeier, Aloys. Christ in Christian Tradition: From the Apostolic Age to Chalcedon (451). Translated by John S. Bowden. New York: Sheed and Ward, 1965.
Guha, Ranajit. "On Some Aspects of the Historiography of Colonial India". In Subaltern Studies 1. Delhi: Oxford University Press, 1982.
Gussner, Robert E. "Śaṅkara's Crest Jewel of Discrimination: A Stylometric Approach to the Question of Authorship". Journal of Indian Philosophy 4 (1977): 265-78.
Haberman, David L. Journey through the Twelve Forests: An Encounter with Krishna. New York: Oxford University Press, 1994.
Hacker, Paul. "Śaṅkarācārya and Śaṅkarabhagavatpāda: Preliminary Remarks Concerning the Authorship Problem". In Philology and Confrontation: Paul Hacker

on Traditional and Modern Vedānta, edited by W. Halbfass. Albany: State University of New York Press, 1995.

Harner, Philip B. "Qualitative Anarthrous Predicate Nouns: Mark 15:39 and John 1:1". Journal of Biblical Literature 92 (1973): 75-87.

Harris, Ischwar. "Radhakrishnan's View of Christianity". In Neo-Hindu Views of Christianity, edited by Arvind Sharma. Leiden: E. J. Brill, 1988.

Hasel, Gerhard F. "The Polemic Nature of the Genesis Cosmology". Evangelical Quarterly 46 (1974): 81-102.

Hatcher, Brian A. Eclecticism and Modern Hindu Discourse. New York: Oxford University Press, 1999.

Healy, Kathleen. Christ as Common Ground: A Study of Christianity and Hinduism.Pittsburgh: Duquesne University Press, 1990.

Heim, S. Mark. The Depth of the Riches: A Trinitarian Theology of Religious Ends. Grand Rapids, Mich.: William B. Eerdmans, 2000.

_______. Salvations: In Search of Authentic Religious Pluralism. Maryknoll, N.Y.: Orbis Books, 1995.

Henderson, John. The Construction of Orthodoxy and Heresy: Neo-Confucian, Islamic, Jewish, and Early Christian Patterns. Albany: State University of New York Press, 1998.

Herman, A. L. Hinduism. Oxford: Westview Press, 1991.

Hick, John, ed. God and the Universe of Faiths. London: Macmillan, 1973.

_______. An Interpretation of Religion: Human Responses to the Transcendent. New Haven, Conn.: Yale University Press, 1989.

_______. The Metaphor of God Incarnate. London: SCM Press, 1993.

_______, and Hebblethwaite, Brian. Christianity and Other Religions. Philadelphia: Fortress Press, 1980.

_______, and Knitter, Paul F. The Myth of Christian Uniqueness. Maryknoll, N.Y.: Orbis Books, 1987.

_______, ed. Truth and Dialogue in World Religions: Conflicting Truth Claims. Philadelphia: The Westminster Press, 1974.

Hirst, J. G. S. "The Teacher and the Avatāra: Mediators of Realisation in Śaṁkara's Advaitin Theology". Ph.D. diss., Cambridge University, 1983.

Hohenberger, A. Rāmānuja—ein Philosoph indischer Gottesmystik. Bonn: Selbstverlag des Orientalischen Seminars der Universität Bonn, 1960.

Howard, Don. "The History That We Are: Philosophy as Discipline and the Multiculturalism Debate". In Anindita Niyogi Balslev, Cross-Cultural Conversation (Initiation), edited by Cleo McNelly Kearns. Atlanta: Scholars Press, 1996.

Hyman, Gavin. "The Study of Religion and the Return of Theology". Journal of the American Academy of Religion 72 (March 2004): 195-219.

Jacob, Colonel J. A. A Concordance to the Principal Upanishads and the Bhagavadgītā. 1891. Reprint. Delhi: Motilal Banarsidass, 1963.

Jaiswal, S. The Origin and Development of Vaiṣṇavism. Delhi: Munshiram Manoharlal, 1967.

Juergensmeyer, Mark, ed. Global Religions: An Introduction. Oxford: Oxford University Press, 2003.

Katz, Ruth Cecily. Arjuna in the Mahabharata: Where Krishna Is, There is Victory. Columbia: University of South Carolina Press, 1989.

Kautzsch, E., ed. Gesenius' Hebrew Grammar. Oxford: Oxford University Press, 1985.

Kelly, J. N. D. Early Christian Creeds. 3rd ed. New York: Longman, 1972.
King, Bruce. New National and Post-Colonial Literatures: An Introduction. Oxford: Clarendon Press, 1996.
King, Richard. Orientalism and Religion: Postcolonial Theory, India and 'The Mystic East'. London: Routledge, 1999.
Kittel, Gerhard, and Friedrich, Gerhard, eds. Theological Dictionary of the New Testament. Translated by Geoffrey W. Bromily. Grand Rapids, Mich.: William B. Eerdmans, 1972.
Klostermaier, Klaus K. In the Paradise of Krishna: Hindu and Christian Seekers. Translated by Antonia Fonseca. Philadelphia: The Westminster Press, 1969.
_______. Indian Theology in Dialogue. Madras: The Christian Literature Society, 1986.
_______. A Survey of Hinduism. Albany: State University of New York Press, 1994.
Knipe, David M. Hinduism: Experiments in the Sacred. New York: HarperCollins, 1991.
Kraemer, Hendrik. Religion and the Christian Faith. London: Lutterworth Press, 1956.
Krašovec, J. Der Merismus im Biblisch-Hebräischen und Nordwestsemitischen. Biblica et orientalia 33. Rome: Biblical Institute Press, 1977.
Krieger, D. The New Universalism: Foundations for a Global Theology. Maryknoll, N.Y.: Orbis Books, 1991.
Krishna, Daya. "Comparative Philosophy: What It Is and What It Ought to Be". In Interpreting Across Boundaries: New Essays in Comparative Philosophy, edited by Gerald James Larson and Eliot Deutsch. Princeton: Princeton University Press, 1988.
Kristensen, W. Brede. The Meaning of Religion: Lectures in the Phenomenology of Religion. Translated by John B. Carman. The Hague: Martinus Nijhoff, 1960.
Küng, H.; Ess, H. van; and Stietencron, H. von, eds. Christianity and the World Religions: Paths of Dialogue with Islam, Hinduism, and Buddhism. London: Collins, 1987.
Leeuw, G. van der. Religion in Essence and Manifestation: A Study in Phenomenology. Translated by J. E. Turner. London: George Allen & Unwin, 1938.
LeSaux, H. Hindu-Christian Meeting Point. Bangalore: National Press, 1969.
Leslie, Julia. Authority and Meaning in Indian Religions: Hinduism and the Case of Valmiki. Burlington, Vt.: Ashgate, 2004.
Lightfoot, J. B., and Harmer, J. R., eds. The Apostolic Fathers: Revised Greek Texts with Introductions and English Translations. 1891. Reprint. Grand Rapids, Mich.: Baker Book House, 1984.
Lipner, Julius J. Brahmabandhab Upadhyay: The Life and Thought of a Revolutionary. Delhi: Oxford University Press, 1999.
_______. "Radhakrishnan on Religion and Religions". In Radhakrishnan Centenary Volume, edited by G. Parthasarathi and D. P. Chattopadhyaya. Delhi: Oxford University Press, 1989.
_______. The Writings of Brahmabandhab Upadhyay: Including a Resumé of His Life and Thought. Vol 1. Bangalore: The United Theological College, n.d.
Loomba, Ania. Colonialism / Postcolonialism. London: Routledge, 1998.
Lyotard, Jean-François. The Postmodern Explained. Translated and edited by Julian Pefanis and Morgan Thomas. Minneapolis: University of Minnesota Press, 1993.
MacDonell, Arthur A. A History of Sanskrit Literature. New York: D. Appleton, 1929.
_______. A Practical Sanskrit Dictionary. London: Oxford University Press, 1969.
MacIntyre, Alasdair. Whose Justice? Which Rationality? Notre Dame: University of

Notre Dame Press, 1988.
Mahadevan, T. M. P. Outlines of Hinduism. Bombay: Chetana, 1984.
Majumdar, R. C.; Raychaudhuri, H. C.; and Datta, Kalikinkar. An Advanced History of India. London: Macmillan, 1950.
Mankad, D. R. Purāṇic Chronology. Anand, Gujarat: Gaṅgājalā Prakashan, 1961.
May, Gerhard. Creatio Ex Nihilo: The Doctrine of 'Creation out of Nothing' in Early Christian Thought. Translated by A. S. Worrall. Edinburgh: T&T Clark, 1994.
May, Peter. "The Trinity and Saccidānanda". Indian Journal of Theology 7, no. 3 (July September 1958): 92-98.
Mayeda, Sengaku. "The Authenticity of the Bhagavadgītābhāṣya Ascribed to Śaṅkara". Wiener Zeitschrift für die Kunde Süd- und Ostasiens 9 (1965): 155-97.
_______. "On Śaṅkara's Authorship of the Kenopaniṣadbhāṣya". Indo-Iranian Journal 10 (1967-1968): 33-35.
_______. "Śaṁkara's Upadeśasāhasrī: Its Present Form". Journal of the Oriental Institute 15 (1966): 252-57.
McDermott, Gerald R. Can Evangelicals Learn from World Religions? Downers Grove, Ill.: InterVarsity Press, 2000.
McKnight, Edgar. Postmodern Use of the Bible. Nashville: Abingdon Press, 1988.
McNeill, John T., ed. Calvin: Institutes of the Christian Religion. 2 vols. Translated by Ford Lewis Battles. Philadelphia: The Westminster Press, 1960.
Messer, Richard. Does God's Existence Need Proof? Oxford: Clarendon Press, 1997.
Miller, Robert J. Born Divine: The Births of Jesus and Other Sons of God. Santa Rosa, Calif.: Polebridge Press, 2003.
Mongia, Padmini, ed. Contemporary Postcolonial Theory: A Reader. London: Arnold, 1996.
Monier-Williams, Sir Monier. A Sanskrit-English Dictionary. Delhi: Motilal Banarsidass, 1990.
Moore, Stephen. Literary Criticism and the Gospels. New Haven, Conn.: Yale University Press, 1989.
Moore-Gilbert, Bart. Postcolonial Theory: Contexts, Practices, Politics. London: Verso, 1997.
Morris, Leon. The Gospel According to John. Grand Rapids, Mich.: Wm. B. Eerdmans, 1971.
_______. New Testament Theology. Grand Rapids, Mich.: Zondervan, 1986.
Mozoomdar, P. C. The Oriental Christ. Boston: George H. Ellis, 1894.
Müller, F. Max, ed. Sacred Books of the East. 50 vols. Reprint. Delhi: Motilal Banarsidass, 1988.
Neill, Stephen. Christian Faith and Other Faiths. London: Oxford University Press, 1961.
Neville, R. Behind the Masks of God: An Essay Toward Comparative Theology. Albany: State University of New York Press, 1991
O'Flaherty, Wendy Doniger. Women, Androgynes, and Other Mythical Beasts. Chicago: The University of Chicago Press, 1980.
Ogden, S. Is There Only One True Religion or Are There Many? Dallas: Southern Methodist University, 1992.
O'Hanlon, Rosalind. "Recovering the Subject: Subaltern Studies and Histories of Resistance in Colonial South Asia". Modern Asian Studies 22, no. 1 (1988): 189-224.
Otto, Rudolf. India's Religion of Grace and Christianity Compared and Contrasted.

Translated by Frank Hugh Foster. London: Student Christian Movement Press, 1930.
Panikkar, Raymond [Raimundo]. "Common Patterns of Eastern and Western Scholasticism". Diogenes 83 (1973): 103-13.
_______. The Intra-Religious Dialogue. New York: Paulist Press, 1978.
Parrinder, Geoffrey. The Christian Debate: Light from the East. New York: Doubleday, 1966.
Pearson, Keith Ansell; Parry, Benita; and Judith Squires, eds. Cultural Readings of Imperialism: Edward Said and the Gravity of History. New York: St. Martin's Press, 1997.
Pinnock, Clark. A Wideness in God's Mercy: The Finality of Jesus Christ in a World of Religions. Grand Rapids, Mich.: Zondervan, 1992.
Prabhavananda, Swami. The Spiritual Heritage of India. London: George Allen & Unwin, 1962.
Pritchard, James B., ed. Ancient Near Eastern Texts Relating to the Old Testament. Princeton: Princeton University Press, 1969.
Pusalker, A. D. Studies in the Epics and Purāṇas. Bombay: Bhāratīya Vidyā Bhavan, 1955.
Quayson, Ato. Postcolonialism: Theory, Practice or Process? Cambridge: Polity Press, 2000.
Race, Alan. Christians and Religious Pluralism. London: SCM Press, 1994.
Rad, Gerhard von. Genesis. Translated by John H. Marks. London: SCM Press, 1963.
Rajappan, D. Immanuel. The Influence of Hinduism on Indian Christians. Jabalpur: Leonard Theological College, n.d.
Ramakantacharya, G. "The Place of Śaṅkara in Hinduism". Proceeding of the All-India Oriental Conference 7 (1935): 359-71.
Ramakrishnananda. Life of Ramanuja. Madras: Sri Ramakrishna Math, 1959.
Raychaudhuri, Tapan. Perceptions, Emotions, Sensibilities: Essays on India's Colonial and Post-Colonial Experiences. New Delhi: Oxford University Press, 1999.
Roberts, Alexander, and Donaldson, James, eds. The Ante-Nicene Fathers. 9 vols. Reprint. Grand Rapids, Mich.: Wm. B. Eerdmans, 1977.
Rooker, Mark F. "Genesis 1:1-3: Creation or Recreation?" Bibliotheca Sacra 149 (October-December): 316-23.
Rooy, J. A. van. "Christ and the Religions: The Issues at Stake". Missionalia 13, no. 1 (April 1985): 3-13.
Rorty, Richard; Schneewind, J. B.; and Skinner, Quentin, eds. Philosophy in History. Cambridge: Cambridge University Press, 1984.
Rukmani, T. S. "The Problem of the Authorship of the Yogasūtrābhāṣyavivaraṇam. Journal of Indian Philosophy 20 (1992): 419-23.
_______. "The Yogasūtrābhāṣyavivaraṇa Is not a Work of Śaṅkarāchārya, the Author of the Brahmasūtrabhāṣya". Journal of Indian Philosophy 26 (1998): 263-74.
Said, Edward W. Culture and Imperialism. London: Chatto & Windus, 1993.
_______. Orientalism. London: Penguin Books, 1985.
_______. The World, the Text, and the Critic. London: Vintage, 1991.
Sailhamer, John H. Genesis. In The Expositor's Bible Commentary. Vol. 2 edited by Frank E. Gaebelein. Grand Rapids, Mich.: Zondervan, 1990.
Samartha, S. J. The Hindu Response to the Unbound Christ. Madras: The Christian Literature Society, 1974.
_______. The Hindu View of History. Bangalore: CISRS, 1959.

Sarna, Nahum M. Genesis. JPS Torah Commentary. Philadelphia: Jewish Publication Society, 1989.
Sharma, B. N. Krishnamurti. "Bhāskara—a Forgotten Commentator on the Gītā". Indian Historical Quarterly 9 (1933): 663-77.
Schaff, Philip. The Creeds of Christendom: With a History and Critical Notes. 3 vols. 1931. Reprint. Grand Rapids, Mich.: Baker Book House, 1985.
_______, ed. The Nicene and Post-Nicene Fathers. First series. 14 vols. Reprint. Grand Rapids, Mich.: Wm. B. Eerdmans, 1974.
_______, and Wace, Henry, eds. The Nicene and Post-Nicene Fathers. Second series. 14 vols. Reprint. Grand Rapids, Mich.: Wm. B. Eerdmans, 1976.
Schmithausen, Lambert, ed. Paul Hacker: Kleine Schriften. Wiesbaden: Franz Steiner Verlag, 1978.
Scott, David, and Selvanayagam, Israel. Re-Visioning India's Religious Traditions. Delhi: SPCK, 1996.
Segovia, Fernando F. Interpreting Beyond Borders: The Bible and Postcolonialism 3. Sheffield: Sheffield Academic Press, 2000.
Sen, K. M. Hinduism. Harmondsworth, England: Penguin Books, 1961.
Sharma, Arvind. "Who Speaks for Hinduism: A Perspective from Advaita Vedanta". Journal of the American Academy of Religion 68 (December 2000): 751-59.
Smart, Ninian. World Religions: A Dialogue. Baltimore: Penguin Books, 1966.
Smith, Bardwell L. Hinduism: New essays in the History of Religions. Leiden: E. J. Brill, 1976.
Smith, W. What Is Scripture? A Comparative Approach. Minneapolis: Fortress Press, 1993.
Speiser, E. A. Genesis. Garden City, N.Y.: Doubleday, 1964.
Srinivasa, Aiyengar, C. R. The Life and Teachings of Sri Ramanujacharya. Madras: R. Venkateshwar & Co., n.d.
Striver, Dan. The Philosophy of Religious Language: Sign, Symbol and Story. Cambridge, Mass.: Blackwell, 1996.
Suchocki, Marjorie Hewitt. Divinity and Diversity: A Christian Affirmation of Religious Pluralism. Nashville: Abingdon Press, 2003.
Sugirtharajah, R. S. Asian Biblical Hermeneutics and Postcolonialism: Contesting the Interpretations. Sheffield: Sheffield Academic Press, 1999.
_______. The Bible and the Third World: Precolonial, Colonial and Postcolonial Encounters. Cambridge: Cambridge University Press, 2001.
_______, ed. The Postcolonial Bible. Sheffield: Sheffield Academic Press, 1998.
_______. Postcolonial Criticism and Biblical Interpretation. Oxford: Oxford University Press, 2002.
_______. Voices from the Margin: Interpreting the Bible in the Third World. London: SPCK / Orbis, 1995.
_______, and Hargreaves, C., eds. Readings in Indian and Christian Theology. Vol. 1. Delhi: ISPCK, 1993
Sugirtharajah, Sharada. Imagining Hinduism: A Postcolonial Perspective. London: Routledge, 2003.
Swain. A. C. "Authenticity of the Bhagavadgītābhāṣya Attributed to Śaṃkarācārya". The Mysore Orientalist 2 (March 1969): 32-37.
Swinburne, Richard. The Christian God. Oxford: Clarendon Press, 1994.
_______. The Coherence of Theism. Oxford: Clarendon Press, 1993.

_______. The Existence of God. Oxford: Clarendon Press, 1991.

_______. Faith and Reason. Oxford: Clarendon Press, 1983.

Tennent, Timothy C. Building Christianity on Indian Foundations. Delhi: ISPCK, 2000.

Thangaraj, M. T. Relating to People of Other Religions: What Every Christian Should Know. Nashville: Abingdon Press, 1994.

Thomas, M. M. The Acknowledged Christ of the Indian Renaissance. London: SCM Press, 1969.

Thompson, E. W. The Word of the Cross to the Hindus. Madras: The Christian Literature Society, 1956.

Torrance, Thomas F. The Christian Doctrine of God: One Being, Three Persons. Edinburgh: T & T Clark, 1996.

_______. Divine Meaning. Studies in Patristic Hermeneutics. Edinburgh: T & T Clark, 1995.

_______. Reality & Evangelical Theology: The Realism of Christian Revelation. Downers Grove, Ill.: InterVarsity Press, 1999.

_______. Space, Time and Resurrection. Grand Rapids, Mich.: William B. Eerdmans, 1976.

_______. Theological Science. London: Oxford University Press, 1969.

Tsumura, David Toshio. "Genesis and Ancient Near Eastern Stories of Creation and Flood". In I Studied Inscriptions from before the Flood: Ancient Near Eastern, Literary, and Linguistic Approaches to Genesis 1-11, edited by Richard S. Hess and David Toshio
Tsumura. Winona Lake, Ind.: Eisenbrauns, 1994.

_______. "The Earth in Genesis 1". In I Studied Inscriptions from before the Flood: Ancient Near Eastern, Literary, and Linguistic Approaches to Genesis 1-11, edited by Richard S. Hess and David Toshio Tsumura. Winona Lake, Ind.: Eisenbrauns, 1994.

Waltke, Bruce K., and O'Connor, M. An Introduction to Biblical Hebrew Syntax. Winona Lake, Ind.: Eisenbrauns, 1990.

Ward, Keith. God, Faith and the New Millennium. Oxford: Oneworld, 1998.

_______. Religion and Creation. Oxford, Clarendon Press, 1996.

_______. Religion and Human Nature. Oxford, Clarendon Press, 1998.

_______. Religion and Revelation: A Theology of Revelation in the World's Religions. Oxford, Clarendon Press, 1994.

Wenham, Gordon J. Genesis 1-15. Word Biblical Commentary. Waco, Tex.: Word, 1987.

Wevers, John William. Notes on the Greek Text of Genesis. Atlanta: Scholars Press, 1993.

Whitney, William Dwight. Sanskrit Grammar: Including both the Classical Language, and the Older Dialects, of Veda and Brahmana. 16th Issue. Cambridge, Mass.: Harvard University Press, 1987.

Wilson, Colin. Afterlife. London: Grafton Press, 1987.

Yandell, Keith. The Epistemology of Religious Experience. Cambridge: Cambridge University Press, 1993.

Young, Richard F. Resistant Hinduism: Sanskrit Sources on Anti-Christian Apologetics in Early Nineteenth Century India. Vol. 8, De Nobili Research Series, edited by G. Oberhammer. Vienna: Indological Institute of the University of Vienna, 1981.

Young, Robert J. C. Postcolonialism: An Historical Introduction. Oxford: Blackwell,

2001.
Zacharias, Ravi. Jesus among Other Gods. Nashville: Word, 2000.
Zaehner, R. C. Hinduism. Oxford: Oxford University Press, 1966.
Zago, Marcello. "Mission and Interreligious Dialogue". International Bulletin of Missionary Research 22, no. 3 (July 1998): 98-101.

# Glossary of Sanskrit Terms

| | |
|---|---|
| Abhāva | negation |
| Abheda | non-difference, non-different, non-differentiated |
| Ācārya | teacher |
| Acetana | non-spiritual |
| Acit | unconsciousness, non-sentient reality |
| Adhyāsa | superimposition—the act of associating with Brahman, something illusory and contrary to Brahman's ultimate being |
| Advaita | non-dualism |
| Āgama | scripture |
| Ahamdhī | I-consciousness |
| Ahaṁkāra | egoism |
| Ajñāna | ignorance |
| Aṁśa | part, aspect |
| Ānanda | bliss |
| Ananta | infinite |
| Antaryāmin | inner-controller, indweller |
| Anumāna | inference or reason |
| Anupalabdhi | non-apprehension |
| Apara brahman | lower Brahman |
| Aparā vidyā | lower knowledge |
| Aparā prakṛti | lower nature (according to Śaṅkara) |
| Apauruṣeya | uncreated |
| Arjuna | name of the warrior hero in the BG |
| Arthāpatti | presumption |
| Asat | non-being |
| Ātman | soul, self |
| Ātmanbrahman | God soul, the Self |
| Avatāra | descent, one who descends |
| Avidyā | ignorance, wrong knowledge |
| Avyakta | unmanifest |
| Avyakta bhūtāni | unmanifest beings |
| Bhagavadgītābhāṣya | a commentary on the Bhagavad Gītā |
| Bhakti | devotion |
| Bhāṣya | commentary |
| Bheda | difference, different, differentiated |
| Bhedābheda | difference and non-difference |
| Bhūtānāṁ Īśvara | Lord of beings |
| Bimbapratibimba | reflection or original / counter-reflection |

| | |
|---|---|
| Brahma | a god |
| Brahma Sūtra-s | a collection of short, esoteric aphorisms written by Bādarāyaṇa concerning the philosophy of the school of Vedānta, summing up the teaching of the Upaniṣads |
| Brahmātmaka | of the nature of Brahman |
| Bṛhattva | greatness |
| Brahman | God |
| Cetana | spiritual |
| Cetanācetanātmaka | sentient and non-sentient beings (reality) |
| Cit | consciousness, sentient reality |
| Dharma | religious duty, virtue, law |
| Divya | divine |
| Divya rūpa | divine form |
| Dravya | substance |
| Dvaita | dualism |
| Guṇa | quality |
| Guṇa-niṣedha | negation of attributes |
| Indra | a god |
| Īśvara | the Lord |
| Īśvarābheda | non-difference from (or in) the Lord |
| Itihāsa | Legend (i.e. the Mahābhārata) |
| Jagat | world |
| Jagat-prapañca | world of appearance |
| Jīva | individual soul |
| Jīva-bahutva-vāda | the teaching of plurality of souls |
| Jīvātman | individual soul, individual self |
| Jñāna | knowledge |
| Kalkī | traditionally the tenth descent of Viṣṇu |
| Karma | action, ceremony, fate |
| Kevalādvaita | absolute monism |
| Kevala-pramāṇa | intuitive sense |
| Kṛṣṇa | name of a god who is an incarnation of Viṣṇu |
| Kṛṣṇāvatāra | Kṛṣṇa in his avatāra (state) |
| Kṣetra | field |
| Kṣetrajña | field-knower |
| Līlā | sport, play |
| Līlā vibhūti | cosmic sport or play |
| Loka | world |
| Mahābhārata | a Hindu epic containing the BG |
| Mahāvākya | great saying |
| Mānuṣī tanu | human form |
| Māyā | power (of God that causes the illusion of the world or the real world) |
| Māyāśakti | the power that is māyā |

| | |
|---|---|
| Mithyā | illusion, unreal, illusory |
| Mokṣa | release, liberation of the soul |
| Mukti | liberation, salvation |
| Mūlaprakṛti | material nature |
| Neti neti | "not this, not this" |
| Nirguṇa | without attributes |
| Nirvikalpa samādhi | the superconscious state |
| Nitya | eternal |
| Pañcabheda | five-fold differences |
| Para brahman | higher Brahman |
| Paramātman | highest Self, supreme Self, Brahman |
| Para bhāva | higher being |
| Parameśvara | higher Lord |
| Parā vidyā | higher knowledge |
| Prakāra | mode |
| Prakṛti | matter, material nature, material world |
| Pramāṇa | valid means of ascertaining truth |
| Pratyagātman | inner Self |
| Pratyakṣa | sense perception, experience |
| Purāṇa-s | religious stories of the heroes and gods of India |
| Puruṣa | soul, person, the cosmic or ancient person |
| Puruṣa para | Supreme Spirit |
| Pūrvapakṣa | opposing argument |
| Pūrvapakṣin | opponent |
| Rajas | passion |
| Rama | a hero, a god |
| Rudra | a god |
| Rūpa | form, nature |
| Śabda | verbal testimony, language |
| Saguṇa | with attributes |
| Sākṣātkāra | intuition |
| Sākṣī | the witness self |
| Śakti | power |
| Sāmānādhikaraṇya | correlative predication; how non-synonymous words sharing the same grammatical case describe the referent that shares the same case |
| Saṁsāra | the cycle of birth, life, death, rebirth |
| Sannyāsin | renouncer |
| Śarāśaropādhi | perishable and imperishable adjuncts |
| Śarīra | body |
| Śarīrin | inner-controller, indweller |
| Sat | being |
| Sattva | goodness |
| Satya | truth |

| | |
|---|---|
| Savikalpa pratyakṣa | determinate perception, knowledge through sense-object contact |
| Smṛti | secondary revelation |
| Śruti | scripture |
| Śuddha | pure |
| Śuddhādvaita | pure non-dualism |
| Sūtrabhāṣya | a commentary on the Brahma Sūtras |
| Sūtrakāra | writer of the BSs |
| Svābhāvika rūpa | essential form |
| Svarūpa | essential nature |
| Tamas | darkness |
| Tat tvam asi | you are That |
| Triguṇātmikā | essence of the three guṇa-s (or constituents) |
| Upamāna | comparison |
| Vaiṣṇava | follower of Viṣṇu |
| Vaiṣnavī māyā | illusive power |
| Vedānta | "end of the Vedas," name of a philosophical school |
| Vedānta Sūtra-s | see Brahma Sūtra-s |
| Vidyā | (correct, ultimate) knowledge |
| Viśeṣa | particularity |
| Viśiṣta | qualified |
| Viśiṣṭādvaita | qualified non-dualism |
| Viṣṇu | name of a god |
| Yuga | age |

# General Index


abhāva 45
abheda 34, 54, 58, 63-70, 81, 86, 90, 93, 95, 102, 113
Abhishiktananda, Swami 228
Aquinas, Thomas 239
Adam, A. K. M. 20
adhyāsa 48, 54-55, 57, 58, 64, 65, 66, 68, 70, 75, 79, 83, 84, 85, 86, 87, 91, 92, 93, 94, 95, 106, 252
afterlife 31, 40, 91, 112, 113, 155, 163, 164, 211, 212, 239-40, 244, 245, 246, 248, 255, 256-59
ajñāna 48, 82, 115, 147
Akhilananda, Swami 9
Alcoff, Linda 17
Aleaz, K. P. 9
Allen, Diogenes 240
Ambrose 182, 191, 192, 205, 209, 210, 213, 215, 216, 217, 218, 219, 220
antaryāmin 63, 78-79, 81, 97, 99, 101, 103, 107-08, 111, 114, 116, 140, 156, 157, 158, 159, 163, 165, 244, 252, 254
anumāna 41-43, 45-46, 48, 49, 51, 52, 53, 54, 55, 56, 57, 58, 59, 60, 61, 62, 63, 70
aparā vidyā 77, 95, 104, 233
Apollinarianism 202, 210, 215, 216
Appasamy, Bishop 227, 249
Arianism 180-81, 202, 205, 209, 210
Athanasius 180-81, 190, 191, 195, 198, 209-10, 212, 213, 215, 217, 218, 220
ātmanbrahman 168, 251, 252
atonement 162, 209, 215, 218, 224, 229, 234-38, 240, 246, 248, 262
Augustine 173, 175, 182-83, 185, 191, 193-94, 198, 201, 202, 210, 212, 217-18, 219
avidyā 48, 51, 54-55, 66, 68, 70, 75, 76, 78, 82, 83, 84, 86, 92, 93, 94, 95, 104, 115, 123, 125, 134, 149, 152, 153, 154, 155, 156, 158, 159, 249
Basil of Seleucia 215
Bassuk, Daniel E. 9, 225, 239
bheda 27, 35, 37, 38, 53, 54, 57, 58, 59, 60, 61, 62, 63-66, 67, 68, 69, 70, 82, 90, 91, 92, 94, 95, 97, 99, 101, 102, 103, 105, 109-11, 115, 154, 163, 256
bhedābheda 38, 87, 90
birth of Christ 203, 210, 220, 231, 245
birth of Kṛṣṇa 29, 31, 118, 121, 122, 123, 124, 126, 129, 130, 131, 149, 153, 165, 166, 168, 231, 249
Bosch, David 260, 261
Boyd, Robin 227, 228
Brockington, John 32, 227, 235, 238, 239, 244
Brown, Harold O. J. 171
Brown, Raymond E. 188, 206, 207, 208
Bruce, F. F. 190, 210
Buitenen, J. A. B. van 42, 50, 63, 119-20, 122, 231
Carman, John B. 3, 21, 22, 26, 27, 48, 71, 98, 99, 114, 122, 159, 160, 161, 162, 236, 245, 246, 261-62
Carson, D. A. 208
Cerinthus 211
Chakkarai, V. 227, 228, 257
Chapman, Mark D. 10
Chatterjee, Chinmayi 21, 22, 23, 232
Cheetham, David 21
Clooney, Francis X. 4, 24, 25, 43, 162, 235, 237, 243
Christian orthodoxy, definition of 2
Colwell, E. C. 206
Cunliffe-Jones, Hubert 172, 178
Cyril of Alexandria 209, 216, 217, 218-19
Cyril of Jerusalem 173, 179
Das, Bhagavan 247
Dasgupta, Surendranath 35, 36, 38, 39, 117
Datta, D. M. 48, 166-67, 241, 242, 263
D'Costa, Gavin 11
Deśika, Vedānta 56, 60, 237
De Smet, Richard 31, 48, 166-67, 241,

242, 252-53, 254, 255, 263
Deussen, Paul 76
Deutsch, Eliot 42, 72, 127, 128, 131, 132, 135, 136, 138, 140, 144
Devanandan, Paul David 75, 76
Dhavamony, M. 122, 129, 130, 144, 225
divya rūpa 27, 98, 100, 102, 104, 122, 125, 156, 158, 159, 160, 161, 162, 163, 168, 240, 241, 244, 245, 250, 252, 257
Dupuis, Jacques 23, 24
Eck, Diana L. 32, 227, 230, 236
Edgerton, Franklin 27-28, 127, 128, 132, 138, 140, 142, 144
Eichrodt, Walther 185, 186, 187, 214
eschatology (see afterlife)
eschaton (see afterlife)
Flood, Gavin 22, 44, 71, 100, 114, 225, 248
Forsthoefel, Thomas A. 52, 55, 61, 65, 233
Foucault, Michel 13
Ganeri, Jonardon 7, 8
George, N. V. 30-33, 34
Ghate, V. S. 35, 72
Gorospe, Vitaliano R. 29, 32, 121, 235
Graves, Kersey 234-35
Gregory of Nyssa 181, 190, 191, 192, 193, 198
Griffiths, Bede 132, 232, 236, 237
Grimes, John 46, 72, 88
Hacker, Paul 48
Harner, Philip B. 206
Healy, Kathleen 32
Hebblethwaite, Brian 239-40
heteroousios 202, 209
Hick, John 224
Hilary of Poitiers 181-82, 190, 198, 202, 205, 209, 210, 213, 215, 216, 217, 218, 219, 220
Hill, W. Douglas P. 119, 123, 124, 125, 127, 128, 132, 138, 140, 142, 144, 148
Hiriyanna, M. 110
homoiousios 209
homoousios 201, 202, 209-10, 246
Huntington, Ronald M. 21-22, 44, 117
Hyman, Gavin 9, 10, 11, 12
identification 8, 12, 29, 35, 38, 39, 102, 145, 158, 159, 162, 163, 165, 167, 168, 169, 210, 229, 241, 242-46, 250, 251, 252, 253, 254, 256, 257, 258
Irenaeus 172, 173, 174-75, 179, 184, 186, 187, 191, 192, 202, 209, 211, 212, 215, 218, 220
Īśvara 47, 54, 63, 72-77, 79, 80, 81, 82, 83, 85, 86, 90, 93, 94, 95, 98, 99, 102, 104, 106, 111, 114, 118, 119, 120, 121, 124, 125, 128, 129, 130, 133, 140, 145, 149, 150, 151, 152, 153, 166, 167, 168, 229, 233, 234, 242, 243, 250, 251, 252, 253
jñāna 67, 68, 95, 119, 120, 121, 233
līlā 83-84, 105-07, 232, 234, 236, 237, 238
kenosis 246
King, Richard 5, 6, 8, 12, 13, 17, 20
Klive, Visvaldis V. 50
Klostermaier, Klaus K. 228
Knipe, David M. 100, 114
Krishna, Daya 5, 43-44
Kristensen, W. Brede 3
Kumar, Frederick L. 43
Lactantius 180, 191, 197, 216
Leo, Pope 209, 210, 215, 216, 217-18, 219, 220
līlā 83-84, 105-07, 232, 234, 236, 237, 238
Lipner, Julius 6, 22, 28, 32, 42, 48-49, 51, 56, 60, 68, 74, 88-89, 102, 104, 114, 123, 160, 161, 162, 163, 225, 226, 229, 231, 235, 236, 237, 247-48, 254, 258, 259
Lott, Eric 23, 25, 26, 27, 28, 36, 38, 41, 61, 74, 103, 112, 115, 160, 167, 225, 233, 240, 242, 243, 249, 251, 255, 256-57
MacDonell, Arthur A. 44
MacIntyre, Alasdair 11
Macquarrie, John 224
Malkovsky, Bradley J. 47-48, 54, 72, 76-77, 119-20, 166, 225, 241, 242, 263
mānuṣī tanu (or human form) 28, 30, 31, 34, 36, 52, 98, 139, 141, 143-45, 150-54, 157-69, 242, 243, 244, 248, 250, 251, 252, 256, 263
Marfatia, Mrudula I. 33, 34
Matilal, Bimal Krishna 46

May, Gerhard 173, 174, 175, 176, 178-79
māyā 33, 34, 47, 54, 63, 68, 73, 76, 77, 78, 79, 81, 82-83, 85, 86, 88, 94, 95, 105-07, 118, 119, 120, 121, 123, 124, 125, 127, 128, 129, 130, 131, 132, 133, 134, 135, 142, 149, 153, 238, 242, 250
Miranda, Prashant 9
Mohammed, Ovey N. 29-30
Mohanty, J. N. 6, 7, 41-42
Monier-Williams, Sir Monier 22, 119, 125, 128, 132, 135, 140, 141, 148, 151, 161
Monophysitism 202-03, 215, 216, 217
Morris, Leon 207, 210
Murty, K. Satchidananda 82, 88, 120, 167
Nayak, G. C. 50, 51
Nestorianism 202, 215, 216, 217, 219
Nestorius 202, 218
Nobili, Roberto de 227, 229
Novatian 173, 177-78, 191, 210, 212, 218
Origen 2, 173, 178-79, 181, 191, 192, 195, 210, 212
O'Hanlon, Rosalind 17
Otto, Rudolf 114, 225, 235
Panikkar, Raimundo 24
parā vidyā 58, 74, 75, 76, 92, 93, 94, 96, 104, 115, 168, 233, 244, 252
Parrinder, Geoffrey 21, 22, 28, 30, 32, 167, 223, 225, 229, 233, 240, 241, 242, 249, 263
Philo 174, 190
postcolonialism 6, 12-21
postmodernism 20, 21
Potter, Karl H. 51, 90
Prabhavananda, Swami 132, 138, 140, 145
Prabhupāda, A. C. Bhaktivedanta 231
pratyakṣa 41, 42, 43, 45, 46-47, 48, 49, 51, 52, 53, 54, 55, 56, 57, 58, 59, 60, 61, 62, 63, 65, 70, 81, 82
Puligandla, R. 45
Quesnell, Quentin 239
Rad, Gerhard von 194
Radhakrishnan, S. 9, 48, 56, 117, 123, 124, 127, 128, 131-32, 133, 138, 140, 142, 144, 148
Raghavachar, S. S. 60, 66, 103, 109
Raju, P. T. 134, 146
Ramachandra, Vinoth 226, 255
Ramakrishnananda, Swami 126, 167-68
resurrection 31, 176, 208, 211, 212, 217, 228, 236, 246, 255, 256, 257, 258, 262
Rooker, Mark F. 187, 194
Sadanandam, C. 125, 129, 167
Said, Edward W. 12-13
Sailhamer, John H. 193, 196
sāmānādhikaraṇya 53-54, 61-62, 65, 67, 68, 70, 90, 101, 108, 109, 110, 111, 112, 159
Samartha, S. J. 13, 14
saṁsāra 77, 79, 87, 92, 96, 112, 113, 115, 123, 129, 131, 143, 150, 229, 232
Sarasvatī, Madhusūdana 121, 124-25, 130
Sarasvati, Swami Satchidanandendra 65, 66, 69, 70, 75, 77, 86, 88
śarīrin 97, 108, 244
Sarna, Nahum M. 194
Satprakashananda, Swami 45, 46, 52, 73, 75, 76, 82, 85, 88, 89, 146
Schaff, Philip 171
Sellers, R. V. 209, 217, 218, 219
semi-Arianism 209
Sharma, Arvind 36, 49, 78, 127, 148, 225
Sharma, B. N. K. 36, 37, 46, 90
Singh, Sundar 227
Smart, Ninian 9, 10, 11, 226
Śrīnivāsa 56, 57, 59, 99, 102, 104, 108, 110, 125, 126, 164, 241, 258
Srinivasachari, P. N. 56, 57, 61
Sugirtharajah, R. S. 7, 12, 13-21, 29
Sugirtharajah, Sharada 13
Tapasyānanda, Svāmī 36, 98, 109
"tat tvam asi" 37, 54, 62, 64, 65, 68, 75, 88, 89, 90, 95, 96, 108-09, 163
Tatian, 173, 175-76
Tennent, Timothy C. 167, 230, 238, 247, 248
Tertullian 173, 177, 184, 210, 212, 216, 219, 220
Thangaraj, M. T. 9
Theodoret 180, 210, 212, 216, 219
Theophilus 172, 173, 176, 191, 195
Torrance, Thomas F. 262, 263
Tsumura, David Toshio 187, 194, 195, 196, 197
Upadhyaya, Brahmabandhava 228, 230, 237, 238, 247

Vempeny, Ishanand 44, 121, 124, 142, 150
vidyā 49, 53, 95
Vidyārṇava, Rai Bahadur Śrīśachandra 50, 53
Vivekananda, Swami 236
Yesurathnam, Regunta 23, 227, 240, 241
Warrier, A. G. Krishna 63, 77, 78, 120, 124, 127, 128, 129, 130, 133, 134, 150, 151, 152, 233
Weil, Simone 240
Wenham, Gordon J. 185, 186, 187, 193, 194
world-formation, doctrine of 174, 176, 182
Xenophon 174
Zaehner, R. C. 27, 127, 128, 131, 132, 134, 136, 137, 138, 139, 140, 142, 143, 144, 148

www.ingramcontent.com/pod-product-compliance
Lightning Source LLC
Chambersburg PA
CBHW070014010526
44117CB00011B/1574